THE WHITE BOOK OF PETERBOROUGH

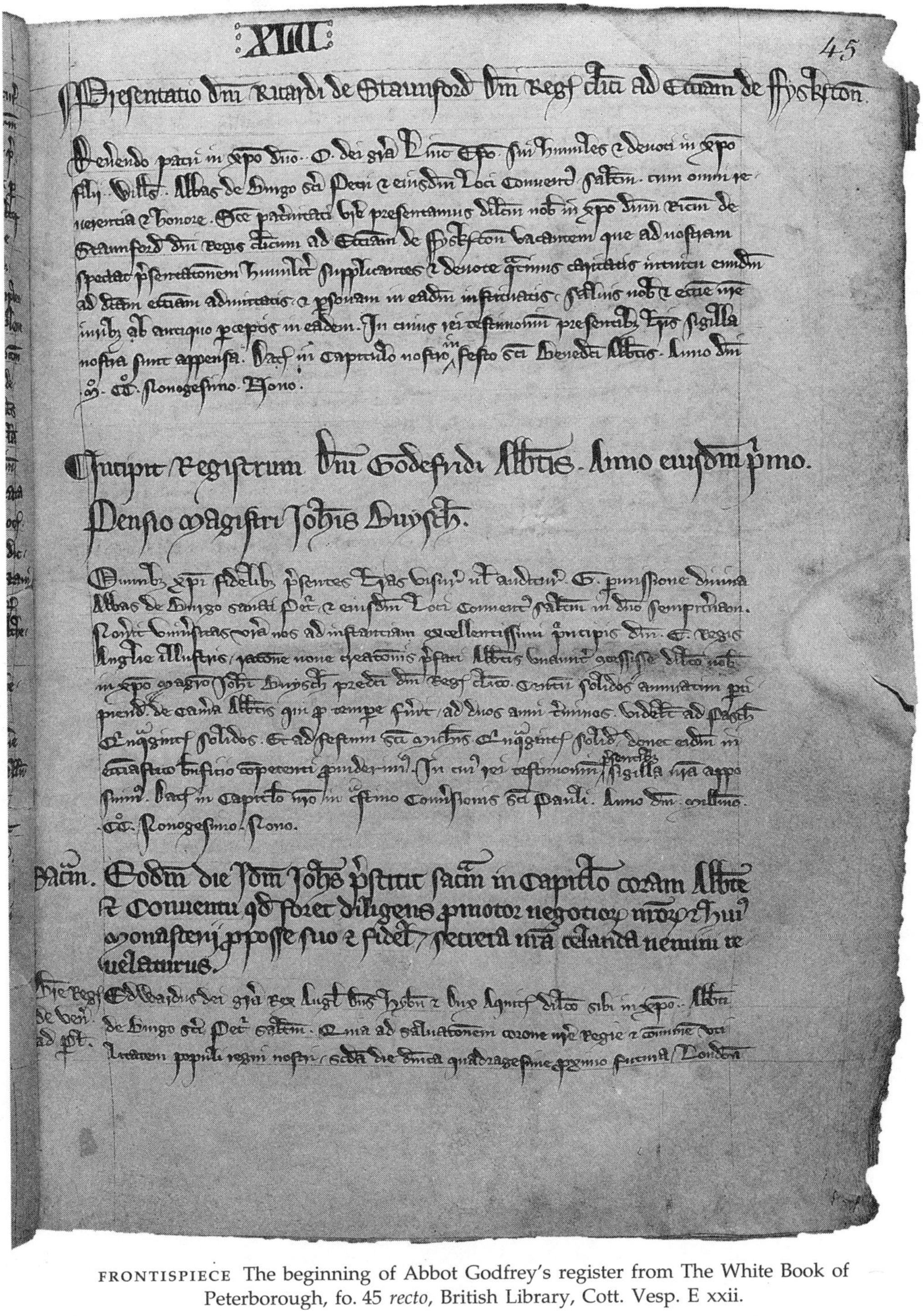

FRONTISPIECE The beginning of Abbot Godfrey's register from The White Book of Peterborough, fo. 45 *recto*, British Library, Cott. Vesp. E xxii.

THE WHITE BOOK OF PETERBOROUGH

The Registers of Abbot William of Woodford, 1295–99 and Abbot Godfrey of Crowland, 1299–1321

EDITED BY SANDRA RABAN
TRANSCRIBED BY CLAIRE DE TRAFFORD AND SANDRA RABAN

Published by the Northamptonshire Record Society
as an Anthony Mellows Memorial Trust volume
on behalf of the Dean and Chapter of Peterborough
2001

Published by the Northamptonshire Record Society, Wootton Hall Park, Northampton, NN4 9AW, on behalf of the Dean and Chapter of Peterborough

Copies of this volume are available from the Chapter Clerk, 12 Minster Precincts, Peterborough PE1 1XS

ISBN 0 901275 62 X

Typeset by Carnegie Publishing Ltd,
Chatsworth Road, Lancaster LA1 4SL.
publishing: www.carnegiepub.co.uk
book production: www.wooof.net

Printed in Great Britain by Bookcraft Ltd, Midsomer Norton

For Marjorie Chibnall
a wise mentor and friend

Contents

Abbreviations

The Black Book	The Black Book, Society of Antiquaries, MS 60
Bodl.	Bodleian Library, Oxford
Cal.Pat.	*Calendar of Patent Rolls*
Chron. Petroburgense	Ed. T. Stapleton, *Chronicon Petroburgense* (Camden Soc., xlvii, 1849)
CUL	Cambridge University Library
Dalderby's Institutions	LAO, Episcopal Register II
Dalderby's Memoranda Register	LAO, Episcopal Register III, calendared in the appendix to C Clubley, 'John Dalderby, Bishop of Lincoln, 1300–1320', unpublished Ph D thesis Hull, 1965
Foedera	Ed T. Rymer, *Foedera, Conventiones, Litterae, et Acta Publica*, vol.I, pt. II (Rec. Comm., 1816)
Henry of Pytchley	Ed. W. T. Mellows, *Henry of Pytchley's Book of Fees* (NRS, ii, 1927)
LAO	Lincolnshire Archives Office
Martin, *Cartularies*	J. D. Martin, *The Cartularies and Registers of Peterborough Abbey* (NRS, xxviii, 1978)
Mon. Angl.	W. Dugdale, *Monasticon Anglicanum*, new edn, ed. J. Caley, H. Ellis, B. Bandinel, 6 vols (London, 1846)
NP and P	*Northamptonshire Past and Present*
NRO	Northamptonshire Record Office
NRS	Northamptonshire Record Society
PRO	Public Record Office
Rec. Comm.	Record Commission
RHS	Royal Historical Society
Sparke	Ed. J. Sparke, *Historiae Anglicanae Scriptores Varii*, 2 vols (London, 1723), vol. II
Sutton's Institutions	LAO, Episcopal Register I
Swaffham	The Book of Robert Swaffham, Peterborough Dean and Chapter, MS, 1, deposited in Cambridge University Library

Taxatio	*Taxatio Ecclesiastica* (Rec. Comm., 1802)
VCH	*Victoria County History*
The White Book	The White Book, BL, Cott. Vesp. Exxii

References to documents in the White Book are by number according to the edited text.

Preface

An undertaking of this sort incurs many debts, not least to earlier generations of historians and antiquarians, without whose labours the task of editing and dating would range from the more laborious to the impossible. Here above all, the collaborative nature of historical scholarship is most evident. The greatest debt in preparing any Peterborough edition is, of course, to William Mellows, without whose own work and generous financial provision, few of the abbey's manuscripts would be in print.

Among contemporary scholars, I am especially indebted to Edmund King for the context provided by his research on the abbey's estates, his assistance in reading the present edition in typescript and his numerous helpful suggestions and references. It has been enormously helpful to be able to call on his expertise for such a specialised text and to benefit from his enthusiastic support. I am also enduringly grateful to Paul Brand for patiently answering a host of queries, drawing my attention to relevant work which would otherwise have escaped my attention and for particular help with legal and administrative texts and documents in French. Errors that remain, whether in Latin or in French, are of my own making. Nicholas Bennett very kindly made his own handlist of Bishop Dalderby's institutions available to me and resolved outstanding queries. Timothy Halliday generously shared his research on local place names and alerted me to visual records of abbey buildings associated with Abbot Godfrey. I have also appreciated help from Jeffrey Denton, Michael Franklin, Katharine Keats-Rohan, Wendy Körner and David Smith. Ron Greenall, who very kindly assisted in the task of proof reading, is owed special thanks.

For much of the time, I have worked from a bound photostat volume, commissioned by William Mellows, on loan from Peterborough Cathedral Library. Visits to the new British Library to consult the manuscript itself proved a pleasure; the architects have created a wonderful working environment for scholars. Staff there and at the University Library in Cambridge, Northamptonshire Record Office, the Bodleian Library in Oxford, the Public Record Office and the Society of Antiquaries have been uniformly helpful. I would also like to thank the British Library for permission to reproduce the folio from the White Book which forms the frontispiece to this volume.

Particular thanks are due to the Anthony Mellows Memorial Trust which made it possible for Claire de Trafford to transcribe the greater part of Abbot Godfrey's register. I thank her too for her speedy work and also Trinity Hall for granting me a year of sabbatical leave. Without both of these, the edition would have been even longer in gestation. I first began work on it in the early 1980s. Ron Greenall, the Society's General Editor has shown an exemplary blend of forbearance and cajolery. I am delighted finally to have an offering with which to appease him and to add another volume to those in memory of Anthony Mellows.

Last, but by no means least, I thank my husband for his unfailing help and support.

Sandra Raban
Cambridge, Michaelmas 2000

Introduction

The great, tenth-century fenland abbeys have left us with an unsurpassed collection of records. Nowhere else in the country has it proved possible to study quite such a concentration of ecclesiastical estates as those held by Peterborough, Ely, Ramsey, Thorney and Crowland. Between them, they dominated the East Midlands to the exclusion of secular landlords of equivalent importance. Each house has been the subject of monographs but, surprisingly perhaps, few of their cartularies and registers have appeared in print.[1] The exception is the cartulary of Ramsey Abbey, published in three volumes in the Rolls Series during the last decades of the nineteenth century, now a very long time ago.[2] That this will be remedied in the case of Peterborough is almost entirely due to W. T. Mellows, formerly Chapter Clerk to the cathedral and a dedicated historian of its medieval predecessor. He embarked on the formidable task of editing the abbey's principal records for publication. The resulting editions included five volumes for the Record Society, of which he was a founding member and, for the eight years before his death, Chairman of its Council. They were *Henry of Pytchley's Book of Fees*, *The Last Days of Peterborough Monastery* (2 vols) and the first two volumes to be published under the general title of *Peterborough Local Administration*. Aware of his fragile health and the immensity of the task, he made provision for its continuation through a trust in memory of his son Anthony, who had been killed on special service with the Maquis in southern France in 1944.[3] Although they appeared after his death in 1950, the first two memorial volumes, *The Book of William Morton* and a third volume of *Peterborough Local Administration*, published in association with the Record Society, were largely his work.[4] They were followed after a long interval by Janet Martin's invaluable handlist of the surviving cartularies and

1 E. King, *Peterborough Abbey 1086–1310: A Study in the Land Market* (Cambridge, 1973); E. Miller, *The Abbey and Bishopric of Ely: The Social History of an Ecclesiastical Estate from the Tenth Century to the Early Fourteenth Century* (Cambridge, 1951); F. M. Page, *The Estates of Crowland Abbey* (Cambridge, 1934); J. A. Raftis, *The Estates of Ramsey Abbey: A Study in Economic Growth and Organisation* (Toronto, 1957); S. Raban, *The Estates of Thorney and Crowland: A Study in Monastic Land Tenure* (University of Cambridge, Department of Land Economy, Occasional Paper, vii, 1977).

2 Ed. W. H. Hart, P. A. Lyons, *Cartularium Monasterii de Rameseia*, 3 vols (Rolls Series, London, 1884–93).

3 NRS, ii, 1927; NRS, xii, 1947; NRS ix–x, 1937–39. Joan Wake's obituary of Mellows in *NP and P*, i, no. 3 (1950), p. 1; Patrick King's bibliography, *ibid.*, ii, no. 5 (1958), pp. 252–5.

4 Trans. W. T. Mellows, ed. P. I. King and C. N. L. Brooke, *The Book of William Morton* (NRS, xvi, 1954); ed. W. T. Mellows, D. H. Gifford, *Peterborough Local Administration: Elizabethan Peterborough* (NRS, xviii, 1956).

registers and an edition of the obedientiaries' accounts, edited by Joan Greatrex.[5] The present edition of the registers of William of Woodford and Godfrey of Crowland, known as The White Book, will thus be the third volume to appear under the terms of the Trust and the fifth in memory of Anthony Mellows.

Historians draw a broad distinction between cartularies, as collections of charters or title deeds, and registers, consisting of copies of documents issued and received by those in whose name the register was made. In practice, many other sorts of documents found their way into both types of compilation if they were considered important enough to merit a copy for future reference or relevant to some piece of current business. This was certainly true of the White Book which contains a wide assortment of material, thereby adding considerably to its interest. One of the objects of this introduction is to set the most important of these documents in their historical context as well as to describe the manuscript and its transmission.

Peterborough Abbey was well provided with cartularies and registers, a good number of which still survive, despite the attrition of time and some near disasters during the Civil War in the seventeenth century.[6] They include, moreover, notably early examples of their kind. The oldest of the cartularies, incorporated in the manuscript known as The Black Book, dates from *c.* 1130. This places it among a handful of early cartularies, although not as early as the doyen among them, the first Worcester Abbey cartulary, compiled in the eleventh century.[7] Registers appeared later on the scene. Those drawn up in religious houses were modelled on bishops' registers, which had become common during the second half of the thirteenth century. That of William of Woodford, abbot from 1295 to 1299, is one of the earliest monastic registers to appear in a fully developed form.[8] It was also the first register to be drawn up at the abbey. Thereafter, keeping them became normal practice, but apart from the register of Godfrey of Crowland, abbot from 1299 to 1321 and his immediate successor, Adam of Boothby, most of the fourteenth-century compilations have disappeared. Those belonging to fifteenth-century abbots, by contrast, have survived almost in their entirety.[9] Mention is also made of a chapter register in a charter of 1305 (184), but nothing further is known about this.

Between them, these two registers present a blend of material ranging from purely domestic matters to those of national, or even international,

5 Martin, *Cartularies*; ed. J. Greatrex, *The Account Rolls of the Obedientiaries of Peterborough* (NRS, xxxiii, 1984).

6 Martin, *Cartularies*, pp. xvi–xvii.

7 G. R. C. Davis, *Medieval Cartularies of Great Britain* (London, 1958), pp. xi, 123.

8 Martin, *Cartularies*, p. xv; D. M. Smith, *Guide to Bishops' Registers of England and Wales* (RHS, London, 1981), p. vii.

9 Martin, *Cartularies*, p. xv.

significance, giving considerable insight into the dealings of the abbey and its relations with the outside world. In addition there are two substantial and important texts, now attached to Abbot Godfrey's register, in which the abbey appears only incidentally and which were probably not part of the original compilation. The earlier of the two in terms of content is the twelfth-century Northamptonshire Survey, for which this is the only surviving text (245). The second is a copy of the 1291 tax assessment of Pope Nicholas IV, with a good deal of material which is absent from the printed edition. To this was added valuations from the 1254 Valuation of Norwich (305), for which this offers one of the two best texts for part of Lincoln diocese.[10]

Yet, for all its considerable interest and value, the White Book does not offer a particularly intimate picture of the abbey. In particular, there is little to reveal the quality of spiritual life at this date. One instance from each abbacy arranges for the transfer of a monk to a Cistercian house, Pipewell Abbey for the first and Garendon Abbey for the second, in order to live a more austere life (5, 147–147A). This might be taken to indicate an unsatisfactory standard of observance at Peterborough, but one should be wary of such an inference. There is a strong element in the Western monastic tradition of individuals progressing towards a more ascetic, and sometimes eremitical, life. That this might be happening at Peterborough perhaps reflects favourably on the ability of the community to foster spiritual growth. Against this, there is mention of murmurings and dissension under Abbot William (20) and something was seriously amiss *c*. 1313.[11] There can be no mistaking, however, the efficiency of the abbey's bureaucratic machine. Both the penmanship and the Latin of the registers are of a high standard and what they record suggests that a tenacious grip was maintained both on the abbey's affairs and its rights.

THE REGISTER OF WILLIAM OF WOODFORD

What, then, do we know about William of Woodford and this early register recording his abbacy? His origins and early life are scantly documented. Virtually the only source is Walter of Whittlesey, the last continuator of the chronicle of Hugh Candidus. This work is urgently in need of a modern critical edition, not least to establish more about Whittlesey himself. Mellows thought he might be identified with the Walter of Whittlesey who was mentioned as sacrist in 1274.[12] This would have made him a very old man in 1321, when his portion of the chronicle ends. Whether or not he wrote of the last decades of the thirteenth century

10 See below, pp. xxxiv, xxxvi–ix.
11 See below, pp. xxviii–ix.
12 *Henry of Pytchley*, p. xxxii.

from personal knowledge, his accuracy as to detail is sometimes questionable, but he is likely to be reliable enough on major points.[13]

He tells us that Woodford was born at *Schelton*, probably Shelton in Bedfordshire, not far from Woodford (Northants.), where he was brought up 'with a certain friend'.[14] He would have been quite elderly when he was elected abbot since he had been entrusted with the abbey's most important business for nearly a quarter of a century. Whittlesey mentions him keeping rolls in the time of Abbot Robert of Sutton, so he was already engaged in some form of abbey administration before 1274.[15] On Sutton's death on 11 March of that year, he was chosen by his fellow monks to negotiate with the crown over custody of the abbey's temporalities during the vacancy. Edward I was in Gascony on a protracted journey home from crusade, so Woodford appeared before the royal council. There he successfully accomplished his mission in return for the payment of 300 marks. Whittlesey describes him as eloquent, endowed with worldly wisdom and expert in canon and civil law, qualities which account for his appearance as a proctor for the abbey in the ecclesiastical courts and as its attorney in the royal courts. From at least 1285, he also held the office of sacrist, in charge of the abbey's most important department. It was during this time that a major building project enlarged the rooms in the convent guest house.[16]

His most important task, while sacrist, was to deal with the affairs of Geoffrey of Southorpe, a member of one of the abbey's ancient knightly families. The sorry tale of his debt and decline had implications for the abbey as well as for Geoffrey and his family because its manors were at risk of falling into hands not of its own choosing. Geoffrey had already sold his manor at Gunthorpe to the abbey in 1277 in return for 550 marks.[17] Two years later he sold manors at Hemmingford and Yelling. By 1280, he had mortgaged other properties, including his last remaining demesne manor of Southorpe, to Stephen of Cornhill, a London draper.[18] Seeking no doubt to rescue his fortunes, he first leased the manors of Torpel and Upton in the Soke from Queen Eleanor of Castile. She in turn had acquired them from her husband, to whom they had been sold by another impoverished Peterborough knight in 1280.[19] Then, between

13 Over the purchase and assignment of Gunthorpe for example, where both the purchase price and date differ from earlier sources. Sparke, pp. 147–8. See below, n. 17.

14 Ibid., p. 151.

15 Ibid., p. 140.

16 *Chron. Petroburgense*, pp. xi–xii, 20, 87, 127–8; Sparke, pp. 151–2; King, *Peterborough Abbey*, p. 89. For the earliest reference to him as sacrist, see Sparke, p. 148. William Salmon appears to have been sacrist *c.* 1280. Ibid., p. 148.

17 *Chron. Petroburgense*, p. 25. 250 marks in Sparke, p. 147.

18 Swaffham, fo. 36v; King, *Peterborough Abbey*, p. 43.

19 King, *Peterborough Abbey* p. 39; J. C. Parsons, *Eleanor of Castile* (New York, 1995), pp. 134, 184–5.

November 1282 and November 1283, Geoffrey and his wife together purchased the wardship of Geoffrey de la Mare, heir to another abbey fee, thereby gaining custody of the two nearby manors of Maxey and Northborough.[20] These remedial measures were in vain, however, because, by 1286, the Queen had resumed Torpel and Upton, arresting Geoffrey for debt, and Stephen of Cornhill had foreclosed on the manor of Southorpe.[21] At this point Woodford stepped in and 'with great labour and expense', recovered Southorpe for the abbey. The intricacies of this operation are set out at length in *Henry of Pytchley's Book of Fees*. It appears that Geoffrey resisted the loss of Southorpe fiercely, and with considerable cunning. He complained to the king that the abbey was seeking to acquire the manor in contravention of the Statute of Mortmain, by acting in collusion with Elias de Bekyngham. This was true, although it was probably intended as an interim measure only. He also appealed to the queen, whose voracious appetite for land was well known, pointing out that Southorpe would be 'exceedingly useful' to her since it lay between Torpel and Upton and, unlike them, had good buildings. He also mentioned that Southorpe lay close to the royal forest which the abbot and his men might destroy. These arguments were well calculated to cause trouble, especially as the king and queen were once more in Gascony, making appeals and verification a long drawn out process. The king eventually found in the abbey's favour, but not before the queen's bailiff at Torpel had scaled the wall and seized the manor in her name. By 1288, William of Woodford was able to take seisin on behalf of the abbey, but its position continued to be challenged until the king granted a licence to acquire the manor in mortmain in 1291. Geoffrey meanwhile was still not reconciled to his loss and inclined to claim that, while in prison, he had been subject to duress. Yet again Woodford demonstrated a safe pair of hands and, 'having respect to his poverty and in order to avoid a scandal, gave Geoffrey ten marks in ready money, and two horses to the value of ten marks'. This enabled him to retire in genteel poverty to the house of the Carmelite friars in Stamford and at last brought an end to the matter.[22]

As well as these worldly services to his house, it is probable that William of Woodford was also responsible for the authorship of the *Chronicon Petroburgense*. When this was edited and published in the mid-nineteenth century, it was attributed to 'some unknown monk', but G. A. Poole writing some thirty years later made a plausible case for identifying Woodford as the most likely candidate. Covering the period 1122–1295, the chronicle becomes distinctive only for the years of Richard of London's abbacy (1274–95), a time when Woodford was deeply involved

20 *Chron. Petroburgense*, pp. 73–5.
21 King, *Peterborough Abbey*, p. 43.
22 Sparke, p. 152; *Henry of Pytchley*, pp. 63–72.

in abbey business. The court cases in which he played such a prominent role are described at length, often with transcripts of the relevant documents. Poole argued that this legal emphasis and the technical exactness of the writing point strongly to Woodford himself and this is now accepted as probable.[23] When Richard of London died on 16 August 1275, William of Woodford was well known to his fellow monks, with a long record of capable service to his credit. This must have recommended him when it came to electing Richard's successor. Indeed, the bishop of Lincoln had already appointed him as coadjutor, or acting abbot, during Abbot Richard's last two years when he was incapacitated by ill health.[24] Despite all this, Woodford may not have been his colleagues' unanimous choice. Whittlesey tells us that he was chosen 'by way of compromise', that is by a committee of electors, an expression often contrasted with election 'by way of the Holy Spirit' and indicating perhaps that the community was not of one mind. On the other hand, an agreement between the abbot and convent in 1297 asserts that he had been elected with the unanimous assent of the whole chapter (29). If there were doubts, it may have been because he was thought to be too old, possibly with failing health himself. Certainly his abbacy lasted only just over four years and he was infirm towards the end.[25] Some monks perhaps sought a more vigorous leader, better able to grapple with problems confronting the house.

These problems were not as pressing as they had been at the time of Richard of London's election two decades earlier. London had then inherited a parlous financial situation from his predecessor, Robert of Sutton, whose strategy during the civil war had proved disastrous. In attempting to steer a course between the warring sides, Sutton had been quite successful in preserving the abbey's estates from seizure and looting, but had provoked both king and barons into levying swingeing fines whenever the tide turned in their favour. Whittlesey estimated that, over the years, these and contingent expenses cost the abbey more than £4,300, a huge financial burden for even a rich house to absorb.[26] Three thousand marks of this was still owing when Richard of London became abbot. Much of it was paid off in twenty years of assertive and careful rule, but some still remained for Woodford to deal with. During the four years of his abbacy, Whittlesey noted that he managed to pay off a further 900 marks, as well as continuing Richard of London's energetic defence of the abbey's rights and liberties.

Encomia of the day tended to count building projects among noteworthy achievements. Here too Woodford was active. In addition to the works

23 *Chron. Petroburgense*, p. vii; G. A. Poole, *Diocesan Histories: Peterborough* (London, 1881), p. 80; A. Gransden, *Historical Writing in England c. 550–c. 1307* (London, 1974), p. 452.

24 Sparke, p. 151.

25 Ibid., p. 153.

26 *VCH, Northants.*, vol. II, pp. 88–9; King, *Peterborough Abbey*, pp. 96–7; Sparke, p. 140.

undertaken for the convent while he was sacrist, he was credited with the lavish refurbishment of his own chapel and a new hay barn, as well as substantial building works at Eye. According to Whittlesey, he was a benign and considerate leader, a model of piety and well respected within the abbey. He also made his mark in the wider ecclesiastical world, where he was elected to preside over the General Chapter of the black monk houses of the southern province.[27] If some of his colleagues had entertained reservations at the time of his election, in the event he appears to have been an excellent choice.

His register contains 115 assorted documents, copied in roughly chronological order. All but four are in Latin and the remainder in French. Many were grants made in conjunction with the convent and sealed with the chapter seal. Among those to which the abbot would normally have appended his own seal, there are two from October 1295 where he used the chapter seal because his own was not yet ready (2, 14). Slightly unusual too was the use of the abbot's seal by Henry of Yaxley, vicar of Warmington, when he appointed a proctor in 1298, because his own would have been unknown (80). In the following year, when the seal of the rural deanery of Nassaburgh was preferred by the rector of All Saints, Irthlingborough in his deed of resignation (99), not in itself an unusual occurrence, the same reason was given.

Some forty deeds antedate William of Woodford's abbacy, most of which can also be found in other Peterborough compilations. The range of subject matter is considerable. As one would expect, a number concern abbey administration. It is with one of these that the register opens; the plea of Geoffrey de la Mare, now of age, claiming the hereditary office of constable of the abbey. The register was sometimes known as the *Registrum Mare* on this account.[28] Several earlier documents relating to this matter, including the writs initiating the case, are recorded in the *Chronicon Petroburgense*.[29] The register picks up the story with the plea, heard in the Court of Common Pleas in the Michaelmas Term 1294, the year before Woodford became abbot, and then records the settlement early in 1296 with Geoffrey's quitclaim to the abbey of the office, along with the right to timber and fuel from Peakirk wood, in return for sixty marks sterling (1, 1A, 1B).

Among other documents illustrating abbey administration, there is a record of the appointment, in September 1298, of John son of Thomas of Oundle as keeper of the liberty of Peterborough during pleasure (87) and an undated copy of ordinances, in French, governing the conduct of

27 Sparke, pp. 151–2; ed. W. A. Pantin, *Documents Illustrating the Activities of the General and Provincial Chapters of the English Black Monks 1215–1540*, 3 vols (Camden Soc., 3rd ser., xlv, xlvii, liv, 1931–37), vol. I, pp. 135, 140, 141n.

28 Martin, *Cartularies*, p. 36; e.g. Bodl., MS Dodsworth, 75, fo. 87v and BL, Harl. 294, fo. 183v.

29 *Chron. Petroburgense*, pp. 130–2.

bailiff of the franchise (24). A second undated document, also in French, perhaps associated with the feudal aid for the knighting of the Lord Edward granted by parliament to Henry III in May 1253, concerns orders to the bailiff of the court of Castor about the conduct of the court (25). Rather more routine are several letters of appointment – of a proctor at the Roman *Curia* in 1298 (79) and attorneys to the bishop of Lincoln's Great Court in Nottinghamshire in 1296 (18) – and documents concerning presentations to abbey livings (12, 68, 84, 94, 99, 106–7).

By far the most interesting of the entries associated with administration are two short inventories and a calculation of the abbey's grain requirements belonging to the mid-thirteenth century (103–5), and extents for the manors of Torpel, Upton and Walcot-on-Humber, drawn up in the 1290s (32, 91). The early inventories are particularly precious because Peterborough Abbey has no surviving account rolls before the 1280s. Professor King links the first of the inventories, dated Michaelmas 1248, with the troubled abbacy of William of Hotot (1246–49). It is clear why a survey of 'the state of the whole abbey' might have been desirable in view of the abbot's undertaking not to alienate the abbey's possessions, sell its woodlands or act in major matters without the knowledge of the convent, promises followed shortly afterwards by his resignation, the voluntary nature of which is the subject of suspicious emphasis.[30] In the event, rather than covering the whole abbey, this inventory was confined to a summary of the abbot's stock and grain, along with a valuation of his treasures and, most significantly, a list of debts totalling 411 marks. The second inventory was drawn up on 11 March 1263, within a few days of the death of Abbot John de Caux, and is rather more detailed than its predecessor. The associated assessment of the abbey's grain needs, which also has a note about the different measures in use, illustrates the sort of calculations that estate administrators were bringing into play during the thirteenth century. The objective appears to have been to estimate whether there was sufficient grain to permit the harvest from outlying manors to be sold.[31]

The extent of Torpel and Upton, dated 11 April 1291, is related to the king's grant of the custody of these two manors, earlier in the year, following the death of Queen Eleanor. The abbey was to hold them during pleasure, for £100 p.a.[32] As the extent was made before Peter of Leicester, an Exchequer official employed on a variety of royal business, it did not originate with the abbey.[33] It is nevertheless easy to see why a copy was kept; the recovery of control over estates in the heartland of

30 E. King, 'Estate Management and the Reform Movement', in ed. W. M. Ormrod, *England in the Thirteenth Century* (Stamford, 1991), p. 7; Sparke, p. 128.

31 King, 'Estate Management', p. 10.

32 Swaffham, fos 294v–5r; King, *Peterborough Abbey*, p. 40; *Cal. Pat., 1281–92*, p. 421; *Cal. Fine Rolls, 1272–1307*, p. 289.

33 M. Prestwich, *Edward I*, 2nd edn (New Haven and London, 1997), p. 340.

the Soke was highly desirable, but it was equally important to determine how much the abbey was paying for the privilege. Although it was not its normal practice, Crowland Abbey, also holding crown estates at farm, made profit and loss calculations in its accounts *c.* 1303–7 for the manors of Holywell (Lincs.) and Stretton (Rutland), then part of Queen Margaret's dower.[34] The valuations in the 1291 extent provided Peterborough with a slightly different means to the same end. By contrast, it is not at all clear why particular importance was attached to the extent of Walcot, drawn up before Abbot William during his second year in office. Walcot-on-Humber was a long established demesne manor, some eighty miles north of Peterborough, but despite its isolation from the rest of the abbey's holdings, it appears to have been well integrated into its administration and not subject to any dispute. The extent is also far less detailed than those for Torpel and Upton, or even another for Walcot itself, made during the vacancy in 1321.[35]

There are surprisingly few documents arising from the abbey's seignorial relationship with its tenants. Among them are a handful relating to homages (11, 60, 61, 89, 90, 92, 92A), two dealing with payment to the abbey for the custody and marriage of the heirs of Andrew Russell (73, 83), two associated with the manor of Lutton (81–81A) and three manumissions granted to abbey villeins. The manumission of William son of Richard of Werrington is intriguing. It was granted by Abbot Richard of London on 4 June 1278 'for the love of Lord Robert, of good memory, once our predecessor as abbot and uncle of the said William, and at the instance of the good man Brother Hugh of Sutton, relative of the said Lord Robert, abbot' (50). Either William came of mixed stock, or Abbot Robert and Brother Hugh of Sutton had servile origins. The other two manumissions both belong to William of Woodford's abbacy and were granted to men wishing to proceed to holy orders (27, 27A, 69, 70). There is also a deed from the first decade of the thirteenth century confirming the grant of William Blund and his family to the abbey in return for two marks, as well as charters confirming the grant of the villein tenement he once held in Stow by Threckingham in Lincolnshire (36–8).

Relatively few charters, in the narrow sense of title deeds, found their way into the register and a significant proportion of them predate William of Woodford's abbacy. The Blund confirmation is one of thirteen deeds collected together under the heading 'Charters of Coldestowe' (33–45), most of which belong to the time of Abbot Akarius (1200–10). Three more then follow under the headings 'Charter of Lady Isabella de Ros' (46) and 'Charters of Walcot-on-Humber' (47–8).

34 S. Raban, 'Mortmain in Medieval England', *Past and Present*, lxii (1974), pp. 7–8. Also in ed. T. H. Aston, *Landlords, Peasants and Politics in Medieval England* (Cambridge, 1987), pp. 207–8.

35 Sparke, pp. 213–14.

There are also relatively few documents reflecting the relationship between the abbot and convent. This was a source of tension in many religious houses where the endowment of the convent often proved inadequate to provide properly for the monks. The register contains grants from earlier abbots, some of which address this perennial problem. Others deal with more routine matters which it was useful to have noted for future reference. Richard of London conceded that the convent might build and repair a granary for their own crops, receive their ancient rations of grain and malt from the abbot's granary and grind their corn without payment of multure. He also granted the monks the future option of building a bakehouse and brewhouse should they so wish (51). In June 1297, Abbot William granted the cellarer a plot of land planted with willows in return for the latter dropping any claim to keep his pigs in a place known as the *Wodeyerd* (30). As was customary at the time, he arranged to augment the convent's endowment, while at the same time providing for his own anniversary. He surrendered 16s 6d *wethersilver*, a customary payment, due to him from the convent's manors at Alwalton and Fletton, one mark of which was to be paid to the convent's receivers to be divided equally between the convent and the poor. The mention of 'murmuring and obloquy' suggests that the background to this arrangement may have been controversial (20). His major assignment came from the income accruing from the manor which he had recovered at Southorpe. In May 1279, the sacrist was enjoined to pay £20 to the convent annually, 40s of which was specifically tied to his anniversary celebrations (29).

Several documents reflect Peterborough's relations with other religious houses. For the most part, these dealt with matters of concern between neighbours and are very similar to documents settling conflicts of interest involving lay lords. An agreement between Peterborough and Thorney Abbey in 1297 over the damming and repair of the watercourse between the River Nene and *Inggewelle* (31) mirrors an agreement with William de Beaumeys in the previous year over access for maintenance of the mill pool at Crowthorp (53) and a promise by Ralph son of Achard, from the beginning of the century, that he would not interfere with the abbey's mill pool at Stamford (55). The extent of ecclesiastical tenure in Lincolnshire and the East Midlands made it inevitable that tenants of other houses would sometimes fall within Peterborough jurisdiction or owe services to the abbey. Thus, in 1279, Peterborough and Ramsey Abbey reached agreement about view of frankpledge in Peterborough's hundred of Polebrook for tenants on the newly purchased Ramsey manors of Barnwell, Hemington, Crowthorp and Littlethorp. Issues relating to Ramsey's competing markets at Barnwell and Elton and common meadow at *Keleseye* (49) were addressed at the same time.[36] In the following year,

36 Raftis, *The Estates of Ramsey Abbey*, p. 237; *VCH, Northants.*, vol. III, p. 73.

there was a similar clarification of the obligations of the tenants of Thurgarton Priory on Peterborough's manor at Collingham in Nottinghamshire (57).[37] Most of these agreements can also be found in the cartularies of the houses in question.

A rather different and particularly interesting group of documents reflects the abbey's relations with dependent religious institutions, principally the nunnery of St Michael in Stamford. Recent work on women religious has thrown much light on a subject where evidence is in short supply.[38] Only nineteen cartularies belonging to their houses have survived and there are very few original charters. The cartularies of St Michael's have been one of the casualties, although nearly three hundred original charters and certain financial documents have been preserved. Notwithstanding this relative *richesse*, Peterborough compilations are the only source of information on some key issues.[39] The abbey has not just served as a conduit for the preservation of evidence however. The relationship between the two communities was significant in itself. Like a number of early nunneries, St Michael's appears to have begun life as an informal group of pious women living under the rather shadowy protection of a male house, in this case Peterborough. Understandably, such irregular arrangements came to worry the church authorities during the reformist era of the twelfth century. The position of St Michael's was therefore formalised. It became a foundation under the authority of the abbey, which appointed one of the monks as warden, or prior, and approved the election of the prioress. Practical signs of the consequent distancing of the two communities appear in the register. The abbey granted the nuns St Michael's church in Stamford in return for the payment of half a mark p.a. towards the repair of its books (95). Also, in an undated document, the bailiff in Stamford was ordered to give them money to buy five cows to replace the cheese they used to receive from the manor of Eye (23). That the abbey's authority may not have been wholly welcome is implied by two documents, probably dating from the 1230s. One is an acknowledgement by the nuns of their subordination (96). The other is an abject plea from the prioress for the assistance of the archbishop of Canterbury in making peace with the monks. The nuns, despite their attempt to argue otherwise, seem to have

37 There are also several documents in William of Woodford's register, antedating his abbacy, which involve Spalding Priory and its parent house of St Nicholas, Angers (47–8) and the priory of Newstead on Ancholme (66). For deeds to which laymen were party, see 28A, 53, 55, 74, 86 and 98.

38 S. Thompson, *Women Religious: The Founding of English Nunneries after the Norman Conquest* (Oxford, 1991); S. K. Elkins, *Holy Women of Twelfth-Century England* (Chapel Hill and London, 1988); B. Golding, *Gilbert of Sempringham and the Gilbertine Order c. 1130–c. 1300* (Oxford, 1995).

39 ed. C. Breay, *The Cartulary of Chatteris Abbey* (Woodbridge, 1999), p. 5; Davis, *Medieval Cartularies*, p. 106; W. M. Sturman, 'The History of the Nunnery of St Mary and St Michael outside Stamford' (unpublished London MA thesis, 1945), pp. 12–20.

tried to assert their independence by means of a papal privilege (97).[40] The importance attached by the abbey to its victory in this matter may be inferred from the inclusion of these documents in all its major cartularies and registers well into the later fourteenth century.

In his supervisory role, Abbot William received Joan de Mortimer into the habit of a nun in 1298 (15). He also enjoyed rights of visitation, conceded by the bishop of Lincoln in 1270, and, in 1297, absolved three nuns whom he had excommunicated following such a visit.[41] One had assaulted a novice. The sins of the other two were unspecified (76). A letter from Oliver Sutton, bishop of Lincoln, setting out penances following his visitation in 1298, shows that the abbot and bishop shared in supervising the nuns' discipline. This double scrutiny does not seem to have guaranteed high standards of observance; Sutton's injunctions reveal the nuns as quarrelsome and incontinent and the house poorly managed and in debt (82). This document is interesting in its own right as one of the few surviving sets of injunctions from the thirteenth century.[42] Less reprehensible, because it was the norm among women religious, was the fact that the bishop wrote to them in French, implying that they were unlikely to have mastered more than liturgical Latin.

The abbey also had the right to appoint wardens to the leper house of St Giles and the hospital of St John the Baptist and St Thomas the Martyr on Stamford bridge. All was not well with the latter either owing to the mental incapacity of its then warden, Hugh de Clisseby, also known as Hugh de Sancto Martino. The abbot and the bishop of Lincoln appear to have differed in their reaction to this, the bishop's pastoral concern contrasting with Woodford's tougher stance. In February 1299, Hugh's friends reported that he was reduced to pawning his clothes in order to survive, since the abbot's servants had taken his goods and he was not receiving any income from All Saints' church. By April, the abbot, at Hugh's own request, had appointed Robert, rector of Northborough, as warden in his place, so that the hospital's affairs could be set to rights (101). The bishop, in his turn, had appointed Walter of Kirmington as Hugh's coadjutor and asked the abbot to restore Hugh's possessions. It appears that by late July, Hugh had recovered sufficiently to resume control and, on 4 August, he acknowledged the return of his property (65).[43] It was not to be a happy ending however, as a visitation shortly after Abbot Godfrey's election revealed (118).[44] Although most of the documents in the register deal with the internal affairs of the monastery

40 Thompson, *Women Religious*, pp. 61–3.

41 Sturman, p. 58; *VCH, Northants.*, vol. II, pp. 98–9.

42 Sturman, pp. 65–8.

43 Ed. R. M. T. Hill, *The Rolls and Register of Bishop Oliver Sutton 1280–1299*, 8 vols. (Lincoln Record Society, 1948–86), vol. VI, pp. 146–7, 150–1, 165–6, 190–1; *VCH, Northants.*, vol. II, p. 164. Hugh was also vicar of All Saints', Stamford.

44 See below, pp. xxix–xxx.

in one way or another, some of the most interesting link the monks to the world far beyond the abbey precincts. One of these is a record of the abbey's payment of pensions amounting to almost fifty pounds p.a. to named judges, clerks and pleaders (10). This was a time when it was considered prudent to have well placed advisers to assist in litigation and business with legal implications. Hugh of Cressingham and John of Berwick had both been officials of Queen Eleanor, a particularly useful connection in view of the Southorpe saga and the subsequent farm of Torpel and Upton. It was equally advantageous to the abbey when its pensioners dealt with cases to which it was party. This happened in 1302, when Thomas son of John de Wengham brought a case of novel disseisin against the abbey in which William Inge was the leading justice (158). Even if the case may only have been a device to gain a secure quitclaim, a friend at court was to be welcomed. Elias de Bekyngham, the abbey's agent in the recovery of Southorpe and another royal justice 'in whom the abbot and convent had great confidence', did not appear on the 1296–97 list, perhaps because he had already been presented to abbey livings at Northborough in 1269 and Warmington in 1281. He did however receive expenses in 1294–95.[45] Among those included on the list, John de Insula and Henry Spigurnel may have recommended themselves because they came from Northamptonshire families.[46] The names of some of the lesser men also point to local origins.

The abbacy of William of Woodford coincided with a period of exceptionally heavy royal taxation which hit the church as hard as it hit the laity and destroyed Edward I's popularity with his subjects. In 1294, the year before Woodford's election, the clergy had given reluctant consent to a massive royal tax of half their assessed wealth, even though they were still liable for the remaining payments on a tenth for each of six years, imposed by the pope in 1291. This huge sum was followed by grants of royal tenths in 1295 and 1297.[47] Small wonder that the abbey carefully copied into its register two versions of the papal bull *clericis laicos* of 1296 (6, 17), forbidding secular taxation of the church without papal permission. It was probably during William of Woodford's abbacy too that the copy was made of Pope Nicholas IV's recent tax assessment, with the earlier assessment of 1254 set alongside.[48] Copies were also made of correspondence relating to the payment of the royal tenths and an undertaking in 1298 to pay a hefty 500 marks towards the ransom of John de St John, the king's lieutenant in Gascony, who had been ambushed

45 King, *Peterborough Abbey*, pp. 133–4; *Henry of Pytchley*, p. 62.

46 King, *Peterborough Abbey*, p. 134.

47 For taxation and the resulting political crisis, see Prestwich, *Edward I*, chap. 16 and app. A; W. E. Lunt, *Financial Relations of the Papacy with England to 1327* (Cambridge, Mass., 1939), p. 346ff; J. H. Denton, *Robert Winchelsey and the Crown 1294–1313: A Study in the Defence of Ecclesiastical Liberty* (Cambridge, 1980), chaps 3–4.

48 See below, pp. xxvii–viii.

and captured by the French in the previous year (3, 63, 72). Less onerous, but no less resented, were the procurations demanded by the pope to cover the expenses of the papal nuncios, the cardinal bishops of Albano and Palestrina. Letters about this were copied also (21).

These financial records are the longest and most complex texts in the register. Like Russian dolls, they contain letters nesting within letters, as each agent in the collecting process cited his immediate authority in a chain reaching back to the pope, king, bishop of Lincoln or archbishop of Canterbury. They throw a good deal of light on the way in which each tax was collected, but give little sign of the political turmoil that accompanied them. Archbishop Winchelsey exhorted the bishop of Lincoln to see that the richer clergy paid the 1297 tenth at once, because of the Scottish invasion, and his letter ordering a meeting of convocation in order to discuss the crisis was also recorded (58), but his bitter wrangling with the crown earlier in the year, and the disaster of William Wallace's victory at Stirling Bridge in September, pass without comment. The only hints in the register are the letter of January 1297 ordering the summons of the clergy of the southern province to a council at St Paul's in London (19) and the cancellation of Hugh of Cressingham's name, without comment, on the list of abbey pensioners after he was killed in the battle.

THE REGISTER OF GODFREY OF CROWLAND

In contrast to William of Woodford, Godfrey of Crowland enjoyed a long period of rule extending over more than twenty years. Characterised by Poole as a 'courtier abbot', he enjoyed royal favour at the beginning of his abbacy.[49] In November 1299, Edward I sent him a silver gilt cup, together with a very cordial message, to celebrate his inauguration (111) and permitted him to delay payment of the one thousand mark fine for custody of the abbey during the recent vacancy.[50] During the following June, the abbey received confirmation of its estates and privileges. In acquiring this, Whittlesey boasts that the abbey had defeated Walter Langton, the royal treasurer, who wished to charge 1000 marks until an appeal directly to the king secured it without payment.[51] Royal favour is also indicated by the grant in 1301 of timber from King's Cliffe, the royal hunting lodge in Rockingham Forest, in order to repair the abbey church and buildings and other concessions associated with the royal forest. In 1305 the abbot was given five bucks and five does to stock his new park and in 1307, at the request of Queen Margaret, he received a licence to create the park at La Biggin (259).[52] Nevertheless, to describe Abbot Godfrey as a 'courtier' is an overstatement. He did not even attend

---

49 Poole, *Diocesan Histories*, p. 85.

50 Sparke, p. 153.

51 *Cal. Charter Rolls, 1257–1300*, pp. 485–6; Sparke, p. 153–4.

52 *Cal. Close, 1296–1302*, p. 416; *1302–7*, p. 243; *Cal. Pat. 1301–7*, p. 507; no. 259.

the magnificent Feast of Swans, held to celebrate the knighting of the Prince of Wales in 1306 (194-A). Both Edward I and Edward II visited the abbey during his abbacy, but neither stayed for more than a day or so. Indeed the two brief visits of Edward II in April and October 1314 appear to have been part of a round trip of the fenland houses.[53]

Close contact with royalty, even of this limited sort, had its advantages, but they came at a high price. On Edward II's earlier visit with Piers Gaveston, before his accession to the throne, Whittlesey recounts a plausible tale of the prince's refusal to accept a costly robe unless Gaveston received one of equal splendour.[54] He further estimated that Edward I's visit alone cost over 250 marks.[55] The abbot of Peterborough was neither the first not the last subject to find the honour of entertaining the monarch a heavy burden. The abbey's location adjacent to the main thoroughfare to the north left it vulnerable to the demands of hospitality. Two cardinals passing through on their way north to mediate between the warring monarchs of England and Scotland also required costly gifts, including an illuminated psalter.[56] Beyond these contacts, however, there is little to suggest that Abbot Godfrey played an active part either in government or court life.

As with William of Woodford, little is known about Godfrey'a life before he became abbot. Once more, Whittlesey is the sole source of information. He records that Godfrey was born, professed and took his name from nearby Crowland (or Croyland).[57] If he did begin his monastic career at the equally ancient, but smaller, abbey there, nothing is known about how he came to transfer to Peterborough. Like Woodford, he was elected from among the ranks of the obedientiaries but, again, nothing is known of his career before he became the pittancer.[58] Symon Gunton, the seventeenth century historian and prebendary of Peterborough, found him 'famous for worthy actions' such that 'there was scarce his like, either before him, or after'.[59] Certainly he was a prodigious builder and improver, both on demesne manors and at the abbey itself, as well as building two new bridges over the River Nene at Peterborough.[60] Like his predecessor, he also spent money on recovering manors and protecting

53 He was at Ramsey on 12 April, Thorney on 14 April and Crowland on 17 April. Similarly, in autumn, he was at Crowland on 27 Oct., Thorney on 29 Oct. and Ramsey as well as Peterborough on 30 Oct. *Cal. Pat., 1301–7*, pp. 25–6; *Cal. Close, 1296–1302*, p. 521 (March 1302). *Cal. Pat. 1313–17*, pp. 104–7, 110, 145–6 (12–14 April 1314), p. 199 (30 Oct. 1314).

54 Sparke, p. 171–2.

55 Ibid., p. 171.

56 Ibid., p. 173

57 Ibid., p. 153.

58 Ibid. Cellarer according to *VCH, Northants.*, vol. II, p. 89 and S. Gunton, *The History of the Church of Peterborough* (London, 1686), p. 39.

59 Gunton, *Peterborough*, p. 39.

60 Sparke, pp. 154–6, 162–6.

the abbey's tenurial interests.[61] Such energy easily shaded into extravagance. He spent liberally on ornaments and plate, especially for the abbey church. He also indulged himself. Gunton claimed that he was the only Peterborough abbot known to have possessed anything like the silver gilt pastoral staff with an image of the Holy Trinity at its head which he acquired for his own use.[62] Whittlesey recounts in vivid detail his lavish purchase of vestments embroidered with religious, naturalistic and animal motifs, so splendid and precious that the abbey was still paying an official to look after them in the sixteenth century.[63]

Although his gifts to the convent included a number of books, personally he seems to have inclined towards worldly rather than spiritual interests. An enthusiasm for hunting is suggested by the creation of his park at La Biggin and a pardon he was granted in 1316 for hunting outside his own precincts.[64] There are also suggestions of pursuits of a less acceptable nature. In February 1313, the bishop of Lincoln testified that the abbot had purged himself of accusations of sodomy with Laurence of Oxford, his chamberlain, as well as adultery with Laurence's wife and three unmarried women from Peterborough. He had also been accused of theft, taking ecclesiastical property from the manor of Eye and inciting guards at the prison in Peterborough to cruelty at the time of his election. Later in the year, the bishop declared that the charges had been laid maliciously during his visitation of the abbey. That Abbot Godfrey was not wholly without blame, however, might be inferred from his pilgrimages to the tomb of St Edmund Rich at Pontigny and St Thomas at Hereford in the midst of this scandal and his visit to Canterbury the following year to atone for his sins and for the sake of his health.[65]

Abbot Godfrey's register takes broadly the same form as that of William of Woodford and, like that of his predecessor, is largely in Latin, with a handful of documents in French. It seems, however, to have been kept less systematically than that of either William of Woodford or Crowland's successor, Adam of Boothby (1321–38).[66] From around 1311, it is noticeably less orderly both in appearance and content. The loss of thirty folios at fo.105r may make it appear less well maintained than it was, but a decline in bureaucratic standards could be a reflection of pressures on the house. The beginning of an abbacy always meant heavy outgoings and it appears that Peterborough borrowed 200 marks from the Templars at that time (162). The high expenditure and possible shortcomings of the abbot himself were an added burden. Whether or not he was guilty of the accusations made by his monks in 1313, they reveal major problems

61 Ibid., pp. 155–8. See also below, pp. xxx–xxxii.

62 Sparke, pp. 154, 156, 163, 169–70, 174; Gunton, *Peterborough*, p. 41.

63 Sparke, pp. 162–4, 167–9; Greatrex, *Account Rolls*, pp. 10, 239, 247.

64 *Cal. Pat. 1301–7*, p. 507; *1313–17*, pp. 475, 480.

65 Dalderby's Memoranda Register, fos 270v, 274v, 285r, 297v.

66 For Boothby's register, see BL, Cott. Vesp. E xxi, fos 48r–106v.

within the community. Much of the trouble apparently centred on Laurence of Oxford, hanged for crimes which are regrettably unspecified. Throughout the summer of 1313, the bishop made strenuous attempts to stamp out a superstitious cult which had developed around Laurence's burial place. This involved monks as well as secular priests and laymen and dissension was reported inside the abbey.[67] When the abbey sought the bishop's permission to appropriate Warmington rectory in 1316, arguments put forward in justification suggest some financial difficulty. The cost of hospitality, wars, 'divers oppressions, exactions and expenses' were all cited. Up to a point, this can be discounted as common form. Similar claims had been made by William of Woodford in an earlier attempt to appropriate the rectory, but the sale of wood in 1306–7, on a scale such that the abbot was able to give the convent 100 marks, is perhaps another straw in the wind.[68] There seem to have been more grants of pensions and corrodies under Abbot Godfrey, even allowing for his much longer abbacy.[69] Although some were patently in return for service to the abbey (148,[70] 253, 296) or were a form of payment (188, 209), a growing number were at the request of members of the royal family (108, 163, 197, 303). Archbishop Winchelsey also made a request on behalf of a probable relative (172). These were an added imposition, hard to evade. Whether, taken together, such hints of financial stringency and lapses of discipline amounted to anything serious in such a prominent house is not clear, but Godfrey of Crowland's abbacy was undoubtedly played out against a background of exceptional hardship for the country as a whole, with extremes of famine, heavy war taxation and misgovernment, combined with official rapacity of ironically ruthless efficiency. It would not be surprising if the abbey had been affected.

As one would expect, some of the more mundane problems recorded in William of Woodford's register continued to exercise his successor. Foundations for which the abbey had responsibility in Stamford were prominent among them. At the hospital of St Thomas Martyr, the custodianship of Hugh de Sancto Martino remained a cause of continuing concern. Under pressure from the bishop, Abbot Godfrey restored him to office in April 1300, on condition that he observed the reform measures put in place following an appalling state of affairs revealed by abbatial visitation. Both the spiritual and practical obligations of the hospital

67 Dalderby's Memoranda Register, fos 276v, 279r, 281v, 283r, 289v.

68 *VCH, Northants.*, vol. II, p. 89; M. J. Franklin, 'The Bishop, the Abbot and Warmington Rectory: A Medieval Church Appropriation Struggle', *NP and P*, vi (1980–1), pp. 199–200; Sparke, p. 163; Dalderby's Memoranda Register, fo. 356r.

69 18 pensions and 10 corrodies in twenty two years in comparison with 3 pensions, other than those paid to legal advisers for which there is no equivalent under Abbot Godfrey, between 1295–9. According to his register, Abbot William agreed no corrodies, but two granted by Richard of London were included (52, 88).

70 Roger de Hegham featured on the 1297 list of legal pensioners (10).

had been neglected, and Hugh had apparently been peculating funds (118–21).

The register is less explicit about administrative shortcomings at St Michael's nunnery. Visitations were carried out in 1300 (137) and 1303 (133), but no injunctions exist to indicate concern. Nevertheless all was not well there either. The monk priors held office for short periods only. William de Stok' resigned in 1302 (164), to be replaced by Stephen de Burgo (165). This new appointment was not wholly successful and Thomas de Sarum was appointed as custodian, with special responsibility for the priory's temporalities. On such matters, his authority overrode that of both the prior and prioress. The matter was temporarily resolved in 1315, when Stephen de Burgo resigned and Thomas de Sarum became prior in his stead. However, he too resigned shortly afterwards.[71] Scandal also continued to dog the house. No hint of this is given in the register, but episcopal records reveal the long saga of Agnes de Flixthorpe's apostasy. It fell to Abbot Godfrey and the archdeacon of Nottingham to retrieve her from Nottingham in 1310 and place her in shackles at Stamford. This was far from the end of the story however. She refused to resume her habit and claimed that she had been married before entering the nunnery. After a period at Cornworthy Priory in Devon, her appeal to return to Stamford was granted in 1318, on condition that she was kept in isolation until she repented.[72] Whether her spirit was finally broken is unrecorded. Closer to home, Godfrey's abbacy opened with an unfortunate incident at the chapel of St Thomas Martyr outside the abbey. Fugitives seeking sanctuary there had been dragged out and blood was shed within its consecrated precincts. The abbot was accordingly charged by the bishop with its purification so that it could once more be used for divine worship (142). This was also a year in which the first rumblings of dissension and revolt within the abbey itself required the bishop's intervention (138).

On a more secular note, the manors of Torpel and Upton continued to present difficulties. Quite apart from complications arising from the death of Queen Eleanor, from whom they were held at farm (152, 232), in 1301 the abbey became involved in long drawn out investigations to clarify tenurial relationships in order to establish whether the crown or the abbot was entitled to the wardship and marriages of the heirs of Geoffrey de Southorpe and Walter de Ufford (149–149F). A few years later, wardships and marriages were again a bone of contention and the abbot was also accused of allowing the manorial buildings at Torpel to fall into disrepair while he held them at farm. The matter was once more put before a jury which, at length *c.* 1310, vindicated the abbot (261). He encountered further challenges to his seignorial rights in 1315 and 1318,

71 Sturman, pp. 252–3; Dalderby's Institutions, fos 5v, 57v.

72 Dalderby's Memoranda Register, fos 164r, 180v, 196v, 201r, 228r, 236r, 302v, 396v.

by which time Torpel and Upton were once again in royal hands. The king responded to his petitions on both occasions by ordering the treasurer and barons of the Exchequer to search their records to see whether the abbot was suffering any injustice (252, 289).

Over-zealous government officials were a perpetual problem. The register contains a number of royal writs, often on petition of the abbot, ordering that his privileges under royal charter be observed. Essentially he was seeking to protect the position whereby his bailiffs, within the liberty and his hundreds elsewhere, should deal with matters which were normally the preserve of the sheriff or especially appointed tax collectors. Chief sources of conflict were the return of writs and the right of the abbot to answer at the Exchequer for any debts owed to the crown (200–1, 203–4, 208). In Stamford, abbey tenants were at constant risk of being tallaged alongside those of the earl of Surrey and this too required action in 1305 (186-A, 283–4). It appears from the register that Abbot Godfrey defended the rights of the abbey with greater vigilance in the early years of his rule. Perhaps this was the case, but appearances can be deceptive. Later measures may not be documented, as is demonstrably the case with certain royal grants. In 1311, the king ordered Hugh le Despenser, justice of the forest south of the Trent, to allow the abbot his long established tithe of venison taken in Northamptonshire. This was duly copied into the register (233), yet it is clear from Chancery records that it was not the only grant of its kind. As it happens, this particular writ was not enrolled on the close rolls, but earlier writs from 1298 and 1301, which were, do not appear in either register.[73] Constant action was required to prevent privileges from erosion, but a less rigorous attitude was sometimes taken towards documenting it.

Debts to the crown, by contrast, are quite well represented, often in the form of copies of Exchequer records. The agreement of 1300 that the 1000 mark fine for custody of the abbey during the vacancy should be paid in annual instalments of 100 marks was recorded (144-A). This was in addition to the king's customary request that one of his clerks, John Bush, should be found a benefice and the need to provide him with a pension of £5 p.a. until this could be done (108).[74] Most debts were incurred through tax liability or the obligation to provide military service. Abbot Godfrey inherited the remains of a £200 fine for service in Scotland (144) and, only in 1311, secured acquittance of a 500 mark fine made by Richard of London with Edward I for service in Gascony. This was conceded on the grounds that the king had not, in the event, gone in person and the service had not generally been performed (237–A). Service in Scotland continued to be a charge on abbey finances under

73 *Cal Close, 1296–1302*, pp. 173–4, 416, 464, 468.

74 Bush was presented to Fiskerton church in 1301 (159). The same request had been made to Abbot William on behalf of John de Drax in 1295 (14).

Edward II, as did the levy of tenths in 1302–3, 1310–11 and 1315 (254, 263, 285–7).

Like Abbot William's register, that of his successor contains very few charters. As a result, Abbot Godfrey's efforts to recover control over abbey fee are represented elliptically through associated documents. Thus, his most important recovery, the manor and advowson of Lullington (Lutton, part of Luddington in Northamptonshire), lies behind the corrody agreements of 1304 and 1306 with John son of Gregory of Lullington, the vendor (188, 209), and consent to the transfer in 1304 by John Marmioun, his immediate overlord (151). The latter was required in order to secure the king's licence to acquire the estate in mortmain. Like other houses in the same situation, the abbey used an agent to handle the transfer, choosing John son of Thomas of Oundle, bailiff of the liberty.[75] Whittlesey, as ever, fills in the details, noting that the whole transaction cost £337 8s 9d and that, as well as the original purchase price, Abbot Godfrey also paid off a 40 mark debt owed by John of Lullington to Walter of Finchingfield, and then paid John himself a further sum in order to reduce his entitlement under the corrody agreement.[76] Separate action was required in 1306 to recover the advowson from the earl of Atholl, to whom it had descended under an enfeoffment of 1248 (81, 190).[77]

There was a less happy outcome to attempts to regain control over the manor and castle of Thorpe Waterville. These, together with holdings at Achurch and Aldwinckle, had fallen through a series of transfers into the hands of Walter Langton, bishop of Coventry and Lichfield and royal treasurer.[78] According to Whittlesey, on Langton's disgrace and the seizure of his estates by the crown, John of Milton, the abbot's bailiff, suggested that he himself should seek custody of the estate because it lay within the liberty. Although the abbot successfully arranged for this, John of Milton died shortly afterwards and the castle was then granted to Earl Warenne. It subsequently passed from one magnate to another according to their fortunes in the fraught politics of Edward II's middle years.[79] The fate of this estate illustrates all too clearly why it was necessary for the abbey to intervene wherever possible to prevent outsiders intruding on abbey fee. All this is hidden from view in the register however. The only hint is given by copies of the accounts rendered at the Exchequer in 1311 by John of Milton's heir, William, for revenue from the time the estates were in his father's keeping (235, 255).

---

75 *Cal. Pat. 1301–7*, pp. 241–2.

76 Sparke, pp. 162–3, 174.

77 *Henry of Pytchley*, p. 48.

78 *Ibid.*, p. 41; A Beardwood, 'The Trial of Walter Langton, Bishop of Lichfield, 1307–1312', *Trans. American Philosophical Society*, NS, liv (1964), pp. 19–20, 33, 35.

79 *Ibid.*, p. 42; Sparke, pp. 172–3.

The register also deals with lesser questions of seignorial interest. In 1300, 90 acres of land and a sheepfold at La Biggin, held at farm by John son of Thomas of Oundle, were exchanged for a life tenancy of 30 acres of demesne land in Oundle (140). Three years later, Geoffrey de la Mare surrendered his claim to a market at Northborough in a negotiated settlement which included remission of his debts to the abbey. This was further secured by a court judgement in 1304 (173, 176). The reason why several earlier deeds (224–5, 239–40) were included in the register is no longer clear. Nor is it evident why the particular scattering of charters dealing with small conveyances to and from the abbey and the record of minor litigation should have merited selection; they are unlikely to have comprised Abbot Godfrey's entire land dealings. Perhaps the most interesting of these minor deeds are two relating to a property in London, held by the abbey from the chapter of St Paul's and situated next to its brewhouse. Part of this tenement was granted in 1308 to Thomas son of Martin de Iseldon' in return for his agreement to pay rent to the canons for the whole site (223-A).

The importance to the abbot of homages and acts of fealty is obvious and they are entered in three major sections (113, 115, 265–77), together with a small number elsewhere in the text (219–222). Entries were normally brief with nothing about the terms on which tenements were held. An interesting exception is the holding of Richard son of Stephen in Irthlingborough for part of which he owed the duty of providing a horse and groom to carry flour for the abbot for 40 days in time of war (113N). Most were taken at the abbey or on its estates, but in March 1300, Geoffrey de Lucy and John Spigurnel paid homage and fealty at the New Temple in full parliament (113D). It is also interesting to note that in 1303 Walter Langton paid homage as well as fealty for his holdings notwithstanding his ecclesiastical status (113O). Despite the missing folios, these records appear to cover the entire abbacy. Blank folios were set aside so that the ceremonies could be entered as they took place, with new sections set aside when the first were full. As one would expect of a longer abbacy, the number of acts of homage and fealty was much greater than those under Abbot William. This was also true of letters to the bishop requesting presentation to abbey livings. Interestingly, however, there were only two manumissions, the same number as under Abbot William, one of which conferred freedom on Richard of Fiskerton, the abbot's chamberlain (166, 179).

A modest sidelight on abbey administration is provided by texts in both Latin and French of the oath required of its officials (168-A), together with a handful of miscellaneous documents.[80] Among these are an undated summary of the rents, farms and customs from abbey manors (154) and

80 For oaths by specific individuals, either servants of the abbey or at the termination of a dispute, see 108A, 183, 185, 205.

a list of the knights' fees of the abbey drawn up *c.* 1200 (246). The latter follows on from the only known text of the Northamptonshire Survey, one of three East Midland county surveys belonging to the early twelfth century.[81] Drawn up originally between 1100–20, it was up-dated in Henry II's reign, making it a complex and difficult document to interpret, although exceedingly useful for a period in which evidence for land-holding is scarce. First printed in translation by J. H. Round in 1902, there is now a Latin edition recently published as part of a prosopographical study of Domesday tenants by K. S. B. Keats-Rohan.[82]

Like its predecessor, Abbot Godfrey's register contains a few grants to the convent. Those of earlier abbots were confirmed in 1301, together with an additional grant of malt and freedom from multure within his jurisdiction, should the convent need to grind corn outside the abbey (155). In 1307, he granted the brothers at Oxney grange 13lbs of cheese p.a. and a weekly supply of milk and butter from his manor at Eye (212). For further information about his augmentation of the convent's endowment, as for so much else, one has to rely on Whittlesey.[83]

Few other religious houses feature in the register of this abbacy. The most important recorded transaction is the permission granted to Sulby Abbey in 1300 to hold the manor of Little Addington (124), where it had been acquiring property on Peterborough fee for the past century.[84] The 10 mark relief payable on the occasion of each vacancy at Sulby and the obligation to pay suit of court at Castor agreed at that time were subsequently remitted by Peterborough in 1308 (125, 131).

The close proximity of Thorney Abbey resulted in continuing friction between the two houses. Abbot Godfrey claimed the right to hunt in the abbot of Thorney's warren at Yaxley and Stanground under a blanket privilege granted by Richard I, but this was surrendered in return for two convenient parcels of pasture land in 1303. At the same time, the two houses agreed to set up boundary marks, agreed by a jury, on the river bank between Fletton and Stanground (174). A more bitter dispute in 1306 concerned a complaint by the abbot of Thorney that a horse had been stolen by the abbot of Peterborough and his men on the footpath between Eye and 'Harlotesford'. A right of way was at issue and the mediation of no less a person than Walter Langton was required before settlement was reached (195-A).

---

81 J. H. Round, *Feudal England* (London, 1895, repr. 1964), pp. 149–81. K. S. B. Keats-Rohan, *Domesday People: A Prosopography of Persons Occurring in English Documents 1066–1166* (Woodbridge, 1999), Apps I and II.

82 Round, *VCH Northants*, vol. I, pp. 365–89; Keats-Rohan, *Domesday People*, App. II, pp. 98–117. It is also available in the form of an interactive CD, *Continental Origins of English Landholders 1066–1166. A Prosopogaphy of Post-Conquest England compiled from the Sources* (Coel Enterprises Ltd, 2000) forthcoming.

83 Sparke, pp. 156, 158–61.

84 *VCH, Northants.*, vol. III, pp. 160–1.

Apart from a letter of 1300 to the abbot of Crowland about relations within the abbey, possibly written, *ex officio*, as president of the General Chapter (122), and an occasion in 1304 when Abbot Godfrey and the sacrist were given custody of two delinquent clerks, pending their judgement by the ecclesiastical courts (177), there is little to show that he played an any more active role in the wider ecclesiastical community than in secular government. The register merely contains the appointments of several proctors (112, 139-A, 143) and a few circular letters from other churchmen. In 1321, the presidents of the General Chapter wrote about the purchase of a house for the Carmelites in Oxford (297). There is also an almost illegible letter from the bishop of Lincoln ordering the excommunication of the unknown assailants of a monk of Crowland. Apparently he had been attacked by 'satellites of Satan' on the road between Frieston and Crowland and, having sought sanctuary in Spalding church, was kept immured there, like a thief, in inhumane conditions (302).

The outside world is also represented by Boniface VIII's letter of 1300 to Edward I rallying support for the recovery of the Holy Land (126), and the long and somewhat specious letter sent by Edward to Boniface in the following year, justifying his claim to lordship over the king of Scotland and complaining about atrocities committed by the invading Scottish army (150). Horror stories involving the cutting off of women's breasts and slaughter of infants are so much a commonplace of war propaganda that the latter should not perhaps be taken on trust. Measures set in place in 1306 to secure the realm before the king left to deal with the rebellion of Robert Bruce are quoted in a letter from the sheriff of Northampton to the bailiffs of the liberty (248). There is also the copy of a royal letter of 1320 addressing problems of law and order, in response to petitions in parliament (301). The suppression of the Templars in England, following the savage attack on the order by Philip IV of France, is echoed in a summons to convocation in 1311 to discuss the accusation of heresy levelled against them (238). The abbey itself was a minor victim of the confiscation of Templar property. The abbot complained that silver vessels pledged as security for a loan of a 100 marks had been forfeit, leaving him without satisfaction for the debt (291).

There is less about the levying of taxes in this register, reflecting the generally less oppressive tax regime of Edward II's reign.[85] There are however orders, in French, for the collection of the twentieth and fifteenth granted shortly after his accession (213). Copies were also made of royal inquisitions held in the three Northamptonshire hundreds of Nassaburgh, Huxloe and Polebrook in 1315 to determine liability for scutage (280–2). Papal taxation is represented by a letter of 1300 from Bartholomew de

85 J. F. Willard, *Parliamentary Taxes on Personal Property: A Study in Medieval Financial Administration* (Cambridge, Mass., 1934), p. 10; Prestwich, *Edward I*, p. 569. The period of heaviest taxation did however coincide with the Great Famine.

Ferentino, canon of St Paul's, claiming £500 from the crusading tenth, levied by Pope Gregory X, which had been deposited with the monks by Geoffrey de Vezano, the papal legate (123). The abbey's continuing lively concern about the burdens imposed by its twin masters is expressed in two documents in which it set out its own tax liability (250–1).

THE *TAXATIO ECCLESIASTICA* OF 1291 AND THE VALUATION OF NORWICH OF 1254

The White Book concludes with 24 folios listing valuations for spiritualities in the archdeaconries of Oxford, Buckingham, Bedford, Huntingdon, St Alban's and part of Northampton from the 1291 *Taxatio* of Pope Nicholas IV, with those of the 1254 Valuation of Norwich set alongside (305–305ZK). The contemporary rubric noted that the rural deanery of Rutland had been omitted from the archdeaconry of Northampton, but other rural deaneries are also missing, including that of Peterborough. It also failed to mention the inclusion of the archdeaconry of St Alban's (305ZG) after the archdeaconry of Huntingdon, possibly because of its small size and distinctive status as a peculiar.[86] The text terminates with the rural deanery of Weldon in the archdeaconry of Northampton. In the seventeenth century, John Vincent noted that 'the remainder of this shire and of Rutland was torn out of ye book'.[87] He was wrong about Rutland which, as the heading makes clear, was never part of the compilation, so he may not be a reliable guide as to the reasons for the missing rural deaneries. It remains an open question therefore as to whether the text of the assessments was subsequently damaged, only partially bound up with the register or simply unfinished.

Although bound into the White Book, the valuations do not seem to have formed part of Abbot Godfrey's register. The hand is similar to those of scribes engaged on the two registers and there is another, and shorter, extract from the *Taxatio* included in Abbot Godfrey's register (146), but the two are very different. The shorter text includes temporalities as well as spiritualities and its coverage is almost completely different. Only places belonging to Peterborough were selected, mostly from the rural deanery of Peterborough itself. Total valuations for the rural deaneries of Lincolnshire and Rutland were appended in what appears to have been an afterthought. Neither feature in 305–305ZK which, unlike the Record Commission text, excludes totals altogether. Both valuations have long been in print, but I have included them in the present edition partly for the sake of completeness, but also as an interim measure because the 1802

86 Six rural deaneries are missing from the Archdeaconry of Northampton: Rothwell, Oundle, Northampton, Haddon, Peterborough and Higham. Risborough in the archdeaconry of Buckingham is also missing. For the archdeaconry of St Alban's see ed. W. Page, *VCH, Herts*, vol. IV, pp. 362–3.

87 BL, Cott. Vesp. E xxi, fo. 34r.

Record Commission edition of the *Taxatio* is widely recognised as inadequate.[88] It was based on a late medieval Exchequer transcript, the defects of which were not entirely overcome by collation with earlier texts from the Exchequer and the Cotton and Harleian collections.[89] As the modern edition for the archdeaconry of Buckingham prepared by Michael Franklin shows, the production of a new and definitive edition of the entire assessment will be a formidable task.[90] However, a major project is now under way to publish such an edition in electronic form.[91] A great many copies of the assessment survive, either in whole or in part, among royal and episcopal records, from the papal Curia and in the archives of religious houses. The task of the editors is further complicated by its long after life as the basis for taxation of the clergy for the rest of the Middle Ages. Copies reflect the different needs of those who made them and later revisions, made both by the crown and papacy, were not always incorporated in subsequent texts.[92] The fact that spiritualities valued at less than six marks were exempt from taxation at the time the earliest Exchequer rolls were compiled has a striking effect on what the Record Commission edition records when compared with the Peterborough text. Franklin calculated that the Record Commission edition for the archdeaconry of Buckingham omitted 24% of the benefices and 50% of the vicarages.[93] An even higher proportion of vicarages were missing from the Record Commission edition for the other archdeaconries.[94] The nineteenth-century text remains superior however in more often recording the names of chapels and totalling valuations. Omissions apart, there is a large measure of agreement between the two texts although valuations in the Record Commission edition occasionally appear mis-transcribed, as in the rural deaneries of Witney (305H) and St Ives (305Y).

The 1254 assessment did not become redundant immediately after the *Taxatio* was drawn up. The crown allowed at least some of the clergy to pay the tenth of 1297–8 on the basis of the earlier valuation and churchmen continued to make use of it for their own purposes.[95] There were therefore practical reasons why the monks of Peterborough might have wished to

88 *Taxatio Ecclesiastica* (Rec. Comm., 1802), pp. 30–9; ed. W. E. Lunt, *The Valuation of Norwich* (Oxford, 1926), pp. 264–314. For the relationship of the valuations to the registers, see below, p. xl.

89 Lunt, *Financial Relations*, p. 666.

90 M. J. Franklin, 'The Assessment of Benefices for Taxation in Thirteenth Century Buckinghamshire', *Nottingham Medieval Studies*, xxix (1985), pp. 73–98.

91 http://irwell.mimas.ac.uk/taxatio/info.html; S. Davnall, J. Denton, S. Griffiths. D. Ross, B. Taylor, 'The *Taxatio* Database', *Bulletin of the John Rylands University Library of Manchester*, 74 (1992), pp. 89–108.

92 Lunt, *Financial Relations*, pp. 350–5.

93 Franklin, *Nottingham Medieval Studies* (1985), p. 83.

94 62% for Oxford; 79% for Bedford; 54% for Huntingdon; 82% for St Alban's; 56% for Northampton.

95 Lunt, *Valuation*, pp. 167–9.

compare the two assessments at this time and it is generally agreed that this was when the text in the White Book was created. There is nevertheless very little internal evidence against which this speculation can be checked. The attribution of a portion from Quainton church in Buckinghamshire to Roger de Viens, whereas Hugh de Vyens was recorded as the former holder in the Record Commission edition may offer a clue, but so far neither man has proved traceable.[96] Welwyn, which appears at the end of the Record Commission text with a note that it was added on 22 November 1318, is incorporated into the body of the Peterborough entry for the rural deanery of Hertford. Although this could be taken to imply that the Peterborough text post-dates 1318, such a late date is unlikely. The discrepancy is more plausibly explained by an earlier exemption of Welwyn for some reason.[97]

Lunt in his edition of the Valuation of Norwich preferred a MS from St Katherine's without Lincoln (designated A) as his principal text for Lincoln diocese because it covered the whole diocese, appeared to be the earlier of the two manuscripts and, unlike the Peterborough text, was not for the most part subordinated to the order of the 1291 Taxatio, but he meticulously collated it with the Peterborough text (designated B).[98] Unfortunately nothing is known about the provenance of the Peterborough version and it cannot be dated with precision. The Valuation was revised in 1255 and 1256.[99] This is reflected in Lunt's A text which gives revised valuations alongside entries in certain rural deaneries especially in the archdeaconry of Oxford.[100] These revised figures generally accord with the valuations of the Peterborough text, but where no revisions are given, either in the archdeaconry of Oxford or elsewhere, the Peterborough text sometimes differs considerably.[101] This suggests that the original from which it was drawn may have recorded valuations which were more extensively revised than those of Lunt's A text. It is still likely to have been an early version however, since the A text has two entries in the archdeaconry of Northampton which were noted as not being part of the original assessment and which are not present in the Peterborough copy either (305ZH and ZJ).

If the present edition does not add appreciably to Lunt's careful work on the Norwich Valuation, it has the merit of making the Peterborough text more accessible, since in Lunt's edition, the points of divergence from his A text are recorded in footnotes and the order in most rural

96 *Taxatio*, p. 34 (305P).

97 *Taxatio*, p. 37 (305ZE).

98 Lunt, *Valuation*, pp. 172–3. Three rural deaneries in Lunt's A text follow the same order as the *Taxatio* (305V, 305ZA, 305ZK). All are in different archdeaconries.

99 *Ibid.*, pp. 84–6, 95.

100 Henley, Aston, Cuddesdon, Woodstock, Witney, and Deddington. Lunt, *Valuation*, pp. 304–10.

101 305A, F, G, I (Oxon.), 305J–N (Bucks).

deaneries is different. There is an added bonus in having the two valuations side by side. It should prove a convenience to modern scholars, just as it was to those who first thought to juxtapose them.

THE MANUSCRIPT AND ITS TRANSMISSION

The abbey's records had a chequered history following the Dissolution. Relatively few remained in the possession of the Dean and Chapter of the newly constituted cathedral and the White Book was no exception. Sir Robert Wingfield, who was one of the commissioners involved in establishing the new see of Peterborough, was probably its first lay owner since it was in the possession of his descendant, another Robert Wingfield, in 1636. In the following year it was in the hands of Sir Christopher Hatton who, according to a note on the fly leaf of the MS, gave it to the Cotton Library, where it is now to be found along with a number of other Peterborough compilations.[102]

In the antiquarian fervour for which the seventeenth and eighteenth centuries were so remarkable, extensive transcripts, either in full or abbreviated form, were made from the White Book. Among those made in the seventeenth century are Bodl. MS Dodsworth 75 (1639) and 86 (1636 and associated with Dean and Chapter MS 17 in Cambridge University Library made in the same year), together with slightly later transcripts made by John Vincent in 1641 and 1659. A century later, David Casley, deputy keeper of the Cotton Library also made copies for John Bridges, whose history of Northamptonshire was published in 1791. White Kennett, bishop of Peterborough from 1718 to 1728, also drew on it.[103] Before his death, William Mellows had transcribed a large portion of the manuscript, along with the others he was preparing for ultimate publication. Most of this work is now gathered together in a single file, but transcriptions of some individual documents are scattered among his other notes, ordered by subject matter. The White Book transcripts passed,

---

102 Cott. Vesp. Exxii. Other Peterborough MSS in the Cotton collection are Cleop. C, i–ii (Great Book of John of Achurch); Nero, C, vii (rentals and surveys of the demesne manors); Faustina, B, iii (register of George Fraunceys); Vesp. E, xxi (register of Adam of Boothby). Otho, A, xvii was destroyed in the Cotton fire of 1731. Other Peterborough MSS are also to be found in other BL collections. Martin, *Cartularies*, pp. xv–xvii and *passim*.

103 Martin, *Cartularies*, p. 36; Vincent's transcripts are in BL, Cott. Vesp. E xxi, fos 3r–31 and Bodl. MS Wood C 3, fos 1r–37v; Casley's in Bodl., MS Top. Northants., c 23, fos 99r–196v. Bodl. MS Dodsworth 86 contains transcripts at fos 1r–9r, 37v, 69r and 71r–102v. Symonds D'Ewes' transcripts are in BL, Harl. 294, fos 183v–5r, Harl. 298, fos 70v–1v and Harl. 312, fos 52r–4r. Those made for White Kennett are in BL, Lansdowne, 991, fos 1r–12r and Lansdowne, 993, fos 3r–42v. Transcripts in the Bodleian Library in particular are more extensive than Martin indicates, not least because the tax assessments and Northamptonshire Survey were often included.

with the rest of his papers, to Northamptonshire Record Office, where they are now indexed and available.[104]

The manuscript itself consists of 146 folios 25.5cm by 18cm, which are pricked and ruled, except where cropping has removed the prickings. The parchment is of good quality with occasional stitching, as at fo.99. A few folios are also imperfectly squared. The first 54 folios are foliated with heavy, contemporary Roman numerals at the top centre. Fos 55–120 are also foliated in Roman numerals in a lighter contemporary hand in the same position. The remainder, principally consisting of the valuations of 1291 and 1254 (305–305ZK), are foliated in later arabic numerals at the top right. The manuscript is currently bound in a Cotton Library binding, but in the transcripts made in 1636, it was referred to as the White Book, presumably indicating an original white leather binding.[105]

As the editor of the Book of William Morton, another Cotton manuscript, found, the tightness of the present binding makes collation extremely difficult. Catchwords appear at the end of quires at fos 12v, 58v, 74v and 132v and possibly 66v, but not otherwise. A single folio is missing between fos 67–8 and five in the quire beginning fo.106. The contemporary foliation also indicates that thirty folios are missing between fos 105–6. These had already disappeared by the seventeenth century as transcripts contain none of the missing material and show the same gap in the contemporary foliation.[106] Both the Northamptonshire Survey (245) and the valuations of 1254 and 1291 (305–305ZK) begin on separate quires. The absence of contemporary foliation on the folios containing the valuations suggests that this part of the text may have been a later addition. The quire containing the Northamptonshire Survey is also distinctive in that, unlike other quires, where the pricking is on the outer edge of the folio, here the pricking is on the inner side of the margins. However, if the Survey was originally separate from the register, the Roman foliation indicates that it must have been incorporated at an early date. Both were certainly part of the White Book by the 1636, so the association of the valuations with the registers antedates the Cotton re-binding.

There is no sharp break in foliation between the registers of Abbot William and Abbot Godfrey, nor is it clear whether the opening of Abbot Godfrey's register, which is the second entry on fo. 45r, is on a fresh quire. Both the contemporary foliation and the references given in Pytchley provide additional evidence that the two registers were closely related from the start.[107] Individual scribes can be identified as having contributed

104 NRO, X7528, File F (c), (The White Book). This is a partial transcript. Transcriptions of other parts of the register can also be found among files dealing with individual aspects of the abbey.

105 Bodl. MS Dodsworth 75, fo. 87v; CUL, Peterborough D and C, MS 17, flyleaf note.

106 Bodl. MD Dodsworth, 86, fos 67v–8r.

107 *Henry of Pytchley*, p. 48; fo. 81r (190).

to both compilations. As one would expect, the registers appear to have grown over time as successive scribes made entries. The heading *anno secundo* across fos 6v–7r reveals a methodical approach to the early compilation. It is the only such example however. A good many documents were added out of sequence, particularly in the later part of Abbot Godfrey's register. It is not always easy to discriminate between the different hands, nor to be sure whether distinctive conventions were employed by a single scribe. However, it is clear that a number of scribes made entries to the registers and that their work is interspersed among that of others rather than each completing a stint. One scribe, writing *c.* 1300 under both Abbot William and Abbot Godfrey, has a particularly idiosyncratic habit of inserting three points before the initial or name of the abbot or comparable ecclesiastical dignitary (e.g. 127–8), but he was not unique in doing this. The same convention was employed a generation later in Adam of Boothby's register.[108] Where documents were added subsequently, some are squeezed in or overlap into the margins (28, 131). Others are in demonstrably later hands (e.g. 64, 151). A number of entries, especially those dealing with grants of land or oaths, have rubrics in large heavy lettering similar to the heavy Roman foliation. Others, often royal or ecclesiastical documents, have no rubrics at all. The remainder have rubrics in letters of varying size, located either above the document to the left, centred or, occasionally, marginated.

The manuscript is generally well written, in clear and accurate hands, although it inevitably has the appearance of a working volume rather than one destined to be an object of beauty in itself. Where there are texts common to the White Book and Swaffham, the White Book often has the more accurate text, although it sometimes records fewer witnesses. It is far less elegant in appearance and systematic in content than the contemporary cartulary known as the Red Book of Thorney, but where they have documents in common, there is nothing to choose between the competence of the scribes. This is the more creditable as the Thorney cartulary obviously had immense care lavished on it, whereas the White Book appears to have been one of many, purely functional, compilations emanating from a large and busy house.

EDITING CONVENTIONS

The text has been edited according to the precepts laid down by R. F. Hunnisett in *Editing Records for Publication*.[109] My principal aim has been to provide a text which is faithful to the original while, at the same time remaining comfortable for a modern reader. Although the general standard of accuracy and legibility throughout the registers is high,

108 E.g. BL, Cott. Vesp. E xxi, fos 49v–51v.
109 Archives and the User 4, British Record Association, 1977.

consistency of spelling and grammar were not familiar concepts. This can present problems when extending words. For example, both *ad Pascha* and *ad Pascham* can be found. Of the two, *ad Pascha* appears the commoner, so I have adopted it throughout when extending. I have extended words where the endings are unambiguous, but especially where it is not clear whether a singular or plural is indicated I have left them unextended. Proper names have not been extended either. Evidence elsewhere in the text would sometimes permit plausible extension, but contemporary variation in spelling makes standardisation questionable. Where they can be identified with a measure of certainty, the modern form of place names has been used for toponyms in the introduction and commentaries. Words such as *Anglie*, where there is a well recognised form, have usually been rendered in full. Where possible, weights and measures and money have been extended in deeds, but provided with standard abbreviations in financial documents. Pounds, shillings, pence, halfpennies and farthings thus appear as *li. s. d. ob. qa.*, marks as *m.*, and quarters, bushels and skeps as *qa. bus. esk'.*

With a few exceptions, spellings have been rendered as they appear in the text. Likely errors have been footnoted or marked [sic] in the text. However, particularly in the long and difficult correspondence dealing with taxation and national affairs, the variations between surviving texts are so numerous that only those affecting the sense of the text have been noted. All editors have to make decisions about particular letters. *Eciam* and *tocius* have been spelt throughout with a *c* rather than a *t*, although practice varied over the text as a whole and it is often possible to distinguish between the two. Similarly, *t* has been preferred to *c*, or vice versa, in words such as *presentatio* or *reverencia* in order to reflect the equivalents in modern English. Scribes appear to have used *i* or *j* fairly randomly in words such as *judicium*. I have preferred *j* in place of the *i* of the text or a *v* in place of *u* where it facilitates understanding. Capitalisation and punctuation have been generally modernised.

There are a considerable number of marginalia, some of which are contemporary or were added later in the middle ages. These have been noted. Most were simple place or personal names, designed to draw attention to the content of particular documents. There are however occasional cross references within the register (195A, 243) and detailed information as to the whereabouts of the original in the royal records (149F, 244). Post medieval annotations have been ignored unless they contain information of interest.

Almost all the documents included in the registers can be closely dated. The exceptions tend to be the early deeds copied into William of Woodford's register. Where no date is recorded, the presence of witnesses can sometimes help. The White Book scribes were usually conscientious in recording these, but occasionally they have been supplied from elsewhere (48). Unusually, document 107 seems to have dated the beginning of the year from 25 December rather than 25 March. No other instance of this can be identified, however, so 25 March has been adopted for dating purposes throughout.

Collation with other texts, especially those in other Peterborough compilations, has been undertaken where possible, but is unlikely to be complete. As with errors, minor differences have not been noted between the White Book and other texts. Papal bulls and other documents of wider importance had such wide currency that they can be found in too many copies to be worth systematic pursuit. Copies that have come to my attention have however been noted. No attempt has been made to collate the texts of the valuations with anything other than the printed texts or to provide detailed notes to accompany the text of the Northamptonshire Survey. To do either would have been to distort the purpose of the edition to an unwarrantable extent and to duplicate the more specialised work embodied in the major new editions.

William of Woodford's register

[fo. 1r] REGISTRUM WILLELMI ABBATIS DE BURGO DE AN[NO] PRIMO[1]

1 Plea in the Court of Common Pleas of Geoffrey de la Mare against the abbot claiming his right to the office of constable as held by his predecessors, with the duties of leading the abbot's men in the royal army in time of war and setting the first dish before each abbot on the occasion of his installation feast and with rights of residence in the abbey and an annual clothing allowance, the use of the gold and silver utensils at the installation feast and the provision of his equipment when on military service for the abbot. The abbot replied that the constableship was incorporeal and not held in demesne, so he should not respond to the writ. [Michaelmas Term 1294]

Placita in banco de termino sancti Michaelis anno regni regis Edwardi xxii. Rotulo xlix[2]

Galfridus de la Mare petit versus abbatem de Burgo Sancti Petri ballivam constabularie abbathie de Burgo Sancti Petri cum pertinenciis, de quo Brianus de la Mare proavus predicti Galfridi, cuius heres ipse est, fuit seisitus in dominico suo ut de feodo die quo obiit. Et unde dicit quod predictus Brianus proavus etc., tempore pacis tempore domini Henrici regis patris regis nunc, fuit seisitus de predictam ballivam etc. in dominico suo ut de feodo, scilicet custodiendi homines ipsius abbatis missos in exercitu domini regis tempore guerre etc. ut constabularius etc. Et assidendi primum ferculum coram abbate loci predicti ad communium installamenti cuiuslibet abbatis etc., capiendo inde expletia, scilicet perhendinando in abbathia predicta pro voluntate sua cum tribus a[rmigeris],[3] sex garcionibus, quinque equis et j dextario et duobus leporariis ad custus abbatis loci predicti ut in pane, vino, cervisia, carnibus, piscibus, feno et avena et aliis necessariis. Et similiter capiendo per annum de camera ipsius abbatis duas robas [vel][3] quatuor libras pro robis illis ac eciam percipiendo ad opus suum proprium in eadem abbathia in quolibet installamento cuiuslibet abbatis eiusdem loci omnia utensilia aurea et argentea coram abbate die comunii installamenti sui ad mensam apposita. Capiendo eciam pro se et uno milite in exercitu regis ratione constabularie predicte de predicto abbate equos, armaturam, et alia sibi necessaria dum in servicio ipsius abbatis in exercitu steterit etc. ad valenciam etc. Et de ipso Briano discendit feodum etc. cuidam Galfrido ut filio et heredi et de ipso Galfrido cuidam Briano ut filio et heredi et de ipso Briano qui obiit sine herede de se discendit feodum etc. cuidam Petro ut fratri et heredi et de ipso Petro qui obiit sine herede de se cuidam Radulfo ut fratri et heredi et de ipso Radulfo qui obiit sine herede de se cuidam Galfrido ut fratri et heredi et de ipso Galfrido qui obiit sine herede de se cuidam Petro ut fratri et heredi et de ipso Petro isti Galfrido qui nunc petit [fo. 1v] ut filius et heres et inde producit sectam etc.

Et abbas per attornatum suum venit et dicit quod non debet ei ad hoc breve respondere. Dicit enim quod res incorporee et non tangibiles non sunt de dominico immo tantum de feodo. Et ex quo predictus Galfridus petit predictam ballivam versus eum que est res incorporea et non tangibilis asserendo per breve suum predictum antecessorem inde obiisse in dominico etc. et supponendo ipsum predictam ballivam habuisse in dominico. Et sic ex tenore brevis resultat contrarietas manifesta etc. Petit judicium de brevi etc. Dies datus est eis de audiendo judicio suo hic in crastino Animarum ut de die in diem etc. Et postea ad diem illum venerunt partes etc. Et datus est eis ulterius de audiendo judicio suo in octabis sancti Hilarii eo quod non dum judicium etc.

1 Folio badly faded, but almost completely legible under ultra violet light.
2 See PRO, CP/40/106, m. 49r.
3 Supplied from PRO text.

1A Quitclaim by Geoffrey de la Mare, for sixty marks sterling, of the office of constable for which he impleaded the abbot in the king's court at Westminster, together with a quitclaim of all his rights in the abbey's wood at Peakirk which provided building wood and fuel for his manors of Maxey, Woodcroft and Northborough. [14 Jan. 1296]

Postea facta est concordia inter partes ut sequitur.

Omnibus Christi fidelibus ad quos presens scriptum pervenerit Galfridus de la Mare miles filius domini Petri de la Mare in Makeseye salutem in Domino. Sciatis me remisisse et omnino de me et heredibus meis quietum clamasse domino Willelmo Dei gracia abbati de Burgo Sancti Petri et eiusdem loci conventui et successoribus suis totum jus et clamium quod habui vel habere potui in balliva constabularie abbatie de Burgo Sancti Petri cum pertinenciis unde predictum abbatem in curia domini regis apud Westmonasterium inplacitavi petendo ab eo predictam ballivam ut jus et hereditatem meam cum pertinenciis subscriptis: scilicet jus custodiendi homines ipsius abbatis missos in exercitu domini regis tempore guerre ut constabularius. Et assidendi primum ferculum coram abbate eiusdem abbathie ad comunium installamenti cuiuslibet abbatis eiusdem abbathie. Et habendi ad opus meum proprium omnia utensilia aurea et argentea coram abbate ad mensam posita. Et perhendmandi in predicta abbathia pro voluntate mea cum tribus armigeris, sex garcionibus, quinque equis, uno dextario et duobus leporariis ad custum abbatis eiusdem domus ut in pane, vino, cervisia, carnibus, et pisce, feno et avena et aliis necessariis. Et capiendi per annum de camera ipsius abbatis duas robas vel quatuor libras [fo. 2r] sterlingorum pro robis illis. Et capiendi pro me et uno milite euntibus in exercitu regis ratione constabularie predicte de predicto abbate equos et armaturam at alia nobis necessaria dum in servicio ipsius abbatis in exercitu regis extiterimus. Que omnia predicta pertinencia predictis abbati et conventui et successoribus suis remisi et de me et heredibus meis quietum clamavi. Ita quod nec ego nec heredes mei nec aliquis nomine nostro aliquid juris vel clamii in predicta balliva vel in predictis pertinenciis vel in aliquibus aliis pertinenciis vel rebus que ratione predicte ballive peti poterunt exigere poterimus inperpetuum. Preterea ego Galfridus remisi et quietum clamavi de me et heredibus meis predictis abbati et conventui et successoribus suis totum jus et clamium quod habui vel habere potui in bosco ipsorum abbatis et conventus de Peychirche ad capiendam sustentationem maneriorum meorum de Makeseye, Wodecroft et Northburg' tam pro reparatione et factione domorum mearum quam pro focali. Ita quod nec ego nec heredes me [sic] nec aliquis nomine nostro aliquid in predicto bosco capere vel aliquid juris exigere poterimus inperpetuum. In cuius rei testimonium presenti scripto sigillum meum apposui. Hiis testibus: dominis Johanne Wake, Hugone Wake, Willelmo de Colevil' militibus, Willelmo de Torp', magistro Galfrido de Mak', Gilberto de Sutton' et aliis. Dat' apud Burgum Sancti Petri anno regni regis Edwardi filii regis Henrici xxiiij^o^ in crastino sancti Hilarii anno supradicti.[1]

[subscribed fo. 1v] Pro ista quieta clamacione dedit predictus abbas predicto domino Galfrido de la Mare sexaginta marcas sterlingorum

1 Marginated *xxiiij^o^ ... supradicti.*

1B Quitclaim by Abbot William and the convent to Geoffrey de la Mare and his heirs of all burdens and services attaching to the office of constable, saving the abbey's rights and the military service owed for the fees held of the abbey. [14 Jan. 1296]

[Marginated] Istam predictam litteram fecit predictus abbas predicto domino Galfrido de la Mare.

Omnibus Christi fidelibus ad quos presentes littere pervenerint Willelmus Dei gracia abbas de Burgo Sancti Petri et eiusdem loci conventus salutem in Domino. Noveritis nos unanimi assensu capituli nostri remisisse et omnino pro nobis et successoribus nostris quantum in nobis est inperpetuum quietum clamasse domino Galfrido de la Mare in Makeseye militi et heredibus suis omnia onera et servicia que occasione ballive constabularie abbathie de Burgo Sancti Petri nobis qualitercumque tenebantur. Salvis ecclesie nostre omnibus articulis ad regalitatem spectantibus. Et salvo ecclesie nostre servicio militari pro feodis que idem Galfridus de nobis tenet. Ita quod nec nos nec successores nostri ratione ballive constabularie predicte vel exactionum seu articulorum ballivam illam qualitercumque contingentium versus eosdem Galfridum vel heredes suos decetero quicquam exigere poterimus vel vendicare. In cuius rei testimonium presenti scripto sigillum commune capituli nostri apposuimus. Dat' apud Burgum Sancti Petri in crastino sancti Hilarii anno regni regis Edwardi filii regis Henrici vicesimo quarto.

2 Grant by Abbot William and the convent of a 40s pension to Master Richard of Northampton, their clerk, until such time as they should provide him to a benefice. If he should refuse such a benefice, the pension shall cease. Sealed with the chapter seal because the abbot did not yet have one. [7 Oct. 1295]

[fo. 2v] Pensio magistri Ricardi de Norhamton'.

Omnibus Christi fidelibus presens scriptum visuris vel audituris frater Willelmus Dei gracia abbas de Burgo Sancti Petri et eiusdem loci conventus salutem in Domino sempiternam. Noverit universitas vestra nos unanimi consensu concessisse dilecto clerico nostro magistro Ricardo de Norhamt' xl s. annue pensionis de camera abbatis de Burgo qui pro tempore fuerit percipiendos ad duos anni terminos; videlicet ad festum sancti Michaelis xx s. et ad Pascha xx s. donec eidem in ecclesiastico beneficio providerimus. Si vero beneficium eidem per nos oblatum recipere noluerit, ex tunc cesset predicte pensionis solutio absque ulteriori calumpnia predicti Ricardi. In cuius rei testimonium quia predictus abbas propter creationis sue novitatem sigillum non dum habuit autenticum, sigillum commune capituli de Burgo Sancti Petri de voluntate predicti abbatis presentibus est appensum. Dat' in pleno capitulo nonas Octobris anno Domini M°CC° nonagesimo quinto

3 Letter from Thomas archdeacon of Northampton to all the rural deans in his archdeaconry, except the dean of Rutland, giving instructions for the payment of the tenth of clerical spiritualities and temporalities granted to the king. The letter includes the text of a letter from the abbot of Osney to the archdeacon, dated 7 January 1296, assigning a date for each deanery to appear at Osney and in turn giving the texts of the royal letter appointing the abbot of Osney and the prior of St

Katherine without Lincoln as collectors, dated 11 December 1295, and the letter of Oliver, bishop of Lincoln giving the abbot his authority in this matter, dated 15 December 1295. [9 Jan. 1296]

Contributio facta regi Anglie per clerum hoc anno.

Thomas archidiaconus Norht' univeris decanis per archidiaconatum constitutis, decano Roteland excepto, salutem in autore salutis. Mandatum religiosi viri domini abbatis Osen' una cum mandatis domini regis et venerabilis patris domini Linc' episcopi recepimus sub hac forma:

Abbas Osen' super decima beneficiorum et bonorum ecclesiasticorum domino Edwardo Dei gracia regi Anglie illustri a prelatis et clero Anglie instanti anno concessa collector deputatus, necnon venerabilis patris domini O[liveri] Dei gracia Linc' episcopi in hac parte commissarius, reverende discretionis viro domino archidiacono Norht' vel eius officiali salutem in Domino. Mandatum dictorum dominorum recipimus in hec verba:

E[dwardus] Dei gracia rex Anglie dominus Hybernie et dux Aquitanie dilectis sibi in Christo abbati Osen' et priori sancte Katerine extra Linc' salutem. Cum prelati et totus clerus de regno nostro decimam beneficiorum et bonorum suorum de quibus decima ultimo in subsidium Terre Sancte concessa fuit data nobis in subsidium nostrum de anno presenti juxta taxationem ultimo inde factam liberaliter concesserint et gratanter, beneficiis ecclesiasticis personarum plura beneficia [fo. 3r] ecclesiastica non habentium per eandem taxationem valorem sex marcarum annuatim non excedentibus dumtaxat exceptis. Ita quod una medietas eiusdem decime primo die Marcii proximo futuro et alia medietas in festo sancte Trinitatis proximo sequente nobis persolvantur. Nos de vestra fidelitate et diligencia confidentes assignavimus vos ad dictam decimam secundum taxationem illam in episcopatu Linc' colligendam adunandam et in tuto loco reponendam et salvo custodiendam donec aliud a nobis inde habueritis in mandatis. Et ideo vobis mandamus rogantes quatinus eandem decimam in forma predicta colligatis adunetis et eam in tuto loco reponatis et custodiatis. Ita quod eam promptam et paratam habeatis juxta equales portiones dictis terminis nobis solvendam et liberandam cum super hoc a nobis fueritis requisiti. Et hoc sicut nostrum et vestrum honorem diligitis nullatenus omittatis. Concesserunt eciam nobis dicti prelati quod clerum suarum dyocesarum auctoritate sua quam vobis per litteras suas patentes prestabunt ad solutionem dicte decime ut premittitur faciendam compellere. Valeatis. In cuius rei testimonium has litteras nostras fieri facimus patentes. Teste me ipso apud Westm' xj^{o} die Decembris anno regni nostri xxiiij^{to}.

O[liverus] permissione divina Linc' episcopus dilecto in Christo filio abbati Osen' salutem graciam et benedictionem. Cum prelati et clerus provincie Cantuar' domino meo regi Anglie illustri decimam tam dignitatum quam beneficiorum et provencium suorum ecclesiasticorum beneficiis ad sex marcas et infra taxatis dumtaxat exceptis secundum ultimam taxationem inde factam primo die mensis Marcii pro una medietate et in octabis sancte Trinitatis pro alia medietate solvendam certis et legitimis ex causis nuper London' duxerint concedendam, idem que dominus rex ad colligendam in archidiaconatibus Bugynghamie, Oxon', Huntingdon', Bedeford et Norht', excepto decanatu Roteland, huius subsidium sibi concessum vos elegerit confidentes ut collectionem ipsam statutis temporibus valeatis efficacius expedire, vobis ad hoc faciendum quantum in nobis est plenam potestatem cum cohercione canonica committimus per presentes. Valete. Dat' apud Bukeden' xviij^{o} kalendas Januarii anno Domini M^{o}CC^{o} nonagesimo quinto.

Horum igitur auctoritate mandatorum vobis cum reverencia tantum qua decet firmiter injungendo mandamus quatinus citetis seu citari facitis omnes religiosos, prebendarios, rectores, vicarios, pensionarios et portionarios infra limites vestri [fo. 3v] archidiaconatus existentes qui ad solutionem dicte decime secundum declarationem superius notatam tenentur quatinus sub pena suspensionis, excommunicationis majoris et interdicti quod compareant coram nobis apud Osen' diebus singulis decanatibus inferius assignatis ad solvendi [sic] primam medietatem decime benficiorum suorum: videlicet de decanatu de Brakele ix^{o} kalendas Marcii; de decanatu de Daventre viij^{o} kalendas eiusdem; de decanatu de Preston' vij^{o} kalendas eiusdem; de decanatu de Weldon' vj^{to} kalendas eiusdem; de decanatu de Rodwelle v^{to} kalendas eiusdem; de decanatu de Undel' iiij^{to} kalendas eiusdem; de decanatu Norht' iij^{o} kalendas eiusdem; de decanatu de Haddon' ij^{o} kalendas eiusdem; de decanatu de Burgo kalendas eiusdem; de decanatu de Hecham iiij^{to} nonas eiusdem. Injungatis insuper decanis et apparitoribus vestris quod prout se optent servare indempnes tam publice et rite citent et moneant omnes supradictos quod nullus per ignoranciam diei sibi prefixi possit se excusare prout retroactis temporibus frequenter plures se excusarunt. Quid autem inde feceritis nos circa festum purificationis beate Marie virginis proximum sequens per litteras vestras patentes harum seriem continentes distinate et aperte certificare curetis. Valete. Dat' apud Osen' vij^{o} idus Januarii anno Domini M^{o}CC^{o} nonagesimo quinto.

Quocirca vobis firmiter injungendo mandamus quatinus inscriptis mandatis supradictis et plenius intellectis juxta formam et tenorem eorumdem omnes religiosos, prebendarios, rectores, vicarios, pensionarios et portionarios qui dictam decimam solvere tenentur prout vestris subjacent decanatibus citatis peremptorie quod sub penis superius annotatis diebus eisdem prout supradictum assignati apud Osen' compareant primam medietatem decime beneficiorum et bonorum suorum soluturam et de eadem plenarie satisfacturam citationem quam feceritis per vos seu apparitores vestros locis omnibus quibus expedit rea diligenter et sollempniter publicantes quod excusationem ignorancie nullus pretendere possit, veri similiter in hac parte et vos ipsos positis servare indempnes. Et quid in premissis feceritis unusquisque vestrum quatenus ipsum tangit nobis constare faciat infra triduum post festum conversionis sancti Pauli proximo futuro per litteras suas patentes harum seriem continentes. Valete. Dat' apud Walden' v° idus Januarii anno Domini supradicto.

3A Note that the abbot and obedientiaries paid the tenth of their spiritualities and temporalities with the clergy and not the laity because the laity were paying an eleventh part of their goods.

[fo. 4r] In ista contributione solverunt abbas et obedientiarii de Burgo decimam tam temporalium quam spiritualium bonorum cum clero et non cum laicis quia laici solvebant tantum undecim partem bonorum suorum.

4 The findings of an inquisition made by Abbot William into the amount of clothing and provisions allowed annually by the abbey to the leper hospital of St Leonard in Peterborough. [Aug. 1295–6]

De hospitali leprosorum.

Hoc[1] anno fecit abbas Willelmus inquirere de rebus assisis quas infirmi hospitalis sancti Leonardi capiunt de abbate per annum. Et compertum est per inquisitionem ut sequitur: Infirmi de hospitali sancti Leonardi capiunt de abbate per annum quadraginta ulnas panni de panno elemosine sicut prebendarii. Item ad festum sancti Martini j petram uncti et j petram sepi. Item in baconibus; videlicet j ad festum natalis Domini et j ad capud Quadragesime et j ad Pascha de carnibus supersanatis. Item totum exitum porcorum supersanatorum. Item iiij cuvatas cervisie; videlicet j cuvatam ad natale Domini. Et aliam ad capud Quadragesime. Et tertiam ad Pascha. Et quartam ad festum apostolorum Petri et Pauli de celario abbatis. Item quolibet mense j eskeppam salis cuius summa per annum est j quarter v eskeppe. Item serviens dictorum infirmorum comedet cum familia abbatis quarter per annum; videlicet ad natale Domini et ad Pascha et ad festum sancti Petri et ad festum Omnium Sanctorum.

[Marginated] iidem capiunt ij multones ad festum apostolorum Petri et Pauli, vel precium in argento xl d videlicet; pro bidente xx d.

1 For commentary, see *VCH, Northants.*, vol. II, p. 162.

5 Letters dimissory from Abbot William concerning the admission of Brother John de Hale into the Cistercian abbey of Pipewell to live a more austere life. [4 May 1296]

Littere dimissorie fratris Johannis de Hale.

Omnibus Christi fidelibus presentes litteras visuris vel audituris frater Willelmus permissione divina monasterii de Burgo Sancti Petri minister humilis salutem in auctore salutis. Cum frater Johannes de Hale monasterii de Burgo monachus ordinis sancti Benedicti nulla que conjecturari potuit levitate seu temeritate ductus, sed ut creditur divinitus inspiratus, religionem affectaverit artiorem, frugem concupiscens vite melioris, ac religiosi viri abbas et conventus de Pippewell' ordinis Cistersiensis eundem fratrem suo ferventi moti desiderio, necnon ex affectione hactenus erga monasterium de Burgo habita specialiter inducti, in sua religiosa congregatione recipere sint parati dictum fratrem Johannem ut ordinem Cistersiensem in predicto monasterio de Pippewell' libere profiteri valeat et observare, de fratrum meorum consilio et assensu licencio per presentes has litteras [fo. 4v] dimissorias eidem de predictorum fratrum consilio et assensu faciens testimoniales. Dat' apud Burgum in crastino ascensionis Domini anno gracie M^{o}CC^{o} nonagesimo sexto.

6 Bull *clericis laicos* of Pope Boniface VIII forbidding churchmen to pay taxes to secular authorities on pain of the excommunication of both parties. [24–25 Feb. 1296]

Bonefacius[1] [servus servorum Dei].[2] Ad perpetuam rei memoriam clericis laicos infestos opido tradit antiquitas, quod et presencium experimenta temporum manifeste declarant[3] dum suis finibus non contenti nituntur invetitum ad illicita frena relaxant, nec prudenter attendunt[4] quam sit [eis][5] in clericos, ecclesiasticas ve personas et bona interdicta potestas ecclesiarum prelatis, ecclesiis, ecclesiasticis que personis, regularibus et secularibus, inponunt onera gravia ipsos que talliant, et eis colectam[6] inponunt[7], ab ipsis suorum proventuum vel bonorum dimidiam, decimam[8] seu vicesimam vel quamvis aliam portionem aut quotam exigunt et extorquent, eos que[9] molliuntur multifarie subicere servituti sue que ditioni submittere, et quod dolentes[10] referimus non nulli ecclesiarum prelati ecclesiastice que persone, trepidantes ubi trepidandum non est, transitoriam pacem querentes, plus timentes majestatem temporalem offendere quam eternam, talium abusibus[11] non tam temerarie quam inprovide adqiescunt sedis apostolice auctoritate seu licencia non optenta. Nos igitur talibus iniquis actibus obviare volentes de fratrum nostrorum consilio apostolica auctoritate statuimus, quod quicumque prelati, ecclesiastice que persone, religiose vel seculares, quorumcumque ordinum [conditionis][12] seu statum, collectas val tallias, dimidiam[13], decimam, [vicesimam seu centesimam][14] suorum que ecclesiarum proventuum vel bonorum [laicis solverint vel promiserint vel se soluturos consenserint, aut quamvis aliam quantitatem, portionem aut quotam ipsorum proventuum vel bonorum][15] estimationis vel valoris ipsorum sub adjutorii mutui, subventionis, subsidii vel doni nomine, seu quovis alio titulo, modo vel quesito colore, absque auctoritate sedis eiusdem; necnon imperatores, reges seu principes, duces vel comites vel barones, potestates, capitanei, officiales vel rectores quocumque nomine censeantur, civitatum, castrorum seu quorumcumque locorum constitutorum ubilibet, et quivis alius cuiuscumque preeminentia,[16] conditionis et status qui talia inposuerint, exigerint vel receperint, aut apud edes sacras deposita ecclesiarum vel ecclesiasticarum personarum ubilibet, arestaverint seysierint seu occupare[17] presumpserint, vel arestari, seysiri aut occupari mandaverint, aut occupata, seysita seu arestata receperint; necnon omnes qui scienter in predictis dederint auxilium, consilium vel favorem, publice vel occulte, eo ipso sentenciam excommunicationis incurrant. Universitates quoque que in hiis culpabiles fuerint, ecclesiastico supponimus interdicto. Prelatis et personis ecclesiasticis supradictis, in virtute obediencie, et sub depositionis pena districte mandantes, ut talibus absque expressa licencia dicte sedis nullatenus adquiescant, quod que pretextu cuiuscumque oblationis, promissionis vel concessionis factarum actenus vel faciendarum in antea priusquam huiusmodi prohibitio constitutio seu preceptum [fo. 5r] ad noticiam ipsorum pervenerint vel solvant, nec supradicti seculares vel quoquo modo recipiant, et si solverint aut predicti[18] receperint, excommunicationis sentenciam incidant ipso facto. A supradictis autem excommunicationis[19] et interdicti sentenciis nullus absolvi valeat preterquam in mortis articulo absque sedis apostolice auctoritate et licencia speciali, cum nostro intentionis existat tam horrendum secularium potestatum abusum nullatenus sub dissimulatione transire, non obstantibus quibuscumque privilegiis sub quibuscumque tenoribus, formis seu modis, aut verborum conceptione, concessis imperatoribus et regibus et aliis supradictis que contra premissa in nullo volumus alicui vel aliquibus suffragari. Nulli ergo omnino hominum [liceat][20] hanc paginam constitutionis nostre, prohibitionis seu precepti infringere vel ei ausu temerario contraire. Si quis autem [hoc attemptare presumpserit, indignationem omnipotentis Dei et beatorum Petri et Pauli apostolorum eius se noverint incursurum.][21] Dat' Rome apud Sanctum Petrum vj kalendas Marcii pontificatus nostri anno secundo.

1 A revised version, dated 21 April 1296 appears at fos 7v–8r, no. 17. For examples of other texts see T. Rymer, *Foedera, Conventiones, Litterae et Cujuscunque Generis Acta Publica*, 3 vols (London 1816–30), vol. I, pt. II, p. 836; ed. G. Digard, M. Faucon, A. Thomas, R. Fawtier, *Les Régistres de Boniface VIII*, 4 vols (Paris 1907–39), vol. I, no. 1567; ed. R. Graham, *Registrum Roberti Winchelsey*, 2 vols (Canterbury and York Soc., li–ii, 1952–6), vol. I, pp. 159–61. For commentary, see Denton, *Robert Winchelsey*, pp. 89–99.

2 Supplied from 17.
3 *declarat* in MS.
4 *advertunt* in 17.
5 Supplied from other texts.
6 *collectas* in other texts.
7 *onera ... inponunt* omitted in 17.
8 *decimam* omitted in 17.
9 *eosdem* in 17.
10 *dolenter* in the papal register.
11 *ab usubus* in MS.
12 Supplied from other texts.
13 *dimidiam* omitted in 17.
14 Supplied from other texts.
15 Added in 17.
16 *preeminentis* in MS.
17 *occupari* in MS.
18 *predicta* in MS.
19 *excommunicationum* in 17.
20 Supplied from other texts.
21 Supplied from 17.

7 Bull *Quorumdam oculos* of Pope Boniface VIII forbidding members of mendicant orders to accept offices outside their own orders in conflict with outside authorities without specific papal licence. [24 Feb. 1296–29 Mar. 1297]

Bonefacius[1] etc. Quorumdam oculos sicut via[2] ambitionis excetat, quod sue quasi professionis inmemores qua contemptis honoribus, abjectis divitiis, sprectis que deliciis, arbitrio proprio subjugato alteri conditioni retro respiciunt ad aratrum manumissa, dum precipitanter ruunt in litigiorum amfractus, causarum strepitibus se involvunt, et extra administrationes proprii ordinis concendere solutionem[3] prelature molliuntur, electionibus [postulationibus][4] seu provisionibus de se in discordia celebratis inprovide prestando consensum, prebendi assensum a suo superiori non numquam exacta[5] licencia, potius quam optenta, ex quo animarum et ecclesiarum dispendia noscimus provenisse et proventura majora [in antea][6] verisimiliter formidamus. Volentes igitur huic pesti salubri remedio obviare, presenti constitutioni censemus[7], ut nullus religiosus predicatorum, minorum, heremitarum sancti Augustini,[8] necnon quorumlibet ordinum mendicantium, electioni, postulationi, provisioni seu vocationi de se facte[9] in discordia, ad aliquam extra administrationes in[10] ordinis prelaturam prestare possit assensum, eciam si magistri ministri priorum[11] generalium suorum ordinum aut inferiorum prelatorum suorum licencia et assensu accederent, absque licencia sedis apostolice speciali faciente plenam et expressam de constitutione huiusmodi mentionem, decernentes irritum et inane, si secus scienter vel ignorantur a quoquam fuerit acceptum. Nulli ergo etc. Dat' Rome apud Sanctum Petrum vj kalendas Marcii pontificatus nostri anno secundo[12]

1 For examples of other texts, see Digard *et al.*, *Les Régistres de Boniface VIII*, vol. I, no. 1577; ed. L. Wadding, *Annales Minorum*, 16 vols (Rome, 1731–6), vol. V, p. 583, no. 28; ed. W. W. Capes, *Registrum Ricardi de Swinfield* (Canterbury and York Soc., vi, 1909), pp. 339–40.
2 *sic vitium* in other texts.
3 *solium* in other texts.
4 Supplied from Wadding's text.
5 *extorta* in other texts.
6 Supplied from Wadding's text.
7 *sancimus* in other texts.
8 *heremitarum, minorum, sancti Augustini* in MS.
9 *sancte* in MS.
10 *sui* in other texts.
11 *seu prioris, promagistri vel prioris gracia* and *seu priores* in other texts.
12 There is considerable variety in the dating clauses attached to this bull. The papal register dates it 29 Mar. 1296. Wadding's text gives 29 Mar. 1297. The Peterborough scribe and Swinfield's register agree on 24–25 Feb. 1296, but it is likely that this has been inadvertently copied from *clericis laicos* with which it is associated in both texts.

8 Sale by Abbot William to Elicia, widow of Richard le Benecok, of the marriage of William, Richard's son and heir, and the wardship of his lands or those of the next heir should William die before reaching his majority. [27 April 1296]

Omnibus Christi fidelibus presens scriptum visuris vel audituris frater Willelmus permissione divina abbas de Burgo Sancti Petri salutem in Domino sempiternam. Noveritis me vendidisse, concessisse et per presentes confirmasse Elicie que fuit uxor Ricardi le Benecok de Burgo pro quadam summa pecunie quam mihi dedit per manibus maritagium Willelmi filii et heredis predicti Ricardi, et wardam terrarum eiusdem Ricardi que per mortem ipsius et minorem etatem predicti heredis ad abbatem de Burgo tanquam [fo. 5v] ad capitalem dominum feodi illius spectant. Tenenda et habenda usque ad plenam et legittimam etatem predicti heredis sine vasto aut destructione facienda, cum liberatione infra abbaciam recipienda ad predictam wardam pertinente. Et faciendo plenarie servicium quod ad predictum feodum pertinet. Et si contingat quod predictus Willelmus ante plenam et legittimam etatem suam in fata discesserit dicta Elicia habebit wardam et maritagium alterius heredis subsequentis usque ad plenam et legittimam etatem suam. In cuius rei testimonium presentibus sigillum meum apponi feci. Dat' apud Burgum die Veneris proxima post festum sancti Marci ewangeliste anno regni regis Edwardi xxiiij^{to}.

9 Cyrograph recording the terms on which Master Geoffrey of Maxey was to serve the abbey.[1] Provision was made that, during his lifetime, he should eat at the abbot's table and have two servants and two horses stabled at the abbey's expense while in residence. He should also receive annually a full set of livery, 40s from the abbot's chamber and 20s from the convent. Provision was set at a reduced level should he become infirm. [Late-thirteenth century]

Cyrographum magistri Galfridi de Makes'.

Omnibus Christi fidelibus etc. Noverit universitas vestra nos unanimi consensu retinuisse magistrum Galfridum de Makeseye clericum in obsequio monasterii nostri, eidem que pro negotiis dicti monasterii gestis et gerendis unanimiter concessisse competentem sustentationem suam in domo nostra quo advixerit percipiendam. Ita videlicet quod victualia percipiat in mensa abbatis qui pro tempore fuerit cum monachis et clericis illuc residentibus. Habebit eciam duos garciones in aula abbatis ad mensam, in comitiva garcionum aliorum clericorum abbatis, victualia sua cum eisdem percipientes cum idem magister Galfridus presens fuerit. Habebit eciam duos equos ad sumptus eiusdem abbatis prout alii clerici habuerint dum residens fuerit infra abbaciam. Percipiet eciam singulis annis plenam robam; videlicet dimidium pannum secundum quod de nundino venerit cum pellura congruenti. Percipiet eciam annuatim quadraginta solidos sterlingorum de camera abbatis ad quatuor terminos usuales. Et viginti solidos de portione conventus ad eosdem terminos. Ista omnia percipiet magister Galfridus quamdiu in negotiis nostris laborare poterit et equitare. Si vero aliquo morbo laboraverit incurabili, tunc sustentationem percipiet corporalem in victualibus comptetentem, sine equis, cum uno garcione tamen, et una roba de sex ulnis panni cum una pellura. Percipiet eciam viginti solidos annuatim ut predictum est de portione conventus. Pro hac autem receptione et perceptione dictus magister Galfridus tactis sacrosanctis evangeliis juravit, promisit et se obligavit quod negotia predicti monasterii diligenter prosequetur procurabit et promonebit sumptibus abbatis vel conventus prout negotia fuerint distinata absque difficultate et dissimulatione. Alioquin de dampnis et jactura predictis abbati et conventui pro suo defectu contingentibus, secundum regem et consuetundinem regni respondebit. Secreta sibi revelata sub sigillo confessionis celatur'. In cuius rei testimonium tam predicti abbas et conventus quam predictus magister Galfridus huic scripto conventionali in modo cirographi confecto alternatim sigilla sua apposuerunt. Dat'.

1 Geoffrey of Maxey was active on abbey business throughout Abbot Godfrey's rule, frequently appearing as a witness and acting as one of his attorneys while he was abroad in 1309 and 1313. Geoffrey was dead by June 1322. Nos 65, 113–113S, 115; *Cal. Pat., 1307–13*, pp. 116, 589; NRO, Milton charter, 265. I am indebted to Professor King for the latter references.

10 Pensions paid to justices, clerks and pleaders. [27 Aug. 1296–29 Aug. 1297]

[fo. 6r] Pensiones tam justiciariorum quam clericorum et narratorum.[1]
Dominus Hugo de Cressingham – lxvj s. viij d. ad Pascha et ad festum sancti Michaelis. Memorandum de arreragiis de tempore abbatis Ricardi.[2]
Dominus Johannes de Berewyk – lxvj s. viij d. ad eosdem terminos. Memorandum de arreragiis.
Willelmus Inge – xl s. ad predictos terminos.
Johannes de Insula – xl s. ad predictos terminos.
Rogerus de Hegham – xl s. ad predictos terminos.
Henricus Spygurnel – xx s. ad predictos terminos.[3]
Clerici
Magister Ricardus de Hereford – c s. ad Pascha et ad festum sancti Michaelis.[3]
Johannes de Drax – c s. ad eosdem terminos.[3]
Ricardus de Staunford – lxvj s. viij d. ad eosdem terminos.
Magister Ricardus de Norht' – xl s. ad eosdem terminos.
Henricus de Jakele capellanus – xl s. ad eosdem terminos.
Priori de Newport – xxvj s. viij d. ad eosdem terminos.
Willelmus de Rasen – xxvj s. viij d. ad eosdem terminos.
Willelmus de Langeleye – xx s. ad eosdem terminos.
Thomas filius domini Walteri de Stirchisle – xl s. ad eosdem terminos.
Johannes filius domini Alani de Chartris – xx s. ad eosdem terminos.[3]
Magister Galfridus de Mak' – xl s. ad eosdem terminos.
Willelmus Loveday – lxvj s. viij d. ad eosdem terminos.
Ricardus de Gosefeld – xx s. ad eosdem terminos.
Ricardus de Coleshille – xx s. ad eosdem terminos.
Ricardus de Ascheby – xx s. ad eosdem terminos.
Johannes de Milton' – xxvj s. viij d. ad eosdem terminos.
Rogerus de Scotere – xx s. ad eosdem terminos.
Johannes Pykard – xx s. ad eosdem terminos.
[Subscribed faintly in a different hand at the foot of the folio] Summa xxxv li. xiij s. iiij d.
Summa uteriusque xl ... li ... s. viij d.
[fo. 6v–7r superscribed] Anno secundo

1 The section listing judges is printed in ed. G.O. Sayles, *Select Cases in the Court of King's Bench* (Selden Soc., lv, 1936) i, p. cxliii. See also King, *Peterborough Abbey*, pp. 133–6.

2 Entry cancelled. Cressingham was killed at the Battle of Stirling Bridge in September 1297.

3 Entry cancelled.

11 Homage of John Wake [6 Nov. 1296]

[fo. 6v] [Marginated] homagium.
Dominus Johannes Wake fecit homagium suum apud Burgum die sancti Leonardi anno regni regis Edwardi xxiiij^to^ incipiente xxv.

12 Surrender of the living of Barnack by Hugh of Nottingham, royal clerk, [*c.* 2 Feb. 1297] and the presentation of Master Nicholas de Appeltre[1] [c. 24 Feb. 1297]

De ecclesia de Bernak.

Hoc anno dimisit dominus H[ugo] de Notingham, clericus regis, ecclesiam de Bernak circa purificationem beate Marie quam quidem ecclesiam tenuit per quadriennium de gracia domini Oliveri Linc' episcopi sine institutione et commendatione. Unde facta denunciatione dicte vacationis abbati et conventui de Burgo per predictum episcopum presentatus fuit magister Nicholaus de Appeltre ad instanciam predicti episcopi circa festum sancti Mathie apostoli anno Domini M^o^CC^o^ nonagesimo sexto.

1 For Nicholas de Appletree's institution on 6 Mar. 1297, see Sutton's Institutions, fo. 272r.

13 Letter of Pope Gregory IX at the request of the abbot and convent forbidding anyone to exact anything from them for the consecration or installation of an abbot. [29 Jan. 1233]

Gregorius IX'.

Gregorius[1] servus servorum Dei dilectis filiis abbati et conventui de Burgo ordinis sancti Benedicti Linc' diocesis salutem et apostolicam benedictionem. Precibus vestris benignum impertientes assensum, auctoritate presentium districte inhibemus, ne quis pro benedictionibus abbatum qui pro tempore fuerint in monasterio vestro vel installandis eisdem, alicuius pretextu consuetudinis, que dici debet potius coruptela, aliquid exigere vel extorquere presumat. Nulli ergo omnino hominum[2] liceat hanc paginam nostre inhibitionis infringere vel ei ausu temerario contraire. Si quis autem hoc attemptare presumpserit, indignationem omnipotentis Dei et beatorum Petri et Pauli apostolorum eius se noverit incursurum. Dat' Anagnie iiij kalendas Februarii pontificatus nostri anno sexto.

1 Also in Swaffham, fo. 80v (old foliation).
2 Swaffham text ends here.

14 Grant by the abbot and convent of 100s p.a. pension to John de Drax, royal clerk, at the request of the king, until they can provide him with a benefice. [11 Oct. 1295]

Pensio Johannis de Drax.

[Marginated] Pensio ratione nove creationis

Omnibus Christi fidelibus presentes litteras visuris vel audituris frater Willelmus Dei gracia abbas de Burgo Sancti Petri et eiusdem loci conventus salutem in Domino sempiternam. Noverit universitas vestra nos ad instanciam excellentissimi principis domini E[dwardi] regis Anglie illustris ratione nove creationis prefati abbatis unamiter concessisse dilecto nobis in Christo Johanni de Drax, predicti domini regis clerico, centum solidos annue pensionis de camera abbatis qui pro tempore fuerit singulis annis percipiendos ad duos anni terminos; videlicet ad Pascha quinqaginta solidos. Et ad festum sancti Michaelis quinquaginta solidos donec eidem in ecclesiastico beneficio competenti providerimus. In cuius rei testimonium quia predictus abbas propter creationis sue novitatem sigillum non dum habuit autenticum [fo. 7r] sigillum commune capituli de Burgo Sancti Petri de voluntate predicti abbatis presentibus est appensum. Dat' apud Burgum in pleno capitulo quinto idus Octobris anno Domini M°CC°nonagesimo quinto.

15 Memorandum that Abbot William received Joan de Mortimer, daughter of Walran de Mortimer, knight, into the habit of a nun of St Michael's Stamford. [25 July 1298]

[Marginated] Memorandum

De monialibus Staunfordie.

Anno Domini millesimo ducentesimo nonagesimo octavo, in festo sancti Jacobi apostoli, abbas Willelmus de Wodeford recepit Johannam filiam domini Walranni de Mortuo Mari militis ad habitum religionis in monasterio monialium sancti Michaelis extra Stanford' suscipiendum. Dat' apud Burgum in aula abbatis juxta cameram suam in presencia monachorum fratris Gilberti de Aylington' et fratris Roberti de Stanford' junioris, domini Willelmi de Wivelesthorp' capellani, Thome de London', Johannis fratris sui et Roberti de Hotoft. Et abbas scripsit priori monialium quod ipse conferret predicte Johanne habitum religionis.

16 Memorandum of the promise of John de Ryseberg, rector of Tinwell, not to harass the abbey, its tenants and officials further concerning the matters over which they had differed at Ingthorpe. [2 Nov. 1295]

De juramento rectoris ecclesie de Tynewell'.

Memorandum quod die Veneris proxima post festum commemorationis animarum anno Domini millesimo CC nonagesimo quinto institit coram nobis W[illelmo] propitiatione divina abbate monasterii de Burgo Sancti Petri et nostro conventu eiusdem Johannes de Ryseberg' rector ecclesie de Tynewell' humiliter cum instancia postularis ut licium materias inter nos et tenentes nostros de Inggethorp' et ipsum, mutuo exortas, salubri consilio curaremus amputare promittens virtute sacramenti sui corporaliter prestiti in verbo sacerdotii et salutis sacris ewangeliis inspectis, quod decetero nos nec nostros tenentes seu servientes quoscunque minime molestabit inquietabit per se nec per alios nomine suo, set fidem et reverenciam malicias adversencium in quantum poterit compescens nobis et successoribus nostris pro toto tempore suo adhibebit, et quod nostro assensu mutuo fuerit ordinatum et in scriptis redactum absque dolo et fraude adimplebit et adimpletum suo perpetuo fideliter conservabit. Nos pium et Deo devotum ab errore desistenti gremium venie aperire reputantes, injurias et offensas personales nobis et nostris per ipsum illatas in caritate duximus eidem remittendas. Acta apud Burgum in presencia dominorum abbatis et prioris et commonacorum nostrorum; videlicet Willelmi de Stokes, Ricardi de Estewik', Galfridi de Carleton', Henrici de Keten', Ricardi de Brampton', Willelmi Saloman, Johannis de Sautre et magistri Galfridi de Makes' et aliorum.

[fo. 7v–8r] **17 Copy of the revised bull** *clericis laicos* **dated 21 April 1296.** See above, no. 6.

17A Letter of Pope Boniface VIII to papal nuncios, the cardinal bishops of Albano and Palestrina, ordering the publication of the bull *clericis laicos* **throughout England and France and the provision of copies to all requesting them. [21 April 1296]**

Item[1] Bonifacius episcopus servus servorum Dei venerabilibus fratribus B[eraldo] Albanen' et S[imoni] Penestr' episcopis sedis apostolice nunciis salutem et apostolicam benedictionem. Constitutionem quam nuper in favorem ecclesiastice libertatis edidimus vobis bulla nostra munitam per dilectos filios magistros Galterum de Raus et Arnaldum de Cantalupo nuncios nostros latores presentium destinamus, fraternitati vestre per apostolica scripta mandantes quatinus vos vel alter vestrum per vos vel per alium seu alios constitutionem predictam per Francie et Anglie regna in eorum locis de quibus expedire videritis auctoritate nostra pupplicare curetis, eius copiam petentibus facientes. Dat' Rome apud Sanctum Petrum xj kalendas Maii pontificatus nostri anno secundo.

1 Also in Graham, *Registrum Roberti Winchelsey*, vol. I, p. 161.

18 Letter of Abbot William appointing Thomas Fraunceys and Walter de Ayston to act on his behalf twice a year at the great court of the bishop of Lincoln at Newark and also elsewhere in the county of Nottingham. [6 Mar. 1296]

Omnibus Christi fidelibus ad quos presentes littere pervenerint Willelmus permissione divina abbas de Burgo Sancti Petri salutem in Domino sempiternam. Noverit universitas vestra nos attornasse et ordinasse Thomam Fraunceys de Colingham et Walterum de Ayston' ad veniendum bis in anno ad magnas curias domini Linc' episcopi apud Newerk'; videlicet semel post festum sancti Michaelis et iterum post Pascham, et ad ibidem et alibi in comitatu Notingham' exigendum et calumpniandum nomine nostro que ad nos et libertates nostras pertinent. In cuius rei testimonium has litteras nostras eisdem fecimus patentes pro voluntate nostra duraturas. Dat' apud Burgum Sancti Petri ij nonas Marcii anno regni regis Edwardi xxiiij^to^.

19 Letter of Robert Winchelsey, archbishop of Canterbury to Richard Gravesend, bishop of London ordering him to summon the clergy of the southern province to a council at St Paul's, London, beginning on 13 January 1297. [27 Nov. 1296]

[fo. 8v] Mandatum pro convocatione cleri.[1]

Robertus[2] permissione divina Cant' archiepiscopus tocius Anglie primas venerabili fratri domino R[icardo] Dei gracia London' episcopo salutem et fraternam in Domino caritatem. Satis per diversa frater conscripte mundi climata perlato rumore diffunditur, et auribus hominum inculcatur[3], sicut nos cotidianis gestorum experimentis, et oculata fide perpendimus, qualiter natale solum in quo peregrinationis presentis dies agimus dispendiosis incomodis atteritur, et variis exteriorum injuriis labescitur.[4] Dum enim gens Anglorum ambiguis fatis guerrarum et horrendis bellorum agressibus non vacabat felici embola personarum excrescentium, et rerum copiosis affluentiis redundabat. Sed nunc pacis emulus et caritatis non ficte perfidus inimicus sic nos et dictam gentem hostium insidiis undique circumcinxit, sicque captiosa tendicula iam tetendit, et innumerabilium aciem bellatorum in nos omnes convertit,atque alia pericula nobis et ecclesie anglicane clero pariter atque regno iminentia fallaciter preparavit, quod patrata strage multorum non sine dampnationis eterne plurium interitu prothdolor animarum, iam decrevit excrescens numerus gentis nostre, fons affluentie rerum exaruit, et quod graviter est gerendum nisi seva sevientium audacia licitis defensionibus reprimatur, et eidem favente Domino competentibus prout convenit remediis occurratur, nos et ecclesiam antedictam, clerum eciam ac ceteros regnicolas ad desolationis irreparabilis detrimentum quod absit perduci posse violenter presumimus et verisimiliter[5] formidamus. Ne igitur flagitiosis et repentinis hostium incursionibus[6] opprimamur, et nostri et ecclesie cleri ac regni predictorum subversionem vel exterminium minus provide patiamur, tutum esse nuper censuimus et consultum casibus huiusmodi quos ut premisimus instantes esse probabiliter committimus[7] et evidenter attendimus quantum licite possumus salubriter obviare. Quocirca fraternitati vestre committimus et mandamus firmiter injungendo quatinus cum celeritate debita omnes et singulos coepiscopos et suffraganeos nostros in nostra Cant' provincia constitutos convocando citetis seu citari peremptorie faciatis ut cessante legitimo impedimento, quod si pretensum fuerit coram nobis, nisi tunc legitime doctum fuerit de eodem, nullatenus admittetur, die sancti Hillarii proximo sequente[8] apud Sanctum Paulum London' ad tractandum et ordinandum nobiscum dicto die et diebus sequentibus proximis, quamdiu videbitur oportunum, qualiter pro tuitione universalis ecclesie anglicane cui non tam in temporalibus quam in spiritualibus una cum regno, clero eiusdem et ceteris regnicolis periculum grande nimis ut prediximus dinoscitur iminere, in necessitatum seu periculorum huiusmodi articulis quantum ad nos at alios viros ecclesiasticos licite pertinet [fo. 9r] salubriter provideri valeat, suam exhibeant presentiam personalem in virtute sancte obediencie qua nobis et ecclesie nostre Cant' juxta sue professionis seriem juramento personaliter prestito sunt astricti, necnon sub pena districtionis canonice, cuius rigorem exercere dante Deo disponimus contra convocationis seu citationis edictum totaliter contempnentes, aut eciam quesitis coloribus sese frustratorie excusantes, electos quoque confirmatos presentes necnon absentium episcporum vel electorum vicarios seu procuratores ad dictos diem et locum sub pena consimili et in forma predicta citetis aut citari peremptorie faciatis. Denunciantes nichilominus prefatis episcopis electis presentibus et tam episcoporum[9] quam electorum absentium vicariis, et eisdem auctoritate nostra districtius injungentes, quatinus quilibet in sua seu sibi commissa diocesi citet aut citari faciat peremptorie omnes decanos, precentores, cancellarios, thesaurarios, archidiaconos et priores cathedralium ecclesiarum, necnon abbates non exemptos ac eciam omnes priores, decanos, prepositos, magistros conventualium et collegiatarum ecclesiarum et alios universos in dignitate constitutos quocumque nomine censeantur, capitula quoque omnium prelatorum[10] et clerum, ut videlicet decani, precentores, cancellarii, thesaurarii, archidiaconi et abbates non exempti, priores, prepositi, magistri et alii ut premittitur in dignitate constituti personaliter, singula vero capitula huiusmodi tam secularium quam religiosorum predictorum per unum, clerus autem cuiuslibet diocesis per duos procuratores ad tractandum et ordinandum nobiscum tractatibus ordinationibus que in premissis et circa premissa seu occasione premissorum faciendis ac omnibus tractatus et ordinationes huiusmodi contingentibus nomine dominorum suorum consentiendum plenam et sufficientem ac specialem potestatem habentes dictis die et loco conveniant seu compareant eodem die et sequentibus oportunis una nobiscum facturi quod superius memoratur, sub pena excommunicationis majoris et interdicti, que merito poterunt formidare, qui in forma prenotata contumaciter omiserint seu contempserint comparere et que contra eosdem qui sic comparere detrectaverint sine delectu personarum intendimus executioni debite demandare. Denuncietis insuper episcopis, electis et vicariis singulis supradictis quod in suis diocesibus omnibus exemptis cuiuscumque fuerint conditionis, ordinis seu professionis notificent manifeste ut[11] prefatis die et loco absque aliquali privilegiorum suorum prejudicio, quibus per hoc non intendimus per hoc [sic] derogare, una nobiscum sufficienter intersint facturi in premissis et ea contingentibus prout superius est expressum, cum commune sit periculum et per consequens communibus absque cuiusque fori privilegio remediis congruis devitandum [fo. 9v] et quod omnes tangit merito debet ab omnibus approbari. Dictis et episcopis, electis et vicariis districtius injungatis ut nos memoratis die et loco singuli certificare procurent per litteras patentes harum seriem continentes, una cum nominibus [omnium][12] ecclesiarum et monasteriorum secundum formam predictam citandorum qualiter presens mandatum in suis diocesibus vel eisdem commissis fuerint executi. Et vos eisdem die et loco et diebus sequentibus similiter personaliter intersitis facturi cum ceteris quod incumbit. De die vero receptionis presentium et quid in premissis feceritis nos distincte et aperte ibidem reddentes inter cetera certiores per litteras vestras patentes harum seriem exprimentes. Valete semper in Christo. Dat' apud Bocking' etc. [v kalendas Decembris anno Domini MCC^mo^ nonagesimo sexto consecrationis nostre tercio][13]

1 In a later medieval hand.

2 Printed in ed. F. M. Powicke, C. R. Cheney, *Councils and Synods with Other Documents relating to the English Church, AD 1205–1313*, 2 vols (Oxford 1964), vol. II, pt. II, pp. 1152–4; Graham, *Registrum Roberti Winchelsey*, vol. I, pp. 144–7.

3 *incillcatur* in MS.

4 *lacessitur* in Winchelsey's register.

5 *veris humiliter* in MS.

6 *incursibus* in MS.

7 *conicimus* in Winchelsey's register.

8 *subsequente* in Winchelsey's register.

9 *ipsorum* in MS.

10 *predictorum* in MS.
11 *et* in MS.
12 Supplied from Winchelsey's register.
13 Idem.

20 Assignment to the convent by Abbot William of 16s 6d *wethersilver* due to his cellarer from the convent's manors of Fletton and Alwalton. Payment to be made annually by the convent cellarer on 29 June, retaining by virtue of his office 3s 2d instead of the profits from the sale of two wethers from the abbot's larder or 3s. Also the assignment of one mark of silver p.a. from the convent cellarer to the convent receivers, to be divided equally between the convent and the poor on the abbot's anniversary. [1295–99]

Carta abbatis Willelmi de wethersilver de Fletton' et Alwalt'.

Notum[1] sit omnibus presens scriptum visuris vel audituris quod cum celerarius abbatis de Burgo recipere solebat annuatim ad festum apostolorum Petri et Pauli de maneriis conventus eiusdem loci, videlicet Alwalton' et Fletton', pro consuetudine de wethersilver sexdecim solidos et sex denarios ut patet in rotulis compoti dictorum officiorum, frater Willelmus monasterii de Burgo Sancti Petri miseratione divina abbas et minister portionem conventus sui cupiens augmentare absque dampno successoribus suis predicti monasterii abbatibus futuris faciendo, advertens eciam statum quorumdam maneriorum ad portionem abbatis spectantium per sui temporis industriam in tantum accrevisse quod bene licuit ei et decuit predicta maneria conventus sui ab omni solutione ac prestatione liberare, non obstante alicuius murmuratione vel obloquio, predictos sexdecim solidos et sex denarios prefato conventui suo assignavit perpetuis temporibus de predictis duobus maneriis per manus celerarii conventus qui pro tempore fuerit in festo apostolorum Petri et Pauli singulis annis recipiendos et possidendos. Ita videlicet quod celerarius conventus qui pro tempore fuerit retineat penes se ratione officii sui tres solidos et duos denarios pro exitibus multonum quos vendicare consuevit de lardario abbatis ad predictum festum vel tres solidos. Ita quod decetero nichil occasione predicta clamare poterit inposterum. Idem vero celerarius conventus liberabit singulis annis ad predictum festum receptoribus conventus unam marcam argenti ad anniversarium predicti Willelmi abbatis tam in solacio conventus quam in elemosina pauperum pro equali portione distribuendam. In cuius rei testimonium etc.

1 Printed in *Mon. Angl.*, vol. I, p. 396, no. 51.

21 Letter from the official of the archdeacon of Northampton to all the rural deans in his archdeaconry arranging for payment of procurations levied for the second year to pay for the papal nuncios Berald, cardinal bishop of Albano and Simon, cardinal bishop of Palestrina. The letter includes a letter from Oliver, bishop of Lincoln, to his archdeacons or their officials, dated 22 Dec. 1296, itself containing a copy of a letter dated 10 Oct. 1296[1] from the nuncios to the bishop ordering collection of the procurations and their surrender to merchants of the society of the Clarenti. This letter in turn contains copies of three papal letters authorising the collection, dated 18–20 Feb. 1295. [after 22 Dec. 1296]

[fo. 10r] Officialis domini archidiaconi Norht' universis decanis per archidiaconatum eiusdem constitutis salutem in autore salutis. Litteras domini Linc' episcopi nuper recepimus formam que sequitur continentes:

O[liverus] permissione divina Linc' episcopus dilectis in Christo filiis universis archidiaconis per Linc' diocesem constitutis, vel eorum officialibus salutem graciam et benedictionem. Litteras venerabilium patrum dominorum B[eraldi] Alban' et S[imonis] Penestr' episcoporum Dei gracia sacrosancte Romane ecclesie cardinalium vj idus Decembris circa horam vesperarum recepimus sub continentia infra scripta:

Miseratione[2] [divina][3] B[eraldus] Alban' et S[imon] Penestr' episcopi venerabilibus fratribus universis et singulis archiepiscopis, episcopis et eorum vicariis in Anglia, Scotia, Wallia constitutis salutem in Domino. Cum in prosecutione negotiorum nobis a sede apostolica commissorum subierimus, et adhuc subire habeamus necessario granda onera expensarum et ob hoc in vestris et regni Francie partibus procurationes nostras pecuniarias in releviatione onerum expensarum huiusmodi pro secundo anno decrevimus exigendas, vobis et vestrum singulis committimus, et nichilominus in virtute sancte obediencie apostolica qua fungimur auctoritate mandamus, quatinus singuli vestrum dictas nostras procurationes pecuniarias vobis ipsis, necnon et abbatibus, prioribus, decanis, prepositis archidiaconis, archipresbiteris et aliis prelatis capitulis et conventibus ecclesiarum parochialium, rectoribus et aliis ecclesiasticis personis, exemptis et non exemptis, Cisterciensis, Cluniacensis, Premonstratensis, sancti Benedicti et aliorum ordinum ac magistris et preceptoribus domorum militie Templi et hospitalis sancti Johannis Jerosolum' in vestris civitatibus et diocesibus constitutis pro secundo anno infra mensem a tempore receptionis presentium inponatis; videlicet pro qualibet marca sterlingorum, quatuor denarios eiusdem monete, ecclesiarum, monasteriorum, prioratuum domorum et aliarum dignitatum seu personatuum quibus dicte persone ecclesiastice preese noscuntur, computatis redditibus et proventibus ecclesiasticis prout in solutione decime computantur, et eas sic inpositas infra duos menses a tempore inpositionis huiusmodi, studeatis per vos vel alium seu alios ydoneos exigere et colligere cum effectu. Nos enim intuemus peremptorie predictas omnes et singulas personas ecclesiasticas quibus huiusmodi procurationes nostras duxeritis inquirendas, eisque sub excommunicationis pena precipimus quam in eis ex nunc ut tunc in hiis scriptis ferimus nisi fecerint quod mandamus, quatinus infra premissum duorum mensium spacium a tempore quo inpositiones per vos sibi factas recipiant numerandum summas ratione procurationum ipsarum per vos eis inpositas nomine nostro, solvant nobis vel eis quos ad receptionem earum duxeritis deputandos. Ipsas autem procurationes sic collectas Johanni Haldebrandini et Johanni Inqueti et Justo Foresii de societate Clarentum de Pistorio, mercatoribus domini nostri pape et nostris vel eorum alteri, seu eorum aut alterius ipsorum procuratori absque more diffugio, nostro nomine et pro nobis reddi et solvi integre dictarum procurationum [fo. 10v] moderatis sumptibus et expensis Lond' faciatis. Contradictores et rebelles auctoritate nostra seu verius apostolica per censuram ecclesiasticam et invocare videritis contra eos auxilium brachii secularis. Quod si in premissis exequendis negligentes quod absit fueritis vel rebelles, nos in singulos vestrum qui in premissis negligentes vel rebelles fueritis ex nunc et ex tunc suspensionis sentenciam promilgamus [sic] que si per mensem sustinueritis, excommunicationis sentenciam auctoritate apostolica nobis in hac parte commissa ex nunc ut ex tunc in vos ferimus in hiis scriptis. Tenores autem litterarum apostolicarum quarum auctoritate, tam presentia vestra quam in absentia, predictas procurationes petere ac peti facere possumus, fecimus presentibus annotari qui sequuntur per ordinem sub hiis formis:

Bonifacius episcopus servus servorum Dei venerabilibus fratribus patriarchis, archiepiscopis et episcopis ac dilectis filiis, electis, abbatibus, prioribus, decanis, prepositis, archidiaconis, archipresbiteris, plebanis et aliis ecclesiarum prelatis et eorum vices gerentibus ac ecclesiaticis personis, religiosis et aliis, ecclesiarum et monasteriorum capitulis et conventibus, exemptis et non exemptis, Cisterciensis, et Cluniacensis, Cartusiensis, Premonstratensis, sancti Benedicti, sancti Augustini, Camaldunensis ac sancti Guibalini ac aliorum ordinum, necnon magistris et preceptoribus militie Templi et hospitalis sancti Johannis Jerosolum' et beate Marie Teutonicorum salutem et apostolicam benedictionem. Cum venerabiles fratres nostros B[eraldus] Albanen' et S[imon] Penestr' episcopos sedis apostolice nuncios viros utique virtutum claritate conspicuos, consilio providos et providencia circumspectos latores presentium ad ultramontanas et Anglicanas partes certis sibi commissis negotiis fiducialiter defonemus, universitatem vestram rogamus et hortamur attente per apostolica vobis scripta districte percipiendo mandantes, quatinus nuncios ipsos cum per partes vestras transitum fecerint, ob reverenciam sedis apostolice et nostram benigne recipientes et honeste tractantes eosdem sibi pro suis et familiarum suarum necessariis de securo conductu, necnon in evectionibus oportunis, si sue in via decesserunt vel defecerint cum super hiis per ipsos vel eorum aliquem in aliquibus locis vel loco interdum moram trahere contigerit, volumus quod non aut ex parte ipsorum fueritis requisiti, in eundo, morando et redeundo liberaliter providere curetis, volumus quod non solum eorumdem eisque vicinarum vel adiacentium partium, sed aliarum eciam sicut eisdem nunciis pro omnibus huiusmodi dividendis et facilius supportandis expedire videbitur remotarum patriarche, archiepiscopi, episcopi, electi, abbates, priores, decani, prepositi, archidiaconi, archipresbiteri, plebani et alii ecclesiarum prelati eorum que vices gerentes, ac persone ecclesiastice, religiose et seculares, ecclesiarum et monasteriorum capitula et conventus, exempti et non exempti, Cisterciensis, Cluniacensis, Cartusiensis, Premonstratensis, sancti Benedicti, sancti Augustini, Camaldinensis, sancti Guibelini et aliorum [ordinum][4], necnon magistri et preceptores militie Templi, hospitalis sancti Johannis Jerosolum' et sancte Marie Teutonicorum et quolibet aliorum locorum ecclesiarum contribuere in subventionibus huiusmodi teneantur. Sic itaque mandatum nostrum efficaciter adimplere curetis, quod positis ex inde non inmerito comendari. Alioquin sentenciam quam iidem nuncii vel eorum quilibet per se vel alium seu alios propter hoc rite tu-[fo. 11r] lerint in rebelles ratam habebimus et faciemus, auctore Domino usquam ad satisfactionem condignam inviolabiliter observari, non obstante si est aliquibus ab eadem sede indultum quod nunciis seu legatis sedis ipsius aliquam procurationem exhibere, vel in ipsa contribuere nisi ad eos declinaverint minime teneantur, seu quod interdici suspendi[5] vel excommunicari non possint per [litteras][6] apostolicas que de indulto huiusmodi totoque tenore ipsius plenam et expressam non fecerint mentionem, sed quibuslibet privilegiis, quibuscumque personis, locis vel ordinibus sub quavis forma verborum ab eadem sede concessis de quibus quorumque totis tenoribus in nostris litteris specialis mentio sit habenda, et per que [presens][6] mandatum nostrum quomodolibet valeat impediri. Dat' Lateran' x kalendas Marcii pontificatus nostri anno primo.

Bonifacius episcopus servus servorum Dei venerabilibus fratribus B[eraldo] Alban' et S[imoni] Penestr' episcopis sedis apostolice nunciis salutem et apostolicam benedictionem. Laudanda vestre circumspectionis industria in magnis et arduis probata multociens instanter inducit et excitat mentem nostram ut vobis utpote diversarum virtutum claritate conspicuis que cordi gerimus fiducia committamus. Cum itaque vos per urgentibus gravibus que negotiis communiter vobis commissis ad ultramontanas partes fiducialiter destinemus, nos ut in terris et in regionibus illarum partium, ad quas et per quas eundo pro negotiis ipsis stando et redeundo, vos vel vestrum quemlibet ire contigerit eo reddamini, amplius graciosi, quo majori fueritis auctoritate nostra muniti, vobis et vestrum cuilibet compellendi quoslibet prelatos cuiuslibet preeminencie vel dignitates extiterint, necnon regulares, Cisteciensis [sic], Premonstratensis, Cluniacensis et aliorum [ordinum][6], magistros quoque preceptores, priores et fratres sancti Johannis Jerosol', militie Templi et aliorum quorumcumque hospitalium sive domorum et alias personas ecclesiasticas cathedralium aliarum, ecclesia sive monasteria, exemptorum et non exemptorum, per censuram ecclesiasticam a procuratoribus in contribuendo vobis debitis, non obstantibus quibuscumque privilegiis et indulgenciis apostolicis per que in hac parte possent quomodolibet se tueri, et de quibus quorum ve totis tenoribus de verbo ad verbum debeat fieri in nostris litteris mentio specialis plenam auctoritate presentium concedimus facultatem. Dat' Lateran' xij kalendas Marcii pontificatus nostri anno primo.

Bonifacius episcopus servus servorum Dei venerabilibus fratribus B[eraldo] Alban' et S[imoni] Penestr' episcopis sedis apostolice nunciis salutem et apostolicam benedictionem. Laudanda vestre circumspectionis industria in magnis et arduis probata multociens instanter inducit et excitat mentem nostram ut vobis utpote diversarum virtutum claritate conspicuis que cordi gerimus secura fiducia committamus. Cum itaque vos pro urgentibus gravibus que negotiis communiter vobis commissis ad ultramontanas partes fiducialiter destinemus. Nos volentes ut eo facilius premissa negotia prosequi valeatis utiliter quo minus fueritis subductis obstaculis inpediti recipiendi huiusmodi negotiorum prosecutione vestra durante, tam in presentia quam in absentia, procurationes a venerabilibus fratribus nostris archiepiscopis et episcopis ac dilectis filiis, electis, abbatibus, [fo. 11v] prioribus, decanis, prepositis archidiaconis, archipresbiteris et aliis ecclesiarum prelatis et ecclesiasticis personis, religiosis et aliis eorum capitulis et conventibus, exemptis et non exemptis, Cisterciensis et Cluniacensis, Premonstratensis, sancti Benedicti et aliorum ordinum, necnon magistris et preceptoribus domorum militie Templi et hospitalis sancti Johannis Jerosol' illarum partium, ad quas et per quas, eundo pro negotiis ipsis stando et redeundo, vos vel vestrum quemlibet ire contigerit, et contradictores per censuram ecclesiasticam appellatione postposita compartendi, non obstantibus constitutione quam felicis recordationis Gregorius papa X, predecessor noster, edidit in concilio Lugdun', et qualibet alia sedis apostolice constitutione seu quibuslibet privilegiis vel indulgenciis quibuscumque personis, locis vel ordinibus sub quavis forma verborum ab apostolica sede concessis de quibus quorum ve totis tenoribus plenam et expressam oporteat in presentibus fieri mentionem, et per que [id][7] quomodolibet valeat inpediri, liberam vobis et cuilibet vestrum concedimus auctoritate presentium facultatem. Dat' Lateran' xij kalendas Marcii pontificatus nostri anno primo.

Act' et dat' Paris' vj[8] idus Octobris anno Domini M^o^CC^o^ nonagesimo sexto, pontificatus domini Bonifacii pape predicti anno secundo.

Ad procurationem igitur predictam singulos quatuor denarios de singulis marcis omnium beneficiorum reddituum et proventuum ecclesiasticorum nostre diocesis juxta taxationem secundum quam reddebatur decima suprascripta ut nobis supra injungitur inponentes, vobis omnibus et singulis in virtute obediencie firmiter injungendo mandamus, quatinus huiusmodi inpositionem procurationis universis personis, religiosis, secularibus et ecclesiasticis prenominatis, redditus et possessiones habentibus quocumque nomine censeantur superius memoratis personaliter inventis et procuratoribus negotiorum gestoribus, servientibus et amicis absentium diebus et locis congruis statim pupplice notificantes, ne a quoquam ignorancia in hoc casu juste valeat allegari, ipsas personas diligenter moneatis, et efficaciter requiratis, seu moneri et requiri per alios faciatis, ut dictam procurationem sit inpositam infra duos menses a tempore notificationis, monitionis et requisitionis huiusmodi, illi scilicet archidiaconi Linc', Leyc', et Stowye ac decanatus Roteland' priori sancte Katerine extra Linc' et religiosi omnes de diocese abbati Oseneye sicut prius in dicte decime solite erat distinctum et servatum, quos ad huiusmodi procurationes colligendas et recipiendas vice nostra certa consideratione duximus deputandos solvere non preponant, sicut sentenciam excommunicationis in non solventes infra tempus sibi statutum latam ut premiattur voluerint evitare. Qualiter autem mandatum nostrum duxeritis exequend' nos litteris vestris patentibus harum seriem et diem receptionis formam ac modum notificationis monitionis ac requisitionis et precipue absentibus factarum in hac parte, ac tempus infra quod eas fecistis sive fieri procurastis plenius continentur. Singuli vestrum certificent tempore oportuno. Valete. Dat' apud Buggeden' xj kalendas Januarii anno supradicto.

1 Possibly 9 Oct., see below, note 8.
2 *miseratione ... secundo* also in ed. W. N. Thompson, *Register of John de Halton*, 2 vols (Canterbury and York Soc., xii–xiii, 1913), vol. I, pp. 90–4. For commentary, see Lunt, *Financial Relations*, vol. I, pp. 553–7.
3 Supplied from Halton's register.
4 Supplied from Halton's register.
5 *suspendi* interlined.
6 Supplied from Halton's register.
7 Idem. Caret in this text.
8 *vij idus* in Halton's register.

22 Plea of trespass against the abbot of Thorney by Ralf Portehors of Polebrook and Walter Carter heard at meetings of Polebrook hundred court. [26 April–25 Sept. 1296]

[fo. 12r] Anno regno regis E[dwardi] xxiiij^{to} in hundredo tento apud Bernewell die Jovis in crastino sancti Marci ewangeliste coram Gilberto de Sutton' tunc capitali ballivo abbatis de Burgo.

Abbas de Thorneye, Odo nomine, attachiatus fuit ad respondendum Radulfo Portehors et Waltero le Carecter de placito transgressionis. Plegii abbatis de respondendo, Thomas filius Radulfi de Kynesthorp' et Willelmus de Keston' de eadem.

Hundredum de Pokebrok' tentum apud Undel' die Jovis in ebdomada Pentecoste anno supradicto.

Abbas de Thorneye versus Radulfum Porthors et Walterum Carectar' de placito transgressionis, per Willelmum de Kyrkeby. [Marginated] Esson'

Hundredum de Pok' tentum apud Undel' die Lune proxima ante festum nativitatis sancti Johannis baptiste anno supradicto.

Abbas de Thorneye defendens versus Radulfum Porthors de Pok' de placito transgressionis per Ricardum filium Walteri de Clopton'. Ad istum diem abbas non fecit se esson' versus Walterum Carectar' et sic fecit defaltam. [Marginated] Esson'

Hundredum de Pok' tentum apud Pottereslyved die Martis proxima ante festum sancte Margarete virginis anno supradicto.

Abbas de Thorn'[1] versus Radulfum Porthors defendens de placito transgressionis per Johannem de Armeston'. Ad istum diem abbas non fecit se esson' versus Walterum Carectar' et sic fecit defaltam. [Marginated] Esson'

Hundredum de Pok' tentum apud Undel' die Lune proxima post festum sancti Petri advincula anno supradicto.

Radulfus Porhors et Walterus Carectar' querentes optulerunt se versus abbatem de Thorn' de placito transgressionis, et abbas attachiatus non venit; ideo consideratum est quod primum plegium predicti abbatis summoneri audiendum judicium suum eo quod non habuerit predictum abbatem quem plegiaverit et predictus abbas distringatur etc.

Hundredum de Pok' tentum apud Undel' die Martis proxima post decollationem sancti Johannis baptiste anno supradicto.

Radulfus Porthors et Walterus Carectar' querentes de placito transgressionis optulerunt se versus abbatem de Thorn' et testatus est per ballivum quod dictus abbas districtus est per unum equum et se non justificat. Ideo consideratum est quod predicta districtio teneatur et melius distringatur.

Hundredum de Pok' tentum apud Undel' die Martis proxima ante festum sancti Michaelis anno supradicto.

Radulfus Porthors et Walterus Carectar' querentes de placito transgressionis non sunt prosecuti versus abbatem de Thorn'. Ideo ipsi et plegii sui de prosequendo in misericordia.

1 Followed by caret, but no omission supplied.

23 Order to the bailiff of Stamford by the abbot to deliver money to the prior or prioress of St Michael's, Stamford to buy five cows in recompense for the tithe of cheese which they used to receive from the manor of Eye. [n.d.]

[fo. 12v] [Marginated] Bayllyf de Estanford' par le abbe de Burk'.

Saluz. Liverez au priour de Seynt Michel ou a la priouresse deners des issues de vostre bayllie pur achater v vaches a le enoytement de la pytaunce le covent en reconpensacioun de la dyme de furmage qe alcune foyz soleyent prendre de la grante le abbe del manere de Eye issi qe des oremes a taunt se teynent saunz plus dyme demaunder.

24 Ordinances for the conduct of the bailiffs of the abbey. [n.d.]

[Marginated] De statu ballivorum abbacie Burgi.

Les bayllyfs de la fraunchise de Burk' Seynt Pere sunt chargez par le serment qe il unt fet a le eglise de Burk', e si com il ne voylent estre atteynt de faus serment, e lur servise perdre, qe lewement se porterunt vers le eglise, e vers chescun du puple qe a le eglise est entendaunt, ou par homage ou par autre subiectioun. E qe le estat e le dreyt de le eglyse susteynderunt, e a chescun du puple dreyture frunt saunz forpryse de persone, ne autre chose ne frunt a nuly pur amur ne pur haunge, ne par doun prendre ne esperer[1] ne chose demaunde desporter, ne estre vye. Les comaundemenz nostre seyngneur le roy e ses justices ausi ben par bref com par precept fet en furme de dreyt lewement furnyrunt e lewement returnerunt par lew respunse fere. Issi qe la fraunchyse seyt sauve saunz peryl, ne nule partye qe est en play en la curt le roy en deu fraunchises sustendrunt cuntre autre, en dyt ne en fet, ne panel de assis' ne de jure, ne de enqueste frunt ne suffrunt estre fet a lur poer plus favorable a lune partye qe a lautre, ne panel a dreyt ordene chaungerunt ne defrunt pur favour dc nuly. E qe les issues de la fraunchyse e le enpruement, lewement coyllerunt, e enterment rendrunt au recevour le abbe saunz paye fere ayllurs, si il ne seyt par bref le abbe ou sun recevour, ne pardoun ne frunt ne respyt de estrete qe lur vent de le eschekere de Burk' saunz garaunt de le abbe especial, si issi ne seyt, qe cely ke tent la curt face pardoun taunt com it est seaunt en curt, e ceo muntaunt a dusze deners par la jurneye. Ne doun ne prendrunt en or, ne en argent, ne en autre chose sauve manger e beyvere e la sustenance de une jurneye. Si il ne seyt par cunge le abbe ou autre home a ky il voudra tel cunge doner e granter. E ke nul home chargerunt par surfetuse venues. Ceo est asaver ne trop sovent ne trop chargaument de menee, mes en la fourme qe il demurent o le abbe. Ceo est asaver le[2] [fo. 13r] chef bayllyf o deus chyvaus e deus garcuns. E le clerk de la fraunchise o un chyval. E le bayllyf erraunt en chescun hundred ne eyt for ke un chyval e un garcoun, e un suthbayllyf saunz plus. E comaunde est a bayllyfs qe deu feez par an facent vewe de acounte a le eschekere de Burk' quel houre qe il seyent garnyz quinze jurs devaunt, ausi ben de la verte cyre com du profyt de lur baillies. E si bayllyf ke rend acunte seit en arrerage de vint souz ou de plus de clere chose, qe il ad leve, le paie tauntost, ou se teygne a la peyne qe ili apent. E si la chose seit a lever, eyt le espace de un moys a lever e paer ceo qe arere est. E si yl ne le face, seyt ordene de ly par bon avysement, si il deyve plus demorer par la defaute de acuns bayllyfs ke avaunt ses houres unt du a le abbe grant aver ke uncore est arere, e ke de graunt chose se unt meyns charge en poynter des roules qe il ne deyvent fere, e de ceo furent apertement atteynz. Ordene est ensement qe si le chef bayllyf va nule part par resun de sa bayllie, ou aylurs par comaundement, qe il preygne ses despenses du recevour, e a ly acunte de ses despenses tauntost a sun returnyr, e ausi le facent tuz les autres ke foreynes bosoygnes espleyterunt. Et si le recevour ne eyt pas argent prest, maunde alcun bayllyf par sun bref qe il livere a un tel par nun certeyne summe de argent par taylle, la quele taylle ensement o le bref seyt mustre sur le procheyn acunte e alowe. Purveu est ensement, qe chescune vewe seyt afure de denz les viij jours. E chescun hundred meyme le jour, e touz affuremenz seyent fes par gent qe connyssent le puple, e qe seyent de bone fey e nent mal queraunz. Issi qe nul bayllyf dunk eyet poer de nuly grever ou desporter a sa volente. E ke le clerk de la fraunchyse, tauntost apres les vewes e les hundres affurez, face estrete de chescune jurneye par sey, et les livere au recevour le abbe, e de suz le seal le recevour seyt maunde le estrete au bayllyf ke face le veue a chescun ke le demaundera, par peryl qe est avenu par bayllyfs ky autrement unt leve, qe ne fu contenu en lur estretes.

[Marginated] Ordinatur per dominum abbatem et consilium suum quod omnes districtiones pro viridi cera facte in hundredo de Nassaburgi ponantur manerio de Burg[obiri] Et de hundredis de Pok[ebroc] et Hokeslaw [in] manerio de Undel'

1 Marginated omission … *robes … nule manere de alliaunce avaunt quat … avant duraunt la bail …*

2 Fo. 12v subscribed *chef bayllyf.*

25 Order to the bailiff of the court of Castor concerning conduct of the court. Marginal reference to aid for the knighting of the king's son. [n.d.]

[Marginated] de auxilio … pro regis filio militem faciendo.

Comaunde est au bayllyf de la curt de Castre ke les somouns tesmoynent a meymes cele curt ke nul assoyne gettent en la curt avaunt dite pur nul home, a nomer eus meymes assoynours, si il ne seyt suz bayllyf pur chef bayllyf de fee escuser ove ky il est. La resun de cest comaundement est tele: ke tort enput est[1] fet au seygnur de la curt ky ad le prowement de defautes. E ensement a la partie, ke par taunt put estre plus delaee en caas de play. De autre part, il est dit comunement ke les bayllyfs de fee tels choses enpernent saunz garaunt pur gayner, e ke force ne frunt de autri damage. E si chef bayllyf de fee desoremes le face, seyt chastie par amerciement, iekes [fo. 13v] a la terce foyz. E puys si il ne se chastie, le fee seyt prise en la meyn le seygnur en noun de destreste, si la ke il se chastie. E si suzbayllyf le face, si al primer amonestement ne se chastye, le bayllyf de la curt remue cely quant a la jurneye, e le office face fere par autre, ou apres la curt tenue devaunt le departyr de suturs, seyt dit a cely ke mes ne est bayllyf, e seyt la verge de ly prise, e dyt seyt a ly, ke il face venyr sun seygnur a la procheyne curt pur le office fere, ou autre presenter en sun lu, ke voylle, pusse e sache tel office parfurnyr.

1 Recte *estre*.

26 Plea of debt by Richard de Ernesby against the abbot in Leicester county court countered by a privilege of Henry III granting that no case could be brought against the abbot in any court other than that of the king or his chief justices without special royal mandate. [6 Dec. 1296]

Comitatus Leycestr'[1] die Jovis in festo sancti Nicholai anno regni regis E[dwardi] xxv[to].

[Marginated] tempore Willelmi de Castello militis tunc vicecomitis eiusdem comitatus ... pro officiar' ...[2]

Ad quem diem Ricardus de Ernesby implacitavit abbatem de Burgo Sancti Petri in comitatu de placito debiti. Et optulit se per esson' suum. Et Gilbertus de Sutton' senescallus ipsius abbatis venit in eodem comitatu et ostendit cartam domini regis Henrici patris domini regis nunc pro predicto abbate in qua continetur quod abbas de Burgo Sancti Petri nec successores sui non respond' in comitatu nec in alia curia de aliqua possessione vel tenemento nec de aliqua re nisi coram domino rege vel capitalibus justiciis domini regis per speciale mandatum domini regis. Et quare placitum est in isto comitatu sine brevi domini regis, ideo consideratum est per totum comitatum quod carta predicti domini regis pro predicto abbate plenarie allocetur. Et quod predictus abbas sit quietus de isto placito et de omnibus placitis hic sine brevi regis. Et dictum est predicto Ricardo quod impetret breve domini regis versus predictum abbatem si voluerit.

1 *Comitatus Leycestr'* marginated.
2 Separate and faded entry

27 Manumission by the abbot and convent of William of Walcot, clerk, by origin their villein, so that he can proceed to full orders and seek an ecclesiastical benefice. [24–27 May 1297]

Manumissio[1]

Universis[2] sancte matris ecclesie filiis presentes litteras inspecturis vel audituris, Willelmus permissione divina abbas monasterii Sancti Petri de Burgo et eiusdem loci conventus salutem in Domino sempiternam. Cum Willelmus de Walecot' clericus, qui de nativis nostris traxit originem, desideret in sacerdotali officio Deo deservire, nolentes ipsum pro cuius morum venustate laudabile testimonium noscitur pro clamare a suo proposito ratione servitutis impediri, caritatis intuitu, eidem concessimus quod possit a domino Linc' episcopo vel alio quocumque ad omnes ordines promoveri, necnon beneficium ecclesiasticum assequendum liberam in domino tribuimus facultatem eidem. In cuius rei testimonium presentibus sigilla nostra sunt appensa. Dat' apud Burgum Sancti Petri in crastino Ascensionis dominice anno Domini M° CC° nonogesimo septimo.

1 In a late medieval hand.
2 Repeated below, no 69. Printed in *Mon. Angl.*, vol. I, p. 395, no. 47.

27A Oath by William of Walcot, clerk, that he will never act against the abbey in secular or ecclesiastical court, nor do anything to show ingratitude. [24–27 May 1297]

Juramentum manumissi[1]

Anno[2] et die supradictis in conventuali capitulo de Burgo Sancti Petri, ego Willelmus de Walecot' clericus, juravi tactis sacrosanctis ewangeliis, quod monasterium de Burgo aut dominos meos abbatem et conventum eiusdem loci numquam inquietabo litigando aut aliquid in foro ecclesiastico vel seculari impetrando, nec aliam notam ingratitudinis contra eosdem perpetrando, jura vel libertates eorum perturbando seu violando. Sed commodum et honorem predicti monasterii et dictorum dominorum meorum omni loco et tempore pro viribus meis procurabo et promovebo. Sic me Deus adjuvet et sancta ewangelia.

1 In a late medieval hand.
2 Entry cramped and written in the bottom margin of the folio. Printed in *Mon. Angl.*, vol. I, p. 395, no. 48.

28 Cyrograph agreement between Henry de Stratton, rector of Cottingham and the abbot concerning view of frankpledge and *husbote* and *haybote* in Cottingham wood. [25 Mar. 1297]

[fo. 14r] Cyrographum domini H[enrici] de Stratton' rectoris ecclesie de Cotingham de husbote et haybote habendo in bosco de Cotingham.

[Marginated] Coting'

Noverint[1] universi presens scriptum visuri vel audituri quod cum controversia moveretur inter abbatem de Burgo Sancti Petri ex parte una et dominum Henricum de Stratton' rectorem ecclesie de Cotyngham ex altera ratione visus franciplegii tenentium predicti rectoris de ecclesia sua predicta, et ratione de housbote et haybote que dictus rector clamabat in bosco predicti abbatis de Cotingham. Demum facta investigatione jur', tam ecclesie sancti Petri de Burgo quam ecclesie de Cotingham, concordati sunt in hunc modum; videlicet quod predictus Henricus pro se et ecclesia sua predicta recognovit predictum visum et omnia que ad visum pertinent esse jus predicti abbatis et ecclesie sue de Burgo. Ita quod omnes tenentes predicte ecclesie singulis annis statutis diebus veniant ad visum predicti abbatis in manerio suo de Cotyngham et ibidem faciant et recipiant omnia que ad visum franciplegii spectant. Dictus eciam Henricus rector recognovit se nullum jus nec warantum habere ad aliquid percipiendum in bosco predicti abbatis de Cotyngham nisi de gracia ipsius abbatis speciali. Pro hac autem recognitione, dictus abbas pro se et ecclesia sua concessit de gracia sua speciali eidem Henrico quamdiu extiterit rector ecclesie de Cotyngham amerciamenta provenientia de hominibus predicti rectoris pro emendis assise panis et cervisie in visu predicto. Ita quod ballivus predicti rectoris recipiat de ballivo predicti abbatis extractas amerciamentorum de tenentibus predicti rectoris quo ad emendas panis et cervisie proven' ad opus predicti rectoris levandorum quamdiu rector extiterit. Concessit eciam idem abbas pro se et successoribus suis de gracia et liberalitate sua speciali predicto Henrico quamdiu extiterit rector ecclesie predicte quandam perceptionem bosci in bosco suo de Cotingham; videlicet rationabilem sustentationem subbosci et spinarum ad comburendum in coquina et pistrina predicti rectoris. Et de arboribus siccis que vocantur Rowurs ad comburendum in aula predicti rectoris. Istam vero perceptionem habebit predictus Henricus per visum et deliberationem custodis predicti bosci de Cotingham sine vasto vel destructione aliqua facienda. Preterea idem abbas remisit eidem rectori et omnibus tenentibus suis omnia amerciamenta ad que amerciati fuerunt in predicto visu a principio mundi usque ad diem confectionis presentis scripti. Ita quod post cessionem vel decessum predicti Henrici, successores sui nichil juris in premissis sibi poterunt vendicare. Sed omnia ad jus et proprietatem ecclesie de Burgo revertantur et remaneant absolute. In cuius rei testimonium presenti scripto in modum cyrographum confecto sigilla abbatis et conventus de Burgo Sancti Petri et sigillum predicti Henrici alternatim sunt appensa. Dat' apud Burgum Sancti Petri in festo annunciationis beate Marie anno Domini M°CC° nonogesimo sexto finiente incipiente septimo.

1 Also in Soc. of Antiquaries, MS 38, fos 39v–40r and BL, Cott. Cleop. C ii, fos 68r–9r.

28A Cyrograph agreement between Henry and William de Stratton and the abbot and convent whereby tenants at Middleton come to Cottingham for view of frankpledge in return for Henry and William gathering wood belonging to the abbot for their use during their lifetimes. [25 Mar. 1297]

[fo. 14v] Cyrographum H[enrici] de Stratton' et Willelmi fratris eius de terra de Middelton'.

[Marginated] Coting'

Noverint[1] universi presens scriptum visuri vel audituri quod Henricus de Stratton' et Willelmus de Stratton' frater eius pro se et successoribus suis concesserunt abbati de Burgo Sancti Petri et eiusdem loci conventui quod omnes tenentes eorumdem Henrici et Willelmi de Middelton' plenarie veniant bis per annum ad visum franciplegii domini abbatis in manerio suo de Cotingham, et quod faciant ibidem quicquid ad eundem visum pertinet inperpetuum. Ita quod predicti Henricus nec Willelmus nec heredes utrorumque nec aliquis nomine eorum de predictis eorum tenentibus nec de aliquo eorum aliquem visum franciplegii teneant nec clamare tenere poterunt inperpetuum. Et pro hac concessione predicti abbas et conventus concesserunt pro se et successoribus suis eisdem Henrico et Willelmo pro se et familia sua apud Middelton' commorantibus tota vita utrorumque ipsorum Henrici et Willelmi rationabilem sustentationem de bosco ipsius abbatis de Cotingham; videlicet in focali de spinis et alio subbosco pro pistrina et coquina, et de bosco qui vocatur Rowurs ad comburendum in aula eorumdem Henrici et Willelmi ibidem per visum et deliberationem custodis bosci sui de Cotingham sine clamio et calumpnia alicuius meremii. Ita tamen quod heredes predictorum Henrici et Willelmi nec aliquis nomine eorum in bosco predicto focale nec aliquid aliud proficuum post decessum predictorum Henrici et Willelmi exigere poterunt nec vendicare in perpetuum. Preterea idem abbas perdonavit eisdem Henrico et Willelmo et tenentibus suis predictis omnimoda amerciamenta ad que amerciati fuerunt in visu predicti abbatis a creatione seculi usque diem confectionis presentis scripti. In cuius rei testimonium presenti scripto cyrograffato tam predicti abbas et conventus quam predicti Henricus et Willelmus sigilla sua alternatim apposuerunt.

Dat' apud Burgum Sancti Petri vicesimo quinto die Marcii anno regni regis Edwardi filii regis Henrici vicesimo quinto.

1 Also in Soc. of Antiquaries, MS 38, fo. 40r–v and BL, Cott. Cleop. C ii, fo. 69r–v.

29 Cyrograph by which Abbot William, following his unanimous election as abbot, assigned the income from the manor of Southorpe, which he had acquired when he was sacrist, to the sacristy with provision for £20 p.a. to be paid to the convent. Of this, 40s was to be divided equally between recreation for the convent and alms to the poor on William's anniversary and the £4 which Alicia de Semark received from the manor of Pilsgate should be allocated to the sacrist. [19 May 1297]

Cyrographum manerii de Suthorp'.

Noverint[1] universi sancte matris ecclesie filii quod cum frater Willelmus de Wodeford abbas monasterii de Burgo Sancti Petri dum in officio sacristie monasterii predicti fuisset constitutus, ac manerium de Suthorp' cum pertinenciis quod pro duobus feodis militarie respondet, non sine corporali labore et mentalibus angustiis, nec absque solutionibus et expensis sumptuosis tantummodo de predicto officio sacristie provenientibus perquisisset. Demum dicto fratre Willelmo in abbatem creato de communi et unanimi assensu tocius capituli de Burgo Sancti Petri per predictum abbatem assignatum est predictum manerium cum pertinenciis [fo. 15r] officio sacristie predicte et integraliter et perpetue annexum. Ita quod sacrista qui pro tempore fuerit singulis annis solvet conventui de Burgo aut receptoribus suis viginti libras sterlingorum ad quatuor terminos anni; videlicet ad natale Domini centum solidos, et ad Pascha centum solidos, et ad festum sancti Johannis baptiste centum solidos, et ad festum sancti Michaelis centum solidos sine dilatione vel diminutione, faciend' eciam tam servicia regalia quam militaria debita et consueta. De predictis autem viginti libris ordinatum est et statutum de communi consensu et voluntate abbatis et tocius conventus quod quadraginta solidi cedant in recreationem conventus et distributionem pauperum ad anniversarium predicti Willelmi abbatis pro equali portione inperpetuum, et vivente predicto abbate singulis annis die statuendo ab eodem fiat distributio predictorum quadraginta solidorum ad profectum tam conventus quam pauperum. De prefatis vero viginti libris allocabuntur sacriste qui pro tempore fuerit singulis annis quatuor libre quas Alicia de Sancto Medardo in Badington' recipit de manerio de Pylesgate quam diu vixerit; videlicet singulis terminis viginti solidos. In cuius rei testimonium presenti scripto in modum cyrographi confecto sigilla predictorum abbatis et conventus sunt appensa. Dat' apud Burgum in capitulo conventuali quartodecimo lalend' [sic] Junii anno Domini M°CC° nonogesimo septimo.

1 Printed in *Mon. Angl.*, vol. I, pp. 395–6, no. 50.

30 Grant by Abbot William to the cellarer of a plot planted with willows, lying between his wall and the water on one side and between the water leading to the water gate at Bolhithe[1] and the cellarer's *curia* on the other, in return for the latter relaxing any claim to a place called Wodeyerd where he used to keep his pigs. [29 June 1297]

Universis sancte matris ecclesie filiis ad quos presens scriptum pervenerit Willelmus permissione divina abbas Burgi salutem in Domino sempiternam. Noverit universitas vestra nos divine pietatis intuitu unanimi tocius conventus nostri assensu concessisse assignasse et presenti carta nostra confirmasse celerarie domus nostre quandam placeam de salicibus plantatam sicut se extendit in longitudine a muro abbatis usque ad aquam et in latitudine ab aqua que ducit ad portam de Bulhid' usque ad curiam celerarie conventualis, habendam et tenendam predictam placeam et cetera cum omnibus aysiamentis dicto celerario qui pro tempore fuerit bene et in pace sine aliquo retenemento nostri vel successorum nostorum inperpetuum. Ita quod celerarius qui pro tempore fuerit nichil decetero clamare poterit vel vendicare infra curiam abbatis que dicitur Wodeyerd ubi celerarius habere solebat porcariam suam. Ut autem hec donationis et concessionis nostre confirmatio perpetuitatis robur optineat in futurorum memoriam presens scriptum sigillis nostris communimus. Teste capitulo nostro in festo apostolorum Petri et Pauli. Anno Domini M°CC° nonogesimo septimo.

1 For the identification of Bolhithe, see E. King, 'The Town of Peterborough in the Early Middle Ages', *NP and P*, vi (1980–1), pp. 192–3 and map p. 188.

31 Agreement whereby the abbot and convent of Thorney may continue to dam and repair a watercourse between the River Nene and Inggewelle[1] in return for an annual payment of half a mark to the abbot and convent at Castor. [24 Aug. 1297]

[fo. 15v] Thorneye.

[Marginated] Thorn' Castr'

Anno[2] regni regis Edwardi vicesimo quinto die sancti Bartholomei apostoli facta est hec conventio inter t'[3] abbatem de Burgo Sancti Petri et eiusdem loci conventum ex parte una et abbatem de Thorn' et eiusdem loci conventum ex altera; videlicet quod dicti abbas et conventus de Thorn' et successores sui decetero sicut actenus consueverunt libere et pacifice possint obstruere et reparare quotiens opus fuerit quemdam cursum aque qui descendit et exit de ripa de Nene usque ad quemdam locum qui vocatur Inggewelle sine aliquo inpedimento predictorum abbatis et conventus de Burgo vel successorum suorum vel hominum suorum imperpetuum. Ita videlicet quod obstructio et reparatio illa fiat sumptibus[4] et expensis abbatis et conventus de Thorney et successorum suorum et de ipsorum terra propria vel lignis et lapidibus sine diminutione vel clamio soli seu alio dampno faciendo in solo abbatis et conventus de Burgo Sancti Petri aut successorum suorum vel hominum suorum imperpetuum, et quod latera illius obstructionis seu reparationis sint cum prato et terra adjacente ex utraque parte equalia, sed in medio ita competenter bassiorum ut cum cursus aque infra abitum ripe sit prata circumadjacentia per nimiam exaltationem illius obstructionis citius non inundentur. Et quod predicti abbas et conventus de Thorney et successores sui a predicto loco de Inggewelle usque ad salices super stagnum ipsorum abbatis et conventus de Thorn' crescentes quotienscumque necesse fuerit defectus si qui per inundationem aquarum emerserint sumptibus suis propriis et de terra sua propria habeant decetero obstruere et reparare. Ita quod dampnum exinde pro defectu reparationis non perveniat abbati et conventui de Burgo vel eorum successorum imperpetuum. Istum articulum promiserunt et concesserunt abbas et conventus de Burgo pro se et successoribus suis predictis abbati et conventui de Thorney et successoribus suis quantum in ipsis est et ad eos pertinet sine prejudicio aliorum. A capite vero salicium usque ad molendina de Neuthon' infra salices super stagnum versus ripam die confectionis presentium crescentes vel infra metas et bundas de consensu partium positas et concessas, nec predicti abbas et conventus de Burgo nec successores sui aliquid juris vel clamii poterint exigere vel vendicare imperpetuum nec eciam predicti abbas et conventus de Thorn' nec eorum successores aliquid extra salices ultra metas et bundas predictas decetero exigere vel clamare poterunt [sic] imperpetuum, sed abbas et conventus de Thorn' et eorum successores de loco qui vocatur Inggewelle usque ad molendina si cursum aque in alveo sustentabunt et obturabunt ne pro defectu competentis sustentationis et reparationis dicti abbas et conventus de Burgo vel eorum successores aut eorum tenentes in pratis circumadjacentibus dampnum incurrant seu jacturam in futurum. Liceat insuper abbati et conventui de Burgo et eorum successoribus quandocumque eis placuerit absque aliqua contradictione vel impedimento predictorum abbatis et conventus de Thorney vel successorum suorum liber' piscari de predicto loco de Inggewelle usque ad barreram in stagno fixam [fo. 16r] die confectionis istius scripti et similiter sub molendino ubi aqua dividit inter terras ipsorum abbatum vel hominum suorum. Pro hac autem conventione quieta clamatione obstructionis et reparationis concessione dicti abbas et conventus de Thorney et eorum successores concesserunt reddere annuatim abbati et conventui de Burgo et eorum successoribus imperpetuum dimidiam marcam argenti solvendam in manerio predictorum abbatis et conventus de Burgo de Castre ad duos anni terminos; videlicet ad festum sancti Michaelis tres solidos et quatuor denarios, et ad Pascha tres solidos et quatuor denarios.[5] Ad quem quidem redditum loco et terminis predictis solvendum predicti abbas et conventus de Thorn' pro se et successoribus suis obligant se et omnes terras et tenementa sua in villa de Makesey ad quorumcumque manus devenerint districtioni predictorum abbatis et conventus de Burgo et successorum suorum. In cuius rei testimonium etc.

1 Inggewelle can be identified with an irregular stream flowing from the Nene downstream from Water Newton mill on the Huntingdonshire side of the river. I am indebted to Mr T. Halliday for this topographical information.
2 also in Soc. of Antiquaries, MS 38, fos 23v–4v; BL, Cott. Cleop. C ii, fos 43r–44v; *Cal. Charter Rolls*, vol. V, p. 82. For the Thorney Abbey text, see CUL Add MS 3021, fos 370v–1r.
3 *t'* omitted in other texts.
4 *sumptubus* in MS.
5 Payment of this sum can be traced in subsequent surviving accounts for Castor under assised rents. E.g. NRO, Fitzwilliam (Milton) a/c roll 2388, m. 4d, for 1300–1. I am indebted to Professor King for this reference.

32 Extent of the manors of Torpel and Upton [11 April 1291]

Extenta maneriorum de Torpel et Upton'.

Extenta terrarum et tenementorum que fuerunt bone memorie Alianore quondam regine Anglie die quo obiit in maneriis de Torpel et Upton' cum suis pertinenciis facta coram Petro de Leyc'[1] apud Leholm die Mercurii proxima ante diem Dominicam in Ramis Palmarum anno regni regis E[dwardi] decimo nono, per sacramentum Johannis de Helpeston', Willelmi de Colevylle milit', Gilberti de Bernak', Willelmi de Northborou, Johannis le Botyller de Castr', Henrici filii Willelmi de eadem, Roberti Feyrfox, Willelmi de Suthorp', Richeri de Kendale, Roberti Peverel de Paston', Rogeri Cordel de Castr', Petri de Bourle juratorum qui dicunt super sacramentum suum quod est ibid unum capitale mesuagium cum gardino quod valet per annum dimidiam marcam. Et sunt ibid in dominico tres carucatate terre in quibus continentur CCCxx acre terre. De quibus CCxl acre terre quelibet valet per annum viij denarios. Summa viij li. Et octoginta et una acra quarum quelibet valet per annum iiij d. Summa xxvij s. Et est ibid apud Loholm quedam cultura que vocatur Hilhawe que domina regina supradicta emit de Galfrido de Suthorp' in qua continentur lxiij acre que modo sunt in dominico de Torpel quarum quelibet valet per annum vj d. Summa xxxj s. vj d.

Summma xj li. v s. ij d.

Sunt ibi quinquaginta acre et una roda prati et valet quelibet acra per annum iiij s. Summa x li. xij d. Et sunt ibi apud Loholm xx acre prati de emptione dicte domine regine de predicto Galfrido quarum xv acre et una roda dimidia prati quelibet valet per annum iiij s. Summa lxj s. Et iiij acre et dimidia et una roda prati quelibet acra valet per annum iij s. vj d. Summa xvj s. vij d. ob.

Summa xiij li. xviij s. vij d. ob.

Sunt ibi xvj acre pasture apud Hilhawe et valet quelibet acra per annum viij d. Summa x s. viij d. Et sunt ibi xviij acre pasture apud le Fen et valet quelibet acra per annum xij d. Summa xviij s. Et sunt ibi viij acre pasture apud Hilhawe de emptione dicte domine regine de predicto Galfrido de Suthorp' et valet quelibet acra per annum viij denarios. [fo. 16v] Summa v s. iij d. Et est ibi unum parcum in quo continentur per estimationem iiij^{xx}ij acrę et valet pastura cuiuslibet acra per annum iij d. Summa xx s. vj d. Et pannagium valet per annum xij d. Et tempore separationis agnorum aliuntur ibid in blado et pastura CC agni. Et valet per annum x s.

Summa lxv s. v d.

Est ibi quoddam molendinum aquaticum quod reddit per annum xv quarteria bladi precium quaterii iij s. Summa xlv s.

Summa patet.

Et sunt ibi libere tenentes qui reddunt per annum de redditu assisa ix li. xj s. ix d. qa. De quibus libere tenentes v reddunt per annum ix capones et valent xviij d. Et iidem v tenentes reddunt per annum v gallinas et valent v d. et xxj gallos et valent ij s. vij d. ob. Et sunt ibi iiij^{or} alii libere tenentes qui faciunt aruram, herciaturam, cariagium feni et bladorum et messuram et valent opera eorum per annum iij s. xj d. Et faciunt sectam curie. Et extenditur infra in placitis et perquisitis. Et omnes libere tenentes tenent per feodum militarie secundum quantitatem tenementorum suorum. Et predicta domina regina per feoffamentum predicti Galfridi de Suthorp' perquisivit ad manerium predictum de Torpel de manerio de Leholm xj li. v s. vij d. ob.

Summa patet.

Summa xxj li. v s. x d. qa.

Est ibi quidam Johannes Trenche qui tenet unum mesuagium et xvj acras terre ad voluntatem domini [et] reddit per annum iiij s. et arrabit et herciabit bis per annum; videlicet dimidiam acram ad semen yemale et dimidiam acram ad semen quadagesimale et valet operatio illa vj d. et dabit domino ad natale Domini unum gallum et ij gallinas et valent v d. ob. Et cariabit ij carectatas busce et valet operatio illa ij d. et falcabit per unum diem pratum domini. Et valet operatio illa ij d. ob. Et cariabit ij carectatas feni et valet cariagium illud ij d. Et fac' unum bedripe ad cibum domini et unum beene sine cibo in autumpno. Et valet operatio illa iij d.

Summa v s. ix d.

Sunt apud Torp' xi villani quorum quilibet tenet unum mesuagium et x acras terre et reddit quilibet eorum per annum ij s. vj d. Summa xxvij s. vj d. Et quilibet eorum dat per annum pro maltsilver et swynespeny per annum v d. Summa iiij s. vij d. Et quilibet eorum arrabit j acram per annum tempore yemali et quadragesimali[2] et valet aratura cuiuslibet per annum v d. Summa iiij s. vij d. Et quilibet eorum herciabit j acram per annum tempore yemali et quadragesimali et valet operatio cuiuslibet j d. Summa xi d. Et quilibet eorum operabitur a festo sancte Trinitatis usque ad festum apostolorum Petri et Pauli; videlicet per unum mensem ut estimatur communibus annis in qualibet per ij dies et valet operatio cuiuslibet in septimana j d. ob. Summa v s. vj d. Et a festo apostolorum Petri et Pauli usque ad gulam Augusti quilibet eorum operabitur in septimana per iij dies. Et sunt xij dies operabiles per idem tempus. De quibus quilibet eorum falcabit per vj dies. Et valet operatio cuiuslibet per diem ij d. ob. Summa xiij s. ix d. Et per alias vj dies quilibet eorum levabit fenum et alia opera facienda, et valet operatio cuiuslibet per diem j d. Summa v s. vj d. Et a gula Augusti usque ad festum sancti Michaelis quilibet eorum operabitur quolibet die in septimana preter dies feriales et Sabbatem. Et sunt xxxvj dies operabiles de quibus quilibet eorum metet per xxvj dies per estimationem. Et valet operatio cuiuslibet iiij s. iiij d. Summa xlvij s. viij d. Et per x dies quilibet eorum operabitur alia opera autumpnalia et valet operatio cuiuslibet x d. Summa x^ti^x s. ij d. Et quilibet eorum fac' iij bedripes in autumpno ad cibum domini cum duobus hominibus in die, et valet operatio cuiuslibet vj d. Summa v s. vj d. [fo. 17r] Et quilibet eorum fac' iij benes ad cibum[3] proprium cum duobus hominibus, et valet operatio cuiuslibet xij d. Summa xj s. Et quilibet eorum metet dimidiam acram frumenti preter alia opera sua predicta, et valet ij d. ob. Summa ij s. iij d. ob. Et quilibet eorum dat pro auxilio et ward per annum ij d. Summa xxij d. Et fuit ibidem in quodam hameletto qui vocatur Ayston' pertinens ad Thorp' vj villani qui tenent in vilinagio iiij^xx^ et xix acras terre. Et quilibet eorum reddit per annum ij s. vj d. ad quinque anni terminos. Et est summa xv s. Et quilibet eorum cariabit duas carectatas busce ad festum sancti Martini et valet cariatio cuiuslibet per annum ij d. Summa xij d. Et quilibet eorum dat pro pannagio j d. Summa vj d. Et quilibet eorum arrabit bis per annum; videlicet ad semen yemale dimidiam acram et ad semen[4] quadragesimale dimidiam acram et valet arrura cuiuslibet v d. Et herciabit quilibet eorum unam acram per annum et valet j d., et est summa arrurarum et herciaturarum per annum iij s. Et quilibet eorum dat ad natale Domini j gallum et iij gallinas. Et valent v d. ob. Summa ij s. ix d. Et quilibet eorum serclabit vel alias opera fac' per ij dies in septimana a festo sancte Trinitatis usque ad festum apostolorum Petri et Pauli; videlicet per unum mensem ut communibus annis estimatur. Et valet operatio cuiuslibet per ebdomadam j d. Summa ij s. Et a festo apostolorum Petri et Pauli usque gulam Augusti quilibet eorum falcabit per vj dies. Et valet operatio cuiuslibet per diem ij d. ob.[5] Summa vij s. vj d. Et quilibet eorum levabit fenum per alios vj dies infra idem tempus. Et valet operatio cuiuslibet per diem j d. Summa iij s. Et quilibet eorum cariabit ij carectatas feni, et valet cariatio cuiuslibet ij d. Summa xij d. Et a gula Augusti usque festum exaltationis sancte Crucis; videlicet per vj septimanas quilibet eorum metet bladum domini qualibet die in septimana preter dies feriales et Sabbatem. Et sunt xxvj dies operabiles. Et valet operatio cuiuslibet per diem ij d. Summa xxvj s. Et quilibet eorum metet dimidiam acram frumenti preter opera sua predicta. Et valet operatio cuiuslibet ij d. ob. Summa xv d. Et a festo exaltationis sancte Crucis usque festum sancti Michaelis quilibet eorum operabitur per iij dies in septimana[6] et valet operatio cuiuslibet per diem j d. Summa iij s. Et quilibet eorum faciet iij bedripes in autumpno ad cibum domini cum duobus hominibus. Et valet operatio cuiuslibet hominis per diem ij denarios. Summa vj s. Et omnes villani predicti dant ad auxilium ad festum sancti Michaelis unam marcam. Et est ibi unus messor de villanis predictis qui debet eligi per liberos homines de Torp' qui dat domino per annum pro officio suo xx s. et ccc ova que valent xij d. Et dant ad auxilium vicecomitis per annum vij d. ob. Summa reddituum et operum villanorum xij li. ix s. ix d. Et est apud Torpel unus cotarius qui tenet unum cotagium et reddit per annum xij d. et ad natale Domini unum gallum et j gallinam et valent ij d. ob. et levabit fenum per vj dies et valet vj d. Et metet in autumpno per vj dies; videlicet[7] iij ad cibum domini et iij ad cibum proprium et valet ix d. Et est apud Ayston' unus cotarius tenens j cotagium qui reddit per annum ij s. et ad natale Domini unum gallum et j gallinam et valent ij d. ob. Et levabit fenum per vj dies et valet vj d. et metet per vj dies in autumpno; videlicet[7] iij ad cibum domini et iij ad cibum proprium, et valet operatio illa ix d.

Summa reddituum coterellorum v s. xj d.

Placita et perquisita valent per annum xx s. Summa patet.

Summa summarum manerii de Torpel: lxvj li. xviij d.[8] ob. qa. et acq' de xx d. de ij li. piperis pro ...' de Hug' de Bernak' et de rector' ecclesie de Offord.[9]

Et est ibi quedam ecclesia apud Ufford cuius advocatio spectat ad manerium de Torpel. Et valet dicta ecclesia per annum l marcas. Leholm in custodia domini regis per mortem Galfridi de Suthorp' qui obiit post mortem dicte regine, cuius heres Johannes de Suthorp' filius predicti Galfridi qui est infra etatem; videlicet etate septem annorum in festo sancti Botulphi proximo venturo. Et est ibi unum mesuagium cum gardino, et valet per annum unam marcam. Et sunt ibi CC acre terre et dimidiam in dominico, quarum quelibet valet per annum x d. Summa viij li. vij s. jd. [fo. 17v] Et sunt ibi xvj acre prati et valet quelibet acra per annum iij s. Summa xlviij s. Et est ibi pastura et valet per annum iij s.

Summa xj li. xj s. v d.

Sunt ibi libere tenentes qui reddunt de redditu assiso xxiij s. iij d. ob. Et faciunt sectam curie et extenditur infra in placitis et perquisitis.

Summa patet.

Sunt ibi septem villani qui tenent in villenagio et reddunt per annum lxxvij s. iij d. ob.

Summa patet.

Placita et perquisita valent per annum ij s.

Summa patet.

Summa summarum tocius custode xvj li. xiiij s. De quibus reddit manerium de Torpel x li.

Et sciendum quod Margeria que fuit uxor Ricardi de Leholm tenet in dotem de herede predicti heredis vj li. ob. qa. terre.

Et predicta Margeria recipere consuevit de domino istius manerii pro recompensatione dotis per annum iij s. v d.

Et apud Thirning' in Comitatu Huntyngdon'[10] sunt de hereditate predicti heredis C s. redditus qui fuit Rois' quondam uxor predicti Galfridi matris predicti heredis qui nuper obiit.

Feoda militaria que tenentur de Torpel

Johannes Fauuel tenet xl solidos terre pro servicium medietatis feodi unius militis faciendo sectam ad curiam de Torpel de iij septimanis in tres septimanas. Willelmus de Colevyle tenet unum mesuagium et dimidiam virgatam terre per servicium viij^ue^ partis feodi unius militar' reddendo inde per annum duas libras que extenduntur supra inter liberos tenentes. Et custodia de Leholm tenetur de Torpel per servicium medietatis feodi unius militis.

[Upton']

Item dicunt super sacramentum suum quod est ibi quoddam capitale mesuagium cum gardinis, et valet per annum x s. Est ibi unum columbarium ad quod columbe non habent accessum, et ideo nichil valet per annum. Sunt ibi due carucate terre in quibus continentur CCiiij^xx^xvij acre dimidiam et dimidiam rodam. De quibus sunt CClxxvij acre dimidiam et dimidiam rodam quarum quelibet acra valet per annum viij d. Summa ix li. v s. ix d. Et de residuo xx acr' quelibet valet per annum iij d. Summa v s.

Summa x li. ix d.

Sunt ibi viij acre prati quarum quelibet valet per annum iij s. Summa xxiiij s. Est ibi unus boscus qui vocatur Suthawe cuius herbagium et subboscus valent per annum xv s. iiij d. Sunt ibi quedam pasture que vocantur Le Haye, Wyndmellebrok' et Le Mormedwe. Et valent per annum vj s. Summa xlv s. iiij d.

Sunt ibi libere tenentes qui reddunt per annum ij s. vj d. et dimidiam libram cymini prec' ob. qa. et nullum aliud servicium.

Summa ii s. vj d. ob. qa.

[fo. 18r] Sunt ibi quinque villani qui tenent in villenagio quinque mesuagia et sexaginta acras terre et quilibet eorum reddit per annum iij s. ix d. Summa xviij s. ix d.

Et quilibet eorum arrabit cum duobus bobus ij arruras per annum, et valet arrura cuiuslibet ij d. Summa x d. Et quilibet eorum dabit ad Natale j gallum et iiij gallinas. Et valent vij d.

Summa ij s. xj d.

Et quilibet eorum dabit ad Natale et ad Pascha pro maltsilver iiij d. Summa xx d. Et quilibet eorum dabit ad Pascha xx^ti ova que valent ob. Summa ij d. ob. Et quilibet eorum operabitur a die sancti Johannis baptiste usque ad festum sancti Michaelis; videlicet per xiij septimanas et quinque dies. Et sunt xxvij dies operabiles per idem tempus in quibus quilibet eorum serclabit per iiij dies et valet operatio cuiuslibet per diem ob. Summa x d. Et quilibet eorum falcabit per unum diem et valet operatio cuiuslibet per diem ij d. ob. Summa xij d. ob. Et quilibet eorum levabit fenum per iij dies ut estimatur[11] et valet operatio cuiuslibet per diem j d. Summa xv d. Et quilibet eorum cariabit ij carectas feni et valet cariatio cuiuslibet ij d. Summa x d. Et quilibet eorum metet in autumpno per xvj dies. Et valet operatio cuiuslibet ij s. viij d. Summa xiij s. iiij d. Et quilibet eorum metet ij bedripes ad cibum domini et ij benes sine cibo. Et valet operatio cuiuslibet xij d. Summa v s. Et quilibet eorum fac' alia opera autumpnalia per ij dies. Et valet operatio cuiuslibet ij d. Summa x d. Et quilibet eorum cariabit j carectatam bladi in autumpno. Et valet cariatio cuiuslibet j d. Summa v d.

Summa xxix s. ij d. xxv s. v d.[12]

Sunt ibi sex villani qui tenent sex virgates terre et continet quelibet virgata xxiiij acras terre et quilibet eorum reddit per annum vij s. vj d. Summa xlv s. Et quilibet eorum arrabit bis per annum semel ad semen yemale et semel ad semen quadragesimale. Et valet operatio cuiuslibet iiij d. Summa ij s. Et quilibet eorum dabit ad Natale unum gallum et quinque gallinas. Et valent viij d. Summa iiij s. Et quilibet eorum dat ad Natale et ad Pascha pro maltsilver viij d. Summa iiij s. Et quilibet eorum dabit ad Pascha xx ova et valent ob. Summa iij d. Et quilibet eorum operabitur a festo nativitatis sancti Johannis baptiste usque festum sancti Michaelis; videlicet in qualibet septimana per tres dies, et sunt xlj dies operabiles per idem tempus, de quibus quilibet serclabit per ix dies. Et valet operatio cuiuslibet iiij d. ob. Summa ij s. iij d. Et quilibet eorum falcabit per iij dies. Et valet operatio cuiuslibet vij d. ob. Summa iij s. ix d. Et quilibet eorum levabit fenum per iij dies. Et valet operatio cuiuslibet iij d. Summa xviij d. Et quilibet eorum cariabit tres carectatas feni et valet operatio cuiuslibet iij d. Summa xviij d. Et quilibet eorum metet per xxvj dies et valet operatio cuiuslibet iiij s. iiij d. Summa xxvj s. Et quilibet eorum fac' ij bedripes ad cibum domini cum iiij hominibus per diem. Et valet operatio cuiuslibet per diem allocato cibo j d. Summa iiij s. Et quilibet eorum fac' ij benes in autumpno ad cibum[13] suum proprium cum iiij hominibus et valet operatio cuiuslibet hominis per diem ij d. Summa viij s.[14] Et quilibet eorum cariabit ij carectatas bladi et valet cariatio cuiuslibet carectate ij d. ob. Summa xv d. Et quilibet eorum dabit ad festum sancti Michaelis unam aucam et valet ij d. Summa xij d. Et omnes predicti villani dabunt de auxilio per annum ij marcas. Et dabunt pro quolibet porco necato per annum ob. et estimatur ad iiij d.

Summa vij li. xvj s. xj d.

Summa reddituum operum et aux' villanorum predictorum ix li. v s.[15] viij li. xviij s. vij d.

[fo. 18v] Sunt ibi quinque coterelli qui tenent cotagia et diversimode fac' opera quorum quidam tenet unum mesuagium et sex acras terre et reddit per annum xviij d. Et dat ad Natale ij gall' et valent iij d. Et dat ad Pascha xx ova et valent ob. Et operabitur a die sancti Johannis baptiste; videlicet per xiij septimanas et quinque dies in qualibet septimana per j diem, et sunt xiiij dies[16] operabiles per idem tempus, quorum serclabit per iij dies et valet operatio illa j d. ob. Et falcabit per unum diem et valet operatio ij d. ob. Et levabit fenum per ij dies et valet ij d. Et metet per viij dies in autumpno. Et valet operatio per diem ij d. Summa xvj d. Et fac' benes in autumpno et valet iiij d. Et fac' ij bedripes ad cibum domini et valet operatio illa cibo allocato ij d. Et contribuet ad auxilium predictum.

Summa iiij s. j d. ob.

Est ibi alius coterellus qui tenet unum mesuagium et unam acram terre et j rodam prati et reddit per annum ij s. et dat ad Natale ij gall' et valent iij d. Et dat ad Pascha xx ova. Et valent ob. Et falcabit per[17] unum diem et valet ij d. ob. Et levabit fenum per unum diem et valet j d. Et fac' ij bedripes ad cibum domini et valet operatio illa ij d. Et fac' ij benes et valet operatio illa iiij d. Summa iij s. j d.

Et est ibi tercius coterellus qui tenet unum mesuagium et reddit per annum xij d. Et ad Natale dat ij gall' et valent iij d. Et ad Pascha xx ova et valent ob. Et levabit fenum per j diem et valet ob. Et fac' ij bedripes ad cibum domini et valet operatio illa ij d. Et fac' ij benes ad cibum proprium et valet operatio illa iiij d. Summa xxj d. ob.

Et est ibi quartus coterellus qui tenet j mesuagium et dimidiam acram terre et reddit per annum ij s. et dat ad Natale ij gall' et valent iij d. Et ad Pascha xx ova et valent ob et levabit fenum per unum diem et valet j d. Et fac' ij bedripes ad cibum domini et ij benes sine cibo et valent vj d.

Summa ij s. x d. ob.

Est ibi quintus coterellus qui tenet j mesuagium et j acram terre et dimidiam rodam prati et reddit per annum xij d. Et dat ad Natale ij gall' et valent iij d. Et ad Pascha xx ova et valent ob. et falcabit per unum diem et valet j d. ob. Et levabit fenum per unum diem et valet j d. Et fac' j bedripe ad cibum domini et j bene ad cibum proprium et valent iij d.

xiij s. vij d. ix d.[18]

Summa redd' et operum coterellorum xvj s. x d. ob.[18]

Summa summarum tocius manerii de Upton' xxij li. vij s. xvj d. qua. xxj d. ob.[19]

Predicta maneria de Torpel et Upton' tenentur de abbate de Burgo Sancti Petri per servicium iiij feodorum milit' et redd' per annum pro manerio de Torpel predicto abbati pro wardo de Rokingham xvj s. Et de auxilio vicecomitis xij s. Et pro visu franciplegii iiij s. Et debet sectam ad curiam de Castre de tribus septimanis[20] in tres septimanas que extenditur ad dimidiam marcam.[21] Et redd' pro manerio de Upton' per annum predicto abbati xlvj s. et magistro Roberto de Scheffeud per annum xij d.

Summa servicia maneriorum predictorum exceptis feodis milit' et cum secta curie lxxix s.[22] iiij li. v s. viij d.

Summa utriusque maneriorum ... viij s. iij d.[23]

1 Peter of Leicester was an Exchequer official. Prestwich, *Edward I*, p. 340.
2 *et valet ... quadragesimale* in margin.
3 *custum* in MS.
4 *semen* interlined.
5 *Et valet car' cuiuslibet iij d. ob.* cancelled.
6 *cum duobus hominibus* cancelled and *operabitur ... septimana* interlined.
7 *videlicet* interlined.
8 *xviij* cancelled.
9 *pro ... Offord* added in cramped hand in the margin.
10 *Huntyngdon* interlined.
11 *ut estimatur* interlined.
12 *xxix s. ij d. xv s. v d.* cancelled.
13 *custum* in MS.
14 *Et quilibet eorum fac' ij benes ... viij s.* added in margin.
15 *ix li. v s.* cancelled.
16 *dies* interlined.
17 *per* interlined.
18 *xiij s. vij d. ix d.* interlined. *vij d. and xvjs. xd.* cancelled. Marginal annotation *pro bet'*.
19 *vij s. xvj d.* cancelled and replaced with *xvj d. ob.*
20 *septimanis* interlined.
21 *que extenditur ad dimidiam marcam* interlined.
22 *lxxix s.* cancelled.
23 *Summa ... iij d.* annotation at the foot of the folio.

[fo. 19r] Carte de Coldestowe

33 Grant by Richard Pykenot with the consent of his wife Edith to Abbot Akarius and the convent of three bovates, five selions of land and three tofts in Stow by Threckingham. [1200–10]

Sciant[1] omnes tam presentes quam futuri quod ego Ricardus Pykenot assensu et voluntate Edith' uxoris mee et heredum meorum concessi et dedi et presenti carta confirmavi Deo et sancto Petro et ecclesie de Burgo et Akario abbati de Burgo et successoribus suis et conventui eiusdem loci in liberam, puram et perpetuam elemosinam in villa de Stowe prope Trikingham, unam bovatam terre cum tofto Ranulfi, quam bovatam Colswanus aliquando tenuit, et aliam bovatam terre cum tofto et pertinenciis quam Willelmus Blund' tenuit aliquando. Et terciam bovatam quam Walterus Godard aliquando tenuit. Et quinque seliones terre que jacent juxta toftum prefati Willelmi Blundi. Et preterea toftum quod fuit Rogeri Roket et Gubbetoft. Habenda et libere, integre et honorifice inperpetuum possidenda absque omni servicio et seculari demanda ad me vel ad meos sive ad quemlibet alium pertinente. Hanc autem terram cum pertinenciis, ego Ricardus Pykenot' et heredes mei warantizabimus ecclesie de Burgo contra omnes homines. Et acquitabimus ab omni seculari servicio vel demanda inperpetuum. Quod ut ratum et stabile perseveret presentem cartam sub sigillo meo ecclesie de Burgo in futurorum memoriam dedi. Et testibus communivi domino Rogero de Torpel, Galfrido filio Gaufridi, Gaufrido filio Gibewyn'[2], Gervasio de Bernech, Willelmo de Mart', Hugone filio Alani, Robert de Ascheby, Gaufrido de Billingburgo, Willelmo de Walecot' Hugone de Trikingham, Gwiton' Foliot, Roberto filio Walter, Gaufrido de Brunna, Rogero filio Andree et aliis

[Marginated] thur'

1 Also in Soc. of Antiquaries, MS 38, fo. 134v and BL, Cott. Cleop. C ii, fo. 33r–v, where only the first witness is given.

2 Recte *Gaufrido Gibewyn*, abbey steward?

34 Confirmation by Robert Marmioun of the grant by Richard Pykenot to the abbot and convent of land in Stow by Threckingham (no. 33). [early thirteenth century]

Confirmatio Roberti Marmioun de terra de Stowe.

Sciant[1] presentes et futuri quod ego Robertus Marmioun ratam et gratam habens[2] donationem quam Ricardus Pykenot fecit Deo et sancto Petro et ecclesie de Burgo et abbati et conventui eiusdem loci de quibusdam toftis et terris cum eorum pertinenciis in villa de Stowe prope Trikingham, eadem tofta et easdem terras cum eorum pertinenciis prefatis abbati et conventui de Burgo in liberam, puram et perpetuam elemosinam confirmavi; videlicet unam bovatam terre cum tofto Ranulphi quam bovatam Colswanus aliquando tenuit. Et aliam bovatam terre cum tofto et pertinenciis quam Willelmus Blundus aliquando tenuit. Et terciam [fo. 19v] bovatam terre quam Walterus Godard aliquando tenuit. Et quinque seliones terre que jacent juxta toftum prefati Willelmi Blundi. Et unum toftum quod fuit Rogeri Roket. Et Gubbetofth, habenda et tenenda libere absque omni servicio et seculari demanda in liberam, puram et perpetuam elemosinam. Et ut hec mea confirmatio perpetuum robur optineat presens scriptum sigilli mei appositione roboravi. Testibus hiis: Almarico de Sabloyl, Willelmo de Osberneby, Willelmo de Newton'. Waltero de Bykethorp', Waltero Frost, Gaufrido de Wymundham tunc decano de Bukingham, magistro Willelmo de Stavenebi, Ricardo fratre eius, magistro Willelmo de Scote' et aliis.

1 Also in Soc. of Antiquaries, MS 38, fos 134v–5r and BL Cott. Cleop. C ii, fos 33v–4r, where only the first witness is given. See also Swaffham fo. 238v for a marginal reference to this confirmation.
2 *habens* twice. The first cancelled.

35 Quitclaim of William de Sudsex to the abbot and convent of a bovate of land formerly held by Colswanus, a toft formerly held by Ranulph and five selions in Stow by Threckingham. [early thirteenth century]

Carta Willelmi de Sudsex per quam dedit et quietumclamavit ecclesie Burgi totum jus et clamium quod habuit in bovata terre in villa de Stowe quam Colswanus aliquando tenuit. Et preterea unum toftum et v seliones terre in eadem villa.

Omnibus[1] Christi fidelibus ad quorum audienciam presens carta pervenerit Willelmus de Sudsex salutem in Domino. Noverit universitas vestra me divine pietatis intuitu dedisse et quietum clamasse Deo et ecclesie sancti Petri de Burgo et conventui ibidem Deo famulanti totum jus et clamium quod in bovata terre cum pertinenciis in villa de Stowe prope Trikingham quam Colswanus aliquando tenuit et ibidem in tofto quod Ranulphus aliquando tenuit et in quinque selionibus terre ibidem que jacent proxime tofto prenominato de me et heredibus meis in perpetuum. Quare volo ut prefati abbas et conventus inperpetuum terras sepedictas cum omnibus pertinenciis habeant et pacifice possideant absque omni reclamatione mei vel meorum heredum libere, pure, integre et honorifice absque omni servicio ad me sive ad heredes meos pertinente. Et ne hec autem memoria ex stantium vel futurorum excidere possit, presentem cartam sigillo meo roboratam eis in futurorum memoriam dedi. Et testibus hiis communivi: domino Rogero de Thorpell', Gaufrido filio Gaufridi, Roberto de Melton', Pagano de Helpiston', Gaufrido de Lehame, Turoldo de Castro, magistro Gileberto de Stowe, magistro Willelmo de Staveneby, magistro Willelmo de Scote', Ricardo filio Umfridi, Gilberto de Manneby, Ricardo de Staveneby, Henrico de Wermington', Radulpho Bachun, Ade de Pillesg' et aliis multis.

1 Also in Soc. of Antiquaries, MS 38, fo. 135r and BL, Cott. Cleop. C ii, fo. 34r–v, where only the first witness is given. See Swaffham, fo. 238v for marginal reference to this quitclaim.

36 Grant by Richard Pikenot of two tofts and a bovate of land in Stow by Threckingham to Abbot Akarius and the convent together with confirmation of the five selions granted by William de Sudsex [1200–10]

[fo. 20r] Item carta Ricardi Pikenot.

Sciant[1] omnes tam presentes quam futuri quod ego Ricardus Pykenot pro anima patris mei et matris mee et antecessorum meorum concessi et dedi et presenti carta confirmavi Deo et sancto Petro et ecclesie Burgi et abbati de Burgo Achario et eiusdem loci conventui duo tofta in villa de Stowe prope de Trikingham; scilicet unum quod fuit Willelmi Blundi et aliud quod fuit Rogeri Roketh. Et unam bovatam terre cum omnibus pertinenciis suis quam prefatus Willelmus Blundus aliquando tenuit in liberam, puram et perpetuam elemosinam, quietam de me et heredibus meis in perpetuum. Hanc autem bovatam terre cum pertinenciis et duo tofta predicta ego Ricardus Pikenoth et heredes mei warantizabimus ecclesie Burgi contra omnes homines et acquietabimus ab omni forensi servicio et seculari demanda. Preterea ego Ricardus Pikenoth hac mea carta confirmo iam dicte ecclesie Burgi quinque seliones terre in eadem villa quas Willelmus de Sudsex homo meus assensu et voluntate mea prescripte ecclesie dedit et carta sua confirmavit sicut ipsius carta quam inde habet ecclesia Burgi testatur. Quod ut perpetue firmitatis robur optineat, presentem cartam eis sub sigillo meo in futurorum memoriam dedi et testibus hiis communivi: Rogero de Torpel, Gaufrido filio Gaufridi, Gileberto de Berneke, Willelmo de Mortune, Hugone filio Alani, Roberto de Ascebi, Gaufrido persona de Billingb', Willelmo de Walec', Hugone de Trikingham, Willelmo de Sudsex, Widone Folioth, Roberto filio Walteri de Thurlebi, Gaufrido filio decani de Thurlebi, Gaufrido de Burne, Rogero filio Andree

1 Also in Soc. of Antiquaries, MS 38, fo. 135r–v and BL, Cott. Cleop. C ii, fos 34v–5r, where only the first witness is given.

37 Confirmation by Richard Pikenoth and Edith his wife of the grant to Abbot Akarius and the convent of William Blund of Stow and his family in return for two marks. [1200–10]

Item carta Ricardi Pikenoth de Willelmo Blundo.

Notum[1] sit omnibus tam presentibus quam futuris quod ego Ricardus Pikenoth assensu et voluntate Edide uxoris mee et heredum meorum concessi et dedi et presenti carta confirmavi Deo et sancto Petro et abbati de Burgo Akario et successoribus suis et eiusdem loci conventui in perpetuum Willelmum Blund' de Stowe prope Trikengham quondam hominem meum cum tota sequela suum [sic] habenda et pacifice possidenda inperpetuum sine omni contradictione vel reclamatione mei vel meorum. Ego autem Ricardus Pikenoth et heredes mei omnibus diebus vite nostre warantizabimus [fo. 20v] ecclesie Burgi contra omnes homines prefatum Willelmum Blund' de Stowe et totam sequelam suam. Pro hac autem mea donatione et confirmatione prefati abbas Akarius de Burgo et conventus eiusdem loci mihi dederunt coram multis viris discretis duas marcas argenti. Quod ut perpetuo ratum maneat et inconcussum presentem cartam sub sigillo meo eis in futurorum memoriam dedi et testibus hiis communivi: Roberto de Braibroc, domino Rogero de Thorpel, Gaufrido filio Gaufridi, Gileberto de Berneke, Hugone filio Alani, Willelmo de Mortune, Roberto de Asceby, Gaufrido persona Billingburgo et aliis.

1 Also in Soc. of Antiquaries, MS 38, fo. 135v and BL, Cott. Cleop. C ii, fo. 35r–v without the witness clause. See Swaffham, fo. 238v for a marginal reference to this grant.

38 Grant by Richard Pikenoth and his wife Edith to Abbot Akarius and the convent of two bovates, three tofts and five selions in Stow by Threckingham. [1200–10]

Item carta Ricardi Pikenoth de terra de Stowe.

Sciant[1] omnes tam presentes quam futuri quod ego Ricardus Pikenoth assensu et voluntate Edithe uxoris mee et heredum meorum concessi et dedi et presenti carta confirmavi Deo et sancto Petro et ecclesie de Burgo et Akario abbati de Burgo et successoribus suis et conventui eiusdem loci in liberam, puram et perpetuam elemosinam in villa de Stowe prope Trikingham unam bovatam terre cum tofto Ranulphi quam bovatam Colswanus aliquando tenuit et aliam bovatam terre cum tofto et pertinenciis quam Willelmus Blundus aliquando tenuit et quinque seliones terre que jacent juxta toftum prefati Willelmi Blundi. Et preterea toftum quod fuit Rogeri Roket' et Gubbetoft.[2] Habenda et libere integre et honorifice possidenda in perpetuum absque omni servicio et seculari demanda ad me vel ad meos sive ad quemlibet alium pertinente. Hanc autem terram cum pertinenciis ego Ricardus Pikenoth et heredes mei warantizabimus ecclesie de Burgo contra omnes homines. Et acquietabimus ab omni seculari servicio vel demanda inperpetuum. Quod ut ratum et stabile perseveret, presentem cartam sub sigillo meo ecclesie de Burgo in futurorum memoriam dedi et testibus communivi: domino Rogero de Torpell', Gaufrido filio Gaufridi, Gaufrido Gibewyn', Gervasio de Bernech'. Willelmo de Mortune, Hugone filio Alani, Roberto de Hasceby, Gaufrido de Billingburgo, Willelmo de Walekot' et aliis.

1 Also in Swaffham, fo. 238v.
2 *Gulbetoft* in Swaffham.

39 Grant by William de Sudsex, with the consent of his lord Richard Pikenoth, to Abbot Akarius and the convent of five selions in Stow by Threckingham. [1200–10]

Carta Willelmi de Sudsex de quinque selionibus terre.

Notum[1] sit omnibus tam presentibus quam futuris quod ego Willelmus de Sudsex assensu et voluntate Ricardi Pikenoth' domini mei concessi et dedi et presentis scripti patrocinio [fo. 21r] confirmavi Deo et sancto Petro et ecclesie Burgi et abbati Akario de Burgo et conventui eiusdem loci in liberam, puram et perpetuam elemosinam in villa de Stowe prope Trikingham quinque seliones terre que jacent directe juxta toftum quod fuit Willelmi Blundi. Habendas et tenendas libere et quiete absque omni seculari servicio, salvo libero exitu meo et heredum meorum sicut antiquitus esse solebat. Has autem quinque seliones ego Willelmus de Sudsex et heredes mei warantizabimus ecclesie Burgi et acquietabimus ab omni seculari servicio inperpetuum. Quod ut stabile et firmum perseveret presenti carte sigillum meum apposui et testibus hiis communivi: Rogero de Torpel, magistro Gaufrido Gibewyn' tunc senescall' Abbathie Burgi et aliis.

1 Also in Soc. of Antiquaries, MS 38, fos 135v–6r and BL, Cott. Cleop. C ii, fo. 35v, with fewer witnesses. See Swaffham fo. 238v for marginal reference to this 'small charter'.

40 Grant by Richard Pikenoth to William de Sudsex of one bovate in Stow by Threckingham. [early thirteenth century]

Carta Ricardi Pikenoth per quam dedit Willelmo de Sudsex unam bovatam terre in villa de Stowe.

Sciant[1] omnes ad quos presens scriptum pervenerit quod ego Ricardus Pikenot assensu Edith' sponse[2] mee dedi et concessi et hac mea carta teste confirmavi Willelmo de Suthsexeya et heredibus suis illam bovatam terre que fuit Colswani cum omnibus pertinenciis exceptis illis que Martinus de ea tenet; scilicet tofto et duabus selionibus, et in orientali parte ville de Stowe toftum quod fuit Ranulphi et quinque seliones que in orientali parte adjaceant propinquiores eidem tofto. Hec autem predicta cum pertinenciis dedi et concessi et hac carta teste confirmavi eidem Willelmo et heredibus suis, tenenda de me et heredibus meis libere quiete honorifice in feodo et hereditate, reddendo annuatim iij solidos pro omni servicio mihi et heredibus meis pertinente, salvo forinseco; scilicet xij d. in festo beati Johannis baptiste et xij d. in festo beati Michaelis et xij d. in purificatione beate Marie. Et sciendum est quod ego Ricardus Pikenot et heredes mei warantizabimus hec omnia prefato Willelmo et heredibus suis contra omnes homines. Hiis testibus et cetera

1 Also in Soc. of Antiquaries, MS 38, fo. 136r and BL, Cott. Cleop. C ii, fos 35v–6r, where the witness clause is also omitted.
2 *uxoris* in other texts.

41 Grant by Thomas son of Martin of Stow to the abbot and convent of two acres in Stow by Threckingham. [early thirteenth century]

Carta Thome filii Martini de terra de Stowe.

Noverint[1] universi ad quos presens scriptum pervenerit quod ego Thomas filius Martini de Stowe concessi et dedi in puram et perpetuam elemosinam [fo. 21v] Deo et beato Petro et abbati et conventui de Burgo duas acras terre mee in campis de Stowe juxta Trikingham; scilicet dimidiam acram que jacet inter terras Walteri Frost de Trikingham et Hugonis clerici de Trikingham que abuttat super viam Hoilondie. Et unam rodam et dimidiam que jacent inter terras Hugonis clerici de Trikingham et filie Durandi de Folkingham et abuttant super predictam viam. Et dimidiam acram in yllatis que jacet inter terras Walteri Frost de Trikingham et Briani filii Swane de Folkingham que abuttat super semitam de Hurbeling'. Et unam rodam et dimidiam in Stangraftes et abuttant super predictam semitam et jacent inter terras Petri de Stowe et Willelmi Skirmiatoris de Trikingham. Et unam rodam in Stangraftes que jacet inter terras abbatis de Burgo et Walteri Fabri de Trikingham. Et ego et heredes mei prenominatas terras warantizabimus predictis abbati et conventui de Burgo contra omnes homines inperpetuum. Et ut hec mea donatio inconcussa et stabilis permaneat presenti scripto sigillum meum apposui. Hiis testibus et cetera

1 Also in Swaffham, fo. 238r, Soc. of Antiquaries, MS 38, fo. 136r–v and BL, Cott. Cleop. C ii, fo. 36r–v, where the witness clause is also omitted.

42 Grant by Robert Bulgard to the abbot and convent of half an acre of meadow in Billingborough. [early thirteenth century]

Carta Roberti Bulgard de dimidia acra prati.

Notum[1] sit omnibus hoc scriptum visuris vel audituris quod ego Robertus Bulgard dedi et concessi et presenti carta confirmavi pro salute anime mee et antecessorum meorum abbati et conventui sancti Petri de Burgo in liberam puram et perpetuam elemosinam dimidiam acram prati in campo de Billingburg', illam scilicet que jacet in prato de Heldgerdung' inter pratum sanctimonialium de Sempringham ex una parte et pratum quod fuit Pagani de Bullingburg'[2] ex altera. Et abuttat super Mukledic. Tenendam et habendam libere et quiete ab omni seculari servicio. Et ego Robertus et heredes mei warantizabimus predictam dimidiam acram dicto abbati et conventui contra omnes homines et feminas. Et de omni servicio tam de forinseco quam de alio acquietabimus. Ut hec autem mea donatio et concessio rata et stabilis permaneat, eis hanc presentem cartam meam feci et sigilli mei inpressione coroboravi. Hiis testibus: domino Alexandro de Poington', domino Stephano de Horbling', Nicholao de Billingborc, Thoma de Stowe, Briano filio Swane, Willelmo de Stowe et aliis

1 Also in Soc. of Antiquaries, MS 38, fos 136v–7r, BL, Cott. Cleop. C ii, fo. 37r and in Swaffham, fo. 238v. None give witnesses.
2 The same variant spelling is found in other texts.

43 Grant by Henry Foliot of Luffenham to Abbot Martin and the convent of two acres in Stow by Threckingham. [1230]

[fo. 22r] Carta Henrici Foliot de duabus acras terre apud Stowe confecta anno ab incarnatione Domini M°CC°xxx° ante festum sancti Michaelis.

Universis[1] sancte matris ecclesie filiis presens scriptum visuris vel audituris Henricus Foliot de Luffenham salutem in Domino. Noverit universitas vestra me divine pietatis intuitu pro salute anime mee et antecessorum meorum dedisse et concessisse et hac presenti carta mea confirmasse Martino Dei gratia abbati de Burgo et eiusdem loci conventui duas acras terre arabilis in territorio de Stowe cum omnibus pertinenciis et libertatibus ad predictam terram pertinentibus. Quarum una jacet super Brochow inter terram Briani de Stowe filii Swane ex parte orientali et terram Hugonis filii Walteri de Trikingham ex parte occidentali, et dimidia acra versus campum de Horbeling' inter terras predicti Hugonis filii Walteri ex parte orientali et occidentali, et alia dimidia acra similiter versus campum de Horbeling' que jacet inter terram prenominati Briani ex parte occidentali et terram Girardi de Stowe ex parte orientali. Habendas et tenendas sibi et successoribus suis libere et quiete et pacifice in puram et perpetuam elemosinam inperpetuum. Ego vero et heredes mei predictas duas acras cum pertinenciis predictis abbati et conventui warantizabimus et defendemus contra omnes homines inperpetuum. Et ut hec mea donatio concessio et confirmatio rata et inconcussa permaneat ad futurorum memoriam huic scripto sigillum meum apposui. Hiis testibus et cetera

1 Also in Soc. of Antiquaries, MS 38, fo. 136v, BL, Cott. Cleop. C ii, fos 36v–7r and in Swaffham, fo. 238r–v, in a slightly abbreviated form. None give witnesses.

44 Grant of John Gowke of Stow to Abbot Richard and the convent of a meadow in Stow by Threckingham. [1274–95]

Carta Johannis Gowke de Stowe de prato.

Sciant[1] presentes et futuri quod ego Johannes Gowke de Stowe dedi concessi et hac presenti carta mea confirmavi domino Ricardo Dei gracia abbati de Burgo Sancti Petri et eiusdem loci conventui in liberam puram et perpetuam elemosinam totum pratum meum sicut jacet quod habui in Boyenge in pratis de Stowe. Quod quidem pratum continet in latitudine duodecim perticatas et dimidiam et quartam partem unius perticate cum omnibus suis pertinenciis et aysiamentis predicto prato spectantibus. Tenendum et habendum dictis abbati et conventui et eorum successoribus [fo. 22v] vel eorum assignatis ut predictum est libere quiete bene et in pace inperpetuum. Et ego Johannes et heredes mei predictum pratum cum omnibus suis pertinenciis predictis abbati et conventui et eorum successoribus vel eorum assignatis warantizabimus acquietabimus et contra omnes gentes inperpetuum defendemus. Et ut hec mea donatio concessio et carte presentis confirmatio in posterum firmitatis robur optineat presentem cartam sigilli mei munimine coroboravi. Hiis testibus et cetera

1 Also in Swaffham, fo. 36v (old foliation), Soc. of Antiquaries, MS 38, fo. 137r and BL, Cott. Cleop. C ii, fo. 37v, where the witness clause is also omitted.

45 Quitclaim of Matilda widow of John Gowke to the abbot and convent of her dower right in Boynge meadow in Stow by Threckingham in return for 10s paid to her in her great need. [later thirteenth century]

Carte Matilde uxoris Johannis Gouke per quam quietum clamavit abbati de Burgo et eiusdem loci conventui totum jus et clamium quod habuit in prato quod vocatur Boynge.

Omnibus[1] Christi fidelibus ad quos presens scriptum pervenerit Matilda que fuit uxor Johannis Gowk de Stowe salutem in Domino sempiternam. Noverit universitas vestra me in legitima viduitate mea concessisse remisisse et omnino quietum clamasse abbati de Burgo Sancti Petri et eiusdem loci conventui totum jus et clamium quod habui in tercia parte cuiusdam prati quod vocatur Boyenge in Stowe, illius scilicet prati quod dicti abbas et conventus habuerunt de dono et dimissione dicti Johannis quondam viri mei. Quam quidem terciam partem clamabam ut dotem meam per mortem dicti Johannis Gowk'. Ita quod ego decetero nichil juris vel clamii in predicto prato seu aliis rebus quibuscumque nomine dotis erga ipsos habere vel clamare potero in perpetuum. Et pro hac concessione et quieta clamancia dedit mihi dictus abbas in magna necessitate mea decem solidos argenti. In cuius rei testimonium huic presenti scripto sigillum meum apposui. Hiis testibus et cetera

1 Also in Soc. of Antiquaries, MS 38, fo. 137r–v and BL, Cott. Cleop. C ii, fos 37v–8r, where the witness clause is also omitted.

46 Grant of King John allowing William de Albiniaco to enclose his park at Stoke Albany and hunt fox and hare in the royal forests. [May 1200-May 1201]

Carta domine Isabelle de Ros.[1]

Johannes Dei gratia rex Anglie et cetera. Sciatis quod concessimus Willelmo de Albaniaco et heredibus suis quod possit claudere parcum suum in Est Stokes qui vocatur Lunda et quod ipse et heredes sui venentur wlponi et leporem cum canibus suis in forestis nostris. Dat' et cetera. Anno regni nostri secundo.

1 Isabella was the daughter and heiress of William de Albini. J. Bridges, *The History and Antiquities of Northamptonshire*, 2 vols (Oxford, 1791), vol. II, p. 339.

[fo. 23r] Carte de Walecote super Humbram

47 Obligation by Prior Nicholas and the convent of Spalding to pay the abbey one mark p.a. rent for land in Alkborough and Walcot. [1186–93[1]]

[Marginated] Walc'

Universis[2] sancte matris ecclesie filiis ad quorum audienciam presens scriptum pervenerit, Nicholaus prior de Spalding' totusque eiusdem loci conventus salutem in Domino. Noverit universitas vestra nos debere solvere singulis annis monasterio sancti Petri de Burgo pro una carucata terre in Haltebarg' et pro una bovata terre in Walecote quas de eodem monasterio[3] tenemus, unam marcam argenti ad firmam de Walecote ad duos terminos; dimidiam marcam videlicet in nativitate Domini et dimidiam marcam in nativitate sancti Johannis baptiste. Et preterea solvemus eidem monasterio singulis annis in passione apostolorum Petri et Pauli apud Burgum tres solidos et tres panes de astivello quod ut perpetue firmitatis robur optineat presenti scripto et sigilli nostri[4] testimonio communivimus.[5]

1 Dated from information in no. 48 about the participation of Hugh, bishop of Lincoln and Benedict, abbot of Peterborough.

2 Also in Swaffham, fo. 193r–v. For the Spalding Priory text, see, BL, Harl., 742, fo. 271r. The original dispute, settled *c.* 1150–55, had involved the church at Alkborough and a chapel at Walcot, which Spalding Priory agreed to build and endow with a bovate of land. Peterborough subsequently surrendered any claim to the church and chapel and granted Spalding Priory one carucate of land in Alkborough and two bovates of land in Walcot. BL, Harl., 742, fos 270r–v.

3 *sancti Petri de Burgo* inserted in Harl. MS.

4 *mei* in Harl. MS.

5 Harl. MS gives as witnesses *Hamone decano et capitulo Linc', Willelmo de Romar' et aliis.* Hamo appears as dean of Lincoln between c. 1189–1196.

48 Confirmation of Abbot William and the convent of St Nicholas, Angers of a transaction between Prior Nicholas and the convent of Spalding and Abbot Benedict and the convent of Peterborough over the church of Alkborough and land in Alkborough and Walcot, whereby Spalding Priory renounced the church of Normanby and acknowledged rents of one mark, three shillings and three barley loaves. [post Mar. 1191[1]]

[Marginated] Walc'

Universis[2] sancte matris ecclesie filiis ad quorum audienciam presens scriptum pervenerit, Willelmus Dei gracia abbas sancti Nicholai Andegavensis totusque eiusdem loci conventus salutem in Domino. Noverit universitas vestra nos ratam habere transactionem factam in presencia domini Hugonis Lincolniensis episcopi inter B[enedictum][3] abbatem Burgi et eiusdem loci conventum et Nicholaum priorem et monachos de Spalding' super ecclesia de Haltebarg' et una carucata terre in eadem villa et duabus bovatis terre in Walecote super quibus iam dicti abbas et conventus Burgi predictos priorem et monachos de Spalding' per litteras bone memorie Clementis pape traxerunt in causam. Ratam eciam habemus renunciationem ecclesie de Normanneby cum omnibus pertinencciis factam a memoratis priore et monachis de Spalding'. Retentis tamen sibi decimis de dominio eiusdem ville quas prius habuerunt sicut scripta coram prefato Lincolniensi episcopo et Lincolniensi capitulo inde confecta testantur. Confirmamus insuper sepedictis abbati et conventui de Burgo annuum redditum ipsius a priore et monachis de Spalding' debitum pro prenominatis carucata terre in Haltebarg' et duabus bovatis terre in Walecote unam scilicet marcam que solvetur ad firmam de Walecote singulis annis in duobus terminis, in nativitate Domini et in nativitate sancti Johannis baptiste. Et preterea tres solidos [fo. 23v] et tres panes de hastivello que solventur monasterio[4] Burgi in passione apostolorum Petri et Pauli annuatim apud Burgum sicut carte inter eos confecte testantur. Quod ut ratum habeatur et inconcussum presentis pagine inscriptione et sigillorum nostrorum appositione duximus corroborandum.[5]

1 Pope Clement died in March 1191.
2 Also in Swaffham, fo. 193v. For Spalding Priory's record of the dispute, including Bishop Hugh's ratification of this agreement, see BL, Harl. 742, fos 270v–1r.
3 Supplied from Harl. MS.
4 *monachis* in Harl. MS.
5 Harl. MS gives as witnesses *Philippo prior, Girardo sacrista monach', de clericis Herberto fratre abbatis Stephano capellano, de laicis Simone de Sancto Lamberto et aliis.*

49 Cyrograph agreement, following litigation in the royal court, between Abbot Richard and the convent of Peterborough and the abbot and convent of Ramsey over view of frankpledge involving Ramsey's tenants at Barnwell, Hemington, Crowthorp and Littlethorp. It was also agreed that Ramsey's market at Barnwell would be suppressed and that, in return, Peterborough would not hinder the creation of a market at Elton. Ramsey would also enjoy common in the meadow at *Keleseye*. [6 Oct. 1279]

Cyrographum inter Ricardum de London' abbatem de Burgo et abbatem de Rameseye.

[Marginated] Und'

Noverint[1] universi quod cum placita et contentiones essent mote in curia domini regis apud Westmonasterium in octabis sancti Michaelis anno regni regis Edwardi septimo inter abbatem de Burgo Sancti Petri ex parte una et abbatem de Rameseye ex altera, concordatum et pacificatum est inter eos in hac forma subscripta; videlicet quod dictus abbas de Rameseye concessit pro se et ecclesia sua quod homines sui de Bernewell' Hemmyngton' Crowethorp' et Parva Thorp' venient coram ballivis predicti abbatis de Burgo ad visum franciplegii bis in anno modo debito et sicut facere consueverunt tempore quo predicte ville fuerunt in manus Berengeri le Moyne et antecessorum suorum per rationabilem et consuetam summonitionem ballivi predicti. Et ballivus dicti abbatis de Rameseye sedebit cum ballivo dicti abbatis de Burgo ad visus predictos si voluerit ad recipiendas extractas medietatis omnium amerciamentorum seu finium aut quorumcumque proficuum de villanis ipsius abbatis de Rameseye[2] quibuscumque de causis in predictis villis emergentium que ad visum franciplegii pertinent, salvis abbati de Burgo redditibus et rebus ab antiquo arentatis, que medietas ipsi abbati de Rameseye et successoribus suis remanebit inperpetuum. Et altera medietas predicto abbati de Burgo et successoribus[3] suis inperpetuum. Nec habebit ballivus predicti abbatis de Rameseye aliam jurisdictionem quam ad recipiendas et levandas predictas extractas medietatis predicte nec propter eius absenciam omittetur quo minus ballivus predicti abbatis de Burgo faciat officium suum. Et salva integre sint eidem abbati de Burgo amerciamenta fines et proficua proveniencia de liberis hominibus ipsius abbatis de Rameseye ad visus predictos. Et similiter integre de villanis ipsius abbatis de Rameseye de forinsecis transgressionibus que ad visum franciplegii pertinent. Amerciabuntur eciam villani predicti abbatis de Rameseye per pares suos proximiores predictarum et vicinarum villarum. Habebit eciam predictus abbas de Burgo et successores sui regalitatem suam integram in predictis villis cum redditibus et rebus arentatis, ita plene sicut ipse et predecessores sui habere consueverunt temporibus predicti Berengeri et antecessorum suorum, salvis abbati de Rameseye concessionibus predictis. [fo. 24r]

Concessit eciam idem abbas de Rameseye pro se et successoribus suis quod mercatum levatum apud Bernewell' cum pyllorio et tumberello prosternatur imperpetuum. Concessit eciam idem abbas de Burgo pro se et successoribus suis et ecclesia sua de Burgo quantum in ipsis est quod predictus abbas de Rameseye levare possit unum mercatum apud Aylyngton' per diem Lune vel Martis sine impedimento vel contradictione ipsius abbatis de Burgo et successorum suorum imperpetuum. Et similiter quod predictus abbas de Rameseye et homines sui habeant pacificam communam in quodam prato quod vocatur Keleseye ita melius et liberius sicut predictus Berengerius et homines sui habere consueverunt. In cuius rei testimonium huic scripto in modum cyrographi confecto sigilla abbatum et conventuum de Burgo et Rameseye alternatim sunt appensa.

1 Also in Soc. of Antiquaries, MS 38, fos 32v–3v, BL, Cott. Cleop. C ii, fos 57r–8r and added in the margins of Swaffham, fos 98v–9r. For the Ramsey Abbey text, see Hart, Lyons, *Cartularium Monasterii de Rameseia*, vol. II, pp. 341–3.

2 *de Rameseye* repeated and cancelled.

3 *et successoribus* interlined.

50 Manumission of William son of Richard of Werrington. [4 June 1278]

Manumissio Willelmi filii Ricardi de Wytherington'.

Omnibus[1] Christi fidelibus ad quos presens scriptum pervenerit Ricardus permissione divina abbas de Burgo Sancti Petri et eiusdem loci conventus salutem in Domino sempiternam. Noverit universitas vestra nos manumisisse et ab omni jugo servitutis liberasse Willelmum filium Ricardi de Wytherington' quem aliquo tempore pro nativo nostro habuimus cum tota sequela sua et omnibus catallis suis, ita quod nec nos nec successores nostri aliquid juris vel clamii in predicto Willelmo sequela sua seu catallis suis exigere seu clamare poterimus, sed ipse Willelmus et tota sequela sua cum omnibus catallis suis liberi et quieti remaneant absque inquietatione exactione seu clamio aliquo nostri et successorum nostrorum ratione alicuius servitutis imperpetuum. Volumus eciam et concedimus quod ipse et heredes sui mesuagia terras redditus et prata in Wytherington' que antecessores sui tenuerunt de nobis et antecessoribus nostris dando et faciendo finem qui appellatur merchet pro filiabus suis maritandis et auxilium de anno in annum pro voluntate nostra decetero habeant et teneant de nobis et successoribus nostris libere quiete pacifice et hereditarie reddendo inde nobis et successoribus nostris annuatim quadraginta solidos sterlingorum ad quatuor anni terminos; videlicet ad nativitate sancti Johannis baptiste decem solidos, ad festum sancti Michaelis decem solidos, ad natale Domini decem solidos et ad Pascha decem solidos pro omni servicio exactione consuetudine et demanda seculari. Salvis tamen nobis sectis curie nostre[2] de Castre de tribus septimanis in tres septimanas wardis et releviis et forinseco domini regis cum acciderint. Et si contingat dictum Willelmum vel heredes suos sine herede aliquo tempore decedere, dicta mesuagia terra redditus et prata cum pertinenciis nobis et successoribus nostris plene et integre [fo. 24v] revertentur. Nec licebit dicto Willelmo vel heredibus suis dicta mesuagia terram redditus prata vel eorum aliquam partem dare vendere alienare invadiare seu aliquo modo incumbrare quo minus dicta mesuagia terra redditus et prata predicta in forma supranominata nobis et successoribus nostris revertantur, quod si secus fecerint factum suum penitus cassetur et quod inde alienatum fuerit nobis et successoribus nostris incurratur. In cuius rei testimonium huic scripto in modum cyrographi confecto ad majorem securitatem sigilla alternatim sunt appensa. Hiis testibus et cetera. Dat' apud Burgum ob amorem domini Roberti bone memorie quondam abbatis predecessoris nostri et avunculi dicti Willelmi et ad instanciam boni viri fratris Hugonis de Sutton' germani dicti domini Roberti abbatis. Anno Domini M° CC° septuagesimo octavo in vigilia Pentecoste.

1 Printed in *Mon. Angl.*, vol. I, p. 394, no. 44. Also in Soc. of Antiquaries, MS 38, fos 41r–2r and BL, Cott. Cleop. C ii, fos 71r–2r, where the witnesses are also omitted.
2 *nostre* interlined.

51 Grant by Abbot Richard of London to the convent of the freedom to build and repair a granary for their own crops and receive their ancient rations of grain and malt, also to build a separate bakehouse and brewhouse if they should wish. [1274–95]

Carta de blado et braseo deliberandis ad granarium conventus.

Universis Christi fidelibus presens scriptum visuris vel audituris Ricardus de Lond' miseratione divina abbas de Burgo Sancti Petri salutem in Domino sempiternam. Noverit universitas vestra nos concessisse ordinasse et statuisse pro nobis et successoribus nostris perpetuis temporibus observand' ad honorem Dei et utilitatem tam hosptialitatis quam elemosine ac religionis augmentum pacem et quietem tam obedienciariorum quam tocius capituli nostri quod conventus decetero habeat granarium per se suis sumptibus construendum et reparandum, et quod custos granarii predicti de communi consilio constitutus recipiat de granario abbatis qui pro tempore fuerit totam liberationem que ad conventum spectare consuevit secundum antiquam assisam frumenti et brasei et[1] cuiuscumque generis bladi fuerit per dictum custodem distribuendum et in usus pios convertendos. Ita quod custos qui pro tempore fuerit habeat electionem tocius frumenti abbatis brasei et pisarum secundum assisam predictam; videlicet de frumento singulis diebus unum quarterium et unum [sic] esk' per mensuram sepedictam[2] et singulis ebdomadis dimidium quarterium et dim' esk' frumenti de assignatione domini Roberti de Lyndeseye quondam abbatis pro octo monachis per ordinationem suam ad conventum augmentatis, preter particulares donationes que distribuuntur in principalibus festis et in die absolutionis ad mandatum et preter alias particulas minutas que sepe contingunt per annum. Idem eciam custos percipiet de braseo singulis ebdomadis quando braciatur de puro ordeo octodecim quarteria et quinque esk' de braseo ordei. Quando autem braciatur de ordeo et drageo, tunc percipiet in ebdomada viginti et unum quarteria et quinque esk' et dim'; videlicet de braseo ordei ad grutmalt vij quarteria et dimidium et de drageo xiiij quarteria j esk' et dimidiam. Quando vero braciatur de maysmalt, quod est pro majori parte avena, tunc percipiet in ebdomada viginti et quatuor quarteria unum esk' [fo. 25r] et dim'; videlicet de braseo ordei vij quarteria et dimidium et de maysmalt xvj quarteria v esk' et dimidiam. Percipiet eciam qualibet ebdomada unum quaterium de braseo ordei ex dono et concessione nostro preter assisam brasei supranotatam. Et si aliquid predictorum frumenti brasei vel pisarum ad opus conventus minus utile fuerit queratur in villa vel alibi quod melius poterit inveniri ad custus abbatis. Volumus eciam ordinamus et statuimus quod conventus decetero habeat omnes proventus et utilitates secundum capituli ordinationem que poterunt provenire de omnibus et singulis supranotatis. Ita quod dictus conventus per abbatem et ministros suos qui pro tempore fuerint omni solacio et quiete gaudeat ut decet suo perpetuo. Et ne aliquis abbas futurus ad ulteriorem liberationem teneatur ex debito nisi aliquid facere voluerit graciose nec ad excusationem predicte liberationis faciende nec retardationem subtractionem seu diminutionem aliquam obstare valeat vacacio abbathie aut caristia vel defectus cuiuscumque bladi quin liberatio predicta custodi granarii conventus ad suam et suorum sustentationem et consuetam hospitalitatem faciendam plene fiat sine aliqua diminutione. Si vero placuerit et oportunum videatur conventui pistrinam et bracinum habere separatum bene liceat eidem nova construere in loco competenti sine contradictione cuiuscumque et famulos sibi in ipsis ordinare et suis sumptibus sustentare. Volumus eciam ut conventus habeat liberam multuram infra abbaciam sicut antiquitus habere consuevit. Et si extra abbaciam propter aliquam necessitatem molere oporteat si ad molendinum qui ad abbatem spectat molere contingat nichilominus a multuro liberi sint.[3] Et ut ista ordinatio et concessio nostra perpetue firmitatis robur optineat, presens scriptum sigilli nostri munimine una cum sigilli capituli appositione roboramus.

1 *et* interlined.

2 *sepedictam* inserted later.

3 *Volumus ... sint* entered at foot of folio in a different hand.

52 Grant by Abbot Richard of London of a corrody to Peter Caumbrey and his son John. [15 Feb. 1274]

Carta Petri Caumbrey et filii eius.

Omnibus[1] Christi fidelibus ad quorum noticiam presens scriptum pervenerit R[icardo] permissione divina abbas de Burgo Sancti Petri et eiusdem loci conventus salutem in Domino sempiternam. Noveritis nos unanimi assensu concessisse Petro Caumbrey et Johanni filio eius primogenito unum corradium; videlict de celario conventus duos panes conventuales et duas lagenas cervisie conventualis de eodem doleo quo monachi bibunt, et duo fercula plenarie de coquina abbatis sicut liberi servientes de familia eiusdem melius habent singulis diebus vite ipsorum ubicumque fuerint percipienda. Ita quod si unus ipsorum moriatur nichilominus alter ipsorum habeat totum predictum corradium quamdiu vixerit absque aliqua contradictione vel calumpnia nostri seu successorum nostrorum. In cuius rei testimonium presenti scripto sigilla nostra duximus apponenda. Dat' in capitulo nostro in crastino sancti Valentini martiris, anno Domini M° CC° septuagesimo tercio.

1 Printed in *Mon. Angl.*, vol. I, pp. 393–4.

53 Grant by William de Beaumeys to the abbot and convent of access to his land at Crowthorp to maintain their mill pool. [25 Nov. 1296]

[fo. 25v] Carta Willelmi de Beaumeys de stagno molendini de Undel'.

[Marginated] Und'

Omnibus[1] Christi fidelibus presens scriptum visuris vel audituris Willelmus de Beaumeys in Crowethorp' juxta Undel' in comitatu Norht' salutem. Noveritis me concessisse abbati et conventui de Burgo Sancti Petri et eorum successoribus pro me et heredibus meis inperpetuum quoddam aysiamentum obstruendi et reparandi cursum aque ad molendinum suum in Undel' super solum meum in Crowethorp' prout commodius pro commodo molendini sui predicti viderint expedire sine calumpnia vel inpedimento mei vel heredum meorum inperpetuum. Ita quod predictus abbas nec successores sui nichil exigere vel clamare poterunt in predicto solo meo nisi tantum modo aysiamentum predictum. Et quod liceat predictis abbati et conventui et eorum successoribus in solo prati mei ibidem manuoperari ad obstructionem et defensionem cursus aque predicte pro commodo molendini sui predicti dum tamen per exitum aque dampnum ibidem non eveniat prato meo. Quod si contingat ad sumptus predictorum abbatis et conventus emendetur. In cuius rei testimonium presenti scripto in modum cyrographi confecto sigilla partium alternatim sunt appensa. Dat' apud Burgum Sancti Petri in festo sancte Katerine virginis anno regni regis Edwardi vicesimo quinto.

1 Also in Soc. of Antiquaries, MS 38, fo. 33v and BL, Cott. Cleop. C ii, fo. 58r–v.

Carte molendini de Stannford'

54 Cyrograph grant by Abbot John and the convent to the prioress and nuns of St Michael, Stamford of their mill at Stamford at fee farm for which the nuns will render ten marks p.a. [Feb. 1258]

[Marginated] Stanf'

Universis Christi fidelibus presens scriptum visuris vel audituris Johannes Dei gracia abbas de Burgo Sancti Petri et eiusdem loci conventus salutem in Domino. Noverit universitas vestra nos unanimi assensu tradidisse ad feodum firmam et concessisse priorisse sancti Michaelis extra Stannford' et monialibus eiusdem loci totum molendinum nostrum cum suis pertinenciis quod habuimus in Stannford', habendum et tenendum de nobis et successoribus nostris dictis priorisse et monialibus et earum successoribus, bene et in pace, libere inperpetuum, reddendo inde annuatim nobis et successoribus nostris decem marcas argenti ad duos terminos anni; scilicet ad festum sancti Michaelis quinque marcas et ad Pascha quinque marcas pro omni servicio exactione et omnimoda alia seculari demanda. Et nos et successores nostri dictis priorisse et monialibus et earum successoribus dictum molendinum cum suis pertinenciis contra omnes gentes per predictum servicium warantizabimus acquietabimus et defendemus inperpetuum. Et si contigerit aliquo casu quod dicta priorissa et moniales vel [fo. 26r] earum successores in solutione decem marcarum predictarum ad terminos predictos defecerint, licebit dictis abbati et conventui et eorum successoribus dictam priorissam et moniales vel earum successores pro voluntate sua distringere per omnes terras suas et omnia bona sua in comitatu Norhampton' et alibi donec de predictis decem marcis dictis abbati et conventui vel eorum successoribus plenarie fuerit satisfactum. In cuius rei testimonium presenti scripto in modum cyrographi confecto sigilla alterutrum sunt apposita. Ita quod parti penes dictam priorissam et moniales residenti sigilla nostra sunt apposita et parti penes nos residenti sigillum dominarum priorisse et monialium est appensum. Dat' anno gracie M^{o} CC^{o} lvii mense Februarii

55 Grant by Ralph son of Achard to the abbot and convent that he will not interfere with the abbey's mill pool at Stamford. [post 2 Feb. 1219]

Sciant[1] presentes et futuri quod ego Radulphus filius Achardi de Stannford' concessi et presenti carta mei confirmavi abbati et conventui de Burgo quod stagnum molendini sui in Stannford' permaneat exaltatum inperpetuum sine inpedimento vel contradictione vel vexatione mei vel heredum meorum sicut fuit in purificatione beate Marie anno tercio Henrici regis Anglie filii regis Johannis. Ita scilicet quod aqua in stagno predicti molendini ante exclusam hanc eiusdem molendini habeat in profundum longitudinem unius ulne regie et dimidie et medietatem quarte partis unius ulne. Et ne ego vel heredes mei aliquam controversiam versus prefatos abbatem et conventum movere possimus inposterum super exaltatione predicti stagni superius expressa pro nocumento vel detrimento prati quod vocatur Leftheynescroft, presens scriptum sigillo meo roboratum eis in futurorum memoriam dedi. Hiis testibus: Briano de la Mare, Galfrido de Leham, Hugone filio suo, Ricardo Pekke, magistro Willelmo de Scotere, magistro Henrico de Stannford', Clemente Vinerario, Willelmo Flemeng, Henrico filio Ysaac, Ricardo filio Seleue, Ketel, Johanne Bottay, Sampsone filio Godrici et aliis.

1 Also in Swaffham, fos 241v–2r in a slightly abbreviated form and without the witness clause.

56 Grant by William son of William de Berc that he and his heirs will abide by the grant of his uncle Ralph son of Achard to the abbot and convent concerning the abbey's mill pool at Stamford. [post 2 Feb. 1219]

Omnibus hoc scriptum visuris vel audituris Willelmus filius Willelmi de Berc salutem. Noverit universitas vestra me ratam et gratam habuisse concessionem et confirmationem quam Radulphus filius Achardi avunculus meus fecit abbati et conventui de Burgo super stagno molendini sui de Stannford' quod dicebatur nocumentum facere prato quod vocatur Leftheynescroft. Et ne ego vel heredes mei predictis abbati et monachis de Burgo movere possimus controversiam super iam dicto stagno contra concessionem et confirmationem prefati Radulphi filii Achardi avunculi mei presens scriptum sigilli mei appositione roboravi. Hiis testibus: Briano de la Mare, Galfrido de Leham, Hugone filio suo, Ricardo Pekke, magistro Willelmo de Scotere, magistro Henrico de Staunford et aliis ut prius.

57 Cyrograph agreement concerning the services owed to the abbot and convent by the tenants of Thurgarton Priory in Danethorpe at the abbey's manor of Collingham. [22 Jan. 1280]

[fo. 26v] De tenentibus prioris et conventus de Thurgerton'.

[Marginated] Thug

Noverint[1] universi presentes litteras visuri vel audituri quod cum tenentes prioris et conventus[2] de Thurgerton' in Dornthorp' de jure debeant et hactenus facere consueverunt abbati de Burgo Sancti Petri et eiusdem loci conventui annuatim servicia et consuetudines subscriptas in manerio suo de Colingham; videlicet unusquisque eorum debet arare per tres dies in anno; scilicet semel ad semen yemale, et iterum ad semen quadragesimale, et tercio tempore warecti. Et habebit quelibet caruca quolibet die quatuor panes et quatuor allecia prout solebant habere secundum antiquam consuetudinem. Item debent metere per duos dies et dimidiam in autumpno, primo die ad cibum domini abbatis consuetum semel in die, secundo die similiter si per totum [sic] diem abbas voluerit habere ipsos, alioquin recedant post horam nonam sine cibo, tercio die non metent nisi usque ad horam nonam sine cibo. Preterea dicti tenentes debent ponere in caulam dicti abbatis omnes oves quas habuerint in eorum possessione vel custodia in yeme exceptis propriis ovibus et filiorum suorum quamdiu fuerint eorum manupasti. Et si oves aliorum quam suorum vel filiorum suorum manupastorum quas in yeme tenuerint vendite vel mortue[3] fuerint vel aliquocumque modo extra eorum possessionem seu custodiam devenerint, invenient totidem alias loco dictarum ovium ad ponendum in caulam dicti abbatis. Et quia ballivi dicti abbatis pro defectibus et transgressionibus in dictis serviciis et consuetudinibus factis distrinxerunt dictos tenentes ad veniendos de curia in curiam ipsius abbatis de Colingham ad respondendum et satisfaciendum ibidem de eisdem, videbatur dicto priori prefatos tenentes suos quandoque magis ex voluntate ballivorum ipsius abbatis quam ex merito eorum gravari. Timens eciam eo pretextu de sectis de tribus septimanis in tres septimanas de dictis tenentibus ad curiam ipsius abbatis exigendis ecclesie sue de Thurgerton' prejudicium posse generari, convenit inter dictos abbatem et priorem quod predicta servicia et consuetudines decetero fiant ut predictum est. Et si defectus seu transgressiones in predictis serviciis et consuetudinibus faciendos inveniantur, tunc attachientur ipsi qui dictos defectus seu transgressiones fecerint per ballivos abbatis veniendos ad curiam ipsius abbatis bis in anno; videlicet ad proximam curiam ante Pascha et ad curiam proximam ante festum sancti Michaelis, et tunc dicti defectus et transgressiones presententur, et inde capientur emende secundum quantitatem delicti in presencia ballivi dicti prioris et ipsorum qui dictos defectus seu transgressiones fecerint si ibidem interesse voluerint. Si vero ibidem venire noluerint seu distulerint, tunc ad curias predictas amercientur per considerationem curie predicte tam pro defaltis quam pro transgressionibus factis secundum legem et consuetudinem regni et leventur amerciamenta ad opus dicti abbatis per ballivos ipsius abbatis. In cuius rei testimonium et cetera [huic scripto in modum cirographi confecto sigilla predictorum abbatis et prioris alternatim fuerunt apponita. Hiis testibus:domino Henrico de Peyrepount, domino Radulpho de Arnhale, domino Roberto de Meringhal', magistro Roberto de Scheffeld, Johanne de Sutton', Fulcone de Hothot, Petro in Venella, Johanne de Herst in Colingham', Willelmo de

Hayde et aliis].[4] Acta in crastino sancti Vincentii anno Domini M° CC lxx nono.

1 For the Thurgarton text see ed. T. Foulds, *The Thurgarton Cartulary* (Stamford, 1994), no. 317.
2 *et conventus* interlined.
3 *vel mortue* cancelled.
4 Supplied from *The Thurgarton Cartulary*.

58 Letter from Robert Winchelsey, archbishop of Canterbury to Richard Gravesend, bishop of London ordering him to summon the clergy to a meeting of convocation to discuss the Scottish invasion. [15 Oct. 1297]

[fo. 27r] R[obertus][1] Dei gracia Cantuar' archiepiscopus tocius Anglie primas venerabili fratri domino R[icardo] Dei gratia London' episcopo salutem et fraternam in Domino caritatem. Casus repentini cuius occasione regni et ecclesie Anglicane magnum timetur periculum iminere recens et inopinatus eventus, nos licet anxios et invitos impellit extra propositum preconceptum prelatos et clerum nostre provincie licet per similia de quo dolemur et angimur sepius fatigatos et pro eiusdem regni et ecclesie atque cleri periculo propulsando cum festinatione consulere et id modis omnibus prout eciam cum quibusdam nostris coepiscopis et aliis sapientibus deliberatione habita censuimus convocare. Nuper siquidem in parliamento London' ubi cum optimatibus et regni proceribus varia tractavimus negotia ut decebat rumor validus atque recens tam per litteras celeriter missas[2] quam eciam per constantem relatum domini comitis de Warrenna principalem custodem per dominum regem Anglie inhibi deputati et aliorum inde celeriter reversorum quorum fida reputatur assercio noviter incurrit quod Scottorum exercitus in multitudine maxima copiosus totum regnum Scotie usque ad fines eiusdem versus Angliam ocupans et cum strage maxima Anglorum etati ac sexui non parcendo iam regnum Anglie veraciter ut dicitur et constanter asseritur est ingressus ipsum regnum Anglie nisi eis bellatorum promptum preparetur obstaculum pro suis viribus vastaturus in tantum quod maxima pars communitatis Northumbr' usque ad villam Novi Castri pretanti[3] timore periculi ad partes certiores[4] se transtulit et bona sua quatenus eis facultas patuit nudata fere patria iam transvexit, propter quod dominus noster filius domini regis karissimus cuius juramento fidelitatis astringimur et regni proceres super hiis artissima revolutione tractantes a nobis et quibusdam nostris coepiscopis ibidem presentibus affectuose petebant, ut in tam grandi et evidenti periculo sicut premittitur iminente nos et ce'teri [sic] prelati aut clerus Anglie quibus sicut ceteris dicitur in hac parte patere necessitas consilium oportunum et efficax presidium impendere curaremus unde cum id fieri aut super hoc congrue responderi non possit illorum quorum interest convocatione debita pretermissa fraternitati nostre[5] committimus et mandamus, quatinus nostros[5] coepiscopos et confratres cum celeritate qua poteritis convocetis et per episcopos ipsos dictum clerum quatenus eis subicitur convocari mandetis; videlicet ut ipsi episcopi et decani ac priores in ecclesiis cathedralibus presidentes personaliter, ceteri vero abbates et priores cuiusque diocesis pro se et conventibus suis per se aut per procuratorem sui ordinis, et reliqua cleri communitas similiter cuiusque diocesis, Wallie videlicet per unum Anglie vero quatenus nostra provincia se extendit per duos, et capitula cathedralium ecclesiarum per unum procuratores ydoneos et instructos die sancti Edmundi regis et martiris una cum diebus sequentibus usque ad finalem expeditionem tractatus apud Novum Templum London' compareant nobiscum et cum ceteris ut premittitur[6] convocandis [fo. 27v] super hiis tractaturi qualiter dicta possunt precaveri pericula provisuri necnon incertam formam inibi providendam concorditer consensuri facturique ulterius quod ad expeditionem ydoneam pertinere videbitur premissorum. Interim vero dicti episcopi cum suis conciliis, ceteri vero prenotati similiter modo quo melius expedire prospexerint plene deliberent et pertractent tam[7] de auxilio licito quam de modo et de hiis omnibus procuratores et alii ut supra mittendi plenius instruantur ut ad diem et ad locum predictos suum possint super hiis deliberatius explicare concilium et quod exigendum[8] extiterit sine mora plenius expedire. Religiosos autem exemptos per diocesanos locorum ad id idem rogari et premuniri congrue demandetis. Et vos ipse dictis die et loco vestram exhibeatis ad premissa presenciam personalem vestros que subditos in forma prescripta faciatis similiter interesse. Denunciatis dictis coepiscopis et per eos suos subditos sic vocandos faciatis ydonee premuniri et vos similiter de eodem premunimus quod absentes in citatione predicta nisi evidens et inevitabile inpedimentum sufficienter probetur tamquam in obedientes graviter puniemus. De die vero receptionis presentium et quid inpremissis feceritis ac de nominibus sic citatur' nos dictis die et loco quatenus ad vos attinet ydonee certificetis per vestras patentes litteras harum seriem continentes et ceteris coepiscopis antedictis ut nos similiter ipsis die et loco singuli singillatim de facto suo certificent injungatis. Valete semper in Christo. Dat' apud Lameheth' idus Octobris anno Domini M° CC^mo^ nonagesimo septimo. Consecrationis nostre quarto.

1 For the text from Winchelsey's Register, see Graham, *Registrum Roberti Winchelsey*, vol. I, pp. 198–200 and Powicke, Cheney, *Councils and Synods*, vol. II, pp. 1178–80.
2 *missas de Scocia* in Winchelsey.
3 Partly illegible. Supplied from Winchelsey.
4 *citeriores* in ibid.
5 *vestre* and *vestros* in ibid.
6 *pretangitur* in ibid.
7 *non* in MS.
8 *agendum* in Whittlesey.

59 Cyrograph grant by the abbot and convent to John, rector of Scotter, of a toft in Scotter next to his messuage for five shillings p.a. [30 Nov. 1297]

Cyrographum rectoris ecclesie de Scotere de quoddam tofto.

[Marginated] Scot'

Anno regni regis Edwardi vicesimo sexto in festo sancti Andree apostoli ita convenit inter abbatem et conventum de Burgo Sancti Petri ex parte una et dominum Johannem rectorem ecclesie de Scoter' ex altera; videlicet quod predicti abbas et conventus tradiderunt concesserunt et dimiserunt predicto rectori quoddam toftum in villa de Scoter' jacens juxta mesuagium predicti rectoris ex parte occidentali quod quidem toftum Henricus ad ecclesiam quondam tenuit, tenendum et habendum predicto rectori et successoribus suis predicte ecclesie rectoribus inperpetuum, reddendo inde annuatim predictis abbati et conventui et eorum successoribus quinque solidos sterlinggorum [sic] ad duos [fo. 28r] anni terminos; videlicet ad Pascha duos solidos et sex denarios et ad festum sancti Michaelis duos solidos et sex denarios pro omnibus serviciis exactionibus et secularibus demandis. Et liceat predictis abbati et conventui et eorum successoribus in predicto tofto districtiones facere si quod absit predictus annuus redditus suis terminis non fuerit persolutus usque ad plenariam satisfactionem omnium arreragiorum. Et si per biennium a solutione dicti redditus fuerit cessatam liceat predictis abbati et conventui et eorum successoribus predictum toftum ingredi et tenere et de eo pro voluntate sua disponere absque contradictione vel clamio predicti rectoris vel successorum suorum inperpetuum. In cuius rei testimonium huic presenti scripto ad modum cyrographi confecto sigilla partium alternatim sunt apposita. Dat' apud Burgum in festo supradicto et anno prenotata.

60 Acknowledgement by Nicholas of Bassingbourn senior that he owes homage to the abbot for four knights' fees. [early thirteenth century[1]]

Carta Nicholai de Bassingburn' senioris.

Universis Christi fidelibus presentes litteras visuris vel audituris Nicholaus de Bassingburn' salutem in Domino. Noverit universitas vestra me tenere de abbate de Burgo Sancti Petri quatuor feoda militum pro quolibet homagium eidem facere debeo sicut predecessoribus suis abbatibus facere consuevi. In cuius rei testimonium has litteras universitati vestre transmitto patentes. Valete in Domino.

1 See *Henry of Pytchley*, p. 77 note.

61 Recognition by Nicholas of Bassingbourn junior to Abbot Walter that he holds a quarter of a knight's fee and that he will in future answer for a total of four fees. [1233–45]

Carta Nicholai de Bassingburn' junioris.

Omnibus[1] hoc scriptum visuris vel audituris Nicholaus de Bassingburn' salutem. Noveritis me recognovisse domino meo Waltero abbati de Burgo et eius successoribus unum quarterium feodi unius militis quod aliquando ei ignoranter dedicebam. Ita videlicet quod decetero dicto abbati et eius successoribus ego Nicholaus et heredes mei de quatuor integris feodis militum plenarie respondebimus. In cuius rei testimonium presenti scripto sigillum meum apposui. Hiis testibus: Thoma filio Roberti de Suthorp', Hugone Fawel militibus, Thoma de Ufford' tunc senescallo, Rogero de Lagrave, Willelmo de Thorp', Ricardo de Emmpingthon', Martino de Paple, Roberto Peverel, Roberto Puttok et tota curia de Castr'.

1 See *Henry of Pytchley*, p. 77 note.

62 Recognition by Ralph parson of Slapton of a debt of nine marks to the abbot. [Easter Term 1298]

[fo. 28v] Cognitio facta coram Johannis de Metingham et sociis suis in termino Pasche anno regni regis Edwardi xxvj et rotulo xliii.

[Marginated] Norht

Radulphus persona ecclesie de Slapton' recognovit se teneri abbati de Burgo Sancti Petri in novem marcas sterlingorum unde solvet eidem abbati ad festum sancti Petri advincula proximo futurum unam marcam, et ad natale Domini proximo sequens unam marcam, et ad Pascha proximo sequens unam marcam, et sic de anno in annum ad eosdem terminos quousque predictum debitum plenarie fuerit solutum. Et nisi fecerit, concedit quod vicecomes fieri faciat de terris et catallis suis ad quorumcumque manus devenerint et cetera.

63 Obligation by the abbot and convent to pay 500 marks sterling to various Italian merchants to raise money for the ransom of John de Sancto Johanne.[1] [9 May 1298]

Obligatio mercatoribus facta pro domino Johanne de Sancto Johanne ad instanciam domini regis.

Universis presentes litteras inspecturis abbas de Burgo Sancti Petri et eiusdem loci conventus salutem in Domino sempiternam. Noveritis quod cum secundum formam sufferencie inter magnificos principes dominum nostrum Edwardum Dei gracia regem Anglie illustrem, adjutores confederatos homines et subditos suos ex parte una et Philippum regem Francie, adjutores confederatos homines et subditos suos ex altera a festo epiphanie Domini proximo preterito usque ad duos annos proximo sequentes super guerra inter eos dudum exorta inite et firmate concordatum fuerit quod omnes capti hinc inde hostagientur, ac inter alios nobilis vir dominus Johannes de Sancto Johanne captus in carcere dicti regis Francie teneatur expeditione reipublice Anglicane. Nos abbas predictus de Burgo Sancti Petri et eiusdem loci conventus considerantes ac eciam attendentes quod pium sit necnon licitum, debitum et honest' pro hostagiamento et liberatione ipsius bona monasterii nostri exponere obligare et si necesse fuerit, distrahere ratione laudabilis defensionis pro utilitate regni et reipublice Anglicane per eum inpense ac servicii per consequens toti ecclesie Anglicane exhibiti in hac parte, presertim cum ad hostagiamentum et liberationem predictam sue non suppetant facultates, Coppe Josep de Societate Friscobaldorum[2], Villano Stoldi de Societate Circulorum Nigrorum, Melior' Pistoleys de Societate Amenatorum de Pistorio, Arbor' Bernadino de Societate Bonseniorum de Cenis, Reyner' Balinzon de Societe Pullicum, Gwidoni Bardi de Societate Spinarum, Philippo Borgu de Societate Mosorum mercatoribus et eorum sociis et societatibus heredibus executoribus et assignatis eorum qui mercatores se pro hostagiamento et liberatione prefati domini Johannis ad mandatum et preces predicti domini nostri regis et nostras predicto regi Francie in viginti milia librarum parvorum Turonen' obligabunt, obligamus nos successores nostros monasterium nostrum bonaque ipsius in quingentis marcis bonorum et legalium sterlingorum [fo. 29r] solvendis vel inde alias ad satisfaciendum eisdem vel alteri eorumdem apud Novum Templum London' infra quinden' purificationis beate Marie anno Domini M° CC° nonogesimo nono sine ulteriori dilatione in eventum si prefatos mercatores vel eorum socios seu societates contigerit obligari vel solvere dicto regi Francie pecuniam antedictam super quilibet obligatione et solucione credatur sepedictis mercatoribus vel uni de societate eorum simplici verbo eorumdem absque alterius onere probationis necnon ad refusionem omnium dampnorum et expensarum et interesse que et quas dicti mercatores vel eorum aliquis aut eorum attornati seu assignati incurrerint et fecerint pro defectum solutionis pecunie predicte sicut eorum aliquis suo simplici verbo tantum sine juramento vel alia probatione dicere voluerit, subicimus eciam nos ecclesiam nostram et successores nostros jurisdictioni et cohercioni auditor' ... arum camere domini pape suique commissar' qui pro tempore fuerit ut possit nos ecclesiam nostram et successores nostros sine strepitu judiciali[3] et figura judicii, sede plena vel vacante, unica tamen monitione premissa omni apellatione postposita per excommunicationis seu interdicti sententias ad omnium premissarum observationem compellere, renunciantes in premissis omnibus et singulis pro nobis ecclesia nostra et successoribus nostris omni juris auxilio canonici et civilis privilegio clericatus et fori omni libertati consuetudini et statuto regie prohibitioni et protectioni conventioni judicium et locorum contradictioni litterarum apostolicarum beneficio restitutionis in integrum novarum constitutionum beneficio in factum actioni conditioni indebiti et sine causa et ex injusta causa omni appellationis remedio omni tempori feriato juri revocandi domum privilegio Anglicis concesso, ne trahantur extra regnum Anglie ad causas per litteras apostolicas petitionem copie presencium litterarum juridicenti nisi creditores probaverint pecuniam in servicium ecclesie esse conversam aliter quam per litteras conventionales quod illitera repetere non possunt. Et specialiter indulgencie si quam habemus vel nos aut successores nostros in futurum habere contigerit quod excommunicari suspendi vel interdici nequeamus aut non nisi in certo loco coram certo judice nec extra regnum Anglie nec citra mare vel extra certam diocesem ad modicum evocari nisi de speciali mandato apostolico faciente plenam et expressam de indubeo huiusmodi mentionem. Omnibus constitutionibus et statutis editis et edendis et precipue constitutioni facte per dominum Bonefacium papam octavum ne aliquis extra suam diocesam trahatur ad causas omni inhibitioni cuiuscumque principis omnibus litteris graciis et privilegiis apostolicis nobis et ecclesie nostre concessis et concedendis juridicenti generalem renunciationem non valere, et omnibus exceptionibus et defensionibus que de jure vel de facto contra premissa vel eorum aliquid ratione aliqua obici possent vel opponi, et que nobis et successoribus nostris possent prodesse et predictis mercatoribus sociis ac eorum heredibus seu eorum alicui aut attornatis seu assignatis suis quoquo modo nocere. In quorum omnium testimonium presentibus sigilla nostra sunt appensa. Dat' in capitulo nostro apud Burgum vij idus Maii anno regni regis Edwardi xxvj°.

1 The king's Lieutenant in Gascony, taken prisoner after ambush in Jan. 1297. Prestwich, *Edward I*, p. 385.
2 Pristorialdorum in MS, see e.g. *Calendar of Patent Rolls 1292–1301*, p. 449.
3 *judiciali* cancelled.

64 Bull of Pope Alexander III to Brand de Fossato concerning the hospital of St John and St Thomas in Stamford. [5 Feb. 1174–78]

[fo. 29v] Alexander[1] episcopus servus servorum Dei dilecto filio Brandoni salutem et apostolicam benedictionem. Dignum est et consentaneum rationi ut eorum justis desideriis animamus qui relictis ponpis [sic] secularibus caritatis operibus intendunt et omnipotenti Domino elegerunt jugi devotione servire. Intelleximus autem extransmissa nobis insinuatione tua quod tu divina inspiratione ductus venundatis omnibus que possidebas hospitale quoddam et capellam ad honorem Dei et beati Johannis et gloriosi martiris Thome quondam Cantuariensis archiepiscopi in capite pontis de Stanford' ex australi parte ad receptionem peregrinorum et pauperum per locum illum frequenter transeuntium. Edificasti ubi elegisti creatori tuo perpetuum famulatum exhibere. Inde est quod nos ob reverenciam Dei et predictorum sanctorum et devotione quam erga ipsos te habere ostendis rationali postulationi tue libencius annuentes prescriptum hospitale capellam cum omnibus que idem hospitale inpresentiarum rationabiliter possidet aut in futurum largitione pontificum oblatione fidelium seu aliis justis modis prestante Domino poterit adipisti sub beati Petri et nostra protectione suscipimus et presentis scripti patrocinio communimus. Statuentes ut predicti capella proprium capellanum cantariam cimiterum et in eodem cimiterio liberam sepulturam debeat sine contradictione qualibet optinere. Decervimus ergo ut nulli omnino homini liceat predictum hospitale temere perturbare vel quibuslibet in debitis vexationibus fatigars [sic] seu hanc paginam nostre protectionis et constitutionis infringere aut ei aliquatenus contraire. Siquis autem hoc attemptans presumpserit indignationem omnipotentis Dei et beatorum Petri et Pauli apostolorum eius se noverit incursurum. Dat' Anagnie nonas Februarii.

1 A later entry. See W. Holtzmann, *Papsturkunden in England,* 3 vols (Berlin and Gottingen, 1930–52), vol. I, p. 130 for date and *V.C.H., Northants.,* vol. II, p. 164 for identification of Brand.

65 Acknowledgement by Master Hugh de Sancto Martino, alias Hugh de Clisseby, warden of the hospital of St Thomas in Stamford of the return of his possessions. [4 Aug. 1299]

[fo. 30r] Aquietancia magistri Hugonis de Sancto Martino custodis hospitalis sancti Thome martiris Stannford'.

Universis[1] sancte matris ecclesie filiis presentes litteras visuris vel audituris, Hugo de Clisseby magister hospitalis sancti Thome martiris juxta pontem Stannford' eternam in Domino salutem. Noverit universitas vestra me recepisse a religioso viro domino W[illelmo] permissione divina abbate de Burgo Sancti Petri domino meo per liberationem magistri Galfridi de Makeseye clerici omnes libros meos, jocalia et omnia utensilia enea et lignea et ceteras res minutas in camera et cistis meis existentes ac eciam in aula celario coquina pistrina in custodia ministrorum dicti domini abbatis dimissa et per ipsos inventa domibus predictis in hospitale predicto et ea omnia plenarie mihi fateor esse restituta, prefatum dominum abbatem et ceteros ipsius ministros huius rerum custodiendos deputatos ab omni actione eisdem inposterum faciendos ea occasione predicta tenore presentium invocans per presentes quietos. In cuius rei testimonium presentibus sigillum meum est appensum. Et ad majorem evidenciam sigillum decanati de Nasso Burgi presentibus procuravi apponi. Dat' apud Stannford' die Martis proxima post festum sancti Petri advincula anno regni regis Edwardi vicesimo septimo.

1 See below, no. 101, which has a marginal cross reference to this document.

66 Grant by Abbot Robert and the convent of a mill and the advowson of a quarter part of Hibaldstow church, together with all the tenements given to the abbey by Robert Fauvel, to the prior and convent of Newstead on Ancholme in return for 8s p.a. [1215–16]

Carta prioris de Novo Loco super Ancolme.

Omnibus[1] Christi fidelibus ad quos presens carta pervenerit, Robertus Dei gracia abbas ecclesie sancti Petri de Burgo et eiusdem loci devotus in Christo conventus salutem in Domino eternam. Noverit universitas vestra nos concessisse et hac carta nostra confirmasse priori et conventui Novi Loci super Ancolme advocationem quarte partis ecclesie de Hybaldestowe et molendinum eiusdem ville et omnia tenementa cum pertinenciis in eadem villa que habent de dono Roberti Fauvel per cartas ipsius Roberti, habenda et pacifice tenenda sicut ea rationabiliter sunt secuti. Ita quidem quod non liceat predictis priori et conventui Novi Loci decetero absque assensu et voluntate nostra terram aliquam sive redditum in feodo nostro emere vel recipere. Pro hac autem nostra confirmatione optinenda prefati prior et conventus Novi Loci solvent nobis singulis annis octo solidos sterlingorum duobus terminis anni scilicet; ad Pentecosten quatuor solidos et in festo sancti Martini quatuor solidos. Et si forte prefati prior et conventus Novi Loci super Ancolme a solutione octo solidorum prefatorum terminis pretaxatis cessaverint, licebit nobis ipsos distringere per averia et catalla que in terris de feodo nostro predicto inventa fuerint donec prefatos octo solidos annuos plene persolverint. Et ut hoc ratum maneat inperpetuum presentem cartam sigillorum nostrorum appositione munitam eis in futurorum memoriam dedimus. Anno ab incarnatione Domini millesimo CC^{o} xv^{mo}. Testibus: magistro Galfrido Gibbewyn et aliis.

1 Also in Soc. of Antiquaries, MS 38, fo. 126r, without the witness clause.

67 Letter of Geoffrey de Vezzano, clerk of the papal camera and nuncio, to Oliver Sutton, bishop of Lincoln, demanding payments due to him under pain of excommunication and interdict. [2 Dec. 1297]

[fo. 30v] O[livero][1] Dei gratia Linc' episcopo Giffredus de Vesano canonicus cameracensis apostolice sedis nuncius salutem cum omne reverencia et honore. Quia sumus circa finem viginti et unus annorum quibus vacavimus circa commissa nobis a dicta sede negotia et de concessis nobis septem solidis diebus singulis per expensas propter inobedienciam multarum ecclesiarum secularium et religiosarum debemus adhuc recipere magnam summam, paternitatem vestram auctoritate apostolice que puplica est et notoria et de qua vobis constat cum reverencia qua decet requirimus quatinus singulas seculares collegiatas ecclesias et singulas ecclesias regulares vestre civitatis et diocesis, Cistersiens' et cuiuscumque ordinis que in auctoritate huiusmodi comprehenduntur et earum personas ex parte nostra immo verius apostolica requiratis et moneatis seu requiri et moneri efficaciter faciatis quod singule ipsarum ecclesiarum et earum persone pro vicesimo primo anno more nostre in Anglie septem solidos et totidem pro singulis annis precedentibus pro quibus non solverunt nobis apud Novum Templum London' infra instans festum Purificationis sub pena excommunicationis in personas et in ecclesias interdicti sine ulteriori dilatione persolvant et certificetis nos per vestras patentes litteras[2] harum seriem continentes qualiter requisitionem nostram immo verius apostolicam fueritis executi providendo si placet si melius expedire videritis quod illi per quos executionem fieri mandaveritis in restribendo veraces existant valeat reverenda paternitas vestra presenti et eterno valore. Dat' Lond' iiij nonas Decembris anno Domini millesimo CC[mo] nonagesimo septimo.

1 For background see Denton, *Robert Winchelsey*, p. 175.
2 *litteras* repeated.

68 Letter from Abbot William and the convent to Oliver Sutton, bishop of Lincoln, asking him to institute Hugh of Nottingham to the church of Bringhurst, together with a note that Hugh declined the presentation. [24 June 1298]

Reverendo patri in Christo domino O[livero] Dei gracia Linc' episcopo sui humiles et devoti in Christo filli W[illelmus] eiusdem dono gracie abbas de Burgo Sancti Petri et eiusdem loci conventus salutem. Et debite reverencie devotam obedienciam sancte paternitati vestre presentamus dilectum clericum nostrum dominum Hugonem de[1] Notingham ad ecclesiam de Brengrest vacantem[2] que ad nostram spectat presentationem, humiliter supplicantes et devote quatinus caritatis intuitu eundem ad dictam ecclesiam admittatis et personam in eadem instituatis, salvis nobis et ecclesie nostre juribus ab antiquo perceptis in eadem. In cuius restimonium [sic] presentibus litteris sigilla nostra sunt appensa. Dat' in capitulo nostro in festo nativitatis sancti Johannis baptiste anno Domini M[o] CC nonogesimo octavo. Dictus[3] dominus Hugo noluit istam ecclesiam recipere sed excusavit se per litteram suam que est in thesaurario[4] annexa predicte presentationi.

1 *de* interlined.
2 *vacantem* interlined.
3 This sentence appended to the main document.
4 *rio* interlined.

69 Manumission of William of Walcot, clerk, by Abbot William and the convent so that he may become a priest and hold a benefice. [24 May 1297]

[fo. 31r] Manumissio Willelmi de Walcote clerici.

Universis[1] sancte matris ecclesie filiis presentes litteras inspecturis vel audituris, W[illelmus] permissione divina abbas monasterii sancti Petri de Burgo et eiusdem loci conventus salutem in Domino sempiternam. Cum Willelmus de Walcot' clericus qui de nativis nostris originem traxit desideret in sacerdotali officio Deo deservire, nolentes ipsum pro cuius morum venustate laudabile testimonium noscitur proclamare a suo proposito ratione servitutis impediri, caritatis intuitu eidem concessimus quod possit a domino Linc' episcopo vel alio quocunque ad omnes ordines promoneri nec non beneficium ecclesiasticum assequendum liberam in Domino tribuimus facultatem eidem. In cuius rei testimonium sigillum capituli nostri commune presentibus est appensum. Dat' apud Burgum Sancti Petri in crastino assensionis Dominice anno Domini millesimo CC° nonagesimo septimo.

1 Repeated above, no. 27.

70 Manumission of Walter son of Geoffrey de Scalthorp' by the abbot and convent so that he can take holy orders. Walter swore his loyalty to the abbey and promised not to prejudice its interests by any act of ingratitude. [23 Nov. 1297]

Manumissio Walteri filii Galfridi de Scalthorp'.

Circa defectum natalium micius agit auctoritas ecclesie et facilius in eo dispensat pro eo quod non a proprio pervenit reatu sed a statu progenitorum quos plus ligat humana constitutio quam divina. Cum igitur Walterus filius Galfridi de Austiby in Scalthorp' qui de nativis nostris traxit originem cupiat in sacris ordinibus omnipotenti Deo deservire, ipsi illud devotissime deprecanti tenore presentium licenciam duximus concedendum quantum ad nos pertinet quod licite possit ad frugem molioris vite connolare aut omnes sacros ordines suscipiendo aut religionem statum ingrediendo, dummodo id faciat infra triennium proximum sequens a confectione presentium. Juravit eciam dictus Walterus tactis sacrosanctis ewangeliis quod fidelis erit et devotus eccclesie de Burgo et dominis suis abbati et conventui eiusdem loci nec aliquam ingratitudinis notam committet per quam eisdem possit dampnum provenire. In cuius rei testimonium has presentes litteras eidem Waltero fieri fecimus patentes. Dat' apud Burgum in festo sancti Clementis martiris anno Domini millesimo ducentesimo nonagesimo septimo.

71 Grant by Henry III to Bishop Hugh and the prior and convent of Ely of all the fines and amercements from their own men, lands and fees. [1229–72]

Carta libertatis de Ely.

[Marginated] Carta de Ely secundum tenorem

H[enricus] Dei gracia archiepiscopis et episcopis et cetera salutem. Noveritis nos intuitu Dei et pro salute anime nostre et animarum antecessorum nostrorum concessisse et hac presenti carta nostra confirmasse Deo et ecclesie sancte Etheldrede de Ely et venerabili patri in Christo Hugoni eiusdem ecclesie episcopo et successoribus suis episcopis eiusdem ecclesie et priori et monachis ibidem Deo servientibus et inperpetuum servituris omnes libertates subscriptas; videlicet quod idem episcopus et successores sui et dictus prior et successores sui habeant inperpetuum pro nobis et heredibus nostris omnes fines et omnia amerciamenta de omnibus hominibus terris et feodis suis postquam aliquis inciderit in misericordiam.

72 Letter from Robert Winchelsey, archbishop of Canterbury, to Oliver Sutton, bishop of Lincoln, asking him to exhort the richer clergy to pay the whole tenth at once because of the Scottish invasion. [4 Dec. 1297]

[fo. 31v] Robertus[1] permissione divina Cantuar' archiepiscopus tocius Anglie primas venerabili fratri in Christo domino O[livero] Dei gracia Linc' episcopo salutem et fraternam in Domino caritatem. Cum post congregationem per nos London' ultimo celebratum moram traheremus ibidem pro arduis expeditionibus rei puplice longiorem cotidianis ac multiplicatis rumoribus prochdolor intelleximus pro constanti quod Scottorum exercitus adeo prodiciosis ac scelerosis actibus contra regnum Anglie et ipsius in colas invalescit quod nisi ipsorum agressibus citiori remedio resistatur toci regno nostro predicto hostium insidiis sicut scitis undique circumcincto irreperabile detrimentum quod absit poterit iminere propter quod per consilium regis nostri tractans satis anixe[2] super periculis huiusmodi caucius evitandis iam extat unanimiter ordinatum quod comites Warenn' Hereford' et Essex' marescallus Norfolch' et Suthfolch'

Glovernie et Warrewich' et dominus Henricus de Percy cum septingentis armaturis strenuorum militum et equitum bellatorum et peditum mutitudine copiosa non parcendo discrimini temporum vel viarum versus Novum Castrum super Tynam quod dicti Scotti nunc[3] obsidere et eo pejora ibidem perpetrare dicuntur celerime dirigant gressus suos quibus fere sex milia marcarum infra duodecim dies et totidem citra Dominicam qua cantatur Letare Jerusalem de decima bonorum ecclesie Anglicane necessario sunt solvenda stipendiis peditum quibus de fisco satisfaciend' erit minime computat'. Nos igitur in tanto necessitatis articulo cum fratribus nostris Lond' tunc presentibus nunc huc nunc illuc per nos et nostros[4] solicite discurrentes et exhausto regis errario cum diversis particularia mutua contrahentes pro prima solutione dictis comitibus facienda personas nostras obligavimus ista vice. Quocirca fraternitatis vestre sinceram devotionem requirimus et rogamus ac vos quantum possumus exhortamur quatinus sine omni more diffugio a potentioribus tam religiosis quam clericis secularibus coram vobis si necesse fuerit personaliter[5] accersitis totam decimam exposita eis primitus dicte necessitatis causa solerter exigere studeatis et pecuniam sic collectam una cum tota portione[6] temporalia et spiritualia vestra contingente ad Novum Templum London' non expectando primum vel secundum terminum salvo et celeriter transmittatis. De ceteris vero religiosis et clericis secularibus qui solvere nequeunt festinanter decimam suis terminis sicut alias ordinavimus plenarie colligatis et ipsam ut premisimus London' oportunis temporibus destinetis. Nam licet inter nos nuper fuisset communiter ordinatum quod quilibet diocesanus in sua diocesi collectam pecuniam detineret et mediante mandato nostro ipsam traderet thesaurario ad hoc inter nos specialiter nominato, tamen propter necessitates et difficultates varias cum consilio regis comitibus predictis et multis regni proceribus nuper plusquam anixe[2] pertractavimus, ordinationem predictam nequimus sine dispendioso circulo quamvis aliud tunc censuerimus observare. Valete semper in Christo. Dat' apud Lamehyth' ij nonas Decembris anno Domini millesimo CC° nonagesimo septimo. Consecrationis nostre quarto.

1 For another text, see Graham, *Registrum Roberti Winchelsey*, vol. I, pp. 213–14. For the background to this tax, see Prestwich, *Edward I*, ch. 16, esp. pp. 429–30.

2 *anxie* in ibid.

3 *iam* in ibid.

4 *ipsos* in ibid.

5 *specialiter* in ibid.

6 *or* of *portione* interlined.

73 The recovery by Abbot William from Geoffrey Russel and Alice the widow of Andrew Russel of 45 marks which they had undertaken to pay Abbot Richard for the marriage of John and Peter, sons and heirs of Andrew Russel, and custody of his lands. [writ: 1294–5; case: Michaelmas Term 1297]

[fo. 32r] [Marginated] Norht

Precipe Galfrido Russel et Alicie que fuit uxor Andree Russel quod juste etc. reddant Willelmo abbati de Burgo Sancti Petri quadraginta quinque marcas quas ei debent et injuste detinent. Et nisi fecerint etc. Tunc sum' per bon' etc. predictos Galfridum et Aliciam quod sint coram justiciariis nostris apud Westm' in octabis sancti Martini ostensuros quare non fecerint etc. et habeas etc. Teste me ipse apud Westm' anno regni nostri xxiij^{o}

Placitum[1] [marginated] versus eosdem de termino sancti Michaelis anno regni E[dwardi] vicesimo sexto incipiente. Rotulo clxxxviij

Galfridus Russel et Alicia que fuit uxor Andree Russel in misericordia pro pluribus defaltis etc.

Iidem Galfridus et Alicia summoniti fuerunt ad respondendum Willelmo abbati de Burgo Sancti Petri de placito quod reddant ei quadraginta quinque libras[2] quas ei debent et injuste detinent etc. Et unde idem abbas per attornatum suum dicit quod cum iidem Galfridus et Alicia in festo Omnium Sanctorum anno regis nunc decimo nono obligassent se teneri cuidam Ricardo abbati de Burgo Sancti Petri predecessori istius abbatis nunc in predictis quadraginta et quinque marcis unde [ei][3] solvisse debuerunt ad Pascha proximo sequens quindecim libras, et ad festum nativitatis Johannis baptiste proximo sequens quindecim libras sine ulteriori dilatione pro maritagio Johannis et Petri filiorum et heredum predicti Andree et custodia terrarum que fuerunt predicti Andree Russel de feodo monasterii Sancti Petri de Burgo existentium. De quibus quidam maritagio et custodia varie demande et petitiones oriebantur inter partes predictas. Iidem Galfridus et Alicia predictos denarios eidem Willelmo abbati semper huc usque ei reddere contradixerunt et adhuc ei reddere contradicunt, unde dicit quod deterioratus est et dampnum habet ad valenciam viginti librarum. Et inde producit sectam etc. et profert scriptum inter eos indentatum quod predictum debitum testatur etc. Et Galfridus et Alicia per attornatum suum venerunt. Et bene cognoscunt predictum scriptum et quicquid in eo continetur. Et quia[4] tenentur predicto abbati in predicto debito. Ideo consideratum est quod predictus abbas recuperet versus eos predictas quadraginta et quinque marcas. Et dampna sua que taxantur per justiciarios ad centum solidos. Et iidem Galfridus et Alicia in misericordia etc.

1 See PRO, CP/40/121, m. 190r.

2 Recte *marcas* as in PRO text.
3 Supplied from PRO text.
4 *quod* in PRO text.

74 A case brought by Bricius le Daneys against Abbot William and others for damage to his sluices, theft of his timber and other offences at Tickencote. [11 Feb. 1296–19 Nov. 1296]

[Marginated left] Rotel' [right] Tynwell'

Si Bricius le Daneys fecerit te etc. tunc pone etc. Willelmum abbatem de Burgo Sancti Petri, Gilbertum de Sutton', Henricum le Clerk', Bernardum de Castr', Willelmum Attetounesende de Ingethorp', Willelmum Bonde, Thomam Lytelsone, Willelmum Fusse, Henricum le Clerk'. Willelmum filium Ade de Tykincote, Simonem Terriessone, Alexandrum de Ingthorp', Henricum Long'ho, Henricum de Clopton', Thomam Alweyn, Walterum in ye Est Lane, Robertum filium Johannis Boleman, Simonem filium Alexandri Alcote, Ricardum Terry, Robertum Boleman, Henricum filium Gilberti, Adam de Tynewell', Robertum Freman, Hugonem Broun, Ricardum Belle, Johannem Bonde, Robertum Aleyn, Hugonem Attegrene, Simonem Bonde, Petrum Davy, Simonem de Cotyngham, Walterum Atteston', Petrum in le Lane, Ricardum filium Ranulphi, Simonem Attecros, Robertum Attewelle, Rogerum filium Gunylde, Petrum de Clopton', Willelmum Broun, Petrum filium Petri in ye Lane, Simonem de Depingg', Simonem Garre, Robertum le Carpent', David Goun, Petrum Aleyn, Petrum le Provost', Johannem Aley, Willelmum Belle, Henricum Attewell', Johannem Davy, Johannem Schecere, Rogerum de Walton', Ricardum de Wadenho, Robertum de Walton, Johannem Brokenhale, Ricardum le Ferur, Radulphum de Thorney, Johannem filium Johannis de Overton', Reginaldum de Thor-[fo. 32v]ney, Rogerum de Creyk', Simonem le Blund, Johannem le Blund', Rogerum le Blund et Galfridum Aynethetoun quod sint coram etc. apud Westm' etc. a die Pasche in xv dies ostensuros quare exclusas ipsius Bricii apud Tykinccote noccantur vi et armis fregerunt et meremium inde ad valenciam xx li. ceperunt et asportaverunt et alia enormia ei intulerunt ad grave dampnum ipsius Bricii et contra pacem nostram et habeas etc. Teste me ipso apud Keten xj die Februarii anno regni nostri xxiiij^{to}.

[*Marginated*] Tynwel

Placitum[1] [Marginated] contra eundem Bricium de termino sancti Michaelis anno regni regis E[dwardi] xxv^{to} incipiente. Rotulo primo

[Willelmus][2] abbas de Burgo Sancti Petri et alii[3] summoniti ad respondendum Bricio le Daneys quare exclusas molendini ipsius Bricii apud Tykencote noccantur vi et armis fregerunt et meremium inde ad valenciam xx li. ceperunt et asportaverunt et alia enormia ei intulerunt ad grave dampnum ipsius Bricii et contra pacem etc. Et unde idem Bricius per attornatum suum queritur quod predictus abbas et alii die Jovis proxima ante festum sancte Katerine anno regni domini regis vicesimo quarto vi et armis, scilicet gladiis arcubus et sagittis, exclusas molendini ipsius Bricii apud Tykencot' fregerunt et meremium inde ad valenciam etc ceperunt et asportaverunt et alia enormia etc. et contra pacem etc. Unde dicit quod deterioratus est et dampnum habet ad valenciam quadr' li. Et inde producit sectam etc.

Et abbas et alii per attornatum suum veniunt et defendunt vim et injuriam quando etc. Et bene defendunt quod ipsi numcquam [sic] a predictis die et anno exclusas [molendini][4] predicti Bricii apud Tykencot' fregerunt nec aliquod meremium inde ceperunt nec asportaverunt nec aliquam transgressionem ei fecerunt sicut eis inponit. Dicunt revera quod ipsi predictis die et anno invenerunt quamdam partem meremii atachiatam in solo ipsius abbatis apud Tynewell' et meremium illud extra solum illud removerunt sicut eis bene licuit. Et de hoc ponunt se super patriam. Et Bricius similiter. Ideo preceptum est vicecomiti quod venire faciat hic in octabis sancti Hillarii xij etc. per quos etc. Et qui nec etc. ad recognoscendum in forma predicta quia tam etc. Ideo postea in octabis sancte Trinitatis anno regni domini regis nunc xxv^{to} venerunt partes et similiter jurati de consensu partium electi qui dicunt super sacramentum suum quod predictus Willelmus[5] et omnes alii preter predictum abbatem predictis die et anno nichil transgressionis fecerunt eidem Bricio in villa de Tyk' sicut idem Bricius quer'. Et dicunt revera quod cum[6] predictus Bricius plantaverat ligna in solo ipsius abbatis predictis exclusis [de Tynewell' pro][2] reparandis ubi predictus Bricius nichil potest plantare vel firmare. Et predictus[7] Gilbertus et alii hoc non permiserunt set ligna illa irredicaverunt et illa projecterunt unde dicunt quod predicti Gilbertus et alii non fregerunt predictas exclusas in predicta villa de T[ykencote][2] sicut idem quer'. Ideo consideratum est quod predictus abbas et alii sine die et Bricius nichil capiat per juramentum istum set sit in misericordia pro falso clamore.

1 See PRO, CP/40/115, m. 1d.
2 Supplied from PRO text.
3 PRO text lists the same names as above in full.
4 *molendini* interlined in PRO text.
5 *Gilbertus* in PRO text.
6 *cum* omitted in PRO text.
7 *predicti* in MS.

75 A case brought by Thomas son of Eustace of Wilsthorpe against Geoffrey Balle of Thurlby and others for damage to his turbary in Thurlby. [14 Oct. 1294 – Michaelmas Term 1297]

[Marginated left, fo. 32v] Lincoln' [right, fo. 33r] Thurl'

Si Thomas filius Eustachii de Wyvelestorp' fecerit te etc. Tunc etc. Galfridum Balle, Robertum Thorald' de Turleby, Galfridum le Swon, Hugonem Akman etc quod sint coram etc. apud Westm' in octabis sancti Martini ostens' quare turbas ipsius Thome ad valenciam x librorum in turbaria sua apud Turleby inventas comminuerunt conculcaverunt et in foveas projecerunt et alia enor-[fo. 33r]mia ei intulerunt ad grave dampnum ipsius Thome et contra pacem nostram. Et habeas etc. teste me ipso apud Westm' xiiij die Octobris anno regni nostri xxij.

Placitum [marginated] contra eundem Thomam de termino sancti Michaelis anno regni xxiiij^o^ finiente. Rotulo primo. De Banco.[1]

Galfridus Balle de Turleby, Robertus Thorald, Hugo Bate, Ivo Attegrene, Johannes Attebek', Ricardus Deye et alii fuerunt atachiati ad respondendum Thome filio Eustachii de placito quare turbas ipsius Thome ad valenciam x li. in turbaria apud Turleby inventas comminuerunt conculcaverunt et in foveas projecerunt et unde idem Thomas per attornatum suum quer' quod predictus Galfridus et alii similiter cum Galfrido le Swon, H ... man et Willelmo Thorald' die Lune proxima post festum sancti Thome martiris anno regni regis nunc vicesimo secundo turbas ipsius Thome ad valenciam x li. in turbaria apud Turleby inventas conculcaverunt comminuerunt et in foveas projecerunt, unde dicit quod deterioratus est et dampnum habet ad valenciam x li. Et inde producit sectam. Et alii per attornatum suum veniunt et defendunt vim et injuriam quando etc. et dicunt quod turbaria predicta in qua etc, est communis villis de Turleby Owethorp' et Wylestorp' quod idem Thomas assensum prebuit predictis Galfrido et aliis quod communicantes in eadem turbaria in quodam certo loco adhoc per eos assignato turbas foderent. Et predictus idem Thomas fodiebat extra predictum locum, predicti Galfridus et alii ipsum Thomam inde inpediverunt sicut eis bene licuit unde petunt judicium. Et Thomas dicit quod ipse[2] numquam prebuit assensum quod communicantes in turbaria predicta foderent in aliquo certo loco sicut predictus Galfridus et alii dicunt et hoc petit quod inquirantur per patriam. Et Galfridus et alii similiter. Ideo preceptum est vicecomiti quod venire faciat hic in crastino purificationis beate Marie xij etc. quorum quilibet etc. per quos etc. qui nec etc. ad recognoscendum in forma predicta quia tam etc. Postea a die sancti Michaelis in tres septimanas anno vicesimo sexto incipiente predictus Thomas petiit licenciam reced' de brevi suo et habet ut patet in rotulo predicto.

1 This reference is to PRO, CP 40/115, m. 1d, the previous document.

2 *ipse* interlined.

76 Absolution from sentence of excommunication by Abbot William to three nuns of St Michael's, Stamford in his capacity as visitor. One had assaulted Emma daughter of Matthew de Eston, a novice. The offence of the other two is not recorded. [29 Sept. 1297]

Absolutio monialium sancti Michaelis extra Stannford'.

Universis sancte matris ecclesie filiis quorum interest innotescat per presentes quod nos Willelmus permissione divina abbas monasterii sancti Petri de Burgo debitum visitationis officium in prioratu beati Michaelis extra Stannford' excertentes dilectas in Christo filias Alexandram de Langetoft et Ceciliam Fleming' ac Margeriam Arketel de Stannford' dicti prioratus moniales a sentencia majoris excommunicationis qua dicte Alexandra et Cecilia propter earumdem commissa et Margeria propter injectionem manuum violentiam in Emmam filiam Mathei de Eston' ad statum monialis receptam exstiterant involute juxta juris exigentiam et sancti Benedicti regulam absolvimus. In cuius rei testimonium presentibus sigillum nostrum apposuimus. Dat' in capitulo dicti prioratus die sancti Michaelis archangeli anno Domini M° CC° nonogesimo septimo.

77 Memorandum from the rolls of the Exchequer concerning a 100s fine levied on John de Assfortheby for taking hunting dogs into the royal forest without warrant, which the abbot falsely claimed under the terms of his liberty. [*c.* 1295–6]

[fo. 33v] Irrotulatio scaccarii.

Memorandum[1] quod cum super compotum Johannis Druel vicecomitis Norht' reddit ad Scaccarium die Mercurii proxima post festum purificationis beate Marie hoc anno exigerentur ab eodem vicecomite C s. qui ei veniunt in sumon' sub nomine Johannis de Assfortheby clerici quod eos redderet. R' statim quidem Rogerus de Clopton quem abbas de Burgo Sancti Petri posuit loco suo coram baronibus de Scaccario ad calumpniandum ibidem nomine ipsius abbatis amerciamenta sua et hominum suorum que clamium habere per libertatem cartarum domini regis et predecesssorum suorum regum Anglie et quibus actenus usus est optulit se pro eodem abbate et calumpniatus est amerciamentum predictum asserens amerciamentum illud ad ipsum abbatem pertinere debere per libertatem predictam eoquod idem Johannes homo est ipsius abbatis et nichil habet extra libertatem predictam per quod debitum illud levari potest. Et dictum est eidem attornato per thesaurarium et barones quod discretius se provideret si amerciamentum illud per libertatem predictam rite calumpniare posset quia forte talia amerciamenta contra tenorem cartarum predictarum calumpniare posset et exigere que cadere possent in prejudicium domini regis et in lesione libertatis predicte. Et predictus attornatus iterato dixit ut prius quod idem Johannes homo est ipsius abbatis et nichil habet extra libertatem etc. Tandem thesaurarius et barones scrutari fecerunt rotulos de Scaccario super amerciamento predicto et compertum est quod idem Johannes amerciatus fuit coram Rogero Exaneo et sociis suis justiciariis ad placita foreste assignatis in comitatu Roteland' ad C s. quia tenuit canes currentes[2] in foresta regis sine waranto et ab eodem comitatu Roteland' remotum fuit debitum illud usque in comitatu Linc'. Et ab eodem comitatu illud usque in comitatu Norht' ubi debitum illud nunc exigitur. Et predictus attornatus positus fuit ad rationem si predictus abbas ullam habet libertatem in predictis comitatibus Roteland' et Lincoln' per quam debitum illud calumpniare possit ibidem. Dixit quod non. Et quia idem attornatus prius dixerat quod idem Johannes nichil habet extra libertatem predictam per quod debitum predictum levari posset et idem Johannes clericus est et beneficiatus in ecclesia de Castr' et plura habet bona ecclesiastica ibidem de quibus debitum illud levari potuit ad opus regis quia eciam idem abbas huiusmodi amerciamenta facta in foresta regis per libertatem cartarum predictarum calumpniare non potest nisi fiat inde specialis mentio in eisdem per quod liquet manifeste quod predictus attornatus amerciamentum predictum calumpniatus est per libertatem predictam in deceptionem curie contra formam cartarum predictarum. Et quia per ipsum non stetit quin dominus rex per huius frivolas calumpnias amerciamentum illud amisisset etc. Concordatum est quod libertas predicta capiatur in manum regis. Et preceptum est vicecomiti etc. Postea thesaurarius et barones replegiaverunt eidem abbati libertatem predictam usque ad quindenam Pasche. Ita quod idem abbas tunc ve-[fo. 34r]niat in propria persona sua satisfacturus de transgressione predicta. Postea xj die Februarii durante compoto predicto predictus attornatus calumpniatus est per libertatem predictam j marca [sic] de fine quem Laurencius Fythun, Elena uxor eius, Willelmus Fythun, Anastia et Emma filie sue, Walterus Fythun, Willelmus filius Johannis le Pestour et alii fecerunt pro disseisina coram A de Crokedayk' et sociis suis justiciariis assignatis ad assisam anno xxiiij^{to}. Et quia predicto abbati non competit actio per libertatem quam habet calumpniandi seu habendi huiusmodi fines quos attornatus suus predictus per libertatem predictam calumpniatus est. Ideo libertas illa iterato capiatur in manu regis. Postea replegiatur ut supra.

1 Also in Soc. of Antiquaries, MS 38, fos 56v–7r and BL, Cott. Cleop. C ii, fos 94v–5v.
2 *currentes* interlined.

78 Cyrograph grant by the abbot to Master Henry Sampson, rector of Fiskerton, that limits on the number of animals permitted to graze on common pasture at Fiskerton and Reepham might be exceeded as long as Gocelin archdeacon of Stowe held the farm of the church. [23 Mar. 1298]

Concessio abbatis facta magistro Henrico Sampson de pastura apud Fyskerton'.

Noverint universi quod cum magister Henricus Sampson rector ecclesie de Fyskerton' tradidisse ad firmam ecclesiam suam predictam magistro Gocelino archidiacono Stowye qui quid archidiaconus ratione predicte ecclesie vendicavit sibi pasturam ad libitum in communa pasture villarum de Fyskerton' et de Repham. Tandem facta diligenti inquisitione per fidedignos juratos utriusque ville, compertum est predictam pasturam ab antiquo fuisse amensuratam et cuilibet bovate terre certum numerum animalium fuisse assignatum et sic hucusque esse usitatum. Sed ad rogatum tam predicti archidiaconi quam predicti magistri Henrici, abbas de Burgo Sancti Petri dominus predictarum villarum de gracia sua speciali concessit quod predictus archidiaconus dum fuerit firmarius predicte ecclesie in tempore predicti magistri Henrici possit habere in pastura predicta animalia ultra numerum predictum, ita quod non intantum oneret eandem pasturam per quod predictus abbas et tenentes sui pasturam sibi competentem amittant. Nec quod aliquis rector ecclesie predicte pretextu dicte concessionis aliquid sibi vendicare possit ultra assisam antiquitus ordinatam. In cuius rei testimonium huic scripto in modum cyrograffi confecto sigilla predictorum abbatis et magistri Henrici alternatim sunt appensa. Dat' apud Burgum Dominica in passione Domini anno regni regis E[dwardi] xxvj^{to}. Et ad majorem securitatem ad instanciam predictorum abbatis et rectoris sigillum archidiaconati Stowye in signum probationis est appensum.

79 Appointment by the abbot and convent of Brother John de Gretham as their proctor in any cases involving the Roman Curia and specifcally regarding the church at Warmington. [24 Mar. 1298]

[fo. 34v] Universis presentes litteras inspecturis abbas et conventus de Burgo Sancti Petri ordinis sancti Benedicti Lincoln' dioc' salutem in Domino sempiternam. Noverit universitas vestra quod nos in omnibus causis et negotiis principalibus et appelationum quas vel que habemus sue habere speramus cum quibuscumque personis coram quibuscumque et in locis quibuscumque in Curia Romana et ad curiam predictam legitime devolutis et in quibus nos ab homine vel a jure legitime constiterit fore citatos, dilectum confratrem nostrum fratrem Johannem de Gretham commonacum nostrum latorem presentium facimus ordinamus et constituimus procuratorem et nuncium specialem, dantes eidem procuratori nostro potestatem agendi defendendi excipendi ponendi positionibus respondendi replicandi appellandi appellatione seu appellationes si quam vel quas seu quivis alius nomine nostro et monasterii nostri interposuerit prosequendi in animas nostras jurandi de calumpnia et de veritate dicenda et prestandi cuiuslibet alterius generis sacramentum crimina et defectus opponendi et illa vel illos contra quoscumque opposita seu oppositos prosequendi status nostri reformationem et inintegrum restitutionis beneficium quociens opus fuerit petendi et optinendi principaliter et eciam incidenter alium procuratorem seu alios procuratores loco sui substituendi et substitutum seu substitutos substituendum vel substituendos quandocumque voluerit seu viderit expedire revocandi et officium procuratoris in se reasumendi et alia faciendi que quomodo libet ad predictam pertinent vel ipsa contingunt volumus tamen et expresse dicimus quod de causis ad Romanam Curiam pro nobis seu contra nos non legitime devolutis et in quibus ab homine vel a jure legitime citati non existimus. Dictus procurator et eius substitutus seu substituti substituendus vel substituendi se nullatenus intermittant nisi in hoc quod possint et debeant articulum tractare utrum causa de qua que' ad Romanam Curiam sit legitime devoluta et super articulo ipso tractando expediendo et terminando eidem procuratori nostro et eius substituto seu substitutis sutbstituendo vel substituendis mandatum damus speciale. Litteras insuper tam de gracia quam de justicia ecclesiam de Wermyngthon' contingentes impetrandi contradicendi necnon in judices consentiendi ratificantes et approbantes expresse omnia et singula acta et gesta et quoscumque processus factos seu faciendos per predictum fratrem Johannem vel eius substitutum vel substitutos substituendum vel substituendos pro eodem eciam procuratori nostro et eius substituto sive substitutis substituendo sive substituendis sub ypoteca rerum nostrorum. Rem ratam haberi judicatum solui exponimus cautiones alia procuratoria quibuscumque in Curia Romana existentibus per nos prius facta revocantes et hoc omnibus quorum interest seu per temporis processum poterit interesse significamus per presentes. In cuius rei testimonium huic procurator' sigilla nostra sunt appensa. Dat' apud Burgum in capitulo nostro in vigilia annunciationis beate Virginis anno Domini millesimo ducentesimo nonagesimo septimo.

80 Appointment by Henry of Yaxley, vicar of Warmington, of Thomas de Barum, clerk, as his proctor in any case involving himself and his vicarage. [26 Mar. 1298]

[fo. 35r] Universis sancte matris ecclesie filiis innotescat per presentes quod ego Henricus de Jakele capellanus ad vicariam de Wermyngton' Linc' dioces' per religiosos viros abbatem et conventum monasterii sancti

Petri de Burgo presentatus in omnibus causis et negotiis principalibus et appelationum me et vicariam dicte ecclesie qualitercumque contingentibus motis seu movendis coram quibuscumque contra quoscumque adversarios meos diebus et locis quibuscumque dilectum mihi in Christo Thomam de Barum clericum procuratorem meum ordino facio et constituo et nuncium specialem, dans eidem procuratori meo potestatem agendi et defendendi, ponendi et positionibus respondendi, replicandi appellandi appellationem seu appellationes prosequendi in animam meam de calumpnia et de veritate dicenda jurandi et cuiuslibet alterius generis sacramentum prestandi status mei reformationem ac inintegrum restitutionis beneficium quociens opus fuerit petendi et recipiendi procur' loco sui substituendi et substitutum revocandi ac officium procuratoris reasumendi. Litteras tam de gracia quam de justicia inpetrandi contradicendi nec non in judices consentiendi et omnia alia faciendi que quodmodo libet ad predicta pertinent vel ipsa contingunt. Rem ratam haberi judicatum solui cautiones pro eodem et eius substituto vel substituendo sub ypotheca rerum expono per presentes. In cuius rei testimonium huic procur' sigillum meum apposui. Et quia sigillum meum est ignotum, sigillum domini mei abbatis de Burgo Sancti Petri presentis est appensum. Dat' apud Burgum Sancti Petri in crastino annunciationis beate Virginis anno Domini M^{mo} CC^{mo} nonagesimo octavo.

81 Grant by Roesia de Doueria, in her widowhood, to William Marmioun and Loretta, his wife and Roesia's daughter, and their joint heirs of her manor of Lutton except for the advowson of the church, rendering annually a pair of gilded spurs or 6d to Roesia and services due to the chief lord of the fee. [7 June 1248]

Sciant[1] presentes et futuri quod ego Roesia de Doueria in pura viduitate et ligia potestate mea dedi concessi et hac presenti carta mea confirmavi Willelmo Marmyoun filio Roberti Marmioun junior' et Lorette filie mee uxori ipsius Willelmi pro homagio et servicio suo totum manerium meum de Ludington' cum omnibus suis pertinenciis simul cum feodo militum in libertatibus et in omnibus aliis, et quicquid in predicto manerio habui vel habere potui sine aliquo retenemento excepta advocatione ecclesie eiusdem manerii. Habendum et tenendum predictis Willelmo et Lorette et heredibus suis de predicta Loretta procreatis de me et heredibus meis inperpetuum libere, quiete et pacifice. Reddendo inde annuatim mihi et heredibus meis unum par calcarium deauratorum ad Pascha vel sex denarios in curia predicti manerii pro omni servicio mihi et heredibus meis pertinenti. Et faciendo capitalibus dominis feodi pro me et heredibus meis omnia alia servicia; videlicet tam in warda castri de Rokingham quam in aliis que ad ipsos pertinent. Et ego Roesia et heredes mei predictum manerium cum omnibus pertinenciis suis sicut predictum est excepta advocatione ecclesie eiusdem manerii predictis Willelmo et Lorette et heredibus suis de predicta Loretta procreatis per predictum servicium contra omnes homines inperpetuum warantizabimus et adquietabimus. Et si forte contingat quod predicta Loretta sine herede de corpore suo procreato [fo. 35v] decedat, totum predictum manerium cum omnibus suis pertinenciis sine aliqua contradictione vel difficultate ipsius Willelmi mihi et heredibus meis integre revertetur. In cuius rei testimonium etc. Dat' ad Pentecost' anno incarnationis Domini millesimo CC° xlviij.

1 Also in *Henry of Pytchley*, p. 48.

81A Memorandum that Isabella de Douere, countess of Atholl made a fine with William Marmioun agreeing that she would acquit him against the abbot of Peterborough for any services due to her from the manor of Lutton on 24 June 1271.

Memorandum[1] de fine levato inter Willelmum Marmioun querentem et Isabellam de Douere comitissam de Asceles per breve de medio quod eadem Isabella adquietaret predictum Willelmum versus abbatem de Burgo Sancti Petri de serviciis etc[2] coram magistro Rogero[3] de Seyton' et sociis suis justiciariis itinerantibus apud Cantuar' in festo sancti Johannis baptiste anno regni regis Henrici filii regis Johannis lv^to^.

1 See *Henry of Pytchley*, p. 48.
2 *pro manerio de Ludington' cum suis pertinenciis* marginated.
3 *Johanne* in *Henry of Pytchley*.

82 Letter of Oliver, bishop of Lincoln, to the prioress and convent of St Michael's, Stamford making arrangements for penances following his visitation of 10 May 1298, with particular instructions about those guilty of incontinence or sharp words and the problem of debt. [16 May 1298]

Oliver par la suffraunce Deu eveske de Nicole a ses cheres filles en Deu priouresse e le cuvent de Seint Michel de hors Estaunford saluz, grace e beneicun ke la visitaciun ke nus feimes en vostre mesun le samadi procheyn apres la feste sein Johan devaunt la porte latin le an nostre seygnur m^l^ cc nonauntime utime ne seit saunz effect, nus enjognum a vus priuresse e suppriuresse en vertu de obedience qe vus teignez en silence tutes celes qe dunk' se sustrestrent de la examinaciun e ne voleient avant venyr pur estre examinees. E ke chescune de eles le vendirdi procheyn apres la receyuere de cestre lettre receyve une displine en chapitle en presence del cuvent e ieune meime le vendirdi en pain potage e cerueyse. E ceste penaunce facent suz peyne de[1] escumengement issi qe vus les teygnez pur escumengees si eles ne la facent. E vus si tost come vus pureiz bonement, nus facez sauer[2] lur nuns.

De autre part de celes deus qe furent atteynt de incontinence par enfaunt porter e par ceo chairent en la sentence qe le eveske Johan dona sur tuz ceus ki nuneines corumpereient pernez bone garde qe eles facent lealment la penaunce qe lur a est enioint de par le abbe de Burgh la quele penaunce[3] nus beinn asauer quele ele fu quant lu e tens serra. Il semble qe eles ne pount estres escusees qe eles ne chairent en le escumengement come parceneres en le crime pur quei la sentence fu dunee, e de ceo ne poeient estre assoussees de autre qe de eveske.

Aliz de Upton' cesse de estre contenciounse e trop aspre vers ses soers e se porte humblement e debonerement vers eles, kar vus devez sauer qe chescune de vus deit porter reuerence a autre sicome estat de religioun demaunde, e de ceo preygnent garde numement les plus joefnes vers les eyneez.

Endreit de ceo qe vus estes [fo. 36r] poure e grefment endetteez ne sauum nus autre remedie fors qe vus portez en patience e mettez peine de vostre estat releuer taunt come vus purrez e sauerez od cunseil e ayde de bone gent en priaunt Deu qe il voylle a ceo mettre sa grace. E vus dussez ben estre de tele conversacioun en religioun gardaunt qe Deus oist vostre priere e donast corage a bone gent de vus ayder.

Vostre acunt ne lessez mie qe il ne seit oi pur sauer certeinete de vostre estat.

De silence meuz garder pensez atteignaument ke nus trouames qe fu malement garde numement en cloistre. Deu vus doint grace de religiun saunz feintise avier e garder, issi qe tutes les choses facez en charite en verite e en chastete. Dune a Buckeden' le venderdi prochein devaunt le Seint Dunstan le an nostre seygnur avaunt dit e de nostre consecracioun diseutime.

1 *de* repeated.
2 *sauer* interlined.
3 *penaunce* interlined.

83 Acknowledgement by Abbot William that Geoffrey Russel has paid his half of the 45 marks owed by Geoffrey and Alice, widow of Andrew Russel for the custody and marriage of John and Peter, sons and heirs of Andrew Russel, which was recovered by the abbot in the court of Common Pleas. [11 July 1298]

Quietaclamatio debiti domini Galfridi Russel.

Noverrint [sic] universi quod ego frater Willelmus permissione divina abbas de Burgo Sancti Petri recepi de domino Galfrido Russel milite estimationem viginti duarum marcarum et dimidiam tam in rebus quibusdam ab eodem receptis quam in relaxatione pecunie facta eidem in partem solutionis pro portione ipsum contingente de quadraginta et quinque marcis quas recuperavi in curia domino [sic] regis in Banco versus eundem dominum Galfridum et dominam Aliciam relictam domini Andree Russel militis defuncti pro custodia et maritagio Johannis et Petri filiorum et heredum predicti Andree Russel. De quibus viginti duabus marcis et dimidia pro portione dictum dominum Galfridum contingente de predictis quadraginta et quinque marcis versus eundem Galfridum et predictam Aliciam ut predictum est recuperatis profiteor et protestor michi plenarie esse satisfactum salvo michi jure super portione predictam Aliciam contingente de debito supradicto. In cuius rei testimonium presentibus sigillum meum apposui. Dat' apud Burgum Sancti Petri die Veneris proxima post translationem sancti Thome martyris anno regni regis E[dwardi] vicesimo sexto.

84 Letter from Abbot William and the convent to Oliver, bishop of Lincoln, requesting him to institute Richard of Hertford to Fiskerton church, currently vacant and to which they have right of presentation. [29 Aug. 1298]

Presentatio domini Ricardi de Herteford'.

Reverendo[1] patri in Christo domino O[livero] Dei gracia Linc' episcopo sui humiles et devoti in Christo filii W[illelmus] eiusdem dono gracie abbas de Burgo Sancti Petri et eiusdem loci conventus salutem. Cum debite reverencie devotam obedienciam et sancte paternitati nostre presentamus dilectum clericum nostrum dominum Ricardum de Herteford' ad ecclesiam de Fyskerton' vacantem, que ad nostram spectat presentationem, humiliter supplicantes et devote quatinus caritatis intuitu eundem ad dictam ecclesiam admittatis et personam in eadem instituatis, salvis nobis et ecclesie nostre juribus ab antiquo perceptis in eadem. In cuius rei testimonium etc. Dat' in capitulo nostro in festo decollationis sancti Johannis anno Domini M° CC° nonagesimo octavo.

1 Richard of Hertford subsequently withdrew. Hill, *Rolls and Reg. Oliver Sutton*, vol. VIII, pp. 30, 226.

85 Memorandum concerning the provision of potage for the convent from the abbot's granary. [n.d.]

[fo. 36v] De potagio conventus.

Memorandum[1] quod conventus capit de granario abbatis singulis annis a festo sancti Michaelis usque ad Dominicam primam Quadragesime singulis diebus septem discos pisarum, de quibus viij disci faciunt j esk'.

Summa per ebdomadam vj esk' j disc'. Et in sex ebdomadis Quadragesime capit eandem mensuram per iiij dies in ebdomada; videlicet die Dominica, die Martis, die Jovis et die Sabbati, quia per diem Lune, diem Mercurii et diem Veneris capit singulis diebus quinque discos albarum fabarum et quinque discos de gruello avenarum. Et post Pascham capit ut supra ante Quadragesimam singulis septimanis usque ad festum apostolorum Petri at Pauli et inter festum predictum et festum sancti Petri advinculam elemosinarius inveniet potagium eidem. Et post idem festum usque ad festum sancti Michaelis abbas inveniet ut supra.

1 Printed in *Mon. Angl.*, vol. I, p. 396, no. 52.

86 Dispute over the status of the church at South Collingham and the right of presentation between the abbot and William de Sancto Botulpho, parson of North Collingham. The case hinged on whether it was a parish church at South Collingham, to which the abbot had right of presentation, or a chapel dependent on North Collingham church. The conclusion is unrecorded. [1274–95]

De divisis ecclesiarum de Colingham.

[Marginated fo. 36v] Notingh' [fo. 37v] Nota [and] Require finem in iii^{o} folio post ad tale signum 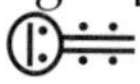[1]

Assisa venit recogn' quis advocatus tempore pacis presentavit ultimam personam que mortua est ad ecclesiam de South Colingham que vacat etc, et cuius advocationem abbas de Burgo Sancti Petri clamat versus magistrum Willelmum de Sancto Botulpho, et unde idem abbas per attornatum suum dicit quod cum quidem Robertus quondam abbas de Burgo Sancti Petri predecessor istius abbatis, tempore pacis tempore H[enrici] regis patris domini regis nunc, presentavit ad eandem ecclesiam per cuius mortem predicta ecclesia modo vacat etc. Et magister Willelmus per attornatum suum venit et dicit quod assisa non debet fieri quia dicit quod ipse est persona de Northcolingh' et persona in eadem personata et advocatione ipsius abbatis. Et tenet capellam de South Colingh' quam predictus abbas dicit esse ecclesiam tanquam capellam ecclesie sue de Northcolingh' pertinentem et annexam, et dicit quod ipse nichil clamat de advocatione predicta nisi tanquam persona etc, unde petit judicium si assisam inter eos precedere debeat. Et abbas dicit quod predictam ecclesiam de Southcolingham est ecclesia per se et non capella pertinens ad dictam ecclesiam de North Colingham et hoc petit quod inquiratur per assisam etc. et petit judicium. Et magister Willelmus dicit quod predicta capella de Southcolingh' quam dictus abbas dicit esse ecclesiam est capella pertinens ad predictam ecclesiam suam de Northcolingh'. Dicit enim quod quidem Galfridus quondam persona ecclesie predicte de

Northcolingham predecessor ipsius Willelmi tempore [fo. 37r] regis J[ohannis] avi domini regis nunc tenuit predictam capellam de Southcolingham annexam predicte ecclesie sue de Northcolingham per longum tempus etc. Et postea quidem Egidius de Alderton persona in eadem ecclesia de Northcolingham in mediate inpersonata similiter tenuit predictam capellam de Southcolingh' toto tempore suo annexam predicte ecclesie sue de Norhcolingham tanquam capellam, post cuius mortem quidem Martinus de Littelbiry quondam persona dicte ecclesie de North Colingham inpersonata in eadem ecclesia similiter tenuit predictam capellam de Southcolingham annexam eidem ecclesie de Northcolingham toto tempore suo tanquam capellam et[2] hoc paratus est verificare per patriam. Et abbas dicit quod predictus Egidius quondam persona predicte ecclesie de Northcolingham tenuit predictam ecclesiam de Southcolingh' non tanquam capellam predicte ecclesie de Northcolingh' pertinentem. Dicit enim quod revera predictus Egidius tenuit utramque ecclesiam predictam, scilicet de Northcolingh' et Southcolingham, sed per diversas presentationes eidem Egidio inde factas diversis temporibus. Et postea vacantibus eisdem ecclesiis per mortem eiusdem Egidii quidem magister Hugo de Colingh', nuper persona ecclesie de Northcol', ad presentationem predicti abbatis predecessoris etc. fuit admissus et institutus in predicta ecclesia de Northcol' etc. et predictus Ricardus de Rowell' similiter admissus et institutus in predicta ecclesia de Southcolingh' ad presentationem predicti abbatis predecessoris etc. per cuius mortem dicta ecclesia de Southcol' modo vacat, et ad evidenc' etc. profert quasdam litteras Walteri quondam archiepiscopi Ebor' loci dioc' que testantur quod idem archiepiscopus per inquisitionem coram officiale suo factam invenit utramque ecclesiarum predictarum esse ecclesiam per se et neutram ab alia dependentem etc. Et dicit quod omnes predecessores predicti abbatis quondam abbates de Burgo Sancti Petri a tempore cuius non extat memoria presentaverunt clericos suos successive ad predictam ecclesiam de Southcolingh' tanquam ad ecclesiam et non tanquam ad capellam pertinentem ad predictam ecclesiam de Northcolingh', unde idem abbas dicit quod predicta ecclesia de Southcolingh' est ecclesia per se non pertinens ad predictam ecclesiam de Northcol' sicut predictus magister Willelmus per rationes suas predictas asserit, et hoc petit ad inquirendum per patriam et magister Willelmus similiter. Ideo inquiratur rei veritas per jur' ass' predicte sed juramentum ponitur in respectum usque a die Pasche in xv dies pro defectu juratorum quia nullus venit et ideo vicecomes habeat corpora etc. Postea ad diem illum venerunt tam predictus abbas quam predictus Willelmus per attornatum ipsius Willelmi et similiter jur' de consensu partium electi qui dicunt super sacramentum suum quod predicta ecclesia de Suthcolingham est ecclesia parochialis per se et non capella pertinens ad ecclesiam de Northcolingh'. Et jur' ques' si predictus Galfridus quondam persona dicte ecclesie de Northcolingh' tenuit predictam ecclesiam de Southcol' [fo. 37v] tanquam ecclesiam per se vel ut capellam annexam predicte ecclesie de Northcol'. Dicunt quod idem Galfridus tenuit ecclesiam illam de Southcolingh' tanquam ecclesiam parochialem per se et non ut capellam pertinentem ad aliam ecclesiam de Northcolingh'. Dicunt eciam precise quod eadem ecclesia de Soutcolingh' a tempore a quo non extat memoria semper hucusque extitit ecclesia parochialis per se et numquam capella pertinens ad ecclesiam de Northcolingh'. Et dicunt quod predictus Robertus quondam abbas predecessor etc. ultimo presentavit ad predictam ecclesiam de Southcolingh' predictum Ricardum clericum suum tanquam ad ecclesiam parochialem per se qui ad presentationem suam fuit admissus et institutus per cuius mortem ecclesia illa modo vacat etc. Et jur' ques' de valore eiusdem ecclesie. Dicunt quod ecclesia illa valet per annum xx marcas. Et si episcopus contulit ad[3] ecclesiam predictam dicunt revera quod tempus sequestr' transiit ad Pascha proximi preter' sed dicunt quod episcopus non contulit ad[3] ecclesiam predictam postea. Quia videtur cur' quod jur' minus sufficienter fuerunt examinati, datus est partibus in crastino ascensionis Domini etc. Et preceptus est vicecomiti quod habeat corpora recogn' ad eundem terminum etc.

1 See below, no. 98.
2 *et* repeated.
3 *ad*? erased.

87 Appointment by Abbot William of John son of Thomas of Oundle as keeper of the liberty of Peterborough during pleasure. [16 Sept. 1298]

Littera Johannis de Undele[1] de custodia libertatis.

Universis sancte matris ecclesie filiis presentes litteras visuris vel audituris frater Willelmus monasterii de Burgo Sancti Petri minister humilis salutem in auctore salutis. Noverit universitas vestra me commisisse dilecto mihi in Christo Johanni filio Thome de Undele clerico custodiam libertatis ecclesie de Burgo cum appendiciis et juribus conservandam, defendendam et sustinendam quibuscumque diebus et locis et coris quibuscumque tam in Curia Regis quam alibi ubicumque pro predicta libertate oportebit respondere vel super aliquo articulo ipsam contingente calumpniam facere. In cuius rei testimonium has litteras meas patentes eidem Johanni feci quamdiu mihi placuerit duraturas. Dat' apud Burgum in festo exaltationis sancte Crucis anno regni regis E[dwardi] xxvj^{to}.

1 For John of Oundle see King, *Peterborough Abbey*, pp. 131–2.

88 Payment by Abbot Richard and the convent to William son of Roger Loueday, for life, of an annual rent of five marks and a robe in the abbey livery. [1281]

[Marginated] Annuus redditus v marcarum et une robe Willelmi Loueday

Omnibus Christi fidelibus presens scriptum visuris vel audituris Ricardus permissione divina abbas de Burgo Sancti Petri et eiusdem loci conventus salutem in Domino sempiternam. Noveritis nos concessisse dilecto et fideli nostro Willelmo Loueday filio domini Rogeri Loueday v marcas argenti annui redditus et unam robam de secta armigerorum nostrorum percipiendas annuatim de domo nostra de Burgo Sancti Petri tota vita ipsius Willelmi ad festum sancti Nicholai. In cuius rei testimonium huic scriptum sigilla abbatis et capituli nostri apposuimus. Dat' in capitulo nostro in octabis sancti Martini anno M°C°C° lxxx primo.

89 Acknowledgement of homage by Geoffrey Russel to Abbot Robert de Sutton for the lands and tenements in the abbot's fee in Paston and Prestgrave formerly held by William Tot. [1262–73]

[fo. 38r] [Marginated] Castr'

Omnibus[1] Christi fidelibus presens scriptum visuris vel audituris Galfridus Russel salutem in Domino sempiternam. Noverit universitas vestra me fecisse homagium domino Roberto de Sutton' abbati de Burgo Sancti Petri pro terris et tenementis que fuerunt quondam Willelmi Tot de feodo domini abbatis in Paston' et Prestegrave cum pertinenciis sub forma tali quod nec ipse abbas nec successores sui teneantur warantizare michi vel heredibus meis dictas terras et tenementa vel aliquam partem dictarum terrarum et tenementorum occasione dicti homagii si aliquo casu vel tempore dictus abbas vel successores sui per me vel heredes meos sint inde vocati ad warantum. Ego autem et heredes mei dictas terras et tenementa de dicto abbate et eius successoribus tenebimus per servicium faciendo sectam ad curiam de Castre de tribus septimanis in tres septimanas et alia servicia forinseca debita et consueta. In cuius rei testimonium huic scripto sigillum meum apposui. Hiis testibus domino Johanne de Helpiston' milite, Roberto de Sheffeud' tunc senescallo Burgi, Roberto Peverel de Paston', Willelmo de Colvile, Hugone de Welyngham, Rogero de Merley, Roberto Peverel de Burgo et aliis.

1 Also in Swaffham, fo. 29r (old foliation), but without the witness clause.

90 Memorandum of homage paid to Abbot William of Woodford by Robert son of Guy of Waterville, knight, for his holding in Orton, by John Spigurnel for his holding in Woodford and Kingsthorpe and by Thomas Ulger for his holding in Polebrook. [2 Aug. 1299]

[Marginated] Homagia et fidelitates

Memorandum quod anno regni regis Edwardi vicesimo septimo et anno domini W[illelmi] de Wodeford' abbatis de Burgo Sancti Petri quarto in festo sancti Stephani martiris dominus Robertus de Watervile miles filius domini Guydonis de Watervile fecit homagium et fidelitatem prefato abbati pro tenemento quod de eo clamat tenere et tenet in villa de Ouerton' in comitatu Huntingt'[1]

Anno eodem et eodem die Johannes Spigurnel fecit homagium et fidelitatem pro tenemento quod de eo tenet et tenere clamat in villa de Wodeford' et Kynestorp'.

Anno eodem et eodem die Thomas Ulger fecit homagium et fidelitatem pro tenemento quod de eo tenet et tenere clamat in Pokebrok'; scilicet de feodo Smert.

Et in presencia subscriptorum fuerunt ista homagia facta et fidelitates; videlicet domini Johannes Druel' vicecomitis Norht', domini Elye de Bekyngham domini regis justiciarii, Rogeri de Hecham, Johannis de Milton', Ade de Haroudon', Johannis de Undel', Gilberti de Sutton', Roberti de Thorp' et aliorum plurimorum.

1 *in comitatu Huntingt'* in a later medieval hand.

91 Extent of the manor of Walcot. [August 1296–97]

[fo. 38v] Extenta[1] manerii de Walcote facta in presencia domini Willelmi abbatis apud Scotere anno eiusdem secundo.

[Marginated] Redd' ass'

Redditus ass' est in dicto manerio cum redd' de Spaldingg' et piscar' de Holflet' cum firma molend' – vj li. xij s. j d. ob.

Sunt ibidem ix^c iiij^or opera quorum Dcc lxviij opera quodlibet valet ob. et C xxxvj quodlibet valet j d. Et est summa utriusque in denariis – xliij s. iiij d.

Sunt ibidem de relax' prati falcand' – xvj d.

Sunt ibidem lxij gall' de cons' que valent – vij s. ix d., prec' cuiuslibet j d. ob.

Sunt ibidem CCClx ova que valent – xiiij d., prec' centum iiij d.

Sunt ibidem per estimationem xvj carucas bondorum ad ij precaria que valent viij s.

Sunt ibidem vj carucas extraneorum ad utrumque semen proven' de v hominibus que valent iij s.

Sunt ibidem xxvij homines qui metent ad j precarium in autumpno ad cibum domini et valent – ij s. iij d.

Sunt ibidem bondi qui dant tallagium pro voluntate domini quod valet communiter – C s.

Sunt ibidem tenentes terram quondam Humfridi de Heytheby qui debent dare ad tallagium – vj s. viij d.

Et franc'pleg' valet per annum – xiij s. iiij d.

Sunt ibidem vj^{xx} viij acre dimid' que valent – vj li. viij s. vj d., prec' acr' xij d.

Sunt ibidem xix acre j rod' prati que valent – xix s. iij d., prec' acr' xij d.

Fines de perquis' curie valent per annum per estimationem – [blank]

Est ibidem quoddam mesuagium quod valet – [blank]

1 For other extents of Walcot, see the Black Book, fo. 129r (1231), fos 233v–5v (1285) and Sparke, pp. 213–14 (1321).

92 Memorandum of homage paid to Abbot William of Woodford by John son of John de Engayne, knight, for his holdings in Pytchley, Hargrave, Hemington and Thorp. [5 Jan. 1299]

[Marginated] Homagium

Memorandum quod anno regni regis Edwardi vicesimo septimo et anno domini Willelmi de Wodeford' abbatis de Burgo Sancti Petri quarto in vigilia Epiphanie apud Fynnesheued'[1] dominus Johannes filius domini Johannis de Engayne miles fecit homagium et fidelitatem prefato abbati pro tenementis que de eo[2] clamat tenere et tenet; videlicet in Pigtesle Haregrave Eymyngeton' Littelthorp'.[3] Hiis presentibus domino Willelmo de Deen, domino Rogero de Huntingfeld', domino Ricardo Basset, Roberto de Potton', Thoma de Sutthorp', Gilberto de Sutton' et Willelmo de Suthorp' et aliis.

1 *apud Fynnesheved* interlined.
2 *eo* interlined.
3 *videlicet ... Littelthorp'* marginated.

92A Memorandum of homage paid to Abbot William of Woodford by John Domer, knight, for his holding in Easton. [5 Mar. 1299]

[Marginated] Homagium

Memorandum quod die Jovis proxima post festum sancti Oswaldi archiepiscopi anno regni regis E[dwardi] xxvij° et anno domini W[illelmi] abbatis iiij^to^ Johannes Domer miles in Eston' fecit homagium et fidelitatem prefato abbati pro tenemento quod de eo tenet et clamat tenere in Eston', presentibus domino Johanne de Veer, Hugone filio Gilberti de Bernak' et aliis multis.

93 Record of assarts in the liberty of Peterborough for which I. le Moyne answers to the Exchequer [n.d.]

[fo. 39r] Particule de assartis de quibus I le Moyne oneratur ad Scaccarium infra libertatem Burgi Sancti Petri.

[Marginated in a different hand] nota pro rege

De Roberto de Pilketon' pro iij acris	ij s.
De Margeria de Stokes pro xj acris et j rod' in Stokes	v s. vij d. ob.
De Ivone de le Brok' pro j acra et di' in Benifeld'	xij d.
De Mauricio Daundelyn pro vij acris in Lyvedon	xiiij s.
De Nicholao de Bassingburn' pro j acra in Suthewyk'	ij s.
De Galfrido de Sancto Medardo milite pro iij acris in Thornhawe	xviij d.
De Stephano de Stokes pro xvij acris in Siberton'	viijs. vj d.
De Simone Blaker pro xix acris di' in eadem	ix s. x d. ob.
De Galfrido de Sancto Medardo clerico pro di' acra et di' rod' in eadem	iij d. ob.
De Radulpho de Caruill' de firma serjancie in Benifeld	ij s.
De Johanne filio Roberti de firma unius acre	iiij d.
De Roberto le Bretoun' de firma iiij^or^ acr' in Siberton' juxta Walmysford'	xviij d.
De Nicholao de Bassingburn' de reffleto	iiij d.
	Summa xlviij s. x d. ob.

94 Letter from Abbot William and the convent to Oliver, bishop of Lincoln, requesting him to institute Simon de Paston as rector of All Saints, Irthlingborough, to which the abbey has right of presentation and which is vacant. [15 Feb. 1299]

Presentatio Simonis de Paston'.

Reverendo in Christo patri ac domino O[livero] Dei gracia Linc' episcopo devoti sui W[illelmus] permissione divina abbas monasterii Beati Petri de Burgo et eiusdem loci conventus salutem obedienciam reverenciam et honorem. Ad ecclesiam Omnium Sanctorum de Irtelingburg' vacantem et ad nostrum patronatum spectantem dilectum nobis in Christo Simonem de Paston' clericum vestre reverende paternitati presentamus ordinandum ad titulum dicte eccelsie in ordines sacros quos dicte ecclesie cura expostulat et requirit, vos exorantes humiliter et devote quatinus dictum clericum ad dictam ecclesiam admittere ac rectorem canonice instituere dignemini in eadem, salvis nobis et ecclesie nostre juribus ab antiquo perceptis in eadem. In cuius rei testimonium presentibus litteris sigilla nostra sunt appensa. Dat' in capitulo nostro die Dominica proxima post festum sancti Valentini martiris anno Domini M°[1] C°C nonogesimo octavo.

1 *M°* interlined.

95 Cyrograph grant by Abbot William of Waterville and the chapter of Peterborough to the nuns of St Michael's Stamford of the church of St Michael, paying an annual pension of half a mark to the abbey for the repair of books. [1155–75]

[fo. 39v] Cyrographum inter abbatem et conventum de Burgo et sanctimoniales beati Michaelis de Stanford' de fundatione et concessione ecclesie earumdem.

[Marginated] Stanf'

Notum[1] sit universis ecclesie filiis quod ego Guillelmus Dei gracia abbbas Burgi totum que capitulum dedimus et presentium auctoritate celebrando[2] concessimus religioni sanctimonialium apud Stanford' commorantium ecclesiam beati Michaelis in perpetuam elemosinam cum omnibus rebus eidem ecclesie pertinentibus bene et in pace et libere ac honorifice possidendam ob remedium et salutem animarum nostrarum in subjectione nostra et consilio [de][3] rebus suis tam interius quam exterius disponendis, tali quidem tenore quod prelatus qui rebus eiusdem monasterii debet providere domini abbatis dispositione et capituli consilio vel ponetur vel deponetur, pari conditione ordinatio priorisse que ceteris in ordine debet preesse in dispositione erit abbatis et capituli consilio. Simili modo suscepio sanctimonialium que ibidem Deo deservient ad imperium pendet abbatis et capituli consilium. Ipse etenim sanctimoniales et omnium rerum suarum ordinationes sunt modis omnibus in dispositione domini abbatis et capituli ita sane ne propter illius monasterii incrementum monasterium Burgi aliquod rerum suarum detrimentum paciatur. Monasterium autem illud recognoscet monasterium Burgi de dimidia marca argenti annua pensione in crastino die post festum sancti Michaelis ad librorum emendationem armario reddenda.

1 Also in Soc. of Antiquaries, MS 38, fo. 154r; CUL, Peterborough D and C, MS 5, fo. 182v. Printed in *Mon. Angl.*, vol. IV, p. 260, no. 2. For Prioress A's recognition of the half mark annual pension, see BL, Cott. Cleop. C ii, fo. 132r–v.
2 *corroborando* in Peterborough D and C, MS 5.
3 Supplied from other MSS.

96 Acknowledgement by Alice, prioress and the convent of St Michael's Stamford of their subordination to the abbot and convent of Peterborough. [pre *c.* 1240][1]

Carta de subjectione ecclesie sanctimonialium sancti Michaelis de Stannf' abbati et conventui de Burgo.

A[licia][2] priorissa et conventus sanctimonialium sancti Michaelis de Stanf' fidelibus ad quos littere presentes pervenerint salutem. Ad noticiam vestram volumus pervenire nos et omnia nostra in dispositione domini abbatis et conventus de Burgo esse in quorum feodo fundata est ecclesia nostra et de quorum beneficiis sustentamur, unde presenti scripto sigillo capituli nostri signato attestamur eos liberam habuisse et habere dispositionem de omnibus rebus et possessionibus nostris secundum quod viderint et eis et nobis expedire, unde fideliter promittimus coram Deo quod numquam ab eorum consilio et dispositione resiliemus sed per omnia eis erimus obedientes.

1 Prioress Alice died *c.* 1240. *VCH, Northants.*, vol. II, p. 100.
2 Also in The Black Book, fo. 154r; Swaffham, fo. 101r; CUL, Peterborough D and C, MS 5, fo. 81v; BL, Cott. Cleop. C i, fo. 130r. For commentary see Thompson, *Women Religious*, pp. 61–2 and above, p. 00.

97 Petition to Richard, archbishop of Canterbury and his suffragans by A. prioress and the convent of St Michael's Stamford asking them to intercede with the abbot and convent of Peterborough for reconciliation after a misconceived privilege obtained on the priory's behalf from the pope. [1173–81 or 1229–31, probably *c.* 1230]

Littere de petitione venie super quodam privilegio male impetrato.

Dilectissimis[1] in Christo patribus et dominis Ricardo Dei gracia Cant' archiepiscopo tocius Anglie primati et apostolice sedis legato eius que suffraganeis, A. priorissa sancti Michaelis de Stanford' humilis que eiusdem loci conventus salutem et orationes in Christo Jesu. In noticiam vestram venire desideramus patres reverendi qualiter clericus quidam nobis et ecclesie nostre [fo. 40r] specialis amicus in Curia Romana dudum constitutus, utilitati domus nostre volens attencius inposterum providere, cum super possessionibus nostris canonice adeptis simplicem tantum confirmationem a domino papa debuisset inpetrasse preter mandatum et conscienciam immo contra communem voluntatem capituli nostri in eisdem litteris confirmationis de habenda littera[2] electione priorisse capitulum inferi fecit quoddam, quod quidem nobis et ecclesie nostre perniciosum est et dampnosum. Presertim cum id aliis privilegiis nostris sit contraium et cartis aliis quas super fundatione domus nostre ab ipsis fundatoribus habemus. Ex huic quidem domini et fundatores nostri abbas et conventus de Burgo rancorem adversus nos et indignationem conceperunt et merito cum sine assensu et voluntate eorum qui locum nostrum fundaverunt et dotaverunt per quos post Deum vivimus nullam electionem priorisse seu institutionem habere debeamus prout ex diligenti inspectione carte eorundem quam super fundatione loci nostri habemus evidenter si placet poteritis cognoscere. Preterea quia et alii sunt articuli unde indignationem dominorum nostrorum abbatis et conventus incurrimus ut pote de ecclesiis quas nobis sub certa pensione contulerunt eis annuatim solvenda, unde a domino papa confirmationes impetravimus nulla pensionis habita mentione, super hoc ipso nos errasse confitemur parate unanimi assensu et hunc et alios articulos eorum arbitrio relinquere corrigendos volentes igitur prout expedit modis quibus possumus in humilitate et omnimoda satisfactione dominorum et fundatorum nostrorum graciam et favorem nobis ad plenum reconciliare mittimus ad pedes vestros. Priorissam nostram cum omnibus cartis et privilegiis ecclesie nostre supplicantes attencius quatinus inspectis eisdem cartis et privilegiis omnem contrarientatem ammoveatis et nos divine miserationis intuitu in plenitudinem pristine dilectionis et gracie dominorum nostrorum restituatis quia sive ipsis universe non possumus sive suffragiis eorum non potest stare ecclesia nostra nec ordo ibidem institutus observari, ut eciam a dominis nostris indignatio adversus nos concepta et omnis nobis[3] tollatur suspicio petimus humiliter et obnixe quatinus rei veritatem quam super hiis vobis scribimus domino pape litteris vestris significare velitis. [Val'][4]

1 Also in The Black Book, fo. 154r–v; Swaffham, fo. 101r–v; CUL, Peterborough D and C, MS 5, fos 80v–81r. For commentary and dating see Thompson, *Women Religious*, pp. 62–3 and above, pp. xxiii–iv.

2 *libera* in Peterborough D and C, MS 5.

3 *omnis a nobis* in the other Peterborough copies.

4 Supplied from Peterborough D and C, MS 5.

98 Conclusion of the dispute over the right of presentation to the church at South Collingham recording the abbot's victory. [Hilary Term 1299]

[fo. 40v] [Marginated] Notingham [1]

Postea a die sancti Hillarii in xv dies anno regni regis nunc vicesimo septimo apud Ebor' venerunt partes per attornatos suos et similiter xij juraturos. Et jur' ques' si predictus Egidius et Martinus quondam persone predicte ecclesie de Northcolingham successive etc tenuerunt predictam ecclesiam de Suthcolingham tanquam capellam eidem ecclesie de Northcolingham annexam vel ut ecclesiam parochialem per se et non ut capellam pertinentem etc. Dicunt quod predictus Egidius tenuit ecclesiam illam de Southcolingh' tanquam ecclesiam parochialem per se et non ut capellam annexam predicte ecclesie de Northcol'. Dicunt eciam quod idem Martinus numquam aliquid habuit in ecclesiis illis. Et que convictum est etc. quod persone etc. temporibus retroactis tenuerunt predictam ecclesiam de Suthcol' tanquam ecclesiam parochialem et non ut capellam pertinentem etc. et quod predictus Robertus quondam abbas etc. ultimo presentavit ad eandem ecclesiam predictum Ricardum clericum suum qui ad presentationem suam fuit admissus etc. Consideratum est quod predictus abbas recuperet presentationem suam etc. et similiter dampna sua ad valorem medietatis ecclesie predicte eoque episcopus non contulit ecclesiam illam etc. Et magister Willelmus in misericordia etc. Et predictus abbas habeat breve archiepiscopo Ebor' quod ad presentationem ipsius abbatis ad predictam ecclesiam idoneam personam admittat etc.

Dampn' x marc'.

1 See above, no. 86.

99 Resignation of Simon of Paston from the rectory of All Saints' Irthlingborough. [27 Feb. 1299]

Resignatio Symonis de Paston'.

Universis sancte matris ecclesie filiis presentes litteras inspecturis vel audituris, Symon de Paston' clericus ad ecclesiam Omnium Sanctorum de Yrtlingburg' Linc' dioc' per religiosos viros abbatem et conventum monasterii sancti Petri de Burgo presentatus salutem in Domino. Noveritis me juri mihi adquisito per presentationem dictorum religiosorum dominorum meorum ad ecclesiam de Yrtlingburg' supradictam, venerabili in Christo patri domino O[livero] Dei gracia Linc' episcopo nuper factam pure sponte et absolute renunciasse nichil juris mihi retinens seu reservans. In cuius rei testimonium presentibus sigillum meum apposui. Et quia sigillum meum pluribus est incognitum, sigillum decanatus de Nassoburgi[1] presentibus in modum collationis apponi procuravi. Dat' apud

Burgum Sancti Petri iij kalendas Martii anno Domini M° C°C nonogesimo octavo.

[note in larger hand] Quere presentationem eiusdem in ij° folio precedente[2]

1 See below, no. 164 for another example of the use of the deanery seal for a resignation.
2 See above, no. 94 for Simon of Paston's institution.

100 Surrender by Robert son of Geoffrey of Gunthorpe of all secular services owed from land in Werrington given to the abbey by Ivo, his father's uncle. [n.d.]

[fo. 41r] Carta Roberti filii Gaufridi de Gunthorp' de terra sua in Witheringthon'.

Notum sit omnibus tam presentibus quam futuris quod ego Robertus filius Gaufridi fil' Gaufridi[1] de Gunthorp' concessi et presenti carta mea confirmavi abbati de Burgo totam terram in Witherington' quam Ivo avunculus iam dicti G[aufridi] patris mei eidem abbacie donavit in liberam et puram et perpetuam elemosinam et carta sua confirmavit. Et ut predicta abbacia de Burgo habeat et teneat prefatam terram in perpetuam elemosinam liberam solutam et quietam ab omni terreno servicio, ego Robertus et heredes mei eandem terram aquietabimus de omnibus forinsecis serviciis et faciemus integre plenarium servicium abbati predicte abbacie quod ad feodum trium militum pertinet inperpetuum. Et ut concessio et confirmatio mea perpetuum robur optineat, presenti scripto sigillum meum apposui. Hiis testibus Rogero de Torpel, Ricardo de Watervile, Briano de la Mare, magistro Willelmo de Scote', Johanne de Salysbiry, Roberto de Scote', Johanne de Walton', Willelmo de Thorp', Thoma de Thorp' et aliis.

1 *fil' Gaufridi* repeated in error?

101 Appointment by Abbot William of Robert, rector of Northborough church, as warden of the hospital of St Thomas Martyr, Stamford at the request of Hugh de Sancto Martino, the existing warden, in order to restore its fortunes. [7 April 1299]

De custodia hospitalis Staunford'.

[Marginated] Quere aquietancia magistri Hugonis de Sancto Martino custodis hospitalis sancti Thome martiris Staunford' in xj folio precedente[1]

Universis Christi fidelibus presentes litteras inspecturis, Willelmus permissione divina abbas monasterii sancti Petri de Burgo salutem in Domino sempiternam. Noveritis nos ad interpellationem magistri Hugonis de

Sancto Martino custodis hospitalis sancti Thome martiris juxta pontem Staunford' nobis litterator' et per nuncium specialem factam custodiam dicti hospitalis a predecessore nostro sibi commissam propter inpotenciam ipsius actualem volentis dimittere desolatam, dilecto nobis in Christo domino Roberto rectori ecclesie de Northburg' curam et custodiam dicti hospitalis cum suis juribus et pertinenciis commisisse et tradidisse, quousque de consilio prefati magistri Hugonis ad feliciores successus altissimo suffragante custode pervenientis de prescripti hospital' custod' aliud duxerimus consultius ordinandum. In cuius rei testimonium sigillum nostrum presentibus apposuimus. Dat' apud Burgum vij idus Aprilis anno Domini M^{o} C^{o}C nongesimo nono.

1 See above, no. 65.

102 Undertaking by Abbot William and the convent to provide William Gacelyn with an annual pension of two marks until they can find him a benefice. [4 Nov. 1297]

Pensio domini Willelmi Gacelyn.

Universis Christi fidelibus presentes litteras visuris vel audituris, W[illelmus] permissione divina abbas de Burgo Sancti Petri et eiusdem loci conventus salutem in Domino sempiternam. Noverit universitas vestra nos caritatis intuitu concessisse dilecto nobis in Christo domino Willelmo Gacelyn clerico duas marcas annue pensionis de camera nostra ad duos anni terminos percipiendas; videlicet ad festum sancti Michaelis unam marcam et ad Pascha unam marcam donec ei in beneficio ecclesiastico providerimus. In cuius rei testimonium presentibus sigilla nostra sunt appensa. Dat' in capitulo nostro die Lune proxima post festum Omnium Sanctorum anno Domini M^{o} C^{o}C nongesimo septimo.

103 Inventory of the abbot's stock, debts and assets. [29 Sept. 1248]

[fo. 41v] Status[1] tocius abbacie Burgi die sancti Michaelis anno tercio domini Willelmi abbatis. Staurum per maneria abbatis xj^{xx}vj equi, eque et pulli. Item CCCC viij boves in carucas. Item ix^{xx}xj vacce. Item CCC et xxj tauri, boviculi, juvence et vituli. Item M^{l} CCC iiij^{xx} et iij oves. Item DCCCl porci.

Item die circumcisionis Domini debuit abbas Ricardo de Hotot vj^{xx} marcas. Item Manser[2] et sociis CC marcas. Item Willelmo preposito Burgi xx li. pro carne et cervisia xvj marcas; Johanni de Wyndesoueres xj li. iij s.; magistro Willelmo de Linc' v marcas; conventui xvj li.; domino S[imone] de Sancto Licio viij marcas.

Summa totalis debiti CCCC xj marcas

Eodem die habuit dominus G. de Aylington' xiiij li. in bursa. Et debentur abbati xl li. Item jocalia abbatis valent xxxvj li. preter vasa que fuerunt predecessoris sui. Item abbas habet frumentum et siliginem ad sufficientiam annuam absque emptione.

1 See King, 'Estate Management' pp. 7, 12.
2 *Mamet* in MS. See King, *ibid.*, p. 12.

104 Inventory of abbey stock and grain. [11 Mar. 1263]

Remanencia[1] staurum et bladi per maneria tocius abbacie anno domini J[ohannis] abbatis xiiij^{o} die Dominica proxima ante festum sancti Gregorii anno domini R[oberti] incipiente primo.

Summa quarter' remanenc' frumenti DC iiij^{xx} vij quart' j esk'.
Summa quarter' siliginis C xiij quart' vij esk'.
Summa quarter' brasei, ordei, drageti et avene DCCCC xxx quart' vij esk' dimid'. Summa quart' avene DC liij quart' vj esk'.
Summa quart' fabe et pise xix quart'.
In granaria Burgi l quart' frumenti, iiij^{xx} quart' brasei de quolibet genere, xvj quart' de avena et iij quart' fabe et pise.
Summa tocius bladi [blank].

Summa equorum et affrorum C et xxxij.
Summa taurorum et boum CCCC liij.
Summa annalium et pullorum xix.
Summa vaccarum C lxxiiij.
Summa boviculorum lvij.
Summa annalium C vj.
Summa vitulorum vj^{xx}vij.
Summa multonum, matricis et hoggastris[2] CCCC iiij^{xx}x[2]; videlicet Ciiij^{xx}xviij de matricibus
Summa agnorum iiij^{xx}xvij.
Summa porcorum DC xxij.
Summa cignorum xxvij.
Summa pavonum ij.
Summa auc' [blank].
Summa anatum [blank].
Summa gallinarum [blank].

1 See King, 'Estate Management', pp. 9, 13
2 *hoggastris* linked with a line to *CCCC iiij^{xx}x*.

105 Assessment of the abbey's annual grain requirements, together with an explanation of the different measures in use. [11 Mar. 1263]

[fo. 42r] Triplex[1] est summa per abbaciam Burgi. Maxima: Hac venditur in foro et dicitur summa regia. Quinque vero summe regie continent sex summas veteres et viij summe regie faciunt ix summas de granario. Parva:

qua liberatur metecorn et hac dicitur vetus summa. Media: qua prepositi mittunt apud Burgum et hac dicitur summa granarii.

Ad sustentationem familie abbatis et conventus et hospitum communibus annis oportet habere infra curiam Burgi singulis annis preter panem et cervisiam aliquando emptis propter necessitatem:

De frumento M^{l} xlviij summas; videlicet qualibet ebdomada xxiiij summas. De avena ad prebendum totidem summas. De avena ad braseum M DCC xl summas; videlicet qualibet ebdomada xl summas. De avena ad pultes et oleia xl quar'. De ordeo ad braseum DCCC iiij^{xx} summas; videlicet in ebdomada xx summas. De fabe per annum lx summas.

Summa omnibus bladi infra curiam iiij^{ml} DCC iiij^{xx} et xvj summe regie per magnum centum. Extra curiam post lxvij carucas oportet habere de semine quadragesimali cum prebenda equorum et boum M^{l} DC et xxx summe. Hoc est ad quamlibet carucam cum prebenda xxx summe.

Summa seminis et metecorn' de omnibus bladis ij^{ml} DCCCC xx summe.

Per abbaciam inter servientes et commedentes ad mensam et famulos capientes metecorn' sunt x^{xx} ad quorum quemlibet per annum pertinent iiij^{or} summe et dimid' de metecorn' de summis regiis. Hoc est per annum DCC et lx summe per magnum centum.

[Marginated] Nota
Si aliquo anno possint haberi vij^{xx} summe de omnibus bladis post unamquamque carucam de lvij carucis que sunt infra Nassum et in partibus occidentalis cum Turleby et de molendinis et wodecoren C lx summe, ita quod respondeant orrea ad predictas carucas pertinentia cum molendino et wodecoren de vijm^{l} et xxx summis regiis per magnum centum, tunc poterit vendi totum bladum de Fyskerton', Colingham, Scotere et Walcote preter semen et metecorn et expensis abbatis et aliorum supervenientium et non oportebit illo anno emere nisi x^{xx} et vj summas de aliquo genere bladi. Nam ad decem carucas que sunt in partibus aquilonis pertinent ad seminandum CCC et xl summe de omnibus bladis et ad xl famulos ibidem manentes cum famulis de Turleby et Stowe pertinent ad metecorn' per annum ix summe regie.

Summa seminis et metecorn' in partibus borialis D summe regie per magnum centum computate.

1 See King, 'Estate Management', pp. 9, 13–14; idem, *Peterborough Abbey*, p. 148.

106 Letter from William of Pickering, archdeacon of Nottingham, in association with the archdeacon of Canterbury and Henry of Nassington, canon of Lincoln, to the abbot and convent of Peterborough about a papal provision for Roger de Scardeburg', incorporating letters from Boniface VIII, dated 9 July 1298, to Roger himself and to William and his associates, charging the abbeys of Peterborough and Bardney with finding a suitable benefice. Authentication by Richard, born Henry de Ganyo, clerk and notary public, in which he noted his correction and omission. [1 June 1299]

[fo. 42v] Willelmus de Pykering' archidiaconus Notinghame in ecclesia Ebor' provisor et executor ad infrascripta una cum venerabilibus viris et discretis archidiacono Cantuarien' ac magistro Henrico de Nassington' canonico Linc' ecclesiarum a sede apostolica deputatus religiosis viris et discretis dominis abbati et conventui monasterii de Burgo Sancti Petri ordinis sancti Benedicti Linc' dioc' salutem et mandatis apostolicis reverenc' in singul' obedire. Litteras sanctissimi patris et domini nostri domini Bonefacii divina providencia pape octavi cum vera bulla plumbea ipsius et integro filo serico rubei et crocei coloris bullatas non viciatas non cancellatas non abolitas non abrasas, nec in aliqua sui parte coruptas, que discreto viro Rogero de Scardeburg' clerico Ebor' dioc' diriguntur ac alias litteras apostolicas nobis presentatas cum vera bulla plumbea eiusdem domini pape et integro filo canap' bullatas similiter non viciatas non cancellatas non abolitas, nec in aliqua sui parte coruptas, sed omni suspicione carentes que dictis collegis nostris et nobis diriguntur cum ea qua decuit reverentia recepimus tenores et formas huiusmodi continentes:

Bonifacius episcopus servus servorum Dei dilecto filio Rogero de Scardeburg' clerico Ebor' dioc' salutem et apostolicam benedictionem. Multiplicia tue probitatis merita super quibus laudabile tibi testimonium fidedigni perhibent nos inducunt ut ad personam tuam apostolice munificencie dexteram extendamus. Volentes igitur tibi huiusmodi meritorum tuorum intuitu, necnon et obtentu, venerabilis fratris nostri archiepiscopi Dublinen' nobis pro te supplicantis gratiam facere specialem beneficium ecclesiasticum cum cura vel sine cura nulli alii de jure debitum consuetum ab olim clericis secularibus assignari, ad collationem vel presentationem dilectorum filiorum de Burgo Sancti Petri aut de Bardenay monasteriorum abbatum et conventuum ordinis sancti Benedicti Linc' dioc' communiter vel divisim pertinens quod duxeris acceptandum si quod in civitate vel diocese Linc' vacat ad presens vel quamprimum illud inibi vacare contigerit conferendum tibi cum omnibus juribus et pertinenciis suis ex nunc donationi apostolice reservamus, districtius inhibentes eisdem abbatibus et conventibus ne de huiusmodi beneficio ante huiusmodi acceptationem quam tibi vel procuratori tuo ad hoc specialiter constituto eciam usque ad unum mensem postquam de ipsius beneficii vacatione tibi vel dicto procuratori constiterit facere liceat disponere vel ordinare quoquomodo presumant, ac decernentes ex nunc irritum et inane si secus de dicto beneficio per quoscumque scienter vel ignoranter contigerit attemptari, non obstante si aliqui super provisionibus sibi faciendis de beneficiis ecclesiasticis ad ipsorum abbatum et conventuum collationem vel presentationem spectantibus, speciales vel generales apostolicas quibus per hoc nullum volumus prejudicium generari litteras impetrarunt, sive si eisdem abbatibus et conventibus a sede apostolica sit indultum, quod ad receptionem vel provisionem alicuius minime teneantur, et ad id compelli non possint, quodque de beneficiis ad eorum collationem seu quamcumque dispositionem [fo. 43r] conjunctim vel separatim spectantibus nequeat alicui provideri per litteras apostolicas non facientes plenam et expressam, ac de verbo ad verbum de indulto huiusmodi mentionem, et qualibet ipsius sedis indulgentia generali vel speciali cuiuscumque tenoris existat, per quam presentibus non expressam vel totaliter non insertam, effectus huiusmodi gracie impediri valeat vel differri, et de qua in nostris litteris, specialis mentio sit habenda. Nulli ergo omnino hominum liceat hanc paginam nostre reservationis inhibitionis et constitutionis infringere, vel ei ausu temerario contraire. Si quis autem hoc attemptare presumpserit indignationem omnipotentis Dei et beatorum Petri et Pauli apostolorum eius se noverit incursurum. Dat' Rome apud Sanctum Petrum vij idus Julii pontificatus nostri anno quarto. Item:

Bonefacius episcopus servus servorum Dei dilectis filiis Cantuarien' et de Notingham Ebor'archidiaconis ac magistro Henrico de Nassington' canonico Lincoln' ecclesiarum salutem et apostolicam benedictionem. Multiplicia probitatis merita dilecti filii Rogeri de Scardeburg' clerici Ebor' dioc' super quibus laudabile sibi testimonium fidedigni perhibent nos inducunt ut ad personam suam apostolice munificencie dexteram extendamus. Volentes igitur eidem Rogero huiusmodi meritorum suorum intuitu, necnon et obtentu, venerabilis fratris nostri archiepiscopi Dublinen' nobis pro ipso supplicantis graciam facere specialem beneficium ecclesiasticum cum cura vel sine cura nulli alii de jure debitum consuetum ab olim clericis secularibus assignari ad collationem vel presentationem dilectorum filiorum de Burgo Sancti Petri aut de Bardenay monasteriorum abbatum et conventuum ordinis sancti Benedicti Lincoln' dioc' communiter vel divisim pertinens quod dictus R[ogerus] duceret acceptandum, si quod in civitate vel diocese Lincoln' tunc vacabat vel quamprimum illud inibi vacare contingeret conferendum eidem Rogero cum omnibus juribus et pertinenciis suis ex tunc donationi apostolice reservavimus, districtius inhibentes eisdem abbatibus et conventibus ne de huiusmodi beneficio ante huiusmodi acceptationem quam sibi vel procuratori suo ad hoc specialiter constituto eciam usque ad unum mensem postquam de ipsius beneficii vacatione ipsi Rogero vel dicto procuratori constaret facere liceret disponere vel ordinare quoquomodo presumerent, ac decernentes ex tunc irritum et inane si secus de dicto beneficio per quoscumque scienter vel ignoranter contingeret attemptari. Non obstante si aliqui super provisionibus sibi faciendis de beneficiis ecclesiasticis ad ipsorum abbatum et conventuum collationem vel presentationem spectantibus speciales vel generales apostolicas quibus per hoc nullum voluimus prejudicium generari litteras impetrassent, sive si eisdem abbatibus et conventibus a sede apostolica esset indultum quod ad receptionem vel provisionem alicuius minime tenerentur, et ad id compelli non possent, quod que de beneficiis ad eorum collationem seu quamcumque dispositionem conjunctim vel separatim spectantibus nequiret alicui provideri per litteras apostolicas non facientes plenam et expressam, ac de verbo ad verbum de indulto huiusmodi mentionem [fo. 43v] et qualibet ipsius sedis indulgentia generali vel speciali cuiuscumque tenoris existeret per quam nostris litteris non expressam vel totaliter non insertam effectus huiusmodi gracie impediri vel differri valeret et de qua in eisdem nostris litteris specialis mentio esset habenda. Quocirca discretioni vestre per apostolica scripta mandamus, quatinus vos vel duo aut unus vestrum per vos vel per alium seu alios huiusmodi reservationem inhihitionem et decretum ad predictorum abbatum et conventuum noticiam deducentes huiusmodi beneficium per nos taliter reservatum si quod tempore huiusmodi nostre reservationis in predictis civitate vel diocese vacabat vel quam cito ipsum inibi vacare contigerit postquam ab eodem Rogero vel dicto procuratore pro eo infra dictum tempus fuerit acceptatum, eidem Rogero cum omnibus juribus et pertinenciis suis auctoritate nostra conferre et assignare curetis, inducentes eum vel dictum procuratorem pro ipso in corporalem possessionem predicti beneficii jurium et pertinenciarum eorumdem et defendentes inductum, facientes sibi de ipsius beneficii fructibus redditibus proventibus et juribus universis integre responderi. Non obstantibus omnibus supradictis, sive si dictis abbatibus et conventibus vel quibuscumque aliis communiter vel divisim a prefata sede indultum existat quod excommunicari aut interdici nequeant vel suspendi, contradictores per censuram ecclesiasticam appellatione postposita compescendo. Dat' Rome apud Sanctum Petrum vij idus Julii pontificatus nostri anno quarto.

Nos igitur Willelmus provisor et executor predictus litteris apostolicis supradictis reverent' receptis huiusmodi mandatum apostolicum nobis et dictis executoribus nostris directum, volentes tanquam obediencie filius juxta sui tenorem exequi ut tenemur, predictas graciam reservationem inhibitionem et decretum factas fuisse per sententiam pontificem ut premittitur ac universa et singula contenta in litteris apostolicis antedictis, vobis abbati et conventui conjunctim et divisim, ac aliis omnibus et singulis quorum interest infirmamus ad vestramque noticiam et aliorum quorum interest tenore presentis deducimus instrumenti collationi et provisioni nostre immo verius apostolice beneficium ecclesiasticum dicto Rogero vel suo procuratori eius nomine conferendum cum omnibus juribus suis et pertinenciis nulli alii de jure debitum consuetum abolim clericis secularibus assignari cum cura vel sine cura ad collationem vel presentationem vestram pertinens communiter vel divisim, si quod tempore reservationis apostolice vel post in dictis civitate vel diocese Lincoln' vacaverat vel vacavit vel nunc vacat, quod idem Rogerus vel procurator suus ad hoc specialiter constitutus duxerit acceptandum usque ad mensem postquam sibi de ipsius beneficii vacatione vel suo procuratori constiterit reservamus. Si vero in dictis civitate vel diocese Lincoln' tale non vacat beneficium, nec vacavit, nos primum vacaturum ibidem ad collacionem vel presentationem vestram pertinens communiter vel divisim quod idem Rogerus vel procurator suus eius nomine usque ad mensem postquam sibi vel procuratori suo constiterit duxerit acceptandum cum omnibus juribus suis et pertinenciis, predicto Rogero conferendum nulli alli de jure debitum consuetum abolim clericis secularibus assignari juxta tenorem mandati [fo. 44r] apostolici supradicti collationi et provisioni nostre immo verius apostolice reservamus, inhibentes vobis abbati et conventui conjunctim et divisim et singul' de conventu, ne beneficium per nos taliter reservatum, vel aliquod jus pertinens ad ipsum beneficium ante acceptationem dicti Rogeri vel sui procuratoris usque ad mensem ut premittitur, vel post acceptationem eiusdem alicui conferre vel assignare vel ad beneficium ipsum infra dictum tempus alium presentare vel quicquam aliud in elusionem mandati nostri immo verius apostolici vel dicti Rogeri prejudicium presumatis attemptare per vos vel per alium seu alios publice vel occulte. Decernentes ex nunc prout ex tunc irritum et inane si secus super hiis scienter vel ignoranter a vobis communiter vel divisim vel quovis alio ante acceptationem dicti Rogeri vel sui procuratoris usque ad mensem a tempore sue noticie vel procuratori sui computandum, vel post acceptationem eiusdem fuerit attemptatum aut infuturum contigerit attemptari. Si enim vos domine abbas et conventus communiter vel divisim vel aliquis de conventu impedimentum prestiteritis in premissis vel premissorum aliquo, alium ante acceptationem dicti Rogeri vel sui procuratoris usque ad mensem ut premittitur vel post acceptationem eiusdem quovis quesito colore presentando, vel beneficium ipsum infra dictum tempus alteri conferendo vel alias quomodolibet reluctando per vos vel per alium seu alios publice vel occulte. In vos abbatem et quoscumque in dicto vestro monasterio officium seu administrationem habentes vel tenentes quocumque nomine censeantur, et in omnes alios et singulos qui se predicits gracie reservationi inhibitioni decreto vel in predictis litteris apostolicis contentorum aliquibus se opponunt quomodolibet vel opponent vel obvia in dictum Rogerum vel elusionem mandati nostri immo verius apostolici machinantur vel machinari presumunt quomodolibet vel procurent, beneficium ante acceptationem dicti Rogeri vel sui procuratoris usque ad mensem ut premittitur vel post acceptationem eiusdem ad presentationem dictorum abbatis et conventus communiter vel divisim recipiendo vel quod jus aliud impedimentum prestando consilio auxilio vel favore directe vel indirecte, clam vel palam, per se vel alium seu alios, vel qui plene in hac parte nostris immo verius apostolicis non perebunt mandatis, et inpresentantes et recipientes beneficium ipsum sub quovis colore quesito vel presentari seu recipi procurantes, necnon et in omnes contradictores singulos et rebelles, qui in premissa vel eorum aliquod reluctare presumpserint quoquomodo, quominus premissa vel eorum aliquid suum expedite sortiantur effectum sentenciam excommunicationis majoris promulgamus in hiis scriptis, monasterium vestrum nichilominus interdicto ecclesiastico supponentes ex nunc si premissis vel eorum aliquibus per vos vel alium seu alios, clam vel palam, obviare presumpseritis quoquomodo. Contra vos et alios quoscumque, cuiuscumque fuerint conditionis ordinis auctoritatis et status, dictum Rogerum vel procuratorem suum impedientes in premissis vel premissorum aliquo ad penas alias processuri prout facti qualitas exegerit et nobis videbitur expedire. [fo. 44v] Presens autem instrumentum cum litteris apostolicis volumus apud dictum Rogerum vel eius procuratorem remanere nec per vos vel alium quemcumque detineri. Immo si aliquis presens instrumentum vel dictas litteras apostolicas per vim vel contra voluntatem dicti Rogeri vel sui procuratoris detinere presumpserit, sentenciam excommunicationis majoris quam ex nunc ferimus in hiis scriptis incurratt [sic] per processus nostros collegis nostris vel eorumdem commissariis prejudicare nolumus, qui ipsi et eorum alter hoc cum nostro servato processu per se vel alium seu alios procedere valeant prout de jure poterunt et debebunt. Retinemus insuper nobis plenam potestatem et liberam addendi, mutandi, corigendi, revocandi, detrahendi, emendandi, exequendi, suplendi, adimplendi, declarandi, interpretandi et faciendi, quicquid per nos minus bene aut minus plene in premissis vel eorum aliquo vel circa premissa vel eorum aliquod factum fuerit neglectum peccatum vel eciam pretermissum, et quicquid ad plenam huiusmodi mandati apostolici executionem viderimus expedire. In quorum omnium testimonium et evidenciam pleniorem nos supradictus Willelmus provisor et executor predictus presens instrumentum nostrum que processum ac omnia et singula suprascripta scribi et publicari mandamus et in publicam formam redigi per notarium infra scriptum nostrumque sigillum apposuimus instrumento presenti. Acta lecta et publicata prolata et pronunciata predicta fuerunt in ecclesia parochiali de Athelyngflet' Ebor' dioc' sub anno Domini ab incarnatione millesimo ducentesimo nonogesimo nono, indictione duodecima, prima die mensis Junii pontificatus domini Bonifacii pape octavi anno quinto. Presentibus domino Radulpho de Haluhgton' rectore ecclesie de Derton' Ebor' dioc', domino Willelmo de Houeden' capellano, Roberto de Suthdalton', Thoma de Athelyngflet', clericis testibus ad hoc specialiter vocatis et rogatis. Et ego Ricardus natus quondam Henrici de Ganyo clericus Couventrens' et Lichefelden' dioc' sacri Romani imperii auctoritate notarius publicus predictis omnibus coram reverendo viro magistro Willelmo de Pykering' archidiacono Notinghame supradicto apud Athelyngflet' actis, una cum dictis testibus, presens interfui et sigillum suum vidi per eum presenti instrumento apponi et predicta omnia de mandato eiusdem magistri Willelmi propria manu scripsi et publicavi, ac in publicam formam redigi et illud interlineare si suprascriptum in terciadecima linea una cum interlinear' redditibus, in tricesima secunda linea descendendo propria manu scripsi corigendo que omiseram per errorem, et postmodum signum meum presenti instrumento apposui consuetum rogatus.

107 Letter from Abbot William and the convent to Oliver, bishop of Lincoln, requesting him to institute Richard of Stamford, royal clerk, to Fiskerton church, to which the abbey has right of presentation and which is vacant. [21 Mar. 1299[1]]

[fo. 45r] Presentatio domini Ricardi de Staunford' domini regis clerici ad ecclesiam de Fyskerton'.

Reverendo patri in Christo domino O[livero] Dei gracia Linc' episcopo sui humiles et devoti in Christo filii Willelmus abbas de Burgo Sancti Petri et eiusdem loci conventus salutem. Cum omni reverentia et honore sancte paternitati vestre presentamus dilectum nobis in Christo dominum Ricardum de Staunford' domini regis clericum ad ecclesiam de Fyskerton' vacantem que ad nostram spectat presentationem, humiliter supplicantes et devote quatinus caritatis intuitu eundem ad dictam ecclesiam admittatis et personam in eadem instituatis, salvis nobis et ecclesie nostre juribus ab antiquo perceptis in eadem. In cuius rei testimonium presentibus litteris sigilla nostra sunt appensa. Dat' in capitulo nostro in[2] festo sancti Benedicti abbatis anno Domini M^{o} C^{o}C nonogesimo nono.

1 If the beginning of the calendar year was calculated from 25 March, neither of the two feast days of Saints Benedict, abbot, are compatible with a letter from Abbot William who was succeeded by Abbot Godfrey in 1299. Either would result in dating this letter to 1300. However, the death of Oliver Sutton in November 1299 and the institution of Richard of Stamford to Fiskerton church on 2 May 1299 confirm 1299 rather than 1300. Hill, *Rolls and Reg. Oliver Sutton*, vol. VIII, p. 30.

2 *in* interlined.

Godfrey of Crowland's register

INCIPIT REGISTRUM DOMINI GODEFRIDI ABBATIS. ANNO EODEM PRIMO.

108 Grant by Abbot Godfrey and the convent of a 100s pension to John Bush, royal clerk, until they can find him a benefice, at royal request on account of the abbot's election. [26 Jan. 1300]

Pensio magistri Johannis Buysch'.[1]

Omnibus Christi fidelibus presentes litteras visuris vel audituris, G[odefridus] permissione divina abbas de Burgo Sancti Petri et eiusdem loci conventus salutem in Domino sempiternam. Noverit universitas vestra nos ad instanciam excellentissimi principis domini E[dwardi] regis Anglie illustris ratione nove creationis prefati abbatis unanimiter concessisse dilecto nobis in Christo magistro Johanni Buysch' predicti domini regis clerico centum solidos annuatim percipiendos de camera abbatis qui pro tempore fuerit ad duos anni terminos; videlicet ad Pascha quinquaginta solidos et ad festum sancti Michaelis quinquaginta solidos donec eidem in ecclesiastico beneficio competenti providerimus. In cuius rei testimonium presentibus[2] sigilla nostra apposuimus. Dat' in capitulo nostro in crastino conversionis sancti Pauli anno Domini millesimo C°C nonogesimo nono.

1 See below, no. 159. For John Bush's employment by the crown and receipt of patronage, see Prestwich *Edward I*, pp. 439, 445, 547; E. L. G. Stones, G. G. Simpson, *Edward I and the Throne of Scotland, 1290–1296*, 2 vols (Oxford, 1978), vol. I, p. 156.

2 *presentibus* interlined.

108A Oath taken by John Bush to promote the abbey's business and observe confidentiality. [26 Jan. 1300]

[Marginated] sacramentum

Eodem[1] die idem Johannes prestitit sacramentum in capitulo coram abbate et conventu quod foret diligens promotor negotiorum nostrorum et huius monasterii proposse et fidelis secreta nostra celanda nemini revelaturus.

1 This entry is written entirely in the larger hand reserved for titles and rubrics.

109 Summons to parliament. [29 Dec. 1299]

[Marginated] Breve regis de veniendo ad parliamentum.

Edwardus Dei gratia rex Anglie dominus Hybernie et dux Aquitanie dilecto sibi in Christo abbati de Burgo Sancti Petri salutem. Quia ad salvationem corone nostre regie et communem utilitatem populi regni nostri, secunda die Dominica quadragesime proximo futura London' [fo. 45v] parliamentum tenere et vobiscum et cum ceteris prelatis necnon magnatibus et proceribus eiusdem regni super negotiis nos et idem regnum contingentibus speciale colloquium habere volumus et tractatum, vobis mandamus in fide et dilectione quibus nobis tenemini firmiter injungentes quod ad predictos diem et locum personaliter intersitis nobiscum et cum ceteris prelatis magnatibus et proceribus predictis super dictis negotiis tractaturi vestrum que consilium impensuri. Et hoc sicut nos et honorem nostrum regnique predicti commodum diligitis nullatenus omittatis. Teste me ipso apud Berewyk' super Twedam xxix die Decembris anno regni nostri vicesimo octavo.

110 Writ of summons for military service. [29 Dec. 1299]

Breve regis de habendo servicium apud Karliolum.

Edwardus Dei gratia rex Anglie dominus Hibernie et dux Aquitanie dilecto sibi in Christo abbati de Burgo Sancti Petri salutem. Quia ad salvationem corone nostre regie communemque magnatum et procerum ac tocius populi regni nostri utilitatem, necnon ad dampna scandala et pericula que ex Scotorum inimicorum et rebellium nostrorum rebellione, si ipsam diutius sustineri contingeret possent accidere, prout tam preteritum tempus quam presens, edocent salubriter precavenda ordinamus et proponimus Domino concedente esse in proximo festo nativitatis sancti Johannis baptiste apud Karliolum cum equis et armis et toto servicio nobis debito ad proficiscendum exinde contra dictos Scotos ad eorum rebellionem perfidiam et nequiciam viriliter et potenter cum Dei auxilio reprimandas. Vobis mandamus in fide et dilectione quibus nobis tenemini firmiter injungentes quod totum servicium quod nobis debetis habeatis ad nos ad predictos diem et locum equis et armis bene munitum et paratum ad proficiscendum nobiscum contra Scotos predictos ad induratas maliciam et rebellionem ipsorum potenter et viriliter conterendas. Et hoc nullatenus omittatis. Teste me ipso apud Berewyk' super Twedam xxi^{o}x die Decembris anno regni nostri vicesimo octavo.

111 Gift to Abbot Godfrey of a silver gilt cup by the king to celebrate his inauguration and so that, in drinking, he may be frequently reminded of the donor. [22 Nov. 1299]

Breve domini E[dwardi] regis missa ad abbatem cum quadam cuppa argentea et deaurata.

Edwardus Dei gratia rex Anglie dominus Hibernie et dux Aquitanie dilecto sibi in Christo abbati de Burgo Sancti Petri salutem. Bene experti sumus affectionem benivolam quam erga nos geritis et habetis et semper hactenus in nostris agendis negotiis habuistis ex quo vobis et domui vestre reputamus specialiter nos teneri. Et quia datum est nobis intellegi quod festum ingressus vestri tenebitis iam in brevi, mittimus vobis per latorem presentium quandam cuppam argenteam deauratam quam ex dono nostro recipere et inde bibere velitis ut saltim ex hoc nos ad vestram memoriam frequentius reducatis. Teste me ipso apud Burton' Archiepiscopi xxij die Novembris anno regni nostri vicesimo octavo.

112 Appointment by Abbot Godfrey of Ralph de Colston' and John Waleys de Eynesham to represent the abbey at the bishop of Lincoln's great court at Newark and elsewhere in Nottinghamshire. [2 Feb. 1300]

[fo. 46r] Omnibus Christi fidelibus ad quos presentes littere pervenerint Godefridus permissione divina abbas de Burgo Sancti Petri salutem in Domino sempiternam. Noverit universitas vestra nos attornasse et ordinasse Radulphum de Colston' et Johannem Waleys de Eynesham ad veniendum bis in anno ad magnas curias domini Linc' episcopi apud Newerk'; videlicet post festum sancti Michaelis et iterum post Pascham et ad ibidem et alibi in comitatu Notinghamie exigendum et calumpniandum nomine nostro que ad nos et libertates nostras pertinent. In cuius rei testimonium presentibus sigillum nostrum fecimus apponi. Dat' apud Burgum Sancti Petri in festo purificationis beate Marie anno regni regis Edwardi vicesimo octavo.

113 Homage and oaths of fealty to Abbot Godfrey. [30 Dec. 1299–1 Dec. 1306]

[Marginated left] homag' [right, bracketed for the rest of the folio] nota[1]
[Marginated] Thomas de Pappelee.[2]
Memorandum quod Dominica proxima post epiphaniam Domini anno regni regis Edwardi vicesimo octavo et anno domini G[odefridi] abbatis primo **[10 Jan. 1300]** Thomas filius et heres Johannis de Pappele fecit homagium et fidelitatem dicto abbati pro tenementis que de eo clamat tenere in Pappele et Achston' in presencia domini Ade de Crok'dayk',

Bernardi de Castre, Gilberti de Sutton', Roberti de Thorp', Johannis de Undele et aliorum.

[Marginated] Johannes de Engayne.[3]
Memorandum quod anno regni regis Edwardi xxviij^{o} et anno domini G[odefridi] abbatis primo in vigilia Epiphanie [**5 Jan. 1300**] apud Blatherwyk' dominus Johannes filius domini Johannis de Engayne miles fecit homagium et fidelitatem prefato abbati pro tenementis que de eo clamat tenere et tenet; videlicet in Pigtesle Haregrave Eymyngton' Littelthorp'. Hiis presentibus: magistro Galfrido de Mak', Roberto de Potton', Johanne de Undele, Roberto de Thorp', Willelmo de Suthorp'. Et aliis.

1 In a different hand.
2 See *Henry of Pytchley*, p. 117.
3 *Ibid.*, pp. 130–2.

113A [Marginated] Rogerus de Heygham.[1]

Memorandum quod anno regni regis E[dwardi] xxviij et anno domini G[odefridi] abbatis primo in crastino sancti Thome martiris [**30 Dec. 1299**] apud Burgum dominus Rogerus de Hegham miles fecit homagium et fidelitatem prefato abbati pro tenemento quod de eo clamat tenere et tenet in villa de Helpeston'. Hiis presentibus: Johanne de Undele, Bernardo de Castr', Roberto de Thorp et aliis.

[Marginated] G. de la Mare.[2]
Anno eodem et eodem die dominus Galfridus de la Mare fecit homagium et fidelitatem prefato abbati pro tenementis que de eo clamat tenere et tenet; videlicet in Makeseye Wodecroft et Thurleby. Hiis presentibus: domino Rogero de Hegham, Johanne de Undele, Roberto de Thorp' et aliis.

[Marginated] Johannes de Ayston'.[3]
Anno eodem et eodem die dominus Johannes de Aschton' fecit homagium et fidelitatem prefato abbati pro tenemento quod de eo clamat tenere et tenet in Aschton'. Hiis presentibus: domino R[ogero] de Hegham, J[ohanne] de Undele, R[oberto] e Thorp' et aliis.

[Marginated] R. de Veer.[4]
Anno eodem et eodem die dominus Robertus de Veer miles fecit homagium pro se et participibus suis pro manerio de Marham. Hiis presentibus: domino R. de Hegham, J. de Undele, R[oberto] de Thorp', Bernardo de Castre et aliis.

1 See *Henry of Pytchley*, p. 149 and note.
2 *Ibid.*, pp. 35–8.
3 *Ibid.*, p. 117.

4 *Ibid.*, p. 43.

113B [fo. 46v] [Marginated bracket for all entries on the folio] Homagia et fidelitates

[Marginated] Petrus de Burlee.[1]
Memorandum quod anno regni regis E[dwardi] xxviij^{o} die Sabbati proxima post festum sancti Mathie apostoli et anno domini G[odefridi] abbatis primo [**27 Feb. 1300**] apud Burgum Petrus de Borley fecit homagium et fidelitatem prefato abbati pro tenemento quod de eo clamat tenere et tenet in villa de Burley. Hiis presentibus: magistro G[alfrido] de Makes', Roberto Fayrfox, Radulpho de Colston' et aliis.

[Marginated] Henricus Tilly.
Memorandum quod die Dominica proxima post festum sancti Mathie apostoli anno ut supra [**28 Feb. 1300**] Henricus filius Henrici Tilly de Wermington' fecit homagium et fidelitatem domino Godefrido abbati pro tenementis que de eo clamat tenere in Wermington'. In presencia fratrum Johannis de Rames', Willelmi de Len, magistri G[alfridi] de Makeseye et Radulphi de Thorneye et aliorum.

1 See *Henry of Pytchley*, pp. 88–9.

113C [Marginated] Nicholas de Semark'.[1]

Memorandum quod in crastino sancti Thome martyris anno regni regis E[dwardi] xxviij^{o} et anno domini G[odefridi] abbatis primo [**30 Dec. 1299**] Nicholas de Semark' fecit homagium et fidelitatem prefato abbati pro tenementis que de eo clamat tenere et tenet in villa de Thornhawe et alibi. In presencia domini Rogeri de Hegham, Johannis de Undele, Roberti de Thorp', Bernardi de Castre et aliorum.

[Marginated] Johannes de Folkisworth'.[2]
Memorandum quod anno eodem et eodem die Johannes de Folkisworth' fecit homagium et fidelitatem domino Godefrido abbati pro tenementis que de eo clamat tenere et tenet in villa de Overton'[3] et alibi. In presencia domini Rogeri de Hegham, Johannis de Undele, Roberti de Thorp' et aliorum.

1 See *Henry of Pytchley*, pp. 22–3.
2 *Ibid.*, p. 53.
3 *Overton'* inserted.

113D [Marginated] G. de Lucy.[1]

Memorandum quod anno regni regis E[dwardi] xxviijo et anno domini G[odefridi] abbatis primo apud Novum Templum London' die Veneris proxima ante festum sancti Gregorii pape **[11 Mar. 1300]** dominus Galfridus de Lucy fecit homagium et fidelitatem prefato abbati pro tenementis que de eo clamat tenere et tenet in villa de Daylington' juxta Norht'. In presencia domini Johannis Lovel, domini Nicholai de Segrave, magistri G[alfridi] de Makeseye, Roberti de Thorp' et Johannis de Undele qui eum inde oneravit.

[Marginated] Johannes Spigurnel.[2]
Memorandum quod die Sabbati in festo sancti Gregorii pape anno regni regis E[dwardi] xxviijo [**12 Mar. 1300**] apud Templum Lond' in pleno parliamento Johannes Spigournel fecit homagium et fidelitatem domino G[odefrido] abbati de Burgo pro tenementis que de eo clamat tenere et tenet in villa de Wodeford'. In presencia magistri G[alfridi] de Makeseye, Roberti de Thorp' et Johannis de Undele et aliorum.

[Marginated] Robertus de Waterville.[3]
Memorandum quod die Lune proxima post festum sancti Augustini apostoli anno regni regis E[dwardi] xxviijo et anno domini G[odefridi] abbatis primo [**30 May 1300**] dominus Robertus de Watervile miles fecit homagium et fidelitatem prefato abbati pro tenementis que de eo clamat tenere et tenet in villa de Overton' Watervile et alibi. Hiis testibus: Johanne Russel de Milton', Roberto de Thorp', Johanne de Undele, Thoma de Thorp' et aliis.

[Marginated] Johannes Russel.[4]
Anno eodem et eodem die Johannes Russel filius domini Galfridi Russel de Milton' fecit homagium et fidelitatem domino G[odefrido] abbati pro tenementis que de eo clamat tenere et tenet in Paston' Milton' et alibi. In presencia domini Roberti de Watervile, Johannis de Undele, Roberti de Thorp' et aliorum.

[Marginated] Johannes Hammond.
Memorandum quod die Martis proxima post festum sancti Augustini apostoli anno regni regis E[dwardi] xxviijo et anno domini G[odefridi] abbatis primo [**31 May 1300**] Johannes Hammond de Stanewygg' fecit homagium et fidelitatem domino abbati pro tenemento quod de eo clamat tenere et tenet in villa de Stanewygg'. In presencia Roberti de Thorp', Johannis de Undele, Rad'i de Thorneye, Willelmi de Suthorp' et aliorum.

1 See *Henry of Pytchley*, pp. 150–1.
2 *Ibid.*, pp. 56, 60 note.
3 *Ibid.*, p. 53.
4 *Ibid.*, pp. 108–10.

113E [fo. 47r] [Marginated bracket for all entries on the folio] Homagia et fidelitates

[Marginated] Robertus Freman.
Memorandum quod die Sabbati in vigilia sancte Trinitatis anno regni regis E[dwardi] xxviij° et anno domini G[odefridi] abbatis primo [**5 June 1300**] apud Burgum Robertus le Freman de Glynton' fecit homagium et fidelitatem prefato abbati pro tenemento quod de eo tenet et clamat tenere in villa de Glynton'. In presencia Roberti Fayrfox, Johannis de Undele, Roberti de Thorp' et aliorum.

[Marginated] Johannes Marmioun.[1]
Memorandum quod die Jovis in festo commemorationis sancti Pauli anno regni regis E[dwardi] xxviij° et anno domini G[odefridi] abbatis primo [**30 June? 1300**] apud Burgum dominus Johannes Marmioun fecit homagium et fielitatem prefato abbati pro tenementis que de eo tenet et clamat tenere in Ludyngton' et Lullington' et alibi. In presencia domini Gregorii de Lullington', Johannis de Undele, Thome de Thorp', Willelmi de Suthorp', Alani de Alkebarue et aliorum.

[Marginated] Willelmus de Kirkeby.[2]
Memorandum quod die Dominica proxima ante festum sancte Margarete virginis anno regni regis E[dwardi] xxviij° et anno domini G[odefridi] abbatis primo [**17 July 1300**] apud Eston' dominus Willelmus de Kirkeby fecit homagium et fidelitatem prefato abbati pro tenementis que de eo tenet et clamat tenere in villis de Cotherstok' Glapthorn' et Brennegrist'. In presencia domini Roberti de Hotot, Johannis de Holc', Henrici de Northwyc', magistri G[alfridi] de Makeseye et Johannis de Undele et aliorum.

[Marginated] Hugo de Bernak'.[3]
Anno eodem et eodem die et in eodem loco Hugo de Bernak' fecit homagium et fidelitatem prefato G[odefrido] abbati pro tenementis que de eo tenet et clamat tenere in Bernak' Badyngton' Cathweyt'. In presencia domini Roberti de Hotot', magistri G[alfridi] de Mak', Johannis de Undel', Henrici de Northwyc' et aliorum.

[Marginated] Henricus de Norwyc'.[4]
Anno die et loco supradictis Henricus de Northwyc' fecit homagium et fidelitatem prefato domino G[odefrido] abbati pro tenemento quod de eo tenet et clamat tenere in Brennegrist'. In presencia domini Roberti de Hotot', Hugonis de Bernak', magistri G[alfridi] de Makes', Johannis de Undele et aliorum.

[Marginated] Abbas de Suleby.[5]
Memorandum quod die Lune in festo sancti Jacoby apostoli anno regni regis E[dwardi] xxviij° et anno domini G[odefridi] abbatis primo [**25 July**

1300] apud Burgum abbas de Suleby fecit fidelitatem prefato abbati pro tenemento quod de eo tenet et clamat tenere in Parva Adyngton'. In presencia fratris Willelmi de Jarewell', Johannis de Undele et Willelmi de Suthorp' et aliorum.

[Marginated] Johannes de Chamberleyn.[6]
Memorandum quod die Mercurii in festo sancti Laurencii martyris anno regni regis E[dwardi] xxviij° et anno domini G[odefridi] abbatis primo [**10 Aug. 1300**] apud Burgum Johannes Chaumberleyn de Wynewyk' fecit homagium et fidelitatem prefato abbati pro tenementis que de eo tenet et clamat tenere in Wynewyk' et alibi; videlicet pro xiii[a] parte feodi unius militis in Wynewyk'. In presencia magistri G[alfridi] de Makes', Johannis de Undele, Thome de Thorp', Roberti de Mythingesby et aliorum.

[Marginated] Nicholas Knyt.[7]
Anno eodem die et loco supradicto Nicholas Knyt' de Stok's fecit homagium et fidelitatem predicto abbati pro tenemento quod de eo clamat tenere et tenet in Stok's; videlicet pro quarta parte feodi unius militis. In presencia supradictorum testium.

1 See *Henry of Pytchley*, pp. 46–9.
2 *Ibid.*, pp. 29–30, 34 note 15, 133–4.
3 *Ibid.*, pp. 124–5.
4 *Ibid.* pp. 133–4.
5 *Ibid.*, p. 75 and no. 124.
6 *Henry of Pytchley*, p. 114.
7 *Ibid.*, pp. 146–7.

113F [fo. 47v] [Marginated bracket for all entries on the folio] Homagia et fidelitates

[Marginated] Walterus de Irland'. [In a different hand] Undele
Memorandum quod die Martis in crastino assumptionis beate Marie anno regni regis E[dwardi] xxviij° et anno domini G[odefridi] abbatis primo [**16 August 1300**] dominus Walterus de Yrland' fecit fidelitatem prefato abbati apud Eye Byri[1] pro tenemento quod de eo tenet et clamat tenere in Undele. In presencia rectoris ecclesie de Peychirche, fratris Johannis de Walkote, Johannis de Undele et aliorum.

[Marginated] Ranulfus de Ry.
Memorandum quod die Jovis proxima post festum exaltationis sancte Crucis anno regni regis E[dwardi] xxviij° et anno domini G[odefridi] abbatis primo [**15 Sept. 1300**] apud Burgum dominus Ranulfus de Ry fecit fidelitatem prefato abbati pro tenementis que de eo clamat tenere et tenet in Thurleby et alibi per uxorem eius. In presencia Johannis de Undele, Roberti de Thorp', Thome de Thorp' et aliorum.

[Marginated] Robertus de Nevyll'.[2]
Memorandum quod die Martis proxima post festum translationis beati Hugonis anno domini G[odefridi] secundo [**11 Oct. 1300**] apud Scote' dominus Robertus de Neville fecit homagium et fidelitatem prefato domino G[odefrido] abbati pro tenementis que de eo clamat tenere in Scotton' Malmeton' et Holm. In presencia fratrum Simonis de Freston', Johannis de Walcot' et Willelmi de Jarewell', domini J. de Aysfortheby, Bernardi de Castre et aliorum.

[Marginated] Johannes de Thevelby.
Memorandum quod Johannes de Thevelby fecit fidelitatem domino G[odefrido] abbati die Mercurii proxima sequent' in presencia testium predictorum apud Scote'. Anno suo secundo [**12 Oct. 1300**].

Memorandum quod dominus Willelmus de Wendovere fecit fidelitatem domino G[odefrido] abbati apud Scote' pro tenementis que de eo clamat tenere in Linc' in presencia testium predictorum. Die Jovis in festo sancti Edwardi anno secundo ut prius [**13 Oct.? 1300**[3]]

[Marginated] Thomas de Novill'.[4]
Eodem die et eodem anno dominus Thomas de Nevill' fecit homagium et fidelitatem domino G[odefrido] abbati apud Scote' pro tenementis que de eo clamat tenere in Cletham in presencia testium predictorum.

1 *Byri* interlined.
2 See *Henry of Pytchley*, pp. 105–6.
3 The feast of the Translation of St Edward fits best with the chronological sequence.
4 *Henry of Pytchley*, p. 79 note.

113G [Marginated] Johannes le Despens'.[1] [In a different hand] Armist'

Memorandum quod Johannes le Despenser de Harmeston' fecit homagium domino G[odefrido] abbati apud La Bigging' pro tenementis que de eo clamat tenere et tenet in Armeston'. In presencia fratrum Alexandri de Wystowe, Johannis de Walcote, Willelmi de Jarewell', Johannis de Undele, Thome de Thorp' et aliorum, die Dominica proxima post festum epiphanie Domini anno eiusdem abbatis secundo [**8 Jan. 1301**].

[Marginated] Johannes de Boys.[2]
Memorandum quod die Mercurii in crastino sancti Valentini martyris anno regni regis E[dwardi] xxix^{o} et anno domini G[odefridi] abbatis secundo [**15 Feb. 1301**] dominus Johannes de Boys miles fecit homagium et fidelitatem prefato abbati apud Eyebyri pro tenementis que de eo tenet et clamat tenere in Wodeford' et Kynesthorp'. In presencia domini Humfridi de Waledene, Johannis Spigournel, Johannis de Undele, Roberti de Thorp' et aliorum.

[Marginated] Willelmus Treilly.[2]
Memorandum quod die Mercurii in crastino sancti Guthlaci martyris anno regni regis E[dwardi] xxix° et anno domini G[odefridi] abbatis secundo [**12 April 1301**] Willelmus Treylli fecit homagium et fidelitatem prefato abbati apud Thorpel pro tenementis que [fo. 48r] de eo tenet in villa de Wodeford' et ...[3] In presencia dominorum Hugonis Wak', Hugonis de Gorham, Rogeri de Heycham, Roberti de Wer de Thrapston', Nicholai de Sancto Marco et aliorum.

1 See Henry of Pytchley, p. 137 note.
2 *Ibid.*, p. 60 note.
3 Gap in the text.

113H [Marginated bracket for all entries on the folio] Homagia et fidelitates

[Marginated] Everard' de Dodesthorp'.[1]
Memorandum quod die Veneris in festo sancti Augustini anglorum anno regni regis E[dwardi] xxix° et anno domini G[odefridi] abbatis secundo [**26 May 1301**] Robertus Everard' de Dodesthorp' fecit homagium et fidelitatem prefato abbati pro j mesuagio et xx acris terre que de eo tenet in Dodesthorp' per homagium et fidelitatem et per servicium vj s. et vj d. In presencia fratris Thome de Wylingho, Johannis de Undele, Roberti de Thorp' et aliorum.

[Marginated] Magister W. de Lincoln'. [In a different hand] nota
Memorandum quod die Lune in vigilia sancti Petri advincula anno regni regis E[dwardi] xxix° et anno domini G[odefridi] abbatis secundo [**31 July 1301**] magister Willelmus de Lincoln' fecit homagium et fidelitatem prefato abbati apud Burgum[2] pro tenementis que de eo tenet in Hibaldestowe. In presencia magistri Galfridi de Makeseye, Johannis de Undele, Willelmi de Suthorp', Thome de Thorp' et aliorum. Scilicet pro j feodo militis.

1 See *Henry of Pytchley*, p. 110 note 8.
2 *apud Burgum* interlined.

113I Memorandum that Griffin, rector of Peakirk, swore an oath not to oppose the abbey, but in future to promote its interests and constrain its adversaries. [n.d.]

[Marginated] Griffinus.
Memorandum quod dominus Griffinus rector ecclesie de Peychirch' prestitit sacramentum corporale de non resistendo seu insurgendo contra abbatem et conventum jura et libertates monasterii de Burgo, set eas et

ea proposse promovebit infuturum, adversarios eorum proposse compescendo. Dat' apud Burgum.

113J Homages and fealties continued.

[Marginated] Wibelottus de Irtelingburg'.
Memorandum quod die Dominica proxima post festum nativitate beate Marie anno regni regis E[dwardi] xxix° et anno domini G[odefridi] abbatis secundo **[10 Sept. 1301]** apud Burgum Wibelottus de Irtelingburg' fecit fidelitatem prefato abbati pro j mesuagio et j bovat' terre que de eo tenet in Irtelingburg' per servicium iij solidorum. In presencia domini Gregorii de Lullington' militis, fratris Petri de Ketene, magistri Galfridi de Makeseye, Johannis de Undele, Roberti de Thorp' et aliorum.

[Marginated] Robertus de Brennegrist'.
Memorandum quod die Dominica in crastino apostolorum Simonis et Jude anno regni regis E[dwardi] xxix° et anno domini G[odefridi] abbatis secundo[1] **[29 Oct. 1301]** dominus Robertus de Brennegrest' capellanus fecit homagium et fidelitatem prefato abbati apud Eye pro j mesuagio et j selion' terre adjacent' que de eo tenet in villa de Burgo Sancti Petri per servicium xij d. In presencia magistri G[alfridi] de Makeseye, fratris Thome de Wylingham, Johannis de Undel', Willelmi de Suthorp', Ricardi clerici et aliorum.

1 If the entry under Robert de Neville (113F) is correct, this should be early in the third year of Abbot Godfrey's rule.

113K [Marginated] Abbas Croyl'.

Memorandum quod die Martis in crastino circumcisionis Domini anno regni regis Edwardi tricesimo et anno domini Godefridi abbatis tercio **[2 Jan. 1302]** apud Burgum Ricardus abbas de Croyland' fecit fidelitatem prefato abbati pro tenementis que de eo tenet in Peykirke et alibi. In presencia prioris Walteri et W. de Winton'[1] supprioris, fratris Petri de Keten' senescalli et multorum aliorum monachorum de conventu et domini Hugonis Wake militis, domini Johannis de Aysfordeby rectoris ecclesie de Castr', Radulphi de Huntingdone, Johannis de Undele, Roberti de Thorp', Willelmi de Suthorp', Bartholomei Broun, Thome Coc', Radulphi de Thorneye, Henrici de Keten', Simonis le Botiler, Ade le Aumoner, Roberti de Mythinggesby et aliorum.

1 *Walteri* and *W. de Winton'* interlined.

113L [fo. 48v] [Marginated bracket for all entries on the folio] Homagia et fidelitates

[Marginated] Willelmus de Kendale.
Memorandum quod die Mercurii in septimana Pentecoste anno Domini M° CCC° secundo et anno domini G[odefridi] abbatis iij° [**13 June 1302**] Willelmus filius et heres Rich' de Kendale de Glinton' fecit homagium et fidelitatem prefato abbati de Burgo Sancti Petri pro tenementis que de eo clamat tenere in Glinton' et Burgo Sancti Petri qui recognovit se tenere j mesuagium et xli acras terre et prati. In presencia fratris Petri de Keten', fratris Willelmi de Jarewell', Johannis de Undele, Henrici le Lord de Castr', Johannis Balle et aliorum.

113M [Marginated] Thomas filius Bate de Refham.

Memorandum quod die Veneris proxima ante festum sancti Johannis baptiste anno regni regis Edwardi xxx^{mo} et anno domini G[odefridi] abbatis iij° [**22 June 1302**] Thomas filius Bate de Refham fecit homagium et fidelitatem prefato abbati de Burgo Sancti Petri pro tenementis que de eo clamat tenere in Refham. In presencia fratris P[etri] de Ketene, Johannis de Undel', Roberti de Thorp', Bernardi de Castre et aliorum.

[Marginated] Priorissa de Gouck'well'.
Memorandum quod die Mercurii proxima post festum nativitate sancti Johannis baptiste anno Domini M° CCC° secundo et anno domini G[odefridi] abbatis de Burgo Sancti Petri iij [**27 June 1302**] Priorissa de Gouckwell' apud Scote' fecit fidelitatem prefato abbati pro tenementis que de eo clamat tenere in Gamelesthorp' et alibi. In presencia fratris P[etri] de Ketene, Johannis de Undele, Bernardi de Castr', Roberti de Mithinggesby clerici et aliorum. Et solvet annuatim vj d. de novo redd' preter content' in conventione inter domos Burgi et Gouck'well'.

[Marginated] Magister Willelmus de Lincoln'.
Memorandum quod die Jovis in vigilia apostolorum Petri et Pauli anno Domini M° CCC° secundo et anno domini G[odefridi] abbatis de Burgo Sancti Petri iij° [**28 June 1302**] apud Scote' magister Willelmus de Lincoln' tannator fecit[1] fidelitatem prefato abbati pro tenementis que de eo clamat tenere in Hybaldestowe.[2] In presencia fratris P[etri] de Ketene, magistrorum G[alfridi] de Makes', T[home] de Freston', Johannis de Undel', J[ohannis] de Thevelby, Bernardi de Castr' et aliorum.

[Marginated] Prior de Novo Loco.[3] [In a different hand] nota
Memorandum quod die Veneris in festo apostolorum Petri et Pauli anno Domini M° CCC° secundo et anno domini G[odefridi] abbatis iij° [**29 June 1302**] apud Scote' prior de Novo Loco juxta Glannfordebrigge fecit fidelitatem prefato abbati de Burgo Sancti Petri pro tenementis que de

eo clamat tenere in Hybaldestowe que quidem tenementa predecessores eiusdem prioris tenuerunt ante confirmationem predecessorum dicti abbatis factam predecessoribus dicti prioris. In presencia fratris P[etri] de Keten', magistri G[alfridi] de Makes', Johannis de Undele, J[ohannis] de Thevelby, B[ernardi] de Castr' et aliorum.

[Marginated] Prior de Thornholm.[4] [In a different hand] nota
Memorandum quod die Sabbati in crastino apostolorum Petri et Pauli eodem anno **[30 June 1302]** et eodem loco prior de Thornholm fecit fidelitatem domino G[odefrido] abbati de Burgo Sancti Petri pro tenementis que de eo clamat tenere de dicto abbate in Messingham et Raventhorp'. Idem prior fac' servicium pro tenementis contentis in conventione inter dictas domos facta; videlicet duas marcas per annum. Idem tenet in Raventhorp' j mesuagium et v bovatas terre per servicium iiij^or^ solidorum pro secta curie per annum et iiij^or^ solidorum et x denariorum pro auxilio vicecomitis per annum et vij denariorum pro vis' franciplegii per annum. In presencia Johannis de Undele, Johannis de Thevelby, Bernardi de Castr', Roberti de Mithingesby clerici et aliorum.

1 *fecit* interlined.
2 See *Henry of Pytchley*, p. 86.
3 *Ibid.*, p. 87.
4 *Ibid.*, pp. 105–6.

113N [fo. 49r] [Marginated] Th[omas] Sorel de Colingham.

Memorandum quod die Mercurii proxima post festum apostolorum Petri et Pauli anno regni regis E[dwardi] xxx^mo^ et anno domini G[odefridi] abbatis iij^o^ **[4 July 1302]** apud Colingham Thomas filius Radulphi Sorel de Colingham fecit homagium et fidelitatem predicto abbati de Burgo Sancti Petri pro tenementis que de eo clamat tenere in Colingham. In presencia magistri Thome de Freston', magistri G[alfridi] de Makes', Bernardi de Castr', Roberti de Mithingesby et aliorum.

[Marginated] Ricardus filius Stephani de Irtlingburg'. [In a different hand] pro . . .
Memorandum quod die Dominica proxima post festum assumptionis beate Marie anno regni regis E[dwardi] xxx^mo^ et anno domini G[odefridi] abbatis iij^o^ **[19 Aug. 1302]** apud Eye Ricardus filius Stephani de Irtlingburg' fecit homagium et fidelitatem prefato abbati pro tenementis que de eo clamat tenere in Irtlingburg'; videlicet pro v virgatis terre per servicium j equi et j garcionis cariant' farinam in guerra pro corpore abbatis ad custus dicti abbatis per xl dies et pro j virgata terre de feodo Gargat[1] in eadem per servicium iiij solidorum per annum, et pro j bovata terre in eadem per servicium j d. et j qa. per annum. In presencia domini Gregorii

de Lullington', J[ohannis] de Undel', Willelmi de Suthorp', Walteri Ballivi et aliorum.

[Marginated] Henricus de Haddon'.
Eodem die et eodem anno supradictis, in presencia testium predictorum, Henricus de Haddon' in Irtelingburg' fecit fidelitatem domino G[odefrido] abbati pro tenementis que de eo clamat tenere in Irtelingburg' per servicium ij caponum solvendum ad festum sancti Michaelis per annum.

[Marginated] Simon filius Henrici de Irtelingburg'.
Eodem die et eodem anno, in presencia testium predictorum, Simon filius Henrici de Irtelingburg' fecit homagium domino G[odefrido] abbati pro tenementis que de eo clamat tenere in eadem; videlicet pro j virgata terre pro [sic] servicium xiij s. iiij d. per annum terminum et pro j cotagio in eadem per servicium ij solidorum per annum.

[Marginated] Willelmus de Hotot'.
Memorandum quod die Martis proxima post festum sancte Katerine virginis anno regni regis E[dwardi] xxx^{mo} primo **[27 Nov. 1302]** dominus Willelmus de Hotot de Clopton' fecit homagium et fidelitatem domino G[odefrido] abbati de Burgo Sancti Petri pro tenementis que clamat tenere de eo in Clopton' per servicium ...[2] per annum. In presencia fratrum J[ohannis] de Rammes' et W[illelmi] de Jarewell', Johannis de Undele, Elie de Cantia, Walteri Ballivi, Roberti de Mythinggesby et aliorum.

[Marginated] Johannis Porthors.
Eodem anno ante festum Omnium Sanctorum **[25 Mar.–1 Nov. 1302]** Johannes filius Johannis Porthors[3] de Pokebrok' fecit homagium et fidelitatem domino G[odefrido] abbati pro tenementis que clamat tenere de eo in Pokebrok'

[Marginated] Aumorius de Nodar'.
Memorandum quod die Veneris in festo Innocentium anno regni regis E[dwardi] xxx^{mo} primo et anno domini G[odefridi] abbatis iiij^{to} **[28 Dec. 1302]** dominus Aumorius de Nodar' de Cestr' juxta Irtelingburg' fecit fidelitatem dicto domino G[odefrido] abbati pro tenementis que clamat tenere de eo in Irtelingburg'; videlicet unum pratum quod vocatur Braddehole pro xvj d. per annum ad gulam Augusti de libera wara. In presencia fratris Thome de [fo. 49v] Stannford', Johannis de Undele, Ricardi le Taillur, Roberti de Mithingesby et aliorum.

1 See *Henry of Pytchley*, pp. 126–7.
2 Sum erased.
3 *Porthors* interlined.

113O [Marginated] Episcopus Couventr' et Lychef'.[1] [In a different hand] Thorp Achirch

Memorandum quod die Martis proxima post festum nativitate beate Marie virginis anno regni regis E[dwardi] xxx^mo^ primo et anno domini G[odefridi] abbatis iiij^to^ **[10 Sept. 1303]** dominus Walterus de Langeton' episcopus Couventr' et Lychef' apud Thorp' Waterville[2] fecit homagium et fidelitatem predicto abbati pro tenementis que de eo clamat tenere in Thorp' Waterville et Achirche et Wadinho.[3] In presencia dominorum Willelmi Tuchet, Hugonis Wake, Hugonis Daundelyn, magistri Galfridi de Makeseye, Johannis de Undele, fratrum Willelmi de Jarewell', Anton' de Spaldingg' et aliorum.

1 See *Henry of Pytchley*, pp. 41–2 and no. 255.
2 *apud Thorp' Waterville* interlined.
3 *et Wadinho* interlined.

113P [Marginated] Robertus de Mithinggesby.[1]

Memorandum quod die Lune in septimana Pasche anno regni regis E[dwardi] xxxij^o^ et anno domini G[odefridi] abbatis quinto **[30 Mar. 1304]** Robertus de Mithingesby fecit fidelitatem predicto abbati apud Burgum Sancti Petri per assignationem Rogeri de Uffington' pro tenementis que clamat tenere de predicto abbate in villa de Burgo Sancti Petri, Walton', Dodesthorp', Newerk', Carton', Thorp' et Eye. In presencia domini Galfridi de Stokes, magistri G[alfridi] de Makes', Nicholai de Sancto Marco, Roberti de Thorp', Bernardi de Castr', Rad'i de Thorneye, Willelmi de Undele clerici et aliorum.

[Marginated] Robertus Dom'.[2]
Memorandum quod die Martis in festo beati Thome martiris in septimana natalis Domini anno regni regis E[dwardi] xxxiij^o^ et anno domini G[odefridi] abbatis vj^to^ **[29 Dec. 1304]** Robertus Domer fecit homagium et fidelitatem predicto abbati apud Burgum Sancti Petri pro tenementis que de eo tenet in Eston'. In presencia fratris Roberti de Spaldingg', domini Johannis de Undele, Johannis de Hotot, Roberti de Mithingesby et aliorum.

1 See *Henry of Pytchley*, pp. 83–4.
2 *Ibid.*, p. 135.

113Q [Marginated] Abbas Croiland'.

Frater Simon de Luffenham abbas Croiland' fecit fideliatem domino Godefrido abbatis de Burgo in manerio de Eye in capella eiusdem manerii die Veneris proxima post festum sancti Bartholomei anno regni regis E[dwardi] xxxiij et anno domini G[odefridi] abbatis vj^{to} **[27 Aug. 1305]** in presencia fratris W. de Walinggford' prioris Burgi, fratris Alexandri de Martheford' monachi Croiland', fratrum W[illelmi] de Jar', R[oberti] de Spaldingg', et R[oberti] de Whiten monachorum Burgi, domini Roberti persone de Undele, Johannis de Milton', Ricardi de Cheiles, Willelmi de Farford', Thome de Thorp', Roberti de Mithingesbi clerici et aliorum; videlicet pro tenementis que de eo clamat tenere in Peichirch'.

113R [Marginated in a different hand] Johanna [sic] Hok [and] Valcot'.

Memorandum[1] quod die Martis proxima ante Pascham anno regni regis E[dwardi] xxxiiij^{o} et anno domini G[odefridi] abbatis septimo **[29 Mar. 1306]** Johanna [sic] Hok fecit homagium et fidelitatem predicto domino Godefrido abbati pro tenementis que de eo clamat tenere in Pilesgat, Suthorp' et Walcot, in presencia fratrum Willelmi Saleman, Johannis de Walcot et Johannis Hok' monachorum, Roberti de Thorp', Ricardi de Holebech', Willelmi de Milton', Johannis de Fletton' et aliorum.

[Marginated] Walterus de Osgotby
Walterus de Osgoteby fecit fidelitatem domino Godefrido abbati apud Burgum pro tenementis que clamat tenere de eo in Walcote; videlicet die Mercurii proxima ante festum sancti Dunstani anno regni regis E[dwardi] xxxiiij^{o} **[18 May 1306]**

[fo. 50r] [Marginated] Dominus W. de Osevill'.
Memorandum quod die Sabbati proxima post festum sanctorum Tiburtii et Valleriani anno regni regis Edwardi tricesimo quarto et anno domini G[odefridi] abbatis septimo **[16 April 1306]** dominus Walterus de Osevill' fecit homagium et fidelitatem predicto domino G[odefrido] abbati apud Stannf' pro portione sua tenementorum que tenet in Bringrist et Draiton' de hereditate domini Willelmi de Kirkeby, in presencia domini Hugonis Wak', Johannis de Milton', domini Ricardi de Osenei, Roberti de Thorp' et aliorum.

1 *Henry of Pytchley* notes John, not Johanna Hook, pp. 70–1.

113S [Marginated] Prior de Novo Loco[1]

Memorandum quod die Martis proxima ante festum epiphanie Domini apud Scote' anno regni regis Edwardi filii regis [Henrici] xxxiiij^{to} et anno domini G[odefridi] abbatis septimo **[4 Jan. 1306]** dompnus Robertus prior Novi Loci super Ancolme fecit fidelitatem domino G[odefrido] abbati de Burgo Sancti Petri pro tenementis que de eo clamat tenere in Hybaldestowe in presencia fratrum Roberti de Spaldingg' et Roberti de Wyten' monachorum, domini Johannis de Undel', magistri Galfridi de Makes', Bernardi de Castr', Roberti de Mithinggesby, Reginaldi de Castr' clerici et aliorum.

[Marginated] Priorissa de Stannf'.[2]
Memorandum quod die Jovis in crastino sancti Andrei apostoli anno regni regis E[dwardi] xxxv et anno domini G[odefridi] abbatis viij° **[1 Dec. 1306]** domina Mabilia le Venur priorissa sancti Michaelis extra Stanford' fecit fidelitatem domino G[odefrido] abbati supradicto apud Eye[3] pro tenementis que de eo clamat tenere, in presencia fratrum Stephani de Burgo tunc prioris dicte domus sancti Michaelis, Roberti de Spaldingg' et Johannis de Witherington' monachorum et dominarum Mirielle de Miriden' et Elizabet de Colingham et aliarum monialium et magistri G[alfridi] de Makes' et Johannis de Milton', domini Ricardi de Oseneie, Roberti de Mithingesby et aliorum.

1 See *Henry of Pytchley*, p. 87.
2 See above, pp. xxiii–iv and nos 96–7.
3 *apud Eye* interlined.

114 Pardon by Abbot Godfrey, at the instance of John de Hotot, of 50s relief owed by Robert Domer on the death of his father, together with 20s aid for the marriage of the king's daughter and 40s scutage, on account of his half knight's fee in Easton by Rockingham. [27 Mar. 1307]

Acquietancia Roberti Domer.

Pateat universis per presentes quod nos Godefridus abbas de Burgo Sancti Petri perdonavimus ad instanciam Johannis de Hotot ex gratia nostra speciali Roberto filio et heredi domini Johannis Domer militis quinquaginta solidos pro relevio suo de morte dicti domini Johannis patris sui pro dimidio feodo militis quod idem dominus Johannes de nobis tenuit in capite in villa de Eston' juxta Rokingham, et viginti solidos pro auxilio ad primogenitam filiam domini regis maritandam, et viginti solidos de scutagio nobis a domino rege concesso de anno vicesimo octavo, et viginti solidos de scutagio nobis a domino rege concesso de anno tricesimo primo. In cuius rei testimonium has litteras nostras eidem Roberto fieri fecimus patentes. Dat' apud Burgum Sancti Petri die Lune in septimana Pasche anno regni regis Edwardi filii regis Henrici tricesimo quinto.

115 Further homages and oaths of fealty to Abbot Godfrey. [11 Mar. 1309–1 Nov. 1312]

[fo. 50v] [Marginated] Ricardus de Croil'.[1]

[References subscribed in a faded later hand at the foot of the folio to other homages] fos cxxxix, xxxviij, lxxxix

Memorandum quod die Martis proxima ante festum sancti Gregorii pape anno Domini millesimo CCC^{mo} octavo et anno regni regis E[dwardi] filii regis E[dwardi] secundo [**11 Mar. 1309**] Ricardus de Croilaund' filius Benedicti de Eye fecit homagium et fidelitatem domino Godefrido abbati de Burgo Sancti Petri in camera sua de Eye pro tenementis cum pertinenciis que clamat tenere de eo in villa de Walton' juxta Burgum, in presencia fratrum Roberti de Spaldingg', Johannis de Witherington' et Roberti de Tanesouere monachorum, domini Nicholai de Tikehull', magistri Galfridi de Makes', domini Roberti rectoris ecclesie de Lullington', domini Thome capellani de capella de Northolm, Johannis de Aylington' clerici, Johannis de Loholm, Johannis filii Martini de Iseldon', Ricardi de Fisk' tunc camerarii dicti abbatis, Walteri filii Bartholomei de Multon' et aliorum.

[Marginated] Willelmus de Senliz[2]
[Marginated separately] homagium respectuatur usque Pascham proxime sa ... frs
Anno Domini M^{o} CCC^{o} nono in festo epiphanie Domini [**6 Jan. 1310**] Willelmus de Senliz fecit fidelitatem domino Godefrido abbati pro tenementis que clamat tenere de eo in Wermington

[Marginated] Johannes de Ayston'.[3]
Memorandum quod die Lune in festo sanctorum Innocentium anno Domini M^{o} CCC^{mo} x^{o} et anno domini G[odefridi] abbatis xij^{o} [**28 Dec. 1310**] Johannes de Ayston' filius domini Johannis de Ayston' et ballivus curie de Castr' fecit fidelitatem predicto domino G[odefrido] abbati pro tenementis que de eo clamat tenere in Ayston', in presencia fratris Roberti de Spaldingg', magistri G[alfridi] de Makeseye, Roberti de Thorp' tunc senescalli Burgi, Bernardi de Castr', Walteri Ballivi et aliorum.

[Marginated with symbol] Johannes de Hegham.[4]
Memorandum quod die Dominica proxima ante festum ascencionis Domini anno regi regis Edwardi filii regis Edwardi quarto et anno domini Godefridi abbatis de Burgo Sancti Petri xij^{o} [**16 May 1311**] Johannes filius domini Rogeri de Hegham fecit homagium et fidelitatem dicto domino abbati in aula sua apud Burgum pro tenementis que de eo tenet et tenere clamat in Helpeston' et pertinenciis, in presencia Roberti de Thorp' tunc senescalli libertatis Burgi, magistri Johannis de Ayllington', Laurencii de Oseneye et aliorum.

[Marginated with symbol]

[Marginated in a later medieval hand] Castre
Radulphus frater et heres Roberti filii Radulphi Abouetoun de Castr' fecit fidelitatem domino Godefrido abbati de Burgo Sancti Petri pro tenementis que de eo clamat tenere in Castr' et alibi, die Omnium Sanctorum anno regni regis E[dwardi] filii regis E[dwardi] sexto [**1 Nov. 1312**]. In presencia fratris Roberti de Spalding', domini Roberti rectoris ecclesie de Pastone, Roberti de Thorp' et Willelmi de Jak' clerici.

[Marginated in a later medieval hand] quere plus fo. cxxxix et precedenti folio xxxviij et fo. lxxxix

1 See *Henry of Pytchley*, pp. 142–3.
2 *Ibid.*, p. 126.
3 *Ibid.*, p. 117 and no. 113A.
4 *Henry of Pytchley*, p. 149 and note and no. 113A.

116 Grant by Abbot Godfrey, at the instance of Walter Langton, of a pension of 100s per annum to Walter de Eylesworth' until he can be provided with a suitable benefice. [6 Feb. 1300]

[fo. 51r] Pensio domini Walteri de Eylesworth'.

Omnibus Christi fidelibus presentes litteras visuris vel audituris G[odefridus] permissione divina abbas de Burgo Sancti Petri et eiusdem loci conventus salutem in Domino sempiternam. Noveritis nos unanimiter concessisse dilecto nobis in Christo domino Waltero de Eylesworth' clerico ad instanciam reverendi patris domini Lich' et Couventr' episcopi et probitatis sue merito centum solidos percipiendos annuatim de camera abbatis qui pro tempore fuerit ad duos anni terminos; videlicet ad Pascha quinquaginta solidos et ad festum sancti Michaelis quinquaginta solidos donec eidem in ecclesiastico beneficio competenti providerimus. In cuius rei testimonium presentibus sigilla nostra sunt appensa. Dat' in capitulo nostro die Sabbati proxima post festum purificationis beate Virginis anno Domini M° CC° nonogesimo nono.

117 Quitclaim by John of Berwick[1] on account of his affection for Abbot Godfrey, of any action that he might have against the abbey and its men because of their activities in Northamptonshire in the time of Abbot William. [23 Mar. 1300]

[Marginated symbol]

Quietaclamatio domini Johannis de Berewyk'.

Universis ad quos presens scriptum pervenerit Johannes de Berewyk' salutem in Domino. Cum diverse dissentiones et contraversie mote fuissent inter fratrem Willelmum quondam abbatem de Burgo Sancti Petri, fratrem Simonem de Freston' commonachum suum, Gilbertum de Sutton', Robertum Fayrfox et quosdam alios homines eiusdem abbatis ex parte una et nos ex altera super diversis transgressionibus et enormiis per predictos abbatem et homines suos in comitatu Norhamt' nobis illatis, nos ex intima cordis nostri affectione quam erga religiosum virum dominum Godefridum Dei gracia abbatem de Burgo eius fama laudabili crebrescente iam concepimus et eciam ob invatam benevolentiam, quam erga conventum eiusdem abbathie meritis suis exigentibus affectuose reportamus, remisimus omnimodam actionem quam erga ipsos abbatem et conventum et homines suos quoscumque habuimus seu habere poterimus occasione quarumcumque transgressionum nobis per eosdem quocumque tempore prius illatarum. Ita quod nos vel aliquis pro nobis seu nomine nostro de predictis abbate et conventu seu hominibus suis quibuscumque ratione transgressionum predictarum nichil de cetero exigere poterimus quoquo modo. In cuius rei testimonium huic scripto sigillum nostrum fecimus apponi. Dat' London' die Mercurii proxima ante festum annunciationis beate Marie virginis anno regni regis Edwardi filii regis Henrici vicesimo octavo.

1 Chief justice in eyre.

118 Letter to Abbot Godfrey from Hugh de Sancto Martino, custodian of the hospital of St Thomas Martyr, Stamford submitting to reform of the abuses found by the abbot on his visitation. [9 April 1300]

[Marginated in a later hand] Stannford

Littera submissionis magistri Hugonis de Sancto Martino de custodia hospitalis sancti Thome Stannford'.

Universis sancte matris ecclesie filiis presentes litteras inspecturis vel audituris Hugo de Sancto Martino Stannford' salutem in Domino sempiternam. Noverit universitas vestra quod cum nuper dominus meus Godefridus permissione divina abbas monasterii Sancti Petri de Burgo [fo. 51v] hospitale beati Thome martyris Stannford' cuius custodie per predecessorem eiusdem in monasterio de Burgo extiti sub certa forma graciose deputatus per suos ministros specialiter destinatos et personas in eodem hospitali commorantes, ex officii sui debito visitasset ac quosdam defectus notorios indebita cantaria et solita exhibitione elemosine pauperibus et peregrinis impendende, necnon sustentatione Roberti Wodefoul conversi in dicto hospitali commorantis per aliquod tempus subtractis per inquisitionem fidelium exhabundanti reperiisset. Volens domino meo et eius jurisdictioni in omnibus parere correctionem et reformationem meorum excessum circa defectus quoscumque personam meam necnon personarum et rerum custodiam dicti hospitalis quomodolibet contingentem subire cum obediencia et suscipere, statum meum et dicti hospitalis custodiam rerum pertinenciarum ad illud ordinationi et potestati domini mei abbatis predicti pure et absolute committo me et omnia dicto hospitali adherentia ordinationi eiusdem diffinitioni et decreto funditus submittens. Cuius ordinationem reformationem et injunctionem virtute sacramenti mei corporaliter prestiti promitto me inviolabiliter durante custodia mea in hospitali predicto suscepturum sponte et conservaturum sub pena depositionis et amotionis a custodia hospitalis suprascripti. In cuius rei testimonium presentibus sigillum meum apposui. Dat' apud Burgum in vigilia Pasche anno Domini millesimo tricentesimo. In presencia domini abbatis, magistrorum Thome de Freston' et Galfridi de Makeseye, Johannis de Undele, Roberti de Thorp', Bernardi de Castre et Ricardi clerici.

119 Memorandum that, following his submission, Hugh de Sancto Martino was readmitted by Abbot Godfrey as custodian for life of the hospital of St Thomas Martyr, Stamford on the representation of John Dalderby, bishop elect of Lincoln, Gocelin, archdeacon of Stowe and John de Scaleby. [9 April 1300]

[Marginated in a later hand] Stannford'

Memorandum quod in vigilia Pasche anno Domini M^{o} tricentesimo accessit ad dominum G[odefridum] permissione divina abbatem Burgi apud Burgum magister Hugo de Sancto Martino Stannford' a custodia hospitalis beati Thome martyris propter varios et notorios defectus subtractiones cantarie et elemosine pauperibus et peregrinis de consuetundine antiqua in dicto hospitali usitata impendendi, a custodia dicti hospitalis per predictum abbatem premissa prius inquisitione solempni articulis certis ipsius depositionem et amotionem exposcentibus per eandem inquisitionem in presencia eiusdem magistri captam inventis et subsequenter propter ipsius inobedienciam et pertinaciam amotus justicia exigente, deferens litteras supplicatorias venerabilis viri magistri Johannis de Alderby Lincoln' ecclesie electi magistri Gocelini archdiaconi Stowie et domini Johannis de Scaleby quibus reverenter receptis et earum concepto tenore prefatus magister Hugo gracie ordinationi diffinitioni et decreto dicti domini abbatis se et omnia dictum hospitale et ipsius contingentia sponte et absolute virtute sacramenti sui corporaliter prestiti submisit in presencia dominorum Hugonis Wake et Roberti de Bauent militum et [fo. 52r] aliorum ibidem presentium, prout ex forma eiusdem submissionis poterit intuenti apparere. Tandem prefatus abbas caritatis intuitu, necnon litterarum domini Lincoln' venerabilis electi et aliorum optentu ad ipsius hospitalis custodiam, salvis sibi et ecclesie Burgi juribus et libertatibus in dicto hospitali antiquitus optentis custodem ordinandi faciendi irrequisito superioris cuiuscumque assensu, necnon ex causa rationabili amovendi sub modis et formis in ordinatione diffinitione et decreto dicti abbatis infra scriptis ad terminum vite eiusdem H[ugonis] admisit.

120 Instructions to Hugh de Sancto Martino, custodian of the hospital of St Thomas Martyr, Stamford, that hospital income should be divided into three equal parts – to maintain the chantry and provide for the religious needs of pilgrims and the infirm; to provide alms through Robert Wodefoul for the inmates and poor pilgrims and to provide for the custodian and his household. Hugh is also enjoined to recover relics lost while in his custody. Hugh undertook on oath to observe the reforms. [14 April 1300]

[Marginated in a later medieval hand] Stannford'

[Marginated in a later hand at the foot of fo. 52v] De hospitali sancti Egidii extra Stanfordiam require in xx^o^v^o^ folio subsequenti de sustentatione sacerdotis per tres dies in ebdomada

In primis ad honorem et gloriam omnipotentis Dei et gloriose Virginis matris sue et beati Thome prothomartyris ordinamus diffinimus et inviolabiliter observari discernimus quod hospitale beati Thome martyris supra pontem Stannford' cum suis juribus et libertatibus per custodem eiusdem hospitalis proposse custodis absque diminutione custodiatur et tueatur. Item quod universa bona ad custodem dicti hospitalis nomine eiusdem hospitalis pervenientia [sic] de terris redditibus necnon obventionibus ex devotione fidelium et industria custodis provenientibus tripliciter dividantur et distribuantur pro equalibus portionibus prout primevo tempore fundationis dicti hospitalis et post de consuetudine loci didicimus veraciter fuisse observatum; videlicet quod una pars sustentationi cantarie continue per sacerdotem ydoneum in dicto hospitali residentem divina celebrantem infirmis ac peregrinis sacramentalia ministrantem, ac inventioni et sustentationi luminaris vestimentorum et aliorum ornamentorum pro divini obsequii ministerio necessariorum in hospitali predicto contribuatur, que per vos magistrum H[ugonem] dicti hospitalis custodem singulis annis precipimus fieri et injungimus vobis sub pena in littera submissionis vestre contenta. Alia pars predictorum bonorum sustentationi elemosine infirmis commorantibus, necnon pauperibus peregrinis ibidem confluentibus ministrande juxta tercie partis divise facultates inpendatur Roberto Wodefoul ad congruam sustentationem prout ipsius forma conventionis requirit in camera sibi antiquitus deputata absque molestia recepto, cui de arreragiis pro annali prestatione dimidiam marcam per vos magistrum H[ugonem] subtracte prefato Roberto debitis, ordinamus et precipimus satisfieri competenter. Tercia parte bonorum sustentationi custodis sue familie necessarie et honeste salva remanente. Ordinamus insuper et diffinimus quod suspecte persone dissipatores bonorum dicti hospitalis provocantes contentiones inter vos prefatum H[ugonem] et vicinos vestros necnon tenentes comitis Warenn' et tenentes nostros per conficta mendacia et falsas detractiones a dicto hospitali et bonorum participatione eiusdem deleantur nec de cetero sustineantur quovismodo de bonis hospitalis antedicti sive parentes fuerint vel extranei sustentatione luminaris in dicto hospitali tam in lampadibus quam in aliis debiti et consueti plenarie restituta que ob reverenciam sanctorum in [fo. 52v] dicto hospitali ante tempus vestre subtractionis honorifice ministrabatur. Reliquias sanctorum in dicto hospitali per vos prius inibi inventas et per vestram simplicitatem vel aliorum maliciam postea ammotas precipimus revocari et restitui cum cura et diligencia debitis prout vobis possibile erit. Ad hec ordinavimus et discernimus quod singula loca in dicto hospitali divino obsequio ac pauperum et infirmorum receptioni antiquitus mancipata inmaculata conserventur, nec rerum aliarum custodiis deputentur, set fiat congruis reformatio per vos custodem vice nostra in personis et rebus dicti hospitalis quod affectiones fidelium trahantur ad antiqui subsidii impensi exemplum et dispersa revocentur, salva retentione congregatorum sane illicte occupationes circa litigia et controversias caritatem perfectam impediunt, necnon bona custodienda consumunt, rancoris calore et aviditate vindicte, ac insurgunt rixe et contentiones ceteros inflammantes et imponentes ira commoti convalescentiam vestri languoris in statum pristinum vel deteriorem esse conversam. Et quod absit evenient posteriora prioribus peiora, volentes vobis et aliis sub districtu nostro existentibus per nostram presentem ordinationem et diffinitionem juris et[1] caritatis intuitu quietem parere et scripulum erroris pro viribus extirpare, ordinamus, discernimus et diffinimus quod materie contentionum inter vos magistrum H[ugonem] et dominum Robertum rectorem ecclesie de Northburg' et ceteros nostros ministros et tenentes quoscumque, cuiuscumque conditionis existant, sub dominice potestatis nostre vel districtu existentes coram quibuscumque judicibus exhorte ex nunc conquiescant, ac per nos amicabili discisione absque strepitu judiciali inordinato, cessante favore, equo labore libramine terminantur, quod si prefati vestri adversarii coram nobis juri ac equitati parere non curaverint vestre prosecutioni coram judice competenter faciende, subsidium impendi faciemus oportunum. Retinemus insuper nobis plenam potestatem premissis addendi, et eorum quodlibet si necesse fuerit mutandi, declarandi, interpretandi, corrigendi, subtrahendi, supplendi seu de novo ordinandi et diffiniendi quotiens et quando nobis visum fuerit expedire. Salvis in omnibus nobis et monasterio nostro juribus et libertatibus circa dispositionem personarum et rerum in dicto hospitali existentium, necnon redditibus et serviciis debitis et consuetis, ac prestationibus personalibus et realibus, subjectionibus universis. Ad suprascripta ordinamus et diffinimus quod si vos magister Hugo contra formam sacramenti vestri prestiti premissis in nostra ordinatione et diffinitione contentis, vel eorum aliquo quod absit minime parere volueritis, premissis ordinationi vel diffinitioni in toto vel in parte reluctando, ex tunc vos a custodia dicti hospitalis, necnon omni comodo bonorum et obventionum eiusdem auctoritate presentis ordinationis et decreti ac sacramenti vestri prestiti decernimus amoveri, potestate nobis de alio custode providendi et eundem in corporalem [fo. 53r] possessionem eiusdem hospitalis et bonorum existentium in eodem introducendi et successoribus nostris salva et libera remanente. In cuius rei testimonium presenti ordinationi, diffinitioni et decreto sigillum nostrum apposuimus. Dat' apud Burgum in festo sanctorum Tyburtii et Valeriani anno Domini M^{o} tricentesimo. Et ego H[ugo] de Sancto Martino suprascriptas reformationes, ordinationes, diffinitiones et decretum sponte et reverenter in toto et in parte suscepi premissis et eorum cuilibet proposse parere, virtute sacramenti mei corporaliter prius prestiti promitto. In cuius rei facti mei testimonium presentibus sigillum meum apposui.

1 *et* interlined.

121 Collation by Abbot Godfrey of Master Hugh, vicar of All Saints in the market of Stamford, to the custodianship of the hospital of St Thomas on the bridge in the same town, on pain of removal should he not abide by the reforms imposed upon him. [14 April 1300]

[Marginated in a later hand] Collatio hospitalis

Universis sancte matris ecclesie filiis presentes litteras inspecturis vel audituris G[odefridus] permissione divina abbas monasterii sancti Petri de Burgo salutem in Domino. Noveritis nos magistro Hugoni vicario ecclesie Omnium Sanctorum in foro Stannford' curam et administrationem hospitalis sancti Thome supra pontem Stannford', ac omnium ad dictum hospitale spectantium caritatis intuitu suo perpetuo graciose commisisse. Ita quod onera hospitalitati incumbentia solita de jure et consuetudine loci inpendenda fideliter agnoscat et sustineat juxta formam nostre ordinationis et diffinitionis, quas idem sponte suscepit, sub pena depositionis et amotionis a custodia antedicta, prout ex forma submissionis et ordinationis plenius poterit apparere. Salvis nobis et successoribus nostris potestate visitandi et corrigendi excessus custodis et aliorum in dicto hospitali commorantium et aliis juribus et libertatibus ad nos et monasterium nostrum de Burgo pertinentibus. In cuius rei testimonium presentibus sigillum nostrum apposuimus. Dat' apud Burgum in festo sanctorum Tyburtii et Valeriani anno Domini M^{o} tricentesimo.

122 Letter from Abbot Godfrey to Richard, abbot of Crowland about the harsh treatment of a monk. [*c.* Mar.–April 1300]

Excellentis[1] religionis viris patri in Christo reverendo ac fratribus amantissimis domino R[icardo] permissione divina abbati Croyland' et eiusdem loci commonachis Deo famulantibus G[odefridus] eadem permissione abbas monasterii sancti Petri de Burgo salutem, et caritatem perfectam pululare extirpatis radicibus detractionis et erroris. Clamosa relatione laycorum et aliorum palam accepimus divulgari, quod quidem confratres vestri zelo versutie inflammati acerbitatem sevicie in confratrem suum et vestrum presidentis indaginem subvertentes, necnon religiosum affectum custodum ordinis et aliorum impedientes cum nimia gravitate nituntur exercere, non absque nostre religionis scandalo et oblocutionem multorum. Volentes super premissis vestre fraternitatis unitatem mutue religionis et affectionis naturalis intuitu premuniri, illicita que conventicula et prosecutiones inordinatas dissolvi, vestre religionis celsitudinem in Christo rogamus, quatinus fame tocius religionis et vestre prout ordo expostulat discipline regularis [fo. 53v] parcentes cum debite correctionis mansuetudine huiusmodi proclamatione aliorum remota suavius agere velitis cum afflicto prout culpe qualitas requirit disciplina canonica inoffensa et fraternalem caritatem reformare ut referitur iam dispersam. In Christo Jesu valete sicut in consimilibus reformandis si iminerit ut quod absit optamus valere.

1 Printed in Pantin, *Chapters of the English Black Monks*, vol. I, p. 141, no. 50. Pantin raises the possiblility that Abbot Godfrey may have succeeded Abbot William briefly as president of the General Chapter and be writing in that capacity. Although he is more inclined to see the letter as an expression of neighbourly concern, the authority with which Abbot Godfrey dissolved the unofficial activities implies more than this. *Ibid.*, n. 2.

123 Letter from Bartholomew de Ferentino canon of London to the abbot and convent of Peterborough concerning the surrender of £500 sterling from the Crusading tenth levied by Pope Gregory X and deposited with them by the papal nuncio Geoffrey de Vezano, incorporating a letter of authorisation dated 5 Feb. 1300 from Pope Boniface VIII to himself and the bishop of Winchester. [19 Mar. 1300]

Bartholomeus de Ferentino canonicus London' et executor ad infrascripta ut inferius plenius continetur religiosis viris dominis abbati et conventui de Burgo Sancti Petri salutem et mandatis apostolicis firmiter obedire. Noveritis nos litteras apostolicas sanas et integras et vera bulla bullatas omni suspicione carentes, quas vobis inspiciendas transmittimus, nobisque fideliter per latorem presentium remittendas recepisse in hec verba:

Bonifacius episcopus servus servorum Dei venerabili fratri episcopo

Wyntoniensis et dilecto filio magistro Bartholomeo de Ferentino canonico London' salutem et apostolicam benedictionem. Gerentes de vestre multiplicis probitatis industria et probate fidei puritate fiduciam in Domino specialem, nostra et ecclesie Roman' negotia vobis secure committimus exequenda, firma credulitate tenentes quod circa executio eorum operose sollicitudinis studium et efficacem solertiam impendetis. Cum igitur totum residuum decime quam felicis recordationis Gregorius papa x predecessor noster in regno Anglie Terre Sancte subsidio deputavit promptum et paratum habere intendamus omnino, et speremus indubie quod huiusmodi negotium per nostram circumspectam prudenciam et sollicitudinem diligentem ad affectum favente Domino celeriter perducetur vobis petendi recipiendi et recolligendi per vos vel nostrum quemlibet residuum supradictum, nostro et eiusdem Romane ecclesie nomine a personis ecclesiasticis et religiosis ac aliis quibuslibet dicti regni apud quas vel eorum loca depositum esse denoscitur residuum memoratum, necnon et contradictores per censuram ecclesiasticam appellatione postposita compellendi. Non obstante si personis eisdem vel aliquibus aliis cuiuscumque conditionis, status, ordinis vel dignitatis existant, communiter vel divisim a sede apostolica sit indultum, quod interdici, suspendi vel excommunicari non possint per litteras dicte sedis non facientes plenam, expressam et determinatam deindulto huiusmodi mentionem, et qualiter alia dicte sedis indulgencia generali vel speciali cuiuscumque tenoris vel expressionis existat per quam presentibus non expressam, vel totaliter non insertam effectus eorum impediri valeat quomodolibet vel differri et de qua plenam et expressam ac de verba ad verbam oporteat in nostris litteris fieri mentionem, plenam et liberam presentium auctoritate concedimus facultatem. Dat' Lateran' nonas Februarii pontificatus nostri anno sexto.

Unde [fo. 54r] nos volentes ut tenemur mandatis apostolicis obdeire auctoritate apostolica nobis in hac parte commissa vos requirimus et peremptorie monemus vobisque ac vestrum singul' districte percipiendo mandantes, quatinus infra duos menses a die presentationes presentium computandos, quod tempus vobis et vestrum singul' pro peremptorio termino assignamus nobis vel college nostro predicto vel nostro seu alterius nostrum commissario, apud Novum Templum London' reddatis et restituatis et assignetis, nomine eiusdem sanctissimi patris et ecclesie Romane integre quingentas libri bonorum novorum et legalium sterlingorum quas in deposito recepistis et habuistis nomine Romane ecclesie et Terre Sancte, a venerabili viro magistro Giffredo de Vezano tunc camere domini pape clerico apostolice sedis nuncio et executore negotiorum Terre Sancte super decima et aliis a dicta sede in Anglia deputato, de pecunia ipsius Terre Sancte concessa subsidio, et cui deposito vos voluntarie obtulistis, pro vestris et monasterii vestri utilitatibus, prout in littera obligatoria vestra que penes nos residet plenius continetur sub pena excommunicationis quam in vos et vestrum quemlibet et interdicti quam in ecclesias vestras proferimus in hiis scriptis, si in premissis vel aliquo premissorum defeceritur quoquomodo. Attendentes quod si in premissis adimplendis negligentes fueritis vel rebelles, quod absit, contra vos elapso dicto termino acrius procedimus. In cuius rei testimonium sigillum nostrum presentibus est appensum. Dat' London' die nonodecimo mense Marcii anno gracie millesimo C°C nonogesimo nono.

124 Cyrograph agreement whereby the abbot and convent of Peterborough give permission for the abbot and convent of Sulby to enter the manor of Little Addington, which Richard son of Gervase of Barnack once held of Humphrey of Bassingbourn, who held of the abbey for one knight's fee. Sulby will render 6s 8d p.a. and suit of court at Castor and will also pay ten marks in relief each time there is a vacancy at Sulby. Peterborough reserves the homage and military service of Humphrey of Bassingbourn. [9 April 1300]

Cyrograffum Abbatis de Suleby.

[Marginated in later medieval hand] Castr'

Pateat[1] universis per presentes quod ita convenit inter abbatem et conventum de Burgo Sancti Petri ex una parte et abbatem et conventum de Suleby ex parte altera; videlicet quod predicti abbas et conventus de Burgo Sancti Petri concesserunt pro se et successoribus suis quantum in ipsis est quod predicti abbas et conventus de Suleby libere et sine impedimento possint ingredi manerium de Parva Adyngton' cum suis pertinenciis. Et illud tenere et habere sui et successoribus suis imperpetuum. Quod quidem manerium Ricardus filius Gervasii de Bernak' aliquando tenuit de Humfrido de Bassyngburn' qui illud tenuit de abbate predicto de Burgo Sancti Petri per servitium feodi unius militis. Et pro hac concessione habenda dicti abbas et conventus de Suleby concesserunt pro se et successoribus suis quod reddent singulis annis predictis abbati et conventui de Burgo Sancti Petri et eorum successoribus sex solidos et octo denarios argenti ad Pascha in manerio suo de Castre et quod facient sectam ad curiam ipsius abbatis de Burgo Sancti Petri de Castre de tribus septimanis in tres septimanas per abbatem de Soleby [sic] qui pro tempore fuerit et eius successores abbates vel eius attornatos imperpetuum. Concesserunt eciam predicti abbas de Suleby et conventus pro se et successoribus suis quod quilibet abbas de Suleby post istum abbatem die confectionis presentium existentem quocumque modo succedens solvet pro [fo. 54v] qualibet vacatione dictis abbati et conventui de Burgo Sancti Petri et eorum successoribus imperpetuum decem marcas argenti nomine relevii apud Burgum Sancti Petri infra octo dies postquam fuerit creatus abbas de Suleby. Et idem abbas de Suleby et successores sui predictis abbati et conventui de Burgo Sancti Petri et eorum successoribus fidelitatem de cetero facient pro predictis tenementis. Et abbas de Burgo Sancti

Petri et eius successores non obstante conventione ista, homagium et scutagium et omnia servitia regalia per manus Humfridi de Bassyngburn' et heredum et assignatorum suorum recipient de predicto tenemento imperpetuum. Et predicti abbas de Suleby et conventus concesserunt pro se et successoribus suis imperpetuum quod predicti abbas et conventus de Burgo Sancti Petri et eorum successores pro voluntate sua in dicto manerio cum pertinenciis distringere possint tam pro predictis decem marcis redditu et secta quam pro aliis quibuscumque serviciis de eodem manerio cum pertinenciis quoquomodo provenientibus et ad ipsos abbatem de Burgo Sancti Petri et conventum et eorum successores inde qualitercumque spectantibus. Et eciam pro serviciis regalibus inde debitis cum aliquid inde arretro fuerit. In cuius rei testimonium huic scripto in modum cyrograffi confecto et penes predictos abbatem et conventum de Suleby remanenti predicti abbas et conventus de Burgo Sancti Petri sigilla sua apposuerunt. Hiis testibus: domino Rogero de Heygham'[2], domino Hugone Daundeleyn, domino Roberto de Veer, militibus, magistro Roberto de Kyuelingworth', magistro Galfrido de Makes', Johanne de Undele, Roberto de Thorp' et aliis. Dat' apud Burgum Sancti Petri die Sabbati in vigilia Pasche anno Domini M° tricentesimo et anno regni regis Edwardi filii regis Henrici vicesimo octavo.

1 Also in Soc. of Antiquaries, MS 38, fos 24v–5r; BL, Cott. Cleop. C ii, fos 44v–5v, without the witness clause and in Swaffham fos 275v–6r as a later addition.
2 *Hiham* in Swaffham.

[Addition to fo. 54r]

125 Acquittance by the abbot and convent of Peterborough of the 10 mark payment in relief due from the abbot and convent of Sulby on the occasion of each vacancy at Sulby. [30 Dec. 1308]

Pateat universis quod cum abbas et conventus de Suleby quandoque se obligassent et successores suos, ac monasterium suum predictum de Suleby in decem marcis sterlingorum solvendis abbati et conventui de Burgo Sancti Petri et eorum monasterio nomine relevii pro qualibet vacatione dicti monasterii de Suleby per singulos abbates post tunc existentem dicti loci abbatem inibi successive creandos, prout in quodam scripto inter dictos abbates et eorum conventus confecto plenius continetur. Ac idem abbas de Suleby nunc ut tunc existens licet ad hoc non teneretur ut premittitur, cupiens cum ex habundanti future dicti monasterii sui utilitati in hac parte previdere solvit et numeravit nobis abbati et conventui de Burgo Sancti Petri decem marcas sterlingorum nomine relevii nobis monasterio nostro suo tempore debiti et pro proximum dicti monasterii de Suleby abbatis nunc existentis successorem abbatem solvendas juxta tenorem scripti supranotati. Quas quidem decem marcas, nos dicti abbas et conventus de Burgo Sancti Petri facemur nos de dicto abbatem de Suleby nunc et tunc existente in futuram exonerationem monasterii sui et abbatis eiusdem proxime sibi successur' recepisse nomine relevii supradicti, ac monasterium suum predictum de Suleby et abbatis eiusdem proximo futurum successorem abbatem tamen[1] de predictis decem marcis modo predicto debitis et solutis acquieta' et quietis' esse clamamus de nobis et successoribus nostris volumus et concedimus[2] per presentis. In cuius rei testimonium presentibus sigillum nostrum ... a cum sigillo prioris nostri est appensum. Dat' apud Burgum Sancti Petri die Lune in crastino translationis beati Thome martiris, anno Domini millesimo tricentesimo octavo.

1 *tamen*(?) interlined.
2 *volumus et concedimus* cancelled.

126 Letter from Pope Boniface VIII to King Edward I about recovering the Holy Land in alliance with the Tartar Khan and the kings of Georgia and Armenia [7 April. 1300]

[marginated in later hand] Rex Anglie christiannissimus a papa appellatur.

Bonifacius[1] episcopus servus servorum Dei karissimo in Christo filio Edwardo regi Anglie illustri salutem et apostolicam benedictionem nova grandia[2] fili karissime, nova felicia, nova utique gaudiis prosequenda precipuis, nuper nobis de orientalibus partibus fidedignis litterarum et nunciorum affactibus illuxerunt, que fidelium ad modum delectant auditum, corda letificant, animosque demulcent. Ideo que tibi veluti Christianissimo principi, et devotissimo ecclesie filio, ea tenore presentium digne quam tocius reserando decernimus[3], ut in eorum perceptione gratissima, jocunderis in Domino, tuique pectoris intima, letitie copiose dulcoribus repleantur, licet iam forsitan, nova eadem, sensibus regiis fame precurrentis assertio revelavit. Sane rex excelsus filius summi regis, qui sua virtuosa potentia in orbe terrarum, mira et stupenda, mortalibus jugiter operatur, quique superborum cornua conterit, enervat vires, molimina vacuat, temerarios ausus frenat, diligenter considerans, et solerter attendens in gentem Christianorum, regum et principum, fideliumque ceterorum desidiam, que prout evidentia facti docet, a longe retro temporibus commissa dinoscitur, circa recuperandam [fo. 55r] de impiorum manibus Terram Sanctam, quam illoram nephanda temeritas, non sine multo, tocius Christianitatis obprobrio, ab olim miserabiliter detinens occupatam, ipsam tandem redegit incinerem et favillam, diebus proximo iam transactis, de sue benignitatis clementia suffocavit[4] spiritum animum tetigit, cor accendit viri magnifici, genti Tartarice dominantis, qui nondum renatus fonte baptismatis, nondum ortodoxe fidei lumine illustratus, ad Christi laudem et gloriam, arma sumens, eiusque prosequens ferventer obsequia, et exponens pro illis totaliter se et sua potenti et copioso excercitu congregato, habito que presidio karissimorum in Christo filiorum nostrorum Jurgianorum et Armenie regum illustrium contra soldanum gentis Babilonice dominum, crucis hostem precipuum et Christiane fidei inimicum, ac mulitudinem Saracenorum inumeram, quam eius soldani dampnata nequitia congregarat duxit hostiliter procedendum, et demum divini favoris auxilio, prefati Tartareorum domini triumphante potentia, eiusque dextera prevalente, Saracenorum ipsorum in estimabili facta cede. Soldanus ipse nimio terrore[5] perteritus, menteque consternatus et animo, ad fuge remedium se convertit, quem idem dominus Tartarorum predictorum regum [munimine][6] circumfultus, per longa terrarum spacia, promptis, animis et victricibus signis explicitis prosequi non quievit, tota terra illarum partium fugientibus incolis, vel verius gladio trucidante subducto restituta, seu reddita Christianis. O inquam inestimabilis pietas. O inmensa benignitas salvatoris, quis meruit quid ve illius induxit clementiam. Ut tante plenitudine gracie, tantique muneris donativo, fidelium populos prosequi, sic que circa illos effundere, sue misericordie multitudine dignaretur, verum quis princeps catholicus non miretur et stupeat, quis fidelis non erubescat obnixius, et rubore non perfundatur uberimo vultus eius, quod Rex Celorum et Dominus, cuius humiliter parent imperio universa, tantam et tam gloriosam victoriam, per ministerium hominis nondum supra petram fidei constituti, voluit modernis temporibus excerceri, cum sicut celsitudo regia non ignorat, tui progenitoris potissime, utpote fide preclari et devotione sinceri, predicte Terre Sancte custodiam excercere continue tueri que potenter ab hostibus, dum temporalis vite cursum peragеretur noscebantur salubriter exponendo, propterea quicquid poterant, quicquid erant, ceteros christianorum reges et principes, ad ea non sine[7] laudum sonoro preconio propensius inducendo. Cum igitur grandi non inmerito cupiamus affectu, nostraque ad id fervens dirigatur intentio, ut Terra Sancta grave jugum Agarenorum effugiat quod iam diutini temporis spacio tolleravit, et de ipsorum celestis[8] manibus liberetur omnino, ea que ad divini numinis glorie exaltationem, fidei, ac tocius Christianitatis honorem vigilantibus studiis in statu prospero conservetur, regalem magnificentiam rogamus et hortamur attente, ac obsecravmus in filio Dei patris, quatinus ob divinam et apostolice [fo. 55v] sedis reverentiam, tueque salutis et exaltationis augmentum, tanquam filius benedictionis et gracie et progenitorum tuorum vestigia clara sequens, tue ample subventionis et potentie brachium circa ipsius terre subsidium, ac succursum solerter extendere non omittas, ut et quod de ipsa terra et aliis ultra marinis regionibus, per christianos solitis retineri recuperandis supersit recuperari valeat, et quod recuperatum est, et recuperabitur, redificari et firmari valeat, ac muniri, ac salubriter retineri, ut cultus divinus inibi observetur, Deo diurne ac nocturne laudes a fidelibus cum devotione solvantur, et multiplicentur, ut augeantur ibidem fides catholica et populus christianus, et ex diversis mundi climatibus, regnis, atque provinciis, ad partes illas fideles concurrant, ad inhabitandum et defendendum partes easdem, et quod adquisitum fuerit dante Domino retinendum, sic te in hiis prout neccesitatis articulus exigit habiturus, quod terra ipsa tuo et aliorum regum et principum adiuta suffragiis, auxiliis circumfulta favente Domino cui nichil impossibile cernitur, ad statum tranquillum et prosperum reducatur, perpetuis futuris temporibus in illo stabiliter permansura. Ceterum te ignorare non volumus quod dictarum terre ac partium statu et conditionibus in maturam deliberationem adductis, nobis temporibus istis non videtur expectandum passagium generale. Licet ad id suo tempore faciendum plenus affectibus intendamus, quia per illud quod dilationem recipit dictis terre et partibus valde dampnosam non succurretur eis tempore oportuno.[9] Ideoque per accelerationem succursus, et ne comoditas ac clementia celesti concessa perdatur, providimus per diversa regna, et ad regiones excitare corda fidelium, qui ante Lugdunense concilium generale ultimo celebratur, vel post illud crucis signaculum assumpserunt, ut in dicte terre succursum cum celeritate qua poterunt generali non expectato passagio personaliter ad terram ipsam se conferant, et reddant inibi altissimo vota sua, ad quod ipsos multum debet excitare devotio, quia loca sancta liberata de Saracenorum manibus poterunt visitare. Providimus quoque quod omnes prelati ecclesiarum terre regionum et partium earumdum, qui sunt citra mare transfretent, et revertantur illuc, necnon persone ecclesiarum earundem indignitatibus seu personatibus constitutis, statuentes ut crucesignati hactenus pro dicte Terre Sancte succursu, et qui ad huc inantea signum vivifice crucis assument, et illuc transibunt personaliter, non expectato passagio generali, et ibi tanto tempore morabuntur, quanto moraturi essent, si transirent in dicto passagio generali, eandem indulgentiam quam haberent si transirent in eodem passagio generali assequantur, sicut hec et alia super hoc ordinata per nos in aliis litteris nostris serio[10] continentur, tu que nobis plenius intimare non differas, quid de tuo procedat consilio in hac parte, qualiter eciam intendas, et velis omnino te super hoc nostris et apostolicis [sic] sedis beneplacitis coaptare. Dat' Latren' [fo. 56r] vij idus Aprilis. Pontificatus nostri anno vj.

1 For other texts see Rymer, *Foedera*, vol. I, pt. II, pp. 919–20; ed. H. T. Riley, *Chronica et Annales: Willelmi Rishanger* (Rolls Series, London, 1865), pp. 465–70.

2 *gaudia* in Rishanger.

3 *decrevimus* in Rymer and Rishanger.

4 *suscitavit* in Rymer and Rishanger.

5 *timore* in Rymer and Rishanger.

6 supplied from Rymer.

7 *sue* in MS.

8 *funestis* in Rishanger.

9 Rishanger text ends here.

10 *seriosus* in Rymer.

127 Cyrograph agreement between Robert of Thorpe and the abbot and convent whereby Robert gave the abbey a plot of land and meadow, part of the tenements known as Hokettescroft by the pond in Boroughbury (in Peterborough), which he held of the abbot and convent and which were formerly held by Benedict Hoket', rendering 9s 8d p.a. In return, the abbot and convent remitted to Robert, his heirs and assigns, 6s 4d p.a. of the rent he owed for the tenements, leaving Robert to pay the remaining 40d at the usual terms. [13 June 1300]

Carta Roberti de Thorp' de stagno de Burbyrr.

Anno[1] regni regis Edwardi filii regis Henrici vicesimo octavo. Die Lune proxima post festum sancti Barnabe apostoli, convenit inter dominum Godefridum abbatem de Burgo Sancti Petri et eiusdem loci conventum ex parte una, et Robertum de Thorp' ex altera; videlicet cum idem Robertus tenuit de predictis abbate et conventu quedam tenementa in villa de Burgo Sancti Petri, que quondam fuerunt Benedicti Hoket', per fidelitatem et servicium novem solidorum et octo denariorum per annum pro omni servicio, predictus Robertus dedit eisdem abbati et conventui, et ecclesie sue de Burgo Sancti Petri quamdam placeam terre et prati in Hokettescroft' de tenemento antedicto, sicut bunde inter terras predicti Roberti et placeam illam posite plenius testantur. Habendam et tenendam predictis abbati et conventui imperpetuum. Pro hac autem donatione, predicti abbas et conventus de Burgo dederunt predicto Roberto de Thorp', heredibus et assignatis suis, sex solidos et quatuor denarios annui redditus, de predicto redditu novem solidorum et quatuor[2] denariorum quos eis reddidit pro tenementis Benedicti Hokett' antedictis, et illum redditum sex solidorum et quatuor denariorum, relaxant et quietum clamant de se et successoribus suis eidem Roberto heredibus et assignatis suis imperpetuum. Reddendo eisdem abbati et conventui et eorum successoribus quadraginta denarios residuos tocius redditus predicti, pro toto tenemento quod fuit Benedicti Hokett' ad quatuor anni terminos usuales. Ita quod ultra illos quadraginta denarios nullum redditum pro tenementis predictis de cetero clamare poterunt vel vendicare. In cuius rei testimonium huic scripto indentato, predicti abbas et conventus parti remanenti penes ipsum Robertum sigilla sua apposuerunt, et parti penes dictos abbatem et conventum residenti idem Robertus sigillum suum apposuit. Hiis testibus, Willelmo de Suthorp', Elya de Cantia, Thoma de Thorp', Ada le Aumouner, Simone le Botiler, Roberto de Mithingesby clerico et aliis.

1 Also in Soc. of Antiquaries, MS 38, fo. 40v and BL, Cott. Cleop. C ii, fos 69v–70r.
2 Recte *octo*.

128 Grant by Henry of Werrington, junior, to the abbot and convent of his plot of land in Hokettescroft by the pond in the abbot's manor of Boroughbury (in Peterborough) for which he was paid 10s. [*c*. 1300]

Carta Henrici de Wytherington' de eodem.

Sciant presentes et futuri quod ego Henricus de Wytherington' junior dedi concessi et hac presenti carta mea confirmavi domino abbati de Burgo Sancti Petri et eiusdem loci conventui quandam placeam terre mee in quodam loco qui vocatur Hokettescroft' super stagnum ipsius abbatis de manerio suo de Burgbyri', que quidem placea continet in latitudine versus orientem juxta terram Simonis le Fevre, triginta pedes, et in longitudine versus austrum viginti et quatuor pedes. Habendam et tenendam predictam placeam predicto abbati et conventui et successoribus suis libere, quiete, integre, bene, et in pace imperpetuum [fo. 56v]. Et ego predictus Henricus et heredes mei predictam placeam cum suis pertinenciis in longitudine et in latitudine ut predictum est, predictis abbati et conventui et successoribus eorumdem warantizabimus, acquietabimus et defendemus imperpetuum. Pro hac autem concessione et warentia dederunt mihi predicti abbas et conventus decem solidos argenti permanibus. In cuius rei testimonium huic presenti carte sigillum meum apposui. Hiis testibus Gilberto de Sutton', Roberto de Thorp', Johanne de Undele, Simone de Paston', Rogero de Catteworth', Stephano de Lotton', Ricardo clerico et aliis.

129 Grant by Simon le Fevere of Peterborough and Petronilla Doraunt, his wife, to Abbot Godfrey and the convent of headlands of three selions, held of the abbey, in Hokettescroft', abbutting on the abbot's pond in his manor of Boroughbury (Peterborough), in return for half a mark. [*c*. 1300]

Carta Simonis le Fevere et Petronille Doraunt de eodem.

Sciant presentes et futuri quod nos Simon le Fevere de Burgo Sancti Petri, et Petronilla Doraunt uxor mea dedimus concessimus et hac presenti carta nostra confirmavimus domino Godefrido abbati de eadem et eiusdem loci conventui, pro dimidia marca argenti quam nobis dederunt permanibus, capita trium selionum terre nostre, in quodam loco qui vocatur Hokettescroft' abuttantes super stagnum ipsius abbatis de manerio suo de Burbyri', que quidem capita continent in longitudine de predicto stagno versus villam viginti et tres pedes, et in latitudine ex utraque parte sex perticatas, et duodecim pedes. Habenda et tenenda predicta capita trium selionum, prefatis abbati et conventui et successoribus suis libere quiete integre bene et pacifice imperpetuum. Et nos predicti Simon et Petronilla et heredes nostri, antedicta capita cum suis pertinenciis, in longitudine et latitudine ut supradictum est, predictis abbati et conventui et eorum successoribus warantizabimus acquietabimus contra omnes et defendemus imperpetuum. In cuius rei testimonium huic presenti carte sigilla nostra apposuimus. Hiis testibus Johanne de Undele, Roberto de Thorp', Simone de Paston', Rogero de Merleye, Simone le Botiler, Ada le Aumoner, Ricardo de Weston' et aliis.

130 Grant by Thomas son of Hugh de Glastone of Peterborough to Abbot Godfrey and the convent of a headland of one selion in Hoketescroft, abutting on the pond in the manor of Boroughbury (Peterborough), in return for 2s 4d. [*c.* 1300]

Carta Thome filius Hugonis de Glastone de eodem.

Sciant presentes et futuri quod ego Thomas filius Hugonis de Glastone de Burgo Sancti Petri dedi concessi et hac presenti carta mea confirmavi domino Godefrido abbati de eadem et eiusdem loci conventui, pro duobus solidis et quatuor denariis argenti quos mihi dederunt permanibus, capud unius selionis terre mee, in quodam loco qui vocatur Hoketescroft', abbutans super stagnum ipsius [abbatis][1] de manerio suo de Burbyri, quod quidem capud continet in longitudine de predicto stagno versus villam, viginti et tres pedes, et in latitudine ex utraque parte duas perticatas et quatuor pedes. Habendum et tenendum predictum capud illius selionis, prefatis abbati et conventui et successoribus suis, libere, quiete, integre, bene et pacifice imperpetuum. Et ego dictus Thomas, et heredes mei, vel assignati mei predictum capud [fo. 57r] dicti selionis cum suis pertinenciis in longitudine et latitudine ut supradictum est, predictis abbati et conventui et eorum successoribus, contra omnes gentes warantizabimus, acquietabimus et defendemus imperpetuum. In cuius rei testimonium huic presenti carte, sigillum meum apposui. Hiis testibus: Johanne de Undele, Roberto de Thorp', Rogero de Merleye, Simone le Botiler, Ada le Aumoner, Bernardo de Castre, Roberto de Mithingesby clerico et aliis.

1 *abbatis* omitted?

131 Cyrograph agreement whereby the abbot and convent of Peterborogh relaxed the obligation of the abbot and convent of Sulby to perform suit of court at Castor in respect of the manor at Little Addington in the fee of the abbot of Peterborough, which Sulby had acquired. In return, Sulby will pay 3s 4d p.a. to the bailiff of Castor. [2 June 1308]

[marginated] Cirograffum abbatis de Suleby de secta curie de Castr' sibi et successoribus relaxata.

[marginated in later medieval hand] Castr'

Universis[1] sancte matris ecclesie filius pateat per presentes quod cum abbas de Suleby teneretur facere sectam ad curiam abbatis de Burgo Sancti Petri de Castre de tribus septimanis in tres septimanas per se vel per suos attornatos imperpetuum virtute cuiusdam conventionis inter dictos abbates et eorum conventos facte super manerio de Parva Adington' cum suis pertinenciis quod dicti abbas et conventus de Suleby nuper adquisiverunt de feodo ipsius abbatis de Burgo Sancti Petri perpetuis temporibus possidendis, tandem ad festum Pentecoste, in anno regni regis Edwardi filii regis Edwardi primo, dicti abbas et conventus de Burgo Sancti Petri volentes parcere laboribus et expensis dicti abbatis de Suleby et successorum eiusdem ac eorumdem quieti in hac parte misericorditer providere concesserunt de gracia sua speciali pro se et suis successoribus quod dictus abbas de Suleby et eius successores quieti fuit imperpetuum de predicta secta ad predictam curiam suam de Castre et ipsam predictam sectam remiserunt, relaxaverunt et quietum clamaverunt predicto abbati de Suleby et eius successoribus pro se et suis successoribus imperpetuum. Pro qua quidem remissione, relaxatione et quieta clamatione, predictus abbas de Suleby et eiusdem loci conventus concesserunt pro se et successoribus suis teneri dictis abbati et conventui de Burgo Sancti Petri et eorum successoribus in tribus solidis et quatuor denariis sterlingorum solvendis annuatim in festo Pasche ballivo suo predicte curie de Castr' qui pro tempore fuerit ipsorum nomine imperpetuum. Pro quibus quidem iij s. et iiij d. si aretro fuerint vel esse contingerint in futurum licebit dictis abbati et conventui de Burgo Sancti Petri et eorum successoribus et eorum ballivis curie predicte qui pro tempore fuerint distringere dictos abbatem et conventum de Suleby et eorum successores in manerio suo predicto de Parva Adington' et districtiones retinere quousque de predicto redditu, dampnis et expensis si que vel quas occasione dicte solutionis minime facte sustinuerint aut incurrerint absque contradictione seu impedimento predictorum abbatis et conventus de Suleby successorum hominum aut ballivorum suorum quorumcumque ad plenum satisfactionem fuerit eisdem alio scripto conventionali inter eosdem religiosos prius super certis serviciis et juribus confecto predicta secta dumtaxat excepta suo robore inviolabiliter duraturo. In cuius rei testimonium parti huius scripti indentati penes dictos abbatem et conventum de Suleby residenti abbas et conventus de Burgo Sancti Petri sigilla sua apposuerunt, et parti penes dictos abbatem et conventum de Burgo Sancti Petri residenti abbas et conventus de Suleby sigilla sua apposuerunt. Dat' in capitulo domus utriusque in festo Pentecoste prenotato.[2]

1 Also in Soc. of Antiquaries, MS 38, fos 25v–6r and BL, Cott. Cleop. C ii. fos 45v–6v.
2 *in festo Pentecoste prenotato* continued vertically up the right hand margin.

132 Grant by Abbot Godfrey to Thomas of London[1], member of his household, of specified food and clothing for the rest of his life, together with 10s for shoes each year. [26 January 1312]

[fo. 57v] [marginated in later medieval hand] Carta Thome de London' de liberat' sua.

Omnibus Christi fidelibus ad quos presens scriptum pervenerit, Godefridus Dei gracia abbas de Burgo Sancti Petri et eiusdem loci conventus salutem in Domino sempiternam. Noverit universitas vestra nos unanimi assensu concessisse dilecto et fideli familio nostro Thome de London' competentem sustentationem in tota vita sua in victu et vestitu in abbathia nostra; videlicet unam robam de secta armigerorum abbatis annuatim percipiendam, et unum panem album et unum panem bissum, et duas lagenas bone cervise de celario abbatis, et unum ferculum integrum cum intermisso secundum varietatem dierum et temporum de coquina eiusdem abbatis cotidie prout libere familie ministratur quamdiu vixerit percipiendos, et decem solidos sterlingorum pro calciatura singulis annis quamdiu vixerit de camera predicti abbatis percipiendos; videlicet ad Pascha et ad festum sancti Michaelis. Concedimus insuper quod predictus Thomas ubicumque fuerit infra abbatia vel extra omnia supradicta libere percipiat, et de hiis pro libito suo disponat. In cuius rei testimonium huic presenti scripto sigilla nostra sunt appensa. Dat' in capitulo nostro die Mercurii in crastino conversionis sancti Pauli anno Domini millesimo CCC^mo undecimo.

1 See nos 15 and 185, where he appears as a witness.

133 Letter from Abbot Godfrey to the prior, prioress and convent of St Michael's, Stamford notifying them of his intention to carry out a visitation of the nunnery on 6 February. [26 Jan. 1303]

[marginated in different hand] Stamford'

G[odefridus] permissione divina abbas monasterii sancti Petri de Burgo dilectis sibi in Christo priori sancti Michaelis extra Stanford' eiusdemque loci priorisse et conventui salutem, que de visceribus emanavit salvatoris. Debitum visitationis officium quod nobis incumbit in prioratu vestro exequendum pro affectu exercere intendenentes vobis mandamus, quatinus die Mercurii proxima post festum purificationis beate Marie virginis in ecclesia vestra conventuali sancti Michaelis, vos, et ceteros congregationis vestre omnes et singulos, qui per nos de jure vel consuetudine visitari debebunt, nobis subjectibiliter exhibeatis paratos, visitationem nostram salubriter subituram. In Christo Jesu per tempora longa valitura.

Dat' apud Eye die Sabbati in crastino conversionis sancti Pauli anno Domino millesimo C°CC secundo

134 Copy of the entry from the fine rolls of the royal Exchequer recording the fine made by the abbot of 300 marks for the service of five knights' fees, through his attorney Brother Simon de Freston'. Also a memorandum to the effect that nothing would be levied unless the king took an army to Scotland. [1299–1300]

In rotulo de finibus ad Scaccarium pro servicio regis debito et recognito in Scotia anno regis Edwardi xxviij°.

[marginated in different hand] Norhampt'

Abbas de Burgo Sancti Petri per fratrem Simonem de Freston', attornatum suum, finem fecit pro servicio quinque feodorum per CCC marcas.

Et memorandum quod in quadam cedula attachiata rotulo predicto continetur quod de huiusmodi finibus nichil erit ad opus regis exactum et levatum nisi rex excercitum suum in Scotia habeat, pro quo excercitu predicti fines facti sunt et recogniti.

135 Grant by Abbot Godfrey to John son of Gilbert of Chesterton, clerk[1], of an annual pension of 40s from his chamber, for the abbot's lifetime or until John can be provided with a benefice. [20 June? 1300[2]]

[fo. 58r] Pensio Johannis filii Gilberti de Cestreton'.

Universis Christi fidelibus presentes litteras visuris vel audituris. Godefridus permissione divina abbas monasterii sancti Petri de Burgo salutem in Domino sempiternam. Noverit universitas vestra nos caritatis intuitu concessisse dilecto nobis in Christo Johanni filio Gilberti de Cestreton' clerico quadraginta solidos sterlingorum nomine pensionis annue de camera nostra ad quatuor anni terminos usuales percipiendos; videlicet ad festum sancti Johannis baptiste decem solidos, ad festum sancti Michaelis decem solidos, ad festum natale Domini decem solidos et ad Pascha decem solidos. Et sic singulis annis ad terminum vite nostre, vel quousque uberius in ecclesiastico beneficio providerimus eidem. In cuius rei testimonium presentibus sigillum nostrum apposuimus. Dat' apud Burgum Sancti Petri die Lune proxima ante festum beati Johannis baptiste anno Domini M° tricentesimo et anno domini G[odefridi] abbatis primo.

1 For Gilbert of Chesterton, a prominent wool merchant, see below, no. 211.

2 Or possibly 22 August, if the other feast day associated with St John the Baptist was intended.

136 Grant by Abbot Godfrey and the convent to Robert of Croyland, clerk, of an annual pension of 5 marks from the abbot's chamber until he can be provided with a suitable benefice. [25 Mar.–7 Oct. 1300[1]]

Pensio Roberti de Croyland.

Universis Christi fidelibus presentes litteras visuris vel audituris Godefridus permissione divina abbas monasterii sancti Petri de Burgo et eiusdem loci conventus salutem in Domino sempiternam. Noverit universitas vestra nos caritatis intuitu concessisse dilecto nobis in Christo Roberto de Croyland' clerico quinque marcas sterlingorum nomine pensionis annue de camera abbatis -[2] ad duos anni terminos percipiendas; videlicet ad festum sancti Michaelis triginta tres solidos et quatuor denarios et ad festum Pasche triginta tres solidos et quatuor denarios. Et sic singulis annis donec eidem in ecclesiastico beneficio competenti providerimus. In cuius rei testimonium presentis litteris sigilla nostra sunt appensa. Dat' in capitulo nostro die Mercurii in festo -[2] beati Johannis baptiste. Anno Domini millesimo tricentesimo et anno domini G[odefridi] abbatis primo.

1 Neither 29 August nor 24 June, the two feast days associated with St John the Baptist, fell on a Wednesday in 1300. Unusual strokes in the text may indicate a faulty original and perhaps a misreading of *in festo* for *ante festum* or *post festum* in the dating clause.
2 Strokes in the text.

137 Letter from Abbot Godfrey to the prior and prioress of St Michael's, Stamford concerning his visitation. [12 July 1300]

[marginated] Stamforde.

G[odefridus] permissione divina abbas monasterii sancti Petri de Burgo dilectis in Christo Priori sancti Michaelis extra Stannford' et eiusdem loci priorisse salutem et religionis salubre incrementum. Quam hac instanti die Mercurii in festo sancte Margarete virginis visitationis officium in prioratu vestro certis excausis disposuimus favente suppremo dispositore extercere super quo vos volumus litteris nostris premuniri, ut vestra solicitudo per justitiam vel dissimulationem in cura vobis commissa, omnem tollat materiam excusationis quesite adventum nostrum ex causa prescripta noticie vestre harum tenore deducimus, ac per vos illis quorum interest insinuari mandamus. Dat' apud Keteringg' die Jovis proxima ante festum sancti Kenelmi regis et martyris anno Domini M^{o} tricentesimo.

138 Letter from John Dalderby, bishop of Lincoln, to the abbot and convent concerning dissension and revolt within the abbey. [21 Aug. 1300]

[fo. 58v] Littera Episcopi Linc' directa abbati et conventui.

Johannes[1] permissione divina Lincoln' episcopus, dilectis in Christo filiis abbati et conventui monasterii de Burgo Sancti Petri salutem graciam et benedictionem. Congregationis vestre nobilis de religionis observantia et unitatis habundantia retroactis temporibus commendate non modicum, famam bonam, integrum quantum in nobis est conservare volentes. Conventui suadendum duximus per presentes, quatinus rebellionibus, et dissensionibus omnimodis, de quarum suscitatione in congregatione predicta aliqua audivimus nobis displicentia procul pulsis, in omni humilitate suo obediat capiti sicut decet, attendens quod sicut obedientia res est optima, sic rebellio res pessima est censenda. Similiter curet abbas cum modestia exequi ea que ad suum officium pertinere noscuntur. Ita tamen quod per remissionem nimiam sua non perinpendatur auctoritas aut vilescat, nec per asperitatem nimiam correctionis impediatur effectus, sed more periti mediti (?) nunc vinum infundat nunc oleum sauciatis. Valete. Dat' apud Lydington' xij[2] kalendas Septembris, consecrationis nostre anno primo.

1 Also in Dalderby's Memoranda Register, fo. 16r.
2 *xj kal'* in Dalderby's Register.

139 Letter from Abbot Godfrey to William, abbot of Malmesbury, president of the General Chapter of Canterbury province, appointing Brother Peter de Ketene as his proctor for the meeting on 21 September, since he is prevented from attending by a variety of urgent business. [14 Sept. 1300]

[marginated in a different hand] procuratorium pro capitulo generali.

Venerabili[1] in Christo patri W[illelmo] Dei permissione abbati de Malmesbyr' generali capitulo ordinis sancti Benedicti Cantuarens' provincie presidenti in presenti, ac universis et singulis confratibus Dei gracia abbatibus et prioribus, et ceteris quibuscumque ordinis predicti in capitulo generali constitutis, Godefridus permissione divina abbas monasterii Sancti Petri de Burgo Linc' diocesis salutem, et mandatis presidentis cum humilitate obedire. Variis et arduis negotiis, nos et monasterium nostrum contingentibus prepediti ad generale capitulum hoc instanti festo sancti Mathei apostoli et evangeliste Oxon' celebrandum accedere non valentes, dilectum in Christo fratrem Petrum de Ketene commonachum procuratorem et excusatorem nostrum ordinamus facimus et constituimus nuncium specialem, dantes eidem potestatem generalem, et mandatum speciale, nomine nostro excusationum causas et absentie allegandi, et super hiis fidem canonicam faciendi, vobiscum insuper tractandi et consentiendi, recipiendi et admittendi, necnon faciendi, quod natura et qualitas negotiorum in capitulo generali ordinandorum, pro utilitate et honestate religionis nostre postulaverint. Ratum habentes et firmum, quicquid idem procurator noster, nomine nostro duxerit faciendum et recipiendum, super omnibus in predicto capitulo articulis pertractandis et expediendis. In cuius rei testimonium presentibus sigillum nostrum est appensum. Dat' apud Burgum Sancti Petri octavodecimo kalendas Octobris. Anno Domini millesimo tricentesimo.

1 Printed in Pantin, *Chapters of the English Black Monks*, vol. I, pp. 141–2, no. 51.

139A Letter from Abbot Godfrey to William, abbot of Malmesbury, president of the General Chapter of Canterbury province, further to his absence from the General Chapter meeting. [*c.* 14 Sept. 1300]

Excellentis[1] religionis viro domino W[illelmo] permissione divina abbati Malmesbyrie generali [fo. 59r] capitulo ordinis sancti Benedicti Cantuarens' provincie presidenti G[odefridus] eadem permissione abbas de Burgo Sancti Petri salutem, et religionis incrementum salubre. Licet ad instans capitulum generale per vos Oxon' celebrandum pro quorumdam expositione negotiorum et precipue pro vestra dilectione optata, indissolubiliter amplectanda, accessisse proposuissemus, ingentis tamen excusationis impedimentum superveniens, per portitorem presentium vobis intimandum, zeli nostri propositum in majoris negotii, nostri monasterii expeditionem necessario convertebat vicinam. Quo circa paternitatis vestre clementiam, cum devotione scincera humilter imploramus, quatinus nostrum excusatorem oportuni favoris presidiis, in hiis que nostre abstentie causas contingunt, habere velitis recommendatum, voluntatem vestram si placet, cui parere intime affectamus nobis demandantes.[2] In Christo Jesu valeat vestra dominatio per tempora longa

1 Printed in Pantin, *Chapters of the English Black Monks*, vol. I, p. 142, no. 52.
2 *voluntatem ... demandentes* omitted from Pantin's text.

140 Grant for life by Abbot Godfrey and the convent to John son of Thomas of Oundle, clerk[1], of 30 acres of demesne land in Oundle, rendering 13s 4d p.a. In return John surrendered 90 acres of land and a sheepfold at La Biggin which he had been granted by Abbot William. [25 Sept. 1300]

De terra Johanni de Undele ad firmam dimissa.

Universis Christi fidelibus presens scriptum visuris vel audituris Godefridus permissione divina abbas de Burgo Sancti Petri et eiusdem loci conventus salutem in Domino sempiternam. Noveritis nos de communi assensu tocius capituli nostri concessisse ac dimisisse Johanni filii Thome de Undele clerico triginta acras terre arabilis de dominicis terre in villa de Undele, quarum vij acre jacent in campo qui vocatur Holm, super le Hulkefurlong', et tres acre super le Brakewang' et x acre in alio campo versus pontem de Ayston' super Smethefeld. Et iij acre super le Netherwelles in tercio campo versus Stok's. Et vij acre super le Ouerewelles, una cum quadam particula prati que vocatur Shakdeles quod continet unam acram et dimidiam, et unam rodam. Habendas et tenendas eidem Johanni toto tempore vite sue de nobis et successoribus nostris per servicium tresdecim solidorum et iiij^{or} denariorum ad quatuor anni terminos usuales solvendorum. Et pro hac concessione dictus Johannes nobis reddidit bercariam de la Bigging' et quaterviginti et decem acres terre quas habuit ex dimissione domini Willelmi abbatis predecessoris nostri. In cuius rei testimonium huic presenti scripto sigilla nostra sunt appensa. Dat' apud Burgum Sancti Petri die Dominica proxima post festum sancti Mathei apostoli et evangeliste. Anno Domini m^{o} tricentesimo. Et anno regni regis Edwardi filii regis Henrici vicesimo octavo.

1 See no. 141, n. 1.

141 Grant by Abbot Godfrey and the convent to John son of Thomas of Oundle, clerk,[1] of an annual pension of 60s from the abbot's chamber until he can be provided with a suitable benefice. [25 Sept. 1300]

Pensio Johannis de Undele.

Universis Christi fidelibus presentes litteras visuris vel audituris Godefridus permissione divina abbas monasterii sancti Petri de Burgo et eiusdem loci conventus salutem in Domino sempiternam. Noverit universitas vestra nos caritatis intuitu concessisse dilecto nobis in Christo Johanni filii Thome de Undele clerico lx solidos sterlingorum nomine [fo. 59v] pensionis annue de camera abbatis qui pro tempore fuerit ad duos anni terminos percipiendos; videlicet ad festum sancti Michaelis xxx solidos et ad Pascha xxx solidos. Et sic singulis annis donec eidem in ecclesiastico beneficio competenti providerimus. In cuius rei testimonium presentibus litteris sigilla nostra sunt appensa. Dat' in capitulo nostro die Dominica proxima post festum sancti Mathei apostoli et evangeliste. Anno Domini M^{o} tricentesimo et anno domini G[odefridi] abbatis primo.

1 Appointed keeper of the liberty 16 Sept. 1298. See no. 87.

142 Letter from John, bishop of Lincoln, to the abbot arranging for the restoration to use of the chapel of the Blessed Thomas the Martyr. It had been placed under interdict by his predecessor following its pollution by the bloodshed caused when fugitives who had sought sanctuary there were dragged forth. [12 Dec. 1300]

Littera domini Linc' episcopi pro capella beati Thome martiris extra portam.

Johannes[1] permissione divina Linc' episcopus dilecto in Christo filio abbati de Burgo Sancti Petri salutem graciam et benedictionem. Cum capella beati Thome martiris juxta monasterium vestrum pro effusione sanguinis in extractione quorumdam confugarum ad dictam capellam et inibi existentium pro ecclesiastica immunitate habenda iampridem temere perpetrata, auctoritate predecessoris nostri supposita fuerit interdicto, donec dicte persone sic abstracte libertati loci predicti forent congrue restituti, eedem que persone impresentiarum sint vel rebus humanis exempte, vel que supersunt prefate capelle reddite sue eciam libertate, nos dictam capellam a divinis laudibus que inibi ut dicitur fieri consueverunt, quantum in nobis est nolentes ulterius manere suspensam, ut ipsam munere consecrationis hactenus nullatenus insignitam, cum aqua per vos exorzizata associatis vobis aliquibus capellanis pro voluntate vestra, cum psalmis primalibus lavare possitis vobis facultatem duximus concedendam, interdictum pretactum veris existentibus que nobis ut premittitur sunt suggesta plenius relaxantes. Valete. Dat' apud Edelington' ii idus Decembris. Anno Domini millesimo tricentesimo.

1 Also in Dalberby's Memoranda Register, fo. 22r–v.

143 Letter from Abbot Godfrey and the convent to John, bishop of Lincoln, appointing Brother William Saleman, the sacrist, and Master Geoffrey of Maxey, clerk, as proctors for the meeting of the convocation of the the clergy of Lincoln diocese in Lincoln cathedral on 9 January. [2 Jan. 1301]

Universis sancte Matris ecclesie filiis presentes litteras inspecturis vel audituris G[odefridus] permissione divina abbas monasterii sancti Petri de Burgo, et eiusdem loci conventus salutem in Domino. Noverit universitas vestra quod nos in hac instanti convocatione cleri, Linc' diocesis per venerabilem in Christo patrem dominum J[ohannem] Dei gracia Linc' episcopum, ad diem Lune proximum post festum epiphanie Domini, in ecclesia cathedrali Linc' facta, dilectos in Christo fratrem Willelmum Saleman, commonacum et sacristam nostram, et magistrum Galfridum de Makes', clericum, procuratores nostros sub alternatione facimus, ordinamus et constituimus per presentes, dantes eisdem, et eorum cuilibet in solidum potestatem specialem et mandatum speciale, nomine nostro et monasterii nostri, negotia per venerabilem patrem supradictum dictis die et loco ex-[fo. 60r]ponenda, reverenter audiendi, et ea ad honorem Dei efficaciter promovendi, tractandi, et consentiendi, una cum venerabili patre supradicto, ipsius ve commissariis ac ceteris in congregatione cleri diocesis antedicte existentibus, faciendi et recipiendi quod utilitati communi ac monasterii nostri de Burgo videbitur expedire. Ratum habentes et firmum quicquid iidem procuratores, vel eorum alter nomine nostro, et monasterii nostri duxerint seu duxerit faciendum in premissis. In cuius rei testimonium presentibus sigilla nostra sunt appensa. Dat' apud Burgum in crastino circumcisionis Domini anno Domini millesimo tricentisimo.

144 Recognition of John de Godesle, keeper of the queen's gold, before the barons of the Exchequer that he had received 100 marks from the abbot and convent as part of the fine of 1000 marks made with the king by the prior and convent for the custody of the abbey during the last vacancy. Also of £20 from the £200 fine which the previous abbot made with the king for service in the army in Scotland. [*c.* 1300]

[Marginated in later hand] Aurum regina.

Johannes de Godesle custos auri regine venit coram baronibus et recognovit se se recepisse ad opus domine regine centum marcas de abbate et conventu de Burgo Sancti Petri pro auro ipsius regine de quodam fine M marcarum, quem prior et conventus eiusdem loci tempore vacationis eiusdem abbatie fecerunt cum rege pro custodia inde habenda tempore ultime vacationis. Et xx li. pro auro domine regine de quodam fine CC li. quem abbas eiusdem domus fecit cum rege pro servicio suo regi debito in exercitu regis Scotie.

144A Grant that the prior and convent might pay the 400 marks remaining from the 1000 mark fine made with the king for custody of the abbey during the vacancy following the death of Abbot William of Woodford in instalments of 100 marks p.a. [Michaelmas Term 1300]

Juratores recognitionis de termino sancti Michaelis anno regni regis Edwardi xxviij° finiente.

Concessum est priori et conventui de Burgo Sancti Petri quod de CCCC marcis que regi aretro sunt de illis M marcis per quas idem prior et conventus finem fecerunt cum rege pro custodia abbatie predicte habenda tempore vacationis eiusdem per mortem fratris Willelmi de Wodeford nuper abbatis ibidem, reddant regi per annum C marcas; unam videlicet medietatem ad Scaccarium sancti Michaelis, et aliam medietatem ad Scaccarium Pasche. Et sic de anno in annum C marcas ad eosdem terminos donec etc.

145 Order from the king to the treasurer and barons of the Exchequer that the abbot and convent be allowed to enjoy the grants and liberties that he had confirmed. [6 Oct. 1300]

[Marginated] Norht'

In rotulo de finibus de termino Pasche anno xxviij°.

Rex thesaurario et baronibus de Scaccario salutem. Cum per cartam nostram confirmaverimus dilectis nobis in Christo abbati et conventui de Burgo Sancti Petri quasdam donationes et concessiones a progenitoribus nostris regibus Anglie per cartas eorum de diversis libertatibus factas, vobis mandamus, quod ipsum abbatem libertatibus predictis coram vobis in Scaccario predicto uti et gaudere permittatur juxta tenorem cartarum et confirmatorum nostre predictarum. Teste me ipso apud Holcolstram' vj die Octobris anno regno nostri xxviij°.

146 Part of the 1291 valuation of the abbey's spiritualities and temporalities, probably associated here with the triennial tenth granted by the pope in 1301[1]

[fo. 60v] Taxatio bonorum spiritualium et temporalium abbatis et conventus de Burgo Sancti Petri sub collecta abbatis et conventus Oseneye existent'.

Ecclesia de Burgo	lv m. decima lxxiij s. iiij d.
Ecclesia de Makeseye	xxij m. decima xxix s. iiij d.
Ecclesia de Wermington'	lv m. decima lxxiij s. iiij d.
Pens' abbatis de Burgo in ecclesia de Castre	C s. decima x s.
Portio eiusdem in eadem	v m. decima vj s. viij d.
Portio eiusdem in Wytering'	ij m. decima ij s. viij d.
Pens' eiusdem in Bernak'	x s. decima xij d.
Portio eiusdem in Thornhawe	xx s. decima ij s.
Portio eiusdem in Helpestone	ij m. decima ij s. viij d.
Portio eiusdem in Etton'	xx s. decima ij s.
Pens' eiusdem in Peykirke	xv s. decima xviij d.
Portio eiusdem in eadem	ii m. decima ii s. viij d.
Pens' eiusdem in Paston'	xiij s. iiij d. decima xvj d.
Portio eiusdem in eadem	xx m. decima xxvj s. viij d.
Pens' eiusdem in Stanewigg'	xx s. decima ij s.
Portio eiusdem in eadem	ij m. decima ij s. viij d.

Portio eiusdem in Wodeford'	v m. decima vj s. viij d.
Pens' eiusdem in Irtelingburg' sancti Petri	xlvj s. viij d. decima iiij s. viij d.
Pens' eiusdem in Cotingham	vj s. viij d. decima viij d.
Pens' eiusdem in Pyteslee	vj s. viij d. decima viij d.
Pens' eiusdem in Wermington'	xxvj s. viij d. decima ij s. viij d.
Pens' eiusdem in Undele	ij m. decima ij s. viij d.
Portio sacriste in Stok'	x s. decima xij d.
Portio eiusdem in Clopton'	ij m. decima ij s. viij d.
Portio eiusdem in Pokebrok'	xx s. decima ij s.
Portio eiusdem in Ufford	ij m. decima ij s. viij d.[2]
Portio eiusdem in Wermington'	v m. decima vj s. viij d.[3]
Portio eiusdem in Irtelingburg'	ij m. decima ij s. viij d.[4]
Pens' in Keteringg'	xl s. decima iiij s.

Summa ij[c] ix m. dim. xx d. que fac' vj[xx] xix li. xviij s. viij d. in libr'

[fo. 61r] Temporalium eiusdem

Abbas de Burgo habet in Castre	xiij li. xj s. vj d.
Idem in Elington'	xv li.
Idem in Wythering'	xiij li. iij s. viij d. ob.
Idem in Walton'	vij li. iiij s.
Idem in Thorp'	viij li. xvj s. j d. qa.
Idem in Eye	ix li. vj s. iij d. ob.
Idem in Burbury	xx li. ij d. ob.
Idem in villa de Burgo	xxij li. vj s. viij d.
Idem in Hundr' de Nasso Burgi	xl s.
Idem in Cotingham	xxiiij li.[5]
Idem in Stanewig'	x li. xj s. x d.
Idem in Irtlingburg'	xij li. xviij s. iiij d.
Idem in Keteringg'	xxvj li. xj s. ix d.
Idem in Wermington'	xxvj li. ij s. viij d.
Idem in Undele et Bigging'	xliiij li. xiiij d.[6]
Idem in Ayston'	x li. xvij s. iiij d.
Idem ibidem in duobus hundredis	v li.
Idem in Aldewyncle	lx s.
Idem habet in Burgo hosp' Infirmorum	vj li.
Camerarius eiusdem domus in Northburg'	vj li. xiij s. iiij d.
Pitanciarius in Paston'	ij m.
Thesaurarius[7] in Botelbrigg'	xxx s.
Infirmarius in Wermington'	vj s.
Elemosinarius in Clopton'	lvj s. viij d.
Idem in Wermington' et Cotherstok'	lxxiij s. iiij d.
Idem in Gunthorp'	xiij li. vj s. viij d.
Idem in Sutton'	vj li. ij s.[8]
Idem in Neuton'	ij s. vj d.
Sacrista eiusdem domus in Suthorp'	xlvj s. viij d.
Idem in Irtlingburg'	x s.

Idem in Pokebrok' vj li. xvj s. viij d.[9]

Summa CCC xxv li. xx d. ob. qa.

[fo. 61v]In Linc'	xiij s. iiij d.	decima	xvj d.
In decanatu de Graham	xx s.	decima	ij s.
In decanatu de Avelund[10]	xx s.	decima	ij s.
In decanatu de Nesso[11]	iiij li.	decima	viij d.
In decanatu de Stanford'	xiiij li. v s. x d.	decima	xxviij s. vij d.
In decanatu Hoylond'[12]	xliij li. ij s. iij d.	decima	iiij li. vj s. ij d. ob. qa.
In decanatu de Coringham	xxx li. xv s. vj d.	decima	lxj s. vj d. ob. qa.
In decanatu de Manlak[13]	xiiij li. ij s. ix d.	decima	xxviij s. iij d. qa.
In decanatu de Lauris[14]	xlvj li. iiij s.	decima	iiij li. xij s. iiij d. ob. qa
In decanatu de Gertre[15]	xxxvij li. iiij s. xj d. ob. qa.	decima	lxxiiij s. vj d.
In decanatu de Roteland'[17]	xxv li. ij s. ob. qa.[17]	decima	l s. ij d. ob. qa.
In decanatu de Neuwerk'[18]	xxj li. iij s. iiij d.	decima	xlij s. iij d.

Summa CC xxxviij li. xiiij s. ob.

1 Although the abbots of Osney were tax collectors on a number of occasions, the position of this extract in the register makes the 1301 tax the most likely. Lunt, *Financial Relations*, pp. 632, 634–7. For the Rec. Comm. text, see pp. 39–40 for spiritualities; pp. 50, 53–5 for temporalities; p. 68 for rural deanery totals.
2 Entry for Ufford omitted from the Rec. Comm. text.
3 Entry for Warmington in the Rec. Comm. text is a pension of £1 6s 8d. *Taxatio*, p. 39b.
4 £2 6s 8d in the Rec. Comm. text, p. 40b.
5 £24 3s in the Rec. Comm text, p. 54a.
6 £44 14s in the Rec. Comm. text, p. 55a.
7 *Thesaurerarius* in MS.
8 Also Bellasise £5 0s 8d in the Rec. Comm. text, p. 53b.
9 The sacrist also has 6s 8d in Warmington in the Rec. Comm. text, p. 55b.
10 Marginated *Stowe*.
11 Marginated ?
12 Marginated *Gosberchurch*.
13 Marginated *Walcot'*.
14 Marginated *Fyskerton'*.
15 Marginated *Eston*.
16 Marginated *Tynewell'*.
17 Farthing omitted in the Rec. Comm. text.
18 Marginated *Colingham*.

147 Letters dimissory from Abbot Godfrey concerning the admission of Brother John de Repynghale into the Cistercian abbey of Garendon to live a more austere life. [18 May 1301]

[Marginated in different hand] Littere dimissorie fratris Johannis de Repynghale.

Omnibus Christi fidelibus presentes litteras visuris vel audituris frater Godefridus permissione divina monasterii de Burgo Sancti Petri minister humiliter salutem in auctore salutis. Cum frater Johannes de Repinghale monasterii de Burgo monachus, ordinis sancti Benedicti, nulla que conjecturari potuit, levitate seu temeritate ductus, set ut creditur divinitus inspiratus, religionem affectaverit artiorem, frugem concupiscens vite melioris ac religiosi viri abbas et conventus de Gerndon' ordinis Cistersiensis eundem fratrem suo ferventi desiderio moti, necnon ex affectione hactenus erga monasterium de Burgo habita specialiter inducti, in sua religiosa congregatione recipere sint perati dictum fratrem Johannem ut ordinem Cistersiensem in predicto monasterio de Gerndon' libere profiteri valeat et observare, de fratrum meorum consilio et assensu licencio per presentes has litteras dimissorias eidem de predictorum fratum consilio et assensu faciens testimoniales. Dat' apud Burgum die Jovis proxima ante festum sancti Dunstani archiepiscopi anno gracie M^{o} tricentesimo primo.

147A Letter from Abbot Godfrey to the abbot and convent of Garendon notifying them that William Saleman, the sacrist, and Master Geoffrey of Maxey, clerk, will be coming as his special envoys in order to expedite the transfer of Brother John de Repynghale in order to live a more austere life. [*c.* 18 May 1301]

Excellentis religionis viris permisione divina domino abbati de Gerndon' et eiusdem loci conventui Cistersiensis ordinis, G[odefridus] eadem permissione abbas monasterii sancti Petri de Burgo salutem, quam sanguis in cruce redemit salvatoris. Cum frater Johannes de Repingale commonachus noster vitam ducere artioris religionis, ac in vestro monasterio juxta sacri ordinis vestri regulam profiteri iam pridem optaverit divinitus inspiratus, cuius devotionem zelo ferventis desiderii conceptam effectui mancipare ut tenemur cupientes, religionis vestre fraternitatem in Christo exoramus, quatinus dilectis nostris in Christo fratri Willelmo Saleman sacriste monasterii nostri, ac magistro G[alfrido] de Makes' clerico nostro nunciis nostris specialibus ad exponendum, prosequendum et promovendum dicti fratris [fo. 62r] negotium vobis transmissis, in hiis que vobis nomine nostro et congregationis nostre duxerint intimanda fidem velitis adhibere indubitatam, caritatis et religionis intuitu exponenda favorabiliter expedientes. In Christo Jesu valeat vestra conversatio religiosa per tempora longa.

148 Undertaking by Abbot Godfrey to provide Roger de Hegham, knight,[1] with a life pension of £10 p.a. from his chamber in return for his past advice and assistance with abbey business and his pledge of future help. [6 Feb. 1300]

Pensio domini Rogeri de Hegham.

Omnibus Christi fidelibus ad quos presentes littere pervenerint G[odefridus] permissione divina abbas de Burgo Sancti Petri salutem in Domino sempiternam. Noveritis nos teneri et per presentes obligari, dilecto nobis in Christo domino Rogero de Hegham' militi pro consilio et auxilio suo prius nobis et ecclesie nostre impenso, et in posterum impendendo, in decem libris sterlingorum ad totam vitam suam de camera nostra de Burgo Sancti Petri annuatim percipiendis ad duos anni terminos; videlicet mediatatem ad Pascha et aliam mediatatem ad festum sancti Michaelis. Et predictus dominus Rogerus concessit et fideliter promisit nobis et ecclesie nostre de Burgo Sancti Petri, quod erit de cetero consulens et auxilians in omnibus negotiis, nos et ecclesiam nostram predictam tangentibus, quotiens et quandocumque ad hoc congrue possit intendere. In cuius rei testimonium presentibus litteris sigillum nostrum apposuimus. Dat' apud Burgum Sancti Petri die Sabbati proxima post festum purificationis beate Marie virginis anno regni regis Edwardi vicesimo octavo.

1 One of the pensioners listed in no. 10. See also King, *Peterborough Abbey*, pp. 135–6, for his services to the abbey.

149 The abbot who has custody of John, son and heir of Geoffrey of Southorpe and Walter, son and heir of Walter of Ufford is challenging the king's claim to their marriage. Letter from King Edward ordering William Carleton' and John Kirkby to hold an inquest in Northamptonshire to determine whether Geoffrey of Southorpe and Walter of Ufford and their ancestors held of the abbey in Peterborough and Stoke Doyle before they held of John de Cameys in Lolham, which is part of the manor of Torpel, now in the king's hand, together with details of their tenure. [23 Feb. 1301]

Maritagia Johanis filii et heredis Galfridi de Suthorp' et Walteri filii et heredis Walteri de Ufford'.

Edwardus Dei gracia rex Anglie, dominus Hybernie, et dux Aquitanie dilectis et fidelibus suis Willelmo de Carleton' et Johanni de Kirkeby' salutem. Quia dilectus nobis in Christo abbas de Burgo Sancti Petri asserit maritagium Johannis filii et heredis Galfridi de Suthorp' et eciam maritagium Walteri filii et heredis Walteri de Ufford', quiquidem heredes sunt in custodia eiusdem abbatis, ad ipsum, et non ad nos pertinere debere, eo quod predicti Galfridus et Walterus de Ufforde et antecessores sui tenuerunt de abbatibus de Burgo Sancti Petri predecessoribus predicti abbatis in villa de Burgo Sancti Petri, et Stok's juxta Undele per servicium militare diu ante quam iidem Galfridus et Walterus quicquam tenuerunt de Johanne de Cameys in Loholm quod de manerio de Torpel tenetur, quod nunc in manu nostra existit, per quod nos super premissis plenius certiorari, et eidem abbati ulterius quod justum fuerit fieri volentes in hac parte, assignavimus vos vel alterum vestrum quem presentem esse contigerit ad inquirendum per sacramentum proborum et legalium hominum de comitatu Norht', per quos rei veritas melius sciri poterit, utrum predicti Galfridus et Walterus de Ufforde vel antecessores sui prius feoffati fuerunt tenendis de abbatibus de Burgo Sancti Petri predecessoribus predicti abbatis, an de [fo. 62v] predicto Johanne vel antecessoribus suis ut predictum est, nec ne, et si de abbatibus de Burgo Sancti Petri tunc a quo tempore, et per quod servicium, et qualiter et quomodo, et si de prefato Johanne vel antecessoribus suis tunc a quo tempore, et per quod servicium, et qualiter et quomodo. Et ideo vobis mandamus quod ad certos dies et loca quos vos ambo vel alter vestrum ad hoc provideritis, inquisitionem inde faciatis in forma predicta. Et eam distincte et aperte factam thesaurario et baronibus nostris de Scaccario sub sigillis vestris, vel alterius vestrum, et sigillis eorum per quos facta fuerit sine dilatione mittatur et hoc breve, mandavimus enim vicecomiti nostro comitatus predicti, quod ad certos dies et loca quos vos ambo vel alter vestrum ei scire faciatis, venire faciatis coram vobis vel altero vestrum tot et tales probos et legales homines de balliva sua per quos rei veritas in premissis melius sciri poterit et inquiri. In cuius rei testimonium has litteras nostras fieri fecimus patentes. Teste meipso apud Lincoln' xxiij die Februarii anno regni nostri vicesimo nono per petitionem de consilio.

149A Royal writ to the sheriff of Northampton, ordering the inquest in 149. [23 Feb. 1301]

Rex vicecomiti Norht' salutem. Quia dilectus nobis in Christo abbas de Burgo Sancti Petri asserit maritagium Johannis filii et heredis Galfridi de Suthorp', et eciam maritagium Walteri filii et heredis Walteri de Ufford, qui quidem heredes sunt in custodia eiusdem abbatis, ad ipsum, et non ad nos pertinere debere, eo quod predicti Galfridus et Walterus de Ufforde et antecessores sui tenuerunt de abbatibus de Burgo Sancti Petri predecessoribus predicti abbatis in villa de Burgo Sancti Petri et Stok's juxta Undele per servicium militare diu antequam iidem Galfridus et Walterus quicquam tenuerunt de Johanne de Cameys in Loholm, quod de manerio de Torpel tenetur, quod nunc in manu nostra existit, per quod nos super premissis plenius certiorari, et eidem abbati ulterius quod fuerit fieri volentes in hac parte, assignavimus dilectos et fideles nostros Willelmum de Carleton', et Johannem de Kirkeby vel alterum ipsorum quem presentem esse contigerit, ad inquirendum per sacramentum proborum et legalium hominum de comitatu tuo per quos rei veritas melius sciri poterit, utrum predicti Galfridus et Walterus de Ufforde vel antecessores sui prius feoffati fuerunt tenendo de abbate de Burgo Sancti Petri predecessore predicti abbatis, an de predicto Johanne vel antecessoribus suis ut predictum est, nec ne, et si de abbatibus de Burgo Sancti Petri, tunc a quo tempore, et per quod servicium, et qualiter et quo modo, et si de predicto Johanne vel antecessoribus suis, tunc a quo tempore, et per quod servicium, et qualiter et quomodo. Et ideo tui precipimus quod ad certos dies et loca quos idem Willelmus et Johannes vel alter ipsorum tibi scire faciatis, venire faciatis coram eis, vel altero ipsorum tot et tales probos et legales homines de balliva tua per quos rei veritas in premissis melius sciri poterit et inquiri. Et habeas ibi hoc breve. Teste meipso apud Lincoln' xxiij° die Februarii anno regni nostri vicesimo nono, per petitionem de consilio.

149B Writ of William de Carleton' to the sheriff of Northampton ordering him to empanel jurors for an inquest on 5 April to establish whether John de Camoys granted the late Queen Eleanor the manors of Torpel and Upton, whether they were held of the abbot or another and on what terms; also to enquire about the enfeoffments of Geoffrey of Southorpe and Walter of Ufford as in 149; also to enquire whether the king's interests would benefit or be damaged it he were to grant the abbot the manors of Torpel and Upton in exchange for the manor of Cottingham. [19 Mar. 1301]

[fo. 63r] W[illelmus] de Carleton' vicecomiti Norhampton' salutem. Ex parte domini regis vobis mando quod venire facias coram me et W[altero] de Gloucestr' et J[ohanne] de Kirkeby apud Torpel die Mercurii in septimana Pasche, lx tam milites quam alios probos et legales homines de visnu de Torpel, Upton', Burgo Sanct Petri, Stokes juxta Undele, Loholm et Cotingham', ad inquirendum per sacramentum eorumdem, si Johannes de Cameys maneria de Torpel et Upton' antequam illa dimisit Alianore quondam regine Anglie consortis regis, tenuit de abbate de Burgo Sancto Petri, vel de alio, et si de predictis abbatibus, tunc per quod servicium, et qualiter et quo modo, prout in brevi domini regis vobis inde directi plenius continetur. Et eciam ad inquirendum utrum Galfridus de Suthorp' et Walterus de Ufforde vel antecessores sui prius feoffati fuerunt, tenendis de abbatibus de Burgo Sancti Petri in eadem villa et Stokes juxta Undele, an de Johanne de Camoys et antecessoribus suis in Loholm quod de manerio de Torpel tenetur. Et si de predictis abbatibus, tunc a quo tempore et per quod servicium, et qualiter et quomodo secundum tenorem brevis regis quod vobis inde venit. Et eciam ad inquirendum si sit ad comodum, vel ad dampnum domini regis aut aliorum si idem dominus rex det et concedat abbati et conventui de Burgo Sancti Petri maneria de Torpel et Upton' cum pertinenciis, habenda et tenenda sui et successoribus suis imperpetuum in escambium pro manerio de Cotingham. Et si sit ad dampnum vel ad comodum domini regis aut aliorum, tunc ad quod comodum, vel quod dampnum secundum tenorem brevis eiusdem domini regis vobis inde directi. Et habeat ibi nomina juratorum, brevia domini regis et hoc breve. Dat' apud Batesford' xix die Marcii.

149C Royal writ to the treasurer and chamberlain notifying them that William de Carleton and John de Kirkeby would be returning the verdict of the inquest ordered in 149 to the Exchequer and also ordering them to search the rolls and memoranda of the Exchequer to discover anything to show which was the prior enfeoffment. [12 May 1301]

Rex thesaurario et camerario suis salutem. Cum nuper assignassemus dilectos et fideles nostros Willelmum de Carleton' et Johannem de Kirkeby ad inquirendum per sacramentum proborum et legalium hominum de comitatu Norhampt', per quos rei veritas melius sciri posset utrum Galfridus de Suthorp' et Walterus de Ufforde et antecessores sui prius feoffati fuerunt tenendis de abbate de Burgo Sanct Petri et predecessoribus suis abbatibus eiusdem loci in villa de Burgo Sancti Petri et Stokes juxta Undele per servicium militare, an de Johanne de Camoys et antecessoribus suis in Loholm quod de manerio de Torpel quod nunc est in manu nostra tenetur, prout in litteris nostris patentibus eisdem Willelmo et Johanni inde confectis plenius continetur, ac iidem Willelmus et Johannes inquisitionem inde fecerint et eam coram vobis returnaverint in Scaccario predicto. Nos nichilominus per vos super premissis plenius certiorari volentes vobis mandamus quod scrutatis rotulos et memoranda Scaccarii predicti id quod inveniri contigerit, una cum inquisitione predicta nobis sub sigillo eiusdem Scaccarii sine dilatione mittatur et hoc breve. Teste me ipso apud Keneseye xij die Maii anno etcetera.

149D Reply to 149C reporting that there is nothing relevant in the rolls and memoranda of the Exchequer. [12 May–30 June 1301]

Responsio istius brevis talis est. Scrutari fecimus rotulos et memoranda Scaccarii juxta [fo. 63v] tenorem istius mandati, nec est aliud compertum de isto mandato contentis, quam in inquisitione quam cum hoc brevi vobis mittimus continetur.

149E Verdict of the inquest ordered in no. 149 and held on 5 April 1301. The verdict of the jurors was that, at his death, Geoffrey of Southorpe held tenements of the abbot in Southorpe, Gunthorpe, Hemington and Stoke Doyle for the service of three knights, and that his ancestors had thus held, time out of mind; also that Geoffrey in the fifth year of Edward I had acquired a mesuage and 2 carucates of land from Ralph of Lolham, part of the manor of Torpel for the service of half a knight's fee and suit of court at Torpel. The jurors also declare that Walter of Ufford, at his death, held a mesuage and half a virgate of land in Peterborough of the abbot for the service of a twentieth part of a knight's fee, and that Thomas of Ufford and his other ancestors had held time out of mind, viz. from the time of Richard I. Also that after the time of Richard I, Thomas of Ufford, steward of Peterborough, acquired various tenements in Ufford, held of the lord of Torpel, rendering 2s and half a pound of cumin p.a., suit of court, scutage of 2s 11d when it is levied at 40s, 7d for sheriff's aid and ward of Rockingham castle. [5 April 1301]

Inquisitio[1] apud Torpel capta coram Willemo de Carleton', Waltero de Glouc', et Johanne de Kirkeby die Mercurii in septimana Pasche; videlicet quinto die Aprilis anno regni regis Edwardi vicesimo nono, super maritagio Johannis filii et heredis Galfridi de Suthorp' et eciam maritagio Walteri filii et heredis Walteri de Offorde, qui quidem heredes sunt in custodia abbatis de Burgo Sancti Petri et quorum maritagia idem abbas asserit ad ipsum, et non ad regem pertinere debere, eo quod predicti Galfridus et Walterus de Offorde et antecessores sui tenuerunt de abbatibus de Burgo Sancti Petri predecessoribus predicti abbatis in villa de Burgo Sancti Petri et Stokes juxta Undele per servicium militare diu ante quam idem Galfridus et Walterus quicquam tenuerunt de Johanne de Camoys in Loholm, quod de manerio de Torpel tenetur, quod nunc est in manu regis utrum videlicet predicti Galfridus et Walterus de Offorde vel antecessores sui prius feoffati fuerunt tenendis de abbatibus de Burgo Sancti Petri predecessoribus predicti abbatis an de predicto Johanne vel antecessoribus suis ut predictum est, et si de abbatibus de Burgo Sancti Petri, tunc a quo tempore, et per quod servicium, et qualiter et quo modo, et si de predicto Johanne vel antecessoribus suis, tunc a quo tempore, et per quod servicium, et qualiter et quo modo, per sacramentum Hugonis de Gorham, Roberti de Veer, Henrici de Tichemersch', Willelmi Jordan, Nicholai de Sancto Marco, Johannis de Folkesworth', Petri de Burlee, Willelmi de Picworth', Henrici le Lord', Willelmi Walrand', Johannis Lucas, et Johannis de Adington' juratorum. Qui dicunt super sacramentum suum, quod Galfridus de Suthorp' tenuit die quo obiit de abbate de Burgo Sancti Petri quedam tenementa in Suthorp', Gunthorp', Hemington' et Stokes per servicium trium feodorum militum, et antecessores predicti Galfridi tenuerunt eadem tenementa de predecessoribus predicti abbatis per eadem servicia, a tempore quo non extat memoria. Et dicunt quod idem Galfridus anno quinto regis nunc perquisivit de quodam Radulpho de Loholm unum mesuagium et duas carucatas terre cum pertinenciis in villa de Loholm per servicium dimidii feodi militis, tenendum de domino manerio de Torpel, et per sectam ad curiam eiusdem manerii de tribus septimanis in tres septimanas. Dicunt eciam quod Walterus de Offorde tenuit die quo obiit de abbate de Burgo Sancti Petri unum mesuagium et dimidiam virgatam terre cum pertinenciis in villa Burgi Sancti Petri per servicium vicesime partis feodi unius militis et quod quidam Thomas de Offord', antecessor dicti Walteri, et alii antecessores sui tenuerunt eadem tenementa de abbatibus predecessoribus predicti abbatis, per idem servicium a tempore quo non extat memoria; videlicet ante tempus regis Ricardi, et postea tempore eiusdem regis Ricardi fuit dictus Thomas senescallus de Burgo Sancti Petri, et tunc temporis perquisivit quedam [fo. 64r] tenementa perticulatim de diversis in villa de Offorde, tenenda de capitalibus dominis feodi manerii de Torpel per servicium duorum solidorum et dimidie libre cymini per annum et per sectam faciendam ad curiam manerii de Torpel de tribus septimanis in tres septimanas. Et ad scutagium, quando scutagium est ad xl solidos, tunc reddet ad scutagium duos solidos et undecim denarios, et ad plus, plus, et ad minus minus. Et vij d. pro custodia castri de Rokingham, et pro auxilio vicecomitis recipiendo per manus ballivorum abbatis de Burgo Sancti Petri qui tenet hundredum de Nasso, quos quidem septem denarios ballivi manerii de Torpel percipient de predicto Waltero et heredibus suis, et eosdem solvent ballivis dicti abbatis in forma predicta. In cuius rei testimonium predicti juratores huic inquisitioni sigilla sua apposuerunt.

1 Enrolled *Cal. Close, 1296–1302*, p. 496, where it is translated in full.

149F Memorandum that this was how the abbot reached an accommodation over the aforementioned marriages and that the inquest was enrolled on the close rolls for June 1301 and that verdict, writs, letters patent and close are filed in the Chancery files.

Et ideo faciat predictus abbas comodum suum de maritagio heredum predictorum.[1] Et memorandum quod ista inquisitio irrotulatur in dorso clausarum in mense Junii anno regni regis Edwardi vicesimo nono. Et ista eadem inquisitio cum brevibus patentibus et clausis affilata est inter inquisitiones in Cancellaria in quarta parte recte in fine.

1 Also on the close rolls following the enrolment of no. 149E.

150 Letter from Edward I to Pope Boniface VIII setting out the history of the kings of England and Scotland in support of his claim to feudal overlordship. He also complained of atrocities committed by the invading Scottish army, including cutting off women's breasts, blocking the doors and setting fire to schools with children inside and the massacre of infants in cradles and mothers in labour. [7 May 1301]

Sanctissimo[1] in Christo patri domino B[onifacio] divina providentia sancte Romane, ac universalis ecclesie summo pontifici Edwardus eiusdem gracia rex Anglie, dominus Hibernie et dux Aquitanie, devota pedum oscula beatorum. Infra scripta, non in forma nec in figura judicii, set omnino extra judicium pro serenanda[2] sancte paternitatis vestre conscientia, vobis transmittimus exhibenda, altissimus[3] inspector cordium nostre scrinio memorie, indelebili stilo novit inscribi, quod antecessores et progenitores nostri reges Anglie juris superioris, et directi dominii ab antiquissimis retro temporibus regno Scotie, et ipsius regibus in temporalibus et annexis eisdem prefuerunt, et ab eisdem regibus, pro regno Scotie et eiusdem regni proceribus, a quibus habere volebant, ligia homagia, et fidelitatis juramenta receperunt, et nos juris et dominii possessionem continuantes, huiusmodi pro tempore nostro, eadem tam a rege Scotie, quam ab ipsius regni proceribus recepimus. Quinimmo tanta juris et dominii prerogativa super regnum Scotie, et eiusdem reges gaudebant, quod regnum ipsum suis fidelibus conferebant, reges eciam ex causis justis amovebant, et constituerunt sub se loco ipsorum alios regnaturos, que procul dubio ab antiquo notoria fuerunt et existunt. Licet aliud forte paternis[4] auribus per pacis emulos et rebellionis filios fuerit falsa insinuatione suggestum, quorum machinosa et imaginaria figmenta vestra providencia quesumus aspernetur.[5] Sub temporibus itaque Ely et Samuelis prophete, vir strenuus quidam, et insignis, Brutus nomine de genere Trojanorum post [fo. 64v] excidium urbis Troie cum multis nobilibus Trojanorum applicuit in quandam insulam tunc Albion vocatam, a gigantibus inhabitatam, quibus sua et suorum devictis potentia et occisis, eam, nomine suo Britanniam, socios que suos Britones appellavit, et edificavit civitatem quam Trinovantum nunccupavit, que modo Londonia nominatur.[6] Et postea regnum suum tribus filiis suis dimisit, scilicet, Locrinio primogenito, illam partem Britannie, que nunc Anglia dicitur, et Albanacto secundo natu, illam partem, que tunc Albania a nomine Albanacti[7], nunc vero Scotia nuccupatur [sic]. Et Cambro filio minori partem illam nomine suo tunc Cambria vocatam, que nunc Wallia vocitatur. Reservata Locrinio seniori regia dignitate. Itaque biennio post mortem Bruti applicuit in Albania, quidam rex Hunorem nomine Humber Albanactum fratrem Locrinii occidit, quo audito, Locrinius rex Britonum persecutus est eum, qui fugiens, submersus est in flumine quod de nomine suo Humber vocatur, et sic Albania revertitur ad dictum Locrinium. Item Dunwallo rex Britonum Staterium regem Scotie sibi rebellem occidit, et terram eius in dedicionem recipit. Item duo filii Dunwallonis scilicet Bellinus et Brennius inter se regnum patris sui diviserunt. Ita quod Belinus senior diadema insule cum Britannia Wallia, et Cornubia possideret. Brennius vero sub eo regnaturus Scotiam acciperet, petebat enim Trojana consuetudo ut dignitas hereditatis primogenito proveniret. Item Arturus rex Britonum, princeps famosissimus, Scotiam sibi rebellem subjecit, et pene totam gentem delevit, et postea quemdam nomine Anguselum in regem Scotie prefecit, et cum postea idem rex Arturus apud Civitatem Legionum festum faceret celeberimum, interfuerunt ibidem omnes reges sibi subjecti, inter quos Anguselus rex Scotie servicium pro regno Scotie exhibens debitum, gladium regis Arturi detulit ante ipsum, et successive omnes reges Scotie omnibus regibus Britonum fuere subjecti. Succedentibus autem regibus Anglis in predicta insula, et ipsius monarchiam et dominium optinentibus subsequenter, Edwardus dictus senior filius Eluredi[8] regis Anglie, Scotorum, Cumbrorum, et Stregwallorum reges sibi tanquam superiori domino subjectos, habuit et submissos. Adelstanus[9] rex Anglie Constantinum regem Scotorum sub se regnaturum constituit, dicens: 'Gloriosus est regem facere quam regem esse', et est dignum memoria quod idem Adelstanus intercedente sancto Johanne de Beverlaco, quondam archiepiscopo Ebor', Scotos rebellantes ei dimicavit, qui gracias Deo devote agens Deum exoravit, petens quatinus interveniente beato Johanne sibi aliquod signum evidens ostenderet quatinus tam succedentes, quam presentes cognoscere possent Scotos Anglorum regno jure subjugari, et videns quosdam scopulos juxta quemdam locum prope Dunbar in Scotia [fo. 65r] prominere, extracto gladio de vagina, percussit in silicem qui lapis ad ictum gladii, Dei virtute agente ita cavatur, ut mensura ulne longitudini possit coruptari[10], et huiusmodi rei hactenus evidens signum apparet, et in Beverlaco ecclesia in legenda sancti Johannis quasi singulis ebdomadis per annum ad laudem et honorem sancti Johannis pro miraculo recitatur. Et de hoc extat celebris memoria tam in Anglia quam in Scotia usque ad presentem diem. Item Constantinus rex Scotorum et Eugenius rex Cumbrorum, ad predictum regem Anglie Adelstanum post aliqualem dissentionem inter eos habitam venientes, se cum suis regnis eidem Adelstano dedidere, cuius facti gracia filium Constantini ipse Adelstanus de sacro fonte suscepit. Item Edredo regi Anglie Scoti sine bello se subdiderunt et eidem regi Edredo tanquam domino fidelitatem debitam juraverunt quodam Yricio rege super ipsos Scotos statuto.[11] Item cum Edgarus rex Anglie regem Scotorum Kinadium et Cumbrorum Malculmum regem plurimarum insularum, Malkum, aliosque quinque subregulos, scilicet Dunenaldum, Tyferth', Huwal, Jacob et Inchil, regem ipsum Edgarum in navi quadam prope proram sedentem per flumen Dehe remigare fecisset, fertur ipsum dixisse successores suos gloriari[12] se reges Anglorum esse cum tanta honore prerogativa fruenter, ut subjectam haberent tot regum potentiam. Post dictum Edgarum, successive successerunt reges Anglie, sanctus

Edwardus martir, Egelredus frater eius, Edmundus dictis Hirneside filius Egelredi, et Knutus[13] qui eorum temporibus regnum Scotie in sua subjectione pacifice tenuerunt, hoc dum taxat, excepto quod anno quindecimo regni Knuti[13] predicti. Idem Knutus[13] Scotiam rebellantem expeditione illuc ducta regem Scotie Malculmum parvo subegit negotio, subditus que est ei idem Malculmus, quibus Haraldus filius Kunti et Hardeknutus frater eius, unus post alium, reges Anglie successerunt, qui eis sic regnantibus sibi subjectionem regni Scotie pacifice habuerunt.
Item sanctus Edwardus rex Anglie regnum Scotie dedit Malcolmo filio regis Cumbrorum de se tenendum. Item Willelmus dictus bastardus rex Anglie, cognatus dicti Edwardi[14], a Malcolmo rege Scotorum tanquam a suo homine subdito, homagium cepit. Item Willelmo Ruffo regi Anglie, predictus Malcolmus rex Scotorum juramento fidelitatis subjectus fuit. Item predictus rex Willelmus Donenaldum de regno Scotie ex justis causis amovit, et loco eius[15] Duncanum filium Malcolmi regem Scotie prefecit, et recepit ab eo fidelitatis juramentum, dicto que Duncano dolose perempto, dictus rex Willelmus prefatum Dunenaldum qui iterum regnum Scotie invaserat, amovit ab eodem, et Edgarum filium dicti Malcolmi regem Scotie constituit, et eidem illud regnum donavit, cui successit Alexander frater eiusdem Edgari, concessu regis Anglie Henrici [fo. 65v] primi fratris dicti regis Willelmi Ruffi. Item Matilldi imperatrici filie et heredi regis Henrici predicti, rex Scotie David fecit homagium et fidelitatem. Item regi Anglorum Stephano Henricus filius dicti regis David homagium fecit. Item Willelmus rex Scotorum pro regno Scotie et David frater suus et comites et barones regni Scotie devenerunt homines Henrici filii regis Anglie Henrici secundi in crastino coronationis predicti Henrici filii Henrici secundi patre vivente, et fidelitatem ei juraverunt contra omnes homines, salva fidelitate debita patri viventi. Anno vero vicesimo regni regis Henrici secundi predicti, dictus Willelmus rex Scotorum rebellare incipiens venit in Northumbr' cum excercitu magno, et excercuit in populo stragem magnam, cui occurrentes milites comitatus Ebor' apud Alnewyk' ipsum ceperunt, et dicto Henrico regi Anglie reddiderunt, anno sequenti, scilicet xv kalendas Marcii[16], est idem Willelmus permissus liber abire. Postea vero apud Ebor' anno eodem xvij kalendas Septembris, idem Willelmus rex Scotorum de consensu prelatorum, comitum, baronum, procerum, et aliorum magnatum, regni Scotie domino suo regi Anglie Henrico filio Matillde imperatricis predicto suis litteris patentibus cavisse noscitur quod ipse et heredes et successores sui reges Scotie, episcopi et abbates[17], comites eciam et barones, et alii homines regni Scotie, de quibus dominus rex habere voluerit, facient regibus Anglie homagium fidelitatem et ligantiam, ut ligio domino contra omnem hominem. Et in signum subjectionis huiusmodi idem Willelmus rex Scotie capellum, lanceam, et cellam suos super altare ecclesie beati Petri Ebor' optulit, que in eadem ecclesia usque in hodiernum diem remanent, et observantur.[18] Item episcopi, comites et barones dicti regni Scotie

conventionaverunt ut verbis eiusdem conventionis utamur, domino regi et Henrico filio suo predictis quod si rex Scotie aliquo casu a fidelitate regum Anglie et conventione predicta recederet, ipsi cum domino rege Anglie tenebunt, sicut cum ligio domino suo contra regem Scotie, quousque ad fidelitatem regis Anglie redeat. Quam quidem compositionem felicis recordationis, Gregorius papa ix[19] in diversis rescriptis regibus Anglie et Scotie directis mandavit firmiter observari, continentibus eciam inter cetera quod Willelmus et Alexander reges Scotorum regibus Anglie Johanni[20] et Henrico ligium homagium et fidelitatem fecerunt que tenentur successores eorum comites et barones regni Scotie ipsis et suis successoribus exhibere, et iterum quod idem rex Scotie homo ligius sit ipsius Henrici regis Anglie, et eidem fidelitatis prestiterit juramentum, quo se principaliter astrinxit, quod in ipsius regis et regni Anglie detrimentum nichil debeat penitus attemptare. Et papa Clemens scribens regi Anglie pro Johanne episcopo sancti Andree, expulso ab episcopatu suo per regem Scotie, inter cetera rogavit, quod Willelmum regem Scotie moneret, et induceret, et si necesse fuerit districtione regali qua ei preminet, et concessa sue regie celsitudini potestate compelleret, ut dicto episcopo, omnem rancorem remitteret [fo. 66r] et episcopatum suum eum habere in pace permitteret. Et post conventionem predictam in ecclesia beati Petri Ebor' coram predictis regibus Anglie et Scotie et David fratre suo et universo populo, episcopi[21], comites, barones, milites de terra regis Scotie juraverunt domino regi Anglie, et Henrico filio suo, et heredibus eorum fidelitatem contra omnem hominem sicut ligiis dominis suis. Et idem Willelmus rex Scotorum ad mandatum regis Henrici predicti venit apud Norhampton' ad parliamentum domini sui, adducens secum omnes episcopos, abbates, priores tocius regni sui. Et venit eciam ad eiusdem regis Anglie mandatum in Normanniam. Et ideo idem rex Willelmus post decessum regis dicti Henrici veniens Cantuar' Ricardo regi Anglie filio et heredi dicti Henrici fecit homagium, quo Ricardo viam universe carnis ingresso sepefatus Willelmus Johanni regi Anglie fratri et heredi predicti regis Ricardi extra civitatem Lincoln' supra quemdam pontem[22] in conspectu omnis populi fecit homagium, et juravit ei fidelitatem super crucem Huberti tunc Cantuarensis archiepiscopi, et eidem Johanni tanquam domino suo per cartam suam concessit quod Alexander filius suus, Henrico filio regis Anglie Johannis, tanquam[23] ligio domino suo contra omnes mortales fidem et fidelitatem tenerent, a quo quidem Willelmo rege Scotorum post modum pro eo, quod desponderat filiam suam comiti Bolonie preter ipsius regis Johannis domini sui assensum pro transgressione et temeraria presumptione huiusmodi debitam satisfactionem accepit. Item Alexander rex Scotorum sororius noster regi Anglie Henrico[24] patri nostro pro regno Scotie et postea nobis homagium fecit. Vacante deinde regno Scotie post mortem Alexandri regis illius et subsequenter post mortem Margarete eiusdem regni Scotie regine et domine neptis nostre, episcopi, abbates, priores, comites, barones, proceres[25], et ceteri nobiles et communitates tocius regni Scotie, ad nos tanquam ad legittimum[26] defensorem ducem, aurigam capitaneum, et dominum capitalem eiusdem regni sic vacantis, gratis et spontanea voluntate accedentes, prout tenebantur de jure, jus nostrum progenitorum et antecessorum nostrorum, ac possessionem superioris et directi dominii in regno eodem, et ipsius regni subjectionem, ex certa scientia pure simpliciter et absolute recognoverunt, et prestitis nobis ab eisdem tanquam superiori et directo domino Scotie debitis et consuetis, fidelitatem juramentis, ac civitatibus, burgis, villis, castris ac ceteris munitionibus regni eiusdem in manu nostra traditis, ad custodiam eiusdem regni, certos jure nostro regio officiales et ministros deputavimus, quibus ipsi tempore vacationis huiusmodi concorditer fuerant obedientes, intendentes in nostris preceptis regiis et mandatis. Postmodum autem diverse persone super successione in dictum regnum Scotie jure hereditario inter se contendentes, ad nos tanquam ad superiorem dominum regni Scotie accesserunt, petentes super jure succedendi in regnum predictum sibi per nos exhiberi justicie complementum. Volentes et expresse consentientes, coram nobis tanquam superiore, et directo domino [fo. 66v] regni Scotie stare juri.[27] Et demum earumdem partium petitionibus et juribus coram nobis tanquam coram superiore et directo domino judicialiter proponitis, ac sufficienter auditis, rimatis, examinatis et diligenter intellectis, in presencia omnium prelatorum et nobilium quasi tocius regni Scotie, et de voluntate et assensu expresso eorumdem procedentes, Johannem de Balliolo debite prefecimus in regem Scotorum, quem tunc in successione eiusdem regni heredem legitimum, et jura habere invenimus potiora, qui quidem prelati, comites, barones, communitates ac ceteri incole eiusdem regni huiusmodi sentenciam nostram expresse omolgarunt[28], acceptarunt et expresse approbarunt et ipsum Johannem de mandato nostro virtute huiusmodi judicii in regem suum admiserunt. Ac idem Johannes rex Scotie pro regno suo, prestito nobis homagio debito et consueto ac fidelitatis juramento, ad parliamenta nostra de mandato nostro veniens[29], eiusdem tanquam noster subditus sicut alii de regno nostro interfuit, et nostris tanquam domini sui superioris dicti regni Scotie paruit beneplacitis et mandatis nobis in omnibus obediens et intendens, quousque idem Johannes rex Scotie et prelati, comites, barones, nobiles, communitates ac ceteri incole majores regni eiusdem ex preconcepta malicia et prelocuta, ac preordinata, proditione, factiones, confederationes, conspirationes[30] et conjurationes in exheredationem nostram, et heredum nostrorum ac regni nostri contra debitum homagii sui ac fidelitatis juramentum inter se inierunt, in crimen lese majestatis nequiter incidendo. Unde cum premissa ex fideli relatione fama publica consenciente, ad aures nostras pervenissent, volentes futuris periculis precavere, que ex hiis et aliis possent nobis regno nostro et regni nostri incolis verisimiliter provenire, pro assecuratione regni nostri accessimus ad confinium regni utriusque pluries mandantes eidem Johanni tunc regi Scotie, quod ad certa loca in confinio predicto ad nos accederet super premissis et aliis pro statu tranquilitate et pace utriusque regni assecurationem facturus et alia per nos et consilium nostrum sibi exponenda auditurus, et super hiis et ea contingentibus justiciam recepturus[31], qui spretis mandatis nostris contumaciter[32] in sua persistens perfidia ad bellicos apparatus, cum episcopis, prelatis et clericis[33], comitibus, baronibus regni Scotie ac eciam aliis exteris conducticiis contra nos regnum nostrum et incolas regni nostri hostiliter se convertens accinxit, et ad hostiles aggressus et incursus procedens regnum nostrum invasit quasdam[34] villas regni nostri Anglie per se et suos depredatus est, easque vastavit incendio, homines nostros interfecit, et non nullis nautis nostris per eos peremptis naves hominum nostrorum regni Anglie comburi fecit, et e vestigio redditis nobis homagio et fidelitate per regem Scotie, tam pro se quam pro aliis quibuscumque regni sui incolis per verba efectum [sic] diffidentie exprimentia[35], comitatus nostros Northumbr', Cumbr' et Westmerl' regni nostri Anglie, congregato ingenti excercitu hostiliter per se et suos invasit, stragem [fo. 67r] innumeram hominum nostrorum, incendia monasteriorum, ecclesiarum, et villarum, in humane perpetrando et patriam undique depopulando, infantes in cunis, mulieres in puerperio decubantes, in misericordi et atroci sevitia[36] trucidarunt, et quod auditu orrendum est, a non nullis mulieribus mamillas atrociter abciderunt, parvos clericulos, primas litteras[37] et gramaticam addiscentes ad numerum circiter ducentorum in scolis existentes, obstructis hostiis scolarum igne supposito concremarunt. Nos que cernentes tot dampna, obprobria, facinora et injurias in exhereditationem nostram et destrutionem populi regni nostri proditionaliter irrogari nec volentes ratione juramenti quo ad conservationem jurium corone regni nostri sumus astricti, tam execranda, detestanda, et nefanda facinora[38] ulterius tolerare nec jura nostra relinquere indefensa, cum idem Johannes et gens Scotorum regni subditi per leges, se justificari minime permisissent, ipso regno Scotie quod a[39] longissimis temporibus sicut superius exprimitur, nobis et progenitoribus nostris feudale extitit, ex causis premissis commisso, deinde bello juxta leges et consuetudines regni nostri contra eos de consilio procerum et magnatum nostrorum indicto, contra dictum Johannem et gentem Scotorum vires potentie nostre extendimus[40], prout de jure nobis licuit et processimus contra ipsos, tanquam notorie proditores, contumaces et publicos hostes nostros. Subacto itaque regno Scotie jure proprietatis nostre ditioni, prefatus Johannes rex Scotie, ipsum regnum Scotie quatenus de facto tenuit sponte, pure, et absolute reddidit in manum nostram proditiones et scelera memorata coram nobis et proceribus regni nostri publice recognoscens. Quo peracto prelati, comites, barones, nobiles et communitates regni Scotie, quos ad pacem nostram regiam suscepimus subsequenter homagia et fidelitates nobis tanquam inmediato et proprio domino eiusdem regni Scotie fecerunt ac eciam prestiterunt ac redditis nobis eiusdem regni civitatibus, villis, castris, munitionibus ac ceteris locis omnibus ad dictum regnum spectantibus officiales nostros et ministros ad regimen eiusdem regni Scotie prefecimus jure nostro. Cumque jure pleni dominii in possessione eiusdem regni existere dinoscamur, omittere non possumus, nec debemus, quin insolentiam subditorum nostrorum rebellium[41], si quos invenerimus, preminencia regia prout justum fuerit et expedire viderimus reprimamus. Quia vero ex premissis et aliis constat evidenter et notorium existit quod prelibatum regnum Scotie tam ratione proprietatis quam possessionis ad nos pertinet pleno jure, nec quicquam facerimus vel caverimus scripto vel facto, sicuti nec possemus, per que juri aut possessioni predictis debeat aliqualiter derogari, sanctitati vestre humiliter supplicamus quatinus premissa provida meditatione pensantes, ex illis, vestri motum animi dignemini informare, suggestionibus contrariis emulorum in hac parte vobis factis fidem, si placet, nullatenus adhibendo quinimmo [fo. 67v] statum nostrum et jura nostra regia subscripta[42] habere velitis, si placet, paternis[43] affectibus commendata. Conservet vos altissimus ad regimen ecclesie sue sancte per tempora prospera et longeva. Dat' apud Kemeseye septimo die Maii anno Domini M° CCC° primo regni nostri vicesimo nono.

1 There is an almost identical text in *Foedera*, vol. I, pt. II, pp. 932–3 and two other texts, which differ considerably, in ed. H. T. Riley, *Chronica et Annales: Willelmi Rishanger* (Rolls Series, London, 1865), pp. 200–8; ed. H. Rothwell, *The Chronicle of Walter of Guisborough*, (Camden Soc., lxxxix, 1957), pp. 338–44. The more important variations from the Peterborough text are noted. The letter is edited and translated in E. L. G. Stones, *Anglo-Scottish Relations 1174–1328: Some Selected Documents* (Oxford, 1970), pp. 192–219. For commentary, Stones, Simpson, *Edward I and the Throne of Scotland*, passim, but especially vol. I, pp. 154–6.

2 *proferanda* in Rishanger.

3 *Guisborough* text begins here.

4 For *procul dubio ... forte paternis* read *proculdubio notoria fuisse, et esse creduntur, apud omnes licet aliud forsan paternis* in *Rishanger* and *Guisborough.*

5 For *vestra ... aspernetur* read *ut vestre sanctitatis oculus avertatur, suppliciter quesumus, et paternam clementiam eccelentiam devotis affectibus exoramus* in *Rishanger* and *Guisborough.* A much shortened early history then follows in *Guisborough.*

6 *edificavit ... nominatur* omitted in *Rishanger.*

7 *a nomine Albanacti* omitted in *Rishanger.*

8 *Alfredi* in *Rishanger.*

9 *Guisborough* text resumes in the same form as the Peterborough text.

10 *coaptari* in other texts.

11 *quodam Yricio ... statuto* omitted in Guisborough.

12 *scilicet ... gloriari* texts in *Rishanger* and *Guisborough* differ from Peterborough and each other.

13 *Hyricus* in Guisborough.

14 *cognatus dicti Edwardi* omitted in *Rishanger.*

15 *et loco eius* omitted in *Rishanger.*

16 *Maii* in *Rishanger.*

17 *priores* included in *Rishanger.*

18 *Et in signum ... observantur* omitted in *Guisborough.* Marginated symbol.

19 *quintus* in *Rishanger.*

20 *Henrico* in *Rishanger.*

21 *episcopi* omitted in *Rishanger*.
22 *montem* in other texts. Either would be feasible given the river and the hill on which the minster is situated.
23 *Alexander ... tanquam*, somewhat fuller text in *Rishanger*.
24 *Henrici* in MS.
25 *proceres* omitted in *Rishanger*.
26 *legittimum* omitted in *Rishanger*.
27 For *regni ... juri* read *in omnibus ordinandis stare et obtemperare* in *Rishanger* and *Guisborough*. The following sentence is fuller here and in *Guisborough*.
28 *omolgarunt* omitted from *Rishanger*.
29 *ad parliamento ... veniens* differs in *Rishanger* and *Guisborough* text, which omit *de mandato nostro*.
30 *proditione ... conspirationes* fuller in *Rishanger* and *Guisborough*.
31 *utriusque regni ... recepturus* fuller in *Rishanger* and *Guisborough*.
32 *contumaciter* omitted in *Rishanger* and *Guisborough*.
33 *et clericis* omitted in *Rishanger* and *Guisborough*.
34 *quasdas* in MS.
35 For *per verba ... exprimentia* read *per litteras eiusdem regis verba offensionum exprimentes, et inter alia, verba diffidationis continentes* in *Rishanger* and a similar, but not identical text in *Guisborough*.
36 *in misericordi ... sevitia* differs in *Rishanger* and *Guisborough*.
37 *primam tonsuram* in *Rishanger*.
38 For *tam ... facinora* read *premissa facinora ulterius concelare* in *Rishanger* and *Guisborough*.
39 *ad* in MS.
40 *deinde ... extendimus* substantially shorter in *Rishanger* and *Guisborough*.
41 *rebellum* in MS.
42 *supradicta* in other texts.
43 *promptis* in *Rishanger* and *Guisborough*.

151 Grant by the abbot and convent to John Marmyon', knight, who holds the manor of Luddington, in Northamptonshire and other tenements in Lincolnshire from them for the service of three knights, suit of court at Castor and a pair of gilt spurs, and who has conceded to them the manor of Lullington, member of the manor of Luddington, which John son of Thomas of Oundle held of him for the service of half a knight. In order not to be disadvantaged by this, John and his heirs may hold the remainder of the tenements for the service of two and a half knights and a pair of gilt spurs alone. The abbey has further undertaken to indemnify John for any demands in respect of suit of court at Castor or service for the manor of Lullington, made by royal ministers during a vacancy. It has also granted that John's name and that of his family be written in the abbey's martyrology so that they may share in its masses and prayers. [3 Aug. 1304]

Universis[1] Christi fidelibus ad quos noticiam hoc presens scriptum pervenerit Godefridus Dei gracia abbas de Burgo Sancti Petri et eiusdem loci conventus salutem in Domino sempiternam. Cum dominus Johannes Marmyon' miles de nobis et predecessoribus nostris manerium de Ludyngton' cum pertinenciis in comitatu Narhamton' [sic] et eciam alia tenementa in eodem comitatu et in comitatu Linc' de fiodo [sic] nostro tenuerit per servicium trium fiodorum militum et sectam ad curiam manerii de Castre de tribus septimanis in tres septimanas et per servicium unius paris calcarum deauratorum, ac idem Johannes de mera et libera voluntate sua nobis concesserit quod manerium de Lullinton' cum pertinenciis quod est membrum predicti manerii de Ludington' quod de eo tenebatur per servicium dimidii fiodi [sic] unius militis de Johanne filio Thome de Undele possimus recipere et nobis et successoribus nostris inperpetuum appropriare. Nos volentes predictum dominum Johannem et heredes suos conservare indempnes concessimus pro nobis et successoribus nostris quod predictus Johannes et heredes sui totum reseduum [sic] tenementorum predictorum quod de fiodo [sic] nostro tenuit in ce ...[2] a brevibus [?] predict' sibi et heredibus suis de nobis et successoribus nostris de cetero teniat [sic] per servicium duorum fiodorum [sic] militum et dimidium tantum et per servicium unius paris calcarium deauratorum. Ita videlicet quod nec nos nec successores nostri de predicto Johanne seu eius heredibus pro predictis tenementis de cetero sectam ad curiam nostram de Castre nec aliquid aliud servicium preter servicium predictum poterimus exigere clamare seu vendicare inperpetuum. Concessimus eciam quod si predictus Johannes vel heredes sui tempore vacationis per ministros domini regis in aliquo graventur seu dampnum incurrerint pro secta curie de Castre seu ratione alicuius alterius servicii dictum manerium de Lullington' contingent quod successores nostri omni ad[3] statum creationis abbatis pervenerint prefato Johanni et eius heredibus ad plenam resitutionem dampnorum suorum et[4] expensarum decetero teniantur [sic]. Preterea concessimus eidem Johanni quod nomen suum et nomen uxoris sue et nomina patris et matris sue et antecessorum suorum et heredum suorum scribantur in martilagio nostro ut specialem tam missarum et orationum quam aliorum beneficiorum in nostro monasterio factorum habeant participatione. Et ne hoc factum nostrum a memoria exstancium sive futurorum decidere possit, presens scriptum sigillis nostris roboravimus. Hiis testibus, domino Rogero de Hecham, domino Johanne de Bosco, militibus, domino Roberto Marmyon', Johanne de Undele, Willelmo de [fo. 68r] Hoveden', Bernardo de Caster, Johanne de Shenlebi [?] et aliis. Dat' in capitulo nostro die Lune proxima post festum sancti Petri advincula anno Domini M° tricentesimo quarto et anno regni regis Edwardi filii regis Henrici tricesimo secundo etcetera.

1 Inserted in a notably later medieval hand. Also in Soc. of Antiquaries, MS 38, fo. 49r–v and BL, Cott. Cleop. C ii, fos 83r–4r, where the witness clause is omitted.

2 *comitatu* interlined. Other texts read *tenuit in comitatu predicto.*

3 *ad* interlined.

4 *et* interlined.

152 Entry from the royal records concerning the abbot's payment of £100 for the farm of Torpel and Upton, formerly held by Queen Eleanor and granted to the abbey at the king's pleasure from 10 Feb. 1291. The abbey does not owe £600 for the preceding nine years because Queen Eleanor's holdings were temporarily handed over to John Bacun and his associates so that her executors could make provision for her soul from the revenues. The Queen had been granted the manors by John de Camoys and the abbot and convent paid the farm to her executors from 9 Feb. 1291 until Michaelmas 1296. In that year, the king took all her holdings into his own hand, as recorded in the memoranda for the following year. The abbey owes £7 2s 7d for part of that year. [29 Sept. 1299–29 Sept. 1300]

In rotulo xxviij regis E[dwardi] filii regis Henrici.[1]

Abbas et conventus de Burgo Sancti Petri reddunt compotum de C li. de firma maneriorum de Thorpel et Upton' cum pertinenciis que fuerunt Alianore regine et consortis regis. Tenenda per talem firmam a x die Februarii anno xix quamdiu rex placuerit sicut continet in originalia anni xix. Reddendo unam medietatem ad Scaccarium Pasche et aliam medietatem ad Scaccarium sancti Michaelis. Et DCCCC li. de eadem de ix annis preter usque annum xix computand'. In Thesauro CCC xlij li. v s. iiij d. per vij tallias. Et debent DC lvij li. xiiij s. viij d.; videlicet de quadam parte huius anni et annorum xix xx xxi xxij xxiij xxiiij. Set non debent summam de DC li. de predictis vj annis per breve regis ad huc inter communia de anno xx in quo continetur quod omnes exitus terrarum et tenementorum que fuerunt in manu Alienore nuper regine consortis regis die quo obiit ex dono regis Henrici vel regis nunc, aut aliunde ex perquisito ipius consortis regis percepti, post mortem ipsius regine liberentur Johanni Bacun et sociis suis, assignato per regem ad recipiendum exitos predictos, et per ordinationem executorum eiusdem in pios usus pro anima eiusdem regine convertendum, et quod thesaurarius et barones de terris et tenementis, aut aliis bonis de exitibus eorumdem, in nullo se intromittant, donec rex aliud inde perceperit. Que quidem regina maneria predicta tempore suo habuit et perquisivit de Johanne de Camoys. Et iidem abbas et conventus predictam firmam predictis executoribus, per manus eiusdem Johannis Bacun et sociorum suorum, reddidit annuatim, a predicto x die Februarii anno xix usque festum sancti Michaelis anno xxiiij factum per predictos vi annos sicut idem Johannem in Scaccario recognovit, quo festo sancti Michaelis rex cepit in manum suam omnes terras et tenementa que fuerunt predicte A[lienore] regine consortis sue sicut continetur in memorand' anni xxv inter commissiones ubi terre que fuerit eiusdem regine committuntur diversis custodibus a tempore predicto. Et debent lvij li. xiiij s. viij d. de parte huius anni. Item reddant compotum de eodem debito. In Thesauro l li. xij s. j d. Et debent vij li. ij s. vij d. Et respondent infra.

1 See PRO, E/372/145. m. 5d.

153 Entry from the pipe roll for Northamptonshire recording that the abbot and convent render account for the remainder of the farm for Torpel and Upton, as above; for a 300 mark fine for service in the royal army in Scotland; for £21 6s 8d for various fines for John of Oundle, their bailiff; for £20 for defaults recorded under Nottingham; for £233 6s 8d outstanding from the 1000 mark fine for custody of the abbey during the vacancy and for 6s 6½d outstanding from the account of John of Oundle in Northamptonshire. Nothing paid because these debts were offset against the £500 from the crusading tenth which the abbey had handed over to the pope on behalf of the king. The abbey has ½d outstanding, which it remits to the king. They are quit. [29 Sept. 1299–29 Sept. 1300]

Abbas[1] et conventus de Burgo Sancti Petri reddunt compotum de vij li. ij s. vij d. de remanentia firme maneriorum de Thorpel et Upton' sicut supra continetur. Et CCC m. de fine pro servicio suo in exercitu regis in Scotia sicut supra continetur. Et xxj li. dim. m. de finibus diversorum pro Johanne de Undele ballivo suo. Et xvij li. xvij s. vj d. de finibus diversorum pro eodem Johanne in Linc'. Et xx li. pro plurimis defaltis que requiruntur supra eundem abbatem in Not'. Et CC xxxiij li. vj s. viij d. de remanentia finis mille marcarum pro custodia abbatie [fo. 68v] eiusdem domus habenda tempore vacationis, quem finem prior et conventus eiusdem domus fecerunt cum rege. Et vj s. vj d. ob. pro Johanne de Undele ballivo suo de remanentia compoti eiusdem Johannis sicut continetur in isto compoto in hoc comitatu. In Thesauro nichil. Et eisdem abbati et conventui in recompensationem quingentarum [librarum] que ad manus regis, de pecunia decime in subsidium Terre Sancte concesse in dicta abbathia deposita devenerunt, et in quibus ipsi abbas et conventus per litteras suas sigillo suo communi signatas pro rege erga summum pontificem se obligaverint, et de quibus eidem summo pontifici pro rege satisfecerunt D li. per breve regis cuius data est xxvij die Decembris[2] anno xxix. In quo continetur quod idem abbas et conventus per petitionem suam coram regis et consilio regis in parliamento regis apud Linc' exhibitam supplicarunt, quod cum ipsi nuper per predictas litteras suas patentes sigillo suo communi signatas pro regi in dictis D li. sterlingorum que ad manus regis de predicta pecunia dicte decime in subsidium Terre Sancte in regno Anglie concesse devenerunt, se erga predictum summum pontificem obligassent. Rexque per litteras suas patentes se obligaverint et successores suos prefatis abbati et conventui et successoribus suis ad plenam et integram eiusdem pecunie solutionem infra duos menses, postquam eisdem abbatis et conventui super hoc rex fuerit requisitus faciend', necnon ad ipsos inde conservandos indempnes, et iidem abbas et conventus virtute obligationis sue predicte de predictis D li. collectoribus dicte decime, per prefatum summum pontificem specialiter deputatis, iam ut asserunt satisfecerunt, rex vellet eisdem pecuniam predictam in debitis que regi debent ad Sccacarium regis predictum allocare. Rex igitur eorum supplicationem annuens in hac parte, mandavit thesaurario et baronibus per breve predictum quod si eis constiterit predictos abbatem et conventum predictas D li. pro rege persolvisse, tunc receptis ab eisdem litteris regis de indempnitate predictis D li. eis ad Scaccarium predictum in predictis debitis allocarent, qui quidem abbas et conventus per Johannem de Undel' ballivum suum predictum restituerunt thesaurario et baronibus predictas litteras regis de indempnitate predicta, necnon et litteras obligatorias ipsorum abbatis et conventus sigillo communi signatas, per quas ipsi summo pontifici, pro predicta pecunia obligati fuerint dampnatas, simul cum quod pupplico instrumento, solutionem predictarum D li. executoribus, ad colligendam et recipiendam dictam decimam per sedem apostolicam deputatis factam plenarie testificantur liberaverunt, que quidem littera regis de indempnitate predicta dampnata cum littera obligatoria et puplico instrumento predictis, dicti thesaurarius et barones in bursa huius compoti posuerunt. Et habent de superplus ob. quem regi remittunt. Et quieti sunt. In Norht' xxviij rotulo regis E[dwardi].

1 See PRO. E/372/145, m. 5d.
2 *Septembris* in PRO text.

154 Summary of the rents, farms and customs from the abbey's manors [n.d.]

[fo. 69r] Summe redditual' maneriorum abbathie Burgi subscriptorum; videlicet:

Burbyr'

Summa tocius redditus firme et consuetudines de termino natalis Domini cum termino sancti Martini	Cxiij s. viij d. ob. qa.
Summa de eisdem de termino Pasche cum termino Purificationis	vj li. x s. viij d.
Summa de eisdem de termino sancti Johannis baptiste	iiij li. xvij s. iij d.
Summa de eisdem de termino sancti Michaelis	xviij li. ij s. v d.
Summa tocius per annum xxxv li. iiij s. ob. qa.	

Eye

Summa tocius redditus, firme et cons' de termino natalis Domini cum termino sancti Martini	xlviij s. ix d. ob. qa.
Summa de eisdem de termino Pasche cum termino Purificationis	lxiiij s. vij d. ob. qa.
Summa de eisdem de termino sancti Johannis baptiste	lxxi s. v d. ob. qa.
Summa de eisdem de termino sancti Michaelis	xi li. vij s. x d. qa.
Summa tocius per annum xx li. xij s. ix d. ob.	

Thorp'

Summa tocius redditus, firme et cons' de termino natalis Domini cum termino sancti Martini	xxxv s. v d. ob. qa.
Summa de eisdem de termino Pasche cum termino Purificationis	lj s.
Summa de eisdem de termino sancti Johannis baptiste	xxiij s. ij d. ob. qa.
Summa de eisdem de termino sancti Michaelis	xj li. iiij s. vj d.
Summa tocius per annum xvj li. xiiij s. ij d. ob.	

Castre

Summa tocius redditus, firme, et consuetud' de termino natalis Domini cum termino sancti Martini	iiij li. xix s. qa.
Summa de eisdem de termino Pasche cum termino Purificationis	vj li. xj s.
Summa de eisdem de termino sancti Johannis baptiste	iiij li. v s. iiij d. qa.
Summa de eisdem de termino sancti Michaelis	xv li. xij s. v d. ob.
Summa tocius per annum xxxi li. viij s. viij d.	

Waltone

Summa tocius redditus, firme, et consuetud' de termino natalis Domini cum termino sancti Martini	xlvj s. x d. ob.
[fo. 69v] Summa de eisdem de termino Pasche cum termino Purificationis	lv s. ob.
Summa de eisdem de termino sancti Johannis baptiste	xxxiij s. ij d. ob.
Summa de eisdem de termino sancti Michaelis	x li. ix s. v d.
Summa tocius per annum xvij li. iiij s. vj d. ob.	

Wytherington'

Summa tocius redditus, firme et consuetudin' de termino natalis Domini cum termino sancti Martini	lxv s. x d. ob. qa.
Summa de eisdem de termino Pasche cum termino Purificationis	iiij li. vj s. vij d. ob. qa.
Summa de eisdem de termino sancti Johannis baptiste	liiij s. j d. qa.
Summa de eisdem de termino sancti Michaelis	xv li. xij s. v d. ob.
Summa tocius per annum xxxiiij li. iij d. ob. qa.	

Glinton'

Summa tocius redditus, firme et consuetudin' de termino natalis Domini cum termino sancti Martini	lxij s. v d. ob.
Summa de eisdem de termino Pasche cum termino Purificationis	iiij li. vj s. ij d.
Summa de eisdem de termino sancti Johannis baptiste	xliij s. iij d. ob. qa.
Summa de eisdem de termino sancti Michaelis	xxiiij li. ix d. qa.

Summa tocius per annum xxxiij li. xij s. viij d. ob. preter firmam piscarie que postea intratur.

Wermington'

[Marginated in same hand] Patria occidentale

Summa tocius redditus, firme et consuetudin' de termino natalis Domini cum termino sancti Martini	ix li. xviij s. x d.
Summa de eisdem de termino Pasche cum termino Purificationis	x li. ix s. qa.
Summa de eisdem de termino sancti Johannis baptiste	vij li. vj s. v d.
Summa de eisdem de termino sancti Michaelis cum Gula Augusti	xxvj li. xvij s. j d.

Summa tocius per annum liiij li. xj s. iiij d. qa. preter iiij d. de Pollardesse

Ayston'

Summa tocius redditus, firme et consuetudin' de termino natalis Domini cum termino sancti Martini	vj li. vj s. iiij d.
Summa de eisdem de termino Pasche cum termino Purificationis	vj li. iij s. iiij d.
Summa de eisdem de termino sancti Johannis baptiste	vj li. vj s. ij d.
Summa de eisdem de termino sancti Michaelis	vj li. xij s. iiij d.

Summa tocius per annum xxv li. viij s. ij d.

[fo. 70r] Undele

Summa tocius redditus, firme et consuetudin' de termino Natalis Domini cum termino sancti Martini	xj li. iiij s. ij d.
Summa de eisdem de termino Pasche cum termino Purificationis	xj li. iiij s. vij d. ob.
Summa de eisdem de termino sancti Johannis baptiste	xj li. iiij s. iij d. qa.
Summa de eisdem de termino sancti Michaelis	xj li. iiij s. iij d. qa.

Summa tocius per annum xliiij li. xvij s. iiij d.

Stanewigg'

Summa tocius redditus, firme et consuetudin' de termino natalis Domini cum termino sancti Martini	iiij li. vij s. ix d.
Summa de eisdem de termino Pasche cum termino Purificationis	iiij li. xix s. ij d. ob. qa.
Summa de eisdem de termino sancti Johannis baptiste	liij s. vj d. ob. qa.
Summa de eisdem de termino sancti Michaelis	x li. xiij s. viij d. ob.

Summa tocius per annum xxij li. xiiij s. iij d.

Irtlingburgh'

Summa tocius redditus, firme et consuetudin' de termino natalis Domini cum termino sancti Martini	vj li. xvj s. j d.
Summa de eisdem de termino Pasche cum Purificationis	vj li. xvij s. ob.
Summa de eisdem de termino sancti Johannis baptiste	vj li. iiij s. v d.
Summa de eisdem de termino sancti Michaelis	xvij li. xviij s. x d. qa.

Summa tocius per annum xxxvij li. xvj s. iiij d. ob. qa.

Keteringg'

Summa tocius redditus, firme et consuetudin' de termino natalis Domini cum termino sancti Martini	x li. xv s. iij d. ob.
Summa de eisdem de termino Pasche cum termino Purificationis	xix li. xiiij s. vj d. ob. qa.
Summa de eisdem de termino sancti Johannis baptiste	vj li. xiij s. j d.
Summa de eisdem de termino sancti Michaelis	xxxix li. ix s. ix d. ob.

Summa tocius per annum lxxvj li. xij s. viij d. ob. qa.

Cotingham

Summa tocius redditus, firme et consuetudin' de termino natalis Domini cum termino sancti Martini	Cxix s. vij d.
Summa de eisdem de termino Pasche cum termino Purificationis	vj li. iiij s. vij d.
Summa de eisdem de termino sancti Johannis baptiste	iiij li. xiij s. ix d.
[fo. 70v] Summa de eisdem de termino sancti Michaelis	xx li. iiij s. v d. ob.

Summa tocius per annum xxxvij li. ij s. iiij d. ob.

Eston'

Summa tocius redditus, firme et consuetudin' de termino natalis Domini cum termino sancti Martini	vj li. xiij s. viij d. ob.
Summa de eisdem de termino Pasche cum termino Purificationis	iiij li. ix s. vij d. qa.
Summa de eisdem de termino sancti Johannis baptiste	vij li. xi d. ob.
Summa de eisdem de termino sancti Michaelis	xix li. vj s. viij d. ob.

Summa tocius per annum xxxvij li. x s. xi d. qa.

Tynewell'

Summa tocius redditus, firme et consuetudin' de termino natalis Domini cum termino sancti Martini	iiij li. xv s. ij d. ob.
Summa de eisdem de termino Pasche cum termino Purificationis	Ciiij s. viij d. ob.
Summa de eisdem de termino sancti Johannis baptiste	lxxvj s. vj d. ob.
Summa de eisdem de termino sancti Michaelis	xiij li. iij d.

Summa tocius per annum xxvj li. xvj s. viij d. ob.

Summa predictorum maneriorum de termino natalis Domini cum termino sancti Martini	iiij^{xx} x li. ix. s. ij. ob. qa.
Summa predictorum maneriorum de termino Pasche cum termino Purificationis	iiij^{xx} xviij li. xij s. viij d. ob.
Summa predictorum maneriorum de termino sancti Johannis baptiste	iiij^{xx} iij li. vij s. j d. qa.

Summa predictorum maneriorum de termino sancti Michaelis	CClxxix li. xviij s. vj d.
Summa tocius redditus de maneriis supradictis per annum	Dlij li. vij s. vj. d. ob.

Redditus maneriorum de partibus borealibus

Fyskertone

De termino natalis Domini cum termino sancti Martini	vj li. xviij s. ij d. ob. qa.
De termino Pasche	vj li. viij s. xj d. ob. qa.
De termino sancti Johannis baptiste cum termino Pentecoste	vj li. iij s. iij d. ob. qa.
De termino sancti Michaelis	vj li. x s. ix d. ob. qa.

Summa tocius redditus de predictis iiij^or terminis xxvj li. xvj d.

De certis firmis cum molend' et incremento redditus de termino natalis Domini	lxj s vij d. ob.
[fo. 71r] Certis firmis de termino Pasche	lxvj s. vij d. ob.
De certis firmis de termino sancti Johannis	lxj s. vij d. ob.
De certis firmis de termino sancti Michaelis cum avantagia de hallebode	lxxj s. iiij d. ob.

Summa tocius firme de predictis iiij^or terminis xiij li. xv d.

Colingham

De termino natalis Domini	vj li. xij s. vj d. ob.
De termino Pasche	vj li. xiij s. vj. ob. qa.
De termino sancti Johannis	vj li. xij s. vj d. ob.
De termino sancti Michaelis	vj li. xiij s. vj d. ob. qa.

Summa tocius redditus de predictis iiij^or terminis xxvj li. xij s. ij d. ob.

Scotere

De termino natalis Domini cum firma aque	vj li. xj s. j d. qa.
De termino Pasche	vj li. xj s. j d. qa.
De termino sancti Johannis	vj li. xj s. j d. qa.
De termino sancti Michaelis	vj li. xv s. j d. qa

Summa tocius redditus de predictis iiij^or terminis xxvj li. viij s. v d.

Walcote

De termino natalis Domini cum redditu prioris de Spaldingg' et firma molend'	xxxiiij s. x d. qa.
De termino Pasche cum firma molend'	xxvij s. xj d. qa.
De termino sancti Johannis cum redd' prioris et firma molend'	xxx iiij s. v d. qa.

De termino sancti Michaelis cum firma molend' xxviij s. ij d. ob. qa.

Summa tocius redditus de predictis iiij[or] terminis vj li. v s. v d. ob.

[In a later hand] Summa tocius redditus de maneriis predicits iiij[xx] xviij li. viij s. viij d.

155 Confirmation by Abbot Godfrey of charters of Abbot William of Woodford and Abbot Richard of London granting the convent allowances of assorted grains, malt, and peas from the abbot's granary, together with wheat granted by Abbot Robert de Lindeseye for the support of eight additional monks. He also confirms Abbot Richard's grant that the convent may build a separate bakery and brewhouse and Abbot William's grant of loaves called *mastini* from the abbot's bakery for specified servants, following a dispute over the allowance of loaves during his rule. He ordains that the grain be rendered according to the customary measures and, for his own part, grants an additional allowance of malt and immunity from toll within his jurisdiction should the convent need to use mills outside the abbey. [20 Nov. 1301]

[fo. 71v] Carta Conventus.

Omnibus Christi fidelibus presens scriptum visuris vel audituris Godefridus miseratione divina abbas de Burgo Sancti Petri salutem in Domino sempiternam. Noverit universitas vestra me inspexisse quasdam cartas bone memorie dominorum Ricardi et Willelmi abbatum predecessorum meorum in hec verba:

Universis[1] Christi fidelibus presens scriptum visuris vel audituris Ricardus de London' miseratione divina abbas de Burgo Sancti Petri salutem in Domino sempiternam. Noverit universitas vestra nos concessisse, ordinasse et statuisse pro nobis et successoribus nostris perpetuis temporibus observandum ad honorem Dei et utilitatem tam hospitalitatis quam elemosine ac religionis augmentum pacem et quietem tam obedientiarioram quam capituli nostri, quod conventus habeat de cetero granarium per se suis sumptibus construendum et reparandum. Et quod custos granarii predicti de communi consilio constitutus recipiat de granario abbatis qui pro tempore fuerit totam liberationem que ad conventum spectare consuevit secundum antiquam assisam frumenti, brasei, cuiuscumque generis bladi fuerit per predictum custodem distribuendam et in usus pios convertendam. Ita quod custos qui pro tempore fuerit habeat electionem tocius frumenti abbatis, brasei et pisarum secundum assisam predictam; videlicet de frumento singulis diebus j quarterium et j eskeppam per mensuram regiam, et singulis ebdomadis dimidium quarterium et dimidiam eskeppam frumenti de assignatione domini Roberti de Lindeseye abbatis pro viij monachis per ordinationem suam ad conventum augmentatis [sic], preter particulares, donationes, que distribuuntur in principalibus festis et in die absolutionis ad mandatum et preter alias particulas minutas que sepe contingunt per annum. Idem eciam custos percipiet de braseo singulis ebdomadis quando braciatur de puro ordeo xviij quarteria et v eskeppas de braseo ordei. Quando autem braciatur de ordeo et drageto, tunc percipiet in ebdomada xxj quarteria v eskeppas et dimidiam; videlicet de braseo ordei ad grutmalt' vij quarteria et dimidium et de drageto xiiij quarteria j eskeppam et dimidiam. Quando vero braciatur de maismalt quod est pro majori parte de avena, tunc percipiet in ebdomada xxiiij quarteria j eskeppam et dimidiam; videlicet de braseo ordei vij quarteria et dimidium et de maismalt xvij quarteria v eskeppas et dimidiam. Percipiet eciam qualibet ebdomada j quarterium de braseo ordei ex dono et concessione nostra preter omnem assisam brasei supra notatam. Et si aliquid predictorum frumenti, brasei vel pisarum ad opus conventus minus utile fuerit, queratur in villa vel alibi quod melius poterit inveniri, ad custus abbatis. Volumus eciam et ordinamus, et statuimus quod conventus de cetero habeat omnes proventus et utilitates secundum capituli ordinationem, que poterunt provenire de omnibus et singulis supranotatis. Ita quod dictus conventus, per abbatem et suos ministros qui pro tempore fuerint omni solacio et quiete gaudeat ut decet suo perpetuo. Et ne [fo. 72r] aliquis abbas futurus ad ulteriorem liberationem teneatur ex debito nisi aliquid facere voluerit graciose, nec ad excusationem predicte liberationis faciende [sic] nec ad retardationem subtractionem seu diminutionem aliquam obstare valeat vacatio abbatie aut caristia vel defectus cuiuscumque bladi, quin liberatio predicta custodi granarii conventus ad suam et suorum sustentationem ac consuetam hospitalitatem faciendam plene fiat sine aliqua diminutione. Si vero placuerit et oportunum videatur conventui pistrinum et bracinum habere separatum, bene liceat eidem nova construere in loco conpetenti sine contradictione cuisuscumque et famulos sibi in ipsis ordinare et suis sumptibus sustentare. Et ut ista ordinatio et concessio nostra perpetue firmitatis robor optineat, presens scriptum sigilli nostri munimine una cum sigilli capituli appositione roboramus.

Quam quidam concessionem, ordinationem et statutum, ego[2] frater Willelmus monasterii predicti minister predicti venerabilis patris domini Ricardi abbatis proximus successor quantum in me est pro me et successoribus meis ratifico et confirmo plene et integre secundum carte tenorem supradicte. Et quia in tempore meo super liberationem xiij panum per diem qui dicuntur mastini controversia movebatur, ego dictus Willelmus abbas mera et spontanea voluntate liberationem vij mastinorum de pistrino abbatis perpetuis temporibus liberandam pro me et successoribus meis gratis assumpsi faciendam; videlicet ij servientibus in ecclesia, ij servientibus in sartrino, et servienti camerarii qui dicitur wodeman, et servienti de pistrino qui dicitur lodisman, servienti refectorarii qui dicitur pincerna. Ita quod celerarius conventus respondeat vj servientibus coquine conventualis de vj mastinis eisdem per diem spectantibus. In cuius rei testimonium presenti scripto sigillum meum una cum sigillo conventus est appensum.

Et[3] ego frater Godefridus monasterii predicti minister predictorum venerabilium patrum dominorum Ricardi et Willelmi abbatum continuus successor, dictam concessionem, ordinationem et statutum, quantum in me est pro me et successoribus meis ratifico, approbo et confirmo plene et integre secundum tenorem cartarum supradictarum. Et ne temporibus futuris fiat calumpnia de mensura antiqua et mensura regia sicut tempore predecessoris nostri actum esse cognoscimus, volumus et concedimus ut custos granarii conventus recipiat totam liberationem frumenti, brasei, et pisarum, ea mensura qua usi fuerunt ante concessionem predictam. Volumus eciam et concedimus motu fraterne caritatis ducti, quod quando conventus recipit liberationem brasei de puro ordeo quod habeat plenarie liberationem suam sicut superius distinctum est, et ubi superius dictum est v esk' nos ex concessione nostra addimus iij eskeppas ut fiat quarterium integrum. Ita quod in qualibet ebdomada recipiat xx quarteria. Quando autem braciatur de ordeo et drageto volumus [fo. 72v] et concedimus quod universa et singula sicut superius dicta sunt effectum sortiantur hoc adjecto quod ubi prius custos granarii conventus recepit de ordeo ad grutmalt' vij quarteria dimidium et de drageto xiiij quarteria j eskeppam et dimidiam ex nunc et in futurum recipiat idem custos de ordeo ad grutmalt' viij quarteria et dimidiam eskeppam et de drageto xiij quarteria et v eskeppas, et hoc ex dono et concessione nostra. Quando vero braciatur de ordeo et maismalt' quod est pro majori parte de avena, recipiet predictus custos viij quarteria et dimidiam eskeppam de ordeo ad grutmalt', et de maismalt' xvi quarteria et j eskeppam. De multura conventus volumus et concedimus quod si aliquando contingat necessitate cogente extra abbathiam molere, ut conventus minimis sit a prestatione tolonei nisi fuerit in locis qui nostre non subjacent jurisdictioni. In cuius rei testimonium huic presenti scripto sigillum nostrum una cum sigillo conventus fecimus apponi. Dat' in capitulo nostro die sancti Edmundi regis et martiris, in anno Domini millesimo tricentesimo primo.

1 Also in Sparke, pp. 145–7.

2 Ibid., p. 152.

3 Ibid., pp. 166–7. The Sparke texts differ in detail and appear less accurate.

156 Quitclaim of Cristiana daughter of Richard Pluket to Abbot Godfrey of any right by inheritance in a messuage, 3 rods of land, 4s rent and any other tenements in Stamford. [31 Dec. 1301]

Scriptum Cristiane Pluket'.

[marginated] Staunford
Noverint universi quod cum placitum erat motum in curia domini regis inter Cristianam filiam Ricardi Pluket' petentem et dominum Godefridum abbatem de Burgo Sancti Petri tenentem de uno mesuagio tribus rodis terre et quatuor solidatis redditus cum pertincenciis in villa de Staunford' per breve de ingressu, dicta Cristiana pro se et heredibus suis quibuscumque concessit, remisit et presens scriptum quietum clamavit domino Godefrido abbati predicto totum jus et clamium quod habuit vel aliquo modo habere potuit in predictis mesuagio, tribus rodis terre et quatuor solidatis redditus, et omnibus aliis mesuagiis, terris, pratis et redditibus quibuscumque in villa Staunford' predicta, que jure hereditario, vel quovis alio titulo sibi vel heredibus suis accrescere possent. Ita scilicet quod nec predicta Cristiana nec heredes sui nec aliquis alius nomine suo vel heredum suorum aliquid juris vel clamii in predictis mesuagio, terris et redditibus et omnibus aliis tenementis in villa de Staunford' quibuscumque ut predictum est exigere vel clamare poterunt inperpetuum. In cuius rei testimonium predicta Cristiana huic scripto quieteclamancie sigillum suum apposuit. Hiis testibus: Nicholao de Burton' de Stanford', Johanne de Wermington' de eadem, Eustachio Malerbe de eadem, Clemente de Melton' de eadem, Henrico Faderman de eadem, Bernado le Bonde de eadem, Petro de Burlee, Simone le Botiler de Burgo, Ada le Aumoner de eadem, Bernardo de Castr' et aliis. Dat' apud Burgum Sancti Petri die Sabbati proxima ante circumcisionem Domini anno regni regis Edwardi tricesimo.

157 Quitclaim of Cecilia, widow of Richard Pluket to Abbot Godfrey of any dower right in all the messuages, lands, rents and tenements formerly held by her husband in Stamford. [31 Dec. 1301]

[fo. 73r] Scriptum Cecilie uxoris Ricardi Pluket'.

Noverint universi quod cum placitum erat motum in curia domini regis inter Ceciliam que fuit uxor Ricardi Pluket petentem et dominum Godefridum abbatem de Burgo Sancti Petri tenentem per breve de dote, dicta Cecilia in libera viduitate sua remisit, et per presens scriptum quietumclamavit, totum jus et clamium quod habuit vel aliquo modo habere potuit nomine dotis in omnibus mesuagiis, terris, redditibus et tenementis que aliquo tempore fuerunt Ricardi viri sui in villa de Staunford'. Ita scilicet quod nec predicta Cecilia nec aliquis alius nomine suo in predictis mesuagiis, terris, redditibus et tenementis exigere vel clamare nomine dotis de cetero poterit imperpetuum. In cuius rei testimonium dicta Cecila huic scripto quieteclamancie sigillum suum apposuit. Hiis testibus: Nicholao de Burton' de Staunford', Johanne de Wermington' de eadem, Eustachio Malerbe de eadem, Clemente de Melton' de eadem, Henrico Faderman de eadem, Bernardo le Bonde de eadem, Petro de Burlee. Simone le Botiler de Burgo, Adam le Aumoner de eadem, Bernado de Castre, et aliis. Dat' apud Burgum Sancti Petri die Sabbati proxima ante circumcisionem Domini anno regni regis Edwardi tricesimo.

158 Quitclaim of Thomas son of John de Wengham to Abbot Godfrey and the convent of all right in the cook's serjeanty, known as *withecok'*, in the convent kitchen, about which a plea of novel disseisin was heard before William Inge and his fellow justices at assizes in the county of Northampton. [2 Jan. 1302]

Scriptum Thome filii Johannis de Wengham.

Universis Christi fidelibus ad quos presens scriptum pervenerit Thomas filius Johannis de Wengham de Burgo Sancti Petri salutem in Domino sempiternam. Noveritis me pro me et heredibus meis remisisse et omnino quietumclamasse domino Godefrido abbati de Burgo Sancti Petri et eiusdem loci conventui totum jus meum et clamium quod habui seu aliquo modo habere potui in quadam serjauntia unius coci que vocatur withecok' in coquina conventuali abbathie de Burgo Sancti Petri, unde placitum assise nove disseisine inter me querentem et predictum abbatem et alios in brevi contentos, coram domino Willelmo Ingge et sociis suis justiciariis domini regis ad assisas in comitatu Norht' capiendas assignatis motum fuerat. Ita quod nec ego nec heredes mei nec aliquis nomine nostro aliquid juris vel clamii in prefata serjauntia vel aliquo alio officio in predicta conventuali coquina de cetero exigere, clamare seu vendicare poterimus nec debemus imperpetuum. In cuius rei testimonium huic presenti scripto sigillum meum apposui. Hiis testibus: domino Hugone Wake, milite, magistro Galfrido de Makeseye, Johanne de Undele, Roberto de Thorp', Bernardo de Castr', Adam le Aumoner, Simone le Botiler, Henrico de Ketene, et aliis. Dat' apud Burgum Sancti Petri die Martis in crastino circumcisionis Domini anno regni regis Edwardi filii regis Henrici tricesimo.

159 Letter from Abbot Godfrey and the convent to John, bishop of Lincoln, requesting that he institute Master John Bush, king's clerk, to Fiskerton church, to which the abbey has right of presentation and which is vacant.[1] [19 Feb. 1302]

[fo. 73v] Presentatio magistri Johannis Buysch' ad ecclesiam de Fiskertone.

[Marginated] b

Reverendo patri in Christo domino J[ohanni] Dei gracia Linc' episcopo sui humiles et devoti in Christo filii Godefridus permissione divina abbas de Burgo Sancti Petri et euisdem loci conventus salutem cum omni reverencia et honore. Sancte paternitati vestre presentamus dilectum nobis in Christo magistrum Johannem Buysch' domini regis clericum ad ecclesiam de Fiskerton' vacantem, que ad nostram spectat presentationem, humiliter supplicantes et devote quatinus caritatis intuitu eundem ad dictam ecclesiam admittatis, et personam in eadem instituatis. Salvis nobis et ecclesie nostre juribus ab antiquo perceptis in eadem. In cuius rei testimonium presentibus litteris sigilla nostra sunt appensa. Dat' in capitulo nostro die Dominica proxima ante festum sancti Petri in cathedra anno Domini M° CCC^{mo} primo.

1 For his institution on 17 Mar. 1302, see Dalderby's Institutions, fo. 84r. He was ordained sub-deacon on the same occasion. See also nos 108–108A.

160 Letter from Abbot Godfrey and the convent to John, bishop of Lincoln, requesting that he institute Master Roger de Scardeburg' to Stanwick church, to which the abbey has right of presentation and which is vacant.[1] [22 Feb. 1302]

Presentatio magistri Rogeri de Scardeburg' ad ecclesiam de Stanewigg'.

[Marginated] a

Reverendo patri in Christo domino J[ohanni] Dei gracia Linc' episcopo, sui humiles et devoti in Christo filii Godefridus permissione divina abbas monasterii de Burgo Sancti Petri et eiusdem loci conventus salutem cum omni reverencia et honore. Sancte paternitati vestre presentamus dilectum nobis in Christo magistrum Rogerum de Scardeburg' clericum ad ecclesiam de Stanewigg' vacantem, que ad nostram spectat presentationem, humiliter supplicantes et devote quatinus caritatis intuitu eundem ad dictam ecclesiam admittatis et personam in eadem instituatis. Salvis nobis et ecclesie nostre juribus ab antiquo perceptis in eadem. In cuius rei testimonium presentibus litteris sigilla nostra sunt appensa. Dat' in capitulo nostro die Jovis in festo sancti Petri in cathedra anno Domini M° CCC^{mo} primo

1 For Roger de Scardeburg's institution on 7 April 1302, see Dalderby's Institutions, fo. 105r.

161 Letter from Abbot Godfrey and the convent to John, bishop of Lincoln, requesting that he institute Robert of Croyland, to Oundle church, to which the abbey has right of presentation and which is vacant *de jure*.[1] [12 Mar. 1302]

Presentatio Roberti de Croylaund' ad ecclesiam de Undele.

Reverendo patri in Christo domino J[ohanni] Dei gracia Linc' episcopo sui humiles et devoti in Christo filii Godefridus eiusdem dono gracie abbas de Burgo Sancti Petri et euisdem loci conventus salutem et debite reverencie devotam obedienciam. Sancte paternitati vestre presentamus dilectum clericum nostrum Robertum de Croylaund' ad ecclesiam de Undele de jure vacantem, que ad nostram spectat presentationem, humiliter supplicantes et devote quatinus caritatis intuitu eundem ad dictam ecclesiam admittatis et personam in eadem instituatis. Salvis nobis et ecclesie nostre juribus ab antiquo perceptis in eadem. In cuius rei testimonium presentibus sigilla nostra apposuimus. Dat' in capitulo nostro die Lune in festo sancti Gregorii pape anno Domini M° CCC° primo.

1 The phrase *de jure* is not a common feature of institutions in Lincoln diocese and its significance is uncertain. It may be associated with benefices held in plurality. I am indebted to Dr Bennett and Dr Brand for these observations. For Richard of Croyland's institution on 2 July 1303, see Dalderby's Institutions, fo. 106r.

162 Letter of obligation from Abbot Godfrey and the convent to William de Lamore, Master of the Templars in England promising to repay 200 marks, which they had borrowed at the New Temple in London for the needs of their house, in the quindene of Michaelmas next. [12 Mar. 1302]

[fo. 74r] Universis Christi fidelibus presens scriptum obligatorium visuris vel audituris frater Godefridus permissione divina abbas de Burgo Sancti Petri, ordinis sancti Benedicti, et eiusdem loci conventus salutem in Domino sempiteram. Noverit universitas vestra nos teneri et firmiter obligari fratri Willelmo de Lamore magistro militie Templi in Anglia et successoribus suis in ducentis marcis bonorum et legalium sterlingorum, quas confitemur nos ab eodem magistro ex causa mutui recepisse et habere in pecunia bene numerata et ponderata, ad ardua et communia domus nostre negotia facienda. Quas quidam ducentas marcas bona fide promittimus et tenemur soluere et reddere dicto magistro vel successoribus suis, aut eorum certo nuncio vel procurator presens scriptum nostrum restituenti apud Novum Templum London', in quindena festi sancti Michaelis proxima futura sine aliquam contradictione vel fraude aut ulteriori dilatione. Et ad hoc observandum, obligamus nos et successores nostros et domum nostram ac eciam omnia bona eiusdem mobilia et immobilia presentia et futura in quibuscumque comitatibus et locis Anglie sive infra libertatem sive extra fuerint inventa districtioni et cohercioni cuiuscumque judicis eccliastici, sive seculari quem dictus magister vel successores sui duxerint eligend', et eciam districtioni quorumcumque ballivorum domini regis et aliorum dominorum. Ita videlicet quod dicti judices et ballivi domum nostram, et omnia maneria ea annexa licite ingredi possint et nos per omnia bona in eisdem inventa artare, usque ad plenam satisfactionem debiti memorati et dampnorum ac expensorum predicti magistri et successorum suorum si que vel quas sustinuerint aut fecerint pro defalto[1] solutionis predicte pecunie quod absit ad terminum prelibatum. Renunciamus in premissis insuper omnibus privilegiis et litteris apostolicis, regiis, protectionibus, statutis et prohibitionibus omnibus libertatibus, immunitatibus, omnibus eciam cavillationibus et omnibus auxiliis et remediis que nobis contra presentem obligationem aut aliquem eiusdem articulum prodesse poterunt et in fraudem predictorum magistri et successorum suorum redundare. In cuius rei testimonium huic scripto sigilla nostra apposuimus. Dat' in capitulo nostro die Lune in festo sancti Gregorii pape anno Domini millesimo tricentesimo primo.

1 *defectu* also possible.

163 Grant by Abbot Godfrey and the convent, at the request of Prince Edward, to Master Henry de Cantebrys of a pension of a 100s p.a. from the abbot's chamber until they can provide him with a suitable benefice. [13 Mar. 1302]

Pensio magistri Henrici de Cantebyrs.

Omnibus Christi fidelibus presentes litteras visuris vel audituris G[odefridus] permissione divina abbas monasterii sancti Petri de Burgo et eiusdem loci conventus salutem in Domino sempiternam. Noverit universitas vestra nos ad instantiam excellentissimi principis E[dwardi] filii illustris regis Anglie unanimiter concessisse dilecto nobis in Christo magistro Henrico de Cantebyrs' [fo. 74v] centum solidos de camera abbatis qui pro tempore fuerit annuatim percipiendos; videlicet ad Pascha quinquaginta solidos, et ad festum sancti Michaelis quinquaginta solidos donec eidem in ecclesiastico beneficio competenti providerimus. In cuius rei testimonium presentibus sigilla nostra sunt appensa. Dat' in capitulo nostro die Martis in crastino sancti Gregorii pape anno Domini millesimo tricentesimo primo et anno domini G[odefridi] abbatis iij°.

164 Letter to John, bishop of Lincoln, from Brother William de Stok' resigning as prior of St Michael's, Stamford on the grounds of old age and infirmity. [31 Mar. 1302]

Resignatio fratris Willelmum de Stok'.

Venerabili in Christo patri domino J[ohanni] permissione divina Lincoln' episcopo devotus in Christo filius frater Willelmus de Stok' prior sancti Michaelis extra Stannfordiam salutem obedienciam reverenciam debitam cum honore. Quin corporali inpotencia inherenti senio et debilitate detentus cure et custodie prioratus sancti Michaelis extra Stannford' prout onus eisdem requirit intendere non valeo prefatum prioratum quantum ad me pertinet manibus sancte paternitatis vestre resigno per presentes. Salvis in omnibus juribus monasterii de Burgo Sancti Petri et libertate. In cuius rei testimonium presentibus sigillum decanatus de Nasso Burgi[1] apponi procuravi. Dat' apud Burgum Sancti Petri die Sabbati proxima post festum annunciationis beate Marie anno Domini millesimo tricentesimo secundo et anno domini G[odefridi] abbatis iij.

1 See above no. 99, for another occasion on which the deanery seal was used.

165 Letter from Abbot Godfrey and the convent to John, bishop of Lincoln, requesting that he institute Brother Stephen de Burgo, monk of the abbey, as prior of the nunnery of St Michael's, Stamford. [9 April 1302]

Presentatio fratris Stephani de Burgo ad prioratum sancti Michaelis Staunford'.

Reverendo patri in Christo domino J[ohanni] Dei gracia Lincoln' episcopo sui humiles et devoti in Christo filii Godefridus eiusdem dono gracie abbas de Burgo Sancti Petri et eiusdem loci conventus salutem cum omni reverencia obedienciam debitam et devotam. Sancte paternitati vestre presentamus dilectum filium in Christo fratrem Stephanum de Burgo monachum nostrum latorem presentium ad prioratum monialium sancti Michaelis extra Staunford' vacantem, qui ad nostram spectat presentationem, humiliter supplicantes et devote quatinus ipsum ad eundem prioratum admittatis, et in eodem instituere velitis, curam si placet prioratus memorati eidem committentes. Salvis nobis et successoribus nostris jurisdictione in eodem juxta morem consuetum, et obediencia prius canonice inpensa. In cuius rei testimonium presentibus sigilla nostra apposuimus. Dat' in capitulo nostro v idus Aprilis anno Domini millesino tricentesimo secundo.

166 Manumission by Abbot Godfrey and the convent of Richard son of William, son of Walter of Fiskerton, the abbot's chamberlain, together with all his family and property. [16 July 1302]

Scriptum Ricardi de Fiskertone camerarii domini G[odefridi] abbatis.

Omnibus Christi fidelibus presens scriptum visuris vel audituris Godefridus permissione divina abbas de Burgo Sancti Petri et eiusdem loci conventus salutem in Domino sempiternam. Noverit universitas vestra quod nos unanimi assensu et voluntate tenore presentium manumittimus Ricardum filium Willelmi filii Walteri de Fiskerton' cum tota sequela sua et peculio [fo. 75r] suo plenam libertatem sibi et sequele sue concedentes. Ita quod nec nos ne successores nostri in ipso Ricardo, nec ipsius sequela, peculio nec catallis aliquid servitutis inposterum clamare vel exigere poterimus. In cuius rei testimonium presentibus sigilla nostra sunt appensa. Dat' in capitulo nostro die Lune proxima post festum translationis sancti Benedicti abbatis anno Domini millesimo tricentesimo secundo.

167 Grant by Abbot Godfrey and the convent to Thomas of Thorpe, clerk, of a pension of 40s p.a. from the abbot's chamber until they can provide him with a benefice. [21 July 1302]

Pensio Thome de Thorp'.

[Marginated] vac' [vacated when he received the benefice]
Universis Christi fidelibus presentes litteras visuris vel audituris Godefridus permissione divina abbas monasterii sancti Petri de Burgo, et eiusdem loci conventus salutem in Domino sempiternam. Noverit universitas vestra nos caritatis intuitu concessise dilecto nobis in Christo Thome de Thorp', clerico, quadraginta solidos sterlingorum nomine pensionis annue de camera abbatis qui pro tempore fuerit ad duos anni terminos percipiendos; videlicet ad festum sancti Michaelis xx solidos, et ad Pascha xx solidos donec eidem in ecclesiastico beneficio providerimus. In cuius rei testimonium presentibus litteris sigilla nostra sunt appensa. Dat' in capitulo nostro die Sabbati proxima post festum beate Margarete virginis anno Domini M^{o} CCC^{o} secundo.

168 Text of the oath of loyalty to be sworn by those serving the abbey

Sacramentum faciendum in capitulo.

Ego N ero fidelis promotor et diligens, verbo et facto, negotiorum monasterii sancti Petri de Burgo jura et libertates eiusdem proposse defendam, salva fidelitate domino regi prestita, consilia et secreta dominorum abbatis et conventus mihi per se, vel per litteras, seu per nuncium manifestata, in dampnum eorumdem vel ecclesie sue antedicte nullatenus pandam infuturum. Et omnia onera et pensiones dicto monasterio de ecclesia michi collata debita vel debitas debitis terminis et certis persolvam.[1] Set ymaginata dispendia a quibuscumque eisdem inferenda, a tempore noticie, debita resistencia impediam et jacturas. Sic Deus me adjuvet, et ista sancta evangelia.

1 *Et omnia ... persolvam* interlined. *terminis et certis* could be marginalia rather than part of the text.

168A The same in French.

Ieo N serai leaus e diligent avancour de bosoignes en dit e en fet del abbe e du covent de Burg' Seint Pierre e de lour eglise a moun poer, sauve la fei nostre seignur le roy, e lour privee conseils monstre a moi par lettre ou par bouche a nuly descoverai en damage de eaus ne de lour eglise avantdite, mes partut desturberai lour damages et lour pertes vers touz iceaus que par mal art ou engyn surquere les vodera countre les dreitz e franchises de lour eglis avantdite, si Dieux me aide e ses seinz e cestes seintes evangiles.

169 Grant by Abbot Godfrey to Master William of Fotheringhay of a pension of 40s p.a. from his chamber for his counsel and protection of the abbey. [10 Mar. 1302/3]

[fo. 75v] [Marginated] Fodringgeye.

Pateat universis quod nos Godefridus Dei gracia abbas monasterii de Burgo Sancti Petri Lync' dyoc' damus et concedimus magistro Willelmo de Fodringgeye, clerico nostro, annuam pensionem quadraginta solidorum sterlingorum de camera nostra annuatim recipiendam pro patrocinio suo nobis et monasterio nostro prestito et consilio suo deinceps prestando, quam annuam pensionem eidem Willelmo vel suo attornato vel procuratori solvere ad duos anni terminos; videlicet in festo Pasche et in festo sancti Michaelis archangeli pro equalibus portionibus tenemur. Et nos ad hoc faciendum tenore presentium obligamus. In cuius rei testimonium sigillum nostrum huic scripto duximus apponendum. Dat' apud Burgum Sancti Petri vj^{o} idus Marcii anno Domini M^{o} trecentesimo secundo.

170 Royal writ addressed to the sheriff of Northampton and Hugh Wake concerning the collection of the aid granted to the king for the marriage of his eldest daughter. The abbot has produced a charter of Henry III and Edward I's own confirmation granting that the abbot's bailiff should collect anything due to the king from the liberty and answer for it at the Exchequer, so the king orders that this be observed. [after 7 Nov. 1302[1]]

[Marginated] Rex

Rex dilectis et fidelibus suis vicecomiti Norht' et Hugoni Wake ad auxilium quadraginta solidorum nobis de singulis feodis militum in regno nostro ad primogenitam filiam nostram maritandam nuper concessum in comitatu predicto levandum et colligendum assignatis salutem. Ex parte dilecti nobis in Christo abbatis de Burgo Sancti Petri nobis est ostensum quod cum ipse per cartam celebris memorie domini H[enrici] quondam regis Anglie patris nostri et confirmationem nostram quas inspeximus hanc habeat libertatem; videlicet quod ballivi predicti abbatis omnia debita nobis debita in omnibus hundredis ipsius abbatis in comitatu predicto, et in omnibus dominiis suis in cuiuscumque balliva sint colligere debeant et respondere per manus suas ad Scaccarium nostrum. Ita quod vicecomes vel ballivi nostri inde se in nullo intromittant, ac predecessores ipsius abbatis tam huiusmodi auxilia quociens aliquibus progenitoribus nostris regibus Anglie fuerint concessa, quam alia debita nobis et eisdem progenitoribus nostris debita in hundredis et dominiis suis predictis a tempore confectionis carte et confirmationis predictarum semper hactenus per ballivos suos proprios colligere, levare, et nobis inde ad Scaccarium predictum respondere consueverint. Vos licet idem abbas huiusmodi auxilium tenentes suos de feodis militar' que tenent in hundredis et dominiis predictis ratione dicte concessionis nobis facte contingens ab eisdem tenentibus per ballivos suos proprios colligere, levare et nobis inde respondere sicut hactenus fieri consuevit sic paratus, tenentes tamen predictos pro huiusmodi auxilio vobis ad opus nostrum prestando graviter distringitis ipsum abbatem et ballivos suos super hoc impediendo minus juste in ipsius abbatis et ecclesie sue predicte prejudicium manifestum et contra tenorem carte et confirmationis predictarum. Nolentes igitur eidem abbati aut dicte ecclesie sue per nos prejudicari in hac parte, vobis mandamus quod si ita sit, tunc predictum abbatem dictum auxilium de tenentibus suis predictis per ballivos suos proprios colligere et levare et nobis inde ad Scaccarium nostrum respondere permittatis, juxta tenorem carte et confirmationis predictarum, et prout huiusmodi auxilia semper hactenus per abbates eiusdem loci et ballivos suos in hundredis et dominiis predictis colligi et levari consueverunt et nobis inde respondere. Teste me ipso apud Sanctum Albanum etc.

1 See Prestwich, *Edward I*, p. 529 for this aid.

170A Royal writ addressed to the sheriff of Northampton and Hugh Wake ordering them not to levy the above aid on the abbey's holdings in free alms, in conformity with the grants of his predecessors and his own confirmation. Anything already levied is to be returned. Like writs to the sheriffs of Lincoln, Nottingham, Leicester, Warwick, Huntingdon and Bedford. [after 7 Nov. 1302]

[fo. 76r] Rex dilectis et fidelibus suis vicecomiti Norhampton' et Hugoni Wake ad auxilium quadraginta solidorum nobis de singulis feodis militum in regno nostro ad primogenitam filiam nostram maritandam nuper concessum in comitatu predicto levandum et colligendum assignatis salutem. Ex parte dilecti nobis in Christo abbatis de Burgo Sancti Petri nobis est ostensum quod cum ipse per cartas progenitorum nostrorum quondam regum Anglie et confirmationem nostram quas inspeximus, diversas terras et tenementa infra comitatum predictum teneat in liberam puram et perpetuam elemosinam per quod idem abbas auxilium aliquod de terris et tenementis illis ratione concessionis predicte nobis facere non debet, vos nichilominus ipsum abbatem pro huiusmodi auxilio de terris et tenementis predictis ac si ea per feoda vel servicia militaria teneret, vobis ad opus nostrum prestando graviter distringitis et ipsum ea occasione multipliciter inquietatis minus juste in ipsius abbatis dampnum non modicum et gravamen et contra tenorem cartarum et confirmationis predictaram, ac contra formam concessionis auxilii supradicti. Nolentes ipsum abbatem in hac parte indebite pregravari, vobis mandamus quod inspectis cartis et confirmatione predictis, ipsum abbatem de auxilio huiusmodi nobis prestando pro terris et tenementis que per easdem cartas et confirmationem in puram et perpetuam elemosinam teneri inveneritis quietum esse permittatis. Et si quid ab eodem abbate de huiusmodi terris et tenementis levari feceritis ad opus nostrum, id eidem abbati sine dilatione restituatis. Teste me ipso etc.

Ista brevia diriguntur vicecomitibus Norhampton', Linc', Notingham, Leyc', Warwyk', Huntingdon', et Bedeford' pro abbate de Burgo Sancti Petri

171 Grant by Abbot Godfrey to John de Nevill' of a pension of 5 marks p.a. from his chamber until he can provide him with a suitable benefice. [13 June 1303]

Pensio domini Johannis de Nevill'.

Universis Christi fidelibus presentes litteras visuris vel audituris Godefridus permissione divina abbas monasterii sancti Petri de Burgo salutem in Domino sempiternam. Noverit universitas vestra nos caritatis intuitu concessisse dilecto nobis in Christo domino Johanni de Nevill', clerico, quinque marcas sterlingorum nomine pensionis annue de camera nostra ad duos anni terminos percipiendas; videlicet ad festum sancti Michaelis triginta tres solidos et quatuor denarios, et ad festum Pasche triginta tres solidos et quatuor denarios. Et sic singulis annis donec eidem in ecclesiastico beneficio competenti providerimus. In cuius rei testimonium presentibus sigillum nostrum apposuimus. Dat' apud Eye juxta Burgum die Jovis proxima post festum sancti Barnabe apostoli anno Domini M° CCC° tercio.

172 Grant by Abbot Godfrey and the convent to Master John of Winchelsey, at the instance of Robert of Winchelsey, archbishop of Canterbury, of a pension of 5 marks p.a. from the abbot's chamber, until they can provide him with a suitable benefice. [4 Oct.[1] 1303]

Pensio magistri Johannis de Wynchelsee.

[Marginated, but partly illegible] vacat quia ad eum ... loco subrogatur [?] magister Willelmus de G ... ham

Universis Christi fidelibus presentes litteras visuris vel audituris G[odefridus] permissione divina abbas monasterii sancti Petri de Burgo et eiusdem loci conventus salutem in Domino sempiternam. Noveritis nos unaniniter [sic] concessisse dilecto nobis in Christo magistro Johanni de Wynchelsee clerico ad instanciam venerabilis patris domini R[oberti] Dei gracia Cantuar' archiepiscopi quinque marcas sterlingorum nomine pensionis annue de camera abbatis qui pro tempore fuerit ad duos anni terminos percipiendas; videlicet ad Pascha [fo. 76v] triginta tres solidos et quatuor denarios, et ad festum sancti Michaelis triginta tres solidos et iiij^or^ denarios. Et sic singulis annis donec eidem in ecclesiastico beneficio competenti providerimus. In cuius rei testimonium presentibus litteris sigilla nostra sunt appensa. Dat' in capitulo nostro die Veneris proxima post festum beati Michaelis anno Domini M° CCC° tercio.

1 Probably the Friday after Michaelmas rather than the other days associated with a Saint Michael.

173 Cyrograph agreement between Abbot Godfrey and convent and Geoffrey de la Mare, whereby Geoffrey has surrendered all claim to a market and fair in Northborough, which he has by grant of King Edward and which damages the abbot's market at Peterborough. Geoffrey has also granted that he will not seek a future market or fair in Northborough and that he will remove all the trappings of the present market and fair. His rights of warren, granted by the same royal charter, are reserved. The abbot and convent grant that Geoffrey and his heirs may have all the amercements in Langdike hundred of his two freemen and one bondman for breaking the assize of ale. All other amercements to be paid to the abbey. The abbey quitclaims to Geoffrey common rights in the pasture called le Hedyk' in Maxey, all his debts to the abbey outstanding at the time of the agreement and grants that he may have his tenants' amercements for breaking the assize of ale in Thurlby outside the abbot's court. [8 Dec. 1303]

[Marginated] compositio facta inter abbatem Godefridum et dominum G[alfridum] de la Mare. [in another hand] nota

Die Dominica proxima post festum sancti Nicholai anno regni regis Edwardi filii regis Henrici xxxij^{o} convenit inter dominum Godefridum Dei gracia abbatem de Burgo Sancti Petri et eiusdem loci conventum ex parte una et dominum Galfridum de la Mare militem[1] ex parte[2] altera; videlicet quod predictus Galfridus de la Mare pro se et heredibus suis imperpetuum renunciavit omni juri et beneficio quod habuit tenendi quoddam mercatum et feriam in villa de Northburg' per cartam domini regis Edwardi sibi concessam, et quod quidam mercatum et feriam predictus abbas asserebat predictum Galfridum levasse ad nocumentum liberi mercati sui, de Burgo Sancti Petri. Et preterea idem Galfridus concessit pro se et heredibus suis, quod nunquam decetero mercatum nec feriam in predicta villa de Northburg' tenebit, et quod omnia judicialia que idem Galfridus occasione predicti mercati seu ferie levavit, prosternet et amoveri faciet et quod remota remanebunt imperpetuum. Et nunquam in predicta villa de Northburg' nec alibi infra Nassum Burgi aliquam libertatem regalem occasione predicte carte, excepta warenna sua clamabit sue vendicabit, nec umquam aliquam cartam de mercato seu feria infra Nassum Burgi habendum impetrabunt. Et predictus abbas et conventus[3] pro se et successoribus suis concesserunt predicto Galfrido et heredibus suis, quod de cetero habeant omnimoda amerciamenta emergentia in hundredum de Langedyk'[4] occasione assise cervisie fracte de duobus liberis tenentibus suis et uno bondo imperpetuum.[5] Ita tamen quod transgressiones assise cervisie omnium tenentium dicti Galfridi in hundredo predicti abbatis plenarie presententur et amerciamenta dictorum trium tenentium ibidem afforantur per sacramentum proborum hominum secundum quod alii braciatores patrie afforantur, et extracte dictorum trium tenentium dicto Galfrido et heredibus suis[6] vel ballivo eorum per ballivum predicti abbatis liberentur. Et si ballivus predicti abbatis vel succesorum suorum qui pro tempore fuerit[7] extractas predictorum amerciamentorum dicto Galfrido seu heredibus suis[8] seu ballivo suo liberare recusaverit, liceat eidem Galfrido et heredibus suis[9] predicta amerciamenta sine contradictione alicuius levare et retinere et in usus proprios convertere[10] et omnimoda alia amerciamenta omnium tenentium dicti Galfridi in turnis et hundredis emergentia, exceptis tribus braciatoribus predictis, sine contradictione dicti Galfridi vel heredum suorum dicto abbati et successoribus suis remanebunt imperpetuum. Et preterea dictus abbas et conventus[11] pro se et successoribus suis remiserunt et quietum clamaverunt dicto Galfrido et heredibus suis totum jus et clamium quod habuerunt vel aliquo modo habere potuerunt communicandi in quadam pastura que vocatur le Hedyk' in Makeseye.[12] Et eciam idem abbas et conventusm remistit [sic] et omnino quietum clamaverunt eidem Galfrido et heredibus suis omnimoda debita in quibus ex quacumque causa eidem abbati vel predecessoribus suis tenebatur, usque ad diem confectionis presentium. Preterea idem abbas et conventusm concesserunt pro se et successoribus suis quod dictus Galfridus et heredes sui bene et pacifice habeant amerciamenta tenentium suorum [fo. 77r] occasione assise cervisie fracte in Thurleby in comitatu Lincoln' extra curiam dicti abbatis, prout alii libere tenentes dicti abbatis infra dominium suum ibidem habent et alibi in comitatu Lincoln'. In cuius rei testimonium presenti scripto ad modum cirograffi confecto sigilla partium alternatim sunt appensa. Hiis testibus: dominis Rogero de Heycham, Hugone Wake, Johanne de Ayston', Hugone Daundelyn militibus, Ricardo Taillard', Willelmo de Northburg', Johanne de Peckebrigg', Johanne de Undele tunc ballivo libertatis predicti abbatis de Burgo, et multis aliis.

1 *militem* interlined.
2 *parte* interlined.
3 *et conventus* interlined.
4 *in hundredum de Langdyk'* interlined.
5 *imperpetuum* interlined.
6 *et heredibus suis* interlined.
7 *vel ... fuerit* interlined.
8 *seu heredibus suis* interlined.
9 *et heredibus suis* interlined.
10 *et retinere ... convertere* interlined.
11 *et conventus* interlined.
12 marginated *nota*.
13 *et conventus* interlined.

174 Cyrograph agreement between Abbot Godfrey and the convent of Peterborough and Abbot Odo and the convent of Thorney whereby the abbot of Peterborough surrenders any claim to hunt hare, fox and wild cat within the abbot of Thorney's warren in Yaxley and Stanground, which he has by virtue of hunting rights throughout the county of Huntingdon conferred by King Richard. In return, Abbot Odo quitclaims all right in two pieces of silt or pasture land over the water, lying between the abbot of Peterborough's pasture at Fletton and the manor of Stanground. They also agree to place boundary marks, as established by a jury, on the river bank between Fletton and Stanground. [7 Dec. 1303]

Die[1] Sabbati in crastino sancti Nicholai anno regni regis Edwardi filii regis Henrici xxxij° convenit inter Godefridum Dei gracia abbatem de Burgo Sancti Petri et conventum loci eiusdem ex parte una, et Odonem eadem gracia abbatem de Thorneye et eiusdem loci conventum ex altera; videlicet quod predictus Godefridus abbas de Burgo Sancti Petri, pro se et successoribus suis remisit et omnino quietum clamavit predicto Odoni de Thorneye abbati et successoribus suis, totum jus et clamium quod habuit vel aliquo modo habere potuit ad fugandum ad leporem, wlpem et catum per concessionem regis Ricardi antecessoris domini regis nunc, predecessori abbatis de Burgo Sancti Petri factam ad fugandum ad leporem, wlpem et catum per totum comitatum Huntingdon'. Ita videlicet quod predictus abbas de Burgo Sancti Petri, nec successores sui, nec aliquis nomine suo unquam decetero occasione predicte carte sive quocumque alio titulo juris aliquod jus vel clamium fugandi infra metas warenne ipsius abbatis de Thorneye per cartam domini regis nunc sibi concessam in villis de Jakele et Staneground' decetero possent exigere vel clamare. Et pro hac remissione et quieta clamatione, predictus Odo abbas de Thorneye pro se et successoribus sui imperpetuum remisit et quietum clamavit predicto Godefrido abbati de Burgo Sancti Petri et successoribus suis totum jus et clamium quod habuit vel aliquo modo habere potuit in duobus hutrellis seu placeis pasture jacentibus ex opposito manerii de Staneground' ex parte de Fletton' ultra aquam que se extendit inter manerium de Staneground' et pasturam abbatis de Burgo Sancti Petri de Fletton'. Ita videlicet quod predictus abbas de Thorneye nec successores sui nec aliquis nomine suo in predictis hutrellis sue placeis unquam decetero aliquod jus vel clamium exigere possent seu vendicare. Concesserunt eciam utrique abbates et bona fide promiserunt quod certe bunde ex utraque parte aque, tam versus Fletton' quam versus Staneground', per visum proborum hominum super ripas aque predicte ponantur. Ita quod nunquam temporibus futuris neutra pars ultra predictas bundas aliquod solum possit occupare seu clamare per quod cursus aque in aliquo possit artari. In cuius rei testimonium presenti scripto ad modum cirograffi confecto sigilla partium alternatim sunt appensa. Hiis testibus: domino Willelmo de Carleton', dominis Rogero de Heycham, Galfrido de la Mare, Hugone Wak', et Hugone Daun-[fo. 77v]delyn, militibus, domino Roberto de Baiocis tunc vicecomite Huntingdon', domino Willelmo de Spanneby, Waltero de Mullesworth', et Roberto de Wassingle et aliis.

1 Also in Soc. of Antiquaries, MS 38, fo. 35r–v and BL, Cott. Cleop. C ii, fos 62v–3r. For the Thorney Abbey text, see CUL, Add. MS 3021, fo. 371r–v.

175 Appointment by Abbot Godfrey of William Poncyn as keeper of the hospital of St Giles extra Stamford, with all its income, for life, on condition that a chantry be observed three days a week in the chapel, the buildings be kept in repair and the customary obligations of the hospital maintained. [25 Dec. 1303]

[Marginated in a later medieval hand] Stanford'

Omnibus Christi fidelibus presens scriptum visuris vel audituris Godefridus permissione divina abbas monasterii sancti Petri de Burgo salutem in Domino. Noveritis nos concessisse et tradidisse Willelmo Poncyn in Stannford' custodiam hospitalis beati Egidii extra Stannford' ad terminum vite sue, una cum edificiis, terris et redditibus et omnibus aliis proficuis ad dictum hospitalem pertinentibus seu ex pia devotione fidelium provenientibus. Ita videlicet quod cantariam in capella beati Egidii tribus diebus per ebdomadam sustinebit, necnon edificia inibi constructa reparabit et sustentabit ac cetera onera dicto hospitali incumbentia de consuetudine antiquam supportabit. Salvis nobis et successoribus nostris juribus et libertatibus in eodem hospitali que ad nos et monasterium Burgi de jure vel consuetudine noscuntur pertinere. In cuius rei testimonium presentibus sigillum nostrum est appensum. Dat' apud Burgum Sancti Petri in festo nathalis Domini anno eiusdem millesimo tricentesimo tercio.

176 Plea in the court of Common Pleas heard at York before Ralph de Hengham and his fellow justices, in which Geoffrey de la Mare was summoned to answer Abbot Godfrey concerning a Wednesday market set up at Northborough during the vacancy following the death of Abbot Richard of London, to the damage of the abbot's Saturday market at Peterborough. Geoffrey is unable to show that his market does not harm that of the abbot, so he is ordered to dismantle it and the sheriff is ordered to proclaim its discontinuance. Geoffrey in mercy. [Hilary Term 1304]

Placita apud Ebor' coram R[adulpho] de Hengham et sociis suis justiciariis domini regis de banco de termino sancti Hillarii anno regni regis Edwardi filii regis Henrici tricesimo secundo.

[Marginated] Norht'

Galfridus[1] de la Mare summonitus fuit ad respondendum Godefrido abbati de Burgo Sancti Petri de placito quare idem Galfridus nuper abbathia de Burgo Sancti Petri per mortem R[icardi] de London' abbatis eiusdem loci vacante et in manu domini regis existente levavit quoddam mercatum in Northburgh' ad nocumentum liberi mercati abbathie predicte de villa de Burgo Sancti Petri in manu predicti Godefridi abbatis nunc existentis ad grave dampnum ipsius abbatis etc. Et unde idem abbas per attornatum suum dicit quod predictus Galfridus nuper [predicta][2] abbathia ut predictum est in manu regis existentur levavit quoddam mercatum in Northburgh' tentum die Mercurii ad nocumentum predicti mercati de Burgo Sancti Petri tenti per diem Sabbati, quod quidem mercatum [de Northburgh'][2] non distat a predicto mercato ipsius abbatis nisi per duas leucas, per quod homines de Holand' et villarum adjacentium veniunt ad predictum mercatum de Northburg' et ibidem mercimonia sua ibidem venditioni exponunt [etc][2] et se subtra[h]unt veniendi ad predictum mercatum ipsius abbatis ad nocumentum etcetera. Unde dicit quod deterioratus est et dampnum habet ad valenciam centum librorum. Et inde producit sectam.

Et Galfridus, per Johannem Maucourneys attornatum suum, venit et non poterit dedicere quin ipse levavit predictum mercatum de Northburgh' ad nocumentum liberi mercati predicti abbatis. Ideo consideratum est quod predictum mercatum de Northburgh' prosternatur. Et predictus abbas gratis remittit dampna sua etcetera. Et preceptum est vicecomiti quod per totam ballivam suam pupplice proclamare [fo. 78r] faciat ne predictum mercatum de Northburgh' plus teneatur, nec sequatur. Et Galfridus in misericordia rotulo lvj^{o}.

1 See PRO. CP/40/150, m. 56r.

2 Supplied from PRO text.

177 Gaol delivery at Peterborough on 26 Feb. 1304 by Henry Spigurnel and Hugh Wake in which Robert of Castor and Robert de Keleseye, clerks, were indicted for theft, found guilty and handed over to Abbot Godfrey, as set out in the bishop of Lincoln's commission of 1 Mar. 1304, in order to be dealt with by the ecclesiastical authorities. The abbot and sacrist are to be responsible for their imprisonment on behalf of the bishop until they come before Roger de Weng'. A letter of 9 March from the bishop to the abbot and sacrist asks them to deliver the clerks to Roger at a suitable place. [26 Feb.–9 Mar. 1304]

Deliberatio gaole facta apud Burgum die Mercurii proxima post festum sancti Mathie apostoli anno regni regis E[dwardi] xxxij° per dominos Henricum Spigurnel et Hugonem Wak' justiciarios per breve domini regis supradictum, quod breve remanet penes dictos justiciarios ad hoc assignatos. Coram quibus Robertus de Castre et Robertus de Keleseye clerici de latrocinio indictati, et per eodem justiciarios inculpati, et per inquisitionem convicti, domino Godefrido abbati de Burgo Sancti Petri, ad exigendum clericos coram eisdem justiciariis potestatem habenti, fuerunt liberati, ut patet per commissionem domini Linc' episcopi que sequitur:

Universis ad quos presentes littere pervenerint, Johannes permissione divina Linc' episcopus salutem in omnium salvatore. Universitati vestre notum facimus per presentes, quod ad exigendum et recipiendum vice et auctoritate nostra secundum libertatem ecclesasticam, et regni consuetudinem approbatam, quoscumque clericos seu alios viros ecclesiasticos pro quocumque crimine seu transgressione captos, et apud Burg' incarceratos et incarcerandos a quibuscumque justiciariis domini regis seu aliis ipsos liberandi habentibus potestatem ut de eis fiat in foro ecclesiastico quod secundum canonicas sanctiones fuerit faciendum, dilectis in Christo filiis domino abbati de Burgo Sancti Petri et sacriste eiusdem loci conjunctim et divisim vices nostras committimus cum cohercionis canonice potestate. In cuius rei testimonium litteras nostras domino abbati et sacriste predictis fieri fecimus has patentes. Dat' apud Lydington' kalendis Marcii anno Domini M° CCC° tercio.

Qui quidem Robertus et Robertus ab eodem abbate quasi in custodia episcopi supradicti admissi in custodia eiusdem abbatis extiterunt a die supradicto usque diem Jovis in festo sancti Gregorii proximum sequenter, quo die episcopus supradictus deliberationem dictorum clericorum per Rogerum de Weng', clericum suum, et per litteram sequentem petiit.

Johannes permissione divina Linc' episcopus dilecto in Christo filio abbati de Burgo Sancti Petri vel sacriste loci eiusdem salutem graciam et benedictionem. Ad recipiendos a vobis Robertum de Castre et Robertum de Kelleseye clericos nuper apud Burg' certis de causis incarceratos, vobisque tamquam commissariis nostri in hac parte, per justiciarios domini regis adjudicandos in foro ecclesiastico nostro nomine liberatos, Rogerum de Weng' clericum nostrum ad vos specialiter destinamus, vos rogantes, quatinus dictum Rogerum facta sibi liberatione dictarum personarum securum conductum usque ad locum competentem prout vos ipsi decreveritis faciatis habere. Valete. Dat' apud Lydington' vij idus Marcii cuius petitioni resistere nolentes, ipsos Robertum et Robertum securum conductum usque Stannford' fac' dicto Rogero delibere fecimus. In presencia Willemi de Wodeston' de Burgo, Johannis Gesthalle de eadem, Radulphii de Berkamstede, Willelmi Wak', Alexandri le Gaunter, et Johannis le Meillour qui eos admisit sub pena qua decebat.

178 Appointment of Brother Thomas de Sarum by Abbot Godfrey to special custody of the nunnery of St Michael extra Stamford, with authority over all its temporal affairs, reserving its spiritual affairs to the prior and prioress. [n.d.[1]]

[fo. 78v] [In a different hand] Stannford'

Universis sancte matris ecclesie filiis presentes litteras visuris vel audituris G[odefridus] permissione divina abbas de Burgo Sancti Petri salutem. Ad vestram noticiam evidenter volumus pervenire quod cum custodia domus sanctimonialium sancti Michaelis extra Stannf' ad abbatem et conventum[2] de Burgo Sancti Petri in temporalibus et in spiritualibus ab antiquo pertinuit et adhuc pertinet de jure et in facto. Nos eandem custodiam animo concupistenti volentes conservare in illius sancte religionis augmentum, constituimus et ordinavimus dilectum confratrem nostrum fratrem T[homam] de Sarum illius domus in temporalibus tantum, custodem specialem, eidem concendentes plenam et liberam potestatem, ordinandi et constituendi, tam infra domum predictam quam extra in omnibus temporalibus, quicquid dicte domui viderit expedire reservata cum priori et priorisse domus supra dicte spirituali dispositione in omnibus dictam domum contingentibus. In cuius rei testimonium etc. Dat' etc.

1 Thomas de Sarum became prior on 27 Oct. 1315. Dalderby's Institutions, fo. 57v.
2 *et conventum* interlined.

179 Manumission by Abbot Godfrey and the convent of William son of Roger Bate of Thurlby, his family and his property. [17 April 1316]

Littera Willemi filii Rogeri Bate de Thurleby.

[marginated in different hand] thurl' [also medieval marginal symbol]

Omnibus Christi fidelibus presens scriptum visuris vel audituris Godefridus permissione divina abbas de Burgo Sancti Petri et eiusdem loci conventus salutem in Domino sempiternam. Noverit universitas vestra quod nos unanimi assensu et voluntate tenore presentium manumittimus Willelmum filium Rogeri Bate de Thurleby cum tota sequela sua et peculio suo, plenam libertatem sibi et sequele sue concedentes. Ita quod nec nos, nec successores nostri in ipso Willelmo nec ipsius sequela, peculio nec catallis aliquid servitutis inposterum clamare vel exigere poterimus. In cuius rei testimonium sigilla nostra presentibus sunt appensa. Dat' in capitulo nostro die Sabbati proxima post festum sanctorum Tiburtii et Valeriani anno Domini millesimo CCC° xvj.

180 Grant by Abbot Godfrey and the convent to Cristiana de Aleby of a messuage and its appurtenances in Peterborough, formerly held by William Marshall, rendering 4s p.a. [30 Mar. 1304]

Omnibus Christi fidelibus presens scriptum visuris vel audituris Godefridus miseratione divina abbas de Burgo Sancti Petri et eiusdem loci conventus salutem in Domino. Noverit universitas vestra nos unanimi asensu dimisisse et presenti scripto concessisse Cristiane de Aleby unum mesuagium cum pertinenciis suis in villa Burgi quod Willelmus Marescallus quondam tenuit de nobis, et jacet inter mesuagium quod Thomas ad ecclesiam quondam de nobis tenuit versus orientem ex una parte et furnum nostrum ex altera, habendum et tenendum de nobis et successoribus nostris et ecclesia nostra, sibi et heredibus suis bene et in pace. Reddendo inde annuatim nobis et successoribus nostris et ecclesie nostre ipsa et heredes sui quatuor solidos argenti ad quatuor anni terminos secundum consuetudines ville constitutos, et faciendo omnia servicia de predicto mesuagio debita et consueta, sicut predictus Willelmus Marescallus et antecessores sui facere debuerunt et plenius consueverunt. Ita tamen [fo. 79r] quod dicta Cristiana nec heredes sui predictum mesuagium vendere invadiare, assignare, vel aliquo modo alienare poterunt sine assensu nostro vel successorum nostrorum. Et ut hec nostra dimissio et concessio quantum ad nos et successores nostros pertinet, rata et stabilis permaneat, presenti scripto sigillum nostrum apposuimus. Dat' apud Burgum Sancti Petri die Martis proxima post festum annunciationis beate Marie anno regni regis E[dwardi] filii regis Henrici xxxii°.

181 Letter from Abbot Godfrey and the convent to John, bishop of Lincoln, requesting that he institute John of Oundle to Scotter church, to which the abbey has right of presentation and which is vacant.[1] [23 Oct. 1304]

Presentatio Johannis de Undele ad ecclesiam de Scote'.

Reverendo in Christo patri domino J[ohanni] Dei gracia Linc' episcopo, sui humiles et devoti in Christo filii Godefridus permissione abbas monasterii de Burgo Sancti Petri et eiusdem loci conventus salutem cum omni reverencia et honore. Sancte paternitati vestre presentamus dilectum nobis in Christo Johannem de Undele, clericum, ad ecclesiam de Scotere vacantem, que ad nostram spectat presentationem, humiliter supplicantes et devote, quatinus caritatis intuitu eundem ad dictam ecclesiam admittatis et personam in eadem instituatis. Salvis nobis et ecclesie nostre juribus ab antiquo perceptis in eadem. In cuius rei testimonium presentibus litteris sigilla nostra sunt appensa. Dat' in capitulo nostro die Veneris proxima post festum sancti Luce evangeliste anno Domini millesimo tricentesimo quarto.

1 For John of Oundle's institution on 4 Dec. 1304, see Dalderby's Institutions, fo. 87r.

182 Letter from Abbot Godfrey and the convent to John, bishop of Lincoln, requesting that he institute William Gascelyn to Northborough church, to which the abbey has right of presentation and which is vacant. [22 Jan. 1305]

Presentatio domini Willelmi Gascelyn ad ecclesiam de Norhtburg'.

[Marginated in different hand] vacat' hic[1]

Reverendo in Christo patri domino J[ohanni] Dei gracia Linc' episcopo, sui humiles et devoti in Christo filii Godefridus permissione divina abbas monasterii de Burgo Sancti Petri, et eiusdem loci conventus salutem cum omni reverencia et honore. Sancte paternitati vestre presentamus dilectum nobis in Christo dominum Willelmum Gascelyn, clericum, ad ecclesiam de Norhtburg' vacantem, que ad nostram spectat presentationem, humiliter supplicantes et devote quatinus caritatis intuitu eundem ad dictam ecclesiam admittatis et personam in eadem instituatis. Salvis nobis et ecclesie nostre juribus ab antiquo perceptis in eadem. In cuius rei testimonium presentibus sigilla nostra sunt apposita vel appensa[2]. Dat' in capitulo nostro die Veneris in festo sancti Vincentii martiris anno Domini M^{o} CCC^{mo} quarto.

1 There is no record of an institution in Dalderby's register.
2 *vel appensa* interlined.

183 Memorandum that on 15 Mar. 1305, Robert de Elmington' of Oundle took an oath before Abbot Godfrey and many others that neither he, nor anyone at his instigation, would act against the interests of the abbey, particularly with regard to the fence at la Biggin.

[fo. 79v] Memorandum quod die Lune proxima post festum sancti Gregorii pape, anno Domini millesimo tricentesimo quarto, et anno domini Godefridi abbatis sexto, Robertus de Elmington' de Undele prestitit corporale sacramentum coram eodem domino G[odefrido] abbate et multis aliis, quod ipse R[obertus] nullo tempore vite sue aliquid in prejudicium Burgensis ecclesie vel eiusdem ecclesie libertatum et precipue ad perturbationem clausture parci de la Bigg' personaliter attemptavit nec per alios attemptari procuravit, nec temporibus futuris vite sue, arte vel ingenio, contra predictum monasterium, nec[1] eius libertates qualitercumque contingentes contraibit nec alios contraire procurabit, set pro viribus suis, quicquid dicto monasterio fuerit necessarium pro posse sue manutenebit, et sustentabit.

1 *nec* interlined.

184 Memorandum recording the life corrody granted by Abbot Godfrey and the convent to Idonia Rivel, consisting of 7s 8d p.a. from the abbot's chamber and food and drink from the abbot's kitchen and cellar. Includes a note that the memorandum will be recorded in the convent's register. [29 Mar. 1305]

Carta Idonie Rivel de corrodio suo.

Memorandum et firmiter tenendum quod die Martis proxima post festum annunciationis beate Marie, anno Domini millesimo tricentesimo quinto, dominus Godefridus Dei gracia abbas de Burgo Sancti Petri et eiusdem loci conventus concesserunt Idonie Ryvel victui necessaria omnibus diebus vite sue sub hac forma; videlicet quod eadem Idonia percipiet singulis annis de camera abbatis qui pro tempore fuerit septem solidos et octo denarios terminum ad Pascha pro herbegagio suo et oblationibus suis, et cotidie de celario abbatis duo panes parvos, unum videlicet album, et alterum bissum, et unam lagenam et dimidiam bone cervise, et unum ferculum de coquina abbatis secundum varietatem dierum. Et ut hec concessio stabilis sit et firma, presens memorandum in registro capituli assensu et voluntate predictorum abbatis et conventus insertur et notatur, et nichilominus presenti memorandum penes dictam Idoniam residenti sigillum predicti domini abbatis est appensum. Dat' in capitulo monasterii de Burgo die et anno supradictis.

185 Memorandum that on 6 Mar. 1306, William of Stanwick, rector of Islip, swore that he would not oppose Abbot Godfrey and the convent in pleas in the royal and episcopal courts against John Strathbogie, earl of Atholl.[1]

Memorandum quod die Dominica proxima ante festum sancti Gregorii pape, anno Domini millesimo CCC^{mo} quinto, dominus Willelmus de

Stanewigg', rector ecclesie de Islep', juravit tactis sacrosanctis ewangeliis, quod ipse numquam per se nec per alium inpedimentum procurabit, nec faciet procurari, contra dominum G[odefridum] abbatem Burgi nec eiusdem loci[2] conventum, in placitis motis in curiis domini regis et domini Linc' episcopi, inter ipsos abbatem et conventum et Johannem Strabolgui comitem Attholie, nec in aliis quibuscumque, jura nec libertates monasterii eorumdem contingentibus. In presencia magistri G[alfridi] de Makes', magistri W[illelmi] de Wermington' junior', Willelmi Jurdan, Ricardi de Croiland', Radulphi de Thorn', Simonis de Gedenei, Thome de London', Roberti nuncii, Ricardi camerarii et aliorum.

1 William of Stanwick had been presented to the disputed church of Lullington by the earl of Atholl. The dispute was settled in the abbot's favour in April 1306. Dalderby's Institutions, fo. 111r. See below, no. 190.

2 *loci* interlined

186 Royal writ to Lambert de Trikingham and Thomas de Burnham, ordering them to cease levying tallage on the abbot's tenants in Stamford and Grafham, because the abbot has shown that they are being tallaged along with the tenants of John de Warenne, earl of Surrey, which is not customary. [28 June 1305]

[fo. 80r] Breve domini regis pro tenentibus abbatis in Stannf' citra pontem.

[Marginated in different hand] Stannford'

Rex dilectis et fidelibus suis Lamberto de Trikingham et Thome de Burnham ad homines villarum de Stannf' et de Graham, qui fuerunt tenentes Johannis de Warenna quondam comitis Surr' defuncti talliandos ad opus nostrum assignatis salutem. Monstravit nobis abbas de Burgo Sancti Petri quod vos quosdam tenentes suos in villis predictis inter predictos tenentes qui fuerunt dicti comitis talliari et pro huiusmodi tallagio nobis reddendo indebite distringi fecistis, ubi iidem tenentes sui inter prefatos tenentes dicti comitis talliari non debent, nec unquam talliari consueverunt. Et quia dicto abbati seu tenentibus suis injuriari nolumus in hac parte, vobis mandamus quod huiusmodi tallagio, super illos quos tenentes dicti abbatis esse in villis predictis vobis constare poterit assidendo supersedeatis et districtionem, si quam ea occasione fieri feceritis sine dilatione relaxari faciatis eisdem. Teste W[altero], Coventr' et Lich' episcopo xxviij die Junii anno regni regis E[dwardi] xxxiij^{o}.

186A Letter of Lambert de Trikingham to Eustace Malerbe and Hugh de Hameldon', collectors of the royal tallage in Stamford, notifying them of the king's order. [*c.* 28 June 1305]

[Marginated] De eodem [and below] Item de eodem in vj^{to} folio sequenti

Lambertus de Trikingham amicis suis, sui gracia Eustachio Mallerbe et Hugoni de Hameldon' ad tallagium domini regis Stannf' colligendum assignatis, salutem in Domino. Quia dominus rex per breve suum testatur, quod tenentes abbatis de Burgo Sancti Petri in villa de Stannf' cum tenentibus de feodo comitis de Warrenn' talliari non debent, nec unquam hactenus talliari consueverunt in eadem villa vobis mando ex parte domini regis quod levationi tallagii super tenentes abbatis predicti de quibus vobis constare poterit assessi in villa predicta supersedeatis omnino juxta mandatum domini regis inde michi directum.

187 Acknowledgement of a debt of £10 to the abbot by William, parson of Achurch. [Michaelmas Term 1305]

[Marginated] Norht'

Willemus persona ecclesie de Achirche cognovit quod debet abbati de Burgo Sancti Petri decem libros. Unde solvet ei ad Pascha proximo futurus centum solidos et ad festum sancti Michaelis proximo sequens, centum solidos. Et nisi fecerit etc concedit quod vicecomes fieri faciat de terris et catallis suis. Et similiter quod episcopus Linc' fieri faciat de bonis ecclesiasticis. Mich' xxxiij finiente rotulo xlvj. Cognitio ista facta in termino Michaelis anno regis E[dwardi] xxiij.[1] Et rotulo xlvj.

1 Recte *xxxiij*?

188 Grant by Abbot Godfrey and the convent to John son of Gregory of Lullington, knight, of support for life for himself, two servants and two horses in the abbey. He is to have his own room and stabling for the horses. He shall eat with the senior members of the abbot's household in the abbot's hall and his servants shall eat with the abbot's servants. Should he become infirm, the food and drink that he should receive from the abbot's cellar is specified and his servants should continue to eat with the abbot's servants. His clothing allowance, fodder for the horses and fuel for his chamber in winter are also specified and he is to receive £10 p.a. The abbey is to fulfil these undertakings or pay a 40 mark penalty. [28 April 1304]

[fo. 80v] Scriptum Johannis de Lullington'.

Omnibus Christi fidelibus presens scriptum visuris vel audituris Godefridus permissione divina abbas de Burgo Sancti Petri et eiusdem loci conventus salutem in Domino. Noveritis nos pro nobis et successoribus nostris concessisse Johanni filio domini Gregorii de Lullington' militis, rationabilem sustentationem in tota vita ipsius Johannis pro se, duobus garcionibus, et duobus equis in abbacia nostra de Burgo Sancti Petri cum camera competenti et stabulo pro duobus equis suis in abbacia nostra predicta. Ita videlicet quod predictus Johannes cum superioribus libere familie abbatis de Burgo et successorum suorum in aula ipsius abbatis ad mensam declinet et admittatur, et garciones sui cum garcionibus ipsius abbatis et successorum suorum in mensa admittantur. Et si contingat quod predictus Johannes causa infirmitatis, vel alia causa necessaria honesta ad mensam in aulam predicti abbatis et successorum suorum accedere nequiverit, volumus et concedimus pro nobis et successoribus nostris, quod idem Johannes recipiat de celario ipsius abbatis et succesorum suorum singulis diebus, duos panes albos, duas lagenas bone cervisie et unum ferculum integrum de coquina abbatis et successorum suorum cum uno intermisso, et garciones sui in aula predicta in victualibus cum garcionibus ipsius abbatis et successorum suorum recipiantur, et quod idem Johannes recipiat pro equis suis cotidie fenum sufficiens et octavam partem quarterii avena in prebenda pro eisdem et focale sufficiens tempore yemali in camera sua, prout alii liberi famuli recipiunt in cameris suis, tempore predicto. Et idem Johannes recipiet singulis annis de garderoba ipsius abbatis et succesorum suorum, duas robas, unam videlicet de meliori secta vallettorum ad festum sancti Martini et aliam ad Pentecosten sibi pro statu suo convenientem, cum fururis decentibus, et decem libras sterlingorum annuatim in abbacia predicta, ad quatuor anni terminos; videlicet ad festum sancti Johannis baptiste quinquaginta solidos, ad festum sancti Michaelis quinquaginta solidos, ad natale Domini quinquaginta solidos, et ad Pascha quinquaginta solidos. Istam conventionem fideliter facere promittunt dicti abbas et conventus pro se et successoribus suis in tota vita ipsius Johannis, sub pena quadraginta marcarum eidem Johanni solvend', cum eos [si] contigerit quod absit, in predicta conventionem eidem Johanni minus plene satisfacere aut desistendo deficere. In cuius rei testimonium huic presenti scripto sigilla nostra fecimus apponi. Dat' in capitulo nostro die Martis proxima post festum sancti Marci ewangeliste anno Domini M^{o} iij^{c} quarto.

189 Letter from Abbot Godfrey and the convent to John, bishop of Lincoln, requesting that he institute Peter of Easton, chaplain, to Bringhurst church, to which the abbey has right of presentation and which is vacant.[1] [*c.* April 1314]

[Marginated] Presentatio Petri de Eston' ad ecclesiam de Brengrist.

Reverendo patri in Christo J[ohanni] Dei gracia Linc' episcopo sui humiles et devoti in Christo filii G[odefridus] eiusdem dono gracie abbas de Burgo Sancti Petri et eiusdem loci conventus salutem et obedientiam debito cum omni reverencia et honore. Sancte paternitati vestre presentamus dilectum nobis in Christo dominum P[etrum] de Eston', capellanum, ad ecclesiam de Brengryst vacantem, que ad nostram spectat presentationem, humiliter supplicantes et devote quatinus caritatis intuitu eundem ad dictam ecclesiam admittatis et personam in eadem instituatis. Salvis nobis et ecclesie nostre juribus ab antiquo perceptis in eadem. In cuius rei testimonium sigilla nostra sunt appensa.

1 Peter of Easton was instituted on 21 April, 1314. Dalderby's Institutions, fo. 208r.

190 Royal writ to John, bishop of Lincoln, ordering him to admit to Lullington church a suitable candidate nominated by the abbot, who has recovered the right of presentation in the royal court from John, son of David, earl of Atholl.[1] [20 April 1306]

[fo. 81r] [Marginated] Breve domini regis pro ecclesia de Lullington'.

Edwardus Dei gracia rex Anglie, dominus Hibernie et dux Aquitanie venerabili in Christo patri J[ohanni] eadem gracia episcopo Linc' salutem. Sciatis quod abbas de Burgo Sancti Petri in curia nostra coram justiciariis nostris apud Westm' recuperavit presentationem suam versus Johannem filium David comitem Atholie ad ecclesiam de Lullington' per defaltam ipsius comitis. Et ideo vobis mandamus quod non obstante reclamatione predicti comitis ad presentationem predicti abbatis ad predictam ecclesiam idoneam personam admittatis. Teste R de Hengham apud Westm' xx die Aprilis anno regni nostri xxxiiij^{o}.

1 For the episcopal record of the dispute, see Dalderby's Institutions, fo. 111r.

191 Royal writ to the sheriff of Rutland ordering him not to demand from the abbot scutage for five knights' fees, levied in the 28th year of Edward's reign for the army in Scotland, because the abbot has fined with him. Also to restore anything distrained without delay. [10 April 1306]

Rex vicecomiti Rotel' salutem. Quia dilectus nobis in Christo abbas de Burgo Sancti Petri finem fecit nobiscum per preceptum nostrum in exercitu nostro Scotie anno regni nostri xxviij^{o} per [sic] servicio quinque feodorum militum quod tunc nobis recognovit, tibi precipimus quod demande quam eidem abbati facis pro scutagio ad opus nostrum pro predictis quinque feodis de exercitu predicto[1] supersedeas et ipsum inde pacem habere permittas. Et distr' si quam eidem abbati ea occasione feceris sine dilatione relaxes eidem. Teste meipso apud Wynton' x° die Aprilis anno regni nostri xxxiiij°.

1 *predicto* interlined.

192 Letter from Abbot Godfrey and the convent to John, bishop of Lincoln, requesting him to institute Robert of Miningsby to Lullington church, to which the abbey has right of presentation and which is vacant.[1] [1 Feb. 1306]

Presentatio Roberti de Mithingesby ad ecclesiam de Lullington'.

Reverendo in Christo patri domino J[ohanni] Dei gracia Linc' episcopo sui humiles et devoti in Christo filii Godefridus permissione divina abbas monasterii de Burgo Sancti Petri et eiusdem loci conventus salutem cum omni reverencia et honore. Sancte paternitate vestre presentamus dilectum nobis in Christo Robertum de Mithingesby, clericum, ad ecclesiam de Lullington' vacantem, que ad nostram spectat presentationem, humiliter supplicantes et devote quatinus caritatis intuitu eundem ad dictam ecclesiam admittatis et personam in eadem instituatis. In cuius rei testimonium presentibus sigilla nostra sunt apposita. Dat' in capitulo nostro die Martis in vigilia purificationis beate Marie anno Domini millesimo CCC^mo^ quinto.

1 For Robert of Miningsby's institution on 4 May 1306, see Dalderby's Institutions, fo. 111r.

193 Grant by Abbot Godfrey and the convent to Master Robert de Bokingham, clerk, of a pension of 5 marks p.a. from the abbot's chamber until they can provide him with a suitable benefice. [2 April 1306]

Pensio magistri Roberti de Bokingham.

Universis Christi fidelibus presentes litteras visuris vel audituris, Godefridus permissione divina abbas monasterii sancti Petri de Burgo et eiusdem loci conventus salutem in Domino sempiternam. Noveritis nos unanimiter concessisse dilecto nobis in Christo magistro Roberto de Bokingham, clerico, quinque marcas sterlingorum nomine pensionis annue de camera abbatis qui pro tempore fuerit ad duos annui terminos percipiendas; videlicet ad Pascha duas marcas et dimidiam, et ad festum sancti Michaelis duas marcas et dimidiam. Et sic singulis annis donec eidem [fo. 81v] in ecclesiastico beneficio providerimus. In cuius rei testimonium presentibus sigillum nostrum fecimus apponi. Dat' in capitulo nostro in vigilia Pasche anno Domini M^{o} CCC^{mo} sexto.

194 Royal writ to the abbot on account of the aid due to the king for the knighting of his eldest son, due to take place on 22 May next. The abbot is ordered to attend on the king and his council at Westminster on 6 June next, or send his proctors or attorneys with full authority to discuss the matter and make decisions. He is to bring the writ. [5 April 1306]

Breve domini regis domino abbati de Burgo directum pro Edwardo filio suo milite faciendo.

Edwardus Dei gracia rex Anglie, dominus Hybernie, et dux Aquitanie dilecto sibi in Christo abbati de Burgo Sancti Petri salutem. Quia ordinavimus quod Edwardus filius noster primogenitus in festo Pentecoste proximo futuro, Deo propitio, militie cingulo decoretur, per quod de jure corone nostre in huiusmodi casu auxilium fieri nobis debet, vobis mandamus in fide et dilectione quibus nobis tenemini firmiter injungentes, quod in crastino sancte Trinitatis proximo futuro sitis in persona propria vestra coram nobis et consilio nostro apud Westm' ad tractandum et ordinandum, una cum aliis prelatis, magnatibus et proceribus de regno nostro de auxilio nobis in casu predicto faciendo, et ad consentiendum hiis que ibidem in hac parte contigerit ordinari, vel procuratores seu attornatos vestros, a vobis sufficientem potestatem habentes, et instructos, ad premissa facienda, tunc ibidem mittatis. Et habeatis ibi hoc breve. Teste me ipso apud Wynton' v die Aprilis anno regni nostri xxxiiij^{to}.

194A Reply by the abbot to the above writ, telling the king that Brother William Saleman, the sacrist, and Robert de Thorp' will come in his place. [23 May 1306]

Responsio predicti brevis.

Excellentisimo in Christo domino suo, domino Edwardo Dei gracia illustri regi Anglie domino Hybernie, et duci Aquitanie, suus si placet capellanus humilis abbas sancti Petri de Burgo, salutem, et votiva orationum suffragia continua, subjectibiliter impendenda. Quoniam hac instanti die Lune in crastino sancte Trinitatis proximo futuro coram vobis et consilio vestro apud Westm' causa impediente legitima, personaliter interesse non valentes; dilectos nostros in Christo, fratrem Willelmum Saleman, commonachum et sacristam nostrum, et Robertum de Thorp', procuratores seu attornatos nostros, ad tractandum et ordinandum una cum magnatibus et proceribus de regno vestro, et ad consentiendum hiis que ibidem ordinari seu fieri debebunt cum mandato et potestate speciali, vestre regie celsitudini transmittimus, ratum promittentes habere et firmum, quicquid pro utilitate et honore regie majestatis vestre, per ipsos vel eorum alterum, ibidem fuerit ordinatum, consensum, statutum seu diffinitum. In cuius rei testimonium presentibus sigillum nostrum apposuimus. Dat' apud Burg' Sancti Petri die Jovis in septimana Pentecoste anno regni vestri xxxiiij[to].

195 Complaint to the justices of the peace in Northamptonshire by William, abbot of Thorney that, on 28 March 1306, Godfrey, abbot of Peterborough, Richard Hunne, harvester of Eye, and Thomas Kideheved, miller of Eye, and others stole a horse valued at £10 on the common path from Eye to a place called *Harlotesford'*[1] on the River Nene.

A[2] les justices nostre seignur le roy de sa pees garder en le cunte de Norhamton' se pleint William abbe de Thorneye que Godefrey abbe de Burgh' saint Pierre, Richard Hunne[3] messer de Eye, Thomas Kideheved mouner de Eye ensembelment oue autres mesconuz a tort vindrent le Mardi en la semeyne penouse en lan du regne notre seygnur le roy Edward trente e quarte en la vile de Eye en un comun chimyn que se ostent [continues foot fo. 82r] de la dite vile deque le ewe de Neen a un gwe que est appelle Harlotesford' et iloeques a force e a armes ceo est asauer espees arqes e seettes pristrount un chival pris de x li e de iloeques lamenerent la ou il voleyent e uncore en sount seysiz, ceo trespas luy firent a tort e encountre la pees nostre seygneur le roy e de denz la semouns de vestre justicerie e a ses damages de xli li.[4]

1 *Harlotesford'* forded the Old Ea Catswater at Thorney mill. I am indebted to Mr T. Halliday for this information.

2 For Thorney Abbey copies in French and English, together with a copy of the court record and jurors' verdict, see CUL, Add. MS 3021, fos 457v–8v; Corpus Christi College, Cambridge, MS 297, fos 177v–8v. See also *Henry of Pytchley*, pp. 3–4.

3 *Humme* in Add. MS 3021.

4 *x li.* in Add. MS 3021.

195A Indentured agreement made at the instigation of Walter Langton, bishop of Coventry and Lichfield, royal treasurer, and other friends, between the abbots of Thorney and Peterborough over a path to Eye in a place on the River Nene called *Herlotesforth'*. Peterborough has granted that Thorney and anyone connected with the abbey may use the path at all times and for all purposes without hindrance. [19 April 1306]

[fo. 82r] Scriptum de chimino concesso abbati et conventui de Thorneie apud molendinum de Thorneye.

[Marginated] infra folio cv.[1]

Universis[2] sancte matris ecclesie filiis pateat per presentes, quod mota discordia inter abbatis de Burgo Sancti Petri, et de Thorneia, de quodam chimino habendo ab uno loco in aqua de Neen, qui vocatur Herlotesforth', usque ad villam de Eye, tandem contentio predicta ad instanciam reverendi patris domini Walteri Coventr' et Lichef' episcopi, tunc temporis illustris regis Anglie thesaurarii et aliorum amicorum communium inter partes easdem, conquievit in hunc modum; videlicet quod predictus abbas de Burgo Sancti Petri et eiusdem loci conventus ex mera voluntate, et speciali sua benivolencia pro mutue religionis caritate augenda et fovenda, concesserunt pro se et successoribus suis, quod predictus abbas de Thorneia et eiusdem loci conventus et eorum successores, et omnes homines eorum, ac alii hospites et familiares apud Thorneye accedentes, decetero habeant predictum chiminum et eo utantur pro voluntate sua omnibus horis anni, ad latitudinem quindecim pedum, cum bigis, carectis, equis, cariagiis propriis et fugacione averiorum et animalium suorum ad mercata, ferias et alibi transeuntum eundo et redeundo sine peturbatione predictorum abbatis de Burgo Sancti Petri, conventus, successorum et hominum suorum inperpetuum. Hoc tamen observato, quod alii quicumque extranei preter quam in forma predicta virtute huius concessionis, nichil juris vel clamii, seu asiamenti in predicto chimino exigere vel vendicare poterunt. In cuius rei testimonium, huic scripto indentato, sigilla dictorum abbatum et eorum conventuum, alternatim sunt apposita. Dat' apud Staunford'[3] die Martis proxima post festum sanctorum Tiburtii et Valeriani anno regni regis Edwardi filii regis Henrici tricesimo quarto.

1 No. 257, an associated quitclaim.

2 Also in Swaffham, fo. 276r–v, Soc. of Antiquaries, MS 38, fo. 111v, BL, Cott. Cleop. C ii, fos 40v–41r and *Henry of Pytchley*, p. 4 note. For Thorney Abbey copies of the agreement and a note about its making, see CUL, Add. MS 3021, fos 371v, 458v and Corpus Christi College, Cambridge, MS 297, fos 178v–9r.

3 Stanground in Add MS 3021. Either is plausible, but no. 257 was concluded at Stamford on the same day.

196 Letter from Abbot Godfrey and the convent to John, bishop of Lincoln, requesting him to institute Philip de Warle, clerk, to the church of Clopton, to which the abbey has right of presentation and which is vacant.[1] [28 Sept. 1311]

Presentatio Philipi de Warl' ad ecclesiam de Clopton'.

Reverendo in Christo patri domino J[ohanni] Dei gracia Linc' episcopo sui humiles et devoti in Christo filii Godefridus permissione divina abbas monasteri Burgo Sancti Petri et eiusdem loci conventus salutem cum omni reverencia et honore. Sancte paternitate vestre presentamus dilectum nobis in Christo Philipum de Warle, clericum, ad ecclesiam de Clopton' vacantem, que ad nostram spectat presentationem, humiliter supplicantes et devote quatinus caritatis intuitu eundem ad dictam ecclesiam admittatis et personam in eadem instituatis. Salvis nobis et ecclesie nostre juribus ab antiquo perceptis in eadem. In cuius rei testimonium presentibus litteris sigilla nostra sunt appensa. Dat' in capitulo nostro iiij^{to} kalendas Octobris anno Domini M^{o} CCC^{mo} undecimo.

1 For Philip de Warle's institution on 12 Oct. 1311, see Dalderby's Institutions, fo. 122v.

197 Grant by Abbot Godfrey and the convent, at the king's request, to Gilbert Goldston, the king's butler, of lifetime support in the abbey, together with a horse and groom. He is to have a decent room and a stable for his horse. He shall eat with the senior members of the abbot's household and his servant shall eat with the abbots's servants. He is to remain in the abbey if he becomes infirm. He is to have 20s and a robe of specified quality and status each year. [13 July 1306]

[fo. 82v] Scriptum Gilberti Goldston'.

Omnibus Christi fidelibus presens scriptum visuris vel audituris Godefridus permissione divina abbas de Burgo Sancti Petri et eiusdem loci conventus salutem in Domino. Noveritis nos per nobis et successoribus nostris ad instanciam domini E[dwardi] Dei gracia illustris regis Anglie, concessisse dilecto nostro Gilberto Golston', butillario eiusdem regis, rationabilem sustentationem in tota vita ipsius Gilberti pro se et uno equo et uno garcione in abbacia nostra cum camera decenti, cum vallettis nostris et successorum nostrorum, et cum stabulo pro uno equo in abbacia nostra predicta. Ita quod predictus Gilbertus cum superioribus familie nostre ad mensam declinet et admittatur, et garcio suus cum garcionibus nostris et successorum nostrorum in mensa admittatur. Et si contingat ipsum Gilbertum quod absit infirmarius, ita quod indigeat per se remanere habebit cameram competentem pro se, et omnia necessaria in abbacia nostra predicta. Idem vero Gilbertus percipiet singulis annis de garderoba nostra et successorum nostrorum unam robam de meliori secta vallettorum nostrorum et successorum nostrorum cum fururo decenti eo tempore quo valetti nostri vel succesorum nostrorum suas robas percipiunt et viginti solidos annuos; videlicet decem solidos ad festum sancti Michaelis, et decem solidos ad Pascha. Et ut ita concessio rata consistat et stabilis, huic presenti scripto sigilla nostra fecimus apponi. Dat' in capitulo nostro die Mercurii proxima post festum translationis sancti Thome martiris anno regni regis E[dwardi] xxxiiij^{to}.

198 Grant by Abbot Godfrey and the convent to William de Gaitington', clerk, of a pension of 4 marks p.a. from the abbot's chamber until they can provide him with a benefice. [26 Oct. 1306]

Pensio Willelmi de Gaitington' clerici.

Universis Christi fidelibus presentes litteras visuris vel audituris Godefridus permissione divina abbas de Burgo Sancti Petri et eiusdem loci conventus salutem in Domino sempiternam. Noverit universitas vestra nos caritatis intuitu concessisse dilecto nobis in Christo Willelmo de Gaitington', clerico, quatuor marcas sterlingorum nomine pensionis annue de camera abbatis qui pro tempore fuerit ad duos anni terminos percipiendas; videlicet ad Pascha duas marcas et ad festum sancti Michaelis duas marcas donec eidem in ecclesiastico beneficio providerimus. In cuius rei testimonium etcetera. Dat' in capitulo nostro die Mercurii proxima ante festum apostolorum Simonis et Jude anno Domini millesimo tricentesimo sexto.

199 Letter from Abbot Godfrey and the convent to John, bishop of Lincoln, requesting him to institute Robert of Miningsby, chaplain, to the church of Paston, to which they have right of presentation and which is vacant.[1] [20 Nov. 1310]

Presentatio domini Roberti de Mithinggesbi ad ecclesiam de Paston'.

Reverendo in Christo patri domino J[ohanni] Dei gracia Linc' episcopo sui humiles et devoti in Christo filii G[odefridus] permissione divina abbas de Burgo Sancti Petri et eiusdem loci conventus salutem cum omni reverencia et honore. Sancte paternitati vestre presentamus dilectum nobis in Christo Robertum de Mithinggesbi', capellanum, ad ecclesiam de Paston' vacantem, que ad nostram spectat presentationem, humiliter supplicantes et devote quatinus caritatis intuitu eundem ad dictam ecclesiam admittatis, et personam in eadem instituatis. Salvis nobis et ecclesie nostre juribus ab antiquo perceptis in eadem. In cuius rei testimonium presentibus litteris sigilla nostra sunt appensa. Dat' in capitulo nostro die Veneris in festo sancti Edmundi regis et martiris. Anno Domini millesimo CCC^{o} x^{o}.

1 For Robert of Miningsby's institution on 10 Dec. 1310, see Dalderby's Institutions, fo. 120v.

200 Royal writ to the sheriff of Cambridge and Huntingdon ordering him to allow the abbot's bailiffs collect the king's debts within the abbot's bailiwick and pay them at the Exchequer, the abbot having shown that he has this right by charter of Henry III, which the present king has confirmed. [2 June 1307]

[fo. 83r] Breve directum vicecomiti Huntingd' pro debitis domini regis levandis per ballivos abbatis de Burgo.

Rex vicecomitibus Cant' et Hunt' salutem. Ex parte dilecti nobis in Christo abbatis de Burgo Sancti Petri nobis est ostensum quod cum per cartam domini H[enrici] regis Anglie patris nostri quam confirmamus, concessum sit abbati de Burgo Sancti Petri qui pro tempore fuerit quod ballivi dicti abbatis colligant omnia debita nobis et heredibus nostris debita in omnibus dominiis suis in cuiuscumque balliva sint, et quod inde respondeant per manum suam ad Scaccarium nostrum, ita quod vicecomites vel ballivi sui inde in nullo se intromittant, quod que ballivi dicti abbatis et predecessorum suorum a tempore confectionis carte et confirmationis predictarum, semper hactenus omnia debita dicto patri nostro et nobis debita in dominiis predictis colligere et inde respondere per manum suam ad Scaccarium predictum, consueverint, tu iam de novo ballivos predicti abbatis quo minus debita nobis debita in dominiis dicti abbatis in comitatu tuo colligere et inde respondere per manum suam ad Scaccarium nostrum sicut predictum est impedivisti et adhuc impedis minus juste in ipsius abbatis dispendium non modicum, et contra tenorem carte et confirmationis predictarum. Et quia nolumus quod prefato abbati injurietur in hac parte, tibi precipimus, quod si ita est, tunc ab huiusmodi impedimentis ballivis dicti abbatis occasione predicta inferrendis desistens ipsos debita nobis in dominiis predicta in comitatu tuo debita colligere, et inde ad Scaccarium nostrum per manum nostram respondere permittas, sicut debita illa colligere et inde ad Scaccarium predictum respondere debent. Et ipsi ac ceteri ballivi dicti abbatis et predecessorum suorum predictorum huiusmodi debita colligere et inde in forma predicta a tempore predicto semper hactenus respondere consueverunt. Teste me ipso apud Karliolum ij die Junii anno regni nostri tricesimo quinto.

201 Royal writ to the treasurer and barons of the Exchequer ordering them to allow the bailiffs of the abbot and monks to respond at the Exchequer for royal debts within their hundreds in Northamptonshire and throughout their domains, in whatever bailiwick, because they have this privilege by charter of Henry III. [20 Mar. 1307]

[Marginated] Breve directum thesaurario et baronibus suis de Scaccario pro abbate de Burgo.

Edwardus Dei gracia rex Anglie, dominus Hibernie et dux Aquitanie thesaurario et baronibus suis de Scaccario salutem. Cum bone memorie dominus H[enricus] quondam rex Anglie pater noster per cartam suam quam confirmavimus, concesserit pro se et heredibus suis, abbati et monachis de Burgo Sancti Petri, quod ballivi predictorum abbatis et monachorum, colligant debita predicto patri nostro et heredibus suis debita in omnibus hundredis dictorum abbatis et monachorum in comitatu Norht' et in omnibus dominiis suis in cuiuscumque balliva sint et quod inde respondeant per manum suam ad Scaccarium predictum. Ita quod vicecomites vel ballivi sui inde in nullo se intromittant, prout in carta predicta plenius continentur, vobis mandamus quod ballivos dictorum abbatis et monachorum debita predicta in hundredis et omnibus dominiis suis in cuiuscumque ballia sint ut predictum est colligere et ad predictum Scaccarium per manus suas respondere juxta tenorem carte predicte permittatis prout ballivi eorumdem [fo. 83v] abbatis et monachorum a tempore confectionis carte et confirmationis predictarum colligere et respondere consueverunt. Teste meipso apud Karliolum xx die Marcii anno regni nostri tricesimo quinto.

202 Royal writ to Hugh le Despenser, justice of the forest south of the Trent, ordering him to permit the abbot, monks and their men to keep unlawed dogs[1] throughout their demesnes, manors and the two hundreds of Nassaburgh in conformity with the charter of Henry III, which the king has confirmed. [20 Mar. 1307]

[Marginated] Breve directum domino H[ugoni] le Despens' justiciario foreste pro abbate de Burgo.

Edwardus Dei gracia rex Anglie, dominus Hibernie, et dux Aquitanie dilecto et fideli suo Hugoni le Despens' justiciario foreste sue ultra Trentam salutem. Cum bone memorie dominus H[enricus] quondam rex Anglie, pater noster, per cartam suam quam confirmavimus, concesserit abbati de Burgo et monachis ibidem Deo servientibus quod habeant canes suos non mutilatos per omnia dominia et maneria sua, similiter milites et francolani et omnes homines de duobus hundredis de Nasso Burgi, habeant canes suos non mitulatos [sic] prout in carta predicta plenius contininetur, vobis mandamus quod ipsos abbatem et monachos per omnia dominia et maneria sua, milites francolanos et omnes homines de duobus hundredis predictis canes suos non mitulatos [sic] habere permittatis prout ipsi et antecessores eorum a tempore confectionis carte et confirmationis predictarum habere consueverunt. Teste meipso apud Karliolum xx die Marcii anno regni nostri tricesimo quinto.

1 For the lawing of dogs, see C. R. Young, *The Royal Forests of Medieval England* (Leicester, 1979), pp. 41, 68.

203 Royal writ to the coroners of Northamptonshire summoning Robert de Veer, sheriff of Northampton, before the barons of the Exchequer at York to answer for his contempt to the king and trespass against the abbot, touching the latter's right to the return of writs within his liberty. [7 May 1302]

Edwardus Dei gracia rex Anglie, dominus Hibernie, et dux Aquitanie, coronatoribus comitatus Norht' salutem. Monstravit nobis abbas de Burgo Sancti Petri, quod cum ipse et predecessores sui per liberatatem cartarum progenitorum nostrorum regum Anglie et confirmationis nostre hactenus habuerunt, et idem abbas habere debeat returna omnium brevium nostrorum de quibus executio fieri debeat infra precintum libertatis sue, Robertus de Veer nunc vicecomes noster comitatus predicti super receptione plurium brevium nostrorum, unde executio fieri debuerat infra libertatem predictam, inportune fingens se returnum huiusmodi brevium nostrorum, ballivis libertatis ipsius abbatis fecisse ad executionem inde faciendam ubi nullum inde dictis ballivis fecerat, coram diversis ministris nostris ubi huiusmodi brevia nostra habuit retornasse maliciose pluries retornavit, quod demandavit executionem huiusmodi brevium nostrorum dictis ballivis ipsius abbatis faciendam, qui nichil inde fecerunt pretextu cuiusdam returni iterato emanarunt brevia nostra dicto vicecomiti directa, quod non omitteret propter dictam libertatem, quin eam ingrederetur et huiusmodi brevium nostrorum faceret executionem in lesionem libertatis cartarum progenitorum nostrorum predictorum et confirmationis nostre antedicte quod nobis cedit in contemptum et exheredationem dicti abbatis manifestam. Et ideo vobis precipimus quod venire faciatis coram baronibus de Scaccario nostro apud Ebor' a die Pasche proxima preterita in unum mensem predictum Robertum vicecomitem nostrum, ad respondendum nobis de contemptu et dicto abbati de transgressionibus supradictis sicut idem abbas rationabiliter monstrare poterit quod inde respondere debeat. Et habeatis ibi tunc hoc breve. Teste W[illelmo] de Carleton' apud Ebor' vij die Maii anno regni nostri tricesimo.

204 Royal writ to the sheriff of Huntingdon, ordering that neither he nor his bailiffs should infringe the right of the abbot and monks, granted by charter of Henry III and confirmation of Edward I, to collect royal debts in their hundreds in Northamptonshire and throughout their domains and to answer for them at the Exchequer, also to pleas of *vee de naam* and return of writs. [7 Mar. 1308]

[fo. 84r] Rex vicecomiti Huntingdon' salutem. Ex parte dilectorum nobis in Christo abbatis et monachorum de Burgo Sancti Petri nobis est ostensum quod cum ipsi per cartas celebris memorie domini H[enrici] quondam regis Anglie, avi nostri, et confirmationem domini E[dwardi] quondam regis Anglie patris nostri quas inspeximus, has habeant libertates; videlicet quod ballivi dictorum abbatis et monachorum colligant debita nostra in omnibus hundredis dictorum abbatis et monachorum in comitatu Norht' et in omnibus dominiis suis in cuiuscumque balliva sint, et quod inde respondeant per manum suam ad Scaccarium nostrum. Ita quod vicecomes vel ballivi sui in nullo inde se intromittant. Et eciam quod habeant placita vetiti namii infra octo hundreda sua in comitatu Norht' et alibi infra libertates dominiorum suorum, cum returna brevium nostrorum ipsos et libertates suas contingentium, ac ballivi dictorum abbatis et monachorum et predecessorum suorum abbatum et monachorum eiusdem loci semper hactenus a tempore confectionis cartarum et confirmationis predictarum debita progenitorum nostrorum quondam regum Anglie et nostra in omnibus hundredis eorumdem abbatis et monachorum in predicto comitatu Northt' et in omnibus dominiis suis in cuiuscumque balliva essent collegerint dicti que abbas et monachi placita vetiti namii infra octo hundreda sua in comitatu Norht' et alibi infra libertates et dominiorum suorum cum returno brevium dictorum progenitorum nostrorum, et nostrorum ipsos et libertates suas contingentium habuerunt. Tu ballivos predictos debita nostra in dominiis dictorum abbatis et monachorum in balliva tua colligere non permittis, nec ipsos abbatem et monachos placita vetiti namii in balliva tua cum returno brevium nostrorum ipsos et libertates suas ibidem contingentium habere facis, set ipsos super hoc iam de novo inpedis minus juste in ipsorum abbatis et monachorum dampnum non modicum et gravamen et contra tenorem cartarum et confirmationis predictarum. Et quia nolumus quod eisdem abbati et monachis injurietur in hac parte, tibi precipimus quod si ita est tunc ballivos predictos debita nostra in omnibus dominiis dictorum abbatis et monachorum in balliva tua colligere permittas, et dicto abbati et monachis placita vetiti namii in balliva tua infra libertates dominiorurm suorum cum returno brevium nostororum tibi directorum et dirigendorum ipsos et libertates suas ibidem contingentium habere facis juxta tenorem cartarum et confirmationis predictarum, et prout ballivi predicti debita illa colligere, et iidem abbates et monachi et predecessores sui, abbates et monachi eiusdem loci placita vetiti namii in balliva tua infra libertates dominiorum suorum cum returno brevium dictorum primogenitorum nostrorum et nostrorum semper hactenus a tempore confectionis cartarum et confirmationis predictarum colligere et habere consueverunt. Teste rege apud Westm' viij die Marcii anno etc. primo.

205 Oath sworn by Master Robert de Bokingham, rector of All Saints, Irthlingborough, before Abbot Godfrey, to be faithful and loyal in his conduct of abbey business. [4 April 1308]

[fo. 84v] Sacramentum magistri Roberti de Bokingham prestitum coram domino Godefrido abbate de Burgo Sancti Petri in capella eiusdem die Jovis in festo sancti Ambrosii anno Domini millesimo CCC^{mo} octavo, presentibus fratre Roberto de Spaldingg', fratre Johanne de Wytherington' monachis, Johanne de Aylington' clerico, publico notario, sub verbis infra scriptis:

Ego Robertus de Bokingham rector ecclesie Omnium Sanctorum de Irtelingburg' ero fidelis promotor et diligens verbo et facto negotiorum monasterii sancti Petri de Burgo jura et libertates eiusdem proposse defendam, salva fidelitate domino regi prestita, consilia et secreta dominorum abbatis et conventus mihi per se vel per litteras seu per nuncium manifestata in dampnum eorumdem, vel ecclesie sue antedicte, nullatenus pandam in futurum, sed ymaginata dispendia a quibuscumque eisdem inferenda a tempore noticie, debita resistencia inpediam et jacturas, sit Deus me adjuvet et ista sancta evangelia.

206 Letter from Abbot Godfrey and the convent to John, bishop of Lincoln, requesting him to institute Master Robert de Bokingham to the church of All Saints, Irthlingborough, to which the abbey has right of presentation and which is vacant.[1] [31 Jan. 1308]

Presentatio eidem[2] magistri Roberti supradicti ad ecclesiam Omnium Sanctorum de Irtelingburgh'.

Reverendo patri in Christo domino J[ohanni] Dei gracia Linc' episcopo sui humiles et devoti in Christo filii Godefridus eiusdem dono gracie abbas de Burgo Sancti Petri et eiusdem loci conventus salutem et debite reverentie devotam obedientiam. Sancte paternitati vestre presentamus dilectum nobis in Christo magistrum Robertum de Bokingham, clericum, ad ecclesiam Omnium Sanctorum de Irtelingburgh' vacantem, que ad nostram spectat presentationem, humiliter supplicans et devote, quatinus eiusdem caritatis intuitu ad dictam ecclesiam admittatis et personam in eadem instituatis. Salvis nobis et ecclesie nostre juribus ab antiquo perceptis in eadem. In cuius rei testimonium presentibus sigilla nostra apposuimus. Dat' in capitulo nostro die Martis proxima post festum conversionis sancti Pauli anno Domini M° tricentesimo septimo.

1 For Robert de Bokingham's institution on 20 Mar. 1308, see Dalderby's Institutions, fo. 113v.
2 *eidem* interlined.

207 Letter from Abbot Godfrey and the convent to John, bishop of Lincoln, requesting him to institute William de Bannewell' to the church of Paston, to which the abbey has right of presentation and which is vacant.[1] [15 April 1308]

Presentatio Willelmi de Bannewell' ad ecclesiam de Paston'.

Reverendo patri in Christo domino J[ohanni] Dei gracia Linc' episcopo sui humiles et devoti in Christo filii Godefridus eiusdem dono gracie abbas de Burgo Sancti Petri et eiusdem loci conventus salutem et debite reverencie devotam obedienciam. Sancte paternitati vestre presentamus dilectum nobis in Christo Willelmum de Bannewell', clericum, ad ecclesiam de Paston' vacantem, que ad nostram spectat presentationem, humiliter supplicantes et devote quatinus caritatis intuitu eundem ad dictam ecclesiam admittatis et personam in eadem instituatis. Salvis nobis et ecclesie nostre juribus ab antiquo perceptis in eadem. In cuius rei testimonium presentibus sigilla nostra apposuimus. Dat' in capitulo nostro die Lune in ebdomada Pasche anno Domini M° CCC^{mo} octavo.

1 For William de Bannewell's institution on 4 May 1308, see Dalderby's Institutions, fo. 114r.

208 Royal writ to an unspecified sheriff ordering him to respect the abbot's right to return of writs and the collection of royal debts within his liberty, which the abbot enjoys under royal charters confirmed by Edward I. [26 Mar. 1308]

[fo. 85r] Rex vicecomiti salutem. Ex parte abbatis de Burgo Sancti Petri nobis est ostensum quod cum ipse per libertatem cartarum progenitorum nostrorum regum Anglie et confirmationis celebris memorie domini E[dwardi] quondam regis Anglie patris nostri habeat returna omnium brevium nostrorum quorum executiones infra libertatem dicti abbatis fieri contingunt. Et quod idem abbas per ballivos suos per extractas summonitionum et brevium nostrorum ei per vicecomites nostros qui pro tempore fuerint liberandas debita nostra que infra predictam libertatem nobis debentur levari et inde super[1] compotum vicecomitis ad Scaccarium nostrum nobis respondere debeat. Et quod nullus vicecomes ingredi debeat predictam libertatem ad aliquas executiones preceptorum nostrorum faciendas absque waranto speciali. Tu per te et ministros tuos dictam libertatem absque waranto intrasti, et debita nostra que nobis in eadem debentur de tenentibus dicti abbatis, et aliis, et que dictus abbas per ballivos suos levasse debuerat per districtiones quam plures minus rite levasti, necnon alias districtiones et indebitas executiones infra eandem libertatem fecisti et facere non desistis in prejudicium libertatis et enervationem concessionis progenitorum nostrorum predictorum. Et ideo tibi precipimus quod ab huismodi gravaminibus et injuriis predicto abbati illatis vel inferendis penitus desistas, ipsum que abbatem libertatibus suis super premissis ut et gaudere permittas, prout ipse et predecessores sui inde plenius uti consueverunt ne amplius clamor ad nos inde perveniat per quod ad te gravi punitione capere debeamus. Teste R de Hegham apud Westm' xxvj die Marcii anno regni nostri primo.

1 *super* interlined.

209 Final charter recording the terms of the life corrody granted by Abbot Godfrey and the convent to John son of Gregory of Lullington, knight. [26 Oct. 1306]

Ultima[1] carta Johannis de Lullingt'.[2]

Omnibus Christi fidelibus ad quos presentes littere pervenerint G[odefridus] permissione divina abbas de Burgo Sancti Petri et eiusdem loci conventus salutem in Domino. Noveritis nos pro nobis et successoribus nostris concessisse Johanni filio domini Gregorii de Lullyngton', militis, rationabilem sustentationem in tota vita sua pro se tantum; videlicet singulis diebus unum panem album et unum panem bissum et unam lagenam et dimidiam bone cervise de celario nostro et successorum nostrorum et unum ferculum integrum grosse carnis, grossi piscis[3] vel allecis secundum varietatem dierum de coquina nostra et successorum nostrorum percipiendum ubicumque fuerit et voluerit tam extra abbaciam nostram quam infra nisi gratis in mensa in aula nostra steterit. Ita tamen quod eo die nichil recipiat de celario nostro nec de coquina nostra nec per eum aliquid exigatur. Et idem Johannes recipiet singulis annis de garderoba nostra et successorum nostrorum unam robam de secta valettorum nostrorum cum furura eo tempore quo valetti nostri vel successorum nostrorum suas robas percipiunt et viginti solidos sterlingorum ad quatuor anni terminos; videlicet ad Natale quinque solidos, ad Pascha quinque solidos, ad festum sancti Johannis baptiste quinque solidos et ad festum sancti Michaelis quinque solidos. In cuius rei testimonium huic presenti scripto sigilla nostra fecimus apponi. Dat' in capitulo nostro die Mercurii proxima ante festum apostlorum Simonis et Jude anno Domini M[l] CCC sexto.

1 See no. 188 and above p. xxxii.
2 Rubric follows on from the previous entry.
3 *pissis* in MS.

210 Letter from Abbot Godfrey and the convent to John, bishop of Lincoln, requesting him to institute Master Robert of Lincoln, chaplain, to the church of Northborough, to which the abbey has right of presentation and which is vacant.[1] [17 May 1306]

[fo. 85v] Presentatio domini Roberti de Linc' ad ecclesiam de Northburgh'.

Reverendo in Christo patri domino J[ohanni] Dei gracia Linc' episcopo, sui humiles in Christo filii Godefridus permissione divina abbas monasterii de Burgo Sancti Petri et eiusdem loci conventus salutem cum omni reverencia et honore. Sancte paternitati vestre presentamus dilectum nobis in Christo dominum Robertum de Linc', capellanum, ad ecclesiam de Northburgh' vacantem, que ad nostram spectat presentationem, humiliter supplicantes et devote quatinus eundem caritatis intuitu ad dictam ecclesiam admittatis et personam in eadem instituatis. Salvis nobis et ecclesie nostre juribus ab antiquo perceptis in eadem. In cuius rei testimonium etcetera. Dat' in capitulo nostro xvi kalendas Junii anno Domini M° CCC° xvj.

1 There is no record of this institution in Dalderby's register.

211 Copy of an entry among the Exchequer memoranda concerning the request by Thomas of Peterborough, parson of Deeping and executor of Gilbert of Chesterton[1], burgess of Stamford, that tallage for 1303–4 owed by Gilbert and by Philip son of Thomas of Grantham, to whom Gilbert was heir and executor, be allocated to the surplus of £223 4s 8d on the account rendered by Gilbert and Elias Russel, citizen of London for wool sent to Holland, Zeeland and Brabant. A sum of £223 4s 8d for the sale of wool, customs on wool, money received from Robert Segre and other things was confirmed from the roll for 1300–1 and the agreement of heirs and executors of Gilbert and Elias as to its equal division recognised. [Michaelmas Term 1312]

Inter memoranda de Scaccario de termino Michaelis anno xj^mo^.

[Marginated in late medieval hand] Stannford'

Memorandum quod exigantur in pipa Linc' de Gilberto de Cestreton viij li. xvij s. x d. de tallagio suo in villa de Stanford' assesso anno xxxij regis E[dwardi] patris regis nunc. Et eciam de Philippo filio Thome de Grantham xvij li. xv s. x d. de consimili' tallagio in villa de Grantham assesso eodem anno. Venit modo Thomas de Burgo, persona ecclesie de Deping', executor testamenti predicti Gilberti defuncti, et petit debita predicta allocari heredibus et executoribus ipsius Gilberti in quodam superplusagio CCxxiij li. iiij s. viij d., quod idem Gilbertus et Elias Russel habent in compoto suo de lanis regis E[dwardi] patris predicti, missis ad partes Holand', Seland', et Brabant' et ibidem venditis etc, asserend' ipsum Gilbertum esse heredem et executorem dicti Philippi etcetera. Et super hoc scrutatis rotulis etcetera. Compertum est in rotulo xxix^{o} dicti regis E[dwardi] regis compotorum, quod Elias Russel civis Lond' et Gilbertus de Cestreton burgensis Stanford' receptores denarios in custodia Roberti Segre existencium, et eciam provenientium tam de lanis et aliis rebus dicti patris regis, in partibus Holand', Seland', et Brabant' existentibus, quam de lanis ipsius regis E[dwardi] ab Anglie usque ad partes predictas transmissis, et denarios provenientes de pacionibus custume lanarum predictarum. Habent de superplusagio in compoto suo, etctera. CCxxiij li. iiij s. viij d. Et super hoc Adam Russel filius, heres et executor testamenti predicti Elie presens etcetera cognovit unam medietatem superplusagii predicti allocari debere heredibus et executoribus dicti Gilberti in debitis que regi debent hic. Et idem Thomas de Burgo', pro se et coexecutoribus suis, similiter cognovit aliam medietatem eiusdem superplusagii allocari debere heredibus et executoribus prefati Elie in debitis que regi etc. Et ideo consideratum est quod predictum superplusagium allocetur heredibus et executoribus predictorum Elie et Gilberti pro equali portione in debitis suis predictis.

1 Gilbert of Chesterton was a prominent wool merchant from Grantham. For this and background to his dealings on behalf of the crown, see T. H. Lloyd, *The English Wool Trade in the Middle Ages* (Cambridge, 1977), pp. 67, 79, 131.

[fo. 86r] blank

212 Grant by Abbot Godfrey to the monks and associated brothers at Oxney of 13 stones of cheese p.a. and ¼ lb butter and 2 gallons of milk per week from his manor of Eye. [2 May 1307]

[fo. 86v] [Marginated in different hand] Oxneye

[Marginated in second hand] Eye

Universis Christi fidelibus presens scriptum visuris vel audituris Godefridus miseratione divina abbas de Burgo Sancti Petri salutem in Domino sempiternam. Inter varias rerum mutationes necessaria sunt litterarum testimonia que fideliter confirmant presencia et representant preterita. Cum igitur nos fines possessionum ecclesie beate Marie de Oxeneya, ac ibidem Deo et ecclesie predicte portiones ministrantium, que pro earum exilitate absque secularium exhibitione requisita minime sufficiunt, conspicientes, indigenciam que religionis pro posse in uberiorem fructum transmutare satagentes, fraterna dilectione et caritate continua commoti, concessimus per nobis et successoribus nostris monachis et confratribus nostris in dicta ecclesia Deo et beate Marie devote famulantibus, singulis annis inperpetuum tresdecim petras casei pro equali portione percipendas, in manerio nostro de Eye, et singulis ebdomadis inter festum inventionis sancte Crucis et festum exaltationis sancte Crucis quartam partem unius petri butiri et duas lagenas lactis ibidem. Ita quod singulis annis perceptio cuiuslibet portionis inter custodem ecclesie supradicte et custodem manerii de Eye plenarie tallietur ut utriumque ignorancia plenius excusetur. Quam vero donationem et concessionem pro nobis et successoribus nostris et ab omnibus firmiter volumus teneri inperpetuum absque diminutione, detentione, seu fraudulenti contradictione nisi nos, seu aliquam successorum nostrorum pro futuris temporibus, terras, possessiones, seu redditus ecclesie supradicte in augmentationem cultus divini et portionis ministrantium ad valenciam nostre presentis concessionis conferre contigerit, que collatio, concessio, seu confirmatio, presentem donationem seu concessionem revocet, diminuat et adnichilet, ultima concessione in suo robore, duratura. In cuius rei testimonium has litteras nostre concessionis fieri fecimus patentes tam sigillo nostro quam sigillo capituli nostri consignatas. Dat' in capitulo nostro vj^{to} nonas Maii, anno Domini millesimo CCC^{mo} septimo, et prelationis nostre octavo.

213 Orders for the collection of the twentieth and fifteenth granted to the king at Northampton on 13 Oct. 1307.

Forma taxationis vicesime et xv^{e}.

Ceo est la furme que les asseours et taxours de vintisme graunte a nostre seignur le roi, a Norht' a la quinzeine de seint Michel lan de soen regne primer, par countes, barouns, francshomes, et les communaltes, de totes les countes du reaume et ensement du quinzime graunte au roi illoqes, en totes les citez, burghs, et les aunciens demeins le roi du mesme le reaume, deivent garder, en mesmes les vintisme et quinzime asseer et leuer, cest a savoir, que les chiefs taxours saunz delai facent venir devaunt eux, de chescune cite, burgh, et autre vile du counte denz fraunchise et de hors de plus loaux hommes et mielz vauez [fo. 87r] de mesmes les lieux, a teu noumbre, dunt les chifs taxours puissunt suffisaument, eslire, quatre, ou, sis, de chescune vile, ou plus si mestier soit, a leur descretion, par les queux la dite taxation et ceo que a ceo apent a faire, melz purra estre fete, et acomplie. Et quant il averunt tieux eslutz, adhuc les facent jurer sur Seintes Euvangiles, ceo est a savoir, ceux de chescune vile per eux que ceux issint jurez loiaument et pleinement enquerront, queux biens chescun de mesmes les viles, avoit le jour de[1] Seint Michel, lan du regne du roi que ore est primer, en mesoun, et de hors, ou que il fussent, saunz nul desporter sour greue forfaiture, et touz ceux biens, ou que ils soient devenutz, depuis en cea par vent, ou en autre manere loiaument taxerent solonc lur verreie value sauve les choses desouz forprises ou ceste fourme, et les ferunt enbrever, et mettre en roule endente tout pleinement le plus en hast que il purrunt, et liverer a chiefs taxours, la une partie, desuz lur seals, et reprendre devers eux lautre partie desuz les seals de chiefs taxours. Et quant les chiefs taxours averunt resceu en tele manere les endentures de ceux que serrunt jurez a taxer, en, citees, burghs, et autres viles, mesmes les chiefs taxours, loiaument, et peiniblement, examinent celes endentures. Et si eux entedent[2] qil yeit ascun defaute, eux tauntost ladrescent issint que rien ne soit concele, ne pur doun, ne pur reward de persone meins taxe, que resoun ne demaunde. Et veut le roi que les chiefs taxours ailent de undret en undret, et de vile, en vile ou mestier serra, a surveer et enquerre que les suth taxours, en les mesmes viles eient pleinement taxe et a eux presente les biens de chescun. Et, si il troesent rien concele, meintenaunt ladrescent, et facent a savoir a tresurer et barouns del eschekere les nouns de ceux qi issint averunt trespassez et la manere de lur mesprise. Et la taxacion de biens de suthtaxours de viles soit fete par les chiefs taxours, et per autres prodeshomes queux il ellirrunt, a ceo faire, issint que les biens de ceux soient taxez bie[3] et loiaument, en mesme la manere, que les autres. La taxatioun de biens a chefs taxours, et de lur clerk soit reserve au tresourer et a barouns del escheker. Et les chiefs taxours, si tost come il averunt resceu presentement de suth taxours, facent lever le vintisme, et quinzime al oeps le roi saunz delai, et saunz desport fere anuli en la fourme que enjointe lour est par commission et facent fere deus roules de la dite taxation acordaunt en touz poinz et retienent lun devers euz, pur leuer la taxacioun, e lautre eient a les cheker le roi a la procheine feste del anunciation nostre Dame, a quel jour il ferunt lur primer paie. Et fet a savoir que les propres biens de prelatz et de [fo. 87v] religiouns e[4] de autres clers, les queux biens sunt issaunz de temporaltez que sount annex a lour eglises et sunt taxes entre lour espiritualtez a la disme ne serrunt mie taxez, en ceste taxation de lays, purceo que les ditz prelatz religiouns, et autres clercs donent au roi le quinzime de lur espiritaltez et temporaltez solonc la taxacion dreinement fete. Nequedent, si prelat home de religion, ou autre clerc, eit terres ou tenementz de heritage, ou de purchaz, ou, a ferme, ou en noun de garde, ou par eschete, ou en autre manere, que ne soit cea en arrere taxe au disme, que la clergie ad done, soit taxacion fete de touz les biens, que leour furunt, en mesmes les lius le jour de Seint Michel de suthdit en la fourme que ceste taxacion se ferra de biens de lais. Ensement[5] les biens de vileins a prelatz gentz de religioun, et autres clercs soent taxez en ceste taxacion, issint que rentes et autres servises, que mesmes le vileins fount a lur seignurs dunt le roi prent quinzime ore apermesmes. Les seignurs seient suztretz en la taxation des biens de vileins et du remenaunt vintisme leve. Et fet a savoir, qen ceste taxacion de biens de la communalte de touz les countez, serrunt forpris armure mounture, jeaux, et robes a chiualers, et a gentifs homes et a lour femmes et lour vessele, dor, dargent et dareime. Et en citez, et en burghs, soient forpris une robe pur le homme et une autre pur la femme, et un lit pur ambedeux, un anel et un fermaile dor, ou dargent, et un ceint de seie qil usent touz le jours et ausint un hanap dargente, ou de mazre dunt il beivent. Et de biens de meseaux, la ou il soient governez par soverein, mesel, ne soient taxez ne prisez, et si il soient meseaux governez par mestre s ... soient lour biens taxez come des autres. Et fait a remembrer, que de biens de gentz de countez hors de citeez, burghs, et de demeins le roi, les queux biens soient trouez, par taxation, que ne passent la value de dis solz, ne soit rien demaunde, ne leve, ne de biens de gentz de citez burghs, ne de demeins le roi, queux biens ne atteignent a la value de quinz solz soit rien leve. Et voelt le roi, que les ditz taxours, par quai qil facent pleinement et loiaument les choses susdites, eient plus suffisalment lor despens' que autres venunt eu en tel cas cea enarrere. Et que les taxours ne lur clercs pregnent rien, pur chapitres liverer, ne pur taille fere.

1 *de* interlined.
2 Recte *entendent*.
3 Recte *bien*.
4 *e* interlined.
5 *nota* marginated.

214 Grant by Abbot Godfrey and the convent to Elias de Cantia of specified food and clothing within the abbey for his lifetime, together with 10s p.a. for footwear, subject to his continuing fidelity in aid and counsel. [28 Oct. 1304]

[fo. 88r] Littera Elie de Cantia.

Omnibus Christi fidelibus ad quos presens scriptum pervenerit G[odefridus] Dei gracia abbas de Burgo Sancti Petri et eiusdem loci conventus, salutem in Domino sempiternam. Noverit universitas vestra nos unanimi assensu concessisse dilecto et fideli nostro Elie de Cantia competentem sustentationem in tota vita sua in victu et vestitu in abbacia nostra; videlicet unam robam de secta armigerorum abbatis annuatim percipiendam, et unum panem album et unum panem bissum et duas lagenas bone cervise de celario abbatis et unum ferculum integrum cum intermisso secundum varietatem dierum et temporum de coquina eiusdem abbatis prout libere familie ministratur quamdiu vixerit percipiendos, et decem solidos sterlinggorum [sic] pro calciatura singulis annis, quamdiu vixerit de camera predicti abbatis percipiendos; videlicet ad Pascha et ad festum sancti Michaelis. Concedimus insuper quod predictus Elias ubicumque fuerit infra abbaciam vel extra, omnia predicta libere percipiet et de hiis pro libito suo disponat ita tamen quod dum laborare poterit consilia et auxilia nobis et nostris fideliter inpendet assueta. In cuius rei testimonium huic presenti scripto sigilla nostra sunt appensa. Dat' in capitulo nostro die Mercurii in festo apostolorum Simonis et Jude, anno Domini M° tricentesimo quarto.

215 Letter from Abbot Godfrey and the convent to John, bishop of Lincoln, requesting him to institute Master Robert of Croyland, chaplain, to the church of Peakirk, to which the abbey has right of presentation and which is vacant.[1] [29 Oct. 1311]

Presentatio magistri Roberti de Croyl' ad ecclesiam de Peychirch'.

Venerabili in Christo patri domino J[ohanni] Dei gracia Linc' episcopo, sui humiles et devoti in Christo filii Godefridus permissione divina abbas de Burgo Sancti Petri et eiusdem loci conventus salutem cum omni reverencia et honore. Sancte paternitati vestre presentamus dilectum nobis in Christo magistrum Robertum de Croyland', capellanum, ad ecclesiam de Peykirk' vacantem, que ad nostram spectat presentationem, humiliter supplicantes et devote quatinus caritatis intuitu eundem ad dictam ecclesiam admittatis et personam in eadem instituatis. Salvis nobis et ecclesie nostre juribus ab antiquo perceptis in eadem. In cuius rei testimonium presentibus litteris sigilla nostra sunt appensa. Dat' in capitulo nostro die Veneris proxima ante festum Omnium Sanctorum anno Domini M° CCC° xj°.

1 For Robert of Croyland's institution on 8 Nov. 1311, see Dalberby's Institutions, fo. 122v.

216 Letter from Abbot Godfrey and the convent to William, archbishop of York and primate of England, requesting him to institute Master Robert of Pinchbeck to the church of All Saints, North Collingham, to which the abbey has right of presentation and which is vacant.[1] [17 Jan. 1312]

Presentatio magistri Roberti de Pyncebek' ad ecclesiam de Northcolingham'.

Reverendo in Christo patri domino W[illelmo] Dei gracia Eborac' archiepiscopo Anglie primati sui humiles et devoti G[odefridus] eiusdem dono gracie abbas de Burgo Sancti Petri et eiusdem loci conventus salutem cum omni reverencia et honore. Sancte paternitati vestre presentamus dilectum nobis in Christo magistrum Robertum de Pincebek' ad ecclesiam

Omnium Sanctorum de Northcolingham' vacantem, que ad nostram spectat presentationem, humilter supplicantes et devote quatinus caritatis intuitu eundem ad dictam ecclesiam admittatis et personam in eadem instituatis. Salvis nobis et ecclesie nostre juribus ab antiquo perceptis in eadem. In cuius rei testimonium presentibus litteris sigilla nostra apposuimus. Dat' in capitulo nostro xvj kalendas Februarii anno Domini millesimo CCC^{mo} xj^{o}.

1 There is no record of this institution in Archbishop Greenfield's register.

217 Grant by Abbot Godfrey and the convent to Adam de Banewell' of specified food and clothing within the abbey for his lifetime and half a mark p.a. from the abbot's chamber for his fee. [n.d.]

[fo. 88v] [Marginated] Carta Ade de Banewell'.

Omnibus Christi fidelibus ad quos presens scriptum pervenerit G[odefridus] Dei gracia abbas de Burgo Sancti Petri et eiusdem loci conventus salutem in Domino sempiternam. Noverit universitas vestra nos unanimi assensu concessisse dilecto et fideli nostro Ade de Banewell' competentem sustentationem in tota vita sua in victu et vestitu in abbacia nostra; videlicet unam robam de secta armigerorum abbatis annuatim percipiendam et unum panem album et unum panem bissum et unam lagenam et dimidiam bone cervise de celario abbatis et unum ferculum integrum cum intermisso secundum varietatem dierum et temporum de coquina eiusdem abbatis cotidie prout libere familie ministratur quamdiu vixerit percipiendos. Concedimus eciam eidem Ade unam dimidiam marcam sterlingorum singulis annis de camera abbatis percipendam pro feodo suo toto tempore vite sue. Concedimus insuper quod predictus Adam ubicumque fuerit infra abbatiam vel extra omnia predicta libere percipiat et de hiis pro libito suo disponat absque aliqua contradictione vel inpedimenti. In cuius rei testimonium presentibus sigilla nostra sunt appensa. Dat' in capitulo etc.

218 Grant by Abbot Godfrey and the convent to Master William de Edington', clerk, of a pension of 5 marks p.a. from the abbot's chamber until they can provide him with a suitable benefice. [23 Dec. 1313]

Pensio magistri Willelmi de Edington'.

Universis Christi fidelibus presentes litteras visuris vel audituris Godefridus permissione divina abbas monasterii[1] de Burgo Sancti Petri et eiusdem loci conventus salutem in Domino sempiternam. Noveritis nos unanimiter concessisse dilecto nobis in Christo magistro Willelmo de

Edington', clerico, quinque marcas sterlingorum nomine pensionis annue de camera abbatis qui pro tempore fuerit ad duos anni terminos annuatim percipiendas; videlicet ad Pascha tringinta et tres solidos et quatuor denarios, et ad festum sancti Michaelis triginta et tres solidos et quatuor denarios, donec eidem in ecclesiastico beneficio compententi provid-erimus. In cuius rei testimonium presentibus litteris sigilla nostra sunt appensa. Dat' in capitulo nostro die Dominica proxima post festum sancti Thome apostoli, anno Domini M° CCC^{mo} tertiodecimo.

1 *monasterii* interlined.

219 Homage of Reginald de Boys to Abbot Godfrey for tenements in Woodford. [31 Mar. 1310]

Reginaldus de Boys fecit homagium domino Godefrido abbati pro tenementis que clamat tenere de eo in Wodeford' in presencia dominorum R[oberti] de Spaldingg' et R[oberti] de Thorneton' monachorum, Roberti de Thorp' tunc senescallo, Roberti de Mithingby, et aliorum; videlicet die Martis proxima post mediam quadragesimam anno regni regis E[dwardi] filii regis E[dwardi] tercio in manerio de Eye.

220 Fealty of Richard, abbot of Barlings to Abbot Godfrey for tenements in Manton. [25 June 1307]

[fo. 89r] [Marginated] abbas de Barling'.

Ricardus abbas de Barlinges fecit fidelitatem domino Godefrido abbati de Burgi Sancti Petri pro tenementis que de eo clamat tenere in Malmeton'; videlicet Dominica in crastino sancti Johannis baptiste, anno regni regis E[dwardi] filii regis Henrici xxxv et anno domini G[odefridi] abbatis predicti viij° in presencia fratrorum Roberti de Spalding' et Johannis de Witherington', Roberti de Mithingesby, et Bernardi de Castre et aliorum.

220A Homage of Thomas Fauvel to Abbot Godfrey for tenements in Scotter. [3 July 1307]

[Marginated] Thom' Fauvel.

Eodem anno die Lune in crastino sancti Suithini, Thomas Fauvel fecit homagium predicto domino G[odefrido] abbati pro tenementis que clamat tenere de eo in Scote' in presencia fratrum Ade de Clipston' et Thome de Wilingham, Johannis de Theveleby et Bernardi de Castr' et aliorum.

221 Homage and fealty of Humphrey of Bassingbourn to Abbot Godfrey for tenements he holds for the service of four knights' fees and for other tenements appurtenant, except for a meadow and fishery in Oundle. Humphrey also recognised that he held a quarter of a knight's fee which he formerly denied and this was recorded in writing. [18 Jan. 1308]

[Marginated in later medieval hand] Humfrid' de Bassingb'

Anno regni regis Edwardi filii regis Edwardi primo dominus Humfridus de Bassingburn' miles fecit homagium et fidelitatem domino Godefrido abbati de Burgo Sancti Petri; videlicet die Jovis proxima post festum sancti Hillarii pro tenementis que de eo clamat tenere; videlicet per servicium quatuor feodorum militum et pro omnibus aliis tenementis eisdem pertinentibus[1] preter pratum et piscariam in Undel'. Idem vero dominus Humfridus recognovit se tenere quartam partem unius feodi militis de parte quatuor feodorum predictorum quam prius dedicebat, et super hoc fecit scriptum suum predicto domino abbati in presencia domini Roberti de Veer de Thrapston' militis, Johannis de Milton' tunc seneschalli Burgi, Willelmi Jurdan de Bernewell', Bernard de Castr', Ricardi de Holebeych' marescalli et aliorum. Act' in scaccario Burgi die et anno supradictis.

1 *eisdem pertinentibus* interlined.

221A Recognition by Humphrey son of Humphrey of Bassingbourn that, contrary to his previous denial, he holds a quarter of a knights' fee of Abbot Godfrey and his successors. [18 Jan. 1308]

Omnibus hoc scriptum visuris vel audituris Umfredus filius domini Umfredi de Bassingburn' salutem. Noverit me recognovisse domino meo Godefrido abbati de Burgo et eius successoribus unum quarter' feodi unius militis, quod aliquando ei ignoranter dedicebam. Ita videlicet quod de cetero dicto abbati et eius successoribus ego Umfredus et heredes mei de quatuor integris feodis militum plenarie respondebimus. In cuius rei testimonium presenti scripto sigillum meum apposui. Hiis testibus: domino Roberto de Veer de Trapston' milite, Willelmo Jordan de Bernewell', Johanne de Milton' tunc dicti domini abbatis senescallo, Johanne de Leholm, Bernardo de Castre, Wiberto de Irtelingburgh' et aliis. Dat' apud Burgum Sancti Petri die Jovis proxima post festum sancti Hillarii anno regni regis Edwardi filii regis Edwardi primo.

222 Homage and fealty of Henry son of Simon of Irthlingborough to Abbot Godfrey for tenements in Irthlingborough and payment of £4 relief. [1299–1321, perhaps 1308]

[Marginated] Henr' fil Simonis de Irtelingburgh'

Henricus filius Simonis de Irtelingburgh' fecit homagium et fidelitatem domino G[odefrido] abbati in presencia domini J[ohannis] de Undele, R[oberti] de Thorn', et Wiberti Ballivi pro tenementis que de eo clamat tenere in Irtelingburgh' et dedit pro relevio suo iiij li.

223 Grant by Abbot Godfrey and the convent to Thomas son of Martin de Iseldon' of part of a site containing a quarter of a rod in the city of London, next to the brew-house of St Paul's, rendering 4s p.a. to the chapter of St Paul's and 18d p.a. to the church of the Blessed Gregory on behalf of the abbey, which owes the rents for the whole site. [8 May 1308]

[fo. 89v] Carta abbatis et conventus de una particula placee sue London'.

Omnibus[1] hoc scriptum visuris vel audituris Godefridus permissione divina abbas de Burgo Sancti Petri et eiusdem loci conventus salutem in Domino. Noveritis nos dedisse et hoc presenti scripto confirmasse Thome filio Martini de Iseldon' quamdam particulam placee nostre in civitate London' juxta bracinam sancti Pauli, in qua quidem particula continetur quarta pars unius rode terre prout patet in longitudine et latitudine mensuratis; videlicet a communi garderoba placee nostre predicte usque ad viam regiam versus austrum et a muro bracine sancti Pauli usque ad placeam Johannis de Waledon'. Habendam et tenendam predictam particulam placee predicte predicto Thome et heredibus suis de nobis et successoribus nostris, imperpetuum et faciendo pro nobis et successoribus nostris pro toto residuo placee nostre predicte capitulo sancti Pauli London' per annum quatuor solidos argenti et ecclesie beati Gregorii per annum octodecim denarios pro omnibus serviciis et seculariis demandis. Et nos Godefridus abbas et conventus predicti et successores nostri predictam particulam placee predicte predicto Thome et heredibus suis per predictum servicium, warantizabimus et defendemus. Et ut hec nostra donatio et concessio firmitatis robur optineat hoc scriptum sigillorum nostrorum munimine roboravimus. Dat' in capitulo nostro die Mercurii proxima post festum inventionis sancti Crucis, anno Domini millesimo CCC^{mo} octavo et anno regni regis E[dwardi] filii regis E[dwardi] primo.

1 Also in Soc. of Antiquaries, MS 38, fo. 213v.

223A Recognition by Thomas son of Martin de Iseldon' that he will not alienate or mortgage the above plot without the abbey's consent and that he is liable for distraint if he defaults on the services agreed. [10 May 1308]

Obligatio pro eadem particula.

Omnibus[1] Christi fidelibus ad quos presentes littere pervenerint Thomas filius Martini de Iseldon' salutem in Domino. Noverit universitas vestra, quod cum dominus Godefridus abbas de Burgo Sancti Petri et eiusdem loci conventus mihi et heredibus meis per cartam suam quamdam particulam placee sue in civitate London' concessissent pro oneribus et serviciis annuis que ad predictam placeam suam pertinent pro eisdm solvendis et sustinendis; videlicet quatuor solidos capitulo sancti Pauli London' per annum et ecclesie beati Gregorii per annum octodecim denarios, fateor me pro me et heredibus meis et recognosco predictam particulam placee predicte, absque assensu et voluntate predictorum abbatis et conventus vel successorum suorum minime posse vendere invadiare, vel aliqualiter alienare. Obligans infra predictam particulam placee predicte eorum potestate et districtioni, quotienscumque et quandocumque, me vel heredes meos in solutione onerum seu serviciorum predictorum deficere contigerit quod absit. In cuius rei testimonium presentibus sigillum meum apposui. Dat' apud Burgum Sancti Petri in presencia dicti domini G[odefridi] abbatis, Willelmi de Bannewell', Petri de Paston', Roberti de Mithingby, Petri de Lullingt', Willelmi filii Johannis de Milton', Ricardi camerarii predicti domini abbatis et Willelmi de Croil'. Die Veneris proxima post festum inventionis sancte Crucis, anno regni regis E[dwardi] filii regis E[dwardi] primo.

1 Also in Soc. of Antiquaries, MS 38, fos 213v–4r.

224 Ancient charter recording the grant by Abbot John de Séez and the convent to Godwin son of Asketill of Collingham of five and a half bovates of land rendering 3s. Godwin formerly held six and a half bovates for the same rent, but gave the monks one bovate for their sustenance in return for association with the abbey. [1114–25]

[fo. 90r] Carta Antiqua.

Frater J[ohannes] abbas omnis que conventus sancti Petri de Burch' omnibus sancte Dei ecclesie filiis salutem et orationes. Noverint omnes ad quoscumque littere iste pervenerint me Johannem abbatem omnem que fratrum congregationem concessisse Godewino filio Asketilli de Colingham inperpetuum pro tribus solidos quinque bovatas terre et dimidiam in capitulo nostro, societatem que nostram atque beneficium pro quadam bovata terre quam Deo et sancto Petro fratribus que in eodem cenobio tam victuris quam viventibus donavit et donando concessit. Prius enim sex bovatas et dimidiam terre habebat pro supradicto censu. Et cum unam dimiserit census tantum diminutus non fuit. Hanc autem concessionem ei fecimus et suis heredibus. Huius rei testes fuerunt, Radulfus Papilio, Willelmus Dapifer', Goffridus Falvel, Ulf presbiter, Outhgrim, Romaldus, Godericus, Osbernus.

225 Ancient writ of Henry I to Abbot Ernulf and Ascelin de Waterville ordering that Godwin be permitted to hold his lands and goods in peace as in the time of Abbot Thorold. [1107–14]

Breve anticum.

H[enricus][1] rex Anglie, Ernulfo abbati et A[scelino] de Walterii villa salutem. Facite ut iste Godewinus ita juste et pacifice teneat terram suam et res suas sicut tenuit tempore Turaldi abbatis. Et nulla injuria ei super hoc fiat. Teste episcopo Salesbirie per Lewinum fratrem Colgrin[2] apud Colingham.

1 Bodl. Dodworth MS 86, fo. 53r has a transcript from the original, then at Peterborough. Calendared in eds. H. W. C. Davis, R. H. C. Davis, H. A. Cronne, C. Johnson, *Regesta Regum Anglo-Normannorum*, 3 vols (Oxford, 1913–68), vol. II, p. 89, no. 924.

2 *Son of Colgrim* in *Regesta*.

226 Letter from Abbot Godfrey and the convent to John, bishop of Lincoln, requesting him to institute William of Melton, chaplain, to the church of Castor, to which the abbey has right of presentation and which is vacant *de jure*.[1] [20 July 1308]

Presentatio domini Willemi de Melton' ad ecclesiam de Castre.

Reverendo patri in Christo domino J[ohanni] Dei gracia Linc' episcopo, sui humiles et devoti G[odefridus] eiusdem dono gracie abbas de Burgo Sancti Petri, et eiusdem loci conventus salutem et tam debitam quam devotam cum omni reverencia obedienciam. Sancte paternitate vestre presentamus dilectum nobis in Christo dominum Willelmum de Meleton', capellanum, ad ecclesiam de Castre de jure vacantem, que ad nostram spectat presentationem, humiliter supplicantes et devote quatinus ipsum ad eandem admittatis et personam in eadem instituatis. Salvis nobis et ecclesie nostre juribus ab antiquo perceptis in eadem. In cuius rei testimonium presentibus sigillum nostrum fecimus apponi. Dat' in capitulo nostro die Lune in festo sancte Margarete virginis anno Domini M^{o} CCC^{mo} viij^{o}.

1 For William de Melton's institution on 24 Oct. 1314, see Dalderby's Institutions, fo. 126v. The entry is vacated. For *de jure*, see no. 106, note 1.

227 Letter from Abbot Godfrey and the convent to John, bishop of Lincoln, requesting him to institute John de Nevill' to the church of Scotter, to which the abbey has right of presentation and which is vacant.[1] [16 Aug. 1308]

Presentatio domini Johannis de Nevill' ad ecclesiam de Scote'.

Reverendo patri in Christo domino J[ohanni] Dei gracia Linc' episcopo, sui humiles et devoti G[odefridus] eiusdem dono gracie abbas de monasterii Burgo Sancti Petri, et eiusdem loci conventus salutem cum omni reverencia et honore. Sancte paternitati vestre presentamus dilectum nobis in Christo dominum Johannem de Nevill' ad ecclesiam de Scote' vacantem, que ad nostram spectat presentationem, humiliter supplicantes et devote, quatinus eundem ad dictam ecclesiam admittatis et personam in eadem instituatis. Salvis nobis et ecclesie nostre juribus ab antiquo perceptis in eadem. In cuius rei testimonium presentibus sigilla nostra fecimus apponi. Dat' in capitulo nostro die Veneris in crastino assumptionis beate Marie anno Domini M^{o} CCC^{mo} viij^{o}.

1 For John de Nevill's institution on 7 Sept. 1308, see Dalderby's Institutions, fo. 92r.

228 Renunciation by Master Geoffrey de Hegham of the living of Northborough to which he had been presented by the abbot and convent, in favour of Walter de Eleswrthe, rector.[1] [29 Aug. 1308]

[fo. 90v] Renunciatio presentationis ad ecclesiam de Northburgh' facta a magistro G de Hegham.

Universis quorum interest pateat per presentes quod ego Galfridus de Hegham ad ecclesiam de Northburgh' tamquam vacantem de jure[2] per veros patronos eiusdem presentatus, omni juri si quod mihi fuerat adquisitum per presentationem dominorum meorum abbatis et conventui de Burgo Sancti Petri pure, sponte, simpliciter, et absolute, necnon liti mote contra dominum Walterum de Eleswrthe rectorem ecclesie antedicte, ratione presentationis antedicte, renuncio per presentes. In cuius rei testimonium presentibus sigillum meum apposui. Dat' apud Burgum die Jovis in festo decollationis sancti Johannis baptiste, anno Domini millesimo tricentesimo octavo. Presentibus magistris Galfrido de Makes', Willelmo de Banewelle rectore ecclesie de Paston', domino Roberto rectore ecclesie de Lullington', Johanne de Aylington' clerico publico notario et aliis.

1 According to Dalberby's register, Walter de Eleswrthe held the living from January 1304 and was replaced in June 1309. Dalderby's Institutions, fos 106v, 116r.
2 See no. 106, note 1.

229 Writ of S. de Grenhil, sheriff of Northampton, to the bailiffs of the abbot's liberty, rehearsing a royal writ of 7 Sept. 1308 ordering that Robert son of Walter of Oxney and his wife Petronilla permit Adam le Aumener to hold a messuage, 10 acres of land and 8s rent in Peterborough, according to the agreement between them. If this is not done, Robert and Petronilla are to be brought before royal justices at Westminster in the Michaelmas Term.

Breve domini regis de uno mesuagio decem acris terre et octo denariis redditus cum pertinenciis que Adam le Aumener habuit de Roberto filio Walteri de Oxeneye et uxore eius.

S de Grenhil vicecomes Norht' ballivis libertatis abbatis de Burgo Sancti Petri salutem. Mandatum domini regis in hec verba recepi: Edwardus Dei gracia etcetera vicecomiti Norht' salutem. Precipe Roberto filio Walteri de Oxeneye et Petronille uxori eius quod juste et sine dilatione teneant Adam le Aumener de Burgo Sancti Petri conventionem inter eos factam de uno mesuagio decem acris terre et octo denariis redditus cum pertinenciis in villa de Burgo Sancti Petri. Et nisi fecerit, et predictus Adam fecerit te securum de clamore suo prosequendo, tunc summone per bonos summonitores predictos Robertum et Petronillam quod sint coram justiciariis nostris apud Westm' in octabis sancti Michaelis ostensurus quare non fecerint. Et habeas ibi summonitores et hoc breve. Teste meipso apud Byfeld vij die Septembris anno regni nostri secundo. Quare vobis mando etcetera.

230 Final concord whereby Robert son of Walter of Oxney and Petronilla his wife recognised that a messuage, 10 acres and 8s rent in Peterborough belonged to Adam le Aumener by their gift. In return, Adam granted the tenements to Robert and Petronilla for their lives, rendering 5s 8d p.a. to Adam and all services due to the capital lords of the fee. [3 Nov. 1308]

Finalis concordia inter predictum Adam et predictum Robertum et uxorem suam.

Hec est finalis concordia facta in curia domini regis apud Westm' in crastino animarum anno regni regis Edwardi filii regis Edwardi secundo, coram Radulpho de Hengham, Willelmo de Berford', Lamberto de Trikingham et Hervico de Stanton' justiciariis et aliis domini regis fidelibus tunc ibi presentibus, inter Adam le Aumener de Burgo Sancti Petri querentem, et Robertum filium Walteri de Oxeneye et Petronillam uxorem eius deforcientes, de uno mesuagio, decem acris terre et octo denariis redditus cum pertinenciis in villa de Burgo Sancti Petri. Unde placitum conventionis summonitum fuit inter eos in eadem curia. Scilicet quod predicti Robertus et Petronilla recognoverunt predicta tenementa cum pertinenciis esse jus ipsius, ut illa que idem Adam habet de dono predictorum Roberti et Petronille. Et pro hac recognitione, fine et concordia idem Adam concessit predictis Roberto et Petronille predicta tenementa cum pertinenciis, et illa eis reddidit in eadem curia. [fo. 91r] Habenda et tenenda eisdem Roberto et Petronille de predicto Adam [sic] et heredibus suis tota vita ipsorum Roberti et Petronille. Reddendo inde per annum quinque solidos et octo denarios ad duos terminos; scilicet mediatatem ad Pascha et aliam medietatem ad festum sancti Michaelis, pro omni servicio, consuetudine et exactione ad predictum Adam et heredes suos pertinente. Et faciendo inde capitalibus dominis feodi illius pro predicto Adam [sic] et heredibus suis omnia alia servicia que ad illa tenementa pertinent. Et post decessum ipsorum Roberti et Petronille predicta tenementa cum pertinenciis integre revertentur ad predictum Adam et heredes suos quiete de heredibus ipsius Petronille. Tenenda de capitalis dominis feodi illius per servicia que ad illa tenementa pertinent inperpetuum.

231 Writ of Edward II to John Langton, bishop of Chichester and royal chancellor, ordering him not to grant protection to Adam de Gernemuth' without the king's special authority, because Adam is using the protection granted to those serving in Scotland to delay the court case between himself and the abbot. [3 Nov. 1308]

Bref le roy pur labbe de Burgh' Seint Piere.

Edward par la grace de Dieu roy d'Engleterre, seignur d'Irlaunde, et ducs d'Aquitaine, al honurable piere en Dieu J[ohn] par la meisme grace evesque de Cicestre nostre chaunceler, salutz. Pur ceo que nous avoms entendu qil yad un ple pendant entre nostre chier en Dieu labbe de Bourgh Seint Piere et Adam de Gernemuth' et que le dist Adam ad delaie le dist ple par la protection nostre chier pere qui Dieus assoile, enfesant suggestion quil feust en son service es parties d'Escoce ou il ne vint unqes, a ceo que hom dit, et qil est ore entour per ses amis de purchacer novele protection de nous, fesaunt suggestion qil va en nostre service as parties d'Escoce avantdites, la quele suggestion nest mie creable. Vous maundoms que vous ne soeffrez que le dit Adam eit protection sanz especial comandement de nous. Don' suz nostre prive seal a Westm' le tierz jour de Novembre lan de nostre regne secunde.

232 Writ of Edward I to the treasurer and barons of the Exchequer ordering that all the revenues from lands and tenements belonging to Queen Eleanor of Castile at her death be surrendered to John Bacoun and Richard de Cantia so that her testament can be executed. [12 Jan. 1292] A note is appended recording that the abbot and convent were allocated the manors of Torpel and Upton at farm under this writ and £600 is entered on roll 38 for Northampton.

Breve de Scaccario domini regis de allocatione DC li.

Edwardus Dei gracia rex Anglie, dominus Hybernie, et dux Aquitanie, thesaurario et baronibus suis de Scaccario salutem. Quia volumus quod omnes exitus terrarum et tenementorum que fuerunt in manu Alianore nuper regine Anglie consortis nostre die quo obiit ex dono celebris memorie domini H[enrici] quondam regis Anglie patris nostri vel nostro, aut aliunde ex perquisito ipsius consortis nostre, liberentur dilectis clericis nostris Johanni Bacoun et Ricardo de Cantia, quos receptores ad recipiendos et custodiendos exitus predictos in Scaccario predicto assignavimus. Ut juxta dispositionem et ordinationem nostram et executorum testamenti predicte consortis nostre convertantur. Vobis mandamus quod omnes exitus quos de terris et tenementis predictis vel aliis bonis dicte consortis nostre post mortem eiusdem recepistis, prefatis Johanni et Ricardo sine dilatione liberetis custodiendos sicut predictum est. Et de terris et tenementis vel aliis bonis predictis aut exitibus eorumdem in nullo decetero vos intro-[fo. 91v]mittatis, donec aliud inde precepimus. Teste me ipso apud Westm' xij die Januarii anno regni nostri vicesimo. Per hoc breve allocantur abbati et conventui de Burgo Sancti Petri in firma maneriorum de Torpel et Upton' DC li. in rotulo xxxviij^{o} in Norht'.

233 Writ of Edward II to Hugh le Despenser, justice of the forest south of the Trent, ordering that the abbot receive a tithe of all game taken in Northamptonshire according to the terms of charters granted by his predecessors. [3 Feb. 1311]

[Marginated] Breve de decima venacionis.

[marginated below in a different hand, refering to both 233 and 234] rex E[dwardus] filius regis E[dwardi]

Edwardus[1] Dei gracia rex Anglie, dominus Hibernie, et dux Aquitanie dilecto et fideli suo Hugoni le Despens' justiciario foreste sue ultra Trentam salutem. Quia dilectus nobis in Christo abbas de Burgo Sancti Petri per cartas progenitorum nostrorum quondam regum Anglie, clamat habere totam decimam tocius venacionis nostre capte in Norhamptonshire, quicumque eam ceperit, ipseque, et predecessores sui abbates eiusdem loci decimam huiusmodi venacionis in comitatu predicto a tempore confectionis cartarum predictarum hactenus habere consueverunt sicut dicitur. Vobis mandamus quod ipsum abbatem decimam tocius venacionis nostre, quam in comitato predicto, a quocumque capi contigerit habere faciatis juxta tenorem cartarum predictarum, et prout ipse decimam illam habere debet, et ipse et predecessores sui predicti a tempore predicto habere consueverunt. Teste meipso apud Berewyc' super Twedam, tercio die Februarii anno regni nostri quarto.

1 For earlier writs to the same effect, see *Cal. Close, 1296–1302*, pp. 173–4 (1298), 416, 468 (1301). This writ was not enrolled.

234 Writ of Edward II to the treasurer and barons of the Exchequer ordering that the abbot be allowed the amercements and chattels forfeit by his men, in accordance with charters granted by his predecessors. [18 July 1310]

[Marginated] Breve de allocatione amerciamentorum.

Edwardus Dei gracia rex Anglie, dominus Hibernie, et dux Aquitanie thesaurario et baronibus suis de Scaccario salutem. Ex parte dilecti nobis in Christo abbatis de Burgo Sancti Petri nobis est ostensum, quod cum ipse per cartas progenitorum nostrorum quondam regum Anglie percipere et habere debeat, et ipse et predecessores sui abbates eiusdem loci semper hactenus a tempore confectionis cartarum predictarum percipere et habere consueverunt catalla hominum suorum fugitivorum et suspensorum et amerciamenta que ex murdro et aliis forisfacturis hominum suorum proveniunt. Vos iam de novo ipsum abbatem quominus huiusmodi catalla et amerciamenta percipere et habere possit impeditis voluntarie et injuste in ipsius abbatis dampnum nonmodicum et ecclesie sue sancti Petri de Burgo exheredationis periculum manifestum. Et quia prefato abbati super jure ecclesie sue predicte in hac parte nolumus injuriari, vobis mandamus quod si vobis constiterit ita esse tunc predictum abbatem catalla et amerciamenta habere permittatis, et ea ei ad Scaccarium predictum allocare faciatis prout ipse ea percipere et habere debet et ipse et predecessores sui predicti ea semper hactenus percipere et habere consueverunt, et prout huiusmodi catalla et amerciamenta predicto abbati et predecessoribus suis ad dictum Scaccarium fuerit hactenus allocata. Teste meipso apud Westm' xviij die Julii anno regni nostri quarto.

Istud breve[1] irrotulatur inter memoranda eiusdem anni. Et preterea est in manibus marescalli.

1 *Istud breve* marginated.

235 Recognition by William son and heir of John of Milton that he will acquit the abbot at the Exchequer for the accounts of the manors of Thorpe Waterville, Thorpe Achurch and Aldwinckle for the period when his father was bailiff of the abbot's liberty and keeper of the said manors; also for the time that William himself had custody of them. Note that this was enrolled on the Exchequer rolls for the Easter Term 1311.

[fo. 92r] Willelmus filius et heres Johannis de Milton' cognoscit se debere acquietare abbatem de Burgo Sancti Petri de compoto maneriorum de Thorp' Watervill', Achirch, et Aldewincle per dominum regem ab eodem abbate exacto de toto tempore quo prefatus Johannes de Milton' fuit ballivus libertatis abbatis predicti et custos maneriorum predictorum, et eciam de toto tempore quo idem Willelmus habuit custodiam eorumdem, et de omnibus demandis custodiam et compotum predictam tangentibus, et ad premissa facienda obligat omnes terras et tenementa sua in quorumcumque manibus devenerunt.

Ista irrotulantur in medio rotuli de recognitionibus in alba parte in Scaccario de termino Pasche anno regni regis E[dwardi] filii regis E[dwardi] quarto.

236 Note that Johanna widow of Peter Tilly, who brought a writ of entry against Roger of Collingham for a messuage and its appurtenances in Cambridge, sought a licence to withdraw it. The case is entered on the 32nd roll for the Michaelmas Term 1311. Abbot Godfrey gave Johanna 40s for this withdrawal.

Johanna que fuit uxor Petri Tilly, que tulit breve de ingressu versus Rogerum de Colingham de uno mesuagio cum pertinenciis in Cantebrigg' petiit licenciam recedendi de brevi suo. Et habet etcetera. Termino Michaelis, anno quinto, rotulo xxxij°. Pro qua recessione Godefridus abbas de Burgo Sancti Petri dedit predicte Johanne xl solidos argenti.

237 Copy from the roll of fines for Gascon service noting that the abbot, among others, was to be quit of debts, by writ under the great seal in 5 Edward II [8 July 1311–7 July 1312].

In rotulo de finibus pro servicio Vascon'.

Memorandum quod non debet fieri executio de subscriptis debitis levandis de diversis, quia sunt inde quieti per brevia de magno sigillo inter communia de anno quinto regni E[dwardi] filii regis E[dwardi]; videlicet de episcopo Norwyc', abbate de Burgo Sancti Petri, abbate sancti Benedicti de Hulmo.

237A Writ of Edward II to the sheriff of Northampton ordering that he should not pursue the abbot for payment of a 500 mark fine which Abbot Richard had made with Edward I, because he had granted that no-one should fine for service in his father's war in Gascony because Edward I had not gone in person, nor was service generally performed. [3 Sept. 1311]

Breve concessum de eadem fine.

Edwardus Dei gracia rex Anglie, dominus Hibernie et dux Aquitanie vicecomiti Norht', salutem. Quia concessimus archiepiscopis, episcopis, abbatibus, prioribus, comitibus, baronibus, et omnibus aliis de regno nostro, qui pro serviciis in guerra domini E[dwardi] nuper regis Anglie patris nostri in Vascon', fines cum eodem patre nostro ad Scaccarium suum fecerunt, quod ipsi ab exactionibus finum predictorum penitus sint quieti, pro eo maxime quod dictus pater noster personaliter non fuit in guerra predicta, nec dictum servicium communiter factum fuit, tibi precipimus, quod districtionem quam per summonitionem Scaccarii predicti, dilecto nobis in Christo abbati de Burgo Sancti Petri pro quingentis marcis per quas Ricardus, quondam abbas loci predicti predecessor suus finem fecit cum dicto patre nostro fieri fecisti occasione predicta, relaxes omnino. Teste me ipso apud London' tercio die Septembris anno regni nostri quinto.

238 Letter from the official of the archdeacon of Northampton to all the rural deans in the archdeaconry concerning letters from the bishops of London and Lincoln and Archbishop Robert Winchelsey of Canterbury, which he is summarising for better effect. Abbots and priors in each deanery are summoned with their convents either in person or by proctors to St Paul's cathedral in London on 23 April 1311 to consider the heresy of the Templars.[1] The clergy of the deanery are also summoned before the bishop of Lincoln in the parish church at Rothwell on 13 April 1311 to choose a proctor for the archdeaconry to appear at All Saints church Northampton shortly after Easter.[2] Each proctor should have a farthing for each mark of the last tax in ready money for the expenses of the proctors at London and Northampton. [early 1311]

[fo. 92v] Officialis domini archdiaconi Norht' universis decanis per dictum archidiaconatum constituti salutem in salutis auctore. Litteras venerabilem virorum Dei gracia London' et Lincoln' episcoporum, verius eciam litteras reverendi patris nostri domini R[oberti] permissione divina Cantuar' archiepiscopi recepimus, ad infra scripta exequenda. Set quia diffusum esset et longum omnes articulos in dictis litteris contentos transcribere, vim et effectum earum quatenus vos contingit, mittimus vobis omnibus et singulis firmiter injungendo, quatinus singuli vestrum abbates et priores, electivos exemptos et non exemptos ac conventus eorum prout in vestris existunt decanatibus, citetis peremptorie, quod iidem abbates et priores personaliter conventusque per eorum abbates et priores seu per alios procuratores quos duxerint eligendos, coram predicto patre domino R[oberto] Cantuar' archiepiscopo una cum ceteris prelatis et procuratoribus provincie Cantuar' in ecclesia cathedrali London' sexta feria post octabas Pasche conpareant super crimine heretice pravitatis singularibus personis ordinis militie Templi inposito tractaturi et ordinaturi sicut alias, nec non et ad alia que in provinciali concilio ordinabuntur, consensum adhibituri, ulteriusque facturi et recepturi in eodem consilio, quod cum prorogatione dierum fuerit faciendum. Ad hec, quisque vestrum clerum sui decanatus peremptorie faciat citari auctoritate nostra, quod die Jovis in septimana Pasche proxime futura in ecclesia parochiali Rowell' coram nobis compareat per procuratorem idoneum qui sufficientem habeat potestatem alium procuratorem pro archidiaconatu nostro eligendi et constituendi ad comparendum coram domino J[ohanne] Dei gracia, etcetera proximo die juridico post octabas Pasche in ecclesia Omnium Sanctorum Norht' seu eius locum tenentibus etcetera. Habeat que dictus procurator in promptu singulos quadrantes de qualiter marca juxta ultimam taxationem pro sumptibus procuratorum tam London' ad predictum consilium, quam Norht' coram predicto patre mittendorum.

1 Dated from eds. F. M. Powicke, C. R. Cheney, *Councils and Synods*, vol 2 (Oxford, 1964), pp. 1299–1300. For commentary on the dissolution of the Templars, see M. Barber, *The Trial of the Templars* (Cambridge, 1978).

2 It is not possible to date precisely the first day for judicial business after Easter week.

239 Confirmation by Robert de Gymeges to Ralph de Gymeges, his brother, of one virgate and its appurtenances in Botolphbridge and a messuage formerly held by William de Engayne, rendering 1d p.a. Ralph holds the virgate and messuage by gift of William de Gymeges, Robert's brother. [n.d.]

[Marginated] Carte terrarum[1] Roberti Gymeges quas nunc tenet S de Drayton'.

Omnibus Christi fidelibus presens scriptum visuris vel audituris Robertus de Gymeges salutem in Domino. Noverit universitas vestra me concessisse et hac presenti carta mea confirmasse Radulpho de Gymeges, fratri meo, unam virgatam terre cum pertinenciis suis in campo de Botolbrige. Et unum mesuagium jacens proximo juxta gardinum dicti Roberti versus austrum, illam videlicet virgatam terre quam Willelmus de Engayne quondam tenuit. Quam quidem virgatam terre et quod mesuagium idem Radulphus habet de dono Willelmi de Gymeges fratris mei. Tenendos et habendos eidem Radulpho et heredibus vel assignatis suis vel cuicumque et quibuscumque, quando ubi dare legare vendere vel assignare voluerit de me et heredibus meis libere quiete hereditarie honorifice et integre cum omnibus pertinenciis, libertatibus et aysiamentis ad predictam virgatam terre cum predicto mesuagio undique spectantibus. Reddendo inde annuatim michi et heredibus meis unum denarium ad Pascha tantum pro omni seculari servicio, consuetudine, secta curie, auxilio warda, relevio, et pro omni exactione et demanda. Et volo illam virgatam terre cum mesuagio et suis pertinenciis tam liberam esse solutam et quietam sicut aliqua terra vel aliquod tenementum melius [fo. 93r] liberius quietius concedi poterit ab aliquo teneri vel haberi. Ita quod nec ego nec heredes mei nec aliquis nomine nostro versus eundem Radulphum aliquod servicium ab eodem Radulpho vel heredibus suis vel suis assignatis nisi tantum illum denarium annui redditus habere nec exigere vel aliquo modo calumpniare decetero possimus nec illum denarium predictum annui redditus alicui dare vendere vel aliquo modi assignare sine spontanea voluntate ipsius Radulphi predicti et heredum suorum vel assignatorum. Et ego Robertus et heredes mei assignati dictam virgatam terre cum dicto mesuagio una cum omnibus pertinenciis suis predicto Radulpho et heredibus vel assignatis suis pro predicto servicio contra omnes homines et feminas warantizabimus et tam in intrinsecis quam in forinsecis acquietabimus et defendemus imperpetuum. Et ut hec mea concessio et carte mee confirmatio perpetue stabilitatis robur optineat imposterum presenti scripto sigillum meum apposui. Hiis testibus domino Galfrido de Gurdeleys milite, Ricardo de Houton'. Waltero de Stachedene, Galfrido filio Roberti, Nicholao Blundo, Ricardo de Conyncton', Nicholao de Boby, Willelmo Takelyn', Henrico le Eyr de Jakele et aliis.

1 *terrarum* interlined.

240 Grant in free alms by Ralph son of William de Gymeges to the abbot and convent, in return for £20, of one messuage and its appurtencances in Botolphbridge and a virgate of land formerly held by William de Engayne, paying 1d p.a. to the capital lord of the fee for all services. [n.d.]

Sciant presentes futuri quod ego Radulfus filius Willelmi de Gymeges concessi dedi et hac presenti carta mea confirmavi abbati de Burgo Sancti Petri et eiusdem loci conventui pro viginti libris michi per manibus pacatis unum mesuagium in villa de Botelbrigge jacens juxta gardinum quod fuit Willelmi patris mei versus austrum, et unam virgatam terre arabilis cum pratis, paschuis, pasturis, libertatibus asiamentis, et omnibus pertinenciis ad me vel heredes meos aliquo modo spectantibus ratione illius tenementi in Botelbrigge et extra, quam quidem virgatam terre Willelmus de Engayne quondam tenuit. Habendos et tenendos de capitali domino feodi predictis abbati et conventui et eorum successoribus in perpetuam elemosinam et cuicumque[1] dictum tenementum cum pertinenciis dare vendere vel assignare voluerint libere quiete bene et in pace imperpetuum. Reddendo eidem capitali domino annuatim unum denarium ad Pascha pro omnibus serviciis consuetudinibus, exactionibus, auxiliis, releviis, wardis et escaetis et sectis curie imperpetuum. Et ego Radulphus et heredes mei predictum tenementum et predictam virgatam terre cum omnibus asiamentis et pertinenciis ut predictum est, predictis abbati et conventui et eorum successoribus et eciam eorum assignatis et heredibus assignatorum suorum pro dicto servicio warantizabimus aquietabimus et contra omnes homines et feminas Christianos et Judeos defendemus de omnibus serviciis tam intrinsecis quam extrinsecis imperpetuum. Ita quod nec ego nec aliquis nomine meo vel heredum meorum aliquid juris, clamii vel servicii in predicto tenemento vel aliquas in parte decetero exigere vel clamare poterimus. In huius rei testimonium huic scripto sigillum meum apposui. Hiis testibus domino Baldewyno de Drayton', milite, Rogero de Luvetot, Hugone de Boby, Johanne de Folkewerthe, Radulpho de Waldechef, Willelmo Cokelyn, Reginaldo Freman et aliis.

1 *cui quando ubi* in MS.

241 Extract from the pipe roll for Northamptonshire recording that, under their charters, the abbot and monks are quit of a ten mark fine due from the township of Peterborough for false presentation. [1232–33]

[fo. 93v] [Marginated] Norht'

Anno[1] regni regis H[enrici] filii regis Johannis in Comitatu Norht' continetur. Idem vicecomes respondet in compoto suo de x marcas de tota villata de Burgo pro falsa presentatione. In Thesauro nichil. Et abbati et monachis de Burgo x marcas per libertatem cartarum regis, et quietus est.

1 See PRO, E/372/77, m. 12d.

242 Extract from Exchequer rolls for Huntingdonshire recording that, under his charters, the abbot is quit of a two mark fine for false presentation at Alwalton and Fletton [1227–28][1], together with a note that on the roll for 1191–92 fines were allocated to the abbot's liberty for concealment and murder in Huntingdonshire.

[Marginated] Hunt'

Anno regni regis H[enrici] filii regis Johannis xij^{o}. In comitatu Hunt' adjudicate fuerunt et reddite ij marce de Scaccario abbati de Burgo quas Alwalton' et Fletton pacaverunt pro falsa presentatione. Et quia barones de Scaccario invenerunt in rotulis tercii anni regis Ricardi abbatem de Burgo fuisse quietum de tali amerciamento per cartas suas, ideo abbatem de predictis duabus marcis quietum adjudicaverunt.

In rotulo tercio regis Ricardi allocatur libertas abbatis de Burgo pro concelamento et murdro in comitatu Hunt' etcetera.

1 For a copy of the related pipe roll entry, see CUL, Peterborough D and C, MS 6, fo. 94v.

243 Note that in 37 Henry III [28 Oct. 1252–27 Oct. 1253], the abbot and convent renewed their charters of liberty and received writs from the Chancery to the treasurer and barons of the Exchequer ordering them to observe them. This writ is to be found in the marshall's purse under 1259–60. The later cross reference is to the Red Book of John of Achurch.

[marginated in later hand] Burg' [and] de ista clausula mentio sit in Achurch' rubio fo lxxxxviij^{o}. Ad tale signo s. σ–o[1]

Anno regni regis H[enrici] filii regis Johannis xxxvij^{o} innovate fuerunt carte libertatis abbatis et conventus de Burgo, et idem abbas tunc habuit breve de cancellario thesaurario et baronibus de Scaccario quod ipsi manuteneant et defendant predictas libertates, et illud breve invenietur in bursa marescalli, anno regni regis eiusdem H[enrici] xliiij^{to}.

1 The Red Book of John of Achurch, CUL, Peterborough D and C, MS6, fo. 94 (modern foliation), which in turn has a marginal reference back to this MS- *quare reg' Godefridi abbatis folio* [interlined] *xciij^{o}*. The text is broadly that of no. 244.

244 An extract from the pipe rolls for Northamptonshire for 20 Edward I recording fines owed for various offences by individuals and townships from which the sheriff had rendered £9 3s 4d to the abbot and monks under their charters of liberty, together with a further note that the sheriff had also rendered three marks to the abbot and monks for offences in Alwalton and Fletton. [1291–92]

In rotulo xx° regis E[dwardi] filii regis H[enrici]. In Norht' in dorso rotuli prope finem.[1]

Idem vicecomes reddit compotum de xx s. de villata de Thornhawe pro concelamento de itinere J[ohannis] de Vallibus.[2] Et de xl s. de villata de Castr' quia non venit sicut continetur ibidem. Et de x s. de villata de Estfeld pro falsa appreciatione ibidem. Et de dimidia marca de decenna Rogeri filii Alicie de Helpeston' pro fuga ibidem. Et de dimidia marca de Willelmo Underwode de Liveden' pro purprestura. Et de dimidia marca de Henrico de Milton' in Undel' et Henrico Talifer de Walmesford' pro vinis venditis contra assisam ibidem. Et de xl d. de Petro Cutteladde de Benigfeld et socio suo pro defalta ibidem. Et de C s. de Galfrido Trailli pro transgressione ibidem. Et de xl d. de Henrico Fabro de Liveden' pro injusta detentione ibidem. Et de xl d. de Willelmo de Thorp' et Johanne filio eius pro disseisina ibidem. Et de dimidia marca de Mabillia que fuit uxor Roberti Aumfrai quia non est prosecuta sicut continetur ibidem. Summa x li. vj s. viij d. De quibus villata de Thornhawe respondet infra de xx s. pro concelamento. Et Henricus Talifer de Walmesford respondet infra de xl d. pro vinis venditis contra assisam. Et debet vicecomes ix li. iij s. iiij d. Idem reddit compotum de eodem debito. In Thesauro nichil. Et abbati et monachis de Burgo Sancti Petri ix li. iij s. iiij d. de eisdem amerciamentis per libertatem cartarum suarum, et per breve regis allocatum abbati de Sancto Edmundo in Norf' in rotulo precedente. Et sicut allocatum est eisdem abbati et monachis de Burgo in rotulo xij° regis H[enrici] in Cant' et Hunt' et in rotulo xvij° eiusdem regis in Norht'. Et quietus est.

Idem vicecomes reddit compotum de ij marcis de villata de Fletton' pro falsa presentatione. Et [j marca][3] de villata de Alwalton' pro eadem et pro murdro. In Thesauro nichil. Et abbati et monachis de Burgo iij marcis per libertatem cartarum regis. Et quietus est.

1 Also copied in CUL. Peterborough D and C, MS 6, fo. 95v. For the PRO text, see E/372/137, m. 12d.

2 For this eyre, see D. Crook, *Records of the General Eyre* (London, 1982), p. 145.

3 Supplied from Peterborough D and C, MS 6.

245 The Northamptonshire Survey [1100–89[1]]

[fo. 94r] Hydar'[2] de comitatu Norhampton'.

1 The basic text of the lost original appears to date from 1100–20 and to have been in the form of a roll. Additions were made as late as Henry II's reign, but were not distinguished from the original in this transcription.

2 Printed in translation in *VCH Northants*, vol. 1, pp. 365–89 and in a modern Latin edition in K. S. B. Keats-Rohan, *Domesday People: A Prosopography of Persons Occurring in English Documents 1066–1166* (Woodbridge, 1999), App. II, pp. 98–117. For commentary, see also above, p. xxxiv and D. Roffe, *Domesday: The Inquest and the Book* (Oxford, 2000), p. 226.

245A Hokeslawe.

Twywelle Albricus camerarius ij hidas de feudo abbatis de Thorneya. Ibidem de feudo comitis David. Ibidem de feudo abbatis Burgi j magnam virgatam. In Slipton' j hidam et unam virgatam de feudo Willelmi de Corcy. Ibidem Ricardus filius Hugonis ij partes unius hide de feudo Burgi. Ibidem Rogerus nepos abbatis terciam partem unius hide de eodem feudo.

In Suburc ij hidas dimidiam de feudo Westmonaster'. In Lofwyc Thomas j hidam et unam virgatam de feudo de Deneford'. Ibidem Radulfus Fleming' j virgatam dimidiam de feudo comitis David. Ibidem Wydo frater eius j magnam virgatam de feudo de Thorneya. In Drayton' Albricus camerarius dimidiam hidam de feudo regis.

In Yslep' idem Albricus ij hidas de feudo regis. Ibidem iiij^or^ sokemanni regis j hidam de feudo Westmonaster'.

In Audewyncle abbas de Burgo iij hidas dimidiam quas Ascelinus de Waterville tenet. Ibidem Galfridus de Glynton' j magnam virgatam de feudo Glovernie pertinens ad Barton'. Ibidem Ricardus filius Wydonis iij hidas dimidiam virgatam minus de feudo regine.

Item in Benifeld Willelmus de Lisurs iij magnas virgatas de feudo regis.

In Bernewell' Robertus de Ferar' vj hidas et j magnam virgatam de feudo regis. Ibidem Reginaldus le Moyne vj hidas de feudo de Rammeseye.

In Lilleford' Willelmus Olyfart v hidas de feudo regis Scotie.

245B Nauesford'.

In Tychemers Robertus de Ferar x hidas. Ibidem Ascelinus de Watervill' iij hidas et j virgatam et tres partes dimidiam hidam de Burgo.

In Thrapston' Radulfus filius Ogeri ij hidas et j virgatam de feudo de Brunne. Ibidem Robertus filius Edeline j hidam et j virgatam de feudo de Clare.

In Torp' et Achirche Ascelinus de Watervill' vj hidas dimidiam de feudo Burgi.

In Clopton' Walterus j hidam et j virgatam de feudo regis. Ibidem iij hidas dimidiam de feudo Burgi. Ibidem Ascelinus dimidiam hidam de feudo Burgi.

Wadenhowe Albricus de Ver ij hidas et j virgatam de feudo regis David. Ibidem Wymunt de Stok' j virgatam de feudo Burgi. Ibidem Rogerus Infans ij parvas virgatas de eodem feudo. Ibidem Wivienus de Chirchefeld' dimidiam hidam de eodem feudo. Ibidem Galfridus de Gonthorp' ij hidas de eodem feudo. In Catteworthe j hidam dimidiam de feudo Burgi.

245C Pokebroc.

In Pokebroc Robertus de Cauz j hidam et j virgatam de feudo regis. Ibidem Walterus de Clopton' ij hidas dimidiam de feudo Burgi. Ibidem Rogerus Marmiun j hidam et j virgatam de eodem feudo.

In Armeston' [?][1] de Burgelay ij hidas dimidiam de eodem feudo. Ibidem Turkil j hidam de eodem feudo. Ibidem Wydo Maufee j hidam de eodem feudo. Ibidem Galfridus de Gunthorp' ij partes dimidie hide de eodem feudo. Ibidem Tedrick iij partes [fo. 94v] de dimidia hida de eodem feodo.[2]

In Pappele j hidam.

In Lullington' j hidam.

In Hemington' Berenger' le Moyne ij hidas dimidiam de feodo de Rammes'. Ibidem Ricardus filius Gilberti j hidam et j virgatam et dimidiam de feodo Burgi. Ibidem Wydo Maufe dimidiam hidam et dimidiam virgatam de eodem feodo. Ibidem Reginaldus le Moyne dimidiam hidam et dimidiam virgatam de eodem feodo.

In Kynesthorp' Walterus de Lodington' j hidam et j virgatam de feodo Burgi. Ibidem Willelmus de Chirchetot' dimidiam hidam de feodo regis.

In Therninge Rogerus Marmioun iij parvas virgatas de feodo Burgi.

In Ayston' abbas de Burgo iiij hidas in dominico. Ibidem Papilun dimidiam hidam de eodem feodo. Ibidem Levenoth dimidiam hidam de eodem feodo.

In Undele abbas in dominico vj hidas. Ibidem Vivien j parvam virgatam.

1 Omission?
2 Spelling changes from *feudo* to *feodo* at this point.

245D Duo hundred' de Nasso.[1]

[marginated in later hand] Duo hundrede de Nasso.

In Stinton'[2] Willelmus de Lisurs ij hidas.

In Bernak' Fulco Paynel iij hidas.
In Wirthorp' abbas Croylaund' ij hidas. Ibidem de feodo Eudonis dapifer j virgatam.
In Eston'[3] Simon j hidam dimidiam.
In Peychirch'. In Etton'. In Northburg' dimidiam virgatam.
In dominico abbatis de Burgo Sancti Petri lxx hidas et iij virgatas et dimidiam.

1 This entry is corrupt and much truncated. A fuller version dealing mostly with Nassaburgh hundred, in which this entry is embedded, can be found in Swaffham, fo. 124r–v (original foliation).
2 Otherwise in Huntingdonshire.
3 Otherwise in Willybrook hundred.

245E Hundred' de Sutton'.

In eadem villa dominus rex habet in dominico iiij hidas. In eadem villa Willelmus de Quency j hidam dimidiam et parvam virgatam terre de comitatu Leycestr'. Ibidem Alfredus viij parvas virgatas de Gilberto de Pinkeny. Ibidem Paganus j hidam et dimidiam et j parvam virgatam de feodo comitis Leycestr'; Robertus filius Osberti tenuit.

In Evenle j hidam et j parvam virgatam de feodo comitis Leyc'.

In Preston' dimidiam hidam de feodo comitis Leyc'.

In Crouelton' iiij^or^ parvas virgatas de feodo comitis Leyc'. Ibidem Seuar' j hidam et ij parvas virgatas de feodo Leyc'. Ibidem Brien filius comitis j hidam dimidiam et ij parvas virgatas de feodo de Walingford'.

In Neubottle Regis de Reynes vj hidas et j parvam virgatam de feodo comitis Leycestr'. Willelmus de Lepyn tenuit.

In Furningho iiij hidas de feodo comitis Leyc'.

In Cherlington' Maynardus j hidam dimidiam et j parvam virgatam. Ibidem Simon Chendut j hidam dimidiam de feodo de Berkamstede et j parvam virgatam. Ibidem Odo dapifer viij parvas virgatas de feodo de Colescestr'.

In Gremesbir' Aunsel' de Chokes ij hidas et iiij^or^ parvas virgatas scilicet quinta pars ij hidarum.

In Middelton' Willelmus Mechin j hidam dimidiam et j parvam virgatam de feodo Willelmi de Curcy.

In alia Middelton' Simon Chendut ij hidas de feodo de Berkamstede.

In Thayniford Mainfenn de Walrenton' j hidam. Ibidem Robertus Basset j hidam de feodo de Walingford.

In Ayno Willelmus de Mandevill' iij hidas.

In Middelton' monachi de Sancto Everaldo ij hidas.

In Walton' j hidam cum ij virgatis. In Sutton' quas Suonild' tenuit.

In Gildeby j hidam et vij parvas virgatas de feodo de Mortal'.

245F [fo. 95r] Hundred' de Albodestowe.[1]

In Chacombe iiij hidas de feodo episcopi Lincoln'.

In Evenl' ij hidas et j parvam virgatam minus, quas Alouf de Merke tenuit.

In Thorp' ij hidas.

In Stanes Gilbertus de Pinkeny ij hidas.

In Colewych' Willelmus ij hidas et iiij parvas virgatas. Ibidem Otuer j hidam.

In Stotebyr' ij hidas quas monachi Norht' tenent.

In Rodeston' ij hidas de feodo comitis Cestr'.

In Wytefeld' Gilbertus de Monte ij hidas et ij virgatas in dominico.

In Merston' Radulfus Murdac iiij hidas de feodo comitis Leyc'.

In Siresham Thomas Sorel j hidam dimidiam. Ibidem comes Leyc' j parvam virgatam. Ibidem Gilo dimidiam hidam. Ibidem Willelmus filius Aluredi iiij parvas virgatas.

In Helmenden' Willelmus de Torewell' iiij hidas de feodo comitis Leyc'.

In Chelverdescote dimidiam hidam idem comitis Leyc'.

In Brackele et Hausho idem comes vij hidas dimidiam.

1 Part of King's Sutton hundred.

245G Hundred de Wardon'.

In Wardon' Ricardus Foliot ij hidas dimidiam et j magnam virgatam, scilicet quarta pars j militis de feodo regis in capite.

In Eston' et Apeltreya Willelmus de Bolonia, vij hidas de feodo comitis de Maundevill'.

In Bottelendon' Fulco Paynel ij hidas una ex illis de feodo Cestr'. Ibidem Willelmus Meschin j hidam. Ibidem j hidam de feodo episcopi Lincoln'.

In Byfeld viij hidas de feodo comitis Leyc'.

In Trapesford' que pertinet ad Byfeld' j hidam et ij parvas virgatas.

In Hinton' de feodo comitis Willelmi ij hidas quas Robertus tenet.

In Farendon' Simon Chendut j hidam dimidiam et j parvam virgatam de feodo de Berchamstede. Ibidem comes Leyc' iiij parvas virgatas.

In Hochecote Rogerus Murdac ij hidas de feodo regis David.

In Wodeford' comes Leyc' ij hidas quas Osemund' tenet.

In Byfeld Rogerus de Reymes ij hidas.

In Aydona Ricardus filius Wale ij hidas de feodo Leyc'.

In Gretteworth' Radulfus de Kaynes ij hidas de feodo suo.

In Solegrave iiij hidas de feodo Gilonis fratris Haschivill'.

245H Graveshende Falewesle.

In Falewesle habet dominus rex ij hidas.

In Chelurdescote ij hidas de feodo comitis Leycestr'.

In Fardingstone iij hidas et j parvam virgatam. Ibidem Hervicus Belet viij parvas virgatas quas Willelmus de Strafford tenet.

In Wedon' monachi de Becco iiij hidas de feodo comitis Leycestr'.

In Charwelton' ij hidas et iiij parvas virgatas de feodo de Berkamstede. Ibidem abbas de Thorneya iiij parvas virgatas antiquo scripto dimidiam hidam. Ibidem Hugo de Chaham dimidiam hidam de feodo comitis Leyc'. Ibidem iiij^or parvas virgatas de feodo Ade de Napton'. Ibidem comes Leyc' iiij^or parvas virgatas.

In Catesby iiij hidas de feodo Willelmi Peverel.

In Eliden' iiij hidas de feodo de Berkamstede.

In Preston' iij hidas ij parvas virgatas minus de feodo Simonis de Wahill'. [fo. 95v] Ibidem Ricardus filius Willelmi j hidam ij parvas virgatas.

In Lichebarue iiij hidas de feodo Hugonis Pol'.

In Everdon' monachi de Bernay ij hidas dimidiam et ij parvas virgatas. Ibidem Hugo vicecomes viij parvas virgatas quas monachi de Daventre tenent. Ibidem Radulfus de Waundevill' iiij parvas virgatas. Ibidem Walterus iiij parvas virgatas.

In Snokescombe iiij parvas virgatas de feodo comitis Leycestr'.

In Stowe Johannes de Armenteres iiij hidas de feodo Gilberti de Gaunt.

245I Hundredum de Aylwoldesle.[1]

In Baddeby et Newenham abbas de Evesham iiij hidas.

In Norton' ij hidas dimidiam et ij parvas virgatas de feodo de Warewyk'.

In Thorp' Stephanus de Turs dimidiam hidam. Ibidem Willelmus de Novo Foro iiij parvas virgatas.

In Beruby ij hidas de feodo Willelmi Peverel.

In Gildesboru episcopus Lincoln' in dominico ij hidas.

In Staverton' Willelmus de Novo Foro j hidam de feodo comitis Leyc'. Ibidem Stephanus de Welton' iij hidas de feodo Rogeri de Moubray.

In Braundeston' Willelmus Trussebot' iij hidas et vj parvas virgatas de feodo Pagani Peverel. Ibidem comes Leycestr' iiij parvas virgatas.

In Daventre Walterus filius Roberti viij hidas de feodo regis Scotie.

In Welton' Willelmus ij hidas dimidiam et ij parvas virgatas de feodo comitis Leyc'. Ibidem Hugo vicecomes v parvas virgatas dimidiam de feodo de Berkamstede; monachi de Daventre tenent. Ibidem Ricardus Maulore ij parvas virgatas.

In Esseby iiij hidas de feodo comitis Leyc'.

In Dodeford' Radulfus de Chanes iij hidas.

In Chelredescote Galfridus de Torevill' j hidam et ij parvas virgatas de feodo comitis Leyc'.

1 Part of Fawsley hundred.

245J Hundredum de Norton'.

In Esseby Stephanus ij hidas et viij parvas virgatas de feodo Hugonis de Lega.

In Mortona Henricus de Pinkeny j hidam et dimidiam.

In Wedona idem Henricus ij hidas et viij parvas virgatas.

In Plomton' Willelmus filius Roberti j hidam dimidiam de feodo Wahill'.

In Slapton' iiij hidas de feodo comitis Leyc'.

In Braddene Paganus j hidam iiij parvas virgatas. Ibidem Vitalis Engayne j hidam iiij parvas virgatas. Ibidem Radulfus de Wandevill' j hidam ij parvas virgatas.

In Parva Blacolvesle Normannus de Sancto Patricio ij hidas de feodo Peverel. Item pertinet ad hidagium de Norton' j hidam et vij parvas virgatas et dimidiam.

In alia Blacolvesle idem dimidiam hidam. Ibidem Rogerus Golofre iij hidas dimidiam et dimidiam parvam virgatam. Ibidem Willelmus de Plumton' ij hidas ij parvas virgatas. Ibidem Gilbertus j hidam dimidiam et j parvam virgatam de feodo de Berkamstede.

Item in Selveston' Otuer' dimidiam hidam de feodo comitis Willelmi. Ibidem Willelmus de Caynes j hidam de feodo de Morton'. Ibidem Henricus de Pinkeny dimidiam hidam.

In Maydeford' Paganus ij hidas ij parvas virgatas.

In Sewewell' Radulfus j hidam vj parvas virgatas.

In Pateshill'[1] iiij^{or} parvas virgatas.

In Norton' et in soca vij hidas et j magnam virgatam.

In Atteneston' [fo. 96r] Galfridus de Turvill' iij parvas virgatas. Ibidem monachi de Becco viij parvas virgatas.

1 Otherwise in Towcester hundred.

245K Hundredum de Toucestr'.

In Gauton' Adnotus de Bettune iij hidas.

In Pateshill' Simon de Wahill' vij hidas. Ibidem Willelmus de Hocton' viij parvas virgatas. Ibidem comes Mauricius de feodo de Botebot ij parvas virgatas.

In Foxleya[1] Simon de Wahill' iiij parvas virgatas. Ibidem comes Mauricius iiij parvas virgatas de feodo de Berkamsted'. Ibidem monachi de Norht' vj parvas virgatas.

In Hinton' Elias ij hidas de feodo comitis Willelmi.
In Wappenham[2] Henricus de Pinkeny ij hidas de feodo.
In Eveleia[2] iiij hidas.
In Grimescote Aunsel ij hidas et iiij parvas virgatas de feodo Rogeri de Moubray. Ibidem monachi de Donestabel' ij hidas de feodo de Wahille.
In Potton' Johannes de Daventre j hidam dimidiam j parvam virgatam.
In Tiffeld' Willelmus de Pery j hidam dimidiam j parvam virgatam de feodo comitis Hugonis. Ibidem Walterus de Fortho j hidam dimidiam et ij parvas virgatas. Ibidem Willelmus de Gaynes vij parvas virgatas.
In Wytlebyr'[1] Ricardus vj parvas virgatas de feodo de Selveston'.
In Toucestr' comes de Arundel vij hidas iiij parvas virgatas. Ibidem Wybertus ad Ecclesiam vj parvas virgatas de feodo sancti Wandragesill'.
In Graftone[3] abbas de Grestenge iiij hidas.

1 Otherwise in Green's Norton hundred.
2 Otherwise in King's Sutton hundred.
3 Otherwise in Cleyley hundred.

245L Hundredum de Cleyle.

In Stok' et in Aldrinton' vij hidas ij parvas virgatas.
In Bassenham j hidam.
In Wyca Mainfein ij hidas de feodo de Wolfrington'.
In Pyria Robertus de Ferrar' iij hidas ij parvas virgatas de feodo comitis de Ferrar'.
In West Pyria iij hidas dimidiam et quinta pars dimidie hide de feodo Willelmi Peverel.
In Forhoue Walterus ij hidas de feodo Ricardi filii Willelmi. Ibidem Willelmus Gernet vij parvas virgatas de feodo de Berkamstede. Ibidem comes Leycestr' iij parvas virgatas.
In Covesgrave Robertus Ryvel viij parvas virgatas. Ibidem Willelmus le Brun vj parvas virgatas. Ibidem Adam ix parvas virgatas.
In Pyria heredes de Salfleto j hidam quinta pars j hide de feodo regis David.
In Pokesl' Robertus Ryvel vj parvas virgatas de feodo comitis Leyc'. Ibidem iiij parvas virgatas de feodo regis David.
In Esteneston' Ricardus de le Estre j hidam dimidiam et j parvam virgatam de feodo de Berkamstede. Ibidem Godefridus et Aldredus viij parvas virgatas de feodo Willelmi Maudut.
In Somereshale Michael' Mauncel vj parvas virgatas de feodo Willelmi Peverel de Hecham. In Wakefeld' iiij parvas virgatas de feodo regis.
In Hertwell' Nicholaus, Hugo, Adam, Radulfus iiij hidas dimidiam j parvam virgatam, scilicet quinta pars dimidie hide de feodo Walkelin Mamyot.

In Esse Robertus filius Anketill' j hidam et ij parvas virgatas de feodo Willelmi Maudut. Ad Hydam Willelmus Ruffi iiij parvas virgatas.

245M [fo. 96v] Hundredum de Wymeresle.

In Middelton' Robertus de Causho et Galfridus v hidas et j virgatam scilicet quarta pars j hide.

In Trop' Ascelinus de Chokes ij hidas dimidiam et $iiij^{ta}$ pars j hide. Ibidem hospital' Norht' dimidiam hidam et $iiij^{ta}$ pars j hide.

In Wotton' ij hidas et ij partes dimidie hide. Ibidem Michael' j hidam et terciam partem dimidie hide.

In Hardingestorn' vij hidas de feodo regis David.

In Blechesworthe et in Cortenhale Peverel vij hidas et iiij parvas virgatas de incremento in Quenton' quas Gilbertus tenuit.

In Quenton' David et Philipus j hidam dimidiam et $iiij^{tam}$ partem j hide.

In Preston' Walterus filius Wymeri j hidam et j virgatam de feodo regis David. Ibidem de feodo de Olneya dimidiam hidam.

In Alecote rex David terciam partem j hide.

In Pidenton' j hidam dimidiam et j virgatam.

In Houcton' Robertus de Pavely j hidam dimidiam virgatam magnam et ij virgatas de feodo Peverel. Ibidem Ricardus David $iiij^{or}$ parvas virgatas quas Osebertus tenuit. Ibidem Simon j hidam et j virgatam.

In alia Houcton' et in Braunfeld' iij hidas dimidiam quas Willelmus de Houcton' tenuit.

In Horton' Alouf de Merk' ij hidas et j parvam virgatam de Wahill'. Ibidem de feodo regis Scotie iij parvas virgatas. Ibidem Turgis de Quenton' vj parvas virgatas de eodem feodo. Ibidem Walterus filius Wynemeri vj parvas virgatas de feodo de Olneya.

In Hakelington' Nortgold' j hidam. Ibidem Turgis de Quenton' dimidiam hidam. Ibidem monachi de Norht' j hidam. Ibidem Willelmus de Lisurs dimidiam hidam de feodo de Olneya. Ibidem Walterus filius Wynemeri viij parvas virgatas de eodem feodo.

In Cugeho Willelmus j hidam dimidiam j virgatam.

In Whiston' Willelmus j hidam dimidiam de feodo abbatis de Rammes'. Ibidem rex David j virgatam magnam.

In Dodington' idem rex j hidam. Ibidem Walterus filius Wynemeri vj parvas virgatas de feodo de Rammeseya. Ibidem Willelmus de Wytendon' x parvas virgatas de abbate de Rammeseye.

In Esseby, et Chaddeston' Willelmus filius Charenbald' iij hidas dimidiam.

In Gerdele et Grendone vij hidas et j virgatam minus de feodo regis David.

245N Hundredum et dimidium de Hecham.

In Eston' et Strixton' Michael de Hamslape iij hidas dimidiam et virgatam magnam. Ibidem Paganus j virgatam magnam.

In Bosesete rex David ij hidas.

In Neweton' Aliiochus de Bidun ij hidas dimidiam minus.

In Wolaston' v hidas dimidiam virgatam de feodo de Chokes. Ibidem Corbelinus ij hidas dimidiam virgatam minus de feodo regis David.

In Haregrave Radulfus de Foleville iij parvas virgatas. Ibidem Ricardus et Rogerus de Costentyn iij parvas virgatas. Ibidem Harold' dimidiam hidam.

In Stanewigge Ascelinus j hidam et j virgatam et dimidiam de feodo Burgi.

In Yrencestre Nicholaus le Sauvage dimidiam hidam de feodo de Wahill'.

In Cotes Gilbertus filius Ricardi j hidam dimidiam et j parvam virgatam de feodo de Deneford'.

In alia Cotes Frumboldus de Deneford dimidiam hidam de eodem feodo.

In Cotes [fo. 97r] Johannes Bidoun j hidam dimidiam et j virgatam et dimidiam.

In Ringstede Gilbertus filius Ricardi iiij parvas virgatas de feodo de Deneford.

In Raundes ibidem Gilbertus iiij parvas virgatas de eodem feodo. Ibidem Robertus filius regis de feodo Glouernie ij hidas dimidiam.

In Knoston' Frumboldus j hidam dimidiam et j magnam virgatam.

In dominico Willelmi Peverel xxxiij hidas dimidiam et dimidiam virgatam.

In Boseyate iij parvas virgatas de feodo Willelmi Peverel.

245O Hundredum de Neubotlegrave.

In Daylington' iiij hidas de feodo abbatis de Burgo.

In Duston' iiij hidas de feodo Willelmi Peverel.

In Upton' dominus rex ij hidas dimidiam.

In Horepol' iiij hidas de feodo de Beuver'. Petrus j hidam dimidiam. Item aliud de feodo Peverel.

In Kyselingbyr' iij hidas dimidiam de feodo Gilberti de Gaunt. Ibidem comes Leyc' dimidiam hidam.

In Buckebrok' iiij hidas de feodo de Morenc'.

In Heyford' iiij hidas.

In Clachetorp' et in Parva Heyford iiij hidas.

In Flora Otuer iiij parvas virgatas de feodo comitis Galfridi. Ibidem Aunsel de Chokes j hidam et virgatam antiquo. Ibidem Radulfus filius

Sewani de feodo Peverel dimidiam hidam. Ibidem Hugo de Chaneys j hidam iiij parvas virgatas de feodo de Kaynes.

In Brockehole et in Musecote[1] Radulfus de Gaynes j hidam de feodo de Gaynes. Ibidem Gervasius Samson j hidam de feodo War'.

In Neubottle et in Brynton' vj hidas.

In Whelton' j hidam de feodo R[ogeri] de Moubray.

In Ravenstorp' et in Cheta iiij hidas de feodo Peverel.

In Haldeneby iij hidas de feodo comitis Leyc'.

In Haddon' idem comes iiij hidas.

In Brampton' idem comes iiij hidas.

In Herleston' iij hidas.

In Holtrop j hidam et j parvam virgatam de feodo de Berkamstede.

1 Otherwise in Fawsley hundred.

245P Hundredum de Gildesboru.

In Gildesboru Willelmus filius Aldredi iij magnas virgatas dimidiam de feodo Peverel. Ibidem presbiter j parvam virgatam de feodo comitis Leyc'.

In Holewelle episcopus Linc' j hidam et tercia pars j hide, Robertus de Dyva tenet. Ibidem comes Leyc' iij parvas virgatas. Ibidem de feodo Peverel v parvas virgatas.

In Nortoft Colemannus dimidiam hidam de feodo Peverel. Ibidem comes Leycestr' ij hidas et j magnam virgatam.

In Cotesbrok' Robertus Botevileyn ij hidas de feodo de Wahill'.

In Creton' Aunsel de Chokes j hidam.

In alia Creton' Herbertus dimidiam hidam de feodo Radulfi de Gaynes.

In Westhaddon' Hugo vicecomes ij hidas j magnam virgatam. Ibidem Peverel j magnam virgatam et dimidiam. Ibidem Aunsel de Chokes j magnam virgatam. Ibidem comes Leycestr' dimidiam hidam. Ibidem Nigellus de Albeny dimidiam hidam de feodo Rogeri de Moubray.

In Watford' iiij hidas de feodo Baldewini filii Gilberti.

In Buckeby Serles de Quency ij hidas dimidiam et j magnam virgatam de feodo Aunsel de Chokes. Ibidem Willelmus filius Alfridi dimidiam hidam de feodo Montis Acuti. Ibidem comes Leycestr' iij magnas virgatas.

In Crek' [fo. 97v] Rogerus de Caunvill' iij hidas dimidiam et j magnam virgatam de feodo Rogeri de Moubray.

In Lilleburn' et Cotes comes Leycestr' iiij hidas. Ibidem Willelmus Alfrid' fil'[1] j magnam virgatam.

In Stanford' abbas de Seleby ij hidas.

In Welleford' Willelmus de Wyvill' iiij hidas et j magnam virgatam de feodo Rogeri de Mounbray de Gildecote. Ibidem Adam j hidam dimidiam de feodo Baldewyni filii Gilberti. In Gelvertoft ij hidas et iij[a] pars j hide de feodo comitis Leyc'. Ibidem Radulfus filius Osmundi dimidiam hidam de feodo Willelmi filii Aluredi.

In Eltesdon' Hugo vicecomes j hidam dimidiam, monachi de Pippewell' tenent. Ibidem Hugo j magnam virgatam de feodo Westmonaster'. Ibidem Hugo de Kaynes iiij parvas virgatas. Ibidem Nigellus de Aubeny ij parvas virgatas de feodo de Welleford'.

In Esseby ij hidas dimidiam de feodo de Coventre. Ibidem Henricus de Mundevill' j magnam virgatam de feodo Peverel. Ibidem Hugo de Kaynes iij magnas virgatas. Ibidem Robertus dimidiam hidam de feodo de Welleford'.

In Wynewyk' iij hidas et j magnam virgatam de feodo de Coventre. Ibidem Robertus Alegod' viij parvas virgatas de feodo Peverel.

In Navesbya vij hidas de feodo Willelmi Peverel.

In Turleby j hidam dimidiam de feodo comitis Leycestr. Ibidem Robertus filius Alegod' j hidam de feodo Peverel. Item ibidem dimidiam hidam per rotulos Wyncestr'.[2]

In Cotes Robertus Halegod' iiij virgatas dimidiam.

1 Recte *filius Alfridi*?

2 Roffe identifies these with an *inquisitio geldi* of 1086. *Domesday*, pp. 110–151.

245Q Hundredum de Mallesl'.[1]

In Houton' de feodo sancti Edmundi j hidam. Ibidem Rocinus j hidam iij virgatas de feodo de Berkamstede. Ibidem j hidam et j virgatam de feodo regis David.

In Langeport Simon Malesoueres iiij hidas de feodo de Wahill'. Ibidem de sokagio sancti Edmundi dimidiam hidam.

In Scaldewell' Albrem de Ver iij magnas virgatas de feodo Oxon'. Ibidem de feodo sancti Edmundi j hidam dimidiam et j magnam virgatam. Ibidem rex David ij hidas dimidiam et j virgatam.

In Walde comes Albemar' iiij hidas et iiij virgatas de feodo Oxonie.

In Faxtone ij hidas dimidiam de feodo de Baillol.

In Waldegrave Henricus iij hidas dimidiam et j magnam virgatam de feodo regis David. Ibidem Henricus de Tracy iij virgatas de sokagio de Foxton'. Ibidem comes Leycestr' dimidiam hidam.

In Brikelesworth' Simon filius Simonis viij hidas dimidiam de feodo de Corcy. Ibidem Alfredus j hidam et j virgatam de feodo de Salesbyrs.

In Thorp' juxta Norht'[2] v hidas j virgatam minus.

In Multon'[2] de sokagio de Torp' j hidam dimidiam et bovatam. Et in Weston'[1] j hidam.

1 Part of Orlingbury hundred.

2 Otherwise in Spelhoe hundred.

245R Hundredum de Speleho.

In Abendon' Unfridus de Bassingburne iiij hidas.

In Weston' Ricardus iiij hidas.

In Parva Billingge iiij hidas.

In Magna Billingge iiij hidas.

In Oveston' Gilbertus de Milers iiij hidas.

In Multon' ij hidas et iiij parvas virgatas de feodo Ricardi de Engayne. Ibidem Wydo de Baillol j hidam dimidiam et j parvam virgatam de feodo [fo. 98r] de Foxton'. Ibidem Ricardus de le Pek' iiij hidas de feodo regis David.

In Boketon' iij hidas et iij parvas virgatas de feodo monachorum sancti Wandragesile.

In Pittesford' Henricus Malesures et Philippus iij hidas dimidiam de feodo de Wahill'. Ibidem comes Leyc' vj parvas virgatas.

In Sprotton' ix parvas virgatas de feodo regis David. Ibidem de feodo Ricardi Basset iij parvas virgatas. Ibidem comes Leyc' ij hidas dimidiam j magnam virgatam.

245S Hundredum de Anfordesho.

In Wenlingburg' [abbas] de Croylande v hidas dimidiam. Ibidem Nicholaus de Cogeho iij magnas virgatas de feodo regis David. Ibidem comes Leyc' j hidam.

In Herdwyk'[1] ix parvas virgatas de feodo regis David.

In Eketon' iiij hidas de feodo comitis de Ferrar', Willelmus de Mungomery tenent.

In Siwell' monachi Norht' et sancti moniales de Aunestowe iiij hidas.

In Holecote Adam ij hidas dimidiam et j parvam virgatam de feodo Willelmi de Curcy. Ibidem j hidam et iiij parvas virgatas de feodo regis David.

In Esseby iiij hidas de feodo regis David.

In Wyleby iiij hidas de feodo regis David.

In Dodington' iiij hidas de feodo regis David.

In Barton' iiij hidas de feodo regis David.

1 Otherwise in Orlingbury hundred.

245T Hundredum de Orlingberge.

In Orlingberg' Fucherus Malesoueres j hidam de feodo de Wahill'. Ibidem j hidam dimidiam de feodo Willelmi de Curcy.

In Wymale j hidam dimidiam et j virgatam de feodo de Wahill'.

In Bateshasel Malesoueres dimidiam hidam de feodo Wahill'.

In Hysham Henricus de Ysham ij hidas et tercia pars j hide de feodo de Daundevill'. Ibidem Thomas Pyel j hidam dimidiam ij parvas virgatas dimidiam de feodo de Rameshe'. Ibidem Galfridus vj parvas virgatas de feodo de Huntingdon'.

In Cranesle Hugo Kyde j hidam dimidiam et j bovatam dimidiam de feodo de Chok'. Ibidem Radulfus Meschin v parvas virgatas de feodo de Geytington'. Ibidem Johannes le Bauld j magnam virgatam. Ibidem Foliot ij hidas dimidiam et j parvam virgatam de feodo de Huntingdon'.

In Pytesle abbas de Burgo v hidas dimidiam set tamen in rotulis Wincestr'[1] vj hidas et iij parvas virgatas. Ibidem Ricardus Engayne iij hidas j virgatam. Ibidem Willelmus filius Gery dimidiam hidam de feodo Mortoin.

In Harudon' Reygold' j hidam de feodo Willelmi de Curcy. Ibidem Galfridus ij hidas et j bovatam minus de feodo de Huntingdon'. Ibidem Nicholaus de Cugeho j hidam de feodo regis. In Haninton' dimidiam hidam de feodo comitis Leycestr'. Ibidem j hidam dimidiam de feodo regis David.

1 See above no. 245P note 2.

245U Hundredum de Stotfolde.[1]

In Maydewell' Alanus iiij hidas ij parvas virgatas de feodo de Wolrington'. Ibidem Robate ij hidas de feodo Rannulfi de Bayouse.

In Keylmers idem dimidiam hidam de feodo sancti Edmundi. Ibidem de feodo de Notingham j hidam dimidiam et dimidiam virgatam. Ibidem de socagio de Geytington' dimidiam hidam et j parvam virgatam. Ibidem Eudo filius Haschul' j hidam [fo. 98v] et j parvam virgatam de sokagio de Rowell'. Ibidem Adam v parvas virgatas de feodo regis David.

In Haselbech' episcopus Salesbir' ij hidas de feodo de Berkamstede. Ibidem comes Leycestr' j hidam de feodo Mor'.

In Clipston' Willelmus Peverel iij hidas dimidiam et j parvam virgatam de feodo Peverel. Ibidem Adam dimidiam hidam et iij parvas virgatas de feodo regis David. Ibidem de socagio de Geytington' v parvas virgatas. Ibidem Mauricius x parvas virgatas de feodo sancti Edmundi. Ibidem de socagio de Rowell' j parvam virgatam.

In Soleby v hidas et j virgatam de feodo Westm'.

In Sibertoft' ij hidas dimidiam et ij partes j virgate de feodo de serjantye regis.

In Oxendon' j hidam et j virgatam de socagio de Rowell'. Ibidem j hidam de feodo regis David.

In Parva Oxendon' Robertus filius Hugonis j hidam et iij partes j virgate de feodo de Berkamstede. Ibidem de socagio de Geytington' ij parvas virgatas. Ibidem Turberd j parvam virgatam.

In Farendon' j hidam et iiij[ta] pars j virgate de feodo de Huntingdon'. Ibidem Robertus filius Hugonis iij virgatas et iij partes j parve virgate de feodo sancti Edmundi. Ibidem Willelmus Meschin j parvam virgatam de socagio de Geytington'

In Boudon' Robertus filius Hugonis ij hidas et j virgatam et terciam partem j virgate de feodo de Berkamstede. Ibidem rex David j hidam et terciam partem j virgate et terciam partem de tertia parte j virgate.

In Thorp' comes Leyc' iiij magnas virgatas et terciam partem j virgate.

In Merston' idem comes j hidam dimidiam et ij partes j virgate quam Osbertus Trussel tenet.

1 Part of Rothwell hundred.

245V Hundredum de Rowell'.

In Hetheringtone Willelmus filius Alvid' vj hidas.

In Braybrok' ij hidas de socagio de Hetherington'. Ibidem Wydo Cocus j hidam. Ibidem Peverel iij partem j hide. Ibidem Ivo ij hidas cum implemento de ij virgatas de terra Peverel et cum dimidia virgata de feodo sancti Edmundi.

In Aringworthe Robertus filius Hugonis et Willelmus filius Albeni ij hidas et ij partes j hide de feodo de Berkamstede. Ibidem Petrus j virgatam.

In Rowell' et in Overton' et in Lodington' Eudo de Haschull' ix hidas et j parvam virgatam. In Lodington Willelmus constabularius iij virgatas quas Robertus le Baud tenet.

In Deseburg' Norman et Reginaldus Race ij hidas et ij partes j hide.

In Pippewell'[1] Robertus filius Hugonis dimidiam hidam et terciam partem j hide. Ibidem Willelmus de Aubeny dimidiam hidam per alium rotulum j hidam et iij partes j hide.

In Riston' Andreas ij hidas dimidiam et terciam partem j hide de feodo regis David. Ibidem Robertus Basset j hidam dimidiam et j parvam virgatam de feodo Willelmi de Aubeny. Ibidem Vitalis Engayne ij partes j hide quas Vitalis Lovet tenuit. Ibidem Siricius Bucar' sextam partem j hide. Ibidem de socagio de Geytington' j parvam virgatam et dimidiam, Rogerus de Cranesle tenuit.

In Bereford' j hidam de socagio de Geytington'.

In Clendon' de eodem socagio dimidiam hidam. Ibidem Siricius Bucar' dimidiam hidam dimidiam virgatam de feodo Willelmi Alur'. Ibidem [fo. 99r] Radulfus Normann' dimidiam hidam dimidiam virgatam de socagio de Rowell'.

In Thorp' Fucherus Malesoueres j hidam et terciam partem j hide de feodo Avenel Willelmi.[2]

In alia Thorp' Hervicus Belet ij partes j hide.

In Drayton' j hidam et dimidiam virgatam de feodo de Rowell'. Ibidem

Corbet dimidiam hidam et iij partes j virgate de feodo regis David. Ibidem Willelmus Durdent j magnam virgatam de feodo Menfelyn de Wolfrington'.

1 Otherwise in Corby hundred.
2 Recte *Willelmi Avenel.*

245W Hundredum de Stokes.[1]

[marginated in later hand] Virgata }magna, parva

In Wilberdeston' et in Stokes Willelmus Daubeny viij hidas et j virgatam.

In Carleton' de socagio regis dimidiam hidam et j parvam virgatam dimidiam. Ibidem Willelmus Daubeny dimidiam hidam et j parvam virgatam et dimidiam. Ibidem Robertus filius Hugonis iij magnas virgatas et j parvam virgatam et dimidiam.

In Brampton' de socagio regis j hidam. Ibidem Basset ij hidas. Ibidem Radulfus filius Eldewyn iiij hidas ij parvas virgatas minus.

In Dingele Alured ij hidas et j virgatam. Ibidem Ricardus Basset j hidam dimidiam et j magnam virgatam in dominico suo.

In Sutton' et Weston' Ricardus Basset vj hidas.

In Assele Radulfus de Beufo ij hidas et ij parvas virgatas de feodo de Beuv'. Ibidem Ricardus Basset iiij parvas virgatas quas Wydo de Watervill' tenuit. Ibidem Willelmus Daubeny vij parvas virgatas. Ibidem Rogerus de Sprotton' j hidam de feodo regis David. Ibidem Berengar' j hidam j parvam virgatam minus quam Wydo de Watervill' tenet de Radulfo de Beufo.

In Cotingham abbas de Burgo vij hidas.

In Banefeld j hidam de feodo.

In Rokingham j hidam de feodo.

1 Part of Corby hundred.

245X Hundredum de Coreby.

In Wakerle ij hidas dimidiam de feodo Eudonis filii Huberti.

In Haringworthe v hidas de feodo regis David.

In Laxinton' et in Hynewyk' Vitalis Engayne j hidam dimidiam. Ibidem Robertus filius Hugonis j magnam virgatam.

In Blatherwyk' Robertus filius Hugonis et Ricardus Dengayne ij hidas.

In Bolewyk' ij hidas.

In Henewyk' Vitalis Lovet dimidiam hidam.

In Deen Radulfus filius Nigelli ij hidas dimidiam de feodo Westm'.

In Neweton' et in Acle ij hidas dimidiam de feodo regis David. Ibidem

Willelmus de Houton' j hidam dimidiam et j magnam virgatam de feodo regis David.

In Parva Acle Willelmus filius Aluredi iij virgatas de feodo Montis Acuti.

In Geytington' dominus rex j hidam et j magnam virgatam. Ibidem j hidam et j magnam virgatam de feodo sancti Edmundi.

In Wycle ij hidas dimidiam de feodo comitis de Warenn' de Morteyn.

In Boketon' j dimidiam [omission ?] de feodo sancti Edmundi.

In Kirkeby j virgatam de feodo Hunfredi de Bassingburn'.

In Stanerne j virgatam dimidiam de socagio de Bristok'.

In Coreby et in Gretton' et in Brixstoke x hidas.

245Y Hundredum de Wylebrok'.

In Lodington Radulfus filius Willelmi ij hidas dimidiam de feodo Burgi. Ibidem abbas de Ramesh' dimidiam hidam.

In Aylington' de socagio Burgi j hidam dimidiam. Ibidem [fo. 99v] Willelmus filius Ketelber' dimidiam hidam de feodo de Rameseye.

In Wermington'[1] abbas Burgi j hidam.

In Elmenton'[2] abbas de Croylaund j hidam.

In Tanesovere Hacvil de Sancto Jacobo v hidas et terciam partem j hide. Ibidem Salomon ij partes j hide de feodo comitis de Warewyk'.

In Sothewyk' cum Jarewell' Willelmus de Lisurs j hidam.

[later marginated symbol] In Fodrengeye vj hidas de feodo regis David.

In Cotherstoke Ricardus filius Hugonis j hidam dimidiam de feodo Burgi. Ibidem Rogerus Infans j hidam dimidiam de eodem feodo.

In Neweton' Robertus de Cerneya iij hidas de feodo Marmiun.

In Eston' Simon de Lindon' ij hidas.

In Weston' Willelmus filius Herewyn ij hidas.

In Nassington' vj hidas.

In Glapthorn' Galfridus de Normanvill j hidam dimidiam. Ibidem Ridel et Hugo dimidiam hidam et j virgatam. Ibidem Fulco de Lisurs iij partes j hide.

In Apethorp' ij hidas.

In Clyva j hidam dimidiam et dimidiam virgatam.

In Dodington' j hidam.

1 Otherwise in Polebrook hundred.
2 Otherwise in Huntingdonshire.

245Z Hundredum de Suthnaveslunt'.[1]

Irtlingburg' v hidas dimidiam et j parvam virgatam de feodo Burgi. Ibidem Reginaldus de la Bataille iij hidas dimidiam de eodem feodo.

Ibidem Simon Basset j hidam Avenel de feodo Burgi. In Adington' Ricardus filius Hugonis iij hidas dimidiam de feodo Burgi. Ibidem Willelmus frater Wydonis dimidiam virgatam de feodo de Croylaund'. Ibidem Willelmus de Huntingdon' j hidam et j virgatam dimidiam de feodo de Gloucestr'.

In Wodeford' viij hidas dimidiam virgatam de feodo Burgi. Ibidem Wydo Treylli j hidam dimidiam de feodo Burgi. Ibidem Reginaldus de la Bataille dimidiam virgatam. Ibidem Willelmus de Houton' dimidiam hidam.

In alia Adington' Albricus camerarius ij hidas de feodo regis. Ibidem j hidam de feodo abbatis. Ibidem Willelmus filius Wydonis ij hidas de feodo abbatis de Croylaund'.

In Thingdene de dominico regis x hidas.

1 Part of Huxloe hundred.

245ZA Northnaveslunt.[1]

In Cranford' Bertram de Wedon' ij hidas et j virgatam dimidiam de feodo Burgi. Ibidem Galfridus camerarius j hidam de feodo Glouernie. Ibidem Ricardus filius Wydonis j hidam de feodo Burgi. Ibidem Mauricius Daundelyn ij hidas dimidiam de feodo Burgi. Ibidem Radulfus filius Rogeri v hidas de Simone filio Petri.

In Barton' Galfridus camerarius v hidas de feodo Gloucestrie.

In Werketon' iiij hidas de feodo sancti Edmundi.

In Keteringe x hidas de feodo Burgi.

In Grafton' Ricardus de Humaz iiij hidas.

In Burtone Ricardus filius Wydonis viij hidas dimidiam. Ibidem Willelmus de Houton' j hidam dimidiam.

1 Part of Huxloe hundred.

246 List of the knights' fee of the abbey. [*c.* 1200].[1]

Feoda militum de Burgo Sancti Petri.

Rogerus Torpel vj milites.

Thornhawe iiij milites et j quarter'.

[fo. 100r] Galfridus de la Mare j miles dim'.

Galfridus filius Galfridi pro Suthorp' et Gunthorp' iiij milites.

Boreville j miles dim'.

Thorp' Waterville iiij milites.

Hugo de Lisurs pro Benifeld', Irtlingburg' et Adington' iiij milites.

Hugo Fauvel j miles dim' scilicet pro Walecot' juxta Castr' j miles et pro Walecot' juxta Humber dim'.

Sutton' ij milites elemosinar'.
Miltone j miles dim'.
Lovetote ij milites. [symbol]
Robertus de Stokes pro Milton' et pro Etton' dim' miles. [symbol]
Torold' de Castre j miles et dim'.
Peverel in Paston' j miles.
Avenel in Irtlingburg j miles.
Almaricus dispensar' in Daylenton' extra Norhampton' ij milites.
Robertus de Toth in Paston' j miles.
Baldewynus Aungein in Chirchefeld'[2] dim' miles
Ivo de Stokes[2]
videlicet Nicholaus Hering' j feod' ut dicitur.
Martinus de Pappele j miles.
Ricardus Engayne iiij quart'.
Henricus Doily dim' mil'.
Mauricius Daundeley in Craneford.[3]
Hugo Gargat in Irtlingburgh et in Wermington'[3] j miles.
Robertus de Dyve in Uptone ij milites.
Robertus Marmiun in Thirningge dim' mil'.
Lucas Maufe in Wodeford' et in Kynestorp' ij milites.
Rogerus filius Pagani in Helpeston' terciam partem j militis.
Willelmus de Walton' in eadem quintam partem j militis.
Walranus de Wodecroft sextam partem j militis.
Galfridus de Caxston' vicesimam partem j militis.
Jacobus de Wynewik' vicesimam partem j militis.
Philippus de Armeston' terciam decimam partem j militis.
Gilbertus de Bernak quartam partem j militis

1 Dated from *Henry of Pytchley*, p. xl.
2 Line from *Chirchefeld'* to *Stokes* and from *Stokes* to *videlicet*.
3 Line from *Craneford'* to *Wermington'*.

[fo. 100v] Blank

247 Royal licence for the abbot and convent to grant the advowson of Normanby church in mortmain to Bishop John Dalderby and the chapter of Lincoln, together with a licence to appropriate. [30 Oct. 1314][1]

[fo. 101r] Littera regia de ecclesia de Normanby.

[marginated in different hand] Walk'

Edwardus[2] Dei gracia rex Anglie, dominus Hibernie, et dux Aquitanie omnibus ad quos presentes littere pervenerint, salutem. Licet de communi consilio regni nostri statutum sit quod non liceat viris religiosis seu aliis ingredi feodum alicuius, ita quod ad manum mortuam deveniat, sine licencia nostra et capitalis domini de quo res illa inmediate tenetur, volentes tamen venerabili patri Johanni episcopo Linc' et capitulo ecclesie beate Marie eiusdem loci graciam facere specialem, concessimus et licenciam dedimus pro nobis et heredibus nostris quantum in nobis est dilectis nobis in Christo abbati et conventui de Burgo Sancti Petri quod ipsi advocationem ecclesie de Normanby dare possint et assignare prefatis episcopo et capitulo. Habendam et tenendam eisdem episcopo et capitulo et successoribus suis in perpetuum. Et eisdem episcopo et capitulo quod ipsi advocationem predictam a prefatis abbate et conventu recipere, et predictam ecclesiam de Normanby apropriare possint sibi et successoribus suis in usus proprios possidendam tenore presentium, similiter licenciam dedimus specialem. Nolentes quod predictus abbas et conventus vel successores, aut predicti episcopus et capitulum seu successores sui ratione statuti predicti per nos vel heredes nostros inde occasionentur molestentur in aliquo seu graventur, salvis tamen capitalibus dominis feodi illius serviciis inde debitis et consuetis.

1 Printed in *Mon. Angl.*, vol. I, p. 394 and *Cal. Pat., 1313–17*, p. 199. A licence granted earlier in the year provides for the crown to make the presentation should there be a vacancy in the bishopric, but makes no mention of appropriation. *Ibid.*, p. 131.
2 For background to this licence,which was associated with the appropriation of Warmington church by the abbey, see Franklin, 'The Bishop, the Abbot and Warmington Rectory', pp. 202–5.

248 Letter from John de Ayston', sheriff of Northamptonshire, to the bailiffs of the liberty, quoting the orders sent to sheriffs by Edward I concerning measures for the maintenance of law and order under the Statute of Winchester and for the arrest of suspects without indictment, while he is in Scotland dealing with the rebellion of Robert Bruce. [6 June 1306]

[fo. 101v] J[ohannes] de Ayston' vicecomes North' ballivis libertatis de Burgo Sancti Petri salutem. Mandatum domini regis in hec verba recipi:

E[dwardus][1] Dei gracia rex etc vicecomiti North' salutem. Cum pro tranquillitate et pace populi regni nostri necnon ad maliciam malefactorum et pacis nostre perturbatorum reprimendum, quoddam statutum apud Wynton' de communi consilio eiusdem regni dudum fecerimus quod pro pace nostra firmius conservandum, et maxime dum ad rebellionem Roberti de Brus inimici et rebellionis nostri per Dei adjutorium refrenandum ad partes Scotie sumus profecturi, valde utile reputamus et quod in omnibus suis articulis firmiter volumus observari ac satis notorium existat quod malefactores et felones ac cetere innumerabiles persone de quibus manifesta suspicio latrocinii et felonie habetur tam in balliva tua quam alibi in diversis comitatibus regni nostri depredationes homicidia et alia enormia nocte dieque, clam et palam contra pacem nostram perpetrantes vagantur discurrunt, receptantur, manutenentur et moram faciunt manifestam quos malefactores receptatores, manutentores et eis consentientes, tu qui pacem nostram in dicta balliva tua specialiter conservare teneris, si pro ea ibidem conservanda, diligentiam apponere curares sicut deberes desicut posse comitatus predicti in quibuscumque huiusmodi necessitatibus ad tuam summonitionem et districtionem est subjectum capere posses et arestare. Tibi firmiter injungendo precipimus quod statutum illud in pleno comitatu tuo necnon in civitatibus, burgis, hundredis, villis mercator' et aliis locis in balliva tua, tam infra libertates quam extra, et ubi expedire videris publice facias[2] recitari et in singulis suis articulis teneri. Preterea quia non est nobis incognitum quod singulorum auribus intitulatur; videlicet qualiter diversi predones et felones coram justiciariis nostris ad felonias et transgressiones in diversis comitatibus regni nostri factas audiendum et terminandum, assignatis, se justificari non permittant, set cum in exigendo ponantur in diversis comitatibus se transferunt et in eis latitantes morantur et ita quod in eis manifesta suspicio felonie aut mali per eorum extraneos adventus, varios que incessus et nocturnos quandoque per eorum voluptuosas expensas haberi potest et habetur. Et licet in statuto nostro Westm' contineatur que nullus capiatur vel imprisonetur nisi prius per sacramentum duodecim juratorum fuerit indictatus et eorum indictamentum per sigilla sua postmodum fuerit testificatum, volumus tamen et precipimus quod omnes tales de quibus manifesta suspicio felonie et latrocinii habetur quos in balliva tua tam infra libertates quam extra inveniri contigerit, quamquam inde sic indictati non fuerint sine dilatione arestari et salvo et secure in prisona nostra custodiri facias donec secundum legem et consuetudinem rengni [sic] nostri de ea deliberentur. Et hec premissa taliter executioni facias demandari sicut te ipsum diligis, et de receptacione et consensu predictorum malefactorum liber esse volumus et inmunis et ne ad te tamquam de predictis maleficiis culpabilem nos capere debeamus. Et talem ac tantam diligentiam [fo. 102r] contra huiusmodi malefactores suspectos et manifeste felones tam per te quam per posse dictorum comitatuum apponas ne tibi post presens mandatum nostrum possit inputari seu debeat, quod per tuam negligenciam et consensum talia intollerabilia infra ballivam tuam amodo perpetrentur volumus eciam quod ex parte nostra precipias et firmiter injungas ballivis comitatus tui omnibus, tam infra libertates quam extra, quod ipsi eandem diligenter pro pacis nostre conservatione nisius custodus apponant, et taliter se habeant in hac parte, ne penam in dicto statuto Wynton' contentam incurrant et nichilominus pro voluntate nostra inprisonentur et ab ea graviter redimantur quod si non fecerint, tu ipse in defectum eorumdem ballivorum libertates illas ingredieris quotienscumque necesse fuerit, et premissa in omnibus informa supradicta strictius fieri facias et facias observari. Et quos hoc mandatum nostrum contempnentes in ipso exequendo remissos seu negligentes vel omnino sequi nolentes inveneris capias et nomina eorumdem justiciariis nostris ad felonias et transgressiones in comitatu tuo contra pacem nostram factas audienda et terminanda, assignatis instanter postquam eos sic ceperis, constari facias ut iidem sic capti nobis de contemptu predicto coram eis veniant responsuri et facturi, quod curia consideraverit in hac parte. Teste me ipso apud Westm' vj die Junii anno regni nostri xxx^mo^ iiij^to^ .

Quare vobis mando quod mandatum istud plene exequamini.

1 The text of the royal writ is printed in translation in *Cal. Close, 1302–7*, pp. 396–7.
2 *facias* repeated.

249 Grant by Abbot William of Woodford and the convent to Richard of Marholm, known as le Taylur, a knight of Bishop Oliver of Lincoln, of sustenance for his lifetime in the abbey, alongside the abbot's knights. [27 July 1296]

[Marginated] Carta Ricardi de Marham.

Omnibus Christi fidelibus presens scriptum visuris vel audituris frater Willelmus de Wodeford' monasterii de Burgo Sancti Petri minister humilis et eiusdem loci conventus salutem in Domino sempiternam. Noverit universitas vestra nos unanimiter concessisse dilecto nobis in Christo Ricardo de Marham, dicto le Taylur, armigero venerabilis patris domini O[liveri] Dei gracia Linc' episcopi, conpetentem sustentationem suam in domo nostra quoadvixerit inter armigeros abbatis de Burgo qui pro tempore fuerit plenarie percepiendam ut in victualibus robis stipendiis curialitatibus et graciis que fuerint annuatim armigeriis abbatis proximioribus. Ita videlicet quod quandocumque dicto Ricardo placuit apud Burgum declinare et in officio armigeri honesto eidem per abbatem qui pro tempore fuerit assignando personaliter ministrare sustentationem predictam percipiet dum minstraverit absque subtractione aliqua vel diminutione. Si vero idem Ricardus debilitate ac infirmitate corporis decentus fuerit quod in officio sui assignato minstrare nequiverit, nichilominus in camera sua eidem Ricardo ut predictum est et prout decebit et oportebit infirmum providebitur. In cuius rei testimonium presentis scriptis sigilla nostra fecimus apponi. Dat' in capitulo nostro die Veneris proximi [sic] post festum sancti Jacobi apostoli anni Domini M^o^ CC^o^ nonagesimo vj^o^.

250 Note of the abbey's liability and payment of a papal tenth. [1293–1317][1]

[fo. 102v] Summa total'[2] taxationis bonorum abbatis de Burgo sub collecta abbatis Oseneye existentium:

CClxxiiij li. xiiij s. vj d. ob. qa.

Inde decima	xxvij li. ix s. v d. ob.
Bona celerarii in Belasise	v li. viij d.
Inde decima	x s. j d.
Item ecclesia de Wermington' cum pensione	xxxvij li.
Inde decima	lxviij s.
Item memorandum quod maneria de Alwalton et Fletton' taxantur ad	xxxvj li. xiij s.
Inde decima	liij s. iiij d.
Summa taxationis bonorum spiritualium et temporalium elemosinarii	lx li. xiiij d.
Inde decima	vj li. j d. ob.
Summa total' bonorum sacriste	lxiiij li. iij s. iiij d.
Inde decima	vj li. viij s. iiij d.
Summa taxationis bonorum camerarii	lij li. xiij s. iiij d.
Inde decima	xiij s. iiij d.
Summa taxationis bonorum pitanciarii	xxvj s. viij d.
Inde decima	ij s. viij d.
Summa bonorum thesaurarii	xxx s.
Inde decima	iij s.
Infirmarius in Wermington'	vj s.
Inde decima	vij d. qa.
Summa total' bonorum supradictorum	CCClxxviij li. viij s. viij d. ob. qa.
Inde decima	xlvij li. xvj s. x d. ob.
Summa tocius decime abbatis de Burgo Sancti Petri facte priori sancte Katerine in plenam solutionem eiusdem decime	xvij li. viij s. x d.
Summa[3] medietatis decime que soluta est per manus recepta abbatis	xiij li. xiiij s. viij d. ob. qa.
Summa tocius decime que soluta est per manus receptur' abbatis	xxvij li. ix s. v d. ob.
Summa decime date pro domibus in civitate Lond'	ij s.

1 The abbot of Osney and prior of St Katherine without Lincoln were deputy collectors for all the papal tenths between 1291 and 1317. Lunt, *Financial Relations*, pp. 632–37.

2 *Summa total'* marginated.

3 The remainder of the document is in a smaller hand.

251 Note of the abbot's liability for payment of a thirtieth. [1306][1]

[fo. 103r] [Marginated] Burgbir'

Abbas de Burgo Sancti Petri habet apud Burgbir' xxx quarteria frumenti, xx quarteria ordei, xl avene, vj pisarum fenum cum fur' xx s.; iiij afros xx s.; viij boves lvi s.; j carrucam cum ij equis xx s. Summa bonorum xviij li. ij s. viij d. Inde tricesime xij s. j d.

[Marginated] Thorp'
Item idem abbas habet apud Thorp' xij quarteria frumenti, viij siliginis, x ordei, viij dragii, x avene, iiij pisarum, fenum cum fur' xiij s. iiij d.; ij afros ix s.; iiij boves xxviij s.; ij sues, iiij porcelli x s.; j caruc' vj s. viij d.; ij equos xvj s. Summa xj li. xix s. Inde tricesime vij s. xj d. ob.

[Marginated] Eye
Item idem abbas habet apud Eye x quarteria frumenti, xij siliginis, xij ordei, xxx dragii, v pisarum, fenum cum fur' xxvj s. viij d.; ij afros prec' cuiuslibet afr' vj s.; vj boves prec' bovis vij s.; xij vaccas prec' vacce v s.; j taurum prec' vi s. viij d.; x boviculos prec' boviculi iiij s.; vij^{xx} ova; j carrucam vj s. viij d.; ij equos prec' equi viij s. Summa xxvij li. iiij d. Inde tricesime xviij s. qa.

[Marginated] Wytherington'
Item idem abbas habet apud Wytherington' x quarteria frumenti, iiij siliginis, vj ordei, xij avene, fenum cum fur' x s.; ij afros prec' cuiuslibet afri v s.; iiij boves prec' bovis vj s. viij d.; j carrucam prec' vj s., iiij vaccas prec' vacce v s.; iij boviculos prec' boviculi iiij s. Summa viij li. viij s. Inde tricesime v s. vij. d. qa.

[Marginated] Walton'
Item idem abbas habet apud Walton' xvj quarteria frumenti, xx avene, ij equos ad carrucam prec' equi vj s. viij d.; j carrucam prec' vij s.; ij afros prec' afri v s.; viij boves prec' bovis vj s. viij d.; fenum cum fur' vij s. Summa viij li. xvij s. iiij d. Unde tricesime v s. xi d.

[Marginated] Glinton
Item idem abbas habet apud Glinton' x quarteria frumenti, iiij siliginis, viij ordei, xvi avene, fenum cum fur' xv s.; ij afros prec' afri v s.; vj boves prec' bovis vj s. viij d.; iiij vaccas prec' vacce v s.; v^{xx} et x ova; vj porcos prec' porci xij d.; j carrucam cum ij equis xx s. Summa xv li. xvij s. viij d. Unde tricesime x s. vij d.

[Marginated] Castre
Item idem abbas habet apud Castre xx quarteria frumenti, viij ordei, xxiiij avene, fenum cum fur' xij s.; iiij afros prec' afri v s.; viij boves prec' bovis vij s.; iiij^{xx} ova; x porcos prec' porci xviij d.; j carrucam cum ij equis xx s. Summa bonorum xvi li. xiij s. viij d. Unde tricesime ix s. xi d. ob.

Summa total' lxx s. vij d.

1 Prestwich, *Edward I*, p. 569. There was no grant of a thirtieth under Edward II. J. F. Willard, *Parliamentary Taxes on Personal Property: A Study in Medieval English Financial Administration* (Cambridge, Mass., 1934), p. 10.

252 Royal writ, at the abbot's request, to the treasurer and barons of the Exchequer ordering them to search their records to ascertain the terms on which the manors of Torpel and Upton are held because, having fallen into the king's hand, their custodians and bailfiffs are unjustly withholding what is due to the abbey. [15 Nov. 1318]

[fo. 103v] [Marginated in a later medieval hand] Torpel and Upton'

Rex thesaurario et baronibus suis de Scaccario salutem. Petitionem dilecti nobis in Christo abbatis de Burgo Sancti Petri coram nobis et consilio nostro exhibitam recipimus continentem, quod cum, maneria de Torpel et Upton' cum pertinenciis in comitatu Norht' de ipso teneantur de ipso et predecessoribus suis abbatibus eiusdem loci, et ecclesia sua de Burgo Sancti Petri teneri consueverint per homagium et servicium quatuor feodorum militum, et alia servicia annua ad valenciam quatuor librorum per annum et per servicium faciendi sectam ad curiam predicti abbatis de Castr' de tribus septimanis in tres septimanas, servicia predicta prefato abbati de toto tempore nostro, quo maneria illa ad manus nostras devenerunt, per custodes et ballivos maneriorum predictorum subtracta exciterunt et detenta in ipsius abbatis et status sui prejudicium, et ecclesie sue exheredationis periculum manifestum super quo idem abbas petiit a nobis per petitionem predictam sibi justicia exhiberi. Nos nolentes eidem abbati injuriari taliter modo hac parte vobis mandamus quod vos per inspectionem rotulorum et memorandorum de dicto Scaccario, et aliis modis, quibus super premissis melius informari poteritis, informetis utrum videlicet maneria predicta de prefato abbate teneantur necne, et si sit, tunc utrum per predicta servicia an alia, et si per alia, tunc per que, et qualiter et quo modo, et predicta servicia tunc a quo tempore, fuerint eidem abbati subtracta, et per quos, vel per quem, et ex qua causa. Et de eo quod inde inveneritis necnon de informatione vestra, nos sub sigillo dicti Scaccarii quamcitius commode, poteritis certiores reddere non omittatis[1] hoc breve nobis remittentes. Teste apud Ebor' xv die Novembris anno duodecimo.

1 *reddere non omittatis* interlined.

253 Grant by Abbot Godfrey and the convent to John of Ulceby, a priest at the papal curia in Rome, a pension of £5 p.a. from the abbot's chamber. [8 April 1314]

Pensio domini Johannis de Ulceby. [in a later medieval hand] Vide cartam[1] factam inde per Edmundum comitem Kant' a° xiij° predicti regis

[Marginated] Ulceby

Universis Christi fidelibus presentes litteras visuris vel audituris Godefridus permissione divina abbas monasterii sancti Petri de Burgo Linc' dioc' et eiusdem loci conventus salutem in Domino sempiternam. Noveritis nos unanimiter concessisse dilecto nobis in Christo domino Johanni de Ulceby, presbitero, in curia Romana commoranti, quinque libros sterlingorum nomine pensionis annue de camera abbatis qui pro tempore fuerit ad unum anni terminum; videlicet infra octab' Pasche in curia Romana singulis annis percipiendos. In cuius rei testimonium, presentibus litteris sigilla nostra sunt appensa. Dat' in capitulo nostro[2] vj idus Aprilis, anno ab incarnatione Domini millesimo CCC^mo quartodecimo.

1 *cartam* interlined.
2 *nostro* interlined.

254 Memorandum of the account rendered by Stephen de Aylington', bailiff of the abbot's liberty, at the Exchequer on 19 Nov. 1318 for £66 13s 4d for the tenth granted by the clergy in the king's eighth year.

[fo. 104r] Memorandum quod super compotus Stephani de Aylington' ballivi libertatis abbatis de Burgo Sancti Petri facto in Scaccario domini regis in octabis sancti Martini anno regni regis E[dwardi] filii regis E[dwardi] duodecimo pro anno xj° allocabatur j tallia continens lxvj li. xiij s. iiij d. de decima regi a clero concessa in anno regni sui octavo. Et invenietur in bursa Norht'

255 Copy from the memoranda roll of the Easter Term 1311 concerning the account rendered by William son and heir of the late John of Milton', former bailiff of the liberty, for revenue from the manors of Walter Langton, bishop of Coventry and Lichfield, at Thorpe Waterville, Aldwinckle and two thirds of the manors of Sudborough and Wittering, in the king's hands from 18 August 1307 until 7 July 1310.

Visus compotus manerii de Thorpwatervill'.

Audito compoto abbatis de Burgo Sancti Petri reddito pro ipso per Willelmum filium et heredem Johannis de Milton' nuper ballivi libertatis eiusdem abbatis de Burgo Sancti Petri defuncti, et executorem testamenti eiusdem, de exitibus maneriorum Walteri de Langeton' Coventr' et Lich' episcopi, de Thorpwatervill', Aldewincl', et duarum terciarum partium maneriorum de Sudburgh' et Wytering' certis de causis in manu regis existentium ab xviij die Augusti anno primo, usque diem Martis proxima post festum translationis sancti Thome martiris anno tercio. Debet CCC iiij^{xx} xix li. xvij s. iij d. ob. Postea assignantur inde Willelmo de Berford' justiciario super feodo suo iiij^{xx} li. Et mandatum est prefato abbati quod pecunia illa liberetur etc. recipiens inde litteras ipsius Willelmi de receptione etc. Et remanet CCC xix li. xvij s. iij d. ob. Postea quia non solvit, preceptum est vicecomiti quod fieri faciat sicut continetur in rotulo brevium de termino sancti Michaelis in memorandis anni sequentis. Postea quoad debitum predictum dictus abbas ostendit hic tria brevia de privato sigilla, et sex indenturas inter Johannem de Milton' et Willelmum de Milton' ballivos maneriorum predictorum de tempore predicto, et Adam de Bray custodem equorum regis de Cvij li. ix s. viij d. ob. solutis eidem Ade ad sustentationem eorumdem equorum de exitibus maneriorum predictorum. Unde restat computare in garderoba regis. Et ostendit iiij^{or} indenturas de recepta Scaccarii de Ciiij^{xx} iiij li. vj s. ij d. liberatis in Thesauro per dictum Johannem de Milton' de exitibus predictis, quarum una continet x li. vj s. ij d., altera lx li., tercia liiij li., et quarta lx li. per quas fient tallie ad Scaccarium. Item restat computare in garderoba regis de vj li. ix s. vj d. qa. quos dictus Willelmus de Milton' ballivus maneriorum predictorum de exitibus predictis [fo. 104v] posuit in expensis Esbeverade Berduc denog' [sic] et aliorum familiarum regis per aliquod tempus perhendinancium in balliva sua per breve regis, et indenturam inter dictum Willelmum et predictos familiares regis. Et debet xxj li. xj s. x d. ob. qa. De quibus ostendit breve de scaccario dat' xv die Julii anno secundo directum Johanni de Milton' custodi terrarum predictarum, quod habere faciat Willelmo Butevyleyn et Johanni de Wyleby taxatoribus et collectoribus xxx^{e} et xx^{e} et xx^{e} et xv^{e} quod iidem Willelmus et Johannis asserunt aretro esse ad opus regis de xxx^{a} et xx^{a} et xx^{a} et xv^{a} de bonis predicti episcopi in maneriis predictis, pretextu cuius brevis asserit se liberasse vij li. xiij s. ob. qa. et ostendit inde litteras Johannis de Wyleby testificantes receptionem etc. que summa restat allocanda in compoto predicto, cuius compertum fuerit quod iidem taxatores onerentur inde in compotis suis secundum particulas eiusdem summe contentas in eisdem litteris. Et debet de claro xiij li. xviij s. x d. Postea pretextu brevium regis que sunt inter communia de anno v^{to} directa baronibus pro Waltero Coventr' et Lich' episcopo supersedetur levacioni debiti predicti.

Ista sunt in rotulo memorandorum regis E[dwardi] filii regis E[dwardi] quarto inter status compoti de termino Pasche.

256 Grant by Abbot Godfrey and the convent to Master Gilbert de Middilton', canon of Lincoln, of a pension of 10 marks p.a. from the abbot's chamber until he can be provided with a suitable benefice. [8 April 1315]

[fo. 105r] Pensio magistri Gilberti de Middilton'.

[At foot of folio in a post medieval hand] 30 leaves torne out![1]

Universis Christi fidelibus presentes litteras visuris vel audituris Godefridus permissione divina abbas monasterii sancti Petri de Burgo et eiusdem loci conventus salutem in Domino sempiternam. Noveritis nos unanimiter concessisse dilecto nobis in Christo magistro Gilberto de Middilton', canonico Linc', decem marcas sterlinggorum [sic] nomine pensionis annue de camera abbatis qui pro tempore fuerit ad duos anni terminos percipiendos; videlicet ad festum Pentecostes quinque marcas, et ad festum natalis Domini quinque marcas, et sic singulis annis donec eidem in ecclesiastico beneficio providerimus competenti. In cuius rei testimonium presentibus sigilla nostra sunt appensa. Dat' in capitulo nostro vj idus Aprilis anno Domini M^{o} CCC^{mo} quintodecimo.

1 This is borne out by the contemporary foliation. See below, no. 260 note.

257 Quitclaim by John Knivet to Abbot Godfrey and the convent of a 20s rent from a meadow which the abbey holds from him in Perio in Southwick. The rubric and cross reference associate this with the footpath between Eye and Thorney. [19 April 1306]

Quietaclamatio Johannis Knivet de redditu viginti solidorum pro chimino apud Eye versus Thorneye.

[Marginated] supra folio lxxxij[1]

Omnibus Christi fidelibus presens scriptum visuris vel audituris Johannes Knyvet dominus de Suthewyk' salutem in Domino sempiternam. Noverit universitas vestra me remisisse, et omnino quietumclamasse pro me et heredibus meis in perpetuum domino Godefrido abbati de Burgo Sancti Petri et eiusdem loci conventui et eorum successoribus totum jus et clamium quos habui vel aliquo modo juris habere potui in viginti solidis annui redditus, et omnibus aliis serviciis exeuntibus de quodam prato quod iidem abbas et conventus de me tenuerunt die confectionis presentium in Pyrihowemor in villa de Suthewyk'. Ita quod nec ego nec heredes mei nec aliquis nomine nostro aliquid de predictis viginti solidis annui redditus, nec aliis serviciis exigere vel vendicare poterimus in perpetuum. In cuius rei testimonium presentibus sigillum meum apposui. Hiis testibus: domino Rogero de Hegham, domino Roberto Peverel, domino

Hugone Wak', domino Johanne Doyly, domino Galfrido de la Mare, domino Nicholao de Wythemal', domino Hugone Daundelyn, Nicholao de Sancto Marco, Roberto de Potton', Johanne de Folkisworth', Galfrido Rydel, et aliis. Dat' apud Stanford' in comitatu Norht' die Martis proxima post quindenam Pasche. Anno regni regis E[dwardi] filii regis H[enrici] xxxiiij^{to}.

1 See no. 195A.

258 Writ of Edward I to the bailiffs of John, bishop of Lincoln, at Newark ordering that they respect the abbot's right to be free of tolls under a charter of Henry III which Edward has confirmed. [25 Aug. 1306]

[fo. 105v] [marginated in a later medieval hand] pro telonio de Colingham non capiendo [and in a second later medieval hand] Newerk'

Edwardus Dei gracia rex Anglie, dominus Hibernie, et dux Aquitanie ballivis Johannis episcopi Linc' de Newerk' salutem. Monstravit nobis dilectus in Christo abbas de Burgo Sancti Petri, quod cum ipse et dominia sua per cartam celebris memorie domini H[enrici] quondam regis Anglie patris nostri quam inspeximus et confirmationem nostram quieta esse debeant, et ipse et predecessores sui abbates eiusdem loci et dominia sua a tempore confectionis carte et confirmationis predictarum, semper hactenus a prestatione theolonii in foris et nundinis, et in omni transitu pontium, viarum et portuum maris in Anglie et extra Anglie, et per omnes terras nostras quieta esse consueverint, vos nichilominus ipsum abbatem et homines de dominio suo de longa Colingham cum bonis et rebus suis ad villam predicti domini vestri de Newerk' venientes, ad theolonium vobis inde prestandum graviter distringetis, et ipsos ea occasione multeripliciter inquietatis et gravatis minus juste, in ipsius abbatis et hominum suorum predictorum dampnum non modicum et contra tenorem carte et confirmationis predictarum. Et quia nolumus quod eidem abbati aut hominibus de dominio suo injurietur in hac parte, vobis precipimus quod ab huiusmodi districtionibus, inquietationibus et gravaminibus prefato abbati aut hominibus de dominio suo occasione predicta decetero inferendis penitus desistentes, ipsum et homines de dominio suo a prestatione theolonii in villa predicta quietos esse permittatis juxta tenorem carte et confirmationis predictarum, et prout inde quieti esse debent, et idem abbas et predecessores sui predicti, et homines de dominio suo a tempore predicto semper hactenus inde[1] quieti esse consueverunt. Et districtionem si quam eidem abbati aut hominibus de dominio suo ea occasione fieri feceritis sine dilatione relaxetis eisdem. Teste meipso apud Neuburgh' in Tyndal' xxv die Augusti anno regni nostri tricesimo quarto.

1 *inde* interlined.

259 Licence of Edward I at the instance of Queen Margaret, for the abbot and convent to enclose and empark their woods at Leyes, Rodes and Tonge at La Biggin in Rockingham forest without interference from his forest officials. [21 Mar. 1307]

Carta domini regis Edwardi de parco de la Bigginge.

[Marginated in a later medieval hand] De boscis infra bundas de Rokyingham

Edwardus[1] Dei gracia rex Anglie, dominus Hibernie, et dux Aquitannie omnibus ad quos presentes littere pervenerint salutem. Sciatis quod, ad instanciam Margarete regine Anglie consortis nostre carissime, concessimus et licenciam dedimus pro nobis et heredibus nostris quantum in nobis est dilectis nobis in Christo abbati et conventui de Burgo Sancti Petri, quod ipsi boscos suos de Leyes, Rodes et Tonge, in comitatu Northamtone qui sunt infra metas foreste nostre de Rokingham includere et parcum inde facere, et boscos illos sic inclusos et parcum inde factum tenere possint sibi et successoribus suis imperpetuum sine occasione vel impedimento nostri vel heredum nostrorum, justiciarorum forestariorum, viridariorum, regardatorum, et aliorum ministrorum nostrorum foreste quorumcumque. In cuius rei testimonium has litteras nostras fieri fecimus patentes. Teste meipso apud Karliolum vicesimo primo die Marcii anno regni nostri tricesimo quinte.

1 enrolled *Cal Pat. 1301–7*, p. 507.

260 Letter of Henry, bishop of Lincoln, to the dean of Gartree ordering him to put John de Preston in possession of the vicarage of Bringhurst to which he has been presented by Master J. de Maidiston', the rector, with the consent of the abbot and convent, patrons of the living and to which the bishop has admitted him, subject to him residing and ministering in person. [30 Nov. 1336]

[fo. 106r][1] H[enricus] miseratione divina Linc' episcopus dilecto in Christo filio decano de Gertre salutem graciam et benedictionem. Cum dilectus in Christo magister J de Maidiston', rector ecclesie de Bringhirst, Johannem de Preston', presbiterum, ad vicarium ecclesie predicte nobis presentaverit, per nos ordinandam ut in toto alteragio consistat excepta decima lane de Eston' et mortuario tocius parochie, ac dilecti in Christo filii abbas et conventus de Burgo Sancti Petri patroni eiusdem ecclesie dicte presentationi suum hac vice probuerunt assensum et nos prefatum presbiterum admisimus ad eandem in dicto alteragio ut premissum est consistentem ipsum que cum onere residendi et personaliter ministrandi perpetuum vicarium canonice instituimus in eadem. Quo circa vobis mandamus quatinus corporalem possessionem dicte vicarie dicto J tamquam vicario habere faciatis in forma prenotata. Valete. Data apud Parcum Stowe pridie kalendas Decembris pontificatus nostri anno septimo decimo.

1 Contemporary foliation now *cxxxiiij et seq.*

261 Account of hearings in which the abbot responded to the king's accusation that, while holding the farm of the manor of Torpel, he had appropriated the wardship and marriages of John of Lolham, William Fauvel and Walter Attekirke and wasted and neglected the manorial buildings incorporating, as evidence in his favour, a letter patent of 11 Mar. 1292 from John of Berwick, one of the executors of Queen Eleanor, who had acquired the manor from John de Camoys, acknowledging that Abbot Richard of London had satisfied him in all respects concerning the wardship of John son of Geoffrey of Southorpe in Lolham and Walter son of Robert Attekirke in Ufford, and citing an inquisition held in April 1301[1] by William de Carleton and John of Kirkby to establish whether the ancestors of John of Lolham and Walter Attekirke held of the abbot or John de Camoys and concluding with the inquisition held not earlier than the Trinity Term 1312[2] which finally found in the abbot's favour.

Abbas de Burgo Sancti Petri attachiatus fuit ad respondendum domino regi, quare ipse tempore quo tenuit ad firmam manerium de Torpel ex commissione domini Edwardi nuper regis Anglie patris domini regis nunc percepturus et habiturus ad firmam illam annuum proficuum predicti manerii ita quod salvo fuissent inde dicto regi Edwardo feoda militum warde et relevia liberorum tenentium qui de eodem manerio tenent in capite, custodie terrarum et tenementorum Johannis de Leham in Leham, Willelmi Fauvel in Suthorp' et Walteri atte Kirke in Ufford, qui de dicto manerio tenent in capite per servicium militare infra etatem existentes, et maritagia eorumdem Johannis, Willelmi et Walteri que ad dictum regem E[dwardum] spectabant sub colore firme predicte sibi apropriavit, et similiter ipsas custodias tempore domini regis nunc occupavit, et eciam quare domos predicti manerii vastavit et deterioravit tempore firme predicte etc. in exhereditacionis domini regis periculum manifestum et dampnum suum. Et unde compertum est per inquisitionem captam super premissis per Nicholaum de Ros, Walrannum de Mortuo Mari et Eustachium Malherbe ad hoc per regem assignatos, eundem abbatem custodias et maritagia predicta appropriasse etc. et domos predictas vastasse et deteriorasse etc. ut premittitur.

Et predictus abbas per attornatum suum venit et defendit quicquid est in exhereditacionem etc. et dicit quod qualitercumque capta fuerit inquisitio super premissis ex officio etc. illa ei prejudicari non debet etc. Et quo ad custodias terrarum et tenementorum dictorum Johannis [fo. 106v] de Leham in Leham et Walteri Attekirke in Ufford, dicit quod vivente domina Elianora quondam regina Anglie matre domini regis nunc que predictum manerium de Torpel perquisiverat de Johanne de Camoys quondam domino eiusdem, qui prius illud tenuit in dominico etc, et que idem manerium cum pertinenciis suis tenuit usque ad obitum suum etc., eedem custodie acciderunt ad manus eiusdem regine que eas tenuit ad obitum suum etc, et quod post eius obitum executores testamenti eiusdem curam et administrationem habentes de bonis et catallis et possessionibus eiusdem regine, ipsas custodias dimiserunt Ricardo tunc abbati de Burgo predecessori suo habendas usque ad legittimam etatem heredum etc. qui quidem Ricardus abbas etc. proinde plene satisfecit eisdem executoribus et super hoc ostendit quasdam litteras patentes quas dicit esse factum Johannis de Berewyk' unius executorum predictorum, in hec verba:

Johannes de Berewyk' clericus domini regis Anglie, et unus executorum celebris memorie domine Alianore nuper regine Anglie omnibus has litteras inspecturis salutem. Sciatis quod dominus Ricardus de London' abbas de Burgo Sancti Petri et eiusdem loci conventus satisfecerunt nobis in omnibus pro custodia terrarum Johannis filii domini Galfridi de Suthorp' in Leham, et Walteri filii Roberti Attekirke in Ufford' usque ad legittimam etatem eorumdem, hoc adjecto quod predicti abbas et conventus invenient predictis Johanni, et Waltero rationabilia estoveria sua usque ad legittimam etatem eorumdem. In cuius rei testimonium has nostras litteras eisdem abbati conventui fecimus patentes sigillo nostro signatas. Dat' London' xj die mensis Marcii anno regni regis Edwardi vicesimo.

Et unde dicit quod ipse custodias illas nullatenus sibi apropriavit etc., nec alium statum inde habet vel clamat quam ex dimissione predictorum executorum etc., ut premittitur tempore dicti regis E[dwardi] nec ipsas custodias tempore domini regis nunc occupavit etc., cum predicti heredes fuissent plene etatis et seisinam habuissent de terris et tenementis suis vivente eodem rege E[dwardo] antequam dominus rex nunc gubernaculum regni sui suscepit etc., et hoc offert verrificare qualitercumque curia etc. Et quo ad maritagia eorumdem Johannis de Leham et Walteri Attekirk' de Ufford dicit et cognovit se ea habuisse etc., sicut bene ei licuit etc., ut de jure ecclesie sue de Burgo etc. ratione videlicet terrarum et tenementorum que antecessores eorumdem heredum tenuerunt de ipso abbate per servicium militare et ratione prioritatis feoffamenti etc., adiciens quod anno regni predicti regis E[dwardi] per inquisitionem captam per Willelmum de Carleton' et Johannem de Kirkeby assignatos per breve eiusdem regis E[dwardi] ad inquirendum utrum antecessores dictorum Johannis de Leham et Walteri prius feoffati fuerunt ad tenendum de abbate de Burgo Sancti Petri an de Johanne de Camoys domino de Torpel' et in Cancellaria eiusdem regis E[dwardi] retornatam, compertum erat quod Galfridus de Suthorp', pater predicti Johannis, tenuit die quo obiit de abbate de Burgo Sancti Petri quedam tenementa in Suthorp', Gunthorp', Hemington' et Stokes per servicium militare, et antecessores eiusdem Galfridi tenuerunt eadem tenementa de predecessoribus predicti abbatis per idem servicium a tempore quo tunc non extitit memoria [fo. 107r] et quod predictus Galfridus anno regni predicti regis E[dwardi] v^to^ perquisivit de quodam Radulpho de Loho ...[3] mesuagium et duas carucatas terre cum pertinenciis in villa de Loholm tenenda de domino manerii de Torpel per servicium dimidii feodi militis. Ac eciam quod Walterus de Ufford qui ut dicit fuit pater predicti Walteri Attekirke tenuit die quo obiit de predicto abbate unum mesuagium et dimidiam virgatam terre cum pertinenciis in villa de Burgo Sancti Petri per servicium vicesime partis unius feodi militis. Et quod quidem Thomas de Ufford antecessor dicti Walteri et alii antecessores sui tenuerunt eadem tenementa de abbatibus predecessoribus predicti abbatis per idem servicium a tempore qua non extitit tunc memoria; videlicet ante tempus regis Ricardi quondam regis Anglie, et postea tempore eiusdem regis Ricardi dictus Thomas de Ufford, tunc temporis senescallus de Burgo Sancti Petri, perquisivit quedam tenementa particulatim de diversis in villa de Ufford, tenenda de domino manerii de Torpel. Et unde dicit quod ratione veredicti inquisitionis illius, tunc dictum fuit eidem abbati quod de maritagiis heredum predictorum faceret comodum suum etc., et inde vocat recordum rotulorum Cancellarie etc. Et quo ad custodiam terrarum et maritagium predicti Willelmi Fauvel dicit quod non apropriavit sibi nec ea habuit, et[4] hoc offert verrificare ut supra.

Et quo ad deteriorationem domorum etc. dicit quod ipse eas in nullo deterioravit nec tempore quo ipse tenuit ad firmam predictam manerium ut predictum est fuerunt deteriorate etc. et hoc offert ut supra.

Et ideo concordatum est quod quo ad custodiam et maritagium Willelmi Fauvel etc. et deteriorationem domorum etc. fiat inquisitio. Et preceptum est vicecomiti quod venire faciat hic in quindenam sancti Hillarii xij tam milites etc de visneto de Torpel et Suthorp' per quos etc. Et idem dies datus est abbati et dictum est ei quod interim sequatur de habendo hic ad eundem diem recordum etc. quod vocat super maritagia dictorum Johannis de Leham et Walteri Attekirke etc. Et quo ad custodias eorumdem Johannis et Walteri quia non constat curia si predicte littere quas idem abbas inde ostendit, fuerunt factum predicti Johannis de Berewyk', seu quo waranto ipse percepit proficuum ipsarum custodiarum post mortem dicte regine, dictum est ei quod sequatur de venire faciendo eundem Johannem ad diem predictum, ad cognoscendum etc. et respondendum inde etc. Postea mandatum est predicto Johani de Berwyk' per breve regis quod ipse sit hic ad diem predictum ad certificandum barones etc. Et eciam mandatum est Cicestrie episcopo cancellario quod certificet barones super dicta inquisitione returnata in Cancellaria quo ad maritagia Johannis de Leham et Walteri Attekirke etc. Postea scilicet ad quindenam sancti Hillarii abbas per attornatum suum venit. Et inquisitio cepit dilationemen pro defalta juratorum usque a die Pasche in xv dies. Et Johannes de Berwyk' non venit ad certificandum barones etc. Et cancellarius Anglie nullum breve retornavit nec certificavit super inquisitionem retornatam in Cancellaria de maritagiis etc. Et mandatum est eis sicut alias, ita etc., ad eundem diem. Et idem dies datus est abbati. Ad quem diem abbas per [fo. 107v] attornatum suum venit. Et vicecomes mandavit quod breve adeo tarde sibi deliberatum fuit quod illud ante diem predictum exequi non potuit. Et Johannes de Berwyk' non venit nec retornavit breve etc. Et Johannes Cicestrie episcopus, cancellarius Anglie misit hic sub pede magni sigilli regis recordum [quod] predictus abbas vocavit super maritagio Johannis de Leham et Walteri Attekirke in hec verba: Inquisitio capta apud Torpel etc. de verbo ad verbum sicut irrotulatur in alio rotulo. Et ideo faciat predictus abbas commodum [sic] suum de maritagia heredum predictorum. Quod quidem recordum remanet hic inter brevia hic retornata pro rege hoc anno. Et quia barones volunt plenius deliberari super premissis, datus est dies predicto abbati hic a die sancti Michaelis in xv dies ad recipiendum quod curia etc. super predicto recordo quo ad maritagia Johannis de Lelham et Walteri Attekirke etc. Et quo ad hoc quod Johannes de Berwyk' non venit etc. Concordatum est quod habeat breve vicecomitis de venire faciendo ipsum etc. Et preceptum est vicecomiti Surreye, ita etc., ad eundem diem etc., Et quo ad inquisitionem capiendam etc., preceptum est vicecomiti Norht' sicut alias quod distringat juratores per omnes terras etc. ita etc. ad diem predictum nisi T de Cantebrigg' baro etc. prius ad partes illas etc. Idem eciam dies datus est abbati ad audiendum veredictum inquisitionis etc. Et quod curia etc., super custodiis dictorum Johannis de Leham et Walteri Attekirke etc. Postea ante diem illum predictus Johannes de Berwyk' presens in curia hic adlocutus per barones super custodiam predictorum Johannis filii Galfridi de Suthorp' in Leham, et Walteri filii Roberti Attekirke in Ufford' etc., cognovit dictam Elianoram reginam Anglie, cuius ipse fuit unus executorum etc. habuisse ipsas custodias. Et predictas litteras ipsius Johannis hic propositas per dictum abbatem de Burgo Sancti Petri de satisfactione earumdem custodiarum esse factum ipsius Johannis etc. Postea die Dominica in crastino assumptionis beate Marie apud Walmesford' coram T de Cantebrig' venit abbas per attornatum suum, et vicecomes tunc ibidem venire fecit milites et alios etc., quorum xij electi et jurati dixerunt quod prefatus abbas non apropriavit sibi custodias nec maritagia Willelmi Fauvel nec domos manerii de Torpel deterioravit nec deteriorari fecit tempore quo ipse illud ad firmam tenuit etc. Ad quem diem abbas per attornatum suum venit et adjornatur ulterius ex prefixione curie in eodem statu quo nunc in crastino purificationis beate Marie. Ad quem diem abbas venit per attornatum suum et adjornatur ulterius in eodem statu quo nunc usque ad quindenam Pasche. Ad quem diem abbas per attornatum suum venit et dictum est ei pro rege quod qualitercumque ipse alias vocaverit recordum super maritagia heredum dictorum Galfridi de Suthorp' et Walteri de Ufford etc., inquisitio inde capta ex officio non prejudicat domino regi quo ad ipsa maritagia cum adverterit jus suum etc. Et abbas dicit quod si videatur curia vocare suum super premissis non sufficere, ipse paratus est verificare qualitercumque curia etc., quod ipsa maritagia ad ipsum de jure spectabant ratione videlicet prioritatis feoffamenti etc. Et concordatum est quod inquiratur super eadem prioritate etc. Et preceptum est vicecomiti quod venire faciat hic in octabis sancti Michaelis nisi R[ogerus] de [fo. 108r] Scotere baro prius etc. xij tam milites gladio cinctos quam alios etc. per quos etc. et qui abbatem nulla affinitate etc. Et idem dies datus est abbati etc. Ad quem diem vicecomes nullum breve misit, ideo sicut alias preceptum est vicecomiti quod venire faciat in octabis sancti Hillarii xij tam milites etc. per quos etc., et qui etc. Et idem dies datus est abbati etc. Ad quem diem abbas per attornatum suum venit et vicecomes nullum breve retornavit. Ideo preceptum est sicut pluries ita etc. in quindenam Pasche nisi aliquis baronum etc. Et idem dies datus est abbati per attornatum suum. Postea ad diem illum W de Norwyco recordatur quod ipse vocato coram ipso dicto abbate precepto per ipsum vicecomiti quod venire faceret coram ipso apud Walmesford' inquisitionem etc., abbas venit ibidem per attornatum suum et inquisitio similiter per Robertum de Ver, Hugonem Daundelyn, Hugonem de Gorham milites et alios qui juratores dicunt super sacramentum suum quod Galfridus pater Johannis de Leham et antecessores sui tenuerunt de abbatibus de Burgo Sancti Petri predecessoribus abbatis nunc quedam tenementa in Suthorp', Gunthorp', Hemington', et Stok' per servicium militare diu ante quam tenuerunt aliqua tenementa de dominis manerii de Torpel. Et quod Walterus pater Walteri Attekirke de Ufford perquisivit quedam tenementa ante tempus regis Ricardi filii Regis Henrici secundi, tenenda de predicto abbate etc. per servicium militare. Et quod postea quidam Thomas de Ufford, antecessor dicti Walteri, videlicet tempore regis Ricardi, perquisivit unum mesuagium et tres virgatas terre per servicium ij solidorum pro scutagio et vij denariorum pro warda castri de Rokingham tenenda de dominis manerii de Torpel per servicium predictum. Et datus fuit tunc dies abbati essendi hic modo ad hunc diem ad audiendum judicium etc. Ad quem diem abbas per attornatum suum venit, et adjornatur ulterius in eodem statu quo nunc, usque octabis sancte Trinitatis. Ad quem diem venit per attornatum etc. Et quia per inquisitionem predictam compertum est quod antecessores Johannis de Leham, et eciam antecessores Walteri Attekirke prius feoffati fuerunt de quibusdam tenementis etc. tenenda de abbatibus de Burgo etc., quam de dominis manerii de Torpel. Et eciam per inquisitionem predictam captam coram T de Cantebrig' est compertum quod dictus abbas non apropriavit sibi custodiam nec maritagium Willelmi

Fauvel, nec domos manerii de Torpel deterioravit, et per testimonium Johannis de Berwyk' habetur quod dictus abbas satisfecit pro custodiis Johannis de Leham et Walteri Attekirke de Ufford' sicut supra continetur, idem abbas super premissis sine die.

1 Dated from no. 149E.
2 John Langton, bishop of Chichester, was chancellor between 18 August 1307 and 6 July 1310. Roger de Scotere was appointed baron of the Exchequer in 17 July 1310 and was dead by 3 March 1312, when W de Norwyco was appointed in his place. *Cal. Pat. 1307–13*, pp. 265, 433.
3 Stain on MS.
4 *et* interlined.

262 Final concord between Philip de Nevill' and Philip son of Philip de Nevill' concerning the manors and advowsons of Scotton and Manton, in which Philip de Nevill' recognised the right of Philip son of Philip by his gift. In return, Philip son of Philip granted the manors and advowsons back to Philip de Nevill' for life, rendering a rose to Philip son of Philip and all services to the lord of the fee. [21 June 1316]

[fo. 108v] Hec[1] est finalis concordia facta in curia domini regis apud Westm' a die sancte Trinitatis in quindecim dies anno regni regis E[dwardi] filii regis E[dwardi] nono coram Willelmo de Berford', Lamberto de Trikingham, Johanne de Bensted', Henrico de Scrop', Johanne Bacoun, et Johanne de Mutford' justiciariis, et aliis domini regis fidelibus tunc ibi presentibus inter Philippum de Nevill' querentem, et Philippum filium Philippi de Nevill' deforciantem, de maneria de Scotton' et Malmeton' cum pertinenciis et advocationibus eorumdem manerii, unde placitum conventionis summonitum fuit inter eos in eadem curia; scilicet quod predictus Philippus de Nevill' recognovit predicta maneria cum pertinenciis et advocationes predictas esse jus ipsius Philippi filii Philippi, ut illa que idem Philippus habet de dono predicti Philippi de Nevill'. Et pro hac recognitione, fine et concordia, idem Philippus filius Philippi concessit predicto Philippo de Nevill' predicta maneria cum pertinenciis et advocationes predictas et illa ei reddidit in eadem curia. Habenda et tenenda eidem Philippo de Nevill' de predicto Philippo filio Philippi et heredibus suis tota vita ipsius Philippi de Nevill'. Reddendo inde per annum unam rosam ad festum nativitatis sancti Johannis baptiste pro omni servicio, consuetudine et exactione ad predictum Philippum filium Philippi et heredes suos pertinente. Et faciendo inde capitalibus dominis feodi illius pro predicto Philippo filio Philippi et heredibus suis omnia alia servicia que ad predicta maneria et advocationes predictas pertinent tota vita ipsius Philippi de Nevill'. Et post decessum ipsius Philippi predicta maneria cum pertinenciis et advocationes predicte integre revertentur ad predictum Philippum filium Philippi et heredes suos quiete de heredibus predicti Philippi de Nevill' tenenda de capitalibus dominis feodi illius per servicia que ad maneria et advocationes predictas pertinent in perpetuum.

1 See *Henry of Pytchley*, p. 105.

[fo. 109r] Blank. Short folio.

263 Memorandum concerning the account rendered at the Exchequer by Stephen de Aylington', bailiff of the abbot's liberty, in 1316 for tenths levied for service in Scotland in 1302–3, 1310–11 and 1313–14.

[fo. 109v] [Marginated] Norht'

Memorandum quod super compotum Stephani de Aylington' ballivo libertatis abbatis de Burgo Sancti Petri factum in Scaccario domini regis apud Westm' anno regni regis E[dwardi] filii regis E[dwardi] ix^o incipiente decimo allocabantur abbati de Burgo Sancti Petri, coram thesaurario et baronibus v^cl m. pro servicio suo in Scotia per iij tallias; videlicet pro servicio suo de anno regni regis E[dwardi] filii regis H[enrici] xxxj C li. per j talliam et pro servicio suo anno regni regis E[dwardi] filii regis E[dwardi] iiij^to CC li. per aliam talliam, pro servicio suo de anno vij^o eiusdem regis C m. per terciam talliam, et ille tallie invenientur in bursa Norht' eiusdem anni et eiusdem compoti.

264 Royal writ to justices of Common Pleas ordering them to not to put the abbot in default for failing to answer their summons. [2 Jan. 1321][1]

Rex justiciariis suis proximo itineraturis ad communia placita apud Turrim London' salutem. Mandamus vobis quod occasione communis summonitionis coram vobis facte de itinere vestro predicto, dilectus nobis in Christo abbas de Burgo Sancti Petri non ponatur in defaltam nec in aliquo sit perdens quia absenciam suam quo ad hoc, ei warantizamus. Teste meipso apud Marlebergh' secundo die Januarii anno regni nostri xiiij^mo per breve de priva sigillo.

1 Edward II was at Marlborough on 2 January 1321. *Cal. Pat., 1313–17*, p. 179.

265 Fealty of Robert, prior of Newstead on Ancholme to Abbot Godfrey for tenements in Hibaldstow. [28 June]

[fo. 110r] Prior de novo loco super Hancholm'.

Robertus prior de novo loco super Hancholm' fecit fidelitatem domino Godefrido abbati apud Scoter' in vigilia apostolorum Petri et Pauli pro tenementis que clamat tenere de eo in Hibaldstowe. In presencia dominorum Humfridi supprioris, Thome de Welingham', et Roberti de Spalding' monachorum, magistri Galfridi de Makeseye, Roberti de Thorp' tunc senescalli Burgi, Bernardi de Castr' tunc ballivi, et Johannis de Thevelby.

266 Fealty of Robert son and heir of Robert le Forester of Scotter to Abbot Godfrey for tenements in Scotter. [29 June]

[Marginated] Robertus Forest'.

Robertus filius et heres Roberti le Forest' de Scoter' fecit fidelitatem predicto domino Godefrido abbati apud Scoter' die apostolorum Petri et Pauli pro tenementis que clamat tenere de eo in Scoter' in presencia predictorum.

267 Homage and fealty of Robert de Hotot of Clopton to Abbot Godfrey for tenements in Clopton. [16 Nov. 1312]

[Marginated] Robertus Hotot.
Memorandum quod die Jovis in festo beati Martini, anno regni regis Edwardi filii regis Edwardi v^to^ et anno domini Godefrido abbatis xiij^o^ Robertus de Hotot de Cloptone fecit homagium et fidelitatem predicto domino abbati pro tenementis que de eo clamat tenere in Clopton', per servicium ...[1] per annum, et per servicium forinsecum.[2]

1 Sum erased.
2 *et per servicium forinsecum* added in a different hand.

268 Fealty of Nicholas son of Robert of Warmington to Abbot Godfrey for tenements in Werrington. [10 Feb. 1313]

Memorandum quod Nicholaus filius Roberti de Wermington' fecit fidelitatem domino Godefrido abbati die Sabbati in festo sancte Scolastice virginis pro tenementis que clamat tenere de eo in Witherington' anno regni regis Edwardi filii regis Edwardi vj^to^ et anno eiusdem domini Godefridi abbatis xiiij^o^. In presencia fratris Roberti de Spaldingg', domini Roberti rectoris ecclesie de Paston', Johannis Puttok' de Witherington', Willelmi de Jakel' clerici et aliorum.

269 Fealty of Philip de Nevill' to Abbot Godfrey for tenements in Scotton and Manton, with a note that homage was delayed until the abbot's coming. [18 May 1314]

Fidelitas domini Philippi de Neville.

[Marginated] homagium respectuatur usque adventum domini abbatis.
Memorandum quod dominus Philippus de Nevill' miles fecit fidelitatem domino Godefrido abbati de Burgo Sancti Petri die Sabbati proximo post festum ascencionis Dominice anno regni regis E[dwardi] filii regis E[dwardi] septimo et anno predicti abbatis xv^{o} pro tenementis que de eo clamat tenere in Scotton' et Malmeton' cum pertinenciis. In presencia fratrum Johannis Sekford' sacriste, Johannis de Rames' tunc senescalli, R[oberti] de Thornton', Hugonis de Stivecle, magistri G[alfridi] Makes', Willelmi Basset vicarii de Langetoft', Roberti de Thorp' tunc senescalli libertatis Burgi, Ricardi de Croyland' et aliorum.

270 Fealty of Thomas son of Hugh Wake to Abbot Godfrey for tenements in Helpston held through his wife. [3 April 1317]

[Marginated] fidelitas T[homas] Wak' pro Helpiston'.
Memorandum quod Thomas filius domini Hugonis Wake fecit fidelitatem domino Godefrido abbati de Burgo Sancti Petri in festo Pasche, anno regni regis E[dwardi] filii regis E[dwardi] x^{mo} pro tenementis que clamat tenere de eo in Helpeston' ratione uxoris sue. In presencia domini Willelmi la Zousch' et aliorum.

271 Homage and fealty of Henry Trailly of Woodford to Abbot Godfrey for tenements in Woodford. [31 Dec. 1316]

[fo. 110v] [Marginated] Henr' Traylli.
Anno Domini millesimo CCC^{mo} xvj^{o} et anno domini Godefridi abbatis xviij^{mo} die Veneris in festo sancti Silvestri Henricus Trailly de Wodeford' fecit homagium et fidelitatem dicto domino Godefrido abbati pro tenementis que de eo clamat tenere in Wodeford'. In presencia fratrum Alexandri de Wystowe, Hugonis de Rysburgh', Roberti de Thornton', Hugonis de Stivecl' monachorum, et domini Roberti rectoris de Paston', Ricardi Scriptor' de Wodeford', et Johannis filii eiusdem in camera dicti domini abbatis apud Burgum.

272 Homage and fealty of John son and heir of John of Folksworth to Abbot Godfrey for tenements in Orton Waterville. [3 Dec. 1317]

[Marginated] Folkesworth'.
Anno Domini millesimo CCC^{mo} septimodecimo et anno domini Godefridi abbatis xix^{mo} die Sabbati proximo post festum sancti Andree apostoli. Johannes filius et heres Johannis de Folkesworth' fecit homagium et fidelitatem dicto domino Godefrido pro tenementis que de eo clamat tenere in Overtonewatervill. In presencia fratris Hugonis de Stivecl', domini Roberti rectoris ecclesie de Paston', Johannis de Haddon', Willelmi de Foddringgeye, Willelmi de Castreton' et Willelmi de Jakel' clerici, in scaccario dicti domini abbatis.

273 Homage and fealty by Ralph of Grendon, son and heir of John of Grendon, to Abbot Godfrey for tenements in Polebrook, Thurning and elsewhere. [17 April 1318]

[Marginated] Grendon'.
Memorandum quod anno Domini millesimo CCC xviij^{mo} et anno domini Godefridi abbatis xix^{mo} Radulphus de Grendon' filius et heres Johannis de Grendon'a die Lune proximo post festum sanctorum Tybertii et Valeriani, fecit homagium et fidelitatem dicto domino Godefrido apud Burgum in domo scaccarii pro tenementis que de ipso clamabat tenere in Pokebrok' et Thirningg' et alibi. In presencia fratris H[ugonis] de Stivecl'[2], domini R[oberti] rectoris ecclesie de Paston, magistri G[alfridi] de Makes', Willelmi de Castreton', Willelmi de Jakel' clericorum, Johannis Porthors de Pok' et aliorum.

1 *filius et heres Johnanis de Grendon'* interlined.
2 *fratris Hugonis de Stivecl'* interlined.

274 Homage and fealty of Thomas Wake, lord of Lydel, to Abbot Godfrey for tenements held of the abbey. [3 Mar. 1319]

[fo. 111r] [Marginated] Dominus T Wak'.
Memorandum quod die Sabbati tercio die mensis Marcii anno Domini M^{o} CCC^{o} xviij^{o} Thomas Wake dominus de Lydel fecit homagium et fidelitatem domino Godefrido abbati de Burgo Sancti Petri, in monasterio de Burgo, videlicet in capella beate Marie virginis, pro tenementis que de ea clamat tenere. In presencia fratris Alexandri de Wystowe prioris eiusdem monasterii, fratris Galfridi de Haddon', fratris Hugonis de Stivecle monachorum et majoris partis conventus dicti monasterii, ac eciam domini Thome rectoris ecclesie sancti Guthlaci de Deping', domini Roberti rectoris de Paston', magistri Galfridi de Makes', domini Johannis

de Heslarton', senescalli dicti T[home] militis, magistri Stephani de Aylington' et aliorum quam plurimum.

275 Homage and fealty of John Bozoun of Woodford to Abbot Godfrey for tenements in Woodford. [8 June 1320]

[Marginated] Johannes Bozoun.
Johannes Bozoun de Wodeford' fecit homagium et[1] fidelitatem suam domino Godefrido abbati de Burgo Sancti Petri die Dominica in festo sanctorum Medardi et Gildardi anno regni regis E[dwardi] filii regis E[dwardi] xiij° pro tenementis que clamat de eo tenere in Wodeford'. In presencia fratrum Roberti de Thornton', Ricardi de Offord monachorum, domini Roberti rectoris ecclesie de Paston', domini Roberti de Thorp' militis, Radulphi de Thorneye et aliorum.

1 *homagium et* interlined.

276 Homage and fealty of John son of Hugh of Barnack to Abbot Godfrey for tenements in Barnack, Cathwaite and Bainton. [6 Feb. 1321]

[Marginated] Johannes filius Hugonis de Bernak'.
Johannes filius Hugonis de Bernak' fecit homagium et fidelitatem suam domino Godefrido abbati de Burgo Sancti Petri apud Burgum ad scaccarium eiusdem, die Veneris in festo sanctorum Vedasti et Amandi, anno eiusdem domini abbatis vicesimo secundo, pro tenementis que de ipso clamat tenere in Bernak', Cathweyt' et Badigton' per servicium quarte partis unius feodi militis. In presencia fratrum Ricardi de Offord', Gilberti de Aslokeby monachorum, Willelmi de Jakel' clerici et aliorum.

277 Homage and fealty of Laurence son and heir of Adam Archebaud' to Abbot Godfrey for tenements in Stanwick. [20 April 1321]

[Marginated] Laur' filius Ade Archebaud.
Anno regni regis E[dwardi] filii regis E[dwardi] xiiij^mo^ et domini Godefridi abbatis xxij° die Lune proximo post festum Pasche, Laurenc' filius et heres Ade Archebaud' fecit homagium et fidelitatem domino Godefrido abbati pro tenementis que de eo clamat tenere in Stanewigg'. In presencia fratrum Ricardi de Offord' et Gilberti de Aslokby, domini R[oberti] rectoris de Paston', Willelmi de Ayscheby et aliorum.

[fo. 111v] **278** [not used. Penstrokes underwriting no. 279, culminating in *F F* [bis]
dd dominum

279 Unfinished and badly faded copy of no. 297.[1]

1 Part of the first sentence, as far as *habentibus*, only.

280 Inquisition to establish those holding knight's fees of the king in Nassabugh hundred for the purposes of scutage. [9 Jan. 1315]

[fo. 112r] [Marginated] Nass [in a later medieval hand] scutagium

Inquisitio capta apud Thrapston' die Martis proxima post[1] epiphaniam Domini anno regni regis Edwardi filii regis Edwardi octavo coram T Wake et J de Wyleby assignatis collectores ad levandum et colligendum scutagium domini Edwardi quondam regis Anglie patris regis qui nunc est, de annis xxviij^{o}, xxxj^{o}, et xxxiiij^{o}. Et ad inquirendum de feodis militum que de eodem rege patre regis nunc diversis modis tenebantur annis supradictis; videlicet per Thomam Cocum de Burgo, Robertum Underwod, Walterum ad Ecclesiam de Ufford', Willelmum Cordel de Castr', Willelmum de Kendal', Willelmum Adam de Marham, Willelmum Teyt de Burgo, Rogerum Payn de Makes', Henricum Wake de Leham, Galfridum filium Radulphi de Sutton', Johannem Godwyne de Castr' et Ricardum le Fouler' de Burgo juratores de hundredo de Nasso Burgi, qui dicunt per sacramentum suum quod Johannis de Somery de Bernak' tenet in Bernak' unum feodum militis de domino rege in capite. Nicholaus de Sancto Medardo tenet in Thornhawe, Wyteringg', Siberton' et Etton' iiij^{or} feoda militum et dimidium feodum[2] unius militis de abbate de Burgo Sancti Petri unde abbas medius versus dominum regem.

In manerio de Thorpel[3] cum membris quod est in manu regine consortis domini regis nunc sunt iiij^{or} feoda dimidium milit' et quarta pars unius feodi militis que ab antiquo tenebantur de abbate de Burgo, et abbas medius ut supra, quousque domina regina mater domini regis nunc manerium illud perquisivit. Galfridus de la Mare tenet in Makes'[4] et Northburg' j feodum militis et dimidium feodi militis de abbate de Burgo, et abbas medius ut supra. Robertus de Ver et participes sui, videlicet Johannes de Tichemers' et Simon de Drayton', tenent in Marham j feodum militis de abbate de Burgo, et abbas medius ut supra. Henricus Torold tenet in Castr'[5] j feodum militis et dimidium feodi militis de abbate de Burgo, et abbas medius ut supra. Fina Fauvel tenet in Walcot'[6] j feodum militis et dimidium feodi militis de abbate de Burgo, et abbas medius ut supra.

Petrus de Burgle tenet in Burgle dimidium fedum [sic] militis de abbate de Burgo, et abbas medius ut supra. Edwardus Charles tenet in Milton' j feodum militis de abbate de Burgo, et abbas medius ut supra. Bartholomeus de Badlismere tenet in Milton' dimidium feodum militis de abbate de Burgo, et abbas medius ut supra. Johannes de Insula, Ricardus de Marham et Johannes de Houton' tenent in Paston' dimidium feodum militis de abbate de Burgo, et abbas medius ut supra. Johannes Peverel tenet in Paston duas partes unius feodi militis de abbate de Burgo, et abbas medius ut supra. Johannes de Hiham tenet in Helpeston'[7] terciam partem j feodi militis de abbate de Burgo et abbas medius ut supra.

Thomas de Goldisburgh' tenet in Wodecroft quartam partem j feodi militis de [fo. 112v] abbate de Burgo, et abbas medius ut supra. Hugo de Bernak' tenet in Bernak' et Cathweyth' quartam partem j feodi militis de abbate de Burgo et abbas medius ut supra.

Ricardus de Croyland' tenet in Walton quartam partem j feodi militis de abbate de Burgo, et abbas medius ut supra. Johannes Marmioun tenet in Castr' sextam partem j feodi militis de abbate de Burgo, et abbas medius ut supra. Et non sunt plura feoda militum infra hundredum de Nasso Burgi. Item dicunt quod abbas de Burgo Sancti Petri tenet diversa tenementa in dominico in hundredo predicto in puram et perpetuam elemosinam per cartas regum Anglie et confirmationem domini regis nunc, et non per servicia militaria. Item idem abbas facit domino regi per feoda que ab eo tenentur in predicto hundredo et alibi in diversis hundredis et comitatibus regni Anglie servicia quinque militum.

1 *Inquisitio ... post* in larger hand.
2 Stain on folio.
3 Marginated in later hand *Torpell.*
4 Marginated in later hand *nota* and in another, later hand *Maxey.*
5 Marginated in later hand *Castr'.*
6 Marginated in later hand *Valcot'.*
7 Marginated in later hand *Helpeston.*

281 Inquisition before the same to establish those holding knights' fees of the king in Huxloe hundred. [*c.* 9 Jan. 1315]

Hundred de Hok': Inquisitio capta coram supradictis ut supra[1] per Robertum de Ver, Johannem de Tolthorp', Johannem Spigurnel milites, Robertum de Craneford', Simonem Greylond', Galfridum de Beumeys, Thomam Curzon, Warinum de Wauton', Henricum de Haddon', Johannem le Fleming', Anton' de Sudburgh', Robertum de Watervill' juratores, qui dicunt per sacramentum suum quod Simon de Drayton tenet de domino rege in Islep', Drayton', Addington Minor', Twywell' et Desburgh' medietatem j feodi militis. Edmund de Plety tenet de domino in Burton' j feodum militis et tenuit tempore regis Edwardi anno xxxj°, xxxiiij° et xxviij°. Hugo Wake, Ricardus le Warde, et Hugo Heroun tenent in Irtlingburgh'[2] j feodum militis de feodo Avenel de abbate de Burgo et abbas medius versus regem. Rogerus de Insula tenet in Irtlingburgh' terciam partem j feodi militis de feodo Gargat de abbate de Burgo, et abbas medius ut supra.

Hugo Daundelyn tenet dimidium feodum militis in Craneford' de abbate de Burgo, et abbas medius ut supra. Rogerus de Boys, Johannes Spigurnel et heres Willelmi Traylly tenent in Wodeford' j feodum militis et dimidium feodum militis de abbate de Burgo, et abbas medius ut supra.

1 *Hundred ... supra* in large hand.
2 marginated *nota*.

282 Inquistion held as above to establish those holding knights' fees of the king in Polebrook hundred. [*c.* 9 Jan. 1315]

Hundred de Pok': Inquisitio capta ut supra[1] per Robertum le Hotot, Johannem Cardoun, Walterum Grymbaud, Robertum filium Johannis de Stok', Robertum de Wyvill', Radulphum filium Andree, Henricum filium Roberti, Willelmum Spanye, Ricardum filium Wydonis, Willelmum filium Johannis de Undel', Willelmum filium Ricardi de eadem [fo. 113r] et Robertum filium Gilberti de eadem juratores, qui dicunt per sacramentum suum quod Hunfridus de Bassingburn' tenet situm castri de Benifeld', et dimidiam virgatam terre in Benifeld' per servicium dimidii feodi militis de domino rege [*abbate* erased]. Idem Hunfridus tenet in Irtlingburg', Benifeld, Addington', Slipton' et Glapthorn iiij^or^ feoda militum de abbate de Burgo, unde abbas medius versus dominum regem. Thomas comes Lancastr' tenet in Thorpwatervill', Achirch', et Tichemers ij feoda militum de abbate de Burgo, et abbas medius ut supra. Abbas de Sautr', dominus Robertus de Hotot, abbas de Thorn'[2], Robertus Porthors, et Thomas Smert tenent in Catteworth', Wynewyk', Clopton'[3] et Pokebrok' ij feoda militum de abbate de Burgo, et abbas medius ut supra. Johannes Marmioun tenet in Ludington' j feodum militis de abbate de Burgo, et abbas medius ut supra. Johannes Chambreleyn et Willelmus filius Stephani de Wynewyk' tenent terciamdecimam partem j feodi militis in eadem, de abbate de Burgo et abbas medius ut supra. Reginaldus le Moygne[4] tenet in Hemington', et Parva Thorp' sextam partem j feodi militis de abbate de Burgo, et abbas medius ut supra.

Johannes Engayne tenet in Hemington' et Parva Thorp terciam partem j feodi militis de abbate de Burgo, et abbas medius ut supra. Philipus Despens' tenet in Armeston' terciamdecimam partem j feodi militis de abbate de Burgo, et abbas medius ut supra.

Johannes de Hemington' tenet in Hemington' tres partes j feodi militis de abbate de Burgo, et abbas medius ut supra. Abbas de Thorn'[2] tenet in Kynesthorp' et Hemington' dimidium feodum militis de feodo Maufe de abbate de Burgo, et abbas medius ut supra. Reginaldus le Moygne et Emma de la Lay tenent in Armiston et Kynesthorp' j feodum militis de abbate de Burgo, et abbas medius ut supra. Johannes de Grendon' tenet in Pokebrok'[5] et Thirning' dimidium feodum militis de abbate de Burgo, et abbas medius ut supra. Thomas de Pappel' tenet in Pappel'[6] j feodum militis de abbate de Burgo, et abbas medius ut supra. Willelmus de Seinlyz tenet in Wermington' ij partes j feodi militis de feodo Gargat[7] de abbate, et abbas medius ut supra. Hugo de Gorham tenet in Chirchefeld[8], Undel' et Wermington' quartam partem j feodi militis de abbate de Burgo, et abbas medius ut supra. Johannes Doyly tenet in Stok' dimidium feodum militis de dicto abbate, et abbas medius ut supra. Nicholaus Knyght de Stok' tenet in Stok' quartam partem j feodi militis de dicto abbate, et abbas medius ut supra. Hugo Wak' tenet in Stok' quartam partem j feodi militis de dicto abbate, et abbas medius ut supra.

[fo. 113v] Radulphus de Camoys tenet in Pilketon' j feodum dimidium militis de abbate de Burgo, et abbas medius ut supra. Et non sunt plura feoda.

1 *Hundred ... supra* in large hand.
2 Marginated in a later hand *Thorney*.
3 Marginated in later hand *Clopton*.
4 Marginated in a different hand *abbas de Ramsey*.
5 Marginated in a later hand *Pokebrok*.
6 Marginated *nota* and in a later hand *Pappele*.
7 Marginated in a later hand *nota*.
8 Marginated in a later hand *Chirchfeld*.

283 Letter of John de Nevill', sheriff of Lincoln, to the bailiffs of the abbot's liberty incorporating a writ of Edward I dated 8 July 1305 about tallage from the burgesses of Stamford, beyond the bridge, and Grafham, and ordering its execution. [July 1305]

[fo. 114r] Johannes de Nevill' vicecomes Linc' ballivis libertatis abbatis de Burgo Sancti Petri salutem. Mandatum domini regis in hec verba recepi:

Edwardus Dei gracia rex Anglie, dominus Hibernie et dux Aquitanie vicecomiti Linc' salutem. Quia dominica nostra per Anglie ad presens fecimus talliari, tibi precipimus quod si burgenses de Stanford' ultra pontem et burgenses de Graham fuerint antiquam dominica nostra vel progenitorum nostrorum quondam regum Anglie et hucusque talliari consueverint, tunc dilecto nobis in Christo abbati de Burgo Sancti Petri de tenentibus suis in burgos predictos rationabile talliagium habere faciatis. Teste meipso apud Cantuar' viij^{o} die Julii anno regni nostri xxxiij^{o}. Quare tibi mando quod mandatum istud diligenter exequaris, et hoc non omittas.

284 Writ of Edward I to Lambert of Threckingham and Thomas de Burnham ordering them not to exact tallage from the abbot's tenants in Stamford and Grafham when they are collecting from the tenants of the late John de Warenne, earl of Surrey. [28 June 1305]

Rex dilectis et fidelibus suis Lamberto de Thrikingham et Thome de Burnham ad homines villarum de Stanford' et Graham qui fuerunt tenentes Johannis de Warenna quondam comitis Surr' defuncti talliandos ad opus nostrum assignatis salutem. Monstravit nobis abbas de Burgo Sancti Petri quod vos quosdam tenentes suos in villis predictis inter predictos tenentes qui fuerunt dicti comitis talliari et pro huiusmodi talliagio nobis reddendo indebite distringi fecistis, ubi iidem tenentes sui inter tenentes predictis dicti comitis talliari non debent, nec unquam talliari consueverunt, et quia dicto abbati seu tenentibus suis predictis injuriari nolumus in hac parte, vobis mandamus quod huiusmodi talliagio super illos quos tenentes dicti abbatis esse in villis predictis vobis constare poterit assidendo penitus supersedeatis et districtionem si quam ea occasione fieri feceritis, sine dilatione relaxari faciatis eisdem. Teste W de Carleton' xxxviij die Junii anno regni regis E[dwardi] xxxiij^{o}.

285 Writ of Edward II to the sheriff of Northampton ordering him to collect 40s scutage from the abbot because he had fined for this sum with Edward I for service in Scotland in 1305–6. [10 Feb. 1315]

Rex vicecomiti Norht' salutem. Quia dilectis nobis in Christo abbas de Burgo Sancti Petri finem fecit cum domino E[dwardo] quondam rege Anglie patre nostro pro servicio suo in exercitu suo Scotie anno videlicet regni ipsius patris nostri xxxiiij^{to} tibi precipimus quod eidem abbati habere facias scutagium predictum de feodis militum que de ipso tunc tenebantur in balliva tua, videlicet quadraginta solidos de scuto pro exercitu supradicto, et hoc nullatenus omittas. Teste meipso apud Westm' x die Februarii anno regni nostri octavo.

286 Writ of Edward II to the collectors of scutage in Huntingdonshire for service in Scotland for the years 1299–1300, 1302–3 and 1305–6, ordering them not to collect from the abbot, other than for fees in the king's hand by reason of feudal incidents. [26 Mar. 1315]

Rex collectoribus scutagii de exercitubus [sic] Scotie de annis regni domini E[dwardi] quondam regis Anglie patris nostri xxviij^{o}, xxxj^{o}, et xxxiiij^{to} in comitatu Huntingdon' salutem. Quia dilectus nobis in Christo abbas de Burgo Sancti Petri finem fecit cum dicto patre nostro pro servicio suo quinque feodorum militum de exercitibus predictis quod tunc eidem patri nostro recognovit sicut per inspectionem rotulorum marescalcie dicti patris nostri de eisdem exercitibus nobis constat, vobis mandamus quod demande quam facitis eidem abbati pro scutagio ad opus nostrum de feodis predictis pro exercitibus supradictis pro quibus scutagium concessum fuit, et de illis que de eodem abbate temporibus exercituum predictorum tenebantur supersedeatis, et si quid inde levaveritis, id ei sine dilatione restituatis, et districtionem si quam ei seu tenentibus suis ea occasione feceritis, sine dilatione relaxetis eisdem. Proviso quod scutagium de feodis militum que idem abbas tenuit de dicto patre nostro temporibus exercituum predictorum ratione honorum, escaetarum seu perquisiti sui, ac eciam hereditatum tunc in manu ipsius patris nostri existentium, prout justum fuerit levetur ad opus nostrum. Teste meipso apud Wyndesore. xxvj die Marcii anno regni nostri octavo.

287 Writ of Edward II to the collectors of the twentieth in Northamptonshire ordering them not to tax the abbot's goods because he had paid a tenth on his temporalities and spiritualities. They are to withdraw the distraint under which he has been placed. [17 April 1315]

[fo. 114v] Rex taxatoribus et collectoribus vicesime in comitatu Norht' salutem. Ex parte dilecti nobis in Christo abbatis de Burgo Sancti Petri nobis est ostensum quod vos occasione vicesime predicte in propriis bonis ipsius abbatis de temporalibus ecclesie sue annexis exeuntibus, que ad decimam inter spiritualia taxantur, et de quibus decima dari consuevit, predictam vicesimam assidere, taxare et levare intenditis minus juste in ipsius abbatis dispendium non modicum et gravamen, et contra formam ordinationis per nos et consilium nostrum inde facte et vobis ex parte nostra liberate. Et quia eidem abbati taliter injuriari nolumus in hac parte, vobis mandamus quod inspecta ordinatione predicta, predictum abbatem in propriis bonis suis que inter spiritualia ad decimam taxantur et de quibus decima dari solet ut predictum est, ratione vicesime predicte non molestetis in aliquo seu gravetis contra formam ordinationis predicte. Et districtionem si qua eidem abbati occasione predicta per vos facta fuerit, sine dilatione relaxari fac' eidem. Teste meipso apud Westm' xvij die Aprilis anno regni nostri octavo.

288 Royal writ to the sheriff of Nottingham ordering him to permit the abbot's bailiffs to have return of writs within his liberty and answer for debts at the Exchequer in conformity with his charters and their confirmation. [n.d.]

Rex vicecomiti Notingham salutem. Ex parte dilecti nobis in Christo abbatis de Burgo Sancti Petri nobis est ostensum quod cum ipse per cartas progenitorum nostrorum quodam regum Anglie et confirmationem nostram habeat returnum omnium brevium nostrorum in omnibus dominicis suis, et executiones et attachiamenta eorumdem per ballivos suos facere ac omnia debita nostra infra eadem dominica sua levare et per manus ballivorum suorum nobis ad Scaccarium nostrum respondere debeat. Ita quod nullus vicecomes seu alius minister noster inde in nullo se intromittat quibus quidem libertatibus idem abbas et predecessores sui abbates loci illius semper hactenus a confectione cartarum et confirmationis nostre predictarum usi sunt sicut dicit, tu nichilominus ipsum abbatem et ballivos suos quominus executiones brevium nostrorum infra dominica sua facere et debita nostra ibidem ac nobis de debitis illis ad Scaccarium nostrum per manus ballivorum eiusdem abbatis respondere possint inpedivistis iam de novo ad dampnum ipsius abbatis non modicum et gravamen, et contra tenorem cartarum et confirmationis nostre predictarum. Et quia eidem abbati injuriari nolumus in hac parte, vobis madamus quod si ita est, tunc ab huiusmodi inpedimentis, eidem abbati aut ballivis suis decetero in hac parte faciendis desistas, ipsum abbatem et ballivos suos executiones brevium nostrorum infra dominica sua in balliva tua facere, et debitis nostra ibidem levare et per manus ballivorum suorum predictorum ad Scaccarium nostrum respondere permittas juxta tenorem cartarum et confirmationis nostre predictarum. Teste etc.

289 Writ of Edward II to the treasurer and barons of the Exchequer, in response to a petition by the abbot because his services from Torpel and Upton had been withdrawn, ordering them to search their records in the presence of the officials of Queen Isabella, to whom the king has granted the manors, and to return their findings to him under exchequer seal. [28 May 1315]

[fo. 115r] Rex thesaurario et baronibus suis de Scaccario salutem. Monstravit nobis dilectus nobis in Christo abbas de Burgo Sancti Petri per petitionem suam coram nobis et consilio nostro exhibitam, quod cum maneria de Torpel et de Upton' cum pertinenciis de ipso abbate teneantur per servicium redditus quatuor librarum per annum et per homagium et fidelitatem ac sectam ad curiam abbatis predicti de tribus septimanis in tres septimanas et per servicium quatuor feodorum militum, ac Johannes de Camoys quondam dominus maneriorum illorum, et omnes antecessores sui quondam domini eorumdem maneriorum omnia servicia predicta pro predictis maneriis a tempore quo non extat memoria omnibus predecessoribus eiusdem abbatis fecerint pro maneriis predictis donec maneria illa ad manus domine Alianore quondam regine Anglie matris nostre per feoffamentum predicti Johannis devenerunt, a quo tempore omnia servicia predicta eidem abbati predicte[1] et successoribus suis omnino hactenus sunt subtracta in ipsorum dampnum non modicum et ecclesie sue exheredationem manifestam, super quo petiit a nobis sibi de congruo remedio provideri. Nos eidem abbati quod justum fuerit fieri volentes in hac parte vobis mandamus quod scrutatis libris et memorandis de eodem Scaccario et inquisita super premissis in presencia ballivorum et ministrorum Isabelle regine Anglie consortis nostre karissime, in cuius manibus maneria illa de dono nostro nunc existunt, ad hoc premuniendorum si interesse voluerint plenius veritate de eo quod inde inveneritis, nos sub sigillo Scaccarii predicti distincte et aperte sine dilatione reddatis certiores, ut extunt inde fieri faciamus quod de jure fuerit faciendum. Remittentes nobis hoc breve. Teste meipso apud Westm' xxviij die Maii anno regni nostri viij°.

1 *predicte* interlined above *successoribus*.

290 Writ of Edward II to the treasurer and barons of the Exchequer ordering them to inspect the enclosed petition from the abbot and to do justice to him on the contents. [24 May 1315]

Rex thesaurario et baronibus suis de Scaccario salutem. Mittimus vobis petitionem dilecti nobis in Christo abbatis de Burgo Sancti Petri coram nobis et consilio nostro exhibitam presentibus interclusam mandates quod inspecta petitionem predictam eidem abbati super contentis in eadem fieri faciatis justicie complementum ne pro defectu vestri querela ad nos inde perveniat iterata. Teste meipso apud Thunderle xxiiij die Maii anno regni nostri viij°.

291 Writ of Edward II to the treasurer and barons of the Exchequer ordering them to do justice to the abbot in respect of silver vessels given to him by William de la More, Master of the Templars, as a pledge for the payment of 100 marks, but which were taken into the king's hands following the seizure of the Templars[1], leaving the abbot without satisfaction for the debt. [post 1312]

Rex thesaurario et baronibus suis de Scaccario salutem. Monstravit nobis dilectus in Christo abbas de Burgo Sancti Petri per petitionem suam coram nobis et consilio nostro exhibitam quod cum ipse fratri Willelmo de la More tempore quo fuit magister militie Templi in Anglia centum marcas mutuasset, idemque Willelmus quedam diversa vasa sua argentea nomine pignoris pro predictis centum marcis eidem abbatis tradidisset, et se prefato abbati ad solutionem predictarum centum marcarum per litteram suam obligatoriam sigillo suo signatam obligasset, omnia vasa predicta statim post tempus captionis Templariorum seisita fuerunt in manum nostram et thes', et baron' de predicto Scaccario qui tunc fuerant ad opus nostrum liberata, eidem abbati de predictis centum marcis in nullo satisfact' in ipsius abbatis dampum non modicum et depossessionem manifestam, super quo petiit sibi de congruo remedio provideri. Nos eidem abbati quod justum fuerit fieri volentes in hac parte, vobis mandamus quod visa littera predicta si per inspectionem eiusdem vobis constare poterit vasa predicta eidem abbati pro predictis centum marcis per prefatum Willelmum ut premittitur fuisse inpignorata, tunc prefato abbati super premissis fieri faciatis quod de jure videritis fore faciendum. Teste etc.

1 See above, no. 238.

292 Grant by Abbot Godfrey to Master Ralph de Wyndesore, clerk, a pension of 5 marks p.a. from the abbot's chamber until he can be otherwise provided for. [16 Mar. 1314]

[fo. 115v] Pensio magistri Radulphi de Wyndesore.

Universis Christi fidelibus presentes litteras visuris vel audituris Godefridus permissione divina abbas monasterii sancti Petri de Burgo salutem in Domino sempiternam. Noverit universitas vestra nos concessisse dilecto nobis in Christo magistro Radulpho de Wyndesore clerico, quinque marcas sterlingorum nomine pensionis annue de camera nostra percipiendas ad duos anni terminos; videlicet ad festum Pasche, triginta tres solidos et quatuor denarios, et ad festum sancti Michaelis triginta tres solidos et quatuor denarios, et sic singulis annis donec uberius eidem providerimus. In cuius rei testimonium presentibus sigillum nostrum fecimus apponi. Dat' apud Eye juxta Burgum xvij kalendas Aprilis anno Domini M° CCC° quartodecimo.

293 Letter from Abbot Godfrey and the convent to John, bishop of Lincoln requesting him to institute Roger de Northburgh', chaplain, to the church of Castor, to which the abbey had right of presentation and which is vacant. [10 Mar. 1316]

Presentatio domini Rogeri de Northburgh' ad ecclesiam de Castr'.

Reverendo patri in Christo domino J[ohanni] Dei gracia Linc' episcopo sui humiles et devoti G[odefridus] eiusdem dono gracie abbas de Burgo Sancti Petri et eiusdem loci conventus salutem, et tam debitam quam devotam cum omni reverencia obedienciam. Sancte paternitati vestre presentamus dilectum nobis in Christo dominum Rogerum de Northburgh', capellanum, ad ecclesiam de Castr' vacantem, que ad nostram spectat presentationem, humiliter supplicantes et devote quatinus ipsum ad eandem admittatis et personam in eadem instituatis. Salvis nobis et ecclesie nostre juribus ab antiquo perceptis in eadem. In cuius rei testimonium sigillum nostrum fecimus apponi. Dat' in capitulo nostro die Mercurii proxima ante festum sancti Gregorii pape anno Domini millesimo CCC^{mo} quintodecimo.

294 Grant by Abbot Godfrey and the convent to Bernard of Castor[1] of clothing and sustenance in the abbey for his lifetime. [8 June 1317]

Carta Bernardi de Castr'.

Omnibus Christi fidelibus ad quos presens scriptum pervenerit, Godefridus permissione divina abbas de Burgo Sancti Petri et eiusdem loci conventus salutem in Domino sempiternam. Noverit universitas vestra nos unanimi assensu concessisse dilecto et fideli[2] nostro Bernardo de Castr' competentem sustentationem in tota vita sua in victu et vestitu in abbacia nostra; videlicet unam robam cum pellura de secta armigerorum abbatis annuatim percipiendam et unum panem album et duos panes bissos et duas lagenas bone cervise de celario abbatis et unum ferculum integrum cum intermisso secundum varietatem dierum et temporum de coquina abbatis cotidie prout libere familie ministratur quamdiu vixerit percipiendos. Concedimus eciam eidem Bernardo quod omnia predicta ubicumque fuerit infra abbaciam vel extra libere percipiat, et de hiis absque aliqua contradictione vel inpedimento nostri vel successoribus nostrorum pro libito suo disponat. In cuius rei testimonium sigilla nostra presentibus sunt appensa. Dat' in capitulo nostro die Mercurii in festo sanctorum Medardi et Gildardi anno Domini millesimo CCC septimodecimo.

1 Bernard of Castor was bailiff of the northern group of manors from 1300–1310. King, *Peterborough Abbey*, p. 136.
2 *et fideli* interlined.

295 Grant by Abbot Godfrey and the convent to Master Richard of Northampton for his lifetime of a room in the abbey, clothing and sustenance at the abbot's table for himself, food and clothing for two servants and stabling for two horses, as provided for the abbot's other senior clerks. [28 Nov. 1317]

[fo. 116r] Littera magistri R[icardi] de Norhampton'.

Universis Christi fidelibus ad quos presentes littere pervenerint Godefridus permissione divina abbas de Burgo Sancti Petri et eiusdem loci conventus salutem in Domino sempiternam. Noverit universitas vestra nos unanimi assensu concessisse dilecto nobis in Christo magistro Ricardo de Norhampton', in tota vita sua, cameram honestam infra abbaciam nostram et sustentationem suam decentem in mensa domini abbatis qui pro tempore fuerit cum honorabilioribus personis, ut in cibis, et potubis et vestura pro se; videlicet dimidium pannum cum pellura, et pro duobus garcionibus suis cum garcionibus dicti domini abbatis in victu et vestitu, et pro duobus equis suis sicut ceterorum clericorum de melioribus abbatis cum stabulo. Et si in camera sua velit seu oporteat morari, concedimus quod habeat pro se duos panes de albioribus, et duas lagenas de meliori cervisa, et de coquina unum ferculum integrum de grossis carnibus seu piscibus cum aliis cibis et ferculis sicut in mensa dicti domini abbatis singulis diebus deservitur, et pro garcionibus suis duos panes bissos et unam lagenam et dimidiam secunde cervise cum uno ferculo de coquina, et pro camera sua focale et candela sicut ceteri supradicti clerici percipiunt. In cuius rei testimonium sigilla nostra presentibus sunt appensa. Dat' in capitulo nostro iiij kalendas Decembris anno Domini millesimo CCC^{mo} septimodecimo.

296 Indentured agreement between Abbot Godfrey and the convent and Robert of Thorpe whereby Robert was granted 100s p.a. from the abbot's chamber until he received land, a tenement or rent to the same annual value in Stamford, or elsewhere on the abbey's demesnes, together with an annual set of the livery worn by the abbot's senior clerks for his lifetime. In return, Robert undertook faithfully to execute the abbey's business as custodian of the liberty. [8 Oct. 1309]

Littera domini Roberti de Thorp' cirograffata.

Universis sancte matris ecclesie filiis presentes litteras visuris vel audituris Godefridus permissione divina abbas de Burgo Sancti Petri et eiusdem loci conventus salutem in Domino sempiternam. Noveritis nos dedisse dilecto nobis in Christo Roberto de Thorp' centum solidos annuos de camera abbatis qui pro tempore fuerit quolibet anno recepiendos ad duos anni terminos; videlicet unam medietatem ad Pascha et aliam ad festum sancti Michaelis donec eidem de terra, tenemento, vel redditu valenc' centum solidos per annum in villa Stanfordie vel alibi infra dominium nostrum providerimus et eidem dederimus, tenendum de nobis ad vitam suam et ex tunc cesset solutio dictorum centum solidorum. Preterea concedimus eidem Roberto singulis annis dimidium pannum de meliori secta clericorum nostrorum cum pellura competenti pro clericis, recipendum de camera abbatis qui pro tempore fuerit tota vita dicti Roberti. Idem vero Robertus concedit per presens scriptum fide media et juramento corporaliter prestito se obligat predictis dominis suis abbati et conventui de Burgo Sancti Petri et eorum successoribus omnibus aliis dominis pretermissis[1] in officio custodie libertatis monasterii eorumdem ac omnibus aliis serviciis consiliis et auxiliis eos ac monasterium suum predictum quoquomodo tangentibus quandocumque opus fuerit aut necessitas exegerit fideliter et inconfuse sumptibus[2] eorumdem deservire. Et ad premissa firmiter observanda, parti huius scripti indentati et versus dictum Robertum remanenti sigillum nostrum et eciam sigillum capituli nostri apposuimus. Et parti penes nos residenti, idem Robertus sigillum suum apposuit. Dat' apud Burgum Sancti Petri die Mercurii proxima ante festum sancti Dionisii anno regni regis E[dwardi] filii regis E[dwardi] tercio.

1 *pretercuissis* in MS.
2 *inconficte sumptubus* in MS.

297 Letter from the presidents of the chapter general of the Benedictine Order, incorporating a letter of 23 Nov. 1320 from John Salmon, bishop of Norwich, about raising money to assist in the purchase of a house in Oxford for the Carmelite brothers. [23–24 Jan. 1321]

[fo. 116v] Littera presidencium pro domibus fratrum de Monte Carmeli apud Oxon' emendis.

Permissione[1] divina de Waleden' et de Rames', capitulo generali ordinis sancti Benedicti presidentes, venerabilibus et religiosis viris abbatibus et prioribus proprios abbates non habentibus per eandem provinciam constitutis, salutem in Domino sempiternam. Litteras reverendi patris domini [Johannis] Dei gracia Norwic' episcopi recipimus in hec verba:

Venerabilibus religionis venerande dominis dominis abbatibus de Rames et de Waleden' presidentibus capitulo generali monachorum ordinis sancti Benedicti provincie Cant' necnon et ceteris abbatibus ac prioribus proprios abbates non habentibus ordinis et provincie predictorum, frater Johannes permissione divina Norwyc' episcopus salutem et sincere dilectionis in Domino continuum incrementum. Vigor exigit rationis omnes et singulos unius professionis vinculis involutos ea appetere opere effectuali subsequente, que comodum et honorem ordinis huiusmodi non mediocriter concernere dinoscuntur. Sane ex fida quorumdam relatione didicimus locum in quo scolares vestri monachi Oxon' studendi et in divina pagina non solum sibi ipsis sed et confratribus suis ac Christicolis universis proficiendi causa moram trahunt, variis inhabitationis incomodis ut de suorum ruinis edificiorum ut pretenditur taceatur, subici hiis diebus pro quibus relevandis vos omnes et singuli nedum ex debito honestatis, sed et vinculo fraterne comunionis quo singuli singulis et singuli universis communi utilitate pensata, cogimini mutuo vobis invicem subvenire, debetis pro viribus manus apponere plurimum adjutrices. Cum itaque fratres de Monte Carmeli suum locum loco dictorum scolarium vestrorum Oxon' contiguum cum suis edificiis iam dimiserint et ipsum totaliter deserendo ac locus ipse vestris commonachis supradictis non tam utilis quam per maxime necessarius existat, prout vestrum quilibet sana conscientia inde poterit esse testis. Vestram in communi requirimus caritatem vos omnes et singulos singulariter totis precordiis exortantes, quatinus pro prefato loco deserto adquirendo et predicto loco scolarium adnectendo contributione facta in communi absque procrastinatione morosa et murmure qualicumque vires apponere effectualiter non tardetis. Nos enim circa expeditionem premissorum religionis optentu ac utilitatis communis ut prefertur, vobis et vestris nunciis assistemus pro viribus cum consilio et presidio in quantum poterimus oportunis. Considerantes si placet quod multa ex inopinato contingere possunt in hoc casu que pium et vestrum Deo gracium desiderium segregare poterunt ab effectu, quod si premissa ad vestram noticiam celeriter deduci nequeant in communi, vos domini presidentes ceteris omnibus nostri [fo. 117r] vestris apicibus dignemini ea quamcitius intimare et quid per vos actum fuerit in premissis. Vos domini presidentes vel saltem alter vestrum dignemini vel dignetur nos expeditis expediendis reddere certiores ad sancte religionis augmentum vos omnes[2] conservet altissimus in prosperitate votiva per tempora feliciter duratura. Scriptum London' ix kalendas Decembris.

Cumque difficile esset vos omnes isto tempore yemali propter hoc alicubi congregare, habito tractatu cum quibusdam vicinioribus vobis abbatibus super huiusmodi negotio et super summa quam iidem fratres exigunt; videlicet octingentis marcis, pro loco et edificiis, una silicet ecclesia, refectorio, dormitorio et quibusdam aliis videbatur nobis in unam contributionem; videlicet quatuor denarios de marca ad presens esse consentiendum ut idem pater habito consensu omnium nostrum de huiusmodi summa in duobus annis solvenda, si fieri poterit securius cum eisdem fratribus tractare possit, et negotium tam fructuosum ordini nostro effectualiter expedire, vos omnes et singulos attente requirimus, quatinus pro dicti patris reverencia ordinis nostri precipui zelatoris, et ipsius ordinis utilitate et honore in prefatam summam consentiatis una nobiscum consensum vestrum et alia que super huiusmodi negotio duxeritis facienda; nobis rescribentes per latorem presencium et litteras vestras clausas, licet non istarum seriem continentes. Conservet vos altissimus ad incrementum religionis et honorem feliciter atque diu. Dat' quo ad nos abbatem de Waledon' x kalendas Februarii Et quo ad nos abbatem de Rames' ix kalendas Februarii anno Domini millesimo CCC^{mo} vicesimo.

1 Printed in ed. H. E. Salter, *Snappe's Formulary and Other Records* (Oxford Historical Society, lxxx, 1924), pp. 379–80. See also no. 279 for the beginning of an earlier copy.

2 *omnes* interlined.

298 Grant by Abbot Godfrey and the convent to John Love of Dogsthorpe of the messuage and three acres of arable in Dogsthorpe which he formerly held of them at farm for 4s p.a. [7 April 1317]

[fo. 117v] Carta Johannis Love.

Sciatis presentes et futuri quod nos Godefridus abbas de Burgo Sancti Petri et eiusdem loci conventus dedimus, concessimus, et hac presenti carta nostra confirmavimus Johanni Love de Dodisthorp' et heredibus suis unum mesuagium cum edificiis supersitis, et tribus acris terre arabilis in crofto adjacentibus in villa de Burgo in hameleta de Dodisthorp' situatis, quod de nobis prius tenuit ad firmam. Habendos et tenendos sibi et heredibus suis predictum mesuagium cum claustura tam versus altam viam quam campum conformiter faciend' cum crofto adjacente et omnibus aliis pertinenciis suis infra villam et extra libere, quiete, jure, et hereditarie, honorifice, bene et in pace in perpetuum. Reddendo inde nobis et successoribus nostris annuatim quatuor solidos tantum ad quatuor anni terminos usuales pro omni seculari servicio consuetudine exactione et demanda. Ita quod nos vel successores nostri nichil aliud juris consuetudinis aut servicii preter annuum redditum predictum, a predicto Johanne et heredibus suis exigere poterimus seu vendicare in futurum. Et nos predicti abbas et conventus omnia predicta tenementa cum suis pertinenciis prefato Johanni et heredibus suis warantizabimus contra omnes gentes in futurum. In cuius rei testimonium huic presenti carte sigilla nostra apposuimus. Hiis testibus: magistro G[alfrido] de Makes' clerico, Roberto de Thorp' tunc senescallo Burgi, Ricardo de Croyland', Johanne Peverel, Roberto Underwod' et aliis. Dat' in capitulo nostro septimo die mensis Aprilis anno regni regis E[dwardi] filii regis E[dwardi] decimo.

299 Grant by Abbot Godfrey and the convent to Walter de Lardar', son of Batholomew de Multon', and Mariota his wife and her heirs of a messuage in Walton and all the lands and tenements in Walton, Paston, Gunthorpe and Werrington, given to the abbey by Robert son of John of Miningsby, paying an annual rent to the convent's treasurer and to Richard of Crowland and John Peverel. [18 Feb. 1309]

[fo. 118r] Scriptum Walteri de Lardar' et Mariote uxoris eius de tenementa in Walton'.

Universis Christi fidelibus presens scriptum visuris vel audituris, Godefridus miseracione divina abbas de Burgo Sancti Petri et eiusdem loci conventus salutem in Domino sempiternam. Noverit universitas vestra nos dedisse, concessisse et hoc presenti scripto confirmasse Waltero filio Bartholomei de Multon' et Mariote uxori eius et heredibus dicte Mariote de se legittime procreatis unum mesuagium in villa de Walton' cum omnibus terris et tenementis, omnibus juribus et suis pertinenciis que et quas habuimus de dono et confirmatione Roberti filii Johannis de Mithingesby in Walton', Paston', Gunthorp' et Witherington'. Habenda et tenenda predictum mesuagium, omnes terras et tenementas predicta cum omnibus suis pertinenciis, libertatibus et aysiamentis predictis Waltero et Mariote et heredibus dicte Mariote libere, quiete, bene, in pace et in perpetuum, faciendo inde annuatim thesaurario conventus nostri, viginti unum solidum [sic] et novem denarios ad quatuor anni terminos; videlicet in festo natalis Domini quinque solidos, quinque denarios et unum quadrantem, in festo Pasche quinque solidos, quinque denarios et unum quadrantem, in festo sancti Johannis baptiste quinque solidos quinque denarios et unum quadrantem, et in festo sancti Michaelis quinque solidos, quinque denarios et unum quadrantem. Et manerio de Walton' quatuor solidos unum denarium et obolum per annum ad predictos terminos. Et manerio de Witherington' sex denarios per annum ad eosdem terminos. Et manerio de Gunthorp' per annum unum denarium obolum, et quadrantem. Et Ricardo de Croyland, duos denarios ad Pascha. Et Johanni Peverel unum denarium ad Pascha pro omnibus serviciis et demandis. Et quia tenementa prius quadam serjantia pro officio curie de Castr' faciendo onerabatur, que per apropriationem eorumdem in manibus nostris fuit extincta, volumus et ordinamus quod predictum officium fiat temporibus futuris per ballivos predicti abbatis et successorum suorum sumptibus suis in perpetuum. Ita quod predictus Walterus, Mariota, nec heredes dicte Mariote ratione illius officii in nullo graventur nec inquietentur. Nec liceat predictis Waltero, Mariote nec heredibus dicte Mariote predicta tenementa ita alienare, vendere, vel invadiare, quominus ballivi et ministri predictorum thesaurar' ad districtionem in predictis tenementis, sine inpedimento vel contradictione poterint evenire si contingat quod absit ipsos vel eorum alterum in solutione predicti redditus terminis predictis deficere quoquomodo. In cuius rei testimonium presentibus sigilla nostra fecimus apponi. Dat' in capitulo nostro octavodecimo die Februarii anno Domini millesimo CCC° octavo.

300 Letter of John Dalderby, bishop of Lincoln, to John de Stratford, his official, Thomas de Langetoft, canon of Lincoln and John de Clipston, canon of Penkridge College concerning visitation and the hearing of ecclesiastical cases. [14 April 1318]

[fo. 118v] Johannes permissione divina Linc' episcopus dilectis in Christo filiis magistro Johanni de Stratford' officiali nostro et Thome de Langetoft canonico ecclesie nostre Linc', necnon domino Johanni de Clipston' canonico in ecclesia collegiata de Pencriche Coventr' et Lich' dioc' salutem graciam et benedictionem. Inter sollicitudines varias nostris humeris incumbentes, illa post ceteris debet esse precipua nobis cordi ut in clero et populo nostre gubernationi a Deo creditis eradicemus vicia, et in ipsis virtutum germina pro viribus propagemus, quin de ipsorum periculo cogimur in extremo judicio reddere rationem, si in eorum excessibus corrigendis negligentes fuerimus vel remissi. Quapropter deliberato consilio nostram diocesem in capite et membris clerum et populum eiusdem per nos alium seu alios decrevimus fore visitandum nostrumque capitulum ecclesie Linc' tam in capite quam in membris, ac eciam civitatem Linc' juxta juris exigenciam primitus fecimus visitari nos huiusmodi visitationis officium in dicta nostra diocese obsistentibus nobis variis inpedimentis et legittimis exercere non valentes, de vestra circumspectione, sollicitudine et diligencia plenam fiduciam reportantes, ad visitandum clerum et populum nostre diocesis, domosque religiosos, monasteria et personas religiosorum tam in capite quam in membris ecclesias parochiales, eciam prebendales, vicarias, cantarias, hospitales, et alia quecumque beneficia ecclesiastica nostre diocesis et personas eorumdem, necnon inquirendum super excessibus quorumcumque subditorum nostrorum, huiusmodique quod excessus ac cetera omnia et singula que in ipsa visitatione sive ad instanciam vel promotionem partium quarumcumque, sive ex officio, correctione et reformatione comperitis seu videritis indigere corrigendum et reformandum, necnon quoscumque a suis beneficiis ecclesiasticiis, et officiis amovendum, si ad amotionem cuiusquam eciam dignitate constituti, a dignitate beneficio vel officio fuerit procedendum, ac contra notatos in visitatione huiusmodi repertos, et alios diffamatos, necnon in causis seu negotiis beneficialibus, matrimonialibus et divorciis, ac aliis quibuscumque ad forum ecclesiasticum spectantibus que in visitatione huiusmodi emerserint procedendum, cognoscendum et ea fine canonico decidendum, ac eciam dies et loca partibus quibuscumque coram vobis qualitercumque procedentibus seu inperitis coram nobis vel vobis, aut aliquo vestrum, seu aliis commissariis nostris, vel commissario infra nostram diocesem prefigendum et assignandum ac cetera omnia et singula facienda, exercenda et expedienda, que circa premissa vel eorum aliqua juxta naturam, et qualitatem negotii cuiuslibet in hac parte communiter vel divisim requiruntur agenda; vobis de consensu coadjuttori nostri conjunctim et divisim, et cuilibet vestrum in solidum, ita quod quilibet vestrum alio non exspectato seu excusato in omnibus et singulis premissis et ea tangentibus procedere, inchoare et finire possitis, et quod unus vestrum inceperit alius continuare valeat ac eciam terminare, vices nostros committimus cum cohercionis canonice potestate. Mandantes quatinus nos de facto vestro distincte et aperte certificetis tempore oportuno. In cuius rei testimonium sigillum nostrum et sigillum coadjutoris nostri predicti presentibus sunt appensa. Et nos subdecanus ecclesie Linc' coadjutor de patris prefatus in signum consensus nostri prefati adhibiti ut premittitur sigillum nostrum fecimus huiusmodi apponi. Dat' apud Parcum Stowe xviij° kalendas Maii anno Domini M° CCCxviij°.

301 Letter patent from the king on the enforcement of law and order following a petition in parliament at Westminster. [27 Nov. 1320]

[fo. 119r] Rex[1] dilectis et fidelibus etc. Cum in parliamento nostro apud Westm'[2] in octabis sancti Michaelis convocato inter ceteras petitiones nobis ibidem porrectas quedam petitio per milites, cives et burgenses pro comitatibus, civibus et burgis regni nostri ibidem existentes liberata fuit, continens diversas felonias et transgressiones enormes in pluribus comitatibus regni nostri perpetratas, colligationes et confederationes illiciter factas esse in lesionem pacis nostre et terrorem populi nostri, super quibus nobis per predictam petitionem supplicatum fuit oportunum remedium adhiberi. Nos igitur volentes huiusmodi malis obviare et perpetrata facinora punire prout decet necnon de malis et gravaminibus, que per conspiratores in dicto regno nostro eveniunt, ut dicitur, providere oportunum remedium, assignavimus vos justiciarios nostros ad inquirendum per sacramentum tam militum quam aliorum proborum et legalium hominum de comitatibus, tam infra libertates quam extra, per quos rei veritas melius sciri poterit malefactores et pacis nostre perturbatores, roberias huiusmodi, homicidia, depredationes et incendia seu alias felonias, a festo sancti Michaelis anno regni nostri sexto in comitatibus predictis perpetrarunt, et qui huiusmodi malefactores scienter receptarunt et eis consentientes vim et auxilium prebuerunt, qui eciam malefactores et pacis nostre perturbatores colligationes seu confederationes aliquas adinvicem fecerunt, ad verberandum, vulnerandum seu male tractandum homines aliquos ad procurationem aliorum seu ad piscandum in vivariis aliorum, vel ad impediendum vi et armis juratores in assisis juratis et recognitionibus positos, quominus ad loca debita pro veredictis eorum dicendis accedere vel coram ministris nostris et locis illis huiusmodi veredicta dicere ibidem morari et exinde pacifice recedere auderent, vel partes negotia sua in curia nostra prosequentes, quo minus ad curiam nostram pro prosecutione negotiorum suorum accedere, ibidem morari et exinde pacifice recedere possent, vel ad conducendum malefactores ad aliquos homines in locis pupplicis vel privatis verberandos vulnerandos seu male tractandos huiusmodi malefactores manutenendo et ad aliquem hominem vi et armis capiendum et usque ad loca extranea vel ignota ducendum seu ad aliquas felonias seu transgressiones perpetrandas seu faciendas, et ad predictas felonias, transgressiones, colligationes et confederationes audiendum et terminandum secundum legem et consuetudinem regni nostri et juxta formam ordinationis per nos et consilium nostrum super hoc in dicto parliamento nostro factam, quod vobis mittimus sub pede sigilli nostri. Et ad inquirendum similiter qui per sacramentum conventiones, colligationes aut alio modo se adinvicem confederarunt quod quilibet eorum alium invaret et sustentaret et in ipsorum negotiis et querelis falsis vel qui maliciose indictare aut falso aquietare aliquos homines, aut falso movendo placita, vel manutenere contra aliquos procurarunt. Et ad huiusmodi confederationes audiendum et terminandum et puniendum secundum legem et consuetudinem regni nostri juxta formam provisionis predicte et ad querelas omnium et singulorum coram vobis conqueri volentium de transgressionibus eis contra pacem nostram ac de confederantibus contra formam provisionis predicte factis recipiendis et de conquerentibus inde justiciam inde faciendum secundum legem et consuetudinem supradictas. Et ideo vobis mandamus, quod ad certos dies et loca quos ad hic provideritis omnia pre-[fo. 119v]missa faciatis et expleatis in forma predicta facturi inde quod ad justiciam pertinet secundum legem et consuetundiem regni nostri. Salvis nobis amerciamentis et aliis nobis inde spectantibus. Mandavimus enim vicecomitibus nostris comitatum predictorum quod ad certos dies et loca, quos eis scire feceritis, venire faciant coram vobis tot et tales tam milites, quam alios probos et legales homines de comitatibus predictis, tam infra libertatem quam extra, per quos rei veritas in premissis melius sciri poterit et inquiri. Et quod vobis quotiens opus si pareant assistant et intendant prout injungetis ex parte nostra. In cuius rei testimonium has litteras nostras fieri fecimus patentes. Teste meipso apud Shene xxvij die Novembris anno regni nostri xiiij^{o}.

1 See *Cal. Pat., 1317–21*, p. 548. Printed in ed. F. Palgrave, *Parliamentary Writs*, 2 vols (Rec. Comm., 1827–34), vol. II:ii, pp. 153–4, where the letter is addressed to Henry Spigurnel, Richard de Rodeneye, John de Bousser and Robert de Maddingle for enquiry in the counties of Wiltshire, Somerset, Dorset and Gloucestershire.

2 Parliament met on 6 Oct. 1320.

302 Letter of John, bishop of Lincoln, to the abbot and other clergy of the diocese and the official of the archbishop ordering the excommunication of the unknown assailants of William de Clipston, monk of Crowland whom they attacked on the road from Frieston to Crowland, via Spalding. William having taken refuge in the parish church of Spalding had been kept prisoner there in inhumane conditions.

Johannes[1] permissione divina Linc' episcopus dilectis filiis abbati monasterii de Burgo Sancti Petri nostre diocesis ac universis et singulis abbatibus, prioribus, archiepiscopis offic', decanis, eccelesiarum rectoribus, vicariis ac capellanis parochialibus, et quibuscumque capellanis aliis per nostram diocesem constitutos salutem graciam et benedictionem. Immense ferocitas excessus ad nostrum nuper pervenit auditum quod non nulli iniquitati filii quorum nomina ignorantur die Sabati in ebdomada

Pentecostes ultimo iam efflux' dum dilectus filius frater Willelmus de Clipston', monachus monsterii de Croyland', ordinis sancti Benedicti, nostre diocesis, de Freston' versus monsterium suum per villam de Spalding' perduct'[?] suum transitum modo pacifico ut decuit peregisset in eundem fratrem Willelmum et fratem Batholomeum de Linc' comonachum suum habitu monachali induct' manua violentes injecerunt et ipsos de equis quibus insidebant in terram crudeliter prostraverunt ac eundem fratrem Willelmum cum baculo et aliis armorum generibus in variis capitis et corporis sui locis verberaverunt et atrociter vulneravunt et alias nephandissime et inhumaniter pertractarunt et dum pro securitate majore sui corporis consequent' ille cum insequent' fugaret ad parochialem ecclesiam dicte ville et ipsius immunitatem caperet et tutelam predicti Sathane satellites insania furientes ipsum fratrem Willelmum vij diebus tanquam latrone in ipsa ecclesia detinuerunt incarceratum pariter et invitum, capam suam, et capellanum[?] cum capum[?] quibus tunc indutuserat ab eo in dicta ecclesia percipuerunt[?] ac inpediverunt et prohibuerunt sibi cibum et potum et alia vite necessaria ministrari et ollas plenas potu quas humanitas et devotio fidelium sibi contulerunt confregerunt et potu huiusmodi effuderunt et sibi alia enormia intulerunt in violatione immunitatis et libertatis ecclesiatice et contra privilegium ordinis clericorum majoris excommuniationis sententias a sacris canonibus et sanctorum Patrum constitutionibus promulgatas in hac parte preter alias penas canonicas dampnabiliter incurrens. Ne igitur tam enorme piaculare flagitium et offensam inde et ecclesie publice perpetratum transeat oculis continentibus inpunitum vobis communiter et divisim in virtute obediencie et sub excommunicationis majoris pena firmiter injungimus et mandamus quatinus omnes et singulos prefatum excessum nephandissimum ut premittitur committentes premissa ve fieri mandantes procurantes seu ea ipsorum nomine facta ratificantes pariter et attemtpantes in dictas excommunicationis sententias incidise et sic excommunicatos fore in singulis ecclesiis vobis subditis omnibus diebus Dominicis et festis intra misa solempnia dum major asseruit populi multitudo campanis pulsatis, cruce erecta, candelis accensis, vestibus sacerdotalibus induti, palam et p ... in genere nuncietis et facietis per alios nunciari. Exinde non cessantis donec delinquentes reatum suum debite agnoserint et beneficium absolutionis premissa satisfactione debita meruerint obtinere aliud que super hoc dederimus in mandatis. Et si quos reclamantes, diffamantes ac culpabiles in huiusmodi inseveritis de quibus per orationem quemlibet inquiri solerter, volumus et mandamus citetis seu citari faciatis peremptorie eosdem pro vicesimo die post citationem huiusmodi si dies juridica fuerit, alioquin proxime die juridico ex tunc sequente compareant, coram nobis in ... ubicumque vel dioc' nostra Linc' tunc fuerimus super prefatis excessibus ...[2]

1 The text is badly faded and, in parts, illegible. Elsewhere, some readings are

questionable. The eighteenth century transcript by David Casley in Bodl., MS Top. Northants c 23, fos 191r–2r is useful, but he too was defeated towards its end.

2 The remainder of the document is too illegible for a useful transcription.

303 Grant by Abbot Godfrey and the convent to William of Fulbourn, at the instance of Queen Isabella, of a pension of 100s p.a. from the abbot's chamber until he can be provided with a suitable benefice. [19 June 1321]

[fo. 120r] Littera domini Willelmi de Fulburn'.

Omnibus Christi fidelibus presentes visuris vel audituris Godefridus permissione divina abbas de Burgo Sancti Petri et eiusdem loci conventus salutem in Domino sempiternam. Noverit universitas vestra nos, ad instanciam excellentissime regine Isabelle Dei gracia regis Anglie consortis, unanimiter concessesse dilecto nobis in Christo domino Willelmo de Fulburn' centum solidos percipiendos annuatim de camera abbatis qui pro tempore fuerit ad duos anni terminos; videlicet ad festum sancti Michaelis L s. et ad festum Pasche proxima sequens L s., donec eidem in ecclesiastico beneficio competenti providerimus. In cuius rei testimonium presentis sigilla nostra apposuimus. Dat' in capitulo nostro die Veneris proxima post festum sancti Botulphi abbatis anno Domini M^{o} CCC vicesimo primo.

304 [fo. 120v] The beginning of a list of contents covering fos 2–21 in a later medieval hand. [not transcribed]

305 Valuation of spiritualities for the archdeaconries of Oxford, Buckingham, Bedford, Huntingdon and Northampton except for the rural deanery of Rutland, from the 1291 tax assessment of Pope Nicholas IV, set alongside those of the 1254 Valuation of Norwich.

[fo. 121r] Taxationes[1] ecclesiarum pensionum et portionum personarum ecclesiasticarum in archidiaconatibus Oxon', Bukingham, Bedeford', Huntindon' et Norhampton' preter decanatus Roteland', per Radulphum et Ricardum de Morton' et de Gillingg' ecclesiarum rectores sub reverendis patribus, dominis O[livero] Dei gratia Lincoln' et J[ohanne] Wynton' episcopis taxatoribus principalibus, a domino Nicholao papa quarto deputatis una cum incremento per retaxationem a supradictis patribus factam superaddito, anno Domini millesimo ducentesimo, nonagesimo, j^{o}

1 For earlier printed editions see above pp. xxxvi–viii. Entries omitted from Lunt and the Record Commission edition of the *Taxatio* are marked *. Figures which differ in either earlier edition are recorded in brackets. For the Valuation of Norwich, collation

has been with the corrected version of Lunt's A text if two valuations are given. Additional material found in the Record Commission edition of the *Taxatio* is supplied in square brackets. This does not include total valuations or marginalia.

305A Decanatus Oxon

	Verus Valor	*Norwycens'*
Ecclesia sancti Petri orientalis cum capellis etc [de Halliwelle et Wolgarcote]	lx m.	l m. (xx m.)
Vicaria eiusdem	C s.	C s.*
Ecclesia beate Marie [Oxon']	xxiij m.	xx m. (x m.)
Ecclesia Omnium Sanctorum dedit[1] pensione	v m. et dim.*	v m. (iiij m.)
Pensiones prioris sancte Fritheswyde[2] in eadem	iij m.	
Ecclesia sancti [sic] Mildrede deducta pens'	iij m.*	iij m. (ij m.)
Pensiones prioris sancte Fritheswyde in eadem	ij m.*	
Capella de Beneseye [pertinens ad priorem sancte Frideswith]	dim m.	
Ecclesia sancti Michaelis australis[2] deducta pens'	iiij m. et dim.*	iiij m. (ij m. et dim.)
Pens' prioris de sancte Fritheswyd' in eadem.	ij m.	
Ecclesia sancti Aldati[2] deducta pens'	iiij m.*	l s. (ij m. et dim.)
Pens' prioris sancte Fritheswyd' in eadem	xx s.	
Pens' [abbatis de] Abindon' in eadem	xx s.	
Ecclesia sancte Ebbe	iij m. et dim.*	xl s. (xx s.)
Ecclesia sancti Petri in Vallio[2,3] deduct' pens'	vj m.*	vj m. (xl s.)
Pens' prioris sancte Fritheswyd' in eadem	iij m.	
Ecclesia sancti Martini[2] deducta pens'	vj m.*	C s. (v m.)
Pens' abbatis Abyndon' in eadem	xxx s.	
Ecclesia sancti Michaelis borialis[2] deduct' pens'	v m.*	v m. (xl s.)
Pens' prioris sancte Fritheswid' in eadem	iij m.	
Ecclesia beate Marie Magdalene	ix m.	xij m. (viij m.)
Vicaria eiusdem	xij m. et dim.*	xx s.
Ecclesia sancti Egidii	x m.	x m. (C s.)
[fo. 121v] Vicaria eiusdem	iiij m.*	v m.
Capella sancti Thome de pauperata	iij m.	v m. (iij m.)

Ecclesia sancti Edwardi, vicaria sancte Frideswyd', ecclesia sancti Clementis et ecclesia sancti Johannis de Merton' vix valent servicium.*

1 Recte *deducta*

2 *indecimabilis* in the Rec. Comm. text.

3 *Ballio* in other texts.

305B Decanatus de Henle[1]

Ecclesia de Henle	xx m.	xv m.[2]
Ecclesia de Herpendene	viij m.	v m.
Ecclesia de Bollehuche	lx s.*	xx s.
Ecclesia de Schipelake	xvij m.	xv m.
Vicaria eiusdem	xxx s.*	
Ecclesia de Caversham [cum capella]	xxv m.	xxx m.
Ecclesia de Mapeldureham ded' port'	xiij m.	xv m.
Vicaria eiusdem	xxx s.*	
Portio abbatis de Becko in eadem	xiij s. iiij d.	
Portio prioris de Lewes in eadem	xv s.	
Ecclesia de Wytchurche ded' port'	xvj m.	xv m.
Portio abbatis de Becko in eadem	ij m.	
Ecclesia de Garingg' deduct' port'	xvj m.	xv m.
Portio abbatis de Becko in eadem	xiij s. iiij d.	
Ecclesia de Stok' Abbatis ded' port'	ix m.	C s.
Portio abbatis de Eynesham in eadem	viij m.	
Ecclesia de Stok' Basset ded' port' cum capellis [de Ispesden et Neunham]	xxxij m.	xxx m.
Portio abbatis de Becko in eadem	iij m.	
Ecclesia de Mungewell' ded' port' et pens'	vj m. et dim.	v m.
Portio prioris Walingford' in eadem	xiij s. iiij d.	
Portio priorisse de Garingg' in eadem	v s.	
Pensio prioris sancti Cutlaci [sic] in eadem	x s.	
Ecclesia de Crowmers	vj m. et dim.	v m.
Ecclesia de Tonfeld deduct' port'	v m. et dim.	x m.
Portio prioris Walingford' in eadem	x s.	
Portio abbatis Dorkcestr' in eadem	v s.	
[fo. 122r] Ecclesia de Swynecumbe' deduct' pens'	vij m.	iiij m.
Pensio abbatis de Becko in eadem	xl s.	
Ecclesia de Rutherfeld' Murdack'	xij m.	x m.
Ecclesia de Rutherfel' Pipard deduct' port'	xj m.	x m. (C s.)[3]
Portio abbatis de Becko in eadem	xiij s. iiij d.	
Ecclesia de Byxegibbewyne	iiij m.*	xl s.
Ecclesia de Bixebrond'	x m.	x m.
Ecclesia de Chakeden'	xvj m.	x m.
Vicaria de Crowmers	xiij s. iiij d.*	
Vicaria de Tonfeld'	xx s.*	
Ecclesia de Nettelbed*		dim. m.[2]

1 Lunt's A text has revised valuations for most of the churches in this rural deanery.
2 Marked *nova* in Lunt's A text.
3 No corrected version in Lunt's A text.

305C Decanatus de Aston'[1]

Ecclesia de Amington'	vj m. et dim.	iiij m.
Ecclesia de Chinnore deduct' port' et pens'	xx m.	xvj m.
Portio abbatis de Becko in eadem	xiij s. iiij d.	
Pens' prioris de Walingforde in eadem	vij s.	
Ecclesia de Crawell'	x m.	xl s.[2]
Ecclesia de Eston deducta portione	xxxij m.	xxx m.
Portio abbatis de Becko in eadem	v m. et dim.	(viij m.)
Vicaria eiusdem	vj m. et dim.	ij m.
Ecclesia de Leukenore deduct' port'	xxx m.	xx m.
Portio abbatis Abyndon' in eadem	xl s.	(iij m.)
Vicaria eiusdem	vj m. et dim.	iiij m.
Ecclesia de Weston' deduct' port'	vj m. et dim.	iiij m.
Portio abbatis Osneye in eadem	xiij s. iiij d.	(x s.)
Ecclesia de Piritone	xxxij m.	xxv m.
Vicaria eiusdem	vj m. et dim.	iiij m.
Ecclesia de Watlington'	xx m.	xxv m.
Vicaria eiusdem non taxatur propter exilitatem.*		
Ecclesia de Schirburn' deduct' port'	xvj m.	xij m.
Portio abbatis Osneye in eadem	ij m.	
[fo. 122v] Vicaria eiusdem	iiij m.*	
Ecclesia de Brytwell'	v m.*	xx s.
Ecclesia de Ewelme	xviij m.	xvj m.
Ecclesia de Chalgrave deduct' port'	xxxij m.	xxx m.[3]
Portio abbatis de Becko in eadem	v m.	
Portio pecunie quam percipiunt ipsi de castro Wallingf'	xl s.	
Ecclesia de Bryttewelle	xxvij m.	xx m.
Ecclesia de Cuxham	viij m.	vij m.
Ecclesia de Ibestan	xl s.*	ij m.
Ecclesia de Werpesgrave deduct' port'	ij m.*	xiij s. iiij d.
Portio Templarii in eadem	xxx s.*	
Ecclesia de Esenden'[4] deduct' pens'	ij m.*	xx s.
Pens' abbatis de Godestowe in eadem	ij m.	
Ecclesia de Wytefeld'	x m.	v m.
Ecclesia de Adewell' deduct' port'	vj m. et dim.	xx s.[5]
Portio abbatis de Becko in eadem	xx s.	
Ecclesia de Stok'Talemach' deduct' port'	viij m.	v m.
Portio abbatis de Tame in eadem	xiij s. iiij d.	

1 Lunt's A text has revised valuations for most of the churches in this rural deanery.
2 Lunt's A text adds *preter decimas monachorum que valeat j m.*
3 Lunt's A text adds *preter decimas prioris iij m.*
4 *indecimabilis* in Rec. Comm. text.
5 Lunt's A text adds *preter portionem prioris x s.*

305D Decanatus de Cudesdon'[1]

Ecclesia de Thame prebendal'	Clxviij m.	
Vicaria eiusdem	xij m.	
Ecclesia prebendalis de Milton'	lx m.	
Vicaria eiusdem	ix m.	
Prebenda consistens in laico feodo ibidem	lxx m.	
Ecclesia de Dorkcestr' cum capellis [prebendal']	lxij m.	xxxij m. (xxxj m.)[2]
Ecclesia de Codesdone	xl m.	xxx m.
Vicaria eiusdem	viij m.	vj m.[3]
Ecclesia de Ambresdon'	xl m.	xxx m.
Ecclesia de Garsindon' deduct' port' et pens'	xx m.	viij m.
Pensio prioris Walingford' in eadem	C s.	
[fo. 123r] Portio prioris sancte Fritheswyd' in eadem	xx s.	
Ecclesia de Newenham deduct' port' et pens'	xix m.	xviij m.
Portio abbatis Abindon' in eadem	xiij s. iiij d.	
Pens' eiusdem in eadem	xxx s.	
Ecclesia de Sanford'	iiij m.*	iij m.[4]
Ecclesia de Wodepyrie[5] deduct' port'	xiij s. iiij d.*	xiij s. iiij d.
Portio abbatis Osneye in eadem	vj s. viij d.	
Ecclesia de Covele	xij m.	x m.
Vicaria eiusdem	ij m.*	xx s.[3]
Ecclesia de Horspath' deduct' port'	x m.	viij m.
Portio abbatis Oseneye in eadem		xiij s. iiij d.
[Capella de Forsthulle deducta portione	j li. vj s. viij d.	
Portio prioris sancte Fritheswyde in eadem	vj s. viij d.]	
Ecclesia de Halenton' deduct' port'	ix m.	viij m.
Portio abbatis Abyndon' in eadem	x s.	
Ecclesia de Waterpyrie	x m.	xij m.
Vicaria eiusdem	ij m.*	
Ecclesia de Waterstock'	viij m.	vj m.
Ecclesia de Aldebur' deduct' port'	v m.*	iiij m.
Portio priorisse de Stodleye in eadem	viij s.*	
Ecclesia de Staunton' deduct' pens'	x m.	vij m.
Pensio abbatis de Eynesham in eadem	xx s.	
Ecclesia de Wodeton'	vij m. et dim.	iiij m.
Ecclesia de Elsefeld	vij m.	xij m.
Vicaria eiusdem non taxatur*		x s.[3]
Ecclesia de Beckele deduct' port'	xv m.	xij m.
Portio abbatis Oseneye in eadem	ij m.	
Portio priorisse de Stodleya in eadem	iij m.*	
Ecclesia de Merton' deduct' pens'	xvij m. x s.	xv m.
Pens' abbatis de Eynesham in eadem	xxx s.	
Ecclesia de Hasele deduct' port'	xxxiij m.	xx m.
Portio abbatis de Becko in eadem	ij m. et dim.	
[fo. 123v] Ecclesia de Iftele	xxij m.	xx m.
Ecclesia de Hedindon'	viij m.	

Vicaria eiusdem	ij m.*	
Ecclesia de Merston'	viij m.	xv m.*
Vicaria eiusdem	ij m.*	

1 Lunt's A text has revised valuations for most of the churches in this rural deanery.
2 Uncorrected in Lunt's A text.
3 Marked *in originali* in Lunt's A text.
4 Identical with the uncorrected valuation in Lunt (A). The corrected figure in the A MS is iiij m.
5 *indecimabilis* in Rec. Comm. text.

305E Decanatus de Wodestock'[1]

Ecclesia de Eynesham cum capellis [de Karsinton' et Erdinton']	xxxij m.	xvi li.
Vicaria eiusdem	iij m.*	xxx s.
Vicaria de Kersington'	ij m. et dim.*	ij m.
Vicaria de Erdington'	ij m.*	xx s.
Ecclesia de Staunton' cum capella [de Suthleye] ded' pens'	xxx m.	xvj li.
Pens' [quam percipit] abbatis Radingg' in eadem	xx m.	(xx m.)
Ecclesia de Coges	xij m.	x m.
Ecclesia de Northleya deduct' port'	xvj m.	vj li.
Portio abbatis Oseneye in eadem	xv s.	
Vicaria eiusdem	ij m.*	
Ecclesia de Wyvelecote vix valet servicium*		
Ecclesia de Stontesfeld	iij m.*	xx s.
Ecclesia de Cumbe deduct' pens'	xij m.	vj li.
Pens' abbatis Evesham in eadem	x s.	
Ecclesia de Haneberg' deduct' pens'	xvij m. x s.	viij li. (viij m.)
Pens' abbatis Radingg' in eadem	xxx s.	
Ecclesia de Bladene cum capellis [de Wodestok et Hensington] ded' port'	xv m.	vij li.
Portio abbatis Oseneye in eadem	v s.	(iiij s.)
Ecclesia de Beckebrok'	iiij m.*	xl s.[2]
Ecclesia de Cudelington'	xl m.	xvj li.
Vicaria eiusdem	ij m.*	
Ecclesia de Schipton'	vj m. et dim.	iiij li.
Ecclesia de Tackele deduct' port'	xxiiij m.	xij li.
Portio abbatis Evesham[3] in eadem	v s.	(x s.)
Portio abbatis Oseneye in eadem	xv s.	
[fo. 124r] Vicaria eiusdem	xxx s.*	ij m.*
Ecclesia de Roulesham	xij m.	C s.[4]
Ecclesia de Stepelaston' deduct' port'	xvj m.	vij li.[5]
Portio prioris de Coldenortone in eadem	xiij s. iiij d.	
Portio vicarii de Northaston' in eadem	v s.*	
Ecclesia de Northaston'	x m.	vj li.

Vicaria eiusdem	xx s.*	x s.
Ecclesia de Dunestywe deduct' port'	xij m.	x m.
Portio abbatis de Oseneya in eadem	xiij s. iiij d.	(j m.)
Vicaria eiusdem	iiij m.*	xx s.
Ecclesia de Magna Barton' cum capellis [de Sanford et Ledewell] ded' port'	xxiiij m.	xv li.
Portio abbatis Colecestr' in eadem	lx s.	
Vicaria eiusdem	ij m.*	xx s.[6]
Vicaria de Saunford'	xx s.*	xv s.
Ecclesia de Barton' Parva ded' pens'	vj m. et dim.	iiij m.
Pens' abbatis de Eynesham in eadem	vj s. viij d.	
Ecclesia de Cudynton'	vj m. et dim.	v m.
Ecclesia de Glimpton' deduct' pens'	viij m. et dim.	C s.
Pens' prioris de Kenilwrth' in eadem	vj s. viij d.	
Ecclesia de Wotton' cum capellis [de Ludewelle et Horedle] ded' pens'	xxx m.	xv li.[7]
Portio abbatis de Oseneya in eadem	vj s.	
Vicaria eiusdem	ij m.*	

1 Lunt's A text has revised valuations for most of the churches in this rural deanery.
2 Marked *nova* in Lunt's A text.
3 *Eynesham* in the Rec. Comm. text.
4 Lunt's A text adds *preter decimas; decime abbatis Oseneie xv s.*
5 Lunt's A text adds *et sunt ibi multe decime separate.*
6 Lunt's A text adds *et j s. ibi deest.*
7 Lunt's A text adds *preter decimas separatas dim. m., item v s., item v s., item iiij s.*

305F Decanatus de Burncestr'

Ecclesia de Burncestr' deduct' port'	xviij m.	xv m. (xij m.)
Portio abbatis de Alneto in eadem	ij m.	
Portio abbatis de Oseneya in eadem	iij m.	
Portio abbatis de Eynesham in eadem	xij s.	
Vicaria eiusdem	iiij m.*	xxx s.*
Ecclesia de Curtlington deduct' port'	xxx m.	xx m.
Portio abbatis de Oseneya in eadem	xiij s. iiij d.	
Vicaria eiusdem	vj m. et dim.	xl s.*
[fo. 124v] Ecclesia de Weston'	xiiij m.	xij m. (x m.)
Vicaria eiusdem vix valet servicium*		
Ecclesia de Blechesdon' deduct' port'	xv m.	x m. (viij m.)
Portio abbatis de Oseneya in eadem	x s.	
Ecclesia de Hampton' Gay	iij m.	xl s. (xx s.)
Ecclesia de Hampton' ad pontem	v m. et dim.*	iiij m. (xl s.)
Ecclesia de Islep	xvj m.	xij m. (x m.)
Ecclesia de Otyndon'	x m.	vij m. (v m.)
Ecclesia de Cherleton' deduct' pens'	xxx m.	xx m.
Pens' prioris de Ware in eadem	iij m.	
Ecclesia de Ake	iiij m. et dim.*	(j m. non

		valet servicium)
Ecclesia de Weldelbur'	x m. et dim.	ix m. (viij m.)
Ecclesia de Cesterton'	xvj m.	xij m. (x m.)
Ecclesia de Langgeton'	xij m.	viij m. (vij m.)
Ecclesia de Godington'	vj m. et dim.	iiij m. (iij m.)
Ecclesia de Ardele ded' pens'[1]	vj m. et dim.	iiij m. (iij m.)
Pensio[1] abbatis de Oseneye in eadem	x s.	
Ecclesia de Midlington'	xv m.	viij m. (C s.)
Ecclesia de Bukenhull' deduct' port'	xv m.	xj m. (x m.)
Pens'[1] abbatis Oseneye in eadem	x s.	
Ecclesia de Stoke Insule	xx m.	xx m. (xvj m.)
Ecclesia de Herdwyk'[2] ded' port'	ij m.*	j m. (x s.)
Port' abbatis in eadem	vj s. viij d.	
Ecclesia de Hethe	x m.	vj m. (iiij m.)
Ecclesia de Cotesford'[2] deduct' pens'	iiij m.*	iiij m. (iij m.)
Pens' prioris de Okeburn' in eadem	xiij s. iiij d.	
Ecclesia de Feringford' deduct' pens'	ix m.	C s. (v m.)
Pens' prioris de Coges in eadem	ij m.	
Ecclesia de Chaldewell'	iiij m.*	xxx s. (xv s.)
Ecclesia de Newenton'	ij m.*	
Ecclesia de Fynemere	xij m.	ix m. (viij m.)
[fo. 125r] Ecclesia de Lillingstan	xij m.	viij m. (vj m. et dim.)
Ecclesia de Mixebur' deduct' port'	xvj m.	xiiij m. (xij m.)
Pens'[1] abbatis Osen' in eadem	xxx s.	
Ecclesia de Toresmere	ix m.	iiij m. (xl s.)
Ecclesia de Fretewell'	xiij m.	x m. (viij m.)
Vicaria eiusdem	xx s.*	xiij s. iiij d.
Ecclesia de Sulthorn deduct' pens'	xv m.	xij m. (x m.)
Pens' abbatis de Eynesham in eadem	C s.	
Ecclesia de Somerton' deduct' port'	x m.	ix m. (C s.)
Portio abbatis Oseneye in eadem	dim. m.	
Ecclesia de Heyfordwaryn[3] deduct' port'	viij m. et dim.	vij m. (v m.)
Portio abbatis Osen' in eadem	xxx s.	
Ecclesia de Heyford' ad pontem habet ij rectores		xij m. (x m.)
Portio rectoris de patronatu Rogeri del Ile	C s.	
Port' rectoris de patronatu abbatis de Eynesham d' p[ens']	C s.	
Pens'[1] abbatis de Eynesham in eadem	xx s.	
Ecclesia de Folewelle*		xl s. (x s.)

1 port' in Rec. Comm. text.
2 *indecimabilis* in Rec. Comm. text.
3 *H* interlined.

305G Decanatus de Dadinton'[1]

Ecclesia de Dadinton'	lx m.	xlv m. (xxx m.)
Ecclesia de Abberbur' deduct' port'	lxx m.	l m. (xxx m.)
Port' abbatis Osen' in eadem	xiij s. iiij d.	
Portio abbatisse de Godestowe in eadem	xviij s.	
Portio abbatis de Eynesham	vj s.	
Port' rectoris de Bereford' in eadem	v s.	
Ecclesia de Bereford' deduct' port'	vj m. et dim.	v m. et dim. (iij m.)
Port' abbatis Oseneye in eadem	xxx s.	
Ecclesia de Newenton'	xvj m.	xv m. (iiij m.)
Ecclesia de Overtone Magna	iiij m. et dim.*	xl s. (xx s.)
Ecclesia de Tademerton' deducta pens'	xij m.	xij m.
Pens' abbatis Abyndon' in eadem	vj m.	
Ecclesia de Magna Tywe	l m.	xl m. (xxx m.)
[fo. 125v] Ecclesia de Wyginton' deducta port'[2]	xiij m.	xv m. et v s. (v m.)
Pens' abbatis de Osen' in eadem	v s.	
Ecclesia de Swaleclive deduct' port' et pens'	xlv m.	xl m. (xxx m.)[3]
Port' rectoris ecclesie de Bannebi' in eadem	vj m.*	
Port' abbatissa de Eluestowe in eadem	iiij m.	
Pens' quam percipit patronus ecclesie in eadem	xxx s.	
Vicaria eiusdem	v m.*	
Ecclesia de Brouhton' deducta pens'	xx m.	xvij m. xl d. (xviij m.)[4]
Pens' abbat[issa] Wyncestr' in eadem	x s.	
Ecclesia de Drayton'	xj m.	C s.
Ecclesia de Hanewell'	xj m.	x m.
Ecclesia prebendalis de Bannebi' ded' port'	xlv m.	
Port' abbatis de Eynesham in eadem	vj m.	
Vicaria eiusdem ded' oneribus	x m.	
Ecclesia de Bloxham deduct' port'	xxxv m.	xxxviij m. (xx m.)
Port' abbatis Westm' in eadem	v m.	
Vicaria eiusdem	x m.	iiij m.
Ecclesia de Wroxstan	x m. (xx m.)	xx m.
Vicaria eiusdem	ij m. et dim.*	xx s.
Ecclesia de Alkrinton'	vj m. et dim.	v m.[5]
Vicaria eiusdem	v m.*	

1 Lunt's A text has corrected figures for the first part of the deanery only.

2 *pens'* in the Rec. Comm text.

3 Lunt's A text adds among the corrections *dicitur in originali: portio rectoris x m.; portio rectoris Ban' xxx s.; portio prioris de Ware x s.; portio abbatisse de Elnestow de decimis separatis xl s.' portio abbatis de Bruern x s.; portio abbatisse de Godestowe vj s.*

4 The uncorrected valuation in Lunt's A text is xv m.
5 The uncorrected valuation in Lunt's A text is iij m. and the corrected valuation *x m. unde portio rectoris v m. et vicarii v m.*

305H Decanatus de Wytteneye[1]

Ecclesia de Wytteneye	lx m. (£10 0s 8d)	l m.
Vicaria eiusdem	vj m. et dim.	v m.
Ecclesia de Bradewell'	xxx m.*	xxiiij m.
Vicaria eiusdem	v m.*	xl s.[2]
Ecclesia de Kenikote deduct' port'	viij m. (£4 12s 8d)	C s.
Port' abbatis Osen' in eadem	viij s. (8s 4d)	(x s.)
Ecclesia de Westwelle	x m. (£6 13s 0d)	C s.
Ecclesia de Boreford deduct' port'	xlv m.	xl m.
Port' abbatis de Ybreyo in eadem	vj m.	(vj m.)
[fo. 126r] Port' prioris de Ministr' in eadem	xiij s. iiij d.	
Vicaria eiusdem	x m.	x m.
Ecclesia de Teynton'	xiij m.	xij m.
Vicaria eiusdem*		xx s.
Ecclesia de Esthalle	x m.	x m.
Vicaria eiusdem	iij m. et dim.*	xl s.
Ecclesia de Ministr'	vij m.	viij m.
Vicaria eiusdem	vij m.	iiij m.
Ecclesia de Dokelingon' deduct' port'	xvj m.	xij m.
Port' abbatis Osen' in eadem	ij m.	(xx s., item x d.)
Port' vicarie de Eynesham in eadem	x s.*	
Ecclesia de Cokthorp'	iij m.	xxx s.
Ecclesia de Mora deduct' pens'	xxij m.	xvj m. et dim.[3]
Pens' rectoris ecclesie de Stanton' in eadem	xiij s. iiij d.	
Ecclesia de Stanlack'	xxiij m.	xx m.
Ecclesia de Bampton' deduct' port'	lxx m.	lx m.
Port' abbatis Osen' in eadem	iij m.	
Port' abbatis de Eynesham in eadem	xiij s. iiij d.	
Vicarius eiusdem que habet tres portionar' [cum portione in Clanefeld]	lx m.	l m.
Ecclesia de Burton'	viij m.	vij m.
Vicaria eiusdem	v m.*	xl s.
Ecclesia de Norton' deduct' port'	xv m.	xxiiij m.
Port' abbatis Osen' in eadem	l s.	
Vicaria eiusdem	vij m.	
Ecclesia de Clanefeld deduct' port'	x m.	x m.[4]
Port' prioris de Ministr' in eadem	xxiiij s.	
Port' rectoris de Alveskote in eadem	dim. m.	

Port' rectoris de Bampton' in eadem	v m.*	
Ecclesia de Eleford	iij m.*	ij m.
Ecclesia de Brouhton' deduct' port'	vij m.	v m.
Port' vicarii de Langgeford in eadem	x s.	
[fo. 126v] Ecclesia de Schulton'	xj m.	x m.[5]
Vicaria eiusdem	iij m. et dim.*	xl s.
Ecclesia de Alveskote	vij m.	v m.
Ecclesia prebendalis de Langeford'	iiij^xx et x m.	
Vicaria eiusdem	C s.	
Prebenda consistens in laico feodo in eadem villa	lx m.	

1 Lunt's A text has revised valuations for this rural deanery.
2 Lunt's A text adds *Templariorum*.
3 Lunt's A text records a portion of ij m.
4 Lunt's A text records a portion of xx s.
5 Lunt's A text adds *Cysterciensis ordinis*.

305I Decanatus de Northon'

Ecclesia de Norton' deduct' pens'	xl m.	xxx m.
Pens' abbatis de Glovernia in eadem	lx s.	
Ecclesia de Hoge Northon'	xxviij m.	xxv m.
Vicaria eiusdem	ij m.*	
Ecclesia de Cestreton'	ix m.	C s.
Vicaria eiusdem	ij m.*	
Ecclesia de Rollendrith Parva[1] ded' pens'	xxx s.*	ij m.
Pens' abbatis de Eynesham in eadem	x s.	
Ecclesia de Ennestan ded' pens' et port'	xxxv m.	xxx m.
Pensio abbatis de Wynchecumbe in eadem	v m.	
Portio eiusdem abbatis in eadem	iij m.	
Ecclesia de Spellesbur'	xx m.	xx m. (xv m.)
Ecclesia de Rollendrith Magna deduct' port'	xvj m.	xv m. (x m.)
Port' abbatis de Eynesham in eadem	dim. m.	
Ecclesia de Schaltford'	iiij m.*	xl s. (xxx s. vix valet servicium)
Ecclesia de Cornwell'	iiij m.*	ij m.
Ecclesia de Kengham	xv m.	x m.
Ecclesia de Cherchull' ded' port'	xx m.	xv m. (x m.)
Port' prioris sancte Fritheswyde in eadem	xiij s. iiij d.	
Ecclesia de Schipton' ded' port' cum capella [de Linham]	xxxij m.	xxx m.
Port' prioris de Pontefracto in eadem	v m.	
Port' abbatis de Brueria in eadem	dim. m.	
Capella de Escote deduct' port'	vj m. et dim.	v m. (iiij m.)
[fo. 127r] Portio prioris sancte Fritheswid' in eadem	dim. m.	

Vicaria de Schipton'	iij m.*	
Ecclesia de Swinebrok'	viij m.	C s.
Capella de Hydebur'	C s.	v m. (iiij m.)
Capella de Fyfhide	vj m.	iiij m.
Capella de Cherlebur' cum capella [Schorthampton] ded' pens' et port'	xxx m.	xx m. (cum capella de Chadlington)
Pens' abbatis de Eynesham in eadem	v m.	
Port' eiusdem abbatis in Podelecote	v s.	
Port' eiusdem abbatis ibidem	iij m.	
Ecclesia de Chadelington'	xv m.	
Ecclesia de Cerceden'[1] ded' pens'	vj m.*	v m.
Pens' abbatis de Eynesham in eadem	xiij s. iiij d.	
Ecclesia de Hethorp'	vj m. et dim.	vj m. (iiij m. et dim.)
Ecclesia de Esterleya	vj m. et dim.	v m. (iiij m.)
Ecclesia de Swereford' [cum capella de Senewell]	x m.	C s.

1 *indecimabilis* in Rec. Comm. text.

Archidiaconatus de Bukingham

305J Deconatus de Bukingham

Ecclesia de Caveresfeld'	x m.	vj m. (v m.)
Vicaria eiusdem	ij m.*	
Ecclesia de Mershe cum portione	xxiiij m.	xviij m. (x m.)
Ecclesia de Achecote[1] deduct' pens'	v m.*	xl s.
Pens' prioris de Longa Villa in eadem	dim. m.	
Ecclesia de Twyford'	xxv m.	xx m. (xv m.)
Ecclesia de Chetwod'	v m.*	iiij m. (iij m.)
Ecclesia de Preston'	x m.	vj m.
Ecclesia de Barton'	iij m.*	ij m. (xx s.)
Ecclesia de Tyngewyck'	xj m.	viij m. (v m. et dim.)
Ecclesia de Schaldeston' deduct' port'	viij m.	vj m. (iiij m.)
Port' abbatis de Oseneya in eadem	ij m.	
Ecclesia de Westbur' ded' port'	x m.	viij m. (v m.)
[fo. 127v] Portio abbatis Osen' in eadem	ij m. dim.	
Vicaria eiusdem	iij m.*	
Ecclesia de Turveston deduct' port'	xij m.	vj m.
Port' abbatis de Eynesham in eadem	iiij s.	
Ecclesia de Stowe	xv m.	xv m. (x m.)
Vicaria eiusdem	iij m.*	
Ecclesia de Lillingstan ded' port'	C s.	v m. (iij m.)

Port' prioris de Longa Villa in eadem	dim. m.	
Ecclesia de Acle[1] deduct' port'	v m.*	iiij m. (ij m.)
Portio prioris de Longa Villa in eadem	ij m. et dim.	
Ecclesia de Bechampton'[1] habet ij rectores: Portio rectoris de patronatu prioris Luffeld	iiij m.*	vj m. (iiij m.)
Port rectoris de patronatu domini ville ded' port'	iiij m.*	
Port' prioris de Longa Villa in eadem	xx s.	
Ecclesia de Thornton' ded' port'	viij m.	C s. (vj m.)
Port' abbatis de Osen' in eadem	x s.	
Ecclesia de Adington' ded' pens'[1]	C s.	xl s.
Pens' hospitalis de Hogsawe in eadem	iij m.*	
Ecclesia de Adestok'	x m.	vj m. (iiij m.)
Ecclesia de Thorneberg' ded' port'	xiiij m.	viij m. (x m.)
Port' abbatis Osen' in eadem	dim. m.	
Vicaria eiusdem	v m.*	
Ecclesia de Padebur'	xviij m.	xvj m. (xiiij m.)
Vicaria eiusdem	iiij m.*	
Capella de Evereshawe	xiij s. iiij d.	x s. (j m.)
Ecclesia de Stepelcleydon'	xiiij m.	xv m. (x m.)
Vicaria eiusdem	iij m.*	
Ecclesia de Hildesdon'	xj m.	ix m. (C s.)
Ecclesia de Morton' ded' port'	viij m.	vj m. (iij m.)
Port' prioris de Longa Villa in eadem	xvij s.	
Ecclesia de Radeclyve deduct' port'	viij m.	v m. (iij m.)
[fo. 128r] Portio abbatis de Osen' in eadem	xiij s. iiij d.	
Ecclesia de Stratford'[1] deduct' port'	v m.*	iiij m. (iij m.)
Portio abbatis Osen' in eadem	xx s.	
Ecclesia de Foxcote	v m.*	v m. (iij m.)
Ecclesia de Lechamstede	xxiiij m.	xx m. (xv m.)

1 *indecimabilis* in Rec. Comm. text.

305K Decanatus de Wendove'

Ecclesia de Wendovere	xxx m. (xxviij li.)	xxx m. (xx m.)
Vicaria eiusdem	viij m.	
Port' prioris de Suwerk' in eadem	xij m.*	
Ecclesia de Donington'	xx m.	xx m.
Vicaria eiusdem	x m.	
Ecclesia de Hampden'	x m.	x m.
Ecclesia de Hadenham	xl m.	xxx m.
Vicaria eiusdem	vj m. et dim.	
Ecclesia de Stone	xviij m.	xvj m.
Ecclesia de Hertwell'	xij m.	x m.
Ecclesia de Huckote	C s.	iiij m.

Ecclesia de Eston' Clynton'	xxx m.	xx m.
Ecclesia de Weston'	xx m.	xvj m. (xv m.)
Ecclesia de Magna Mussenden'	xv m.	xij m.
Ecclesia de Parva Mussenden'	xj m.	xij m. (x m.)
Vicaria eiusdem	ij m. et dim.*	
Ecclesia de Eselburg' ij habet portiones; portio rectoris ded' pens'	x m.	xx m.
Portio[1] prioris de Sanwell' in eadem portione	ij m. et dim.	
Item alia portio eiusdem prioris	x m.	
Ecclesia de Magna Kinehell' ded' port'	xviij m.	xvj m. (xv m.)
Portio prioris de Wallingford' in eadem	dim. m.	
Vicaria eiusdem	ij m. et dim.*	
Ecclesia de Parva Kinehell' deduct' pens'	vij m.	v m.
Pensio abbatis de Sancto Albano in eadem	xxx s.	
[fo. 128v] Ecclesia de Horsindon'	v m. et dim.*	iiij m.
Ecclesia de Ryseberge Comit'	xxij m.	xx m.
Ecclesia de Bledelawe deduct' pens'	xxx m.	xxvj m. (xx m.)
Pens' abbatis de Gresteyn in eadem	l s.	

1 *Pens'* in Rec. Comm. text.

305L Decanatus de Wycumb'

Ecclesia de Wycumb' ded' pens'	xxx m.	lx m. (xl m.)
Pensio prioris de Becko in eadem	xij m.	
Vicaria eiusdem	x m.	
Ecclesia de Wouburn' deduct' port'	xvj m.	xxv m. (xv m.)
Portio abbatisse de Eluestowe in eadem	l s.	
Ecclesia de Edesore	ij m.*	xl s. (xx s.)
Ecclesia de Parva Merlawe ij habet rectores		xxviij m. (xx m.)
Portio rectoris de patronatu de Bello Campo deduct' pens'[1]	xj m.	
Pens' priorisse de Merlawe in eadem	xx s.*	
Portio altera de patronatu de Danvers	xij m.	
Ecclesia de Magna Merlawe	l m.	l m. (xl m.)
Ecclesia de Medmeham	xij m.	xv m. (x m.)
Vicaria eiusdem	v m. et dim.*	
Ecclesia de Hamelden'	xxxv m.	lv m. et dim. (xxx m.)
Ecclesia de Falleya	xvij m.	xv m.
Ecclesia de Tyrefeld'	xij m.	xij m. (x m.)
Vicaria eiusdem	v m.*	
Ecclesia de Tynghurst	viij m.	x m. (C s.)
Ecclesia de Radenach' ded' pens'[1]	x m.	x m. (v m.)
Pens' Templarii in eadem	xiij s. iiij d.*	

Ecclesia de Haveringdowne cum port' de Morton'	xl m.	xl m. (xxx m.)
Ecclesia de Bradenham	iiij m.*	v m. (iij m.)
Ecclesia de Huchendon'	xxx m.	xxx m. (xx m.)
Vicaria eiusdem	vj m. et dim.	
Ecclesia de Sandresdon' sancti Nicholai	viij m.	x m. (v m.)
[fo. 129r] Ecclesia de Sandresdon' sancte Marie	viij m.	C s. (v m.)

1 *indecimabilis* in Rec. Comm. text.

305M Decanatus de Burmham

Ecclesia de Burnham	xlv m.	l m.
Vicaria eiusdem	xvj m.	
Ecclesia de Stok'	xviij m.	xv m. (xij m.)
Vicaria eiusdem	v m.*	
Ecclesia de Dorneya	x m.	C s. (v m.)
Ecclesia de Farnham	xxiiij m.	xx m.
Ecclesia de Hucham	vj m. et dim.	C s. (v m.)
Ecclesia de Tappelowe	x m.	x m. (C s.)
Ecclesia de Upton' ded' port'	xx m.	xv m. (x m.)
Portio[1] abbatisse de Eluestowe in eadem	xx s.	
Vicaria eiusdem	v m.*	
Ecclesia de Eton'	xvj m.	x m. (C s.)
Ecclesia de Dachet cum capella [de Folmere]	xx m.	xv m.
Ecclesia de Horton'	xxj m.	xv m.
Ecclesia de Wyrardebur' et ecclesia de Langel'	l m.	xl m. (xxx m.)
Ecclesia de Evere	l m.	xxv m.
Ecclesia de Wexham	x m.	vj m. (iiij m.)
Ecclesia de Denham	xxiij m. (xvj li)	xx m. (xv m.)
Ecclesia de Chalfonte sancti Petri	xviiij m.	xx m. (xv m.)
Vicaria eiusdem	viij m.	
Ecclesia de Chalfounte sancti Egidii	xx m.	xv m.
Ecclesia de Penna	xx m.	xviij m. (xv m.)
Ecclesia de Bekenesfeld'	xxiij m.	xx m.
Vicaria eiusdem	v m. et dim.*	
Ecclesia de Amondesham deducta pens'	lx m.	lx m. (xl m.)
Pensio abbatis de Waleden in eadem	v m.	
Pensio prioris de Hurnle in eadem	iij m.	
Ecclesia de Iselhampstede	vij m.	vj m. (v m.)
[fo. 129v] Capella de Iselhampstede	ij m. et dim.*	
Capella de Hugele	xl s.*	iij m. (ij m.)
Capella de Cippeham	xij m.	x m. (C s.)
Ecclesia de Chesham s. portio abbatis de Wouburn' [deduct' pens']	xxx m.[2]	lx m. (l m.)
[Pens' abbatis de Sancto Albano in eadem	15s 0d]	

[Item pens' prioris de Dunstaple in eadem	£2 0s 0d]	
Vicaria eiusdem	v m. dim.*	
[Item alio] Portio [que est] abbatis Leycestr' in eadem ecclesia	xxx m.	
Vicaria eiusdem portionis	v m. dim.*	
Capella sancti Leonardi	ij m.*	xx s. (j m.)
Capella prebendalis de Aylesbur'	xC m.	
Vicaria eiusdem ded' oneribus	xv m.	
Capelle de Burton', Querndon' etc [Stock' et Bocland]	iiij^{xx} m.	
Prebenda de Sutton' cum ecclesiis de Buck' et Hurnle	Cclx m.	
Vicaria eiusdem [deducta oneribus]	x m.	

1 *Pens'* in Rec. Comm. text.

2 This figure tallies with the Rec. Comm. text when the pensions recorded there as belonging to the abbot of St Alban's and the prior of Dunstable are added to the church valuation.

305N Decanatus de Mursle

Ecclesia de Horewode ded' pens' et port'	xv m.	xv m. (x m.)
Pens' prioris de Longa Villa in eadem	iij m.	
Portio eiusdem prioris in eadem	xx s.	
Ecclesia de Waddon'	xv m.	xij m.
Vicaria eiusdem	iiij m.*	
Capella de Toterho	xiij s. iiij d.	x s.
Ecclesia de Mursle ded' pens' et port'	xv m.	x m.
Pens' prioris de Eton' in eadem	iij m.	
Port' prioris de Luffeld in eadem	xx s.	
Ecclesia de Drayton' Passelewe	xv m.	x m.
Ecclesia de Sulebur' deduct' pens'	xx m.	xv m.
Pens' prioris de Tykeford' in eadem	v s.	
Ecclesia de Linchelad' deduct' port' [Chikesond]	xij m.	ix m.
Portio prioris de Newenham in eadem	xiij s. iiij d.	
Vicaria eiusdem	ij m.*	
Ecclesia de Grava	iiij m.*	xl s. (xx s.)
Ecclesia de Schapton' deduct' port'[1]	xviij m.	xv m. (x m.)
[fo 130r] Portio Willelmi de Hameldon' in eadem	ij m. et dim.*	
Ecclesia de Kerslowe ded' pens'	vij m.	ij m. dim
Pens' Hospit' in eadem	dim. m.*	
Ecclesia de Dodington'	iiij m.*	ij m. et dim.
Ecclesia de Edelesbur'	xlv m.	xxx m.
Ecclesia de Ivxngho	lv m.	xxx m.
Ecclesia de Messewrth' ded' port' et pens'	xiiij m.	xij m.
Pens' archid' Buck' in eadem	x s.	

Port' cerofar' Ecclesie Linc' in eadem	ij m.*	
Port' abbatis Osen' in eadem	vj m. et dim.	
Vicaria eiusdem	iiij m.*	
Ecclesia de Pichelesthorn	xvj m.	xij m.
Ecclesia de Swaneburn'	xiij m.	x m.
Vicaria eiusdem	ij m.*	
Ecclesia de Schetingdon'	x m.	ix m. (C s.)
Ecclesia de Wenge	xl m.	xl m.
Vicaria eiusdem	vj m. dim.	2
Ecclesia de Drayton' Beuchamp ded' pens'	xiij m.	x m.
Pens' abbatis de Gresteyn in eadem	xiij s. iiij d.	
Ecclesia de Mentemore	xij m.	ix m.
Vicaria eiusdem	iij m.*	
Ecclesia de Wengrave	xxv m.	xx m.
Vicaria eiusdem	iiij m.*	
Ecclesia de Stivecle	xviij m.	xv m.
Vicaria eiusdem	iij m.*	
Ecclesia de Hogeston'	x m.	C s.
Ecclesia de Cobelington' ded' pens'	vj m. dim.	ij m. dim.
Pens' prioris de Dunstapl' in eadem	ij m.	
Ecclesia de Herdwyck'	xvj m.	xij m. (x m.)
Ecclesia de Wytchurch'	xx m.	xvj m.
Ecclesia de Haurugg'	xiij s. iiij d.*	x s.
[fo 130v] Ecclesia de Chelwoldesbur' non taxatur pro exilitate*		(x s.)

1 *indecimabilis* in Rec. Comm. text.

2 No valuation in Lunt's A text although the vicarage is entered.

305O Decanatus de Neuportpaynel

Ecclesia de Neuport cum capella de Linford' [Parva]	xxx m.	xx m.
Vicaria eiusdem	vij m.	
Ecclesia de Chele	ix m.	vij m.
Vicaria eiusdem	iiij m.*	
Ecclesia de Estwode	x m.	vij m.
Vicaria eiusdem	v m.*	
Ecclesia de Bradewell' deducta portione	iiii m.	iij m.
Port' prioris de Longa Villa in eadem	xiij s. iiij d.	
Vicaria eiusdem	ij m.*	
Ecclesia de Wylie	iij m. et dim.	iij m.
Vicaria eiusdem	ij m. et dim.*	
Ecclesia de Molesho[1] ded' port'	v m.*	iiij m.
Portio abbatisse de Eluestowe in eadem	xxx s.	
Portio prioris de Longa Villa in eadem	xiij s. iiij d.	
Portio priorisse de Garingg' in eadem	lx s.	
Ecclesia de Raveneston'	xv m.	xv m.

Vicaria eiusdem	C s.	
Ecclesia de Gahurst	viij m.	v m.
Ecclesia de Clifton'	xiij m.	x m.
Ecclesia de Harmede ded' port' et pens'	viij m.	C s.
Portio prioris de Tykeford' in eadem	ij m.	
Pensio prioris de Merton' in eadem	xx s.	
Ecclesia de Woleston' Minor'	vj m. dim.	ij m.
Ecclesia de Lathebur'	xv m.	ix m.
Ecclesia de Pettesho	iiij m. dim.*	ij m.
Ecclesia de Hampslap	lx m.	xxx m.
Vicaria eiusdem	x m.	
Ecclesia de Stantton'	vij m.	vj m.
[fo 131r] Vicaria eiusdem	iiij m.*	
Ecclesia de Wolverton'	xvj m.	xiij m.
Vicaria eiusdem	vj m. dim.	
Ecclesia de Lavenden' deduct' pens'[1]	viij m.	vj m.
Pens' magistri Johannis Norht' in eadem	xiij s. iiij d.*	
Vicaria eiusdem	ij m.*	
Ecclesia de Loutton Magna[1] deduct' port'	iiij m. dim.*	xl s.
Port' prioris de Longa Villa in eadem	xx s.	
Ecclesia de Louton' Parva ded' port'	ij m. dim.*	xx s.
Port' prioris de Bradewell' in eadem	xx s.	
Ecclesia de Newenton' Longevile ded' pens'	viij m.	v m.
Pens' prioris de Longa Villa in eadem	ij m.	
Ecclesia de Schenle ded' port'	xviij m.	x m.
Port' prioris de Dunstapl' in eadem	ij m.	
Ecclesia de Crable	xxx m.	xv m.
Ecclesia de Parva Brichulle	vj m. et dim.	iiij m.
Vicaria eiusdem	ij m. dim.*	
Ecclesia de Haversham ded' port'	xx m.	xij m.
Port' prioris de Lenton' in eadem	iiij m.	
Ecclesia de Middelton' Kaynes ded' port'	xv m.	x m.
Port' prioris sancti Albani in eadem	iij m.	
Ecclesia de Bolbrichull' ded' port'	viij m.	iiij m.
Port' prioris de Longa Villa in eadem	xx s.	
Ecclesia de Magna Brichull' ded' pens'	xj m.	x m.
Pens' prioris de Dunstapl' in eadem	xx s.	
Ecclesia de Schirington'	xx m.	x m.
Ecclesia de Blechell' ded' pens'	xx m.	xij m.
Pens' prioris de Longa Villa in eadem	xx s.	
Ecclesia de Tyringham	xx m.	x m.
Ecclesia de Stok' Goldingtone	xx m.	x m.
Ecclesia de Wavendene	xv m.	x m.
[fo 131v] Ecclesia de Calverton'	xxij m.	xiij m.
Ecclesia de Newenton' Blosmevill'	viij m.	iiij m.
Ecclesia de Emberton' ded' pens'	xv m.	x m.
Pens' rectoris ecclesia de Olneya in eadem	ij m.	
Ecclesia de Filegrave	vij m.	iij m.
Ecclesia de Olneya	l m.	xxv m.

Ecclesia de Magna Lymford'	xv m.	x m.
Ecclesia de Magna Woleston'	vij m. et dim.	iij m.
Ecclesia de Seweneston'	viij m.	vj m.
Ecclesia de Wokenton'	x m.	vj m.
Ecclesia de Walton'	viij m.	vj m.
Ecclesia de Braunfeld	iij m. et dim.*	iij m.
Ecclesia de Brouhton'	ix m.	iiij m.
Ecclesia de Stokhamund'	xij m.	vj m.
Ecclesia de Ekeneye*		dim. m.

1 *indecimabilis* in Rec. Comm. text.

305P Decanatus de Wottesdon'

Ecclesia de Wottesdon' habet tres portiones equales quelibet qualiter valet	x li.	xxx m.
Portio abbatis de Becko in eadem	x m.	C s.*
Ecclesia de Quenton' ded' port'[1]	xxx m.	xiiij m.
Portio Rogeri de Viens[2] in eadem	iij m.	
Ecclesia de Hoggeshawe[3] ded' pens' et port'	x m.	(vj m.)
Pens' Hospitalitatis Jerosolim in eadem [marginated] superfluit	dim. m.*	
Port' prioris de Beremundeseye in eadem [marginated] superfluit	xx s.	
Ecclesia de Schobinton' ded' pens'	xij m.	x m.
Pens' abbatis de Becko in eadem	x s.	
Vicaria eiusdem	iij m.*	
Ecclesia de Picheton' ded' pens'	viij m.	v m.
Pens' prioris de Malvernia in eadem	vj s.	
Ecclesia de Ovingg' ded' pens'	vj m. et dim.	iij m.
Pens' Hospitalitatis Jerosolim in eadem	iiij m.*	
[fo 132r] Ecclesia de Norhtmerston' ded' pens'	x m.	C s.
Pens' prioris de Dunstapl' in eadem	xx s.	
Ecclesia de Estcleydon' ded' pens'	x m.	C s.
Pens' prioris de Walingford' in eadem	x s.	
Ecclesia de Grendon'	x m.	v m.
Ecclesia de Ikeford' ded' pens'	x m.	C s.
Pens' rectoris ecclesie de Mershe in eadem	ij m.	
Ecclesia de Ilmere	vj m. et dim.*	v m.
Vicaria eiusdem	ij m. et dim.*	
Ecclesia de Eston' Sanford'	vij m.	iiij m.
Ecclesia de Eya Regis	x m.	C s.
Vicaria eiusdem	iij m. et dim.*	
Ecclesia de Fletemerston' ded' pens'	vj m. et dim.	iij m.
Pens' rectoris ecclesie de Chalgrave in eadem	iiij m.	
Ecclesia de Wotton' ded' port'	viij m.	vj m. (v m.)
Portio[1] prioris de Longa Villa in eadem	ij m.	
Ecclesia de Parva Cleydon'[4] ded' pens'	v m.*	iij m.

Pens' prioris de Lenton' in eadem	x s.	
Ecclesia de Wynchindon' Superior'	viij m. et dim.	C s.
Vicaria eiusdem	iij m.*	
Ecclesia de Wormehale	vij m.	vj m.
Vicaria eiusdem	iij m.*	
Ecclesia de Crendon' cum capella [de Wynchedon Infer' et Chardesl'] ded' port'	xxx m.	xx m.
Port' rectoris de Ikeford' in capell' de Cherdesle	xx s.	
Ecclesia de Chilton' cum capella de Durton'	xj m.	ix m.
Ecclesia de Esindon'	ix m.	C s.
Ecclesia de Acle cum capella [capellis de Brehulle et Borstale]	xl m.	xxx m.

1 *pens'* in Rec. Comm. text.
2 *Portio que fuit Hug' de Vyens* in Rec. Comm. text.
3 *Lotegarsale* (Ludgershall) in Rec. Comm. text.
4 *indecimabilis* in Rec. Comm. text.

305Q [Decanatus de Ryseberg'[1]

Ecclesia de Ryseberge Monachorum	£16 13s 4d
Ecclesia de Neuuton' cum pens'	£26 13s 4d
Portio prioris de Walingford' in eadem	£1 0s 0d
Ecclesia de Halton'	£10 0s 0d]

1 Omitted completely from the Peterborough text and Lunt's A text of the Valuation of Norwich.

Archidiaconatus Bedeford'

305R Decanatus de Eton'

Ecclesia de Etone	xxxiij m.*	xx m.[1]
Vicaria eiusdem ded' pens'	vj m. et dim.	
[fo 132v] Pens' vicarie debit' hospit' in eadem	x m.*	
Ecclesia de Robesdon'	xv m.	x m.
Vicaria eiusdem	vj m. et dim.	
Ecclesia de Bereford'	xx m.	x m.
Vicaria eiusdem	iiij m.*	
Ecclesia de Ronhale	viij m.	v m.
Vicaria eiusdem	ij m. et dim.*	
Ecclesia de Ravenesdon'	vij m.	iiij m.
Vicaria eiusdem	ij m.*	
Ecclesia de Wylden'	xx m.	x m.
Ecclesia de Colingworth'	xiij m.	vj m.
Ecclesia de Stotton'	C s.	iiij m.

Ecclesia de Bollehurst ded' port'	vij m.	x m.
Port' abbatis de Thorneya in eadem	viij m. ix s.	2
Ecclesia de Lega	xv m.	x m.
Ecclesia de Cayso	xvj m.	x m.
Vicaria eiusdem ded' pens'	v m.*	
Pens' prioris de Chikesond in [vicaria] eadem[3]	iij m.	
Ecclesia de Pertenhale	x m.	v m.
Ecclesia de Schelton'	x m.	iij m.
Ecclesia de Givelden'	xv m.	iiij m. (iij m.)
Ecclesia de Rissele	xvj m.*	x m.[1]
Ecclesia de Tillebrok'	xvj m.	v m.
Ecclesia de Dena	xiiij m.	viij m.
Ecclesia de Melcheburn'	viij m.	v m.
Vicaria de Risele	vj m. et dim.	

1 Lunt's A text adds *Hospitalariorum.*

2 Lunt's A text adds *cum portione abbatis de Torneya,* but gives no valuation.

3 *indecimabilis* in Rec. Comm text.

305S Decanatus de Clopham

Ecclesia de Charnebrok' ded' port'[1]	xx m.	xij m.
Pens' sacriste ecclesie cathedral' Linc' in eadem	C s.*	
Pens' archid' Bedeford' in eadem	xx s.	
Vicaria eiusdem	iiij m.	
[fo 133r] Ecclesia de Acle cum capella [de Clopham] ded' pens'	xviij m.	xij m.
Pens' abbatis [Oseneye][2] in eadem	vj m. et dim.	
[Ecclesia[2]] de [Fulmersham[2]] cum capella [capellis de Pabeham et Radwell]	xl m.	x m.
[Ecclesia[2]] de Sta[che]dene	xv m.	x m.
[Ecclesia[2]] de Burnham	vj m. et dim.	iiij m.
(Vicaria) eiusdem	ij m.*	
[Eccles][2]ia de Podington'	xv m.	x m.
Vicaria eiusdem	vij m.	
Ecclesia de Farndis	C s.	iij m.
Ecclesia de Knottingg'	x m.	iij m.
Ecclesia de Bletchesho [que est integ']	xiij m.	x m.
Ecclesia de Middilton' ded' port'	C s.	iiij m.
Portio abbatisse de Eluestowe in eadem	x s.	
Vicaria eiusdem	xx s.*	
Ecclesia de Wyminton' ded' pens'	xv m.	iij m.
Pens' prioris de Dunstapl' in eadem	xx s.	
Ecclesia de Stiventon'	ix m.*	viij m.
Vicaria eiusdem	ij m.*	
Ecclesia de Harewolde	ix m.*	viij m.
Vicaria eiusdem	xiij s. iiij d.*	

Ecclesia de Wodhull'	xx m.	x m.
Ecclesia de Sulthorp'	C s.	iij m.
Ecclesia de Charlton'	vij m.	iij m.
Ecclesia de Thorneya[3] habet ij rectores. Portio prioris sancti Neothi	xiij m.	x m.
Portio alterius rectoris	xiij m.	
Chelmynton'	v m.*	iij m.

1 *pens'* in Rec. Comm text.
2 Illegible in the Peterborough text.
3 Recte the church of Turvey, cf. *Tureneya* in the Rec. Comm. text.

305T Decanatus de Bedeford'

Ecclesia sancti Pauli Bedeford'	ix m.	v m.
Ecclesia sancti Petri de Dunstapl'[1]	ij m.*	xx s.
Pens' prioris [de] Dunstapl' in eadem	dim. m.	
[fo 133v] Ecclesia sancte Marie Bedeford'[1] ded' pens'	xxiiij s.*	xx s.
Pens' prioris de Dunstapl' in eadem	xx s.	
Ecclesia sancti Petri de Merton' in Bedeford'	ij m. et dim.*	(x)[2] s.
Ecclesia sancti Cuthberti in Bedeford'	ij m.*	[?] m.
Ecclesia omnium Sanctorum in Bedeford'[1] ded' pens'	xv s.*	x s.
Pens' prioris de Newenham in eadem	xij s.	
Ecclesia sancti Johannis in Bedeford'	dim. m.*	dim. (m.)[2]
Ecclesia de Goldington'	iiij m.	iij m.
Vicaria eiusdem	xx s.*	
Ecclesia de Kerdington'	xv m.	x m.
Vicaria eiusdem	iij m.*	
Ecclesia de Wotton'	xv m.	viij m.
Vicaria eiusdem	ij m.*	
Ecclesia de Houcton' habet duos rectores Portio unius	vij m.	viij m.
Portio alterius ded' pens'	vij m.	
Pens' prioris de Newenham in eadem	dim. m.	
Ecclesia de Bydenham ded' port'	vj m. et dim.	v m.
Portio prioris de Newenham in eadem	dim. m.	
Portio prioris de Caldewell' in eadem	x s.	
Ecclesia de Willeshampstede ded' port'	v m.	v m.
Portio prioris de Bello Loco in eadem	xiij s. iiij d.	
Vicaria eiusdem	ij m.*	
Ecclesia de Eluestowe habet duos rectores Portio unius	vij m.	viij m.
Portio alterius	vij m.	
Ecclesia de Wyliton'	iiij m.	iij m.
Vicaria eiusdem	ij m.*	
Ecclesia de Coupol	C s.	v m.

Vicaria eiusdem	ij m.*	
Ecclesia de Kemston'	xv m.	x m.
[fo 134r] Vicaria eiusdem	iij m.*	
Prebenda Linc' dicta minor in villa Bedef'	vj m. et dim.	
Prebenda dicta major in eadem villa cum portione de Kirkeby[3]	xij m.	

1 *indecimabilis* in Rec. Comm. text.
2 Illegible in this text.
3 *cum portione de Kirkeby* omitted from Rec. Comm. text.

305U Decanatus de Dunstapl'

Ecclesia de Dunstapl'	xix m.	xv m.
Ecclesia de Stodham	xv m.	xv m.
Vicaria eiusdem	iiij m.*	
Capella de Wybesnade	v m.	iij m.
Ecclesia de Toterho	vij m.	v m.
Vicaria eiusdem	v m.*	
Ecclesia de Chalgrave	xij m.	x m.
Vicaria eiusdem	vj m. et dim.	
Ecclesia de Eyton'	xxv m.	xv m.
Vicaria eiusdem	viij m.	
Ecclesia de Tuleswrthe	viij m.*	v m.
Vicaria eiusdem	xx s.*	
Ecclesia de Hocclive	xij m.	vj m.
Ecclesia de Batelesdon' ded' port'	viij m.	iiij m.
Port' prioris de Longa Villa in eadem	xx s.	
Ecclesia de Middilton'	x m.	v m.
Ecclesia de Todington' ded' port'[1]	xv m.	xx m.
Portio de Bare in eadem	v m.*	
Portio de Chalton' in eadem	iiij m.*	
Portio de Todington' in eadem	iij m. et dim.*	
Ecclesia de Luton'	C m.	C li.
Vicaria eiusdem	xxiiij m.	
Ecclesia de Houcton'	xxv m.	xix m. (xx m.)
Vicaria eiusdem	xxiiij s.*	
Ecclesia de Potesgrave	v m. et dim.	v m.
Vicaria eiusdem	xx s.*	
[fo 134v] Ecclesia de Sonendone deducta portione	vj m. et dim.	iiij m. et dim. (v m.)
Port' monachorum de Struguile in eadem	xx s.	
Vicaria eiusdem	xx s.*	
Ecclesia de Stratteleye ded' port'	v m.	vj m.
Portio prioris de Swanehuwe in eadem	xiij s. iiij d.	
Portio leprosorum sancti Juliani de Sancto Albano	xiij s. iiij d.*	
Ecclesia de Cadingdone	xxiiij m.	xxiiij m.

Vicaria eiusdem	vj m. et dim.	
Prebenda de Esterbur' in Cadindon'	v m.	
Altera prebenda in Cadindon'	xl s.	
Ecclesia de Hiham ded' pens'	vij m.	x m.
Pens' priorisse de Markyate in eadem	v m.	
Ecclesia de Barton' ded' pens'	xviij m.	xij m. (x m.)
Pens' abbatis de Rameseye in eadem	xx s.	
Ecclesia prebendalis de Leytone Bussard	Cxliij m. et dim. (xCiij li. xiij s. iiij d.)	
Vicaria eiusdem deduct' oneribus	vj m. et dim.	

1 *indecimabilis* in Rec. Comm. text.

305V Decanatus de Flitte[1]

Ecclesia de Huseburn'	vj m. et dim.	v m.
Vicaria eiusdem	ij m.*	
Ecclesia de Seggenho	xij m.	x m.
Vicaria eiusdem	iij m.*	
Ecclesia de Flettewick'	vj m. et dim.	v m.
Ecclesia de Pellokeshull'	viij m.	vj m. (v m.)
Vicaria eiusdem	ij m.*	
Ecclesia de Flitte deducta portione[2]	xij m.	xij m.
Portio leprosorum sancti Juliani de Sancto Albano in eadem	ij m.*	
Vicaria eiusdem	xl s.*	
Ecclesia de Westone	vj m. et dim.	vj m. (v m.)
Vicaria eiusdem	xv s.*	
Ecclesia de Mellebrok'	vj m. et dim.	v m.
Vicaria eiusdem	xiij s. iiij d.*	
[fo 135r] Ecclesia de Clophulle ded' port'	vj m. et dim.	v m.
Portio prioris de Walingford' in eadem	xxx s.	
Ecclesia de Ametull'	iiij m.	iiij m. (iij m.)
Portio prioris de Bellovero in eadem	viij s.*	
Vicaria eiusdem	v m.*	
Ecclesia de Haunes ded' port'	x m.	ix m.
Port' prioris de Newenham[3] in eadem	ij m.	
Vicaria eiusdem ded' pens'	xx s.*	
Pens' prioris de Chikesond in eadem[4]	xv s.	
Ecclesia de Saleford'	vj m. et dim.	v m.
Vicaria eiusdem	xx s.*	
Ecclesia de Everesholt ded' port'	vij m.	v m. viij d. (v m.)
Portio prioris de Newenham in eadem	ij m.	
Ecclesia de Aspele	vij m.	v m.
Ecclesia de Holecote[2] ded' pens'	iij m.*	xx s.
Pens' prioris de Newenham in eadem	v s.	

Ecclesia de Craunfeld	xxx m.	xv m.
Ecclesia de Merston'	xxv m.	xx m.
Ecclesia de Littlingdon'	xvij m.	xv m.
Ecclesia de Stepengel'[2] ded' pens'	iiij m.*	iij m.
Pens' prioris de Dunstapl' in eadem	xiij s. iiij d.	
Ecclesia de Craveneshurst	iiij m.*	iij m.
Ecclesia de Herlingdone	xv m.	vj m.
Ecclesia de Tingrith'	iij m.*	xxx s.
Ecclesia de Maldon'	vij m.	v m.
Ecclesia de Birchemore	ij m.*	ij m. (xx s.)

1 Lunt's A text lists churches in this rural deanery in the same order as the *Taxatio.*
2 *indecimabilis* in Rec, Comm. text.
3 Newnham cancelled in Rec. Comm. text and Chicksands substituted.
4 *Portio prioris de Chikesond in vicaria eiusdem indecimabili* in Rec. Comm text.

305W Decanatus de Schefford'

Ecclesia de Schitlingdon' ded' pens'	lx m.	xl m.
Pens' abbatis de Rames' in eadem	x m.	
Pens' prioris de Newenham in eadem	xiij s. iiij d.	
Ecclesia de Holewell'[1] deducta pens'	v m.*	iij m.
[fo 135v] Pens' abbatis Westmon' in eadem	x s.	
Ecclesia de Meptishale deducta pens'	xvj m.	xiij m.
Pens' prioris de Lenton' in eadem	dim. m.	
Ecclesia de Henlowe ded' pens'	xviij m.	xiij m.
Pens' monachorum de Wenge in eadem	xxij s.	
Pens' hospitalis sancti Juliani de Sancto Albano in eadem	xvj s.*	
Vicaria eiusdem	v m.*	
Ecclesia de Alricheseye	xviij m.*	xiij m.
Vicaria eiusdem	v m.*	
Ecclesia de Chikesond'	iiij m.	iij m.
Vicaria eiusdem	xiij s. iiij d.*	
Ecclesia de Stondon'[1] ded' pens'	xx s.*	xiij s. iiij d.
Pens' prioris de Merton' in eadem	viij s.	
Ecclesia de Bluham	xxx m.	xx m.
Ecclesia de Themesford' ded' pens'	xij m.	xj m. (C s.)
Pens' prioris de Walingford' in eadem	dim. m.	
Pens' prioris de Sancto Neoto in eadem	vj m.	
Ecclesia de Camelton' ded' pens'	vj m. et dim.	v m.
Pens' prioris de Bello Loco in eadem	xl s.	
Ecclesia de Clifton'	xj m.	x m. (viij m.)
Ecclesia de Wardon'	xiij m.	ix m.
Ecclesia de Berkford' ded' port'	xiij m.	vij m.
Portio rectoris ecclesie de Eynesbur' in eadem	dim. m.	
Port' prioris de Sancto Neoto in eadem	dim. m.	
Ecclesia de Suth Givele ded' pens'[1]	xviij m.	xv m.

Pens' leprosorum de sancto Juliano in eadem	iiij m. et dim.*	
Vicaria eiusdem	v m.*	
Ecclesia de Langeford'	xxv m.*	xx m.[2]
Vicaria eiusdem	v m.*	
Ecclesia de Donnicton[1] ded' port'	xij m.*	x m.
Portio prioris de Wallingford' in eadem	xl s.	
[fo 136r] Vicaria eiusdem	l s.*	
Ecclesia de Potton' ded' port'	xxx m.	xvj m.
Port'[3] prioris sancti Andree Norht'[4] in eadem	v m.	
Ecclesia prebendalis de Bikeleswad'	lxx m.	
Vicaria eiusdem	v m.*	
Ecclesia de Stotfold ded' port'	xviij m.	xiij m.
Port' prioris de Newenham in eadem	dim. m.	
Vicaria eiusdem	iiij m.*	
Ecclesia de Estwyk'[1] ded' pens'	v m.*	iiij m.
Pens' prioris de Chikesond in eadem	xiij s. iiij d.	
Pens' leprosorum sancti Juliani de Sancto Albano in eadem	x s.*	
Ecclesia de Edwrth'	ix m.	v m.
Ecclesia de Eywrth'	vij m.	v m.
Ecclesia de Sutton'	xx m.	x m.
Ecclesia de Wrastlingwrth' ded' pens'	vij m.	v m.[5]

1 *indecimabilis* in Rec. Comm text.
2 Lunt's A text adds *Templariorum.*
3 *pens'* in Rec. Comm text.
4 *Norht'* interlined.
5 The Rec. Comm. text and Lunt's A text continue with a pension of 3s belonging to the prior of Newnham and entries for Sandy, Cockayne Hatley and Northill.

Archidiaconatus Huntingdon

305X Decanatus Huntingdon

Ecclesia beate Marie Huntingdon' [deduct' port' vicarie]	vij m.	x m.[1]
Ecclesia omnium Sanctorum Hunt'[2] ded' pens'	iiij m.*	v m. (iiij m. paupera[1])
Pens' abbatis de Thorn' in eadem	x s.	
Pens' prioris de Huntingdon' in eadem	x s.	
Ecclesia sancti Andree	xl s.*	
Ecclesie sancti Edmundi, sancti Petri, sancti Johannis,[3] sancti Martini, sancte Trinitatis, sancti Clementis, sancti Benedicti,[4] et sancti Laurencii vix valent servicium[5]		
Ecclesia prebendalis de Brampton'	vij m. (xxxv li. vj s. viij d.)	
Vicaria eiusdem	vij m.	

1 Included among churches recorded as *non valent servicium* in Lunt's A text.
2 *indecimabilis* in Rec. Comm text.
3 Valued at iij m. in Lunt's A text.
4 Marked *respondet* and *vix valet servicium* in Lunt's A text.
5 Lunt's A text includes At Andrew's and St Bartholomew's church and records them as *non valent servicium*. All are omitted from the Rec. Comm. text.

305Y Decanatus Sancti Ivonis

Ecclesia de Wardeboys deducta pens'	xxx m.	xxiiij m.
Pens' abbatis de Rameseie in eadem	xl s.	
Ecclesia de Brouhton' ded' pens'	xx m.	xv m.
[fo 136v] Pens' abbatis Rames in eadem	j m.	
Ecclesia de Someresham	l m.	xxx m. (xxiiij m.)
Ecclesia de Bluntesham	xx m.	xv m.
Ecclesia de Houcton, Witton ded' pens'	l m.	xxij m.
Pens' abbatis Rameseye in eadem	xx s.	
Ecclesia de Hertford'	xiij m.	x m.[1]
Vicaria eiusdem	v m.*	
Ecclesia de Stivecle Majore ded' pens'	xxiij m.	xx m.[1]
Pens' prioris sancti Andree Norht' in eadem	xxxvj s. viij d.	
Vicaria eiusdem	vj m. et dim. (iiij li. vj s. iiij d.)	
Ecclesia de Stivecle Minor'	xvj m. (x li. xiij s. viij d.)	xij m.
Ecclesia de Haliwell'	xx m.	xviij m. (xx m.)
Ecclesia de Wystowe deduct' pens' et port'[2]	viij m.	xij m. (x m.)
Pens' abbatis Rames' in eadem. Portio eiusdem taxatur cum ecclesia de Byri'[3]	dim. m.	
Ecclesia de Ripton' Regis	xiij m.	x m.
Ecclesia de Ripton' Abbatis	xxxv m.	xx m.
Ecclesia sancti Ivonis cum C s. annuis abbatis Rameseye et [in] vicaria eiusdem	xxxvij m. et dim.	xxiiij m.[1]
Vicaria eiusdem	C s.	
Ecclesia de Rameseie parochialis	ix m.	
Ecclesia de Biri' cum capella [capellis de Wystowe Upwode et Revele]	xxxiiij m.	

1 Marked *respondet* in Lunt's A text.
2 *et port'* omitted from Rec. Comm. text.
3 *Portio ...Byri'* omitted from Rec. Comm. text.

305Z Decanatus de Jakele

Ecclesia de Jakele ded' pens'	liij m.	xxviij m. (xxv m.)
Pens' abbatis de Thorn' in eadem	ij m.	
Ecclesia de Stangrund deduct' pens'	xxx m.	xxv m.
Pens' abbatis de Thorn' in eadem	vij m.	
Ecclesia de Fletton'	x m	viij m.
Ecclesia de Wodeston' ded' pens'	xij m.	ix m. (x m.)
Pens' abbatis de Thorn' in eadem	dim. m.	
[fo 137r] Ecclesia de Botelbrigg' ded' pens'[1]	viij m.	xij m. (x m.)
Pens' Templariorum in eadem	v m.*	[2]
Ecclesia de Overton' Lungevile ded' port'	x m.	ix m.
Portio prioris de Huntingdon' in eadem	xxx s.	
Ecclesia de Folkesworth' ded' pens'	x m.	vj m. (v m.)
Pens' abbatis de Croyland' in eadem	dim. m.	
Pens' prioris de Northwode in eadem	j m.	
Ecclesia de Overton' Watervile ded' port'	xv m.	xij m. (x m.)
Portio prioris de Huntingdon' in eadem	xx s.	
Ecclesia de Alwalton'	xiiij m.	xij m.
Ecclesia de Cestreton' ded' pens' et port'	xviij m.	xvj m. (xiiij m.)
Pens' prioris de Cruce Roys in eadem	xl s.	
Port' prioris de Huntingdon' in eadem	xx s.	
Port' abbatis de Thorn' in eadem	xxx s.	
Ecclesia de Stibinton' ded' pens' et port'	xviij m.	xvj m.
Pens' abbatis de Thorn' in eadem	j m.	
Port' elemosinarii de Thorn' in eadem	xx s.	
Ecclesia de Neweton' ded' pens'	x m.	viij m.
Pens' abbatis de Thorn' in eadem	xxix s. viij d.	
Ecclesia de Ailington' ded' pens'	xxxv m.	xxvj m. (xxiiij m.)
Pens' abbatis de Rameseie in eadem	v m.	
Ecclesia de Haddon' ded' pens'	xvj m.	x m. (viij m.)
Pens' abbatis de Thorn' in eadem	v s.	
Ecclesia de Moreburn' ded' pens'	x m.	viij m.
Pens' abbatis de Croyland' in eadem	ij m.	
Ecclesia de Wassingle ded' port'	x m.	viij m.
Port' prioris de Huntingdon' in eadem	j m.	
Ecclesia de Caldecote[1] deducta portione	v m.*	iiij m. (iij m.)
Portio prioris de Huntingdon' in eadem	dim. m.	
Ecclesia de Denton'	vij m.	iiij m.
Ecclesia de Stilton' ded' port'	x m.	x m. (C s.)
[fo 137v] Portio prioris de Huntingdon' in eadem	x s.	
Ecclesia de Glatton' ded' pens' et port'	xxxj m. et x s.	xx m.
Pens' abbatis de Mussenden' in eadem	vj m.	
Port'[3] abbatis de Brunn' in eadem	xxx s.	
Ecclesia de Conington'	xxx m.	

		xx m. (xviij m.)
Ecclesia omnium Sanctorum de Saltreia	xij m.	viij m.
Ecclesia sancti Andree de Saltreia ded' port'	x m.	vij m. (vj m.)
Port' prioris de Huntingdon in eadem	xx s.	
Ecclesia de Waltone	x m.	(viij m.)

1 *indecimabilis* in Rec. Comm text.
2 *una cum xl s. quos habent Templarii in eadem* in Lunt's A text.
3 *Pensio* in Rec. Comm. text.

305ZA Decanatus de Leytonestan[1]

Ecclesia de Elington' ded' port'	xxxv m.	xxx m. (xi m.)
Portio prioris de Huntingdon' in eadem	x s.	
Ecclesia de Grafham ded' port'	x m.	viij m.
Port' prioris de Hunt' in eadem	v s.	
Portio abbatis de Thorn' in eadem	v s.	
Ecclesia de Kinebauton' ded' port'	xxxiiij m.	xxx m. (xxv m.)
Port' prioris de Beremundeseye	vj m.	
Ecclesia de Swynesheved	vij m.	v m.
Ecclesia de Kestan	xxviij m.	xx m.
Ecclesia de Covington'	xij m.	viij m.
Ecclesia de Cattewrth'	xxv m.	xviij m.
Ecclesia de Moleswrth' ded' port'	vij m.	v m.
Port' prioris de Hunt' in eadem	xx s.	
Ecclesia de Brimpton' cum capell'	xlv m.	xxx m.
Ecclesia de Teringg'	xij m.	ix m.
Ecclesia de Hamerton' ded' pens'	vij m.	xxj m. (x m.)
Pens' abbatis de Colecestr' in eadem	xvj m.	
Ecclesia de Wynewyk'	xij m.	x m.[2]
Vicaria eiusdem	vij m.	
Ecclesia de Giddingg' Parva	viij m.	v m.
Ecclesia de Stepilgiddingg'	ix m.	vj m. (v m.)
[fo. 138r] Ecclesia de Copmanford'	vij m.	v m.
Ecclesia de Bukwrth'	xxviij m.	xx m. (xvj m.)
Ecclesia de Upton'	x m.	x m.
Ecclesia de Wlueye	C s.	v m.
Ecclesia de Alkumbir'	l m.	xl m.[2]
Vicaria eiusdem	x m.	
Ecclesia de Gyddingg' Magna ded' port'	xx m.	xvj m. (xv m.)[2]
Port' rectoris ecclesie de Blaterwyk' in eadem	xx s.	
Vicaria eiusdem	vij m.	
Vicaria de Spaldwyk'	vj m. et dim.	
Prebenda de Leyton que consistit in laico feodo	lxx m.	

Ecclesia prebendalis de Stowe cum capell'	lxxiij m. et dim. (lxiij li. vj s. viij d.)	
Vicaria eiusdem	viij m.*	
Ecclesia prebendalis de Leyhton'	liij m.	
Vicaria eiusdem	vij m.	

1 Lunt's A text lists churches in this rural deanery in the same order as the *Taxatio*.
2 Marked *respondet* in Lunt's A text.

305ZB Decanatus de Sancto Neoto

Ecclesia sancti Neoti'	xxxij m.	xxx m.[1]
Vicaria eiusdem	C s.	
Ecclesia de Eynesbi' s. portio rectoris	xv m.	xv m.
Port' prioris sancti Neoti in eadem	x m.	
Pens' prioris de Newenham in eadem	j m.	
Ecclesia prebendalis de Buckeden' [inclusa port' de Scotton' tax' ij li.]	lx m.	
Vicaria eiusdem	xl s.*	
Ecclesia de Hemingford' Prioris ded' port'	xvij m.	xv m.[1]
Port' prioris de Hatfeld in eadem	iij m.	
Ecclesia de Overton'	xvij m.	xvj m. (xv m.)[1]
Ecclesia de Abbotesle ded' port'	xxxvj m.	xxx m.
Port' prioris de Huntingdon' in eadem	xxx s.	
Ecclesia de Wersle	xx m.	xv m.
Ecclesia de Grantesden' ded' pens'	l m.	l m. (xl m.)
Pens' abbatis sancti Augustini de Bristoll' in eadem	x m.	
[fo. 138v] Ecclesia de Hemingford' Abbatis deducta pens'	xxv m.	xx m.
Pens' prioris sancti Ivonis in eadem	iij m.	
Ecclesia de Gillingg' ded' port' et pens'	xviij m.	xv m. (x m.)
Port' prioris Huntingdon' in eadem	xx s.	
Pens' prioris de Merton' in eadem	vj m.	
Ecclesia de Gormucestr'	lx m.	xl m.[1]
Vicaria eiusdem	xij m.	
Ecclesia de Offord Cluny	xx m.	xv m. (xij m.)
Ecclesia de Offord Dacy ded' pens'	viij m.	v m. (C s.)
Pens' prioris de Huntingdon' in eadem	l s.	
Ecclesia de Stocton' ded' portionibus que alibi includuntur	xl m.	xxx m.
Ecclesia de Suho ded' port'	xxiiij m.	xv m. (xxiiij m.)
Port' prioris de Newenham in eadem	iiij m.	
Port' prioris de Huntingdone in eadem	xx s.	
Ecclesia de Dodington'	xvij m.	xv m. (xij m.)
Ecclesia de Staunton'	xlv m.	xxx m.

Ecclesia de Paxton' cum capella [inclusa port' in Scotton' supra et exclusa port' vicarie Lincoln indecimabili]	xl m.	xl m.[1]
Vicaria eiusdem	C s.	
Vicarie de Hemingford' Prioris, de Overton' et de Dodington' vix valent servicium*		

1 Marked *respondet* in Lunt's A text.

305ZC Decanatus de Berchamstede

Ecclesia sancti Petri de Berchamsted' ded' pens'	xv m.	xiiij m.
Pens' abbatis de Grestein in eadem	xij m.	
Ecclesia beate Marie de Northberchamsted' ded' pens'	xxj m.	xviij m.
Pens' abbatis de Gresteyn in eadem	iij m.	
Ecclesia de Treng' cum capell' [de Wyginton']	lv m.	xl m.
Ecclesia de Puttenham	x m.	C s. (v m.)
Ecclesia de Aldebure	ix m.	viij m.
Ecclesia de Gattesden' Parva	ix m.	vij m. et dim. (v m.)[1]
Ecclesia de Magna Gattesden'	xx m.	xviij m.
Ecclesia de Keneswrth'	xv m.	xij m.[1]
[fo. 139r] Vicaria eiusdem	iiij m.*	
Ecclesia de Flamsted'	xxx m.	xxv m.
Ecclesia de Westhamsted' ded' port'	xx m.	viij m.
Port' abbatis Westm' in eadem	xxx m.	xxx m.[2]
Ecclesia de Northmimmes	xxv m.	xiiij m.
Ecclesia de Schenle	xx m.	xv m. (xvj m.)
Ecclesia de Aldenham ded' pens'	xix m.	xviij m.
Pens' sacriste Westm' in eadem	xiij s. iiij d.	
Vicaria eiusdem	v m.*	
Ecclesia de Langel' Regis	xx m.	xv m.
Ecclesia de Hemelhamsted'	l m.	xl m.
Vicaria eiusdem	C s.	
Ecclesia de Wykinton'*		iij m.

1 Marked *respondet* in Lunt's A text.
2 Lunt's A text adds *s. portio persone; portio monachorum xxxii m. Respondet pro medietate.*

305ZD Decanatus de Hicche

Ecclesia de Hicche cum capellis [de Dynesle et Wymundele]	lx m.	l m. (xl m.)[1]
Vicaria eiusdem	vj m. et dim.	
Vicaria capelle de Dinesle ded' pens', de		

Wymundele Magna et Parva et de Piritone vix valent servicium[2]*		
Pens' abbatisse de Eluestowe in eadem [in vicaria de Dynesle indecimabili]	ij m.	
Ecclesia de Gravele	x m.	x m.
Ecclesia de Waleden' Regis ded' pens' et port'	xxx m.	xxx m.[1]
Pens' capell'i[3] ecclesie Linc' in eadem	v m.	
Pens' abbatisse de Eluestowe in eadem	xx s.	
Portio abatis de Sancto Albano in eadem	iij m.	
Ecclesia de Lynleye	viij m.	viij m. (vij m.)
Ecclesia de Stichenach' ded' pens'	xl m.	xxxvj m. (xxv m.)
Pens' abbatis Westm' in eadem	l s.	
Ecclesia de Parva Wymundele	vij m.*	vj m. (v m.)[1]
Ecclesia de Offeleye	xxxij m.	xxx m.
Ecclesia de Piriton'	xxxij m.	xxx m.[1]
Pens' prioris de Hertford' in vicaria eiusdem ecclesie[4]	xxij s.	
[fo. 139v] Ecclesia de Knebbewrth'	xij m.	xij m.
Ecclesia de Kymington' ded' port'	xxv m.	xxx m.[1]
Portio prioris de Hertford' in eadem	xx s.	
Vicaria eiusdem	C s.	[5]
Ecclesia de Lecchewrth' ded' pens'	xij m.	viij m. (vij m.)
Pens' abbatis de sancto Albano in eadem	xiij s. iiij d.	
Ecclesia de Chivesfeld	vij m.	v m.

1 Marked *respondet* in Lunt's A text.
2 In Lunt's A text, Temple Dinsley church was valued at xl s. and Great Wymondley church at xxx s. Both were marked *respondet*.
3 *capitulum* in Rec. Comm. text.
4 *indecimabilis* in Rec. Comm. text.
5 The vicarage is noted in Lunt's A text, but neither text gives a valuation.

305ZE Decanatus de Hertford'

Ecclesia de Esenden' cum capella [de Beyford]	xxvj m.	xx m.
Vicaria eiusdem	xl s.*	
Ecclesia de Watton'	xxiij m.	xx m.
Ecclesia monachorum de Hertford'	iiij m. et dim.	iiij m.
Ecclesia de Stepelford'	x m.	C s.
Ecclesia de Sauecompe	x m. et dim.	x m. (C s.)
Ecclesia de Brancesfeld ded' pens'	x m.	ix m.
Pens' abbatis de Sancto Albano in eadem	ij s.	
Ecclesia de Digneswell'	x m.	v m. (iiij m.)
Ecclesia de Attemunfichet	vj m. et dim.	vj m.
Ecclesia sancti Andree de Hertford'	x m.	viij m.
Ecclesia omnium Sanctorum de Hertford'	xiij m.*	x m.[1]

Pens' abbatis de Waltham in vicaria eiusdem ecclesie	xx s.*	
Ecclesia de Berchamsted' Parva ded' pens'	ix m.	viij m.
Pens' prioris de Lewes in eadem	x s.	
Ecclesia de Beningho	xv m.	xij m.[1]
Ecclesia de Hatfeld	lv m.	xl m.
Capella de Tateringg'	v m.	iiij m.*
Ecclesia sancti Laurencii de Ayete	vij m.	vj m. (v m.)
Ecclesia de Twing'	xj m.	x m.
Ecclesia de Welewes[2]	xxv m.	xx m.
Ecclesia sancti Nicholai[3] de Hertford'	v m.*	v m.
Pens' prioris de Wyleford' in eadem	xx s.	
[fo. 140r] Ecclesia de Hertfordingbur'	xij m.	x m.
Ecclesia de Dachewrth'	x m.	ix m.
Ecclesia beate Marie de Parva Hertford'	v m.*	xxx s. (j m.)
Vicarie monachorum de Hertford', de Hertford Omnium Sanctorum, et de Beningho vix valent servicium*		

1 Marked *respondet* in Lunt's A text.
2 The Rec. Comm. text, which records Welwyn at the end of the deanery, has a note that it was inserted on 22 Nov. 1318, p. 37.
3 *indecimabilis* in Rec. Comm. text.

305ZF Decanatus de Baudack'

Ecclesia de Aston ded' port' et pens'	xvij m.	xv m.
Pens' abbatis de Redingg' in eadem	xx s.	
Port' abbatis de Colecestr' in eadem	iij m. et dim.	
Ecclesia de Parva Munden'	xvij m.	xv m.
Ecclesia de Magna Munden'	xxxij m.	xxv m.
Ecclesia de Benington'	xxx m.	xxv m.
Ecclesia de Westmilne ded' port'	xxij m.	xx m.
Port' prioris sancte Trinitatis London' in eadem	ij m.	
Ecclesia de Asspeden'	xij m.	x m.
Ecclesia de Wylie ded' port'	xx m.	xvj m.
Portio prioris de Willeford' in eadem	ij m.	
Ecclesia de Walkeleye	vij m.	iij m.
Ecclesia de Throckingg'	vj m. et dim.	(v m.)
Ecclesia de Walkern'[1] ded' pens' et port'	xx m.	xv m.[2]
Pens' abbatis Colecestr' in eadem	j m.	
Port' abbatis eiusdem in eadem	iiij m.	
Port' abbatis de sancto Albano in eadem	iij m.	
Ecclesia de Erdeleya	xviij m.	xx m.[3]
Vicaria eiusdem	iiij m.*	
Ecclesia de Codreth	xij m.	xx m.
Ecclesia de Rissenden'	xvj m.	xv m. (x m.)

Ecclesia de Wellington' ded' port'	xij m.	x m.
Portio abbatis de sancto Albano in eadem	xx s.	
Ecclesia de Sandon'	xxij m.	xvij m. (xv m.)[3]
Vicaria eiusdem	iij m. et dim.*	
Ecclesia de Therefeld	l m.	xl m.
[fo. 140v] Ecclesia de Keleshull'	xx m.	xv m.
Ecclesia de Assewell'	xl m.	xl m.[3]
Vicaria eiusdem ded' pens'	xv m.	
Pens' abbatis Westm' in eadem	xxxj s. viij d.	
Ecclesia de Henxewrth'	xviij m.	xv m.
Ecclesia de Caldecote	vj m. et dim.	v m. (iij m.)
Ecclesia de Radewell'	vj m. et dim.	v m.
Ecclesia de Beygrave	xv m.	xv m.
Ecclesia de Clohale	xxij m.	xx m.
Ecclesia de Bradefeld	xx s.*	xiij s. iiij d.
Ecclesia de Weston'[4] cum capell'	xlvj m.*	xlj m. (xx m.)[3,5]
Vicaria de Weston'	vj m. et dim.	

Vicaria de Walkern' vix valet servicium*

1 St Neot's in Rec. Comm. text.
2 *quia inferius* cancelled in Lunt's A text.
3 Marked *respondet* in Lunt's A text.
4 *indecimabilis* in Rec. Comm. text.
5 Lunt's A text adds *Templariorum.*

305ZG Archidiaconatus de Sancto Albano

Ecclesia sancti Petri cum capellis etc [de Sanrug et la Rugg' sancti Andree et Norhale cum octo marcis quas percipit priorissa de Marckyate]	iiij^{xx} et x m.
Vicaria eiusdem ded' pens'	C s.
Pens' infirmarii sancti Albani in eadem	viij m.
Ecclesia de Watford' s. portio monialium de Markzat' ded' port'	xviij m.
Port' refectorarii sancti Albani in eadem	xiij m.
Port' vicar' de Lazaret	iiij m.*
Vicaria de Watford' ded' pens'	vij m.
Pens' refectorarii sancti Albani in eadem	xij m.
Ecclesia de Herteshevede' s. portio rectoris ded' pens'	xiiij m.
Pens' abbatis de sancto Albano in eadem	ij m. et dim.
Pens' priorisse de Markzate in eadem	xx s.
Ecclesia de Rikemereswrth'	xxiiij m.
Vicaria eiusdem ded' pens'[1]	v m.*
Pens' sacriste de sancto Albano in eadem	x m.

Ecclesia de Langgeleye	xvij m.
Vicaria eiusdem ded' pens'[1]	iiij m.*
[fo. 141r] Pens' camerarii sancti Albani in eadem	l s.
Ecclesia de Redburn' ded' port'	xxvj m.
Port' scriptor' sancti Albani in eadem	ij m.
Vicaria eiusdem ded' pens'[1]	iiij m.*
Pens' camerarii sancti Albani in eadem	l s.
Ecclesia de Aston' ded' pens'[1]	v m.*
Pens' coquinarii sancti Albani in eadem	lx s.
Pens' leprosorum sancti Juliani in eadem	xx s.*
Ecclesia de Wynselowe cum capellis etc [de Horwode et Greneberwe]	xxvij m.
Vicaria eiusdem ded' pens'[1]	v m.*
Pens' camerarii de sancto Albano in eadem	xiij s. iiij d.
Vicaria de Parva Horewode	iij m.*
Vicaria de Greneborwe ded' pens'[1]	iiij m.*
Pens' camerarii sancti Albani in eadem	ij s.
Ecclesia de Norton'	x m.
Vicaria eiusdem	iij m.*
Ecclesia de Newenham	x m.
Vicaria eiusdem	xx s.*
Ecclesia de Heuxeneston'	xij m.
Vicaria eiusdem	iij m.*
Ecclesia de Waleden'	xv m.
Vicaria eiusdem ded' pens'[1]	iij m.
Pens' refectorarii sancti Albani in eadem	iij m.
Pens' monialium beate Marie de Pratis in eadem	j m.*
Pens' leprosorum sancti Juliani in eadem	ij m.*
Ecclesia de Schephale	viij m.
Ecclesia de Codicote	v m.*
Vicaria eiusdem	v m.*
Vicaria de Sanrugg' ded' pens'[1]	iiij m.*
Pens' infirmarii sancti Albani in eadem	iiij m.
Ecclesia de Kyngebur'	xv m.
[fo. 141v] Vicaria eiusdem ded' pens'[1]	iiij m.*
Pens' sacriste sancti Albani in eadem	x m.
Ecclesia sancti Stephani de Sancto Albano	xiij m.
Vicaria eiusdem ded' pens'[1]	iiij m.*
Pens' coquinarii sancti Albani in eadem	x m.
Ecclesia leprosorum sancti Juliani'	C s.
Portiones leprosorum in ecclesiis de Kingebi' et de sancto Stephano	xxx m.*
Vicaria de la Rugg'	iij m.*
Ecclesia de la Barnat	x m.
Ecclesia de Thidelvestr'	iij m.*
Pens' elemosinarii[2] sancti Albani in capella de Northawe[1]	C s.

Port' elemosinarii sancti Albani per particulas infra archidiaconatum eiusdem videlicet in Sanrugg, Langeleye, Redburn, Tytenhangre[3], Aspa, Wynselowe, Heuxeneston', Neuham, Norton', Walden', Codicote etc [et alie parve particulares]	xviij m.

1 *indecimabilis* in Rec. Comm. text.
2 *sacriste* in Rec, Comm. text.
3 Omitted from the list in the Rec. Comm. text.

Archidiaconatus Norht'

305ZH Decanatus de Brackele

Ecclesia de Brackel'	xxxvj m.	xxvj li. (xxv li.)[1]
Vicaria eiusdem	x m.	
Ecclesia de Wedon' Pynkeneye	xv m.	x m.
Vicaria eiusdem	vj m. et dim.*	iiij m.
Ecclesia de Wappenham ded' port'	xxiiij m.	xvj m
Port' prioris de Wedon' in eadem	xiij s. iiij d.	
Ecclesia de Slapton'	vij m.	v m. (vij m.)
Ecclesia de Bradden'	vij m.	v m. (vij m. et dim.)
Ecclesia de Norton'	xxx m.	x li.
Ecclesia de Toucestr' ded' port'[2]	xl m.	xxij m.
Port' prioris de Bradenestok' in eadem	xxxv s.	
Ecclesia de Tiffeld	ix m.	iiij li.
Ecclesia de Gayton'[3] ded' pens'	xvj m.	x m.
Pens' abbatisse de Pratis in eadem	j m.	
[fo. 142r] Ecclesia de Pateshull' habet duos rectores.		
Portio unius s. prioris de Dunst'	ix m.	xvj m.
Portio alterius s. abbatisse de Godestowe	ix m.	
Due vicarie in eadem utraque per se	xl s.*	iij li.
Ecclesia de Hiham s. port' prioris de Dunstapl'	vj m. et dim.	C s.
Port' alterius	vj m. et dim.	
Ecclesia de Blakilvesle[4]	xx m.*	x li.[5]
Vicaria eiusdem	vj m. et dim.	xl s.
Ecclesia de Plumpton'	vij m.	xx s.
Ecclesia de Sulgrave	ix m.	v m.[6]
Vicaria eiusdem	vj m.*	ij m.
Ecclesia de Stutesbi'[4] ded' pens'	xl s.*	xx s.
Pens' prioris sancti Andree Norht' in eadem	dim. m.	
Ecclesia de Helmeden' ded' pens'	xvj m.	x m.

Pens' magistri [hospitalis sancti] Johannis de Norht' in eadem	xl s.	
Ecclesia de Syresham ded' pens'	xv m.	x m.
Pens' abbatis Leycestr' in eadem	dim. m.	
Ecclesia de Wytefeld	ix m.	v m.
Vicaria eiusdem	xl s.*	(v m., sed vicaria non taxatur in originali)
Ecclesia de Evenle	xx m.	x li.
Vicaria eiusdem	iij m. et dim.*	xl s.
Ecclesia de Crowelton' ded' pens'[4]	xviij m.	x li.
Pens' magistri hospitalis de Aynho in eadem	xij s.*	
Ecclesia de Aynho ded' port'	xxv m.	viij li.
Portio prioris de Hurnle in eadem	ij m.	
Ecclesia de Neubotle deducta portione	xiiij m.	viij li.[7]
Portio[8] prioris de Ware in eadem	xx s.	
Vicaria eiusdem	vij m.	v m.
Ecclesia de Thorp'	C s.	iiij m.
Vicaria eiusdem	xl s.*	
Ecclesia de Chaucumbe	xv m.	viij li.
[fo. 142v] Vicaria eiusdem non taxatur*		
Ecclesia de Middelton ded' port' et pens'	xxv m.	xx m.
Pens' prioris de Ware in eadem	xxiiij s.	
Portio [decimar'] eiusdem prioris in eadem	xx s.	iiij m.*
Ecclesia de Gruttewrth'	v m. et dim.	(iiij m.)[9]
Ecclesia de Thenford'[4] habet duos rectores s. portio unius	v m.*	viij m.
Portio alterius s. prioris de Colde Norton'	v m.	
Pens' prioris de Bradewell' in eadem	xiij s. iiij d.	
Portio abbatis de Osen' in eadem	xx s.	
Ecclesia de Farningho ded' pens'	xx m.	xij li.
Pens' abbatis Leycestr' in eadem	iiij m.	
Ecclesia de Stenes	viij m.	iiij li.
Ecclesia de Hinton'	xij m.	viij m.
Ecclesia de Merston'	xxxvj m.	xx li.
Vicaria eiusdem ded' pens'	xv m.	viij li.
Pens' prioris de Ware in eadem	xx s.	
Ecclesia de Colewrth' ded' port'	xx m.	xiij m.[10]
Portio prioris de Esseby in eadem	xl s.	
Ecclesia de Maydeford'	ix m.	C s.
Ecclesia de Hochecote	xv m.	x m.
Ecclesia de Wardon'	xxiiij m.	xvij m.
Ecclesia de Aston'	xv m.	viij li.
Ecclesia de Botindon' habet duos rectores		
Portio de patronatu prioris de Tikeford' ded' pens'	xj m.	x li.
Pens' eiusdem in eadem	xiij s. iiij d.	

Portio alterius s. portio de patronatu de Chacumb'	vj m.	
Ecclesia de Bifeld	xxx m.	xij li.
Ecclesia de Wodeford' ded' pens' et port'	xx m.	xvj m.
Pens' prioris de Roucestr' in eadem	xl s.	
[interlined in later medieval hand] Portio prioris Roff ...*		xiijs iiij d.*
Portio Willelmi de Holecote in eadem	dim. m.	
Ecclesia de Eydon ded' port'	xij m.	vj li.
Ecclesia[11] prebendalis de Sutton' cum capell'	Cclx m.*	
Vicaria eiusdem	x m.*	
Firma capituli Linc' in Merschton'	xx m.*	
[fo. 143r] Portio prioris de Ware in eadem	xiij s. iiij d.	
Portio magistri Willelmi Brokedys in eadem	iij m.	
Ecclesia de Morton' ded' pens'	xv m.	x m.[10]
Pens' prioris de Esseby in eadem	iij m.	
Ecclesia de Esseby [Canonicorum] cum vicaria que est in esculentis	xv m.	viij li.[10]
Prebenda de Merston' que est in laico feodo	xviij m.	
Ecclesia prebendalis de Croprith cum capell'	C m.	
Vicaria eiusdem	xxvij m.	

1 Marginated *abb' Leic'* in a later medieval hand.
2 *pens'* in Rec. Comm. text.
3 *Eyton* in Rec. Comm. text.
4 *indecimabilis* in Rec. Comm. text.
5 Marginated in a later medieval hand *prior (?) hosp'*.
6 Marginated in a later medieval hand *Andr'*.
7 Illegible margination in a later medieval hand.
8 *Portio ... Chaucumbe* and the entry for Middleton Cheney church appear at the end of the entry for the deanery in the Rec. Comm. text.
9 Corrected from iiij li. in Lunt's A text. No valuation is given in the Peterborough text.
10 Marginated in a later medieval hand prior *Esseby*.
11 *Ecclesia prebendalis ... Merschton'* are added in a later medieval hand at the foot of the folio.

305ZI Decanatus de Daventre

Ecclesia de Daventre ded' pens'	xxviij m.	xx m.
Pens' prioris de Ware de capella de Walton'	xiij s. iiij d.	
Vicaria eiusdem cuius major pars in esculentis	ij m.*	
Vicaria capelle de Waltone	v m.*	
Ecclesia de Norton' ded' pens'	xvj m.	xij m.
Pens' prioris de Warmenton' in eadem	xij s.	
Vicaria eiusdem	x m.	
Ecclesia de Staverton'	xiij m.	x m.
Vicaria eiusdem	vj m. et dim.	
Ecclesia de Falewesle	xj m.	x m.

Vicaria eiusdem	v m.*	
Ecclesia de Preston'[1]	ix m.	C s.
Vicaria eiusdem	lx s.*	
Ecclesia de Cattesby ded' pens'	x m.	C s.
Pens' prioris de Brommesfeld in eadem	dim. m.	
Vicaria de Cattesby	vij m.	
Ecclesia de Braundeston'	xx m.	xij m.
Ecclesia de Kildesby	x m.	C s.
Ecclesia de Esseby ded' pens'[2]	xv m.	viij m.
Pens' prioris de Ware in eadem	ij m.	
Vicaria eiusdem	iiij m.*	
Ecclesia de Beroby ded' pens'[3]	xx m.	xj li.
[fo. 143v] Pens' magistri sancti David extra Norht' in eadem	dim. m.*	
Ecclesia de Charwalton' ded' pens'	xiij m.	x m.
Pens' prioris sancti Oswaldi in eadem	j m.	
Ecclesia de Baddeby	xx m.	xij m.
Ecclesia de Wedon'	xv m.	xj m.
Vicaria eiusdem	lx s.*	
Ecclesia de Stowe	xviij m.	x m.
Ecclesia de Fardingston'	viij m. et dim.	vj m.
Ecclesia de Dodeford'	xiiij m.	x m.
Vicaria eiusdem	vj m. et dim.	
Ecclesia de Everesdon'	xvj m.	x m.
Ecclesia de Lichebarwe	xij m.	x m.

1 *prior Daventr'* added in a later medieval hand.
2 *Wodegar'*(?) added in a later medieval hand.
3 *indecimabilis* in Rec. Comm. text.

305ZJ Decanatus de Preston'

Ecclesia de Grendon'	xx m.	vj li.
Ecclesia de Esseby	xxv m.	vj li.
Ecclesia de Wyston'	vij m. et dim.	iiij li. (iiij m.)
Ecclesia de Jordele	xxv m.	vj li.
Ecclesia de Braunfeld	xv m.	viij m. et dim.
Vicaria eiusdem	iij m.*	
Ecclesia de Parva Houcton'	xv m.	vij m.
Vicaria eiusdem	iiij m.*	
Ecclesia de Cugeho	vij m. et dim.	v m.
Ecclesia de Magna Houcton'	xxx m.	x m.[1]
Ecclesia de Horton' ded' pens'	vj m. et dim.	v m.
Pens' prioris sancti Andree Norht' in eadem	dim. m.	
Vicaria eiusdem	xx s.*	
Ecclesia de Pydington'	xviij m.	x m.
Ecclesia de Preston'	viij m.	v m.
Vicaria eiusdem	ij m.*	

Ecclesia de Quenton'	iij m. et dim.*	xl s.
[fo. 144r] Ecclesia de Wotton'	xx m.	viij m.[2]
Ecclesia de Colentre	vij m.	v m.
Ecclesia de Middilton'	vj m. et dim.	v m.
Ecclesia de Thorp'	ix m.	vj li.
Vicaria eiusdem	ij m.*	
Ecclesia de Blisewrth' ded' port'	x m.	vj li.[3]
Portio prioris de Lenton' in eadem	xvj s.	
Ecclesia de Cortenhale	ix m.	viij m.
Ecclesia de Rode cum portione abbatis sancti Jacobi extra Norht'	v m.	v m. (vj li.)
Ecclesia de Stokebruer'	xx m.	vij li. (C s.)
Ecclesia de Esteneston'	x m.	vij m. et dim. (vij li.)[4]
Ecclesia de Westpirie	xxiiij m.	x m.
Ecclesia de Aldrington'	iiij m.*	(xl s.)[5]
Ecclesia de Grafton'	viij m.	C s.
Ecclesia de Estpirie	xvj m.	x m.[6]
Ecclesia de Fortho	ij m.*	ij m.[7]
Ecclesia de Covesgrave	x m.	iiij li.
Ecclesia de Passenham ded' pens'	xv m.	vj li.[8]
Pens' abbatis Cirencestr' in eadem	iiij m.	
Ecclesia de Wykedyve ded' port'	vj m. et dim.	iiij li.[9]
Portio abbatis Oseneye in eadem	ij m.	
Ecclesia de Wikehamund	xx s.*	xx s.

1 Lunt's A text adds *preter decimas monachorum que valent xx s.*
2 Lunt's A text adds *preter decimas monachorum que valent iiij s.*
3 Lunt's A text adds *preter decimas monachorum que valent xxv s.*
4 Lunt's A text adds *cor' preter decimas religiosorum que valent ij m.*
5 Marked *non est in originali* in Lunt's A text.
6 Lunt's A text adds *preter pensionem et decimas monachorum viij m.*
7 Lunt's A text adds *preter decimas monachorum que valent dim. m.*
8 Lunt's A text adds *preter pensionem iiij m. quas monachi de Cirncestria [habent].*
9 *preter decimas de Oseneia que valent ij m.* in Lunt's A text.

305ZK Decanatus de Weldon'[1]

Ecclesia de Wakerle	xij m.	vij m.
Ecclesia de Blatherwyk' Trinitatis	xij m.	viij m.
Ecclesia de Blatherwyk' Magdalen'	iiij m.*	xl s.
Ecclesia de Laxton'	iiij m.	xl s.
Ecclesia de Bolewyk'	xiij m.	C s.
Vicaria eiusdem	v m.*	(v m.)
[fo. 144v] Ecclesia de Deen	xx m.	x li.
Ecclesia de Weldon' habet duos rectores, s. portio prioris de Landa	x m.	viij li.
Portio alterius rectoris	x m.	

Ecclesia de Corby	x m.	iiij li.
Ecclesia de Brickestock'	xvj m.	viij li.
Vicaria eiusdem	vj m. et dim.	v m.
Ecclesia de Parva Akele	ij m. et dim.	xx s.
Ecclesia de Geytinton'[2]	l m.	xx li.
Ecclesia de Wycle ded' pens'	xj m.	vj li.
Pens' monachorum de Ses in eadem	xv s.	
Vicaria eiusdem	v m. et dim.*	v m.
Ecclesia de Haringwrth'[3]	xv m.	viij li.
Vicaria eiusdem	v m. et dim.*	v m.
Ecclesia de Rokingham	vj m. et dim.	iij li.
Ecclesia de Cotingham ded' pens'	xij m.	C s.
Pens' abbatis de Burgo in eadem	dim. m.	
Ecclesia de Carlton'	vij m. et dim.	v m.
Ecclesia de Wilberston'	x m.	viij m.
Vicaria eiusdem	v m. et dim.*	v m.
Ecclesia de Stok' Daubeneye ded' port'	vj m. et dim.	xl s.
Portio prioris de Beaver in eadem	xl s.	
Ecclesia de Brampton' ded' pens'	xij m.	x m.
Pens' monachorum de sancto Neoto in eadem	C s.	
Ecclesia de Dingele	vij m.	vij m. (vj m.)
Ecclesia de Weston'	xiij m.	vj li.
Vicaria eiusdem	v m.*	v m.
Ecclesia de Assele	x m.	vij m.
Prebenda de Gretton'	lxx m. (£40 0s 0d)	
Vicaria eiusdem	x m.	

1 Lunt's A text lists churches in this rural deanery in the same order as the *Taxatio* with one minor exception.
2 Marginated in later medieval hand *vicaria x li.*
3 *abbatisse Eluestowe* added in later medieval hand

306 Letter from A de Nodariis, sheriff of Northampton, to the bailiffs of the abbot's liberty, quoting a writ of Edward II dated 10 Jan. 1307, ordering him to supply animals for the coronation feast, and ordering the bailiffs to contribute their share. [10 Jan.–2 Feb. 1307]

[fo. 144v] A de Nodariis vicecomes Norht' ballivis libertatis abbatis de Burgo Sancti Petri salutem. Mandatum domini regis in hec verba recepi:

Edwardus Dei gracia rex Anglie, dominus Hibernie et dux Aquitanie vicecomiti Norht' salutem. Cum coronationis nostre solempnia quam die Dominica proxima post festum sancti Valentini proxima iam ventura Deo propitio volumus celebrare tam de victualibus quam aliis, grandes et varios exigant apparatis; tibi firmius quo poterimus injungend' precipimus quod statim visis presentibus de exitibus ballive tue infra eadem ballivam tuam ubi ad manus commodum nostrum et ad minus gravamen populi ballive tue predicte fieri poterit emas et provideas xxiiij boves vivos, xxiiij porcos vivos, quatuor braones vivos et xl bacones de melioribus et pinguioribus pro expensis hospitii nostri magis competentibus, quos in partibus illis vendendos, potis invenire ita quod eos habeas apud Westmon' ad quindenam purificationis beate Marie proximo futur' ad ultimum illi vel illis quem vel quos ad huiusmodi providentias recipiend' ibidem duxerimus assignandos per indenturam inter te et ipsum vel ipsos tam de pretio quam de munero rerum predictarum soficiendam, liberandos, attendens pro certo nullatenus vos latere quod provisiones predicte in forma predicta fieri poterunt absque injuria cuiquam inferenda. Propter quod si super illo clamor ad nos perveniat, nos ad te punctione gravissima capiemus. Volumus insuper et tibi precipimus, quod quicquid de bobus, porcis, braonibus vel baconibus huiusmodi competentibus pro expensis hospitii nostri predicti penes te habes, inter cetera bona et catalla Walteri de Langeton' Coventr' et Lichef' episcopi, que in manu nostra et in tua custodia per preceptum nostrum certis de causis existunt, habeas una cum providentiis supradictis per te ut premittitur faciend' ad predictos diem et locum liberandos in forma predicta. Et de custubus [sic] quos circa premissa apposueris, volumus quod in garderoba nostra computes, et ibidem inde allocationem habeas competentem. Teste Waltero Reginald' thesaurario nostro apud Westm' x die Januar' anno regni nostri primo.

Quare vobis mando quod statim visis presentibus, emas et provideas sex boves vivos, sex porcos vivos, unum braonem vivum et decem bacones de pinguioribus quos invenire poteris infra ballivam tuam ad opus domini regis, ita quod omnia predicta sint parata ad festum purificationis beate Marie secundum tenorem mandati domini regis London' mittend'. Et hoc nullo modo omittas.

[fo. 145r] blank

Bibliography

PRIMARY SOURCES CITED

Unpublished

Cambridge University Library, Add MS 3020–1 (The Red Book of Thorney)
Peterborough D and C, MS 1 (The Book of Robert Swaffham)
Peterborough D and C, MS 6 (The Red Book of John of Achurch)
Peterborough D and C, MS 17 (transcripts from The White Book)
Lincolnshire Archives Office, Episcopal Register I (Bishop Oliver Sutton's register)
Episcopal Registers II–III (Bishop John Dalderby's registers)
London, British Library, Cott. Vesp. Exxii (The White Book)
Cott. Vesp. E xxi, fos 1–34 (transcripts from The White Book), fos 45–106 (The Register of Adam of Boothby)
Cott. Cleop. C, i, fos 35–157; ii, fos 1–165 (copy of The Great Book of John of Achurch)
Harl. 742 (Spalding Priory cartulary)
Public Record Office, CP/40 (plea rolls)
E/372 (pipe rolls)
Society of Antiquaries, MS 38 (The Great Book of John of Achurch)
MS 60 (The Black Book)
NRO, X7528, File F (c), (Mellows transcripts of The White Book)
Oxford, Bodleian Library, MS Dodsworth, 75 (transcripts from The White Book)
MS Dodsworth 86 (transcripts from The White Book)
MS Top. Northants., c 23 (transcripts from The White Book)
MS Wood C 3 (transcripts from The White Book)

Published

The Account Rolls of the Obedientiaries of Peterborough, ed. Greatrex, J. (NRS, xxxiii, 1984)
Anglo-Scottish Relations 1174–1328: Some Selected Documents, ed. Stones, E. L. G. (Oxford, 1970)
Annales Minorum, ed. Wadding L., 16 vols (Rome, 1731–6)
The Book of William Morton, eds. King, P. I. and Brooke, C. N. L., trans. Mellows, W. T. (NRS, xvi, 1954)
Calendar of Charter Rolls, 1226–1516, 6 vols (HMSO, 1903–27)
Calendar of Close Rolls, 1272–1509, 47 vols (HMSO, 1900–63)
Calendar of Fine Rolls, 1272–1509, 22 vols (HMSO, 1911–62)
Calendar of Patent Rolls, 1232–1582, 71 vols (HMSO, 1906–86)
Cartularium Monasterii de Rameseia, ed. Hart, W. H. and Lyons, P. A., 3 vols (Rolls Series, London, 1884–93)
The Cartulary of Chatteris Abbey, ed. Breay, C. (Woodbridge, 1999)

Chronica et Annales: Willelmi Rishanger, ed. Riley, H. T. (Rolls Series, London, 1865)
The Chronicle of Walter of Guisborough, ed. Rothwell, H. (Camden Soc., lxxxix, 1957)
Chronicon Petroburgense, ed. Stapleton, T. (Camden Soc., xlvii, 1849)
Councils and Synods with Other Documents relating to the English Church, AD 1205–1313, ed. Powicke, F. M., Cheney, C. R., 2 vols (Oxford, 1964)
Documents Illustrating the Activities of the General and Provincial Chapters of the English Black Monks 1215–1540, ed. Pantin, W. A., 3 vols (Camden Soc., 3rd ser., xlv, xlvii, liv, 1931–7)
Foedera, Conventiones, Litterae et Cuiuscunque Generis Acta Publica, ed. Rymer, T., 3 vols (London 1816–30)
Henry of Pytchley's Book of Fees, ed. Mellows, W. T. (NRS, ii, 1927)
Historiae Anglicanae Scriptores Varii, ed. Sparke, J., 2 vols in 1 (London, 1723)
The Last Days of Peterborough Monastery, ed. Mellows, W. T. (NRS, xii, 1947)
The Lindsey Survey in ed. Keats-Rohan, K. S. B., *Domesday People: A Prosopography of Persons Occurring in English Documents 1066–1166* (Woodbridge, 1999), App. I, pp. 77–90
The Northamptonshire Survey in ed. Keats-Rohan, K. S. B., *Domesday People: A Prosopography of Persons Occurring in English Documents 1066–1166* (Woodbridge, 1999), App. II, pp. 98–110
Parliamentary Writs, ed. F. Palgrave, 2 vols (Rec. Comm., 1827–34)
Peterborough Local Administration, vols I–II, ed. Mellows, W. T. (NRS, ix–x, 1937–9)
Peterborough Local Administration: Elizabethan Peterborough, eds. Mellows, W. T. and Giffard, D. H. (NRS, xviii, 1956)
Regesta Regum Anglo-Normannorum, eds. Davis, H. W. C., Johnson, C., Cronne, H. A., Davis, R. H. C., 4 vols (Oxford, 1913–68)
Register of John de Halton, ed. Thompson, W. N., 2 vols (Canterbury and York Soc., xii–xiii, 1913)
Les Régistres de Boniface VIII, ed. Digard, G., Faucon, M., Thomas, A., Fawtier, R., 4 vols (Paris, 1907–39)
Registrum Ricardi de Swinfield, ed. Capes, W.W. (Canterbury and York Soc., vi, 1909)
Registrum Roberti Winchelsey, ed. Graham, R., 2 vols (Canterbury and York Soc., li–ii, 1952–56)
The Rolls and Register of Bishop Oliver Sutton 1280–1299, ed. Hill, R. M. T., 8 vols, (Lincoln Record Society, xxxix, xliii, xlviii, lii, lx, lxiv, lxix, lxxvi, 1948–86)
Select Cases in the Court of King's Bench ed. Sayles G. O. (Selden Soc., lv, 1936)
Snappe's Formulary and Other Records, ed. Salter, H. E. (Oxford Historical Society, lxxx, 1924)
Taxatio Ecclesiastica (Rec. Comm., 1802)
The Thurgarton Cartulary, ed. Foulds, T. (Stamford, 1994)
The Valuation of Norwich, ed. Lunt, W. E. (Oxford, 1926)

Electronic

CD *Continental Origins of English Landholders 1066–1166. A Prosopogaphy of Post-Conquest England compiled from the Sources* (Coel Enterprises Ltd, forthcoming) (Northamptonshoire Survey)

http://irwell.mimas.ac.uk/taxatio, website for the forthcoming Taxatio database

SECONDARY WORKS CITED

Published

Barber, M., *The Trial of the Templars* (Cambridge, 1978)

Beardwood, A., 'The Trial of Walter Langton, Bishop of Lichfield, 1307–1312', *Trans. American Philosophical Society*, NS, liv (1964), pp. 3–45

Bridges, J., *The History and Antiquities of Northamptonshire*, 2 vols (Oxford, 1791)

Crook, D, *Records of the General Eyre* (London, 1982)

Davis, G. R. C., *Medieval Cartularies of Great Britain* (London, 1958)

Davnall, S., Denton, J., Griffiths. S., Ross, D. B., Taylor, B., 'The *Taxatio* Database', *Bulletin of the John Rylands Library*, lxxiv (1992), pp. 89–108

Denton, J. H., *Robert Winchelsey and the Crown 1294–1313: A Study in the Defence of Ecclesiastical Liberty* (Cambridge, 1980)

Dugdale, W., *Monasticon Anglicanum*, new edn., ed. Caley, J., Ellis, H., Bandinel, B., 6 vols (London, 1846)

Elkins, S. K., *Holy Women of Twelfth-Century England* (Chapel Hill and London, 1988)

Franklin, M. J., 'The Bishop, the Abbot and Warmington Rectory: A Medieval Church Appropriation Struggle' *NP and P*, vi (1980–1), pp. 197–206

Franklin, M. J., 'The Assessment of Benefices for Taxation in Thirteenth Century Buckinghamshire' *Nottingham Medieval Studies*, xxix (1985), pp. 73–98

Golding, B., *Gilbert of Sempringham and the Gilbertine Order c.1130–c.1300* (Oxford, 1995)

Gransden, A., *Historical Writing in England c.550–c.1307* (London, 1974)

Gunton, S., *The History of the Church of Peterborough* (London, 1686)

Holtzmann, W., *Papsturkunden in England*, 3 vols in 4 (Berlin and Göttingen, 1930–52)

Hunnisett, R. F., *Editing Records for Publication* (Archives and the User, 4, British Records Association, 1977)

King, E., *Peterborough Abbey 1086–1310: A Study in the Land Market* (Cambridge, 1973)

King, E, 'The Town of Peterborough in the Early Middle Ages', *NP and P*, vi (1980–81), pp. 187–95

King, E., 'Estate Management and the Reform Movement', in ed. W. M. Ormrod, *England in the Thirteenth Century* (Stamford, 1991), pp. 1–14

King, P., bibliography of the works of W. T. Mellows *NP and P*, ii, no. 5 (1958), pp. 252–5

Lloyd, T. H., *The English Wool Trade in the Middle Ages* (Cambridge, 1977)

Lunt, W. E., *Financial Relations of the Papacy with England to 1327* (Cambridge, Mass., 1939)

Martin, J. D., *The Cartularies and Registers of Peterborough Abbey* (NRS, xxviii, 1978)

Miller, E., *The Abbey and Bishopric of Ely* (Cambridge, 1951)

Parsons, J. C., *Eleanor of Castile: Queen and Society in Thirteenth-Century England* (New York, 1995)

Poole, G. A., *Diocesan Histories: Peterborough* (London, 1881)

Prestwich, M., *Edward I*, 2nd edn (New Haven and London, 1997)

Raftis, J. A., *The Estates of Ramsey Abbey: a Study in Economic Growth and Organisation* (Toronto, 1957)

Raban, S., 'The Estates of Thorney and Crowland: A Study in Medieval Monastic Land Tenure' (*University of Cambridge, Department of Land Economy, Occasional Paper* 7, 1977)

Raban, S., 'Mortmain in Medieval England' *Past and Present*, lxii (1974), pp. 3–26. Also in ed. T. H. Aston, *Landlords, Peasants and Politics in Medieval England* (Cambridge, 1987), pp. 203–26

Roffe, D., *Domesday: the Inquest and the Book* (Oxford, 2000)

Round, J. H., *Feudal England* (London, 1895, repr. 1964)

Smith, D. M., *Guide to Bishops' Registers of England and Wales* (RHS, London, 1981)

Stones. E. L. G., Simpson, G. G., *Edward I and the Throne of Scotland, 1290–1296*, 2 vols (Oxford, 1978)

Thompson, S., *Women Religious: The Founding of English Nunneries after the Norman Conquest* (Oxford, 1991)

The Victoria History of the County of Hertford, ed Page, W., 4 vols (London, 1902–14)

The Victoria History of the County of Northampton, eds Serjeantson, R. M., Adkins, W. R. D., Page, W. and Salzman, L. F., 4 vols (London and Oxford, 1902–37)

Wake, J, obituary of W. T. Mellows *NP and P*, i, no. 3 (1950), pp. 1–5

Willard, J. F., *Parliamentary Taxes on Personal Property: A Study in Medieval Financial Administration* (Cambridge, Mass., 1934)

Young, C. R., *The Royal Forests of Medieval England* (Leicester, 1979)

Unpublished

Bennett, N., personal handlist of John Dalderby's institutions from Lincolnshire Archives Office, Episcopal Register II

Clubley, C., John Dalderby, Bishop of Lincoln, 1300–1320, unpublished Hull PhD thesis, 1965

Sturman, W. M., The History of the Nunnery of St Mary and St Michael outside Stamford, unpublished London MA thesis, 1945

Index

County boundaries are those obtaining in the Middle Ages. Settlements in the abbey's liberty of Nassaburgh in Northamptonshire are recorded as within the Soke. The text is indexed by document number.